Exam 70-643: TS: Windows Server 2008 Applications Infrastructure, Configuring

OBJECTIVE	CHAPTER	LESSON
DEPLOYING SERVERS		
Deploy images by using Windows Deployment Services.	1	1, 2
Configure Microsoft Windows activation.	1	4
Configure Windows Server Hyper-V and virtual machines.	1	3
Configure high availability.	2	2
Configure storage.	2	1
CONFIGURING REMOTE DESKTOP SERVICES		
Configure RemoteApp and Remote Desktop Web Access.	4	3
Configure Remote Desktop Gateway (RD Gateway).	4	2
Configure Remote Desktop Connection Broker.	3	2
Configure and monitor Remote Desktop resources.	4	1
Configure Remote Desktop licensing.	3	1, 2
Configure Remote Desktop Session Host.	3 4	1, 2 1
CONFIGURING A WEB SERVICES INFRASTRUCTURE		
Configure Web applications.	5 6	2 2
Manage Web sites.	5 6	2 1
Configure a File Transfer Protocol (FTP) server.	7	1
Configure Simple Mail Transfer Protocol (SMTP).	7	2
Manage the Web Server (IIS) role.	5	1, 2
Configure SSL security.	6	2
Configure Web site authentication and permissions.	6	1, 2
CONFIGURING NETWORK APPLICATION SERVICES		
Manage the Streaming Media Services role.	8	1
Secure streaming media.	8	1
Configure SharePoint Foundation options.	9	1
Configure SharePoint Foundation integration.	9	1

Exam Objectives The exam objectives listed here are current as of this book's publication date. Exam objectives are subject to change at any time without prior notice and at Microsoft's sole discretion. Please visit the Microsoft Learning website for the most current listing of exam objectives: http://www.microsoft.com/learning/en/us /exams/70-643.mspx.

Microsoft

MCTS Self-Paced Training Kit (Exam 70-643): Configuring Windows Server® 2008 Applications Infrastructure (2nd Edition)

J.C. Mackin
Anil Desai

PUBLISHED BY
Microsoft Press
A Division of Microsoft Corporation
One Microsoft Way
Redmond, Washington 98052-6399

Library of Congress Control Number: 2011928628
ISBN: 978-0-7356-4878-4

Printed and bound in the United States of America.

3 4 5 6 7 8 9 10 11 QG 7 6 5 4 3 2

Microsoft Press books are available through booksellers and distributors worldwide. If you need support related to this book, email Microsoft Press Book Support at mspinput@microsoft.com. Please tell us what you think of this book at http://www.microsoft.com/learning/booksurvey.

Microsoft and the trademarks listed at http://www.microsoft.com/about/legal/en/us/IntellectualProperty /Trademarks/EN-US.aspx are trademarks of the Microsoft group of companies. All other marks are property of their respective owners.

The example companies, organizations, products, domain names, email addresses, logos, people, places, and events depicted herein are fictitious. No association with any real company, organization, product, domain name, email address, logo, person, place, or event is intended or should be inferred.

This book expresses the author's views and opinions. The information contained in this book is provided without any express, statutory, or implied warranties. Neither the authors, Microsoft Corporation, nor its resellers, or distributors will be held liable for any damages caused or alleged to be caused either directly or indirectly by this book.

Acquisitions Editor: Jeff Koch
Developmental Editor: Karen Szall
Project Editor: Carol Dillingham
Editorial Production: nSight, Inc.
Technical Reviewer: Mitch Tulloch; Technical Review services provided by Content Master, a member of CM Group, Ltd.
Copyeditor: Kerin Forsyth
Indexer: Lucie Haskins
Cover: Twist Creative • Seattle

[2012-01-27]

Contents at a Glance

Contents

What do you think of this book? We want to hear from you!

Microsoft is interested in hearing your feedback so we can continually improve our
books and learning resources for you. To participate in a brief online survey, please visit:

www.microsoft.com/learning/booksurvey/

What do you think of this book? We want to hear from you!

Microsoft is interested in hearing your feedback so we can continually improve our books and learning resources for you. To participate in a brief online survey, please visit:

www.microsoft.com/learning/booksurvey/

Introduction

This training kit is designed for information technology (IT) professionals who support or plan to support Windows Server 2008 R2 networks and who also plan to take the Microsoft Certified Technology Specialist (MCTS) 70-643 exam. It is assumed that before you begin using this kit, you have a solid, foundation-level understanding of Windows client and server operating systems and common Internet technologies.

The material covered in this training kit and on the 70-643 exam relates to the technologies in a Windows Server 2008 R2 network that support remote access to operating systems, web content, media, and applications. The topics in this training kit cover what you need to know for the exam as described on the Skills Measured tab for the exam, which is available at *http://www.microsoft.com/learning/en/us/Exam.aspx?ID=70-643&locale=en-us#tab2*.

By using this training kit, you learn how to do the following:

- Deploy Windows servers and clients across a network by using Windows Deployment Services and the Windows Automated Installation Kit (AIK) for Windows 7
- Configure Hyper-V
- Configure an activation infrastructure
- Configure high-availability storage solutions for servers
- Configure and manage Remote Desktop Services in Windows Server 2008 R2
- Configure and manage Internet Information Services 7.5
- Configure Windows Media Services
- Configure Microsoft SharePoint Foundation 2010

Refer to the objective mapping page in the front of this book to see where in the book each exam objective is covered.

Hardware Requirements (Hyper-V)

You should use the Hyper-V virtualization platform on a single physical computer as the computer lab environment for this training kit. Hyper-V is a feature of Windows Server 2008 and Windows Server 2008 R2 and is a topic that is covered on the 70-643 exam. Because the task of setting up this computer lab environment in Hyper-V helps you develop knowledge and skills required for the 70-643 exam, using an alternative virtualization software platform such as VirtualBox is not recommended.

You need only one physical computer to perform the exercises in this book. This physical host computer should meet the following minimum hardware requirements:

- An x64-based processor that includes both hardware-assisted virtualization (AMD-V or Intel VT) and hardware data execution protection. (On AMD systems, the data execution protection feature is called the No Execute or NX bit. On Intel systems, this feature is called the Execute Disable or XD bit.) These features must also be enabled in the BIOS.

- 4.0 GB of RAM (more is recommended).
- 90 GB of available hard disk space.
- DVD-ROM drive.
- Internet connectivity.

Software Requirements

The following software is required to complete the practice exercises:

- Windows Server 2008 R2. You can download an evaluation edition of Windows Server 2008 R2 at the Microsoft Download Center at *http://www.microsoft.com/downloads*.
- The Windows Automated Installation Kit (AIK) for Windows 7. You can download the Windows AIK for Windows 7 at the Microsoft Download Center at *http://www .microsoft.com/downloads*. This kit is installed on top of Windows Server 2008 R2 on the Server1 computer.

Practice Setup Instructions

After you have installed Windows Server 2008 R2 on your physical computer and have established an Internet connection, you are ready to begin the practice setup. This setup occurs in five phases. In the first phase, you install the Hyper-V server role and create a virtual network named contoso.local. In the second phase, you create three virtual machines. Figure I-1 shows the virtual hardware configuration of the virtual machines as they appear after this second phase.

> **IMPORTANT   DOWNLOAD REQUIRED SOFTWARE**
>
> Before you begin preparing the practice computers, you must have a copy of Windows Server 2008 R2 (either as an .iso file or as a DVD) and the Windows Automated Installation Kit (either as an .iso file or as a DVD).

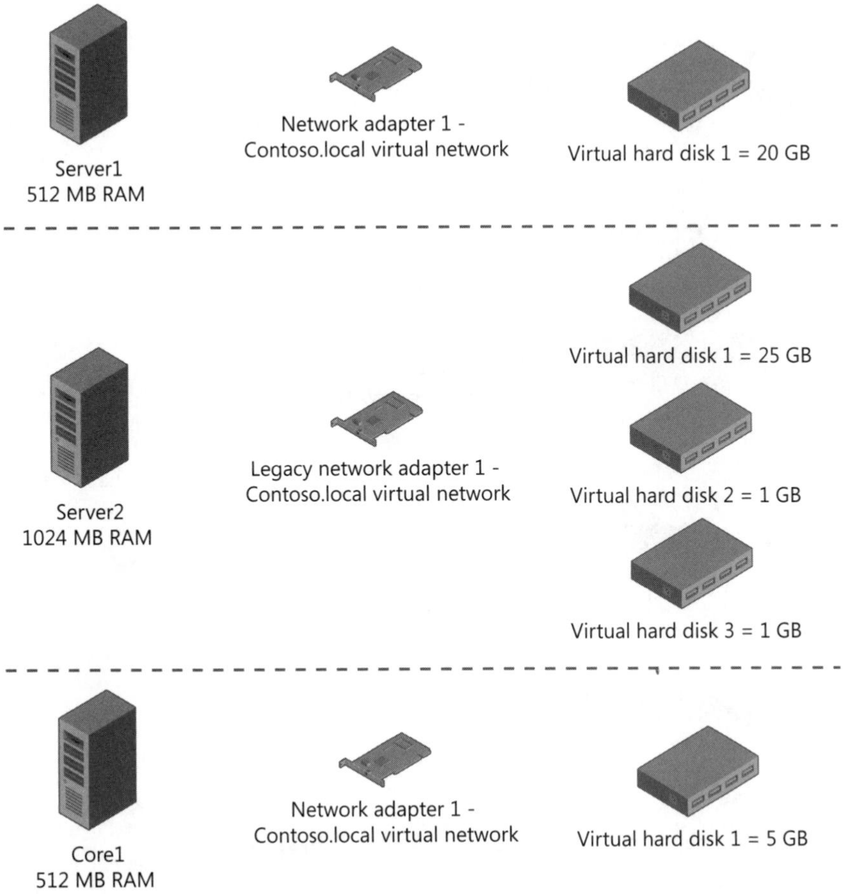

Server1
512 MB RAM

Network adapter 1 -
Contoso.local virtual network

Virtual hard disk 1 = 20 GB

Virtual hard disk 1 = 25 GB

Server2
1024 MB RAM

Legacy network adapter 1 -
Contoso.local virtual network

Virtual hard disk 2 = 1 GB

Virtual hard disk 3 = 1 GB

Core1
512 MB RAM

Network adapter 1 -
Contoso.local virtual network

Virtual hard disk 1 = 5 GB

FIGURE I-1 Hardware configuration for the three computers in Hyper-V.

In the third phase of the practice setup, you configure the software for the Server1 and Core1 machines. (No software configuration is necessary for Server2 because this computer must be left as a virtual bare-metal machine.)

The fourth phase of practice setup describes the configuration necessary to provide an Internet connection for all computers. By performing these steps, you add a second virtual network adapter to Server1 and configure Network Address Translation (NAT) across its two adapters, as shown in Figure I-2.

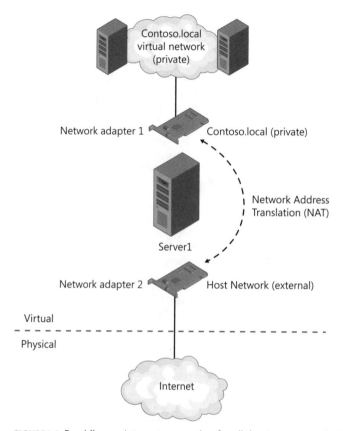

FIGURE I-2 Providing an Internet connection for all three computers in Hyper-V.

In the fifth and final phase of the practice setup, you activate the Server1 and Core1 servers over the Internet.

Phase 1: Install and Configure the Hyper-V Server Role on the Host Server

Perform the following steps to create and prepare the virtual environment for the lab computers.

Add the Hyper-V Server Role

On the host computer running Windows Server 2008 R2, click Add Roles in the Initial Configuration Tasks window and then add the Hyper-V server role.

After Hyper-V is installed, use the Hyper-V Manager administrative tool to open Virtual Network Manager and add the following two networks:

- Virtual Network 1
  - Type = Private
  - Name = Contoso.local
- Virtual Network 2
  - Type = External
  - Name = Host Network
  - Select an external adapter with Internet access

Phase 2: Create the Virtual Machines

Perform the following steps to create the virtual machines for this training kit.

Create the Server1 Virtual Machine

In Hyper-V Manager, right-click the local server node in the console tree, click New, and then click Virtual Machine to launch the New Virtual Machine Wizard. Use the New Virtual Machine Wizard to specify the following settings:

- Name: Server1
- RAM: 512 MB
- Connection: Contoso.local
- Create a virtual hard disk
- Virtual hard disk size: 20 GB
- Install an operating system later
- Do not add a second adapter yet

Create the Core1 Virtual Machine

Use the New Virtual Machine Wizard to create a second virtual machine. Configure all settings identically to those of the Server1 machine, except in the following two cases:

- Name: Core1
- Virtual Hard Disk Size: 5 GB

Create the Server2 Virtual Machine

Use the New Virtual Machine Wizard to create the third virtual machine. Configure all settings identically to those of the Server1 machine, except in the following cases:

- Name: Server2
- RAM: 1024 MB
- Hard Disk Name: Server2DiskA.Vhd
- Hard Disk Size: 25 GB
- Connection: Not Connected

> **IMPORTANT   USE A LEGACY NETWORK ADAPTER FOR SERVER2**
>
> Server2 needs a Legacy Network Adapter for you to perform the exercises related to Windows Deployment Services found in Lesson 2 of Chapter 1, "Implementing and Configuring a Windows Deployment Infrastructure."

Replace the Default Network Adapter with a Legacy Network Adapter

The default network adapter assigned in Hyper-V is incompatible with network-based installations. For this reason, you must replace the default adapter with the Legacy Network Adapter. Right-click Server2 in Hyper-V manager and click Settings. In the Settings For Server2 dialog box, select the hardware named Network Adapter and then click Remove. Click Add Hardware, select Legacy Network Adapter, and click Add. You should see a new Legacy Network Adapter in the list of hardware. Select the new Legacy Network Adapter, assign it to the Contoso.localnetwork from the drop-down list, and click Apply.

Attach a Second and Third Hard Disk to Server2

In Hyper-V Manager, right-click Server2 and then click Settings. In the Settings For Server2 window, select IDE Controller 0 in the list of hardware, select Hard Drive, and then click Add. Click New to start the New Virtual Hard Disk Wizard.

In the New Virtual Hard Disk Wizard, specify the following:

- Dynamically Expanding
- Name: Server2DiskB.vhd
- Location: Browse To The \Virtual Machines\Server2\ folder
- Create A New Blank Virtual Hard Disk
- Size: 1 GB

In the Settings For Server2 window, select IDE Controller 1. Repeat the same process to create and attach a third 1 GB virtual hard disk named Server2DiskC.vhd. Click Apply to save the changes.

Configure Startup Order in the BIOS Setting

In the Settings For Server2 window, click BIOS in the list of hardware. Change the startup order so that Legacy Network Adapter is listed first. Click Apply to save the changes.

After you have finished creating and configuring the Server2 virtual machine, the Settings window should look like the one shown in Figure I-3.

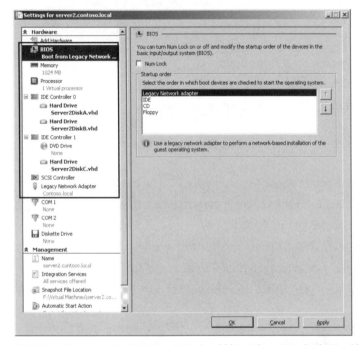

FIGURE I-3 The Server2 virtual machine should have three attached virtual hard disks and a Legacy Network Adapter. It should be configured to start from the Legacy Network Adapter.

When you are finished, click OK to save the changes you have made in the Settings For Server2 window.

Phase 3: Configure the Operating Systems on Server1 and Core1

Use the following instructions to configure the Server1 and Core1 computers.

Configure Server1

Server1 will be used as a DHCP server, DNS server, and Active Directory domain controller for the contoso.local domain. Server1 must also have the Windows AIK for Windows 7 installed. Perform the following steps to meet the configuration requirements for the server.

1. In Hyper-V Manager, right-click Server1 and click Settings.

2. In the Settings For Server1 window, click DVD drive.

3. In the Media section, do one of the following:

   - Click Physical CD/DVD Drive and specify the physical CD/DVD-ROM drive on the host machine in which you will place the Windows Server 2008 R2 media.

   - Click Image File and browse to an ISO file that contains a disc image of the Windows Server 2008 R2 media.

4. Click OK to close the Settings For Server1 window.

5. In Hyper-V Manager, right-click Server1 and then click Connect.

6. In the Server1 On Localhost window, click Start on the menu bar. (This button is round and blue-green.)

   The Server1 computer starts, and the Windows Server 2008 R2 installation process begins.

7. Perform a default installation of Windows Server 2008 R2. Use the following guidelines:

   - If desired, choose a language and keyboard corresponding to your region.

   - Do not enter a product key at this time.

   - Choose Windows Server 2008 R2 Enterprise (Full Installation).

   - Install Windows in the default location (Disk 0 Unallocated Space).

   - Use a strong password of your choice when logging on as Administrator for the first time.

8. Configure the Local Area Connection on Server1. You can perform this step by using either the Initial Configuration Tasks window or a command prompt.

   If you prefer to use the Initial Configuration Tasks window, click Configure Networking, open the properties of the Local Area Connection, and then configure the properties of Internet Protocol version 4 (TCP/IPv4) with the following options and values:

   - Select Use The Following IP Address.

     - IP Address: 192.168.10.1

     - Subnet Mask: 255.255.255.0

     - Default Gateway: Leave blank

- Select Use The Following DNS Server Addresses.
  - Preferred DNS server: 192.168.10.1
  - Alternate DNS server: Leave blank

To configure these same IP settings at a command prompt instead, type the following two commands in succession:

```
netsh interface ipv4 set address "local area connection" static 192.168.10.1
255.255.255.0
netsh interface ipv4 set dns "local area connection" static 192.168.10.1
```

9. Configure the computer name. You can perform this step by using either the Initial Configuration Tasks window or a command prompt.

   In Initial Configuration Tasks, click Provide Computer Name And Domain. Click Change and specify the computer name as Server1. Do not specify a domain at this time.

   To set the computer name at the command prompt instead, type the following command:

```
netdom renamecomputer %computername% /newname:Server1 /reboot
```

10. Use the Run box from the Start menu to run Dcpromo and configure Server1 as a domain controller in a new Active Directory domain named contoso.local. Specify the following options in the Active Directory Domain Services Installation Wizard:

    - Create a New Domain In A New Forest.
    - FQDN Of The Forest Root: contoso.local.
    - Forest Functional Level: Windows Server 2008 R2.
    - Additional Domain Controller Options: DNS Server (Default).
    - If you are warned that the computer has a dynamically assigned IP address, click Yes.
    - If you are warned that a delegation for this DNS server cannot be created, click Yes.
    - Locations for database, log files, and Sysvol: Leave defaults.
    - Directory Services Restore Mode Administrator Password: Any strong password of your choice.

11. After the Active Directory Domain Services Installation Wizard completes, restart Server1 immediately and then log on to the contoso.local domain from Server1 as CONTOSO\Administrator.

> **IMPORTANT   HOW DO YOU LOG ON TO A COMPUTER IN HYPER-V?**
>
> Note that in Hyper-V, you must use the *Ctrl+Alt+End* command to enter the Ctrl+Alt+Del keystroke. You can also choose Ctrl+Alt+Delete from the Action menu.

12. Add the DHCP Server role. In the Initial Configuration Tasks window, click Add Roles. Use the Add Roles Wizard to add the DHCP Server role with the following options:

- Network Connection Bindings: Default. (Leave 192.168.10.1 selected.)
- IPv4 DNS Server Settings:
  - Parent Domain: contoso.local
  - Preferred DNS Server IPv4 Address: 192.168.10.1
  - Alternate DNS Server IPv4 Address: Leave blank
- WINS Server Settings: WINS is not required.
- Add a DHCP scope with the following specifications:
  - Scope Name: Contoso.local
  - Starting IP Address: 192.168.10.2
  - Ending IP Address: 192.168.10.10
  - Subnet Mask: 255.255.255.0
  - Default Gateway: 192.168.10.1 (This assumes an Internet access configuration as described in Phase 3 of the practice setup instructions.)
  - Subnet Type: Wired
  - Activate This Scope: Leave selected
  - DHCPv6 Stateless Mode: Leave default
  - IPv6 DNS Server Settings: Leave default
  - Authorize DHCP Server: Leave default

13. Create and name three domain administrator accounts. To do so, use the following step-by-step instructions.

    a. In the Active Directory Users And Computers administrative tool, expand the *contoso.local* node in the console tree and then select the Users folder.

    b. Right-click the Users folder, point to New on the shortcut menu, and then click User.

    c. In the New Object – User dialog box, type **ContosoAdmin1** in the Full Name and User Logon Name text boxes and then click Next.

    d. Enter a password of your choice, click Next, and then click Finish.

    e. In the Active Directory Users And Computers console, locate the ContosoAdmin1 account you have just created in the details pane. Right-click the account and then click Add To A Group from the shortcut menu.

    f. In the Select Groups dialog box, type **domain admins** and then press Enter. In the Active Directory Domain Services message box, click OK.

    g. Create two additional domain administrator accounts, named ContosoAdmin2 and ContosoAdmin3, respectively, by using steps **b** through **f**.

    h. If desired, create an additional domain administrator account with your name.

14. Enable file sharing on Server1.

    a. In the Search Programs And Files box of the Start menu, type Manage Advanced Sharing Settings and then press Enter.

    b. In the Advanced Sharing Settings window, select the Turn On File And Printer Sharing option and then click Save Changes.

15. Install the Windows Automated Installation Kit for Windows 7 (Windows AIK) by using the Windows AIK DVD or .iso file you have downloaded from the Microsoft Download Center. To do so, use the following step-by-step instructions.

    a. Use the Settings For Server1 window in Hyper-V to mount the Windows AIK for Windows 7 .iso file as a DVD drive.

    b. In the AutoPlay window, use the Windows AIK for Windows 7 Setup link to install the Windows AIK for Windows 7 and any prerequisite components if necessary.

Configure Core1

Core1 will act as a member server in the contoso.local domain. Use the following instructions to configure the Core1 server.

1. In Hyper-V Manager, right-click Core1 and click Settings.

2. In the Settings For Core1 window, select DVD Drive from the list of hardware.

3. In the Media section, do one of the following:

- Click Physical CD/DVD Drive and specify the physical CD/DVD-ROM drive on the host machine in which you will place the Windows Server 2008 R2 media.

- Click Image File and browse to an ISO file that contains a disc image of the Windows Server 2008 R2 media.

4. Click OK to close the Settings For Core1 window.

5. In Hyper-V Manager, right-click Core1 and then click Connect.

6. In the Core1 On Localhost window, click Start on the menu bar. (This button is round and blue-green.)

The Core1 computer starts, and the Windows Server 2008 R2 installation process begins. Perform a default installation by using the following guidelines:

- If desired, choose a language and keyboard corresponding to your region.

- Do not enter a product key at this time.

- Choose Windows Server 2008 R2 Enterprise (Server Core Installation).

- Install Windows in the default location (Disk 0 Unallocated Space).
- To log on for the first time, specify a user of Administrator with a strong password of your choice.

7. Verify the IP configuration. At the command prompt, type **ipconfig /all** to ensure that Core1 has received an IP configuration from Server1.

8. At the command prompt, type **sconfig**.

9. Use option 2 in the Server Configuration utility to change the computer name to Core1 and then agree to restart the computer.

10. Log on to Core1 as Administrator and type **sconfig** at the command prompt to start the Server Configuration utility again.

11. Use option 1 in the Server Configuration utility to join Core1 to the Contoso.local domain and then agree to restart the computer.

Phase 4: Configure Internet Access for the Contoso.local Network

In this phase, you add to Server1 a second adapter that is bound to a physical network adapter on the physical host machine. You then configure network address translation (NAT) on Server1.

Add and Configure a Second Virtual Adapter on Server1

Complete the following steps to add and configure a second virtual adapter on Server1.

1. Shut down Server1. Open Server1 settings in Hyper-V Manager.

2. In the Settings For Server1 dialog box, select Add Hardware, select Network Adapter, and then click Add. When the new Network Adapter appears in the list of hardware, assign it to the network named Host Network.

   The physical adapter on the host computer should already have its own IP address and be able to communicate with the Internet.

3. Start and log on to Server1.

4. In Server Manager, click Add Roles. Use the following information to complete the Add Roles Wizard:

   - Select Server Roles: Network Policy And Access Services
   - Select Role Services: Routing And Remote Access Services (Do not select any other role services at this time.)

Configure NAT on Server1

Use the following step-by-step instructions to configure NAT on Server1.

1. After you have installed the Routing And Remote Access Services role service, open the Routing And Remote Access administrative tool through the Start menu.

2. In the Routing And Remote Access console tree, right-click the *Server1* node and then click Configure And Enable Routing And Remote Access.

3. Specify the following settings in the Routing And Remote Access Server Setup Wizard:

   - On the Configuration page, click Network Address Translation (NAT).

   - On the NAT Internet Connection page, select Local Area Connection 2 as the public interface to connect to the Internet.

4. In Server Manager, select the *Server Manager* node. In the Security Information area of the details pane, click Configure IE ESC. Select the option to turn IE ESC off for Administrators.

5. Open Internet Explorer and select Internet Options from the Tools menu. Set the home page to an Internet-based webpage of your choice.

6. Verify Internet connectivity in Internet Explorer by clicking the Home icon.

Phase 5: Activate the Servers (Recommended)

Perform the following steps if you have product keys for both Server1 and Core1.

1. Activate Server1. Open the System Control Panel and select the option to change the product key. Type the product key when prompted and click Next.

   Windows automatically activates over the Internet.

2. Activate Core1 by using the following step-by-step procedure:

   a. Log on to contoso.local from Core1 as a domain administrator and then type the following command to install the new product key, where *productkey* is your product key (with dashes):

   ```
   slmgr -ipk productkey
   ```

   b. When you receive a message indicating that the product key was installed successfully, type the following command to activate Windows:

   ```
   slmgr -ato
   ```

EXAM TIP

You need to know these last two commands for the 70-643 exam.

---

c. After you receive a message indicating that the product has been activated successfully, you can shut down Core1 by typing the following command:

```
shutdown /s /t 0
```

Using the Companion CD

A companion CD is included with this training kit. The companion CD contains the following:

- **Practice tests** You can reinforce your understanding of how to configure Windows Server 2008 R2 by using electronic practice tests you customize to meet your needs from the pool of Lesson Review questions in this book. Alternatively, you can practice for the 70-643 certification exam by using tests created from a pool of 200 realistic exam questions, which give you many practice exams to ensure that you are prepared.

- **Webcasts and Videos** To supplement your learning, the CD includes Microsoft-sponsored webcasts and videos from experts. These webcasts and videos are lectures and demonstrations that provide additional information about subjects covered in the book.

- **An eBook** An electronic version (eBook) of this book is included for when you do not want to carry the printed book with you. The eBook is in Portable Document Format (PDF), which is viewable by using Adobe Acrobat or Adobe Reader, and in XML Paper Specification (XML).

> **NOTE   COMPANION CONTENT FOR DIGITAL BOOK READERS**
>
> If you bought a digital-only edition of this book, you can enjoy select content from the print edition's companion CD. Visit *http://go.microsoft.com/FWLink/?Linkid=220878* to get your downloadable content.

How to Install the Practice Tests

To install the practice test software from the companion CD to your hard disk, do the following:

1. Insert the companion CD into your CD drive and accept the license agreement.

   A CD menu appears.

> **NOTE   IF THE CD MENU DOES NOT APPEAR**
>
> If the CD menu or the license agreement does not appear, AutoRun might be disabled on your computer. Refer to the Readme.txt file on the CD-ROM for alternate installation instructions.

2. Click Practice Tests and follow the instructions on the screen.

How to Use the Practice Tests

To start the practice test software, follow these steps.

1. Click Start\All Programs\Microsoft Press Training Kit Exam Prep.

A window appears that shows all the Microsoft Press training kit exam prep suites installed on your computer.

2. Double-click the lesson review or practice test you want to use.

> **NOTE LESSON REVIEWS VS. PRACTICE TESTS**
>
> Select the (70-643) Configuring Windows Server 2008 Applications Infrastructure (2nd Edition) lesson review to use the questions from the "Lesson Review" sections of this book. Select the (70-643) Configuring Windows Server 2008 Applications Infrastructure (2nd Edition) practice test to use a pool of 200 questions similar to those that appear on the 70-643 certification exam.

Lesson Review Options

When you start a lesson review, the Custom Mode dialog box appears so that you can configure your test. You can click OK to accept the defaults, or you can customize the number of questions you want, how the practice test software works, the exam objectives to which you want the questions to relate, and whether you want your lesson review to be timed. If you are retaking a test, you can select whether you want to see all the questions again or only the questions you missed or did not answer.

After you click OK, your lesson review starts.

- To take the test, answer the questions and use the *Next* and *Previous* buttons to move from question to question.

- After you answer an individual question, if you want to see which answers are correct—along with an explanation of each correct answer—click Explanation.

- If you prefer to wait until the end of the test to see how you did, answer all the questions and then click Score Test. You will see a summary of the exam objectives you chose and the percentage of questions you got right overall and per objective. You can print a copy of your test, review your answers, or retake the test.

Practice Test Options

When you start a practice test, you choose whether to take the test in Certification Mode, Study Mode, or Custom Mode.

- **Certification Mode**   Closely resembles the experience of taking a certification exam. The test has a set number of questions. It is timed, and you cannot pause and restart the timer.

- **Study Mode**   Creates an untimed test in which you can review the correct answers and the explanations after you answer each question.

- **Custom Mode**   Gives you full control over the test options so that you can customize them as you like.

In all modes, the user interface when you are taking the test is basically the same but with different options enabled or disabled, depending on the mode. The main options are discussed in the previous section, "Lesson Review Options."

When you review your answer to an individual practice test question, a "References" section is provided that lists where in the training kit you can find the information that relates to that question and provides links to other sources of information. After you click Test Results to score your entire practice test, you can click the Learning Plan tab to see a list of references for every objective.

How to Uninstall the Practice Tests

To uninstall the practice test software for a training kit, use the Programs And Features option in Windows Control Panel.

Support & Feedback

The following sections provide information on errata, book support, feedback, and contact information.

Errata

We have made every effort to ensure the accuracy of this book and its companion content. Any errors that have been reported since this book was published are listed on our Microsoft Press site at oreilly.com:

http://go.microsoft.com/FWLink/?Linkid=220879

If you find an error that is not already listed, you can report it to us through the same page.

If you need additional support, please email Microsoft Press Book Support at *mspinput@microsoft.com*.

Please note that product support for Microsoft software is not offered through the addresses above.

We Want to Hear from You

At Microsoft Press, your satisfaction is our top priority, and your feedback our most valuable asset. Please tell us what you think of this book at:

http://www.microsoft.com/learning/booksurvey

The survey is short, and we read every one of your comments and ideas. Thanks in advance for your input!

Stay in Touch

Let us keep the conversation going! We are on Twitter: *http://twitter.com/MicrosoftPress*.

Preparing for the Exam

Microsoft certification exams are a great way to build your résumé and let the world know about your level of expertise. Certification exams validate your on-the-job experience and product knowledge. While there is no substitution for on-the-job experience, preparation through study and hands-on practice can help you prepare for the exam. We recommend that you round out your exam preparation plan by using a combination of available study materials and courses. For example, you might use the Training kit and another study guide for your "at home" preparation, and take a Microsoft Official Curriculum course for the classroom experience. Choose the combination that you think works best for you.

Note that this Training Kit is based on publicly available information about the exam and the author's experience. To safeguard the integrity of the exam, authors do not have access to the live exam.

Microsoft
C E R T I F I E D
Technology
Specialist

CHAPTER 1

Implementing and Configuring a Windows Deployment Infrastructure

Windows deployment has changed dramatically since Windows Server 2003. New deployment technologies have appeared, such as ImageX and Windows Deployment Services, along with new considerations such as deploying virtual machines and implementing a Windows activation infrastructure. Consequently, there is much to learn about the seemingly elementary topic of Windows deployment, even for experienced Windows administrators. This chapter introduces you to the many new deployment technologies and concepts you need to understand for both real-world deployment and the 70-643 exam.

> **IMPORTANT**
> ### *Have you read page xxx?*
> It contains valuable information regarding the skills you need to pass the exam.

Exam objectives in this chapter:

- Deploy images by using Windows Deployment Services.
- Configure Microsoft Windows activation.
- Configure Windows Server Hyper-V and virtual machines.

Lessons in this chapter:

Before You Begin

To complete the lessons in this chapter, you must have:

- A domain controller named Server1.contoso.local with at least 3 GB of free space on any partition or volume.

- A computer or virtual machine with no operating system installed and at least 1024 MB of RAM. (This bare-metal computer will be used for Server2.)

- Downloaded the Windows Automated Installation Kit (AIK) for Windows 7 from the Microsoft Download Center (*http://www.microsoft.com/download*) and installed the Windows AIK on Server1.

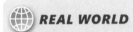

REAL WORLD

J.C. Mackin

There are certain times when the exam world and the real world diverge in a big way, and that's certainly the case with Windows deployment. It's not tested on the 70-643 exam, but the Microsoft Deployment Toolkit 2010 (MDT 2010) is a great free download that is frequently used to automate the deployment of Windows onto many client computers. MDT 2010 sets up distribution shares with optional customizations, and then it helps you create a boot CD that automatically connects to those shares and starts installing Windows with your applications. MDT 2010 is actually one of the easiest ways to deploy Windows in a small or medium-sized organization, and you can make the process even easier by combining MDT 2010 with Windows Deployment Services for increased automation.

If you need to deploy Windows in your organization, or if you just want to find out more about MDT 2010, I highly recommend that you watch the two MDT-related videos in the Videos folder of the companion CD, SMB_AutomatedInstallation.wmv and WDS_MDT2010.wmv (in that order). Be sure to visit *http://technet.microsoft .com/en-us/windows/dd320282.aspx* for other great videos related to Windows deployment. And to download MDT 2010, visit *http://download.microsoft.com*. (At the time of writing, the latest version of this solution accelerator is MDT 2010 Update 1.)

Lesson 1: Deploying Windows in a Windows Server 2008 R2 Environment

You can deploy new Windows clients and servers in a number of ways. All Windows deployment methods since Windows Vista, however—including basic installation from CD—are now based on imaging technology. To deploy Windows images, you can use the installation media (DVD), Windows imaging tools such as ImageX and Microsoft System Center Configuration Manager 2007 R3, or the Windows Deployment Services server role built into Windows Server 2008 R2.

> **After this lesson, you will be able to:**
>
> - Understand the tools that can help you manage, edit, and deploy Windows images.
> - Understand the various methods to deploy Windows 7 and Windows Server 2008 R2.
> - Create a Windows PE CD.
>
> **Estimated lesson time: 50 minutes**

Windows Deployment Fundamentals

Since Windows Vista, operating system deployment in Windows networks relies on a set of deployment tools and processes based on a file format called Windows Imaging Format (WIM) and a lightweight version of Windows called Windows PE. Many of these new tools, such as ImageX, Windows SIM, and Copype.cmd, are made available in a free toolkit called the Windows Automated Installation Toolkit (AIK). In Windows 7 and Windows Server 2008 R2, support for WIM images and Windows PE has been expanded through a new tool called Dism.exe.

Understanding WIM Files

A *WIM file* contains one or more disk images in the WIM format. Windows images are *file-based*. This type of image isn't a sector-based snapshot of disk data, as is common with most disk image types. Instead, Windows images are copies of the complete set of files that make up a volume. The main advantage of file-based images over sector-based images is that you can modify them before, during, and after deployment.

Besides storing file data, WIM files include XML-based metadata describing the files and directories that make up each image. This metadata includes access control lists (ACLs), short/long file names, attributes, and other information to restore an imaged volume. Figure 1-1 shows the metadata associated with a specific WIM file.

FIGURE 1-1 Viewing WIM file information.

WIM files offer a number of advantageous features for Windows deployment, including the following:

- Because the WIM image format is hardware-agnostic, you need only one image to support many hardware configurations or hardware abstraction layers (HALs). (Separate images, however, are needed for x86 and 64-bit operating systems.)

- WIM files enable you to customize images by using scripts or automate them by using answer files upon installation.

- The WIM image format enables you to modify the contents of an image offline. You can add or delete certain operating system components, updates, and drivers without creating a new image.

- WIM files need to keep only one copy of disk files common to all the images stored in the file. This feature dramatically reduces the amount of storage space required to accommodate multiple images.

- You can start a computer from a disk image contained in a WIM file by marking an image as bootable.

- The WIM image format allows for nondestructive deployment. This means that you can leave data on the same volume to which you apply the image because the application of the image does not erase the disk's existing contents.

- A WIM file image uses only as much space as the files that comprise it. Therefore, you can use WIM files to capture data on a volume with empty space and then migrate the data to a smaller volume.

- A WIM file can span multiple CDs or DVDs.

- WIM files support two types of compression—Xpress (fast compression) and LZX (high compression)—in addition to no compression, which is fastest.

Understanding Boot and Install Images

The \sources folder on every Windows product DVD since Windows Vista contains two images: a default boot image (Boot.wim) and a default install image (Install.wim). A *boot image* is a relatively small Windows image (.wim) file you can use to start a bare-metal client computer and begin the installation of an operating system. By contrast, an install image contains the actual Windows operating system to be installed. Whether you deploy Windows through installation DVDs or over the network, you can customize these boot and install images to suit the needs of your organization and network.

The default boot and install images found on the Windows Server 2008 R2 product DVD are shown in Figure 1-2. Note the difference in the sizes of these two files.

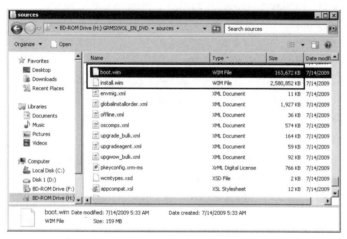

FIGURE 1-2 The default boot and install images are found in the \sources folder on the Windows Server 2008 R2 DVD.

Windows Automated Installation Kit Tools

The latest version of the Windows AIK is called the Windows AIK for Windows 7, which you can download from the Microsoft Download Center at *http://www.microsoft.com/downloads*. The Windows AIK for Windows 7 provides tools and documentation for performing unattended installs of Windows Vista, Windows 7, Windows Server 2003 R2 SP2, Windows Server 2008, and Windows Server 2008 R2. You can also use the Windows AIK for Windows 7 to help deploy Windows 7 SP1 and Windows Server 2008 R2 SP1, as long as you do not want to modify the default boot.wim and winre.wim files on these operating systems. To create custom images of Windows 7 SP1 and Windows Server 2008 R2 SP1, you should install an optional add-on called the Windows Automated Installation Kit (AIK) Supplement for Windows 7 SP1, also available from the Microsoft Download Center.

The Windows AIK includes several important deployment tools, including the following:

- **Windows Preinstallation Environment (Windows PE) 3**   The Windows AIK for Windows 7 helps you create a Windows PE 3.0 CD by using tools such as Copype.cmd and Oscdimg.exe. (If you install the Windows AIK Supplement for Windows SP1, the version is Windows PE 3.1.) Windows PE is a lightweight and customizable version of Windows with which you can start a computer from a CD/DVD, from a removable USB drive, or from a network source. Installations of Windows PE vary in size, but a typical installation requires about 200 MB of storage space.

   The main purpose of Windows PE is to provide an environment from which to capture or apply a Windows image, but you can also use it to troubleshoot or recover an installed operating system or to perform any specialized function. Windows PE can run many familiar (typically command-line) programs and even communicate over IP networks. If you start a computer from a typical Windows PE disk, a command prompt appears from which you can run built-in tools and other programs you have made available through customization.

> **NOTE** **WINDOWS SETUP AND WINDOWS PE**
>
> The default Boot.wim file on a Windows product DVD includes a version of Windows PE. Whenever you start from the product DVD and run the Setup program, Windows PE is actually running in the background.

   Although Windows PE starts from the CD drive, Windows PE 3 does not actually run from the CD when it is fully started. Windows PE 3 instead creates a RAM disk (a portion of RAM used as a drive), loads the operating system into that drive, and then runs from that RAM disk. This RAM disk is assigned the drive letter X by default. From this command prompt, you can then run various tools and utilities, many of which can be added through optional packages.

- **ImageX**   ImageX is a command-line utility you can use to capture, modify, and apply WIM images for deployment. The main function of ImageX is to enable you to capture a volume to a WIM file image and apply a WIM file image to a volume. For example, to capture an image, you can start Windows PE and use the *Imagex.exe /capture* path *wimfilename.wim "Image_Name"* command, by which "path" is the path to the file. To apply an image to a volume, use *Imagex /apply* path*wimfilename.wim 1*. (In this case, the value *1* indicates the index number of a particular image stored in the wimfilename.wim file.)

- **Windows SIM**   Windows System Image Manager (SIM) is the tool used to create unattended Windows Setup answer files. In Windows Vista, Windows 7, Windows Server 2008, and Windows Server 2008 R2, answer files are XML-based documents used during Windows setup to supply information needed by the Windows installation. For example, you can use Windows SIM to create an answer file that partitions and formats a disk before installing Windows or that changes the default setting for the

Internet Explorer home page. By modifying settings in the answer file, you can also use Windows SIM to install third-party applications, device drivers, language packs, and other updates.

> **NOTE WINDOWS SIM VS. SETUP MANAGER**
>
> As a means to create answer files for unattended installations, Windows SIM replaces the Setup Manager tool used in Windows XP, Windows Server 2003, and earlier versions of Windows.

Windows SIM uses catalog (.clg) files along with Windows images (WIM files) to display the available components and packages that can be added to an unattended answer file. Catalog files and WIM files contain configurable settings that you can modify after the component or package is added to an answer file. Figure 1-3 shows the Windows SIM tool.

FIGURE 1-3 Windows SIM.

Sysprep

Sysprep is a tool in the *%SystemRoot%*\System32\Sysprep folder of every Windows installation since Windows Vista. The purpose of Sysprep is to generalize a model computer installation image so that it can be used on many other computers. Sysprep achieves this generalization by removing only those settings of the model installation that should not be shared by other computers—settings such as the computer name, its domain membership, the time zone, the product key, the security identifier (SID), and various other user and machine settings. When you run Sysprep on an installation of Windows, a Sysprep image is generated, and the installation is said to be *Sysprepped*.

After you run Sysprep, the computer shuts down. The Sysprepped installation then resides on the hard disk, ready to be captured by ImageX or Windows Deployment Services into a WIM file and deployed to other computers.

The settings removed by Sysprep need to be replaced on each computer that uses the Sysprepped image. Some of these settings (such as the computer SID) are automatically regenerated when the installation starts for the first time after Sysprep has run. Other settings might be provided by an answer file you configure in advance and supply when the Sysprepped image first starts. All remaining settings the system needs are provided by the user in an interactive wizard that appears during the first restart after Sysprep is run.

Deployment Image Servicing and Management (Dism.exe)

Dism is a command-line utility that is new in Windows 7 and Windows Server 2008 R2. It enables you to modify Windows images before deployment. With Dism, you can mount an image offline and then add, remove, update, or list the features, packages, drivers, or international settings stored on that image. You can also use certain Dism commands to service an online image—in other words, the current (active) operating system. As a utility, Dism consolidates and replaces the features of PEimg, Intlcfg, and Package Manager, which were available on earlier versions of Windows AIK.

Dism is a powerful utility with many functions and options. The following list presents some of its main uses:

- Mount, unmount, or get information about a Windows image

  You can use /Mount-Wim to mount a Windows image in the Windows file structure. After it is mounted, you can make changes to the image. For example, the following command mounts the first image within a WIM file named install.wim in the C:\test\ offline directory.

  ```
  Dism /Mount-Wim /WimFile:C:\test\images\install.wim /index:1 /MountDir:C:\test\
  offline
  ```

  After servicing an image, you might want to save any changes you have made while the file is still mounted in the file structure. To do so, use /Commit-Wim. For example, the following command commits changes made to the image mounted in C:\test\offline.

  ```
  Dism /Commit-Wim /MountDir:C:\test\offline
  ```

  To unmount an image, use /Unmount-Wim. You can also specify the /Commit or / Discard argument to save or discard unsaved changes made to the image when it was mounted. The following example unmounts the file mounted in C:\test\offline and commits any changes made since the image was last saved.

  ```
  Dism /Unmount-Wim /MountDir:C:\test\offline /commit
  ```

  To get information about an image or WIM file, use /Get-WimInfo. The following example gets information about the first image in a file named install.wim.

  ```
  Dism /Get-WimInfo /WimFile:C:\test\offline\install.wim /index:1
  ```

- Add a package to or remove a package from an image

  Packages are .cab files that can be installed into a Windows image and that add feature sets to that image. If you have installed Windows AIK, you can find many such packages built for Windows PE images in the C:\Program Files\Windows AIK\Tools\ PETools\amd64\WinPE_FPs\ folder. Packages in this folder include WinPE-WMI.cab, which enables some system diagnostics for a Windows PE image through the Windows Management Instrumentation interface, and WinPE-WDS-Tools, which adds Windows Deployment Services tools to the image.

  To add a package, use /AddPackage. For example, the following command adds the Package1.cab package to the image mounted in C:\test\offline.

  ```
  Dism /image:C:\test\offline /Add-Package /PackagePath:C:\packages\package1.cab
  ```

  To remove a package, use /RemovePackage. For example, the following command removes the Package1.cab package from the image mounted in C:\test\offline:

  ```
  Dism /image:C:\test\offline /Remove-Package /PackagePath:C:\packages\package1.cab
  ```

- Add or remove a device driver

  You can use the *Dism* command with the /Add-Driver option to add third-party device drivers to a Windows image. When you use the /Driver option to point to a folder, INF files that are not valid driver packages are ignored. If you point to a path and use /Recurse, all subfolders are queried for drivers to add. For example, the following command adds all the drivers found in the C:\test\drivers directory and its subdirectories to the image mounted in C:\test\offline. Invalid driver packages will be ignored.

  ```
  Dism /image:C:\test\offline /Add-Driver /driver:C:\test\drivers /recurse
  ```

  To remove a third-party device driver, use /Remove-Driver. When they are added to an image, third-party device drivers are named Oem0.inf, Oem1.inf, and so on. To remove a third-party driver, you must specify such a name. For example, the following command removes the second third-party driver added to the system:

  ```
  Dism /image:C:\test\offline /Remove-Driver /driver:oem1.inf
  ```

- Modify international settings

  You can use /Set-UILang with the *Dism* command to set the default user interface language. The language must also be installed in the Windows image, or this command will fail. Use the following command, for example, to set the default user interface language to French on the image mounted in C:\test\offline.

  ```
  Dism /image:C:\test\offline /Set-UILang:fr-FR
  ```

MORE INFO **LEARN MORE ABOUT** *DISM*

For more information about the features and functions of *Dism*, visit *http://technet .microsoft.com/en-us/library/dd744256(WS.10).aspx*.

Windows Deployment Methods

Deployment technologies in a Windows Server 2008 R2 network help deploy both Windows clients and Windows servers. The following section discusses deployment methods that relate to both Windows client and server technologies.

Windows 7 and Windows Server 2008 R2 are typically deployed in one of four ways: by means of the product DVD, a network share (optionally with the help of Windows AIK and, potentially, Microsoft Deployment Toolkit 2010), Windows Deployment Services, or System Center Configuration Manager 2007 R3. Each of these four methods offers an increasing level of automation, but each method also requires an increasing amount of resources, expertise, and preparation. The most suitable method for you to use depends on the resources you have available, the size of your organization, and the number of deployments you need to make.

Installing from the Product DVD

Often, the easiest way to deploy Windows onto a single computer is to run the Setup program from the Windows product DVD. You can automate installation from a DVD by supplying an answer file named Autounattend.xml at the root of an accessible USB Flash Device (UFD) drive or floppy disk when you begin the program. This deployment method is most suitable when no high-bandwidth connection to the destination computer is available (as might be the case in a branch office), when you are deploying Windows to a small number of computers, and when no IT personnel are available at the site of the target computer. Compared to other automated forms of deployment, this deployment method also requires the least amount of technical preparation, resources, and expertise at both source and destination sites.

Deploying Windows by means of the product DVD does have significant limitations, however. First, it requires more interaction on the part of nontechnical end users than is ideal for operating system installations. Even if you send users an answer file through email, for example, the users must be guided to place this answer file at the root of a UFD or floppy disk and restart the computer with that disk and the product DVD loaded. A second limitation of the media distribution method is that it does not allow for any additional drivers or updates (called configuration sets) to be installed as part of Setup without significant technical expertise at the site of the end user. Finally, the physical media must be distributed to every target computer, so installation can occur simultaneously on only as many computers as the number of product DVDs you have available.

Network Share Distribution

You can deploy installations of Windows Vista, Windows 7, Windows Server 2008, and Windows Server 2008 R2 from a network share by using the Windows Setup program, by applying a WIM file image, or by using Microsoft Deployment Toolkit 2010.

In the first method, the contents of the Windows product media are stored on the network share. You can then either keep the default version of Install.wim or replace it (and associated catalog files) with an image of your own custom-configured master installation. Setup is then launched from the command prompt in Windows PE on the local computer. You can use the /unattend switch to specify an answer file if desired. For example, if you have mapped a drive Y to the network share containing the installation files and saved a deploy_unattend.xml answer file in the same share, you could start the local computer by means of Windows PE and type the following: **Y:\setup.exe /unattend:deploy_unattend.xml**.

In the second method, you store a captured WIM file image of a Sysprepped master installation on a network share. You can then keep an answer file inside the installation in the following location: *%SystemRoot%*\Panther\Unattend. (The name of the answer file must be Unattend.xml or Autounattend.xml.) Finally, on the target computer, you can apply the Windows image by using Windows PE and ImageX. For example, if you have mapped a drive Y to the network share containing the WIM file images, you would start the local computer by using Windows PE and type the following: **Imagex /apply Y:\myimage.wim 1 c:**.

In the third method, you download Microsoft Deployment Toolkit 2010 Update 1 (MDT 2010) from the Microsoft website and install this software on a selected computer (called a *technician computer*) that stores deployment files on network shares. MDT 2010 includes a Deployment Workbench interface that helps configure installations through network shares and enables you to include extra applications, packages, and drivers as part of an automated network deployment. Finally, MDT 2010 enables you to create a boot CD for clients that automatically connects to the technician computer and makes installation relatively easy for nontechnical users.

Deploying Windows through a network share is a suitable solution when sufficient bandwidth exists to copy very large files across the network, when you need to deploy only a small number of computers (between five and 20), and when the network environment does not include an Active Directory domain service (AD DS) domain or the System Center Configuration Manager 2007 R3 network management application.

The main disadvantage of this method is that it is not completely automated: It requires someone to be present at the site of the target computer who will start Windows PE and either run appropriate commands or, in the case of MDT 2010, choose appropriate selections and enter appropriate credentials in the deployment wizard. Unlike Windows Deployment Services (WDS), this solution does not automatically begin deployment from starting a bare-metal computer without using a special CD and without knowing any network credentials. Unlike System Center Configuration Manager 2007 R3, this solution does not allow an administrator to push an operating system automatically to a remote computer without anyone present at that computer.

Windows Deployment Services

WDS enables an end user without any technical expertise to start a computer with no operating system and simply select a Windows image to install from a menu. To achieve this, the computer relies on a pre-startup execution environment (PXE) startup process. PXE is a technology that uses Dynamic Host Configuration Protocol (DHCP) to locate a specially configured network server during a computer's startup phase.

WDS is a far more scalable and manageable solution than is simply storing WIM files on a network. However, WDS does have fairly extensive infrastructure requirements:

- **AD DS**   A Windows Deployment Services server must be either a member of an Active Directory domain or a domain controller for an Active Directory domain. The Active Directory domain and forest versions are irrelevant; all domain and forest configurations support Windows Deployment Services.

- **Dynamic Host Configuration Protocol**   You must have a working DHCP server with an active scope on the network because Windows Deployment Services uses PXE, which in turn uses DHCP. The DHCP server does not have to be on the Windows Deployment Services server, but it (or a DHCP relay agent) does need to be on the same subnet as the client.

- **Domain Name System**   A working Domain Name System (DNS) server on the network is required to run Windows Deployment Services. The DNS server does not have to be running on the Windows Deployment Services server.

- **NTFS volume**   The server running Windows Deployment Services requires an NTFS file system volume for the image store.

- **A high-speed, persistent connection between the WDS servers and the target computers**   Such a connection is necessary because of the size of the images being distributed to the target computers. In addition, these servers should be on subnets adjacent to the target computers to ensure high-speed connectivity.

Aside from the extensive infrastructure requirements of WDS, another limitation of this deployment solution is that it requires end-user participation. The administrator cannot simply choose to push an operating system to any computer in the organization.

As a result of these limitations, WDS does not scale well to the largest corporate networks with multiple Active Directory domains, IP subnets, or physical sites.

Quick Check

- What are the server and infrastructure requirements for WDS?

Quick Check Answer

- Windows Server 2008 with WDS installed; Active Directory directory service; DNS; DHCP; an NTFS volume; and a persistent, high-speed connection.

System Center Configuration Manager 2007 R3

When used in conjunction with the other deployment methods, System Center Configuration Manager 2007 R3 enables you to create a fully managed deployment solution for large organizations. Unlike other deployment options, System Center Configuration Manager 2007 R3 allows for a completely unattended operating system deployment to remote computers.

System Center Configuration Manager 2007 R3 assists with the many tasks involved when you apply automated procedures to multiple servers and client computers, tasks such as:

- Selecting computers that have the hardware necessary for a given operating system and that you are ready to support.
- Distributing the operating system source files to all sites, including remote sites and sites without technical support staff.
- Monitoring the distribution to all sites.
- Providing the appropriate user rights for the upgrade.
- Automatically initiating the installation of software packages, with the possibility of having users control the timing.
- Resolving problems related to the distributions or installations.
- Reporting on the rate and success of deployment.
- Verifying that all computers in your organization have received the standardized operating system configuration.

Deploying Windows 7 or Windows Server 2008 R2 with System Center Configuration Manager 2007 R3 requires a high-speed, persistent connection between the servers and target computers used in the deployment process. Such a connection is necessary because of the large size of the images being distributed to the target computers.

Among the disadvantages of System Center Configuration Manager 2007 R3 is, first, that unlike the other deployment methods mentioned, it is a separate product requiring a purchase beyond Windows Server 2008 or Windows Server 2008 R2. In addition, installing and configuring a System Center Configuration Manager 2007 R3 infrastructure requires significant technical expertise. A third disadvantage of System Center Configuration Manager 2007 R3 is that, unlike WDS, you can't use it to deploy an operating system onto a bare-metal system without using bootable media. The target system requires the System Center Configuration Manager 2007 client software or is booted by using other bootable media. (Because of this last limitation, in fact, System Center Configuration Manager 2007 R3 is typically used in conjunction with WDS and not as a replacement for it.)

In this practice, you create a bootable Windows PE CD from which you can capture or apply native Windows images. This practice requires you to have installed the Windows AIK on the C drive on Server1.

EXERCISE   Creating a Windows PE CD

In this exercise, you create a Windows PE CD with which you can later start a computer and use tools such as ImageX.

1. On Server1, click Start, All Programs, and Windows AIK; right-click Deployment Tools Command Prompt and then select Run As Administrator.

2. At the Windows PE Tools command prompt, type the following:

   ```
   copype amd64 C:\WinPE_amd64
   ```

> **NOTE** **CREATING A WINDOWS PE CD FOR USE ON AN IA64 OR X86 COMPUTER**
>
> The syntax for the preceding command applies only to a system with an AMD64 compatible processor. If your computer is running on an Itanium 64 processor, you should type the following command instead: copype ia64 C:\WinPE_ia64. In this case, you should also replace all instances of "amd64" with "ia64" in the following steps. Note also that, in this context, you are creating the Windows PE CD for use on a computer that can host Windows Server 2008 R2, which must be a 64-bit machine. However, if you need to create a Windows PE CD for an x86 system, you can type the following command instead: copype x86 C:\WinPE_x86.

The Copype.cmd script creates the following directory structure:

```
\WinPE_amd64
```

```
\WinPE_amd64\ISO
```

```
\WinPE_amd64\Mount
```

The root WinPE_amd64 directory contains the base Windows PE image, or .wim file, which is named winpe.wim. The ISO subdirectory contains the eventual contents of the Windows PE CD and includes only startup information by default. The Mount directory is empty by default. It mounts the winpe.wim image into the Windows file structure so that you can modify it by adding or removing files, by adding or removing packages, or by changing settings.

3. Mount the base WinPE.wim image in the Mount folder by typing the following command at the Windows PE Tools command prompt:

   ```
   dism /Mount-Wim /WimFile:C:\WinPE_amd64\winpe.wim /Index:1 /MountDir:C:\WinPE_amd64\mount
   ```

Wait for the image to be mounted. After it is mounted, you can add packages to the mounted image.

4. Type the following command to add disk tools for Windows Deployment Services:

```
dism /image:C:\WinPE_amd64\mount /Add-Package /PackagePath:"C:\Program Files\
Windows AIK\Tools\PETools\amd64\WinPE_FPs\winpe-wds-tools.cab"
```

The package takes a few moments to be installed on the mounted image.

5. Unmount the image and commit the changes by typing the following command:

```
dism /Unmount-Wim /MountDir:C:\WinPE_amd64\mount\ /Commit
```

The process of saving the changes and unmounting the image takes several moments to complete.

6. Copy the newly customized WIM file to the ISO\sources folder by typing the following command:

```
copy C:\WinPE_amd64\winpe.wim C:\WinPE_amd64\ISO\sources\boot.wim
```

Now, you can add any additional tools you want to include on the Windows PE CD.

7. Add the ImageX utility to the ISO folder by typing the following command:

```
Copy "C:\Program Files\Windows AIK\Tools\amd64\imagex.exe" C:\WinPE_amd64\
ISO
```

8. In Notepad, create an empty file named **Wimscript.ini** and save it to the C:\WinPE_amd64\ISO folder.

9. Enter the following text into Wimscript.ini and then save the file again.

```
[ExclusionList]
ntfs.log
hiberfil.sys
pagefile.sys
"System Volume Information"
RECYCLER
Windows\CSC

[CompressionExclusionList]
*.mp3
*.zip
*.cab
\Windows\inf\*.pnf
```

The [ExclusionList] section in the Wimscript.ini file specifies which files should not be captured when you are performing an image capture by using the ImageX tool. The [CompressionExclusionList] section of Wimscript.ini specifies which files or file types should not be compressed when you are compressing an image by using the ImageX tool.

Now you can make the .iso file.

10. At the Windows PE Tools command prompt, type the following line:

```
Oscdimg -n -bC:\WinPE_amd64\etfsboot.com C:\WinPE_amd64\ISO
C:\WinPE_amd64\WinPE_amd64.iso
```

The *Oscdimg* command makes an .iso file of the specified ISO directory. The –b switch makes the eventual Windows PE CD bootable ble to start by specifying the location of the boot sector file, etfsboot.com. There is no space after the –b switch. (The *C* that follows the switch is the drive letter in the path to etfsboot.com.) Finally, the –n switch in *Oscdimg* enables long file names in the .iso file.

> **NOTE USE EFISYS.BIN FOR IA64**
>
> If you are creating the Windows PE CD for use on an IA64 system, type the following command instead: `Oscdimg -n -bc:\WinPE_ia64\efisys.bin c:\WinPE_ia64\ISO c:\WinPE_ia64\WinPE_ia64.iso.`

11. (Optional) Insert a blank CD-R into a local disc drive and then burn the new .iso file to a CD by right-clicking the WinPE_amd64.iso file and selecting Burn Disc Image. (If this option does not appear in the shortcut menu, choose Open With and then select Windows Disc Image Burner.)

Lesson Summary

- In a network made up of clients running Windows Vista or Windows 7 and servers running Windows Server 2008 or Windows Server 2008 R2, you can deploy new clients and servers in a number of ways, and all these methods—including basic installation—are based on WIM files.

- A WIM file is a file containing one or more disk images in the native Windows imaging format. WIM files are file-based and, therefore, can be modified before, during, and after deployment.

- The Windows AIK is an ISO file you can download from the Microsoft website; it includes several important deployment tools, including Windows PE, ImageX, and Windows SIM.

- Sysprep is a tool found in the *%SystemRoot%*\System32\Sysprep folder of a Windows Vista or Windows Server 2008 installation. The purpose of Sysprep is to generalize a model computer installation image so that it can be used on many other computers.

- Dism is a new command-line utility in Windows 7 and Windows Server 2008 R2 that enables you to mount images in the Windows file structure and service them by modifying settings, adding or removing packages, or adding or removing drivers.

Lesson Review

The following questions are intended to reinforce key information presented in this lesson. The questions are also available on the companion CD if you prefer to review them in electronic form.

> **NOTE ANSWERS**
>
> The answers to these questions and explanations of why each answer choice is correct or incorrect are located in the "Answers" section at the end of the book.

1. Which of the following tools can be used to generalize a master installation to prepare it for having its image captured for use in image-based deployment?

    A. Windows PE

    B. ImageX

    C. Sysprep

    D. Windows SIM

2. You want to modify an existing Windows image by adding a third-party device driver. Which tool should you use?

    A. ImageX

    B. Windows SIM

    C. Windows PE

    D. Dism

3. Which of the following is not a network requirement for the Deployment Server role service of Windows Deployment Services?

    A. Public key infrastructure

    B. Active Directory Domain Services

    C. DHCP server

    D. DNS server

Lesson 2: Configuring Windows Deployment Services

WDS is a server role in Windows Server 2008 and Windows Server 2008 R2 that enables you to deploy Windows easily over the network. When you configure WDS, a bare-metal client with a PXE-compatible network adapter will automatically connect to the WDS server and display a menu of operating systems available for installation.

WDS was introduced in Windows Server 2008 as an improved version of Remote Installation Services (RIS). In Windows Server 2008 R2, WDS is improved even more by the addition of new features such as driver deployment.

After this lesson, you will be able to:

- Deploy Windows images by using Windows Deployment Services.

Estimated lesson time: 120 minutes

Introducing Windows Deployment Services

WDS is a server-based technology for deploying Windows over the network and onto bare-metal computers. The WDS server stores Windows images, and bare-metal clients locate the WDS server during the startup phase by using either remote client boot disks or PXE, a DHCP-based technology most network cards use. You can also use WDS to manage and customize images, which makes WDS a good choice for organizations that have high-volume deployments requiring a lot of customization.

NOTE **WHAT IS PXE?**

PXE enables you to start a computer from a network card and to have that network card immediately begin broadcasting DHCP-based queries as the computer starts. When the DHCP server gives the network card an address, it can also refer the PXE client to a WDS server, which then makes an operating system available to the client over the network.

Comparing WDS to Windows AIK Tools

WDS provides a graphical user interface that eliminates the need to use some Windows AIK tools directly. For example, you can use WDS (instead of ImageX) to capture and deploy images onto computers. However, familiarity with the Windows AIK tools increases the power of WDS. You can use Windows SIM, for instance, to create answer files to automate your WDS deployments.

Performing automated Windows deployment by using the Windows AIK requires a large degree of manual configuration and customization. Alternatively, WDS provides an easy-to-use management console that simplifies many of these configuration and customization tasks. Also, by using the Wdsutil command-line utility, you can automate many WDS tasks by scripting them. Finally, as a server-based solution, WDS makes it easy to manage large numbers of customized boot and install images. Windows AIK, by comparison, provides no native framework for managing such images—you must create and maintain this framework manually.

Advantages of WDS

WDS has several advantages that can make it a good choice for a deployment solution for many organizations. First, as a server-based solution, WDS makes it easier to centralize and manage all aspects of the deployment process, including capturing, customizing, maintaining, updating, and installing images. Such centralization helps reduce the complexity of the deployment process, and can therefore also help reduce the cost and effort of such deployments. Second, the Windows Server 2008 R2 version of WDS supports deploying any of the following operating systems: Windows Server 2008 R2, Windows Server 2008, Windows 7, Windows Vista with SP1, Windows Server 2003, and Windows XP. If you have a mixed environment containing both current and earlier Windows platforms, you need only one deployment infrastructure to maintain them. Third, the Windows Server 2008 R2 version of WDS includes enhancements to the Trivial File Transfer Protocol (TFTP) and multicast support that enable very large environments to deploy Windows without overwhelming ordinary network usage.

Understanding WDS Infrastructure Components

Before you deploy the Windows Deployment Services server role in your environment, you must take steps to prepare your environment. These steps differ, depending on which WDS role service you are deploying. During installation of the Windows Deployment Services server role, you have a choice of two role services:

- **Deployment Server** This role service provides the full functionality of WDS and enables you to create and customize images and deploy them remotely onto bare-metal systems. If you choose to deploy this role service, you must first have deployed Active Directory Domain Services (AD DS), a DNS server, and a DHCP server on your network. (You can install these services on a single server, but if you include a DHCP server on the WDS server, you will have to choose a special option during WDS installation.)

- **Transport Server** This role service provides only a subset of WDS functionality and can be used to create custom solutions using stand-alone deployment servers and multicast addressing. You do not require AD DS, a DNS server, or a DHCP server to support this role service.

  Although the Transport Server role service has fewer infrastructure requirements than the Deployment Server role service does, the Transport Server role service is intended for advanced scenarios and requires special customization to function as a deployment solution. This chapter, therefore, focuses only on using the Deployment Server role service of WDS for deploying Windows.

- **Server components** These are located on the WDS server itself and include an image repository that contains boot images, install images, and other files needed for remote installation over a network; a PXE server to enable the remote computer to start remotely with no operating system; a TFTP server to enable the remote computer to download and install an operating system image from the image repository; a networking layer that includes support for multicasting image files over the network; and a diagnostic component that ties into the Windows eventing infrastructure of Windows Server 2008 R2.

- **Client components** These include a graphical user interface that runs within Windows PE and enables a user to select the operating system image to be installed on the remote computer. After the selection is made, the client components then request and download the appropriate image from the image repository on the WDS server.

- **Management components** These include the Windows Deployment Services console found in the Administrative Tools program group, the Wdsutil command-line utility, and other tools.

Installing WDS

The simplest way of installing the WDS role is to use the Add Roles Wizard. To launch this wizard from Server Manager, right-click the *Roles* node and then select Add Roles. If the Before You Begin page appears, click Next. When the Select Server Roles page appears, select the Windows Deployment Services option and click Next (Figure 1-4).

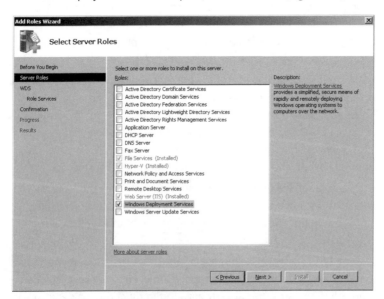

FIGURE 1-4 Adding the Windows Deployment Services role.

The Overview Of Windows Deployment Services page appears next; it provides a brief overview of what WDS is about and includes links to additional information on installing, configuring, and managing the role.

Clicking Next brings up the Select Role Services page (Figure 1-5). This is where you can specify whether your WDS server will function as a deployment server or as a transport server. If you choose the Deployment Server option, you must also select Transport Server because the former role depends upon the latter for its operation.

To finish the wizard, click Next, review the changes that will be made on your server, and then click Install to begin the installation.

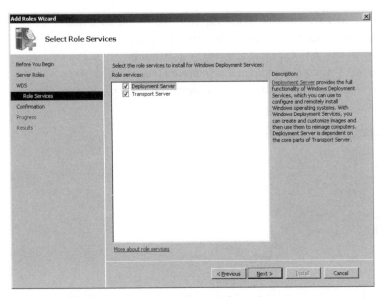

FIGURE 1-5 Installing the Deployment Server role service.

Configuring WDS

To begin deploying Windows over the network, you must configure the WDS server. The following sections describe some of the more common WDS configuration tasks, including performing initial server configuration, adding default startup and install images, and configuring the boot menu.

Performing Initial Server Configuration in the WDS Console

To perform the initial configuration of your WDS server, open the Windows Deployment Services console from the Administrative Tools program group, right-click the node representing your server, and select Configure Server (Figure 1-6). This launches the Windows Deployment Services Configuration Wizard, and you simply follow the steps in this wizard to complete the configuration of your server.

FIGURE 1-6 Windows Deployment Services needing configuration.

Configuring your server does several things. First, it creates the image store where your startup and install images will be stored. By default, the wizard suggests the *%SystemDrive%* RemoteInstall location as an image storage location (Figure 1-7), but for performance reasons, you might want to use a different partition on a dedicated hard drive for this purpose. However, the only requirements for your image store location is that the partition be formatted by using NTFS and have sufficient free space to hold your images.

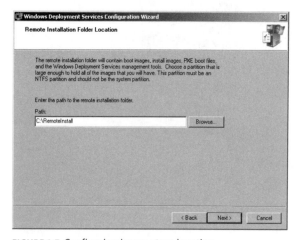

FIGURE 1-7 Configuring image store location.

Next, if your WDS server is also a DHCP server, the configuration wizard presents you with special configuration options, shown in Figure 1-8. The first option enables you to avoid a port conflict between WDS and DHCP by instructing the WDS server not to listen on port 67. If the local DHCP server is a Microsoft DHCP server, you should also select the Configure DHCP Option 60 To 'PXE Client' option. This second option configures the local DHCP server to refer PXE requests to the WDS service. If the local DHCP service is a third-party application, you will need to configure this option manually in that application.

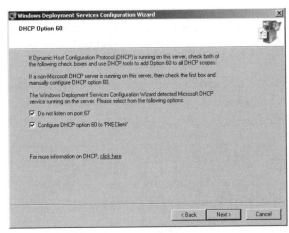

FIGURE 1-8 You must select both these options if the local server is an active Microsoft DHCP server.

During initial server configuration, you must now configure the answer policy for your server. This means you specify the kind of client computers to which your WDS server will respond (Figure 1-9).

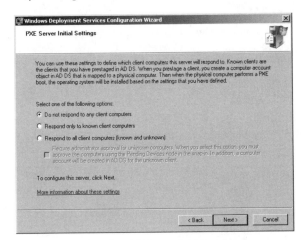

FIGURE 1-9 Configuring PXE Server initial settings.

Depending on how you configure your server, your settings can be:

- **Do Not Respond To Any Client Computers**   Leaving WDS in this state means that no installations will be performed. You can think of this as parking your WDS server until it is needed.

- **Respond Only To Known Client Computers**   A known client computer is one whose computer account has been pre-staged in Active Directory. Configuring WDS this way prevents your WDS server from responding to installation requests from unstaged and rogue systems.

- **Respond To All (Known And Unknown) Client Computers** An unknown computer is one whose computer account has not been pre-staged, so selecting this configuration option means that your WDS server will respond to any client system that makes an installation request.

After this point, the configuration settings you have chosen are applied to the new server, and the image store is created. When this process is finished, the Windows Deployment Services Configuration Wizard is complete.

 Quick Check

1. Which setting should you configure on your WDS server if you don't want PXE-enabled client computers to try to connect to your server automatically and download an image?

2. Which setting should you configure on your WDS server if you plan on pre-staging your client computer accounts in Active Directory?

Quick Check Answers

1. Select Do Not Respond To Any Client Computers on the PXE Response Settings tab of your WDS server Properties sheet.

2. Select Respond Only To Known Client Computers on the PXE Response Settings tab of your WDS server Properties sheet.

Adding Boot and Install Images

When the Windows Deployment Services Configuration Wizard is complete, you are presented with an option to add both boot and install images to the image store. This option is selected by default, as shown in Figure 1-10.

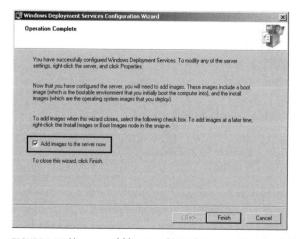

FIGURE 1-10 You can add boot and install images after the initial configuration of WDS is complete.

If you leave this option selected, clicking Finish opens the first page of a new wizard: the Add Image Wizard. On the Image File page, the wizard prompts you to point to the root of an installation DVD that contains boot and install images, as shown in Figure 1-11.

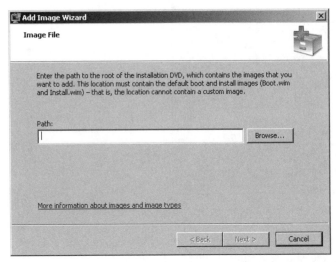

FIGURE 1-11 Specifying an installation DVD for copying boot and install images.

You can specify the Windows Server 2008 R2 product DVD as the image source, but the boot image on this DVD is only useful for 64-bit computers on the network. If you want to use WDS to deploy Windows to 32-bit computers on your network, you must add a 32-bit boot image, such as one found on a 32-bit version of Windows 7. Note also that the install images found on the Windows Server 2008 R2 product DVD are useful only if you want to deploy Windows Server 2008 R2 through WDS. In most environments, you will want to add Windows 7 images or other WIM files that you have customized for your particular clients.

> **IMPORTANT   USE THE RIGHT BOOT IMAGE!**
>
> You need one boot image for each processor architecture (x64 or x86) of your client computers. In addition, you should use the latest operating system possible for the boot image because this will ensure compatibility with the latest operating systems and WDS features.

Next, you are prompted to create or specify the image group that will contain your install images. An image group is a folder within the image repository of WDS. File resources are shared across an image group and are single-instanced, which makes image groups more storage-efficient than storing images individually on your server. Also, you can set security permissions on each image group separately so that, for example, when users in various departments connect to WDS from a bare-metal computer, they will only see images within specific image groups.

During initial configuration, WDS suggests a default name of ImageGroup1 for the first image group. (See Figure 1-12.)

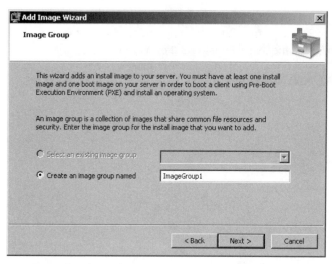

FIGURE 1-12 Creating an image group.

At this point, WDS scans your DVD to detect images. The results of this detection are displayed on the Review Settings page, shown in Figure 1-13.

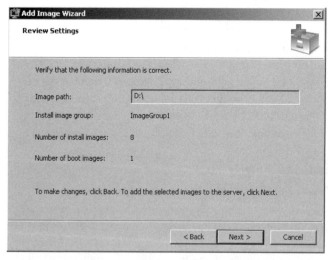

FIGURE 1-13 The Add Image Wizard scans your product DVD for boot and install images to add.

The new images are then imported into the appropriate folders in the image store. Figure 1-14 shows eight install images from the Windows Server 2008 R2 DVD copied to the Install Images folder in WDS. After an image is imported, you can right-click it to perform management functions such as *Export Image*, *Replace Image*, and *Create Multicast Transmission*.

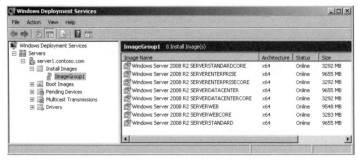

FIGURE 1-14 Images copied from the Windows Server 2008 R2 DVD can be deployed to WDS clients on the network.

It is likely that you will need to import more images after the initial WDS configuration phase. For example, you should import at least one boot image for each architecture type (x64, x86, and ia64). You might also need to import install images from different operating systems so that you can deploy more than one Windows version through WDS. To import another boot image, right-click the Boot Images folder in the WDS console and then click Add Boot Image. To add more install images, right-click the Install Images folder and then click Add Install Image.

Configuring the Boot Menu

Another configuration task you must perform is to configure the boot menu. When a PXE-enabled computer that has no operating system starts, it contacts the PXE server on your WDS server, obtains an IP address, and downloads the WDS client. The WDS client then displays a boot menu, which presents a list of the boot programs available, typically for different architecture types (x86, x64, and ia64). The WDS boot menu uses the same Boot Configuration Data (BCD) menu structure Windows 7 and Windows Server 2008 R2 use.

The boot menu is displayed only if there is more than one supported boot image on your WDS server. In other words, if you add only the default boot image to your server, no boot menu is displayed on the client computer. One reason to add several boot images to your server is to provide different functions to clients through each image. For example, you can use one boot image to launch Windows Setup to install Windows in unattended mode, another boot image to launch the WDS Image Capture Wizard so you can capture the image of a master computer to use as an install image for future installations, and a third boot image to repartition and reformat a system's hard drives to support BitLocker Drive Encryption before installing Windows on them.

After you've added several boot images to your WDS server, you can then use the *Bcdedit. exe* command to modify the boot menu behavior by editing the Default.bcd file. This file is found in the *Path*\RemoteInstall\Boot*architecture* folder on your server. (The RemoteInstall folder is found on the NTFS partition you choose during WDS configuration.) For help using this command, type **bcdedit /?** at a command prompt.

Configuring Server Properties

You can adjust a number of settings for the WDS server after the initial configuration. To configure these server-level settings in the Windows Deployment Services console, right-click your *server* node, select Properties, and then select the tabs you want to configure (Figure 1-15). The following section describes the configuration options available on each of the nine server-level properties tabs.

- **General** Shown in Figure 1-15, this tab displays server name, mode, and location of the remote installation folder where images are stored.

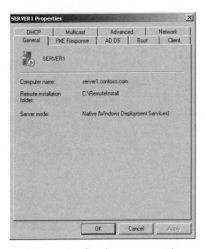

FIGURE 1-15 Configuring server settings.

- **PXE Response** This tab enables you to specify which types of computers (known or unknown) can download and install images from the server. In WDS, known computers are pre-staged with a pre-created computer account in AD DS. You can configure the WDS server not to respond to any computers, to respond only to known computers, or to respond to both known and unknown computers. If you choose the last option, you can also require administrator approval for unknown computers. In this case, service requests by WDS clients appear in the WDS console in the *Pending Devices* container. An administrator must approve an individual request (by right-clicking it and selecting Name And Approve) before the corresponding client can receive an image from the WDS server.

  Finally, in the PXE Response Delay configuration area, this tab also enables you to determine the PXE boot delay in seconds (zero by default). The PXE Response tab is shown in Figure 1-16.

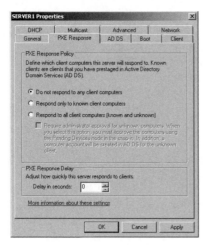

FIGURE 1-16 Configuring PXE Response Policy and PXE Response Delay.

- **AD DS** This tab is shown in Figure 1-17. Use the Client Naming Policy section to choose an automatic naming format for WDS clients in AD DS. (This setting applies only to WDS clients that are unknown or unidentified. For pre-staged WDS clients, you first manually create a named computer account in AD DS before deployment, as demonstrated in Exercise 4 in the Practice section of this lesson.) The Computer Account Location section enables you to specify where new accounts for unknown WDS clients will be stored in Active Directory. To prevent a computer account from being created in AD DS, use the Client tab.

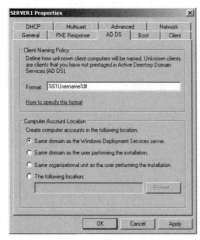

FIGURE 1-17 Configuring automatically generated computer account names and locations in AD DS.

- **Boot** On this tab, shown in Figure 1-18, you can specify the default network boot image for each architecture type (x86, x64, and ia64) and the PXE Boot Policy settings for known and unknown clients. For both categories of clients, you can require the user to press F12 to continue the PXE boot as opposed to continuing the PXE boot (without pressing F12), or continue the PXE boot unless the user presses the ESC key.

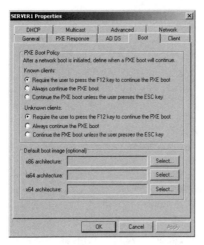

FIGURE 1-18 Configuring PXE Boot Policy and the default network boot image.

- **Client**   Use this tab, shown in Figure 1-19, to enable and configure unattended installation of the WDS clients. The client tab is also used to specify that WDS clients do not join a domain after installation and to enable client logging.

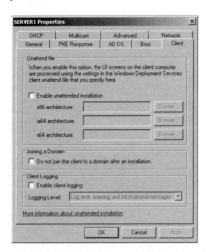

FIGURE 1-19 Configuring unattended installations for WDS clients.

- **DHCP**   This tab, shown in Figure 1-20, controls the same settings as those on the DHCP Option 60 page (shown in Figure 1-8) of the Windows Deployment Services Configuration Wizard. If you have a DHCP server running on your WDS server, you must select the option not to listen on port 67. If the DHCP server is a Microsoft server, you should also select the option to configure DHCP Option 60.

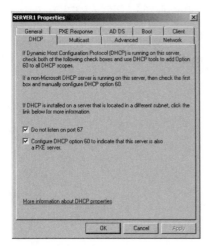

FIGURE 1-20 Configuring WDS for use with a local DHCP server.

- **Network** Shown in Figure 1-21, this tab enables you to specify the UDP port ranges WDS uses. You can use the Network Profile area in Windows Server 2008 only (not in Windows Server 2008 R2) to specify the bandwidth of your network: 10 Mbps, 100 Mbps, 1 Gbps, or a custom bandwidth. In Windows Server 2008 R2, the Network Profile setting is not configurable because it is determined automatically.

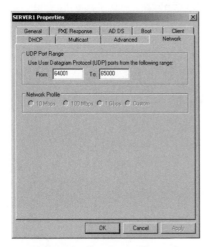

FIGURE 1-21 Configuring WDS ports.

- **Multicast** The Multicast tab and its settings are new to Windows Server 2008 R2. You can use this tab (shown in Figure 1-22) to configure IPv4 and IPv6 multicast address ranges when performing multicast deployments. Also use this tab to configure multicast transfer settings. Transfer settings enable you to select one of four options for handling multicast clients that connect at greatly varying speeds. First, you can keep all multicast clients in a session at the same (slowest) speed. Second, you can separate clients into three sessions (slow, medium, and fast). The third option is to separate clients into two sessions (slow and fast). Finally, you can opt to automatically disconnect clients who fall below a threshold speed of your choice (specified in KBps).

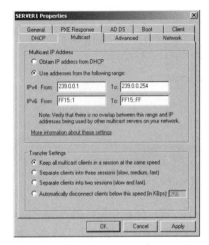

FIGURE 1-22 Configuring multicast address ranges and transfer settings.

■ **Advanced** This tab is shown in Figure 1-23. Use these settings to authorize your WDS server in DHCP and either to specify a domain controller and global catalog or to allow WDS to discover them on its own.

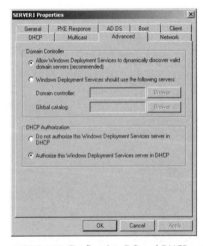

FIGURE 1-23 Configuring DC and DHCP settings for WDS.

Capturing Images with WDS

After you have installed and configured WDS, you create and customize the boot and install images you will use later to install Windows onto destination (also known as client) computers, which are bare-metal systems. You can use WDS to deploy many versions of Windows, but the explanation here focuses on deploying Windows Server 2008 R2.

A *boot image* starts the client computer to begin the process of installing Windows. Boot images contain Windows PE and the WDS client, and they display a boot menu on the client computer that enables you to select which operating system image you want to install on the computer. Boot images can be added to the image store in WDS, and they can be customized. You can also use boot images as a basis for creating two special types of boot images: capture images and discovery images.

A *capture image* is a special boot image you use to start a master computer. (Recall that a master computer is a system that has a master installation installed on it—a customized installation of Windows that you plan to duplicate on one or more destination computers.) To use a capture image, you first prepare your master installation by configuring Windows, installing applications, and performing any other customizations needed. Then, you sysprep your master computer to remove any machine-specific information from your master installation. After sysprep shuts the computer down, you restart the system by using the capture image, which launches a wizard that captures an install image from the computer and saves it as a .wim file to a location you specify. After you've captured an image of your master installation, you can then add the image to your image store as a new install image that you can then deploy to your destination computers by using WDS.

A *discover image* is a boot image you can use to deploy an install image onto a computer that is not PXE enabled. Discover images can be useful in a number of scenarios. For example, you can use a discover image to deploy Windows to an older computer system that does not support PXE startup by creating the discover image, saving it to bootable media (CD or DVD media or a USB flash drive), and then start the client computer by using the media to start the installation process. Alternatively, you might use discover images in an environment in which PXE is not allowed for policy reasons. You can also use discover images in an environment in which you have multiple WDS servers, and configure each discovery image to connect to a different WDS server for initiating deployment.

Creating a Capture Image

To create a new capture image, begin with the default boot image found in the Boot Images folder of the Windows Deployment Services console. Right-click the default boot image and select Create Capture Image to launch the Create Capture Image Wizard. On the first page of this wizard, you specify an image name, image description, file name, and file location for the capture image (Figure 1-24). It is best not to accept the default name and description. Instead, be sure to designate the image as a capture image so that you can recognize it. The location should be a folder on a local hard drive on your WDS server. Finally, remember that if you have chosen an x64-based image on which to base your capture image, you will not be able to use that image on x86-based computers.

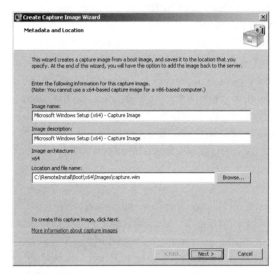

FIGURE 1-24 Creating a capture boot image.

Clicking Next causes the Create Capture Image Wizard to extract the image from the source file (the default boot image) and capture it to the destination .wim file you specified. On the final page of the wizard, select the option to add the image to the Windows Deployment Server now. Otherwise, you can right-click the Boot Images folder in the WDS console, select Add Boot Image, and add your new capture image to the image store. (See Figure 1-25.)

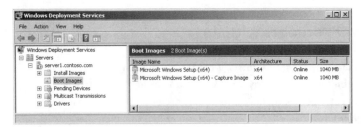

FIGURE 1-25 Default and capture boot images.

Creating a Discover Image

To create a new discover image, right-click the default boot image as before, but this time, select Create Discover Boot Image. The first page of this wizard requires you to specify an image name, image description, file name, and file location for storing the discover image. It also requires you to specify the WDS server with which the discover image will connect the client (Figure 1-26). Clicking Next causes the wizard to extract the image from the source file and capture it to the destination .wim file you specified, and then you can add the new discover image to the image store as before. If you need to create boot media (CD or DVD media or a USB flash drive) with this image, you can use the *Oscdimg* tool in the Windows AIK to do this. (Using *Oscdimg* was demonstrated in the Lesson 1 practice, "Creating a Windows PE CD," earlier in this chapter.)

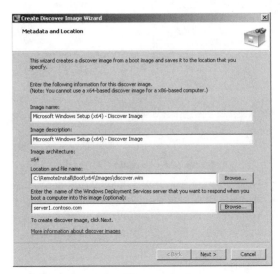

FIGURE 1-26 Creating a discover boot image.

EXAM TIP

For the TK 70-643 exam, you must understand the purpose of all WDS image types: boot, install, capture, and discover.

Deploying Driver Packages with an Image

Through a new feature called *dynamic driver provisioning*, Windows
Server 2008 R2 enables you to add driver packages to WDS and deploy them
to chosen clients along with the install image. To deploy driver packages, you must
first configure a *driver group* in the WDS console that will hold a specific collection of packages you want to deploy to certain computers. You use the properties
of each driver group to configure filters that match only the client computers you
choose. More specifically, you can configure a driver group by filtering WDS clients
by computer manufacturer, Bios Vendor, Bios Version, Chassis Type, UUID, OS
Version, OS Edition, and OS Language, as shown in Figure 1-27.

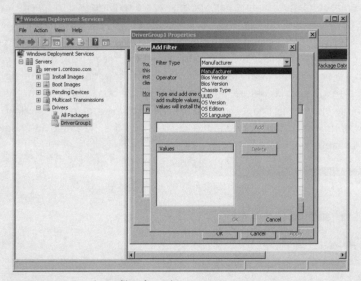

FIGURE 1-27 Creating a filter for a driver group.

After you configure a driver group by creating its filters, you can add driver packages to that group. To add a driver package, right-click the chosen driver group
container in the WDS console and then click Add Driver Packages To This Group.
Use the Add Driver Packages dialog box to search for and locate packages by attributes, as shown in Figure 1-28, and then click Add.

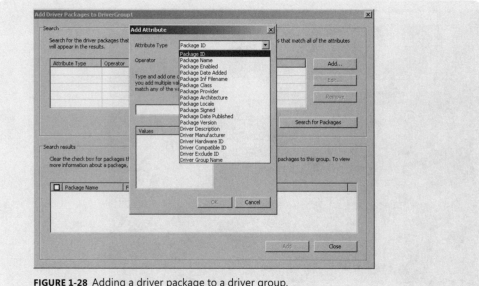

FIGURE 1-28 Adding a driver package to a driver group.

Deploying Images with WDS

After you have configured your WDS server, added boot images, captured an install image from a customized master installation, and added this install image to your store, you are ready to begin deploying Windows to your client computers. To do this, your client computers must have at least 512 MB of RAM (so they can load and run Windows PE boot images in RAM), and they must have their BIOS configured so that the PXE-compatible network card is first in the boot order (unless you are starting them from media by using bootable discover images).

You can use WDS to deploy images both manually and in automated fashion by using answer files. Manual deployment requires the least preparation on your part, but needs the most attention at the client end. Automated deployment requires using the Windows SIM to create an answer file.

Manually Deploying an Image with WDS

To deploy an install image manually to a client computer, start by turning on the client computer and then pressing F12 when prompted to do so. If more than one boot image is available, the Windows Boot menu appears, and you select the boot image you want to use to start the system and begin the installation. (See Figure 1-29.)

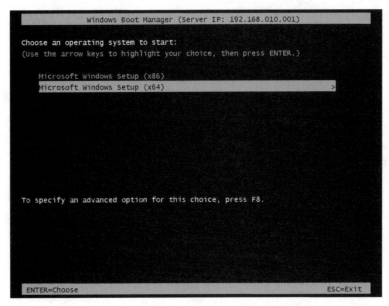

FIGURE 1-29 Selecting a boot image during manual deployment.

After the boot image has been downloaded from the TFTP server, the client computer starts Windows PE, and you are prompted to choose the locale in which you want Windows Setup to run.

When you are prompted to do so, enter your domain administrator credentials to connect the client computer to the image store on your WDS server. After a connection is established, a list of install images you can install is displayed. Select the customized image you captured from your master installation (Figure 1-30).

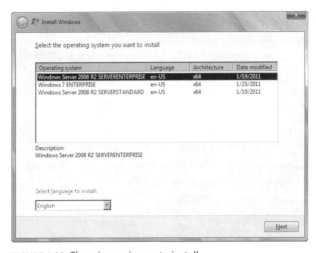

FIGURE 1-30 Choosing an image to install.

When you click Next, you are prompted to select a drive on which to install Windows, and after this is done, the server initiates a session with the client computer, and the customized install image is downloaded and installed onto your client computer. After this process has been completed, the destination computer restarts and Setup finishes its work.

Understanding What Happens During Deployment

It's worthwhile to understand what's going on during the preceding deployment scenario to provide a good foundation for troubleshooting issues when something goes wrong. Here's a quick summary of what's happening at the network level when a PXE-enabled client computer connects to a WDS server to download and install an image:

1. The client computer broadcasts a DHCP discover message to locate a DHCP server.

2. The DHCP server responds with a DHCP offer message offering an IP address to the client.

3. The client sends a DHCP request message requesting to lease the IP address contained in the previous DHCP offer message.

4. The DHCP server responds with a DHCP acknowledgment message indicating that the client has successfully leased the address.

5. The client broadcasts a second DHCP request message to locate a PXE server (that is, the WDS server).

6. The PXE server responds with a DHCP reply message that contains the ServerHostName (the WDS server name) and BootFileName (pxeboot.com for a manual install initiated by pressing F12 on the client).

7. The client now uses TFTP to download the boot file from the TFTP server (that is, the WDS server). This involves a lot of UDP traffic.

8. After the boot file is downloaded, the client then downloads the Windows Boot Manager Bootmgr.exe by using TFTP.

9. The client then displays the boot loader menu from which you choose your boot image.

10. The boot image is then downloaded from the server by using TFTP, and is loaded into memory.

11. At this point, Windows PE is now running in a RAM disk, and after you've selected the install image you want to install on your computer and specified any other information needed, the server uses Server Message Block (SMB) to download the install image so it can be applied to your computer.

PRACTICE **Configure Windows Deployment Services**

In this practice, you install and configure the Windows Deployment Services role on Server1 and then use WDS to deploy Windows Server 2008 R2 on Server2. For this practice, you need at least 3GB of free space on an NTFS partition on Server1. Server2 must be a PXE-boot compatible computer, located on the same physical or virtual network as Server1, that has no operating system installed. (Note: In Hyper-V, be sure to use an earlier network adapter on Server2.)

EXERCISE 1   Adding the Windows Deployment Server Role

In this exercise, you install the Windows Deployment Services role on Server1.

1. Log on to Server1 as a domain administrator and then open Server Manager.

2. In the Server Manager console tree, select the *Roles* node and then, in the details pane, click Add Roles.

   The Add Roles Wizard appears.

3. On the Before You Begin page, click Next.

4. On the Select Server Roles page, select Windows Deployment Services and then click Next.

5. On the Overview Of Windows Deployment Services page, read all the text on the page and click Next.

6. On the Select Role Services page, verify that both role services are selected and then click Next.

7. On the Confirm Installation Selection page, click Install.

8. When the Installation Results page appears, click Close.

9. Close Server Manager and proceed to Exercise 2.

EXERCISE 2   Performing Initial Server Configuration

In this exercise, you configure your WDS server by creating a RemoteInstall folder for your image store and configuring the PXE boot settings for your server.

1. While you are logged on to Server1 as a domain administrator, launch Windows Deployment Services from the Administrative Tools program group.

2. Expand the console tree until the *local server* node appears beneath the *Servers* node.

3. Right-click the *local server* node and then click Configure Server.

   The Windows Deployment Services Configuration Wizard launches, displaying the Before You Begin page.

4. On the Before You Begin page of the Windows Deployment Services Configuration Wizard, read all the text on the page and then click Next.

5. On the Remote Installation Folder Location page, read all the text on the page.

6. In the Path text box, leave the default path and folder name of C:\RemoteInstall.

   In a production environment, you should modify this path as necessary to specify an NTFS partition with 3 GB of free space or more. It is preferable (but not necessary) to choose a drive other than the Windows system volume.

7. On the Remote Installation Folder Location page, click Next.

8. If a warning message appears indicating that the volume you selected is also the Windows system volume, click Yes to continue.

9. On the DHCP Option 60 page, read all the text on the page.

   This page appears when a DHCP server is installed on the local computer.

10. On the DHCP Option 60 page, select both check boxes and then click Next.

11. On the PXE Server Initial Settings page, read all the text on the page.

12. On the PXE Server Initial Settings page, select the Respond Only To Known Client Computers option and then click Next.

13. When the Operation Complete page appears, clear the Add Images To The Server Now check box.

14. Click Finish.

EXERCISE 3 Adding the Default Boot and Install Images

In this exercise, you add the default boot image and the default install image from your Windows Server 2008 R2 media to your image store.

1. While you are logged on to Server1 as a domain administrator, open the Windows Deployment Services console if it is not already open.

2. In the Windows Deployment Services console tree, expand the *local server* node under *Servers* if necessary until the various folders contained in the server's image store are displayed.

3. Insert your Windows Server 2008 R2 DVD into the DVD drive of your WDS server. (Alternatively, you can mount the Windows Server 2008 R2 ISO file as a drive.) If the AutoPlay dialog box opens, close it.

4. Right-click the Boot Images folder and select Add Boot Image.

   The Add Image Wizard launches.

5. On the Image File page, click Browse and browse the file system to select the Boot. wim file in the \Sources folder on your product DVD. Click Open to begin adding the default Boot.wim boot image from your Windows Server 2008 R2 product DVD to the image store on your WDS server.

6. On the Image File page, click Next.

7. On the Image Metadata page, accept the default image name and description for your boot image and then click Next.

8. On the Summary page of the wizard, read all the text and then click Next.

   The Task Progress page appears while the boot image from your product DVD is added to your image store. This can take a number of minutes to complete.

9. When the image is successfully added to your server, click Finish.

   Now that you have added your default boot image to WDS, you should add your default install image from your product DVD.

10. In the WDS console, right-click the *Install Images* node and then select Add Install Image.

    The Image Group page of the Add Image Wizard appears, prompting you to create a new image group on your server.

11. Accept the default name for this image group and then click Next.

12. On the Image File page, browse to locate the default Install.wim install image on your product DVD and then open the image to begin adding it to your image store.

13. On the Image File page, click Next.

14. On the List Of Available Images page, review the available images. Clear all images except for SERVERSTANDARD and SERVERENTERPRISE and then click Next. (Normally, these images are first and third in the list.)

15. On the Summary page, review the information provided on the page and then click Next.

    The Task Progress page appears while the images are added to the store. This process can take 15 minutes or more.

16. When the image is successfully added to your server, click Finish.

EXERCISE 4 Pre-Staging the Client Computer in the Contoso Domain

In this exercise, you pre-stage the Server2 computer by adding its account to Active Directory and entering a 32-byte value associated with its MAC address. This procedure is necessary because you have configured Windows Deployment Services to respond only to known client computers.

To perform this exercise, Server2 must be a new virtual machine in Hyper-V configured with Legacy Network Adapter. No operating system or other software should be installed on Server2.

1. On your host (physical) computer, open Hyper-V Manager in the Administrative Tools program group.

2. In the list of virtual machines, right-click Server2 and select Settings.

3. In the Settings For Server2 window, select BIOS in the list of hardware on the left.

4. In the Startup Order area on the right side of the window, verify that Legacy Network Adapter is at the top of the list. If necessary, use the arrows to move Legacy Network Adapter to the top of the list.

   In Hyper-V, only Legacy Network Adapter is PXE-boot compatible.

5. In the list of hardware on the left, select Legacy Network Adapter. On the right side of the window, ensure that the network selected is Contoso.local. In the MAC address area, select Static and note the 12-character MAC address assigned to the virtual machine.

6. Click Apply. Leave the Settings For Server2 window open.

7. Switch to Server1, and if you have not already done so, log on to Server1 as a domain administrator.

8. On Server1, open Active Directory Users And Computers from the Administrative Tools program group.

9. In the Active Directory Users And Computers console tree, expand the *Contoso.local* node.

10. In the console tree, right-click the Computers container, select New, and then click Computer.

    The New Object - Computer page appears.

11. In the Computer Name text box, type **Server2** and then click Next.

    The Managed page appears.

12. On the Managed page, read all the text on the page and then select This Is A Managed Computer.

13. In the Computer's Unique ID (GUID/UUID) text box, type 20 zeroes followed by the 12-character MAC address of Server2 that is shown in the Settings For Server2 window. For example, if the MAC address of Server2 is 00 03 FF 9F B5 36, you should type **0000000000000000000003FF9FB536**.

14. On the Managed page, click Next.

15. On the Host Server page, read all the text on the page and then, leaving the default selection, click Next.

16. On the New Object - Computer page, click Finish.

17. On the host (physical) computer, click OK to close the Settings For Server2 window.

EXAM TIP

Understand pre-staging for the 70-643 exam and remember that in Hyper-V, only legacy network adapters work with WDS.

EXERCISE 5   Deploying Windows Server 2008 R2 through WDS

In this exercise, you deploy Windows Server 2008 R2 to Server2. To perform this exercise, you must ensure that Server2 is located in the same broadcast domain (physical subnet or virtual network) as Server1.

1. On your host (physical) computer, open Hyper-V Manager.

2. In the list of virtual machines, right-click Server2 and then click Connect.

3. In the Server2 On Localhost window, click Start. (This button is blue-green and appears beneath the Action menu.)

   After a few moments, the PXE boot process begins, and the local DHCP client immediately seeks and obtains an IP address for Server2. After an address is obtained, you are prompted to press F12 to begin a network service startup.

4. Press F12 on Server2. You have only a few seconds to perform this step. If you miss the opportunity, reset Server2 and try again.

   You see a message indicating that Windows is loading files as the boot image is loaded from Server1. This process can take five minutes or longer.

   After the boot image is loaded, a graphical user interface appears and then the Windows Deployment Services page of the Install Windows Wizard appears.

5. On the Windows Deployment Services page, choose an appropriate locale and keyboard for your region and then click Next.

   You are prompted to enter credentials for the domain.

6. Type the user name and password corresponding to a domain administrator in the Contoso.local domain and then click OK. Be sure to enter the user name in the contoso\username format.

7. On the Select The Operating System You Want To Install page, choose Windows Server 2008 R2 SERVERENTERPRISE and then click Next.

8. On the Where Do You Want To Install Windows page, ensure that Disk 0 is selected and then click Next.

   Windows installation begins. This process can take 30 minutes or more, during which time the server restarts.

9. When the Set Up Windows page appears, select the appropriate options for your country or region, time and currency, and keyboard layout and then click Next.

10. On the Please Read The License Terms page, review the license terms, click the I Accept The License Terms check box, and then click Start.

11. When prompted to press Ctrl+Alt+Del to log on, either press Ctrl+Alt+End or select Ctrl+Alt+Del from the Action menu of the Server2 On Localhost window.

12. Type the credentials of a domain administrator account and then press Enter.

    A desktop appears, and then the Initial Configuration Tasks window appears.

13. Take a few moments to review the computer information displayed on the Initial Configuration Tasks page.

    The full computer name is listed as Server2.contoso.local, and the domain is listed as contoso.local.

14. Click Set Time Zone to adjust the time zone if necessary.

15. In the Search Programs And Files box of the Start menu, type **Manage Advanced Sharing Settings** and then press Enter.

16. In the Advanced Sharing Settings windows, select Turn On Network Discovery and Turn On File And Printer Sharing and then click Save Changes.

17. Shut down Server2 and then shut down Server1.

Lesson Summary

- Windows Deployment Services is a server-based technology for deploying Windows images onto bare-metal computers.

- When a PXE-enabled computer that has no operating system starts, it contacts the PXE server on your WDS server, obtains an IP address, and downloads the WDS client. The WDS client then displays a boot menu, which presents a list of operating systems that can be installed on the system.

- A *boot image* is a Windows image (.wim) file you can use to start a bare-metal client computer to begin the deployment of an operating system to the computer. When deploying images with WDS, you can use the default boot image from the \sources folder on the Windows Server 2008 R2 DVD.

- An *install image* is an image of the Windows Vista or Windows Server 2008 R2 operating system itself that you plan on deploying onto the client computer. The simplest way of using WDS is to deploy the default install image included in the \sources folder on your Windows Server 2008 R2 product DVD.

- A *capture image* is a special boot image you use to start a master computer and upload an image to a WDS server.

- A *discover image* is a boot image you can use to deploy an install image onto a computer that is not PXE enabled.

Lesson Review

The following questions are intended to reinforce key information presented in this lesson. The questions are also available on the companion CD if you prefer to review them in electronic form.

> **NOTE ANSWERS**
>
> Answers to these questions and explanations of why each answer choice is correct or incorrect are located in the "Answers" section at the end of the book.

1. Which of the following is not a component of Windows Deployment Services?
    - **A.** Image store
    - **B.** Trivial File Transfer Protocol (TFTP) server
    - **C.** Windows System Image Manager (Windows SIM)
    - **D.** Pre-boot execution environment (PXE) server

2. You want to use WDS to deploy Windows 7 to 50 x86-based, PXE-enabled client computers in your domain. You have not pre-staged any of the client computers in the domain. Which of the following tasks should you NOT perform?

   A. Create a *Path*\RemoteInstall folder on a disk volume formatted by using FAT32.

   B. Configure the PXE Response Settings to allow both known and unknown client computers.

   C. Add the Boot.wim file from the *Path*\Sources folder of your Windows 7 media to your image store.

   D. Add the Install.wim file from the *Path*\Sources folder of your Windows 7 media to your image store.

3. You want to use Windows Deployment Services to deploy a custom image of Windows 7 to 100 PXE-compatible computers. On a computer named Win7-01, you install Windows 7 and configure all the applications and settings you need for client computers in your organization. You then run Sysprep to generalize the image. What should you do next?

   A. Create a boot image based on the installation of Win7-01.

   B. Create an install image based on the installation of Win7-01.

   C. Create a capture image based on the installation of Win7-01.

   D. Create a discover image based on the installation of Win7-01.

Lesson 3: Deploying Virtual Machines

Computer virtualization enables you to emulate physical computers in software. This technology is becoming widespread because of the advantages it offers as a means to consolidate physical computers, reduce energy expenses, support earlier operating systems on newer hardware, and facilitate testing and server management.

Windows Server 2008 and Windows Server 2008 R2 both include the Hyper-V server role, a native virtual environment you can use to run multiple operating systems as self-contained computers on a single physical server.

> **After this lesson, you will be able to:**
> - Understand the benefits of computer virtualization.
> - Understand the features of Hyper-V.
> - Configure virtual machines in Hyper-V.
> - Attach a VHD file as a drive on a physical machine.
>
> **Estimated lesson time: 60 minutes**

What Are Virtual Machines?

A virtual machine (VM) is a software emulation of a physical computer. With VMs, you can run several operating systems simultaneously on a single physical computer, as shown in Figure 1-31.

FIGURE 1-31 Several VMs running on a Windows desktop.

Virtualization software works by providing a software environment for an operating system that is indistinguishable from that of a physical computer. The operating system running in the virtualized environment is known as the *guest*, and the operating system on which the virtualization software is running is known as the *host*. Within the host operating system or on top of a hardware virtualization layer, each guest VM runs its own operating system with its own installed applications, as shown in Figure 1-32.

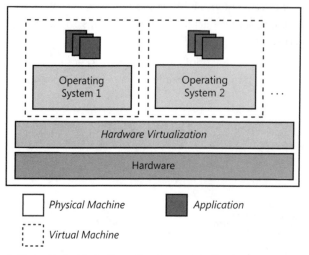

FIGURE 1-32 An illustration of hardware virtualization.

Why Use Virtual Machines?

You can deploy VMs or migrate physical servers to VMs to provide the following functions or benefits:

- **Consolidate production servers** Virtualization is most commonly used to consolidate the workloads from a large number of underused physical servers onto a smaller number of physical servers. In enterprise networks, the hardware usage rates for physical servers can often be as low as 5 or 10 percent of server capacity. By migrating physical servers to a virtual environment, efficiency increases, and the costs associated with powering, cooling, and maintaining the physical servers are greatly reduced. Physical space is also saved, which is a critical factor in many data centers.

- **Support earlier applications and operating systems** Virtual machines often host applications requiring an earlier operating system, such as Windows NT. By hosting the operating system and application in a virtual environment, you no longer have to dedicate an entire physical server for this purpose.

- **Software test and development** VMs can easily be isolated from a corporate network, and they can quickly be repurposed. Because of this flexibility, you can use VMs to test and model operating systems, applications, or security.

- **Maximize server uptime** With virtualization, you can isolate applications in their own machines and prevent one application from affecting the performance of another in a production environment. For example, if a VM hosting one application crashes, no other server applications will be affected. Another way virtualization improves server uptime is by reducing or eliminating hardware conflicts. Virtual machines with their generic hardware drivers provide a stable environment for applications; as a result, applications tend to function reliably in a virtual environment.

- **Efficient server management and maintenance** By using management tools such as Microsoft System Center Virtual Machine Manager, you can manage VMs remotely and even migrate a VM from one physical server to another with minimal downtime. These features simplify management and allow you the flexibility of adjusting server workloads in response to current demands.

Understanding Hyper-V

Hyper-V is a hypervisor virtualization technology provided by the Hyper-V server role in Windows Server 2008 and Windows Server 2008 R2, and by the stand-alone Hyper-V Server 2008 R2 product. A *hypervisor* is a thin layer of software that runs beneath the host operating system and provides all installed operating systems, both host and guests, with equal access to the hardware of the physical computer. In Hyper-V, each allocation of resources given to a VM is called a partition. The host operating system runs in the parent partition, and each guest VM runs in a child partition, as illustrated in Figure 1-33.

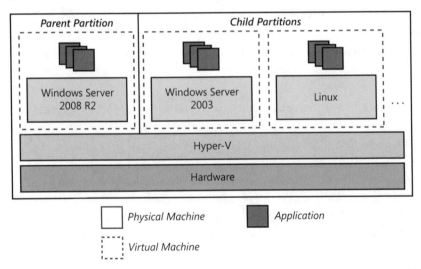

FIGURE 1-33 Hyper-V divides a host computer's resources into a parent partition and child partitions.

In Windows Server 2008 and Windows Server 2008 R2, Hyper-V is managed through the Hyper-V Manager administration tool, shown in Figure 1-34.

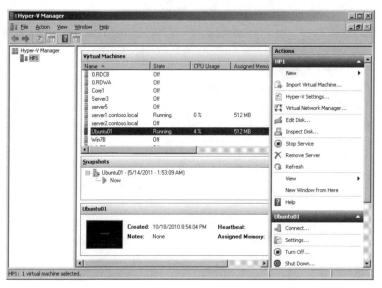

FIGURE 1-34 Hyper-V Manager.

The following list describes some of the specific features and benefits of Hyper-V:

- **Both 32-bit and 64-bit guest support**   Hyper-V supports both 32-bit and 64-bit operating systems in child VMs.

- **Multicore and multiprocessor guest support**   On a Hyper-V enabled server, each guest VM can be assigned up to four processors (depending on the guest operating system).

- **High performance**   The hypervisor technology, as well as the support for multiple CPUs and increased memory, results in excellent performance for VMs in the Hyper-V environment.

- **Snapshots**   Hyper-V provides the ability to take snapshots of a running virtual machine. A snapshot is a saved copy of the state of a virtual machine at any given point, including all data and configuration settings. After you create a snapshot of a VM, you can apply that snapshot to the VM at any later point. You can also choose the Revert function, which discards all changes on the active VM since the last snapshot was taken.

> *NOTE* **LIMITATIONS OF SNAPSHOTS**
>
> Snapshots are a useful feature for testing, but they have limitations in a production environment. First, they are not an alternative to backups because a backup provides protection that is not provided by snapshots. Second, snapshots of domain controllers are not supported by Microsoft, so a change on any computer that results in a change in AD DS is not eligible for snapshots. Third, snapshots reduce the performance of their associated virtual hard disks. Finally, snapshots require substantial storage space—as

much as 50 percent or more of the virtual hard disk space required by a virtual machine. You can delete snapshots to free up space, but deleted snapshot files are not removed from the physical storage until the virtual machine is shut down, turned off, or put into a saved state. For more information about snapshots, visit *http://technet.microsoft.com /en-us/library/dd560637(WS.10).aspx*.

- **Dynamic VM storage** New to Hyper-V in Windows Server 2008 R2 is support for hot plug-in and hot removal of storage.

- **Quick migration** Hyper-V in both Windows Server 2008 and Windows Server 2008 R2 supports quick migration. Quick migration saves the state of a running guest virtual machine, moves the storage connectivity from one physical server to another, and then restores the guest virtual machine onto a second server.

- **Live migration** New to Hyper-V in Windows Server 2008 R2 is a live migration feature, which enables you to move a virtual machine between two host servers without any disruption of service or perceived downtime.

- **Integration Services** Also called Integration Components, Integration Services in Hyper-V are software additions that greatly improve performance and help integrate a virtual machine with the physical hardware and parent operating system. Integration Services are automatically preinstalled with Windows guest operating systems in Hyper-V. However, you must install the Integration Services manually to support virtual machines running non-Windows operating systems. Another reason you might need to install Integration Services manually is if you have upgraded the host Windows Server 2008 operating system to Windows Server 2008 R2 or Windows Server 2008 R2 SP1. In this case, you should upgrade the Integration Services to take advantage of new Hyper-V features such as dynamic memory.

NOTE **INSTALLING INTEGRATION SERVICES**

To install Integration Services, select Insert Integration Services Setup Disk from the Action menu when the VM is running. A virtual CD-ROM containing the Integration Services installation program is then attached to the VM.

 Quick Check

- What is a hypervisor?

Quick Check Answer

- A hypervisor is a thin layer of software that runs beneath the parent operating system and grants both host and guest operating systems equal access to the hardware. A hypervisor essentially turns all locally installed operating systems into virtual machines.

Hyper-V Hardware and Software Requirements

Hyper-V has strict hardware requirements that relate to the processor. Specifically, Hyper-V requires an x64-based processor that includes both hardware-assisted virtualization (AMD-V or Intel VT) and hardware data execution protection. (On AMD systems, the data execution protection feature is called the No Execute, or NX, bit. On Intel systems, this feature is called the Execute Disable, or XD, bit.) In addition, these features must be enabled in the BIOS. (By default, they are often disabled.)

The software requirements of the Hyper-V server role are for an x64 version of Windows Server 2008 or Windows Server 2008 R2. Hyper-V can run on a server core installation and on the full installation of Windows Server 2008 or Windows Server 2008 R2.

Hyper-V is also available in the free product called Hyper-V Server 2008 R2. Hyper-V Server 2008 R2 is essentially a version of the Server Core installation option of Windows Server 2008 R2 that has all server roles disabled except for Hyper-V.

Use the following procedure to install Hyper-V on a full installation (as opposed to a Server Core installation) of Windows Server 2008 R2.

Install Hyper-V

1. Ensure that your system meets the hardware requirements for Hyper-V and that both hardware-assisted virtualization and data execution protection have been enabled prior to installation. If BIOS reconfiguration changes were made to enable these hardware features, you must complete a full power cycle before proceeding.

2. In Server Manager, add the Hyper-V role. To do this, click Add Roles under Roles Summary and then select Hyper-V in the Add Roles Wizard, as shown in Figure 1-35.

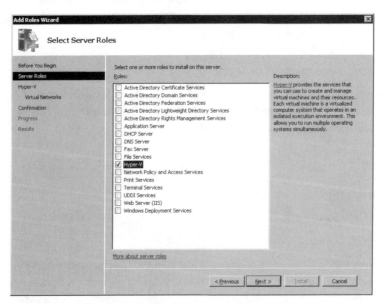

FIGURE 1-35 Adding the Hyper-V role.

3. Follow the on-screen instructions to complete the Add Roles Wizard.

4. At the end of the Add Roles Wizard, you must restart the system for the Hyper-V role to be enabled.

5. Upon restart, log on with the same account used to install the Hyper-V role.

6. Confirm the installation of the Hyper-V role by expanding the *Roles* node in Server Manager, selecting the *Hyper-V* node, and verifying that the Hyper-V services are running, as shown in Figure 1-36.

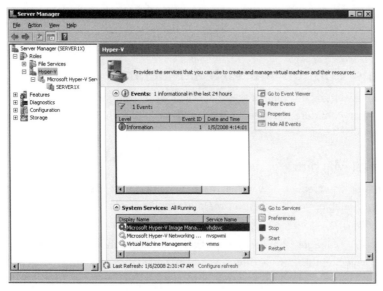

FIGURE 1-36 Hyper-V services.

NOTE **HYPER-V SERVERS SHOULD BE DEDICATED TO THAT ROLE**

It is recommended that no other server role be enabled on the host system if the Hyper-V role is enabled.

Use the following procedure to enable Hyper-V on a Server Core installation of Windows Server 2008 and Windows Server 2008 R2.

Enable Hyper-V on a Server Core Installation

1. Type **start /w ocsetup Microsoft-Hyper-V** to enable the Hyper-V role.

2. Restart when prompted.

> **IMPORTANT   REMOTE ADMINISTRATION OF SERVER CORE**
>
> To manage Hyper-V installed on a Server Core installation, you can connect remotely to the server by using Hyper-V Manager on a different system. To allow remote computers to connect through Windows Firewall, type the following at the command prompt on the server core computer: **Netsh advfirewall firewall set rule group="remote administration" new enable=yes**.

After you have installed Hyper-V, you can create virtual machines. Use the following procedure to do so.

Creating and Configuring Virtual Machines in Hyper-V

You can create a new virtual machine in Hyper-V Manager by using the New Virtual Machine Wizard. You can then configure the virtual hardware devices of a VM through its associated Settings window.

Create a Virtual Machine

In Hyper-V Manager, you create a new virtual machine by using the New Virtual Machine Wizard. This wizard enables you to create a simple VM with a single virtual network adapter and virtual hard disk.

1. Open Hyper-V Manager from the Administrative Tools program group and then select the server object in the console tree.
2. From the Actions pane, click New and then click Virtual Machine.
3. Proceed through the pages of the New Virtual Machine Wizard to specify the following:
   - A name for the VM.
   - A storage location for the VM.
   - The amount of physical RAM you want to assign to the VM.
   - The virtual network, if any, to which you want to connect the default network adapter assigned to the VM.
   - The name, size, and location of the VHD you want to create for the VM, if any. Alternatively, you can attach an existing VHD or not attach any VHD.
   - The media containing the installation files for an operating system, if any. You can choose to install an operating system later or specify a CD/DVD-ROM drive, an ISO file, a virtual floppy disk, or a network-based installation.
4. After you have finished configuring the virtual machine, click Finish.

Configure Virtual Hardware Devices

After you create a VM, you can open its settings (as shown in Figure 1-37) to configure its virtual hardware devices such as RAM, processors, virtual hard disks, and virtual network adapters.

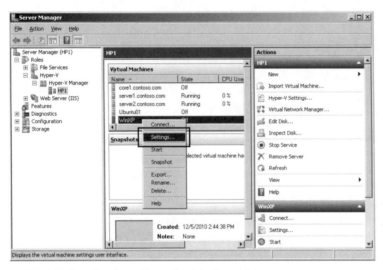

FIGURE 1-37 Opening the settings of a virtual machine.

Adding Virtual Hardware

The Settings window for a virtual machine is shown in Figure 1-38. If you select Add Hardware on the left side of the window beneath Hardware, you can select one of at least three types of devices to add: a SCSI controller, a network adapter, or a legacy network adapter. In addition, in Service Pack 1 for Windows Server 2008 R2, you can add RemoteFX 3D Video Adapter if your physical host computer includes a video card that can support this technology. RemoteFX enables high-performance graphics in VMs and Remote Desktop connections.

If you want to add a virtual hard disk, select a particular IDE or SCSI controller instead of selecting Add Hardware. Then, on the right side of the window, select Hard Drive and click Add.

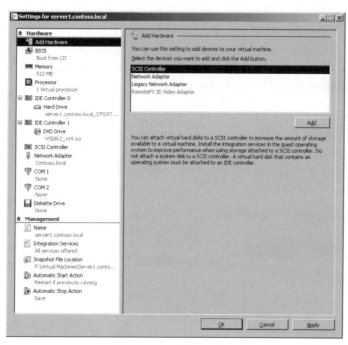

FIGURE 1-38 Settings for a virtual machine.

Configuring BIOS Settings and Device Boot Order

When you select BIOS, beneath Hardware in the Settings window, the Startup Order area on the right side of the window enables you to configure the boot order of the hardware devices in your VM. In Hyper-V, you can start from a CD (physical or ISO file), an IDE hard disk, a virtual floppy, or a legacy network adapter. The BIOS settings are shown in Figure 1-39.

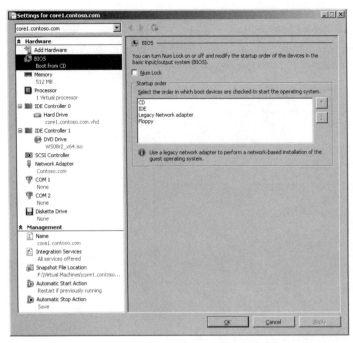

FIGURE 1-39 Configuring the order of startup devices in the BIOS of a VM.

Configuring Memory (RAM)

In Windows Server 2008 and the original (RTM) version of Windows Server 2008 R2, the memory that you assign a VM is a fixed amount of physical RAM that cannot be used by the host operating system when the VM is running. In addition, you can adjust the amount of RAM allocated to a VM only when that VM is stopped.

However, Service Pack 1 for Windows Server 2008 R2 introduces a new feature in Hyper-V called dynamic memory, by which you specify a range for the amount of RAM assigned to a VM, and Hyper-V then adjusts RAM allocations continually in real time among your running VMs as needed.

Dynamic memory settings in Windows Server 2008 R2 SP1 are indicated in Figure 1-40. In the Startup RAM text box, you enter the minimum amount of RAM needed to start and run the VM. The Maximum RAM setting defines the upper limit of RAM that you want to be allocated to the VM at any given time. The Memory Buffer setting defines how much extra RAM beyond the committed RAM Hyper-V should attempt to allocate to the VM. For example, if a VM currently requires 1000 MB of RAM to run its workload, and you leave the Memory Buffer setting at the default of 20%, Hyper-V will attempt to allocate 1200 MB to the VM. The Memory Weight setting determines the priority a VM should be given relative to other VMs running on the host when Hyper-V determines how to distribute RAM.

Note that only the following guest operating systems are compatible with dynamic memory allocation in Hyper-V: Windows Vista Enterprise SP2 and Windows Vista Ultimate SP2,

Windows 7 Enterprise and Windows 7 Ultimate SP1, Windows Server 2003 SP2, Windows Server 2008 SP2, and Windows Server 2008 R2 SP1. In addition, if the VM was created before Windows Server 2008 R2 SP1 was installed on the host system, the Integration Services on the VM must be upgraded on the system to the most recent version.

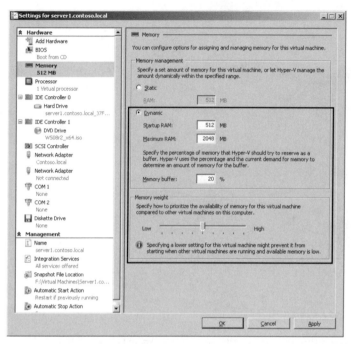

FIGURE 1-40 Allocating dynamic RAM to a VM in Windows Server 2008 R2 SP1.

Configuring Virtual Processor(s)

To configure processor settings for a VM, select Processor in the Settings window beneath Hardware, as shown in Figure 1-41. The Processor configuration area on the right side of the window enables you to assign a guest VM to up to four of the available CPUs on the physical host machine. (These virtual CPUs are not reserved exclusively for use with the VM, but are shared with the physical host system and any other VMs running on the system.) You can also use the Resource Control area to balance virtual processor resources among your hosted VMs. Finally, the Processor Compatibility area provides two options that improve the compatibility of the VM. The first option, new to Windows Server 2008 R2, prepares the VM for migration to another host physical computer with a different CPU. The second option restricts virtual CPU features to improve their compatibility with older guest operating systems, such as Windows NT.

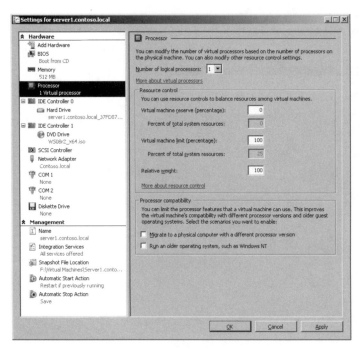

FIGURE 1-41 Configuring virtual processors in a VM.

Configuring IDE Devices

A VM in Hyper-V contains two IDE controllers: 0 and 1. By default, IDE Controller 0 hosts a single virtual hard disk, and IDE Controller 1 hosts a single DVD drive. You can use the Add button (shown in Figure 1-42) to add another virtual hard disk or DVD drive to either of these IDE controllers. However, each IDE controller can host only two devices total, one at location 0 and another at location 1, as shown in Figure 1-43. Although the number of controller locations is limited compared to a SCSI device, the advantage of an IDE controller over a SCSI controller is that you can start from an IDE device.

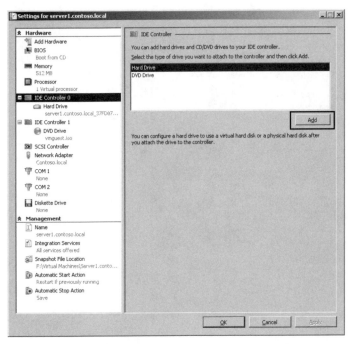

FIGURE 1-42 Adding an IDE device.

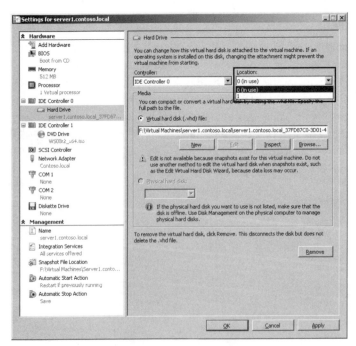

FIGURE 1-43 Each IDE controller in Hyper-V includes two locations (0 and 1) to which you can attach devices.

Configuring SCSI Devices

In general, you can add or remove hardware in a VM only when the VM is stopped (shut down), but there is one useful exception: You can add a new SCSI hard drive to an existing controller on a live VM. To do so, select SCSI Controller in the Hardware list, select Hard Drive on the right side of the window, and then click Add, as shown in Figure 1-44.

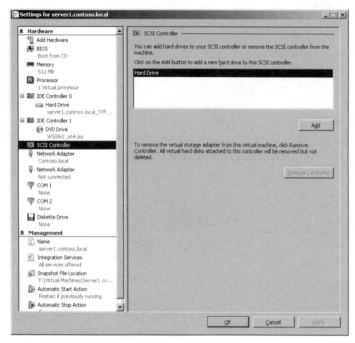

FIGURE 1-44 Adding a SCSI hard drive to a live VM.

For both IDE and SCSI controllers, you also have the option of attaching a physical hard disk to the VM. When a physical disk is reserved for use with a VM in this way, the disk is known as a *pass-through disk*. To configure a pass-through disk, first use the Disk Management console to verify that the desired physical disk is offline. Then, after choosing to add a new hard drive, select Physical Hard Disk and specify the disk, as shown in Figure 1-45.

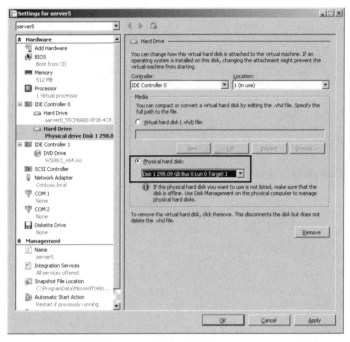

FIGURE 1-45 Configuring a pass-through disk.

Configuring Network Adapters

By configuring Network Adapters or Legacy Network Adapters in the Settings window of a VM, you can change the virtual networks to which these adapters are attached. You can achieve this by selecting the adapter in the Settings window beneath Hardware and then selecting the desired network from the Network drop-down list on the right side of the window. Note also that you can perform this task even when the VM is running, just as you can switch network cables on a live physical machine.

The MAC Address configuration area provides another group of settings related to virtual network adapters. By default, the Dynamic option is selected, which enables Hyper-V to assign a unique MAC address to the virtual machine as the VM starts. If you choose Static, you must specify a fixed MAC address or simply agree to the one suggested. The option to enable spoofing of MAC addresses is new to Windows Server 2008 R2. This option provides Hyper-V with more flexibility in dealing with MAC addresses internally, and you must enable it to configure certain advanced features such as Network Load Balancing with VMs.

The last feature you can configure for a virtual network adapter in the Settings window is virtual LAN (VLAN) identification. VLANs are broadcast domains in Ethernet that are customized in a manner that is independent of the physical topology. VLANs are typically used in large networks and rely on special adapters, switches, and software. In a VLAN, physical network adapters are tagged with a VLAN ID that represents the particular LAN to which the adapter belongs.

Hyper-V enables you to assign virtual network adapters to particular VLANs on your physical network. Each virtual network adapter assigned to a VLAN must be assigned its own exclusive physical network adapter on the physical host. In addition, that physical network adapter must be VLAN compatible and must be configured with the correct VLAN ID. To assign a network card in a virtual machine to a VLAN, select the option to enable LAN identification and type the appropriate VLAN ID.

The virtual network adapter settings are shown in Figure 1-46.

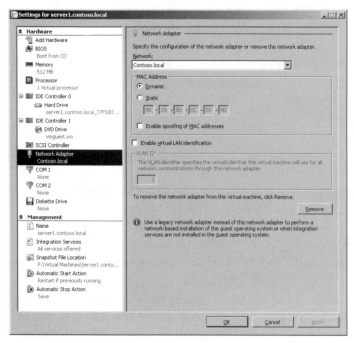

FIGURE 1-46 Configuring virtual network adapter settings.

Create and Manage Virtual Disks

Like many other virtualization products, Hyper-V uses VHD files for virtual hard disks. You can create a new virtual disk in Hyper-V Manager by right-clicking the *server* object in the console tree, selecting New, and then selecting Hard Disk, as shown in Figure 1-47. This step opens the New Virtual Hard Disk Wizard, which prompts you to specify a disk type, size, and location for the new VHD.

FIGURE 1-47 Creating a new VHD.

You can choose to create any of three VHD types: dynamically expanding, fixed, and differencing.

- **Dynamically expanding**   Dynamically expanding virtual hard disks provide storage capacity as needed to store data. The size of the VHD file is small when the disk is created and grows as data is added to the disk. The size of the VHD file does not shrink automatically when data is deleted from the virtual hard disk. However, you can compact the disk to decrease the file size after data is deleted by using the Edit Virtual Hard Disk Wizard.

- **Fixed**   Fixed virtual hard disks provide storage capacity by using a VHD file that is the size specified for the virtual hard disk when the disk is created. The size of the VHD file remains fixed regardless of the amount of data stored. However, you can use the Edit Virtual Hard Disk Wizard to increase the size of the virtual hard disk, which increases the size of the VHD file.

- **Differencing**   A differencing virtual hard disk is a virtual hard disk associated with another virtual hard disk in a parent-child relationship. The differencing disk is the child, and the associated virtual disk is the parent. The parent disk can be any type of virtual hard disk. The differencing disk (the child) stores a record of all changes made to the parent disk and provides a way to save changes without altering the parent disk. In other words, by using differencing disks, you ensure that changes are made, by default, to the differencing disks and not to the original virtual hard disk. You can, however, elect to merge changes from the differencing disk to the original virtual hard disk when it is appropriate to do so. You can also use many differencing disks that share a single parent. This method saves storage space if you need to have multiple virtual hard disks based on a single image.

Modifying a Virtual Disk

You can change certain properties of a disk by using the Edit Virtual Hard Disk Wizard. To open this wizard, click Edit Disk on the Actions pane in Hyper-V Manager. The wizard enables you to perform one of three actions on a VHD, as shown in Figure 1-48: Compact, Convert, or Expand.

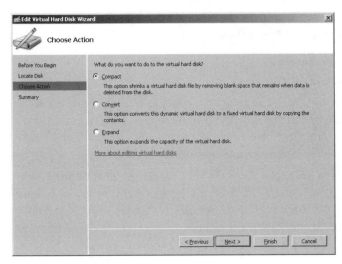

FIGURE 1-48 Changing the size or type of a VHD.

Compacting a virtual hard disk makes a VHD file smaller by removing blank space on the disk. The Convert option enables you to convert a hard disk to a fixed VHD. The Expand function enables you to expand the capacity of a virtual hard disk.

Inspecting a Virtual Hard Disk File

You can determine the properties of a VHD file by choosing Inspect Disk from the Actions pane in Hyper-V Manager. After you select a VHD file to inspect, a dialog box like the one in Figure 1-49 appears, displaying basic properties about the disk such as disk type and size.

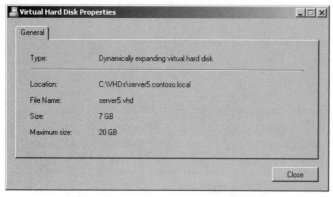

FIGURE 1-49 Inspecting a VHD file.Using VHD Files on Physical Computers.

Using VHD Files on Physical Computers

Windows 7 and Windows Server 2008 R2 introduce the ability to attach (mount) a VHD file as a disk and create lettered volumes on that disk. This process can be used just as easily for physical computers as it can for virtualized computers. To attach a VHD file, you can use the Disk Management console or the Diskpart command-line utility.

To attach a VHD file as a disk in Disk Management in Windows Server 2008 R2, right-click the *Disk Management* node and click Attach VHD from the shortcut menu, as shown in Figure 1-50. In the Attach Virtual Hard Disk dialog box that opens, simply browse to and select the desired VHD file. After you click OK, the file appears as a new drive in Disk Management. You can then initialize the disk and create new volumes in it as you can with any disk.

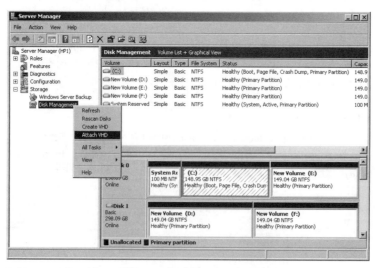

FIGURE 1-50 Attaching a VHD to a physical system in Disk Management.

To perform the same process by using the Diskpart utility, use the *attach vdisk* command. In the following example, a file named windows7.vhd is attached as a drive to the local machine, and then a single partition (volume) is created on this drive, assigned the letter v, formatted, and labeled.

```
diskpart
create vdisk file=c:\windows7.vhd maximum=25600 type=fixed
select vdisk file=c:\windows7.vhd
attach vdisk
create partition primary
assign letter=v
format quick label=vhd
exit
```

After you create a partition on a VHD file, you can make the VHD bootable by marking the partition as active, applying a bootable image to that partition by using ImageX, and then editing the boot menu by using the Bcdedit utility. This option can be used for disaster recovery or for the quick distribution and launch of a sysprepped operating system.

When using attached VHD files, be aware of certain limitations:

- BitLocker cannot be used on volumes contained inside a VHD.

- An attached VHD cannot be configured as a dynamic disk. (Dynamic disks are covered in Chapter 2, "Configuring Server Storage and Clusters," Lesson 1.)

- Native VHD boot does not support hibernation of the system, although sleep mode is supported.

MORE INFO MAKING A VHD FILE BOOTABLE

For more information about making a VHD file bootable on a physical computer, watch the demonstration titled "Windows7VHDBoot.wmv," found in the Videos folder of the companion CD.

Creating Virtual Networks in Hyper-V

When you first add the Hyper-V server role by using the Add Roles Wizard, you are given an opportunity to create a separate virtual network for each physical network adapter on the host computer. The networks you create in this step are virtual in the sense that they are used in the Hyper-V platform, but they are essentially extensions of the physical networks to which your host computer is connected. After installation, these networks appear as options to which you can connect virtual network adapters in any virtual machines you create.

You can create additional virtual networks at any time after you add the Hyper-V server role. To do so, in Hyper-V Manager, click Virtual Network Manager in the Actions pane, as shown in Figure 1-51.

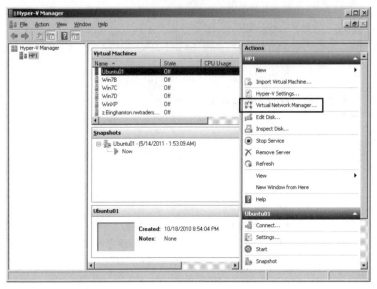

FIGURE 1-51 Opening Virtual Network Manager.

Then, in the Virtual Network Manager window, select the type of virtual network you want to create and click Add, as shown in Figure 1-52. You can create any of three network types: external, internal, and private.

- **External** An external virtual network binds to the physical network adapter so that virtual machines can access a physical network. For example, if there is a DHCP server on the physical network, virtual machines connected to an external network will receive a DHCP address from that network server.

  When you add the Hyper-V server role, you can create an external network for each hardware network adapter connected to the computer.

- **Internal** An internal virtual network can connect all the virtual machines with the local physical computer. This type of virtual network cannot provide access to a physical network connection.

- **Private** A private virtual network can only connect virtual machines to other virtual machines running on the local physical computer. It cannot connect to the local physical computer itself.

Afterward, when you create a new virtual machine by using the New Virtual Machine Wizard, you can connect the new machine to any virtual networks you have already created, as shown in Figure 1-53.

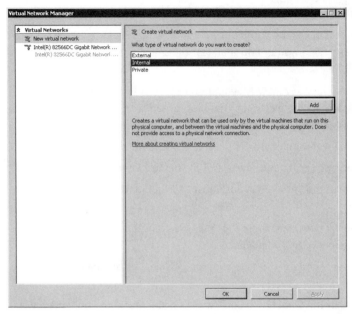

FIGURE 1-52 Creating a new virtual network.

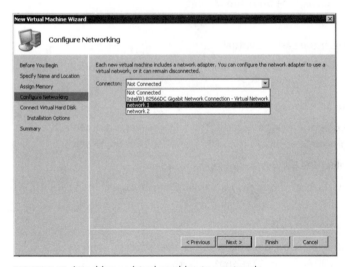

FIGURE 1-53 Attaching a virtual machine to a network.

PRACTICE Use Snapshots in Hyper-V

In this practice, you use the host computer running Hyper-V to take snapshots of the Server2 computer.

EXERCISE Creating, Applying, and Reverting to Snapshots

The snapshot feature in Hyper-V saves the complete state of a computer. In this exercise, you take snapshots of the Server2 computer and then test the snapshots with the *Revert* and *Apply* functions.

1. On your host computer, open Hyper-V Manager and connect to Server2. If necessary, start the Server2 virtual machine by clicking the blue-green *Start* button in the Server2 On Localhost - Virtual Machine Connection window.

2. Log on to the Contoso.local domain from the Server2 computer.

3. On the desktop of Server2, create and save a TXT file named **Snapshot1**.

4. From the Action menu of the Server2 On Localhost - Virtual Machine Connection window, select Snapshot.

5. In the Snapshot name window, type **Snapshot1**. If you do not finish typing the name, you can edit the name in Hyper-V Manager.

6. On the desktop of Server2, create and save another TXT file, this one named **Snapshot2**.

7. From the Action menu of the Server2 On Localhost - Virtual Machine Connection window, select Snapshot.

8. In the Snapshot name window, type **Snapshot2**.

9. Delete the Snapshot2.txt file.

10. In Hyper-V Manager, select the Server2 virtual machine.

11. From the Action menu of the Server2 On Localhost - Virtual Machine Connection window, select Revert.

12. In the Revert Virtual Machine dialog box, click Revert.

    The Server2 virtual machine window goes black. Then, after several moments, the desktop reappears with both Snapshot1.txt and Snapshot2.txt on the desktop.

13. In Hyper-V Manager, select the Server2 virtual machine again.

14. In the Snapshots pane, right-click the Snapshot named Snapshot1 and then click Apply from the shortcut menu.

15. In the Apply Snapshot dialog box, click Apply.

    The Server2 virtual machine window goes black. Then, after several moments, the desktop reappears with only Snapshot1.txt on the desktop.

IMPORTANT **DO NOT REVERT TO OLD SNAPSHOTS ON DOMAIN CONTROLLERS**

You should not apply old snapshots to domain controllers because the resulting lack of time synchronization with other domain controllers can cause AD DS to become unstable.

Lesson Summary

- A virtual machine is a software emulation of a physical computer. Virtual machines are used (among other reasons) to help consolidate physical servers, support earlier applications and operating systems, and assist in testing and development.

- Hyper-V is a hypervisor technology, which is a thin layer of software that runs on top of the hardware and provides the host and all guest operating systems with equal access to the hardware.

- You can configure virtual machines with various hardware, including fixed, dynamically expanding, and differencing hard disks; network adapters and earlier network adapters; and up to four processors.

- You can create three types of networks in Hyper-V: external networks, which are bound to a physical adapter on the host; private networks, which cannot communicate with the host or the external network; and internal networks, which can communicate with the host but not with the external network.

- In Windows 7 and Windows Server 2008 R2, you can mount a VHD file as a drive in the file system by using the Diskpart utility and the *attach vdisk* command. If the VHD file contains boot data, you can start from the VHD by marking the drive as active and editing the boot menu with the *Bcedit* command.

- Service Pack 1 for Windows Server 2008 R2 includes a dynamic memory allocation feature in which you define a range of memory that you want to assign to a VM and allow Hyper-V to assign RAM as needed in real time.

Lesson Review

The following questions are intended to reinforce key information presented in this lesson. The questions are also available on the companion CD if you prefer to review them in electronic form.

> **NOTE ANSWERS**
>
> Answers to these questions and explanations of why each answer choice is correct or incorrect are located in the "Answers" section at the end of the book.

1. You use Hyper-V to create a new virtual machine named Client01 on a network with a server named WDS1 that is running Windows Deployment Services. You want to use Windows Deployment Services to deploy Windows 7 to Client01. Client01 contains a single, earlier network adapter, but the computer does not look for WDS1 upon starting. What should you do to fix the problem?

    A. Add enough RAM to the virtual machine to support Windows 7.

    B. Configure the BIOS settings in Hyper-V to start from the network card.

C. Replace the earlier network adapter in Hyper-V with a later network adapter.

D. Create a discover CD and start from the CD.

2. You are installing a new management server as a virtual machine in Hyper-V. You want the server to be accessible to other computers on your company's private network. To which type of network should you connect the network adapter in Hyper-V?

A. Internal

B. Private

C. External

D. Either internal or private

3. A database server running on Windows Server 2008 R2 in Hyper-V has been compromised. You make a copy of the server's virtual hard disk (VHD) files and then send these files to a security expert for forensic analysis. The security expert has a computer with an x86 processor and normally analyzes hard disks offline on a USB drive. How should you instruct him to investigate the server's VHD files?

A. Instruct the expert to use the Diskpart utility and the *attach vdisk* command to attach the VHD files as drives.

B. Instruct the expert to use the Diskpart utility and the *create vdisk* command to create a new drive from the VHD file.

C. Instruct the expert to attach the VHD files as hard disks in Virtual PC on his system.

D. Instruct the expert to mount the VHD files in Hyper-V on his system.

Lesson 4: Implementing a Windows Activation Infrastructure

A volume license key is a product key that validates multiple copies of software, typically for medium-sized or large organizations. With Windows XP and Windows Server 2003, volume license keys needed to be entered during installation, but these installations didn't need to be activated. This earlier volume license activation policy first changed with Windows Vista and Windows Server 2008 so that now even volume-license deployments of operating systems must be activated within 30 days of installation. Activation, as a result, must now be considered an integral part of corporate deployment.

This lesson describes the new options, procedures, and technologies to activate volume-license editions of Windows.

> **After this lesson, you will be able to:**
> - Describe the difference between MAK and KMS licensing.
> - Describe the scenarios in which MAK or KMS licensing is preferable.
> - Install and configure a KMS host.
>
> **Estimated lesson time: 50 minutes**

Product Activation Types

There are three basic types of product activations for Windows 7 and Windows Server 2008 R2: OEM, retail, and volume. OEM activation is the BIOS-bound, out-of-the-box activation performed automatically on computers preinstalled with an operating system. Retail activation must be performed if you purchase Windows 7 or Windows Server 2008 R2 through a software retailer. These purchases include a retail license key that typically applies to one computer only. After entering this retail license key, you can activate the software online or over the telephone.

Volume activation is more complex; it provides customers with the following two types of keys, including three methods of activation.

- *Multiple Activation Key* (MAK)
  - MAK independent activation
  - MAK proxy activation
- *Key Management Service* (KMS) key
  - KMS activation

All customers are free to purchase and use a MAK, but a KMS key can be used only by organizations that can activate 25 virtual or physical computers (for Windows 7) or five virtual or physical computers (for Windows Server 2008 R2). These keys and activation methods are described in the following sections.

> **NOTE** **EXTENDING THE GRACE PERIOD BEFORE ACTIVATION WITH** *SLMGR.VBS*
>
> You can use the *Slmgr.vbs -rearm* command to manually extend the grace period of a Windows installation before activation is required. This command works on Windows Vista, Windows 7, Windows Server 2008, and Windows Server 2008 R2. The number of days you can extend the grace period and the number of times you can rearm the installation depends upon the product license type, but you can type **slmgr.vbs - dlv** to find out how many more times the installation can be rearmed and how many days are left in the current grace period.

Implementing MAK Activation

MAKs are typically used in environments with fewer than 25 computers. With MAK activation, you use a product key to activate a specific number of Windows installations. This product key does not need to be entered during installation because, as with all versions of Windows 7 and Windows Server 2008 R2, you have a 30-day grace period to enter the product key and activate Windows. The Windows activation is then valid until there is a significant hardware change on the computer.

In general, there are two ways to activate computers by using a MAK.

- **MAK online activation** In online (or independent) activation, two steps are required. First, you must enter the MAK on each computer to be activated. You can perform this step during operating system installation or afterward. After installation, you can enter the key on the client locally by using the Change Product Key Wizard or remotely by connecting to the computer over the network with Volume Activation Management Tool (VAMT) 2.0.

> **MORE INFO** **WHERE CAN YOU OBTAIN THE VAMT?**
>
> VAMT 2.0 can be downloaded from the Microsoft Download Center at *http://www .microsoft.com/download*.

After you enter the MAK, you can then activate each computer by using either the VAMT or the telephone, as illustrated in Figure 1-54. (To activate a computer remotely by using the VAMT, you must first create an inbound firewall rule allowing Windows Management Instrumentation on that computer.)

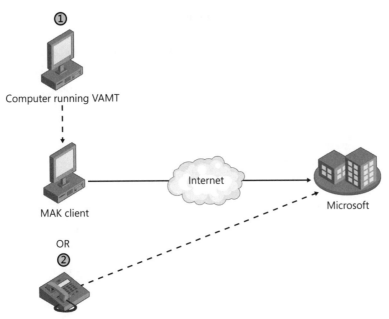

Computer running VAMT

MAK client

Internet

Microsoft

OR

FIGURE 1-54 You can perform MAK independent activation by using the VAMT on another computer or by telephone.

In general, you can think of online activation as the method for activating any number of MAK clients that have an Internet connection or a very small number (one to three) of MAK clients not connected to the Internet.

> **IMPORTANT ACTIVATING SERVER CORE**
>
> To activate a Server Core installation of Windows Server 2008 R2 with a MAK or retail key, use the *Slmgr* command to perform the following two steps. First, if you have not entered the key during Windows setup, type **slmgr.vbs -ipk [product_key]** at a command prompt, where *[product_key]* is your product key including the four dashes. (If you already entered the product key during Windows Setup, you can skip this first step.) Then, type **slmgr.vbs -ato** to perform the actual activation.

- **MAK proxy activation** Activating clients by telephone is a time-consuming process. If you have a fair number (4–24) of computers on your network that are isolated from the Internet, it would not be desirable or practical to activate them all in this fashion. MAK proxy activation provides a simpler method to activate such groups of computers that have no Internet access.

  With MAK proxy activation, on a computer that can connect to the isolated computers, you use the VAMT to collect the Installation IDs (IIDs) of those computers and save those IIDs in an XML file. Then, on a computer that has Internet access, you again use the VAMT to connect to Microsoft and obtain the Confirmation IDs (CIDs) associated with those IIDs. (If necessary, you can move the XML file manually from one computer to another to complete this process.) Those CIDs are then saved to the same XML file. Finally, you again use the VAMT to connect to the isolated computers and use the updated XML file to activate them.

The MAK proxy activation procedure is illustrated in Figure 1-55.

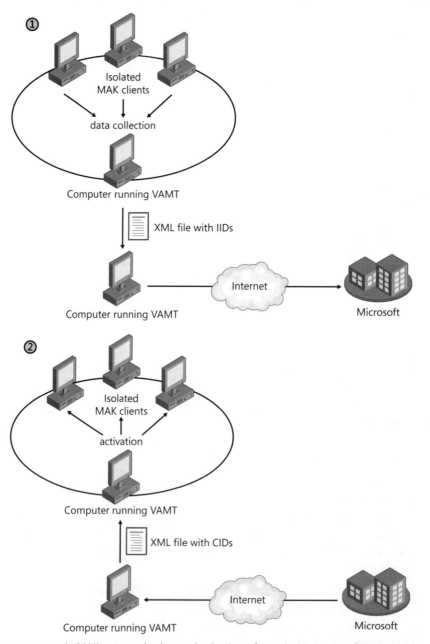

FIGURE 1-55 In MAK proxy activation, activation is performed with the aid of an XML file.

Advantages and Disadvantages of MAK Licensing

When you need to activate a relatively small number of computers, MAK licensing is easy. It requires no infrastructure to be set up. You can use the VAMT to facilitate the process, but you also have the familiar option to enter the product key and activate locally as you would with any retail key. In addition, after you activate a MAK Windows installation, that installation remains activated forever unless the local hardware changes significantly.

However, if you have a large number of clients to activate, MAK licensing would be difficult from an administrative point of view. Typing in product keys 250 to 2,000 times, keeping track of the number of times each key has been activated, and then keeping track of the computers that have been activated would be a time-consuming process.

For such large networks, it would be preferable to have an option for activation that did not require you to enter any product key on the local computer, and on which activation for clients was performed automatically without user intervention. That option is available in KMS licensing.

Implementing KMS Activation

KMS licensing enables clients in a large network to be activated automatically without contacting Microsoft. In a KMS infrastructure, there is only one key on the network—the KMS key—and that key is installed on a single computer, known as the KMS host. Of all the computers on the network, only this KMS host activates directly with Microsoft, and this step is performed only once. Beyond the initial activation, a KMS host never again needs to communicate with the Microsoft Activation servers.

Computers running volume license editions of Windows 7 and Windows Server 2008 R2 (KMS clients) automatically attempt to activate by connecting to a KMS host machine. Clients not yet activated attempt to connect to the KMS host every two hours. Upon activation, KMS clients must reactivate periodically; this is an essential difference between KMS activation and other forms of activation. KMS clients must, in fact, renew their activation at least once every 180 days (or 210 days if you include the grace period). Activated KMS clients attempt to reconnect to the KMS host every seven days and, if successful, renew the full 180-day activation life span. If clients are unable to contact a KMS server after the 180-day activation life span ends, they have an additional 30-day grace period to complete activation or reactivation. Clients not activated within this time period go into Reduced Functionality Mode (RFM).

Figure 1-56 depicts a basic KMS infrastructure.

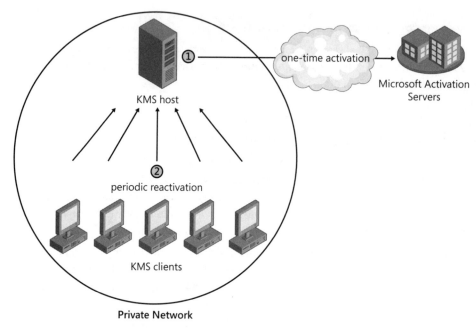

Private Network

FIGURE 1-56 KMS clients are activated periodically by contacting a KMS host on your network.

Minimum KMS Client Numbers (Thresholds)

KMS activation requires a minimum number of computers (virtual or physical) to connect to the KMS host before activation can occur. This minimum number is known as the KMS activation threshold, which is a nonconfigurable threshold that helps ensure that the delegated activation service is used only in an enterprise environment and serves as a piracy protection mechanism.

The KMS host counts activation requests and responds to each valid request with the count of how many systems have contacted the KMS host in the past 30 days. If the count meets or exceeds the KMS activation threshold, that KMS client self-activates.

The threshold for Windows Server 2008 R2 and Windows 7 differs, and is calculated in the following manner:

- For a Windows Server 2008 or Windows Server 2008 R2 installation to activate successfully, at least five KMS virtual or physical client computers must request activation on the KMS host.

- For a Windows Vista or Windows 7 client to activate, at least 25 physical KMS virtual or physical client computers must request activation on the KMS host.

- The thresholds can be achieved by activation requests from any Windows operating system, including Windows Vista or later.

The KMS host itself does not contribute to the count.

KMS Host Discovery

For KMS-based activation, clients must be able to locate a KMS host on a network. Clients can locate the KMS host by using one of two methods: *Autodiscovery*, in which a KMS client uses DNS records to locate a local KMS host automatically; or *direct connection*, in which a system administrator specifies the KMS host location and communication port.

- **Autodiscovery** By default, a KMS client discovers a KMS host by querying a DNS server for an SRV record named _vlmcs._TCP. If a client wants to discover a KMS host, therefore, the DNS server with which the client communicates needs to contain an SRV record named _vlmcs._TCP that points to the KMS host.

  The KMS host automatically attempts to create this SRV record by using dynamic DNS. For KMS autodiscovery to work properly, DNS servers must support both dynamic DNS registrations and SRV resource records. Versions of Microsoft DNS included with Windows 2000 Server, Windows Server 2003, and Windows Server 2008 and BIND DNS versions 8.2 and later all support this functionality.

  If the DNS entry for KMS appears to be missing, first try to force dynamic DNS registration of this record by restarting Software Licensing Service, slsvc.exe. You can do this by using the Services console or by typing **net stop slsvc && net start slsvc** at an elevated command prompt on the KMS host.

  If the attempt to force dynamic DNS registration for KMS is still unsuccessful, you should create the SRV record manually in DNS. The full name of the record should be _vlmcs._TCP.*DNSDomainName*, where *DNSDomainName* is the name of the local DNS domain. The time to live (TTL) for these records should be 60 minutes. The KMS host address and port (1688/TCP) should also be included in each record.

- **Direct connection** You can use *Slmgr.vbs* to specify a KMS host on the client and bypass the autodiscovery process. To configure this type of direct connection, type the following command on the KMS client, where *KMS-host* is the DNS name or IP address of the KMS host:

```
slmgr.vbs -skms KMS-host
```

EXAM TIP

For the 70-643 exam, know how to force dynamic registration of the DNS records for KMS, how to configure SRV records manually on a DNS server, and how to specify a direct connection to a KMS host.

Installing and Configuring a KMS Host

All the tools required for KMS host operation are already included in Windows Vista, Windows 7, Windows Server 2008, and Windows Server 2008 R2. You simply need to use the *Slmgr.vbs* script first to install and then enable the KMS key. After performing these steps, the KMS host can begin servicing activation requests from KMS clients.

To configure a KMS host, perform the following steps on a computer running Windows Vista, Windows 7, Windows Server 2008, or Windows Server 2008 R2.

1. Install an enterprise volume license key by running the following command in an elevated command prompt window, where *Key* is the enterprise volume license key:

   slmgr.vbs -ipk *Key*

2. Activate the KMS host by using the Internet by running this script:

   slmgr.vbs -ato

3. To activate the KMS instead by telephone, start the Windows Activation Wizard by running this executable:

   slui.exe

   Click Activate Windows Online Now and then click Use The Automated Phone System To Activate.

4. Ensure that the KMS port (the default is 1688/TCP) is allowed through all firewalls between the KMS host and KMS client computers.

> **IMPORTANT** **KMS HOST SECURITY**
>
> Do not provide unsecured access to KMS hosts over an uncontrolled network such as the Internet. Doing so can lead to exposure to penetration attempts and unauthorized activation by computers outside the organization.

5. Make any configuration changes required for the environment.

   By using the *Slmgr.vbs* script and editing the KMS host's registry, you can customize the configuration of KMS. For example, you can configure KMS to register SRV resource records on multiple DNS domains, not to register with DNS at all, to use nonstandard ports, and even to control client renewal intervals.

EXAM TIP

Expect to see questions on the 70-643 exam requiring you to know different options used with Slmgr.vbs. At a minimum, know all the options covered in this lesson. For more information about all of the options available with Slmgr.vbs, type **slmgr** at the command prompt. (The dialog box that appears is the first of four. Click OK to bring up the next in the series.)

Advantages and Disadvantages of KMS Licensing

KMS licensing is generally preferable to MAK licensing because it requires no user intervention. The KMS host automatically registers its address in DNS, and the KMS client then automatically uses DNS to locate the KMS host.

The disadvantages of KMS licensing are its significant infrastructure requirements. First, the KMS client threshold requires at least 25 KMS clients for Windows 7 and five KMS clients for Windows Server 2008 R2. In addition, all KMS clients must be able to connect to a KMS host at least once every 180 days. In contrast, MAK licensing has no such requirements; after a MAK client is activated, it is activated forever unless the hardware is significantly changed.

Because of the diverse topology of large, multisite networks, many large organizations need both MAK and KMS licensing.

Activation Infrastructure Example

Because KMS activation is preferable to MAK activation, the general rule for designing an activation infrastructure for large organizations is simply to use KMS licensing wherever possible and to use MAK everywhere else. This principle is illustrated in Figure 1-57, which shows a private network with four sites.

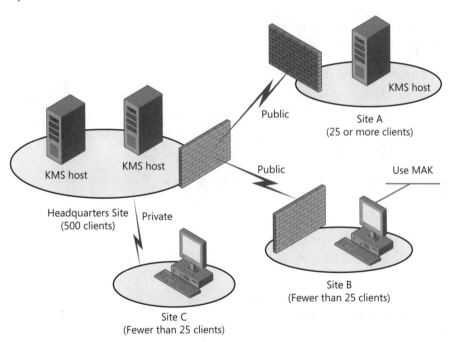

FIGURE 1-57 Multisite networks typically need both KMS and MAK licensing.

This figure shows a private network with four sites. At the Headquarters site, 500 clients are sufficient to support KMS licensing, so KMS activation is used. (The two servers shown in the diagram can be used either to support activation for two DNS domains or merely to balance the request load between two servers.) At Site A, the 25 or more clients are enough to support a local KMS host, so a local KMS host is used. At Site B, there are not enough clients to support a local KMS host. In addition, the clients at the site are not able to connect to a KMS host elsewhere on the private network. In such a case, KMS licensing is not an option, so MAK licensing should be used instead. At Site C, there are not enough clients to support a local KMS host, but the clients at the site are able to connect to a KMS host at the Headquarters site. In this case, KMS licensing is the best option.

 Quick Check

- Why would you ever need to create SRV records to help activation?

Quick Check Answer

- KMS clients query for an SRV record in DNS to discover the address of a KMS host. If the local KMS host has not automatically created this SRV record on the DNS server, you must create the record manually.

PRACTICE **Activate Windows**

In this practice, you use the Change Product Key Wizard to activate Server2 on the Internet. You then watch a video on KMS host configuration.

EXERCISE 1   Activate Server2

In this exercise, you use the System Control Panel to activate Server2. Before beginning this exercise, you must ensure that Server2 can connect to the Internet.

1. Log on to Contoso.local from Server2 as a domain administrator.
2. In Control Panel, click System And Security and then click System.
3. In the Windows Activation area of the System window, click the link to activate Windows now.

   The Activate Windows Now page of the Windows Activation Wizard appears.
4. Click Activate Windows Online Now.
5. If you are prompted to enter a product key, type the key in the space provided and then click Next.

   The Windows Activation Wizard indicates that activation was successful, and a Windows Activation message box appears, informing you that you need to restart your computer.
6. Click Close to close the Windows Activation message box.
7. Click Close to close the Windows Activation Wizard.
8. Shut down Server2.

EXERCISE 2 Watch a Video on Configuring a KMS Host

You must have a volume license key to configure a KMS host. To learn about the procedure, you can watch a demonstration. In the Videos folder of the companion CD, watch the video titled, "Set Up a KMS Host on a Windows Server 2008 R2 Machine.wmv."

Lesson Summary

- Both retail and volume license versions of Windows 7 and Windows Server 2008 R2 need to be activated within 30 days of installation.

- For Windows 7 and Windows Server 2008 R2, two types of volume licenses are available: Multiple Activation Key (MAK) licenses and Key Management Service (KMS) licenses. Each of these licenses is associated with a different method of activation.

- MAKs are typically used in environments with fewer than 25 computers. With MAK activation, you use a product key to activate a specific number of Windows installations.

- KMS licensing enables clients in a large network to be activated automatically without contacting Microsoft. In a KMS infrastructure, there is only one key in the network—the KMS key—and that key is installed on a single computer known as the KMS host. Computers running volume license editions of Windows 7 and Windows Server 2008 R2 (KMS clients) automatically attempt to activate by connecting to a KMS host machine.

Lesson Review

The following questions are intended to reinforce key information presented in this lesson. The questions are also available on the companion CD if you prefer to review them in electronic form.

> **NOTE ANSWERS**
>
> Answers to these questions and explanations of why each answer choice is correct or incorrect are located in the "Answers" section at the end of the book.

1. You are an administrator for a corporate network. At a branch office, you want to deploy Windows 7 to 21 client computers and Windows Server 2008 R2 to four servers. For which operating systems is the branch office eligible for KMS licensing?

   A. Windows 7

   B. Windows Server 2008 R2

   C. Both Windows 7 and Windows Server 2008 R2

   D. Neither Windows 7 nor Windows Server 2008 R2

2. Which of the following is the most efficient way to activate 15 volume-license comput-ers running Windows 7 on a research subnet that has no Internet access?

   A. MAK online activation

   B. MAK proxy activation

   C. KMS host activation

   D. Retail key activation

3. Which of the following is not a step for configuring a KMS host?

   A. Running the *slmgr.vbs –ipk* command

   B. Running the *slmgr.vbs –ato* command

   C. Configuring a firewall exception for TCP port 1688

   D. Configuring a firewall exception for TCP port 1723

Chapter Review

To practice further and reinforce the skills you learned in this chapter, you can:

- Review the chapter summary.
- Review the list of key terms introduced in this chapter.
- Complete the case scenarios. These scenarios set up real-world situations involving the topics of this chapter and ask you to create solutions.
- Complete the suggested practices.
- Take a practice test.

Chapter Summary

- You can deploy Windows 7 and Windows Server 2008 R2 by using the product DVD, by using tools included in the Windows Automated Installation Kit (AIK), or by using Windows Deployment Services (WDS). The main methods to deploy Windows 7 and Windows Server 2008 R2 are based on a new native Windows imaging WIM format. WIM files (.wim) contain file-based (as opposed to sector-based) images that can be modified before, during, and after deployment.
- You can use WDS to deploy Windows 7 or Windows Server 2008 R2 to bare-metal computers. With WDS, a PXE-enabled computer contacts the WDS server and down-loads a menu of available operating systems. An end user can then choose an operating system to install from this menu.
- A virtual machine is an emulation of a physical computer that can be used in server consolidation, testing, and hosting earlier applications.
- Hyper-V is a server role in Windows Server 2008 R2 that installs a hypervisor beneath the parent operating system. Hyper-V gives parent and guest systems equal access to the hardware.
- Even volume license versions of Windows 7 and Windows Server 2008 R2 must be activated. There are two volume licensing options: Multiple Activation Key (MAK) licensing and Key Management Service (KMS) licensing. MAK licensing is for environments of fewer than 25 computers. KMS licensing provides larger networks with a more automated solution for activation.

Key Terms

Do you know what these key terms mean? You can check your answers by looking up the terms in the glossary at the end of the book.

- boot image
- capture image
- discover image

- guest operating system
- host operating system
- hypervisor
- install image
- Key Management Service (KMS)
- Multiple Access Key (MAK)
- WIM file

Case Scenarios

In the following case scenarios, you apply what you've learned in this chapter. You can find answers to these questions in the "Answers" section at the end of this book.

Case Scenario 1: Deploying Servers

You are a network administrator for Contoso.local. You must design a deployment solution for a rollout of 200 installations of Windows 7 and 25 installations of Windows Server 2008 R2.

1. Management requests the ability to deploy operating systems remotely from a central location. Which deployment solution should you use to meet this requirement?

2. You have only six available servers on which to deploy eight installations of Windows Server 2008 R2. Four servers in the company are hosting Windows Server 2003 and SUSE Linux applications, and the usage rates of those servers average 15 percent of capacity. Given this scenario, how can you use virtualization to reduce the costs associated with deploying Windows Server 2008 R2?

Case Scenario 2: Creating an Activation Infrastructure

You work in IT support for Northwind Traders, and you are part of the deployment team. Northwind Traders is planning to deploy 500 installations of Windows 7 and 30 installations of Windows Server 2008 R2. You have been asked to design the activation infrastructure for the new operating systems.

Northwind Traders includes three sites. At the Headquarters site in New York, you plan to deploy 400 Windows 7 clients and 23 installations of Windows Server 2008 R2. Among its 400 clients, Headquarters includes an isolated research network of 20 Windows 7 clients. The research network has no connection to the Internet or to the rest of the Nwtraders.com network.

The second Northwind Traders site is located in Binghamton, NY. This branch office network includes 80 Windows 7 clients and five servers running Windows Server 2008 R2. The Binghamton office network is connected to the Headquarters network by a virtual private network (VPN).

The third site is located in Syracuse, NY. This branch office network is composed of 20 Windows 7 clients and two servers running Windows Server 2008 R2. There is no VPN network connection from the Syracuse site to either of the other two company network sites.

1. How should you design the activation infrastructure for the Headquarters site?
2. How should you design the activation infrastructure for the Binghamton site?
3. How should you design the activation infrastructure for the Syracuse site?

Suggested Practices

To help you successfully master the exam objectives presented in this chapter, complete the following tasks.

Deploy Images by Using Windows Deployment Services

Use these practices to solidify your understanding of Windows deployment.

- **Practice 1** Create and customize an installation of Windows 7 that includes Microsoft Office or any other software you need in your daily work. Then, use the Sysprep utility to generalize the installation and prepare it for imaging. Use a capture image to turn the Sysprepped installation into a WIM file, upload the new image to WDS, and then deploy the image to a PXE-enabled client.

- **Practice 2** Visit *http://technet.microsoft.com* and perform a search for "TechNet Virtual Lab Express: Windows 7: Modifying Windows 7 Operating Systems with DISM." Follow the link to perform the virtual lab.

- **Practice 3** Visit *http://technet.microsoft.com* and perform a search for "TechNet Virtual Lab: Windows 7: Introduction to Deploying Windows 7 Using the Windows Automated Installation Kit." Follow the link to perform the virtual lab.

Configure Hyper-V and Virtual Machines

As with any technology, Hyper-V is best understood by working with it hands-on. Use a high-speed Internet connection to perform the following virtual lab with Hyper-V.

- **Practice** Visit *http://technet.microsoft.com* and perform a search for "TechNet Virtual Lab: Implementing Citrix XenDesktop 4 on Hyper-V R2." Follow the link to perform the virtual lab.

Take a Practice Test

The practice tests on this book's companion CD offer many options. For example, you can test yourself on just one exam objective, or you can test yourself on all the 70-643 certification exam content. You can set up the test so that it closely simulates the experience of taking a certification exam, or you can set it up in study mode so that you can look at the correct answers and explanations after you answer each question.

> **MORE INFO** **PRACTICE TESTS**
>
> For details about all the practice test options available, see the "How to Use the Practice Tests" section in this book's introduction.

CHAPTER 2

Configuring Server Storage and Clusters

Storage area networks (SANs), host bus adapters (HBAs), and logical unit numbers (LUNs) were once the sole domain of storage specialists, far removed from the expertise of your average Windows administrator. However, the arrival of new technologies, such as the Windows Virtual Disk service and Internet SCSI (iSCSI), along with the increasingly complex realities of enterprise storage, has brought these once-specialized topics into the realm of Windows Server 2008 administration. To be an effective Windows server administrator today, you still need to know the difference between the various RAID levels, but you also need to know quite a bit more about advanced server storage technologies.

This chapter introduces you to the basics of disk management in Windows Server 2008 R2, along with more advanced storage technologies such as SANs. The chapter then builds upon this storage information to introduce the various clustering technologies available in Windows Server 2008 R2.

Exam objectives in this chapter:

- Configure storage.
- Configure high availability.

Lessons in this chapter:

Before You Begin

To complete the lessons in this chapter, you must have:

- A computer named Server2 that is running Windows Server 2008 R2. Beyond the disk on which the operating system is installed, Server2 must be equipped with two additional hard disks of equal size.
- A basic understanding of Windows administration.

Lesson 1: Configuring Server Storage

A variety of server storage solutions is available for corporate networks, and Windows Server 2008 R2 connects to these technologies in new ways. This lesson introduces you to the major server storage types and the tools built into Windows Server 2008 R2 you can use to manage them.

After this lesson, you will be able to:

- Understand the basic features of direct-attached storage, network-attached storage, and storage-area networks.
- Know the function of the Virtual Disk service.
- Understand the features of simple, spanned, striped, mirrored, and RAID-5 volumes.
- Use the Disk Management console to create the various volume types.

Estimated lesson time: 80 minutes

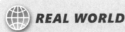 **REAL WORLD**

J.C. Mackin

Although you cannot create them in Windows, the RAID levels known as RAID 0+1 and RAID 1+0 are becoming increasingly common in the real world. A RAID 0+1 (or 01) is a *mirror of stripes*, essentially twin copies of a striped volume. This type of RAID is constructed by creating RAID 0 sets and then mirroring them. A RAID 1+0 (or 10), alternatively, is a *stripe of mirrors* in which the data is striped across multiple mirrored sets. You construct this type of RAID by first creating a series of mirror sets and then building a RAID 0 set across the mirror sets.

Both of these solutions allocate 50 percent of the disks for fault tolerance, and both offer excellent read and write performance. RAID 1+0, however, offers a better chance for recoverability if more than one disk fails.

Note also that the naming conventions for these two RAID levels are not firmly established. Some companies (including Microsoft) might generally refer to both RAID 01 and 10 as 0+1. If you need to clarify your requirements to vendors, you are better off specifying either a *mirror of stripes* or a *stripe of mirrors*.

Understanding Server Storage Technologies

As the demand for server storage has grown, so too has the number of new storage technologies. Over the years, the range of server storage options has broadened from simple direct-attached storage (DAS) to network-attached storage (NAS) and, most recently, to Fibre Channel (FC) and iSCSI SANs.

Direct-Attached Storage

DAS is storage attached to one server only. Examples of DAS solutions are a set of internal hard disks within a server or a rack-mounted RAID connected to a server through a SCSI or FC controller. The main feature of DAS is that it provides a single server with fast, *block-based* data access to storage directly through an internal or external bus. (Block-based, as opposed to file-based, means that data is moved in unformatted blocks rather than in formatted files.) DAS is an affordable solution for servers that need good performance and do not need enormous amounts of storage. For example, DAS is often suitable for infrastructure servers, such as DNS, WINS and DHCP servers, and domain controllers. File servers and web servers can also run well on a server with DAS.

The main limitation of DAS is that it is directly accessible from a single server only, which leads to inefficient storage management. For example, Figure 2-1 shows a LAN in which all storage is attached directly to servers. Despite the web and App2 servers having excess storage, there is no easy way for these resources to be redeployed to either the Mail or App1 server, which need more storage space.

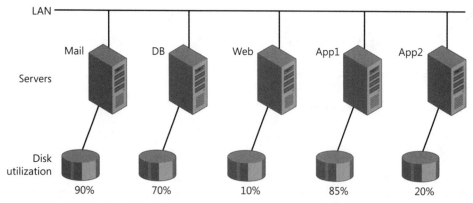

FIGURE 2-1 A network with only a DAS solution.

The main tool used for managing DAS in Windows is the Disk Management console. This tool, which you can access in Server Manager, enables you to partition disks and format volume sets. You can also use the Diskpart.exe command-line utility to perform the same functions available in Disk Management and to perform additional functions as well.

Network-Attached Storage

NAS is self-contained storage that other servers and clients can easily access over the network. A NAS device or appliance is a preconfigured server that runs an operating system specifically designed for handling file services. The main advantage of NAS is that it is simple to implement and can provide a large amount of storage space to clients and servers on a LAN. The downside of NAS is that, because your servers and clients access a NAS device over the LAN as opposed to over a local bus, access to data is slower and file-based as opposed to block-based. NAS performance is, therefore, almost always slower than that of DAS.

Because of its features and limitations, NAS is often a good fit for file servers, web servers, and other servers that don't need extremely fast access to data. In addition, NAS appliances come with their own management tools, which are typically web-based.

Figure 2-2 shows a network in which clients use a NAS appliance as a file server.

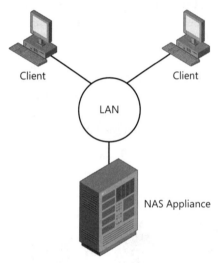

FIGURE 2-2 A LAN with a NAS appliance.

Storage-Area Networks

SANs are high-performance networks dedicated to delivering block data between servers and storage subsystems. From the point of view of the operating system, SAN storage appears as if it were installed locally. The most important characteristic that distinguishes a SAN from DAS is that in a SAN, the storage is not restricted to one server but is, in fact, available to any of a number of servers. (SAN storage can be moved from server to server, but outside of clustered file system environments, it is not accessible by more than one server at a time.)

A SAN is made up of special devices, including SAN network adapters, called HBAs, on the host servers, cables and switches that help route storage traffic, disk storage subsystems, and tape libraries. These hardware devices that connect servers and storage in a SAN are called the *SAN fabric*. All these devices are interconnected by fiber or copper. When connected to the fabric, the available storage is divided up into virtual partitions called logical unit numbers (LUNs), which then appear to servers as local disks.

SANs are designed to enable centralization of storage resources while eliminating the distance and connectivity limitations posed by DAS. For example, parallel SCSI bus architecture limits DAS to 16 devices at a maximum (including the controller) distance of 25 meters. Fibre Channel SANs extend this distance limitation to 10 km or more and enable an essentially unlimited number of devices to attach to the network. These advantages enable SANs to separate storage from individual servers and to pool unlimited storage on a network where that storage can be shared.

SANs are a good solution for servers that require fast access to very large amounts of data (especially block-based data). Such servers can include mail servers, backup servers, streaming media servers, application servers, and database servers. The use of SANs also enables efficient long-distance data replication, which is typically part of a disaster recovery (DR) solution.

Figure 2-3 illustrates a simple SAN.

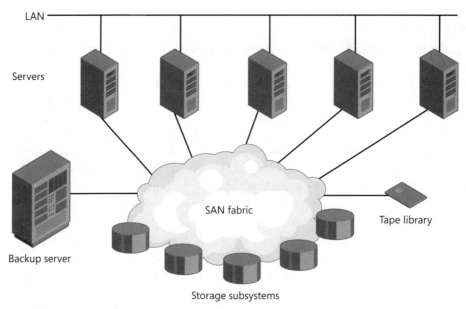

FIGURE 2-3 A sample storage area network (SAN).

SANs generally occur in two varieties: Fibre Channel and iSCSI.

FIBRE CHANNEL SANS

Fibre Channel (FC) delivers high-performance block input/output (I/O) to storage devices. Based on serial SCSI, FC is the oldest and most widely adopted SAN interconnect technology. Unlike parallel SCSI devices, FC devices do not need to arbitrate (or contend) for a shared bus. Instead, FC uses special switches to transmit information between multiple servers and storage devices at the same time.

The main advantage of FC is that it is the most widely implemented SAN technology and has, at least until recently, offered the best performance. The disadvantages of FC technology are the cost of its hardware and the complexity of its implementation. Fibre Channel network components include server HBAs, cabling, and switches. All these components are specialized for FC, lack interoperability among vendors, are relatively expensive, and require special expertise.

ISCSI SANS

Internet SCSI (iSCSI) is an industry standard developed to enable transmission of SCSI block commands over an Ethernet network by using the TCP/IP protocol. Servers communicate with iSCSI devices through a locally installed software agent known as an *iSCSI initiator*. The iSCSI initiator executes requests and receives responses from an *iSCSI target*, which itself can be the end-node storage device or an intermediary device such as a switch. For iSCSI fabrics, the network also includes one or more Internet Storage Name Service (iSNS) servers that, much like DNS servers on a LAN, provide discoverability and zoning of SAN resources.

By relying on TCP/IP, iSCSI SANs take advantage of networking devices and expertise that are widely available, a fact that makes iSCSI SANs generally simpler and less expensive to implement than FC SANs.

Aside from lower cost and greater ease of implementation, other advantages of iSCSI over FC include:

- **Connectivity over long distances** Organizations distributed over wide areas might have a series of unlinked SAN islands that the current FC connectivity limitation of 10 km cannot bridge. (There are new means of extending Fibre Channel connectivity up to several hundred kilometers, but these methods are both complex and costly.) In contrast, iSCSI can connect SANs in distant offices by using in-place metropolitan area networks (MANs) and wide-area networks (WANs).

- **Built-in security** No security measures are built into the Fibre Channel protocol. Instead, security is implemented primarily through limiting physical access to the SAN. In contrast to FC, the Microsoft implementation of the iSCSI protocol provides security for devices on the network by using the Challenge Handshake Authentication Protocol (CHAP) for authentication, and the Internet Protocol security (IPsec) standard for encryption. Because these methods of securing communications already exist in Windows networks, they can be readily extended from LANs to SANs.

> *NOTE* **ISCSI SAN FABRIC**
>
> **An iSCSI SAN can use dedicated devices for its fabric, or it can rely on an organization's existing LAN, MAN, or WAN infrastructure. For both security and performance, a dedicated iSCSI network separating network traffic from storage traffic is recommended.**

The main disadvantage of an iSCSI SAN is that, unless it is built with dedicated (and expensive) 10 Gbps Ethernet cabling and switches, the I/O transfer of iSCSI is slower than an FC-based SAN can deliver. And if you do choose to use 10-GB equipment for your iSCSI SAN instead of the much more common choice of gigabit Ethernet, the high cost of such a 10-GB solution would eliminate the price advantage of iSCSI relative to FC.

EXAM TIP

Vocabulary terms you should understand for the exam include LUNs, HBA, iSCSI initiator, iSCSI target, SAN fabric, and iSNS.

Configuring a SAN Connection with iSCSI Initiator

You can use the iSCSI Initiator built into Windows Server 2008 and Windows Server 2008 R2 to connect to an iSCSI SAN, configure the features of this iSCSI connection, and provision storage. To configure a SAN connection with iSCSI Initiator, select the tool from the Administrative Tools group in the Start menu. This step opens the Targets tab of the iSCSI Initiator Properties dialog box, as shown in Figure 2-4.

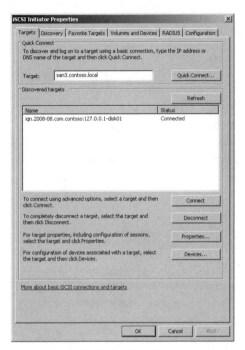

FIGURE 2-4 iSCSI Initiator Properties.

To connect to an iSCSI SAN, specify an iSCSI target by name in the Target text box and then click Quick Connect. (Quick Connect is a new feature in Windows Server 2008 R2.) The Targets tab also provides access to Multipath I/O (MPIO) settings through the *Devices* and *Connect* buttons. MPIO enables you to configure multiple simultaneous connections to an iSCSI target so that if one adapter fails, another connection can continue processing I/O without any interruption of service. To enable MPIO, use the Add Features Wizard to add the Multipath I/O feature.

After you establish a connection to an iSCSI target, you can use the following tabs to configure the connection:

- Discovery

  On this tab, you can discover targets on specified portals and choose iSNS servers.

- Favorite Targets

  Use this tab to ensure that connections to selected iSCSI targets are restored every time the local computer restarts.

- Volumes And Devices

  This tab enables you to provision volumes and devices on targets and bind to them so they are readily available on system restart.

- RADIUS

This tab enables you to specify a RADIUS server and shared secret for the authentication of the iSCSI connection.

- Configuration

  This tab enables you to require negotiation of the CHAP authentication protocol and IPsec encryption for all connections to the local iSCSI Initiator. The tab also provides a unique identification number for the iSCSI Initator, which you can specify on a remote iSCSI target to configure a connection to the local machine.

EXAM TIP

For the 70-643 exam, you need to be familiar with the various configuration options available for iSCSI Initiator, including MPIO, favorites, RADIUS, and IPsec.

Other Tools for Managing SANs

Windows Server 2008 and Windows Server 2008 R2 include the Virtual Disk service (VDS), an application programming interface (API) that enables FC and iSCSI SAN hardware vendors to expose disk subsystems and SAN hardware to administrative tools in Windows. When vendor hardware includes the VDS hardware provider, you can manage that hardware within Windows Server 2008 and Windows Server 2008 R2 by using iSCSI Initiator and other tools, such as Disk Management, Storage Manager for SANs (SMfS), Storage Explorer, or the command-line tool, DiskRAID.exe.

- **Storage Manager for SANs**   SMfS is available in Windows Server 2008 and Windows Server 2008 R2 as a feature you can add by using the Add Features Wizard. You can use SMfS to manage SANs by provisioning disks, creating LUNs, and assigning LUNs to different servers in the SAN.

- **Storage Explorer**   Storage Explorer is available by default in Windows Server 2008 and Windows Server 2008 R2 through the Administrative Tools program group. You can use Storage Explorer to display detailed information about servers connected to the SAN and about fabric components such as HBAs, FC switches, and iSCSI initiators and targets. You can also use Storage Explorer to perform administrative tasks on an iSCSI fabric.

- **DiskRAID**   DiskRAID is a command-line tool that enables you to manage LUNs in a VDS-enabled hardware RAID.

Managing Disks, Volumes, and Partitions in Windows Server 2008 R2

The main tool you can use to manage disks, volumes, and partitions in Windows Server 2008 and Windows Server 2008 R2 is Disk Management. With Disk Management, you can initialize disks, bring disks online or offline, create volumes within disks, format volumes, change disk partition styles, extend and shrink volumes, and create fault-tolerant disk sets.

To access Disk Management, you can type **Diskmgmt.msc** in the Run box, select Disk Management beneath the *Storage* node in Server Manager, or select the *Disk Management* node in the Computer Management console (accessible through Administrative Tools).

Disk Management is shown in Figure 2-5.

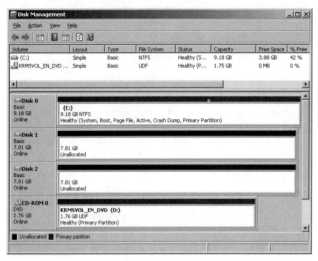

FIGURE 2-5 Disk Management in Windows Server 2008 R2.

Understanding Basic and Dynamic Disks

Disk Management enables you to manage both basic and dynamic disks.

By default, all disks are basic disks. A basic disk is a physical disk that contains primary partitions, extended partitions, or logical drives. The number of partitions you can create on a basic disk depends on the disk's *partition style*. On disks that use the master boot record (MBR) partition style, you can create up to four primary partitions per basic disk, or you can create up to three primary partitions and one extended partition. Within the one extended partition, you can then create unlimited logical drives. On basic disks that use the GUID partition table (GPT) partition style, you can create up to 128 primary partitions. Because GPT disks do not limit you to four partitions, you do not need to create extended partitions or logical drives. GPT disks are recommended for disks larger than 2 terabytes (TB) and for disks on 64-bit systems.

> **NOTE PARTITION STYLES**
>
> Partition styles refer to the most elemental disk structure visible to the operating system. Partition styles do not affect file formats within partitions, such as NTFS or FAT32. Basic and dynamic disks can occur on either partition style.

Dynamic disks provide advanced features that basic disks do not: features such as the ability to create an unlimited number of volumes, volumes that span multiple disks (spanned and striped volumes), and fault-tolerant volumes (mirrored and RAID-5 volumes). There are five types of dynamic volumes: simple, spanned, striped, mirrored, and RAID-5.

In previous versions of Windows, you needed to convert a basic disk to a dynamic disk before you could create any of these volume types. When you use Disk Management in Windows Server 2008 R2 to create any of these volume types, however, basic disks are automatically converted to dynamic disks during the process. As a result, the question of whether a disk is basic or dynamic has become less important from an administrative point of view. Despite this development, it is still important to know for dual-boot configurations that many earlier versions of Windows (such as Windows NT, Windows 98, and Windows ME) cannot access dynamic disks. Also relevant for dual-boot configurations is the fact that dynamic disks are only compatible with Windows operating systems.

EXAM TIP

Even though basic disks are automatically converted to dynamic disks when necessary, you still need to know which volume types require dynamic disks for the 70-643 exam.

Creating Volumes

You can use Disk Management or the Diskpart command-line utility to create the following volume types in Windows Server 2008 R2.

- **Simple or basic volumes**   Simple volumes are basic drives that are not fault tolerant. A simple volume can consist of a single region on a disk or multiple regions that are on the same disk and linked together.

  To create a simple volume in Disk Management, right-click unallocated space on a disk and then click New Simple Volume, as shown in Figure 2-6. (This process is identical whether you are creating the volume on a basic or dynamic disk, even though on a basic disk, the new volume is technically called a partition or basic volume.) Note that first you might need to right-click the disk and select Online.

  To create a simple volume by using the Diskpart utility, use the utility to select the disk and then, on a dynamic disk, type the **create volume simple** command. To create a new volume (partition) on a basic disk, type **create partition**. You can use **create volume ?** or **create partition ?** to learn the specific syntax associated with these commands.

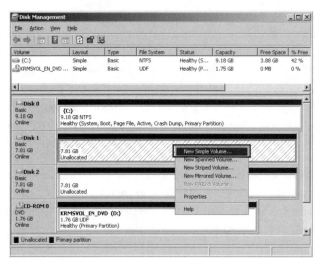

FIGURE 2-6 Creating a simple volume.

- **Spanned volumes** A spanned volume is a dynamic volume consisting of disk space on more than one disk. If a simple volume is not a system volume or boot volume, you can extend it across additional disks to create a spanned volume, or you can create a new volume as a spanned volume by using unallocated space on more than one disk.

  To create a new spanned volume, in Disk Management, right-click unallocated space on one of the disks where you want to create the spanned volume and then click New Spanned Volume. This step opens the New Spanned Volume Wizard, which allows you you to add space to the spanned volume from the disks available.

  Figure 2-7 shows a spanned volume, assigned drive letter E. Notice how the drive uses space from Disk 1 and Disk 2, but appears as only a single volume with a capacity of 7.32 GB.

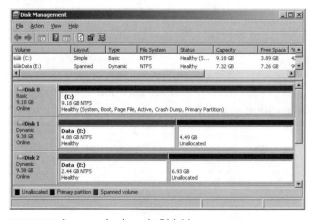

FIGURE 2-7 A spanned volume in Disk Management.

- **Striped volumes** A striped volume, which is also known as RAID 0, is a dynamic volume that stores data in stripes across two or more physical disks. Striped volumes offer the best performance of all the volumes available in Windows, but they do not provide fault tolerance. If a disk in a striped volume fails, the data in the entire volume is lost.

Figure 2-8 shows how data in a striped volume is written across a set of disks.

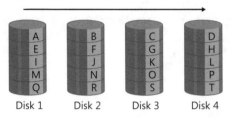

FIGURE 2-8 A RAID 0, or striped volume, stripes data across disks.

When should you use a striped volume? A striped volume is the best storage solution for temporary data that does not need fault tolerance but does require high performance. Examples of such temporary data include page files and Temp folders. To create a new striped volume in Disk Management, right-click unallocated space on a disk and then click New Striped Volume.

A striped volume in Disk Management is shown in Figure 2-9. The volume uses 1.46 GB of space from both Disk 1 and Disk 2 and appears as a single volume E with a total capacity of 2.93 GB. Note how the volume is being used to store temporary data (the Page File).

NOTE **RAID DISKS**

As with all RAID solutions, a striped volume is built with disks of equal size.

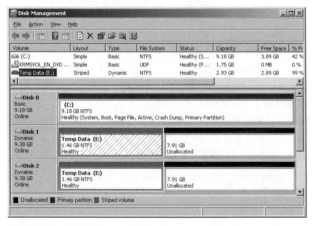

FIGURE 2-9 A RAID 0, or striped volume, in Disk Management.

- **Mirrored volumes** Also known as a RAID 1, a mirrored volume is a fault-tolerant volume that provides data redundancy by using two copies, or mirrors, of the same volume. All data written to the mirrored volume is written to both volumes, which are located on separate physical disks. If one of the physical disks fails, the data on the failed disk becomes unavailable, but the system continues to operate by using the unaffected disk.

Figure 2-10 illustrates how data is stored on a mirrored volume. Because data is duplicated, no data is lost if either disk fails.

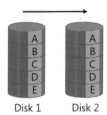

Disk 1   Disk 2

FIGURE 2-10 A RAID 1, or mirrored volume, copies all data onto a second disk.

> **NOTE TRIPLE MIRRORING AND BEYOND**
>
> Although mirrored volumes configured in Windows Server 2008 and Windows Server 2008 R2 are limited to two disks, mirrors created through third-party solutions can be created out of three disks or more. In a triple mirror configuration, for example, the contents of one disk are duplicated on two additional disks. Multiple mirrors degrade write performance but improve fault tolerance. They are good solutions for mission-critical data.

As a fault-tolerant solution, a mirrored volume has advantages and disadvantages. One advantage of a mirrored volume is that it offers very good read performance as well as fairly good write performance. In addition, mirroring requires only two disks, and almost any volume can be mirrored, including the system and boot volumes. The disadvantage of a mirrored volume is that it requires 50 percent of a disk's total storage capacity to be reserved for fault tolerance. Overall, if you need a fault-tolerant storage solution, a mirror is a good choice if you have only two disks; if you need good read and write performance; or if you need to provide fault tolerance for the system volume, the boot volume, or other mission-critical data.

To create a mirrored volume, you can either add a mirror to an existing volume or create a new mirrored volume. To add a mirror to an existing volume in Disk Management, right-click the existing volume and then click Add Mirror, as shown in Figure 2-11.

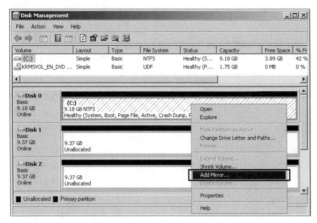

FIGURE 2-11 Adding a mirror to the System partition.

To create a new mirrored volume in Disk Management, right-click unallocated space on a disk and then click New Mirrored Volume. A new mirrored volume is shown in Figure 2-12. The drive uses 5.86 GB of space from both Disk 1 and Disk 2 and appears as a single volume E with a total capacity of 5.86 GB.

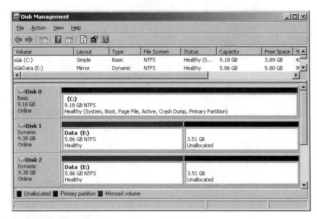

FIGURE 2-12 A RAID 1, or mirrored, volume.

- **Raid-5 volumes** A RAID-5 volume is a fault-tolerant volume that combines areas of free space from at least three physical hard disks into one logical volume. RAID-5 volumes stripe data along with *parity* (evenness or oddness) *information* across a set of disks. When a single disk fails, Windows uses this parity information to re-create the data on the failed disk. RAID-5 volumes can accept the loss of only a single disk in the set.

Figure 2-13 shows a RAID-5 volume made up of four disks. Data written to the volume is striped across these disks from left to right. For each stripe across the set of disks, one disk is used to hold parity information about the evenness or oddness of the other data in the stripe. In the simplified example shown in Figure 2-13, parity is set to 1 when the sum of the values in the stripe is odd, and parity is set to 0 when the sum of the remaining values is even. By using this parity information along with other disk data, if any one (and only one) disk fails, Windows can reconstruct the complete contents of that failed disk. The data of the failed drive can be re-created in real time as users request it. The party information can also be re-created live on a new disk after the failed disk has been replaced.

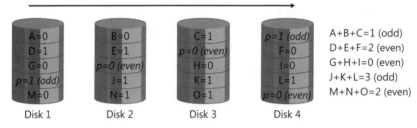

FIGURE 2-13 A RAID-5 volume calculates parity (evenness or oddness) for fault tolerance.

Space approximately equivalent to one disk is always used for fault tolerance in a RAID-5 volume. For example, if you create a RAID-5 out of four 120-GB disks, the total storage space available in that RAID-5 is 360 GB.

When should you use a RAID-5 volume? A RAID-5 volume is characterized by very good read performance, relatively poor write performance, and optimal use of storage space in a fault-tolerant solution. Therefore, consider using a RAID-5 volume when good write performance is not a priority, or when you need a fault-tolerant storage solution that makes the best use of available storage. Note also that you cannot assign the system or boot partition to a RAID-5 volume created in Windows Server 2008 or Windows Server 2008 R2.

NOTE **SOFTWARE AND HARDWARE RAIDS**

A RAID-5 volume created in Disk Management is an example of a software RAID because the RAID is created by the operating system. Some vendors, however, sell disk enclosures that include their own built-in RAID setup utility. If you configure a RAID-5 with this vendor software, the storage appears to Windows as a single local volume. A RAID configuration such as this, which is transparent to the operating system, is known as a hardware RAID. Although software RAID has lower performance than hardware RAID does, software RAID is inexpensive and easy to configure because it has no special hardware requirements other than multiple disks. If cost is more important than performance, software RAID is an appropriate solution.

To create a RAID-5 volume in Disk Management, right-click unallocated space on one of the dynamic disks on which you want to create the RAID-5 volume and then click New RAID-5 Volume and follow the instructions in the New RAID-5 Volume Wizard.

To create a RAID-5 volume by using the Diskpart utility, use the *create volume raid* command. You can use the *help create volume raid* command to learn the exact syntax.

EXAM TIP

For the 70-643 exam, make sure you understand RAID levels and the different volume types.

Extending a Volume

You can add more space to existing simple or spanned volumes by extending them into unallocated space on the same disk or on a different disk. To extend a volume, it must either be formatted with the NTFS file system or unformatted. To extend a volume in Disk Management, right-click the simple or spanned volume you want to extend and then click Extend Volume.

NOTE EXTENDING BOOT AND SYSTEM VOLUMES

You cannot extend a boot or system volume onto another disk.

Shrinking a Volume

You can decrease the space used by simple or spanned volumes by shrinking them into contiguous free space at the end of the volume. For example, if you need to increase the amount of unallocated space on a disk to make room for a new partition or volume, you can attempt to shrink the existing volumes on the disk. When you shrink a partition, any ordinary files are automatically relocated on the disk to create the new unallocated space. There is no need to reformat the disk to shrink the partition.

The amount of space you can gain from shrinking a volume varies greatly. In general, the greater the percentage of unused space on the volume and the fewer the bad clusters, the more you can shrink the volume. If, however, the number of bad clusters detected by dynamic bad-cluster remapping is too great, you will not be able to shrink the volume at all. If this occurs, consider moving the data and replacing the disk.

> **CAUTION** **DO NOT SHRINK RAW PARTITIONS THAT CONTAIN DATA**
>
> If a partition is not formatted with a file system but still contains data (such as a database file), shrinking the partition can actually destroy the data.

To shrink a volume in Disk Management, right-click the simple or spanned volume that you want to shrink and then click Shrink Volume, as shown in Figure 2-14.

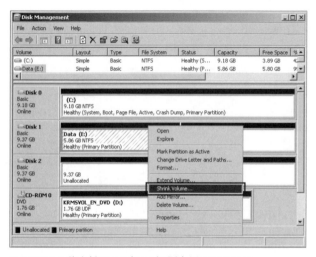

FIGURE 2-14 Shrinking a volume in Disk Management.

EXAM TIP

Shrinking is a new feature in Windows Server 2008 and Windows Server 2008 R2. Expect to see a question on this topic on the 70-643 exam.

Configuring a Mount Point

A mount point is a folder in a volume that acts as a pointer to the root directory of another volume. For example, if you need to make more storage space available to the system or boot disk, you can create a new volume on another disk and then mount that volume in a folder in the system volume.

This arrangement is illustrated in Figure 2-15. In this scenario, the original disk capacity of the C drive is 9.18 GB. By mounting a 3.51-GB volume in a folder named MountedVolume in C, you are able to access more disk space through C even though you have not changed the capacity of the disk.

FIGURE 2-15 A new volume mounted in the system volume.

You can create a mount point in Disk Management by creating a new volume and then choosing the option to mount the volume in an empty NTFS folder, as shown in Figure 2-16.

> **NOTE   EXTENDING THE SYSTEM OR BOOT VOLUME**
>
> Because you cannot extend a system volume onto another disk, mount points are the only way you can make more space available to the system volume without replacing hardware.

You can also create a mount point for an existing volume by right-clicking the volume and then selecting Change Drive Letter And Paths. In the Change Drive Letter And Paths dialog box, click Change and then choose the option to mount the volume in an empty NTFS folder.

EXAM TIP

Understand mount points for the 70-643 exam.

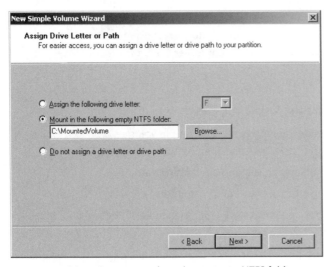

FIGURE 2-16 Mounting a new volume in an empty NTFS folder.

✓ **Quick Check**

1. Can you extend a mirrored volume?

2. True or False: A hardware RAID-5 volume cannot act as a system volume in Windows Server 2008 R2.

Quick Check Answers

1. No

2. False. Although a *software* RAID-5 cannot be used as a system volume in Windows Server 2008 R2, a *hardware* RAID-5 volume can indeed be used as the system volume because a hardware RAID would be transparent to the operating system. The limitation for RAID-5 volumes affects what you can configure from within the Windows operating system. You cannot add the system or boot partition to a software RAID-5 volume, and you cannot install an operating system on a RAID-5 volume that you create in Windows. (Note also that installing an operating system on a hardware RAID-5 volume, although possible, is discouraged because of the poor write performance associated with RAID-5.)

PRACTICE Work with Disk Sets

In this practice, you create various volume types in Disk Management.

> **NOTE** **HOW MANY DISKS DO YOU NEED FOR THESE EXERCISES?**
>
> These exercises require Server2 to have two unpartitioned disks (Disk 1 and Disk 2) of equal size. These disks must be separate from the system disk (Disk 0) on which you have installed Windows Server 2008 R2. If you have not done so already, you should now create these two new virtual disks by using Hyper-V Manager. (You can specify a size of 1 GB each.) You should then use the Settings For Server2.contoso.local dialog box in Hyper-V Manager to add one of these virtual disks to IDE Controller 0 and the other to IDE Controller 1.

EXERCISE 1 Working with Disks and Simple Volumes

In this exercise, which you perform on Server2, you create simple volumes on Disk 1 while switching first between dynamic and basic disks and then between MBR and GPT disks.

1. Log on to Contoso.com from Server2 as a domain administrator.

2. In the Run box, type **diskmgmt.msc** and then press Enter.

3. If the Initialize Disk dialog box appears, select MBR (Master Boot Record) and then click OK to initialize Disk 1 and Disk 2.

4. In Disk Management, in the top pane, ensure that C is the only lettered volume that is visible. If necessary, back up data and then delete all other volumes. (You may ignore any volume named "System Reserved.")

   In the bottom pane of Disk Management, three disks should be displayed: Disk 0, Disk 1, and Disk 2.

5. Right-click the unallocated space on Disk 1 and then click New Simple Volume.

   The New Simple Volume Wizard opens.

6. On the Welcome page of the New Simple Volume Wizard, click Next.

7. On the Specify Volume Size page, read all the text on the page and then click Next.

8. On the Assign Drive Letter Or Path page, read all the text on the page and then click Next.

9. On the Format Partition page, read all the text on the page, verify that Perform A Quick Format is selected, and then click Next.

10. On the Completing The New Simple Volume Wizard page, click Finish.

    After the creation and formatting are complete, the new volume appears in Disk Management.

11. In Disk Management, in the bottom pane, right-click the Disk 1 tile and then click Convert To Dynamic Disk.

12. In the Convert To Dynamic Disk dialog box, verify that Disk 1 is selected and then click OK.

13. In the Disks To Convert Dialog box, click Convert.

14. In the Disk Management dialog box, read all the text and then click Yes.

    After several moments, the new volume changes from blue to green.

15. Right-click the Disk 1 tile and then answer the following questions:

    Question: Can you convert Disk 1 back to a basic disk?

    Answer: No, because the option is grayed out.

    Question: Can you convert Disk 1 to the GPT partition style?

    Answer: No, because the disk contains volumes, so the option is unavailable.

16. Right-click the new volume you have created on Disk 1 and then click Delete Volume. Click Yes when prompted to confirm.

17. After the volume has deleted, answer the following question:

    Question: Is Disk 1 now listed as Basic or Dynamic?

    Answer: Basic. By default, disks with no volumes are basic.

18. Right-click Disk 1 and choose the option to convert Disk 1 to a dynamic disk. Then, after the conversion has completed, right-click Disk 1 to convert it back to a basic disk.

When a disk contains no volumes, you can convert it freely between basic and dynamic. However, when a disk contains volumes, you can convert only from basic to dynamic.

19. Right-click Disk 1 and then click Convert To GPT Disk.

20. After a few moments, right-click Disk 1 again and then click Convert To MBR Disk.

When a disk contains no volumes, you can convert it freely between MBR and GPT partition styles. However, you cannot convert the partition style of a disk when it contains any volumes.

21. Leave Disk Management open and proceed to Exercise 2.

EXERCISE 2 Creating Mount Points

In this exercise, which you perform on Server2, you mount two volumes as folders in volume C.

1. While you are logged on to Contoso.com from Server2 as a domain administrator, in the root of volume C, create two new folders named **MountVol1** and **MountVol2**, respectively.

2. In Disk Management, right-click the unallocated space in Disk 1 and then click New Simple Volume.

3. On the Welcome To The New Simple Volume Wizard page, click Next.

4. On the Specify Volume Size page, in the Simple Volume Size In MB text box, type a value that represents approximately half of the available space. For example, if 1021 MB are available, type 500 and then click Next.

5. On the Assign Drive Letter Or Path page, select Mount In The Following Empty NTFS Folder. Type **C:\MountVol1** in the associated text box (or use the *Browse* button to select that folder) and then click Next.

6. On the Format Partition page, in the Volume Label text box, replace the "New Volume" text by typing **Mounted in C**.

7. On the Format Partition page, verify that Perform A Quick Format is selected and then click Next.

8. On the Completing the New Simple Volume Wizard page, click Finish.

After a few moments, the new volume appears in Disk Management. It is not assigned a drive letter, but it is labeled Mounted In C.

9. In the Start menu, select Computer.

In the Computer window, only the C drive is visible. You cannot directly access the new drive you have just created.

10. Open the C drive.

In the C drive, the MountVol1 folder is marked by a special icon. It is also associated with a large size, even though the volume is empty.

11. Open the properties of MountVol1.

    In the MountVol1 Properties dialog box, the type is listed as Mounted Volume.

12. In the MountVol1 Properties dialog box, click Properties.

    The Mounted In C (C:\MountVol1) Properties dialog box opens. The dialog box displays the same information you would find in the properties sheet of a volume.

13. Click OK to close the Mounted In C (C:\MountVol1) Properties dialog box and then click OK to close the MountVol1 Properties dialog box.

14. In Disk Management, create a new simple volume on Disk 1 by using the same process described in Exercise 1. Use all the remaining space on Disk 1 for the new volume and do *not* select the option to mount the volume in an NTFS folder. Type **Mounted In C (2)** as the name for the volume and choose the option to perform a quick format.

    After the new volume is created, it appears in Disk Management, assigned a drive letter such as E.

15. In Disk Management, right-click the Mounted In C (2) volume and then click Change Drive Letter And Paths.

16. In the Change Drive Letter And Paths dialog box, click Remove and then click Yes to confirm.

    You can mount an existing volume only if you first remove any drive letter associated with it.

17. In Disk Management, right-click the Mounted In C (2) volume again and, again, click Change Drive Letter And Paths.

18. In the Change Drive Letter And Paths dialog box, click Add.

19. In the Add Drive Letter Or Path dialog box, click Mount In The Following Empty NTFS Folder and then type or browse to C:\MountVol2.

20. In the Add Drive Letter or Path dialog box, click OK.

21. Click Start and then Computer to verify that Mounted In C (2) has been configured as a mount point in the folder named MountVol2 in the C drive.

22. In Disk Management, delete both the Mounted In C and the Mounted In C (2) volumes. Verify that only unallocated space remains on Disk 1.

23. Close all windows except for Disk Management and then proceed to Exercise 3.

EXERCISE 3   Add and Break a Mirror

In this exercise, which you perform on Server2, you create a new volume on Disk 1 and then add a mirror on Disk 2.

1. While you are still logged on to Contoso.com from Server2 as a domain administrator, in Disk Management, create a new simple volume on Disk 1, using all the available space on the disk. Complete the New Simple Volume Wizard by using all the default options.

2. Right-click the new E volume on Disk 1 and then click Add Mirror.

3. In the Add Mirror dialog box, select Disk 2 and then click Add Mirror.

4. In the Disk Management dialog box, read all the text and then click Yes.

    A new volume is created on Disk 2, and then, after both Disk 1 and Disk 2 are converted to dynamic disks, the new volume on Disk 1 is also assigned the drive letter C. The status of the twin volumes is then shown as Resynching while the mirror is created. This process of resynchronization varies, depending on the size of the volumes.

5. After the mirror volume has finished resynchronizing, take a few moments to browse Disk Management, noting the single volume listed in the top pane and the capacity of the drive.

6. On Disk 2, right-click volume E. Use the options available on the shortcut menu to answer the following questions:

    Question: Which option on the shortcut menu should you choose if you want to turn the mirrored volume into two separate volumes?

    Answer: Break Mirrored Volume. You should choose this option when one of the disks fails or becomes corrupted.

    Question: Which option on the shortcut menu should you choose if you want to delete the mirror on Disk 2 immediately?

    Answer: Remove Mirror.

7. On the shortcut menu, click Remove Mirror.

8. In the Remove Mirror dialog box, select Disk 2 and then click Remove Mirror.

9. In the Data Management dialog box, click Yes to confirm.

    In Disk Management, Disk 2 once again appears as a basic disk with only unallocated space.

10. Delete Volume E on Disk 1.

11. Leave Disk Management open and proceed to Exercise 4.

EXERCISE 4   Creating a Spanned Volume

In this exercise, you create a spanned volume on Disk 1 and Disk 2. You need two unpartitioned dynamic disks for this exercise.

1. In Disk Management, right-click the unallocated space in Disk 1 and then click Create New Spanned Volume.

    The New Spanned Volume Wizard opens.

2. On the Welcome To The New Spanned Volume Wizard page, read all the text on the page and then click Next.

3. On the Select Disks page, verify that only Disk 1 is visible in the Selected area.

4. In the Select The Amount Of Space In MB text box, type an amount that is equal to approximately half of the available space. For example, if the default number in the box is 1021, replace that amount by typing **500**.

5. On the Select Disks page, select Disk 2, which is shown in the Available area, and then click Add to move Disk 2 to the Selected area.

6. In the Selected area, click to select Disk 2.

7. In the Select The Amount Of Space In MB text box, type an amount that is equal to approximately 25 percent of the available space. For example, if the default number in the box is 1021, replace that amount by typing **250**.

8. On the Select Disks page, click Next.

9. On the Assign Drive Letter Or Path page, click Next.

10. On the Format Volume page, in the Volume Label text box, replace the text by typing **Spanned Volume**.

11. On the Format Volume page, verify that the Perform A Quick Format check box is selected and then click Next.

12. On the Completing The New Spanned Volume Wizard page, click Finish.

13. If the Disk Management dialog box appears, read all the text and then click Yes.

    After the creation and formatting complete, the new spanned volume appears in Disk Management. The new volume spans disks 1 and 2.

14. Spend a few moments browsing the information related to the new volume in Disk Management. Note, for example, the capacity of the volume and the fact that it is assigned a single drive letter.

15. Leave Disk Management open and proceed to Exercise 5.

EXERCISE 5   Creating a Striped Volume

In this exercise, you create a new striped volume in the remaining space on Disk 1 and Disk 2.

1. While you are logged on to Contoso.com from Server2 as a domain administrator, in Disk Management, right-click the unallocated space in Disk 1 and then click New Striped Volume.

   The New Striped Volume Wizard appears.

2. On the Welcome page of the New Striped Volume Wizard, click Next.

3. On the Select Disks page, note that only Disk 1 appears in the Selected area.

4. On the Select Disks page, select Disk 2 in the Available area and then click Add to move Disk 2 to the Selected area.

   The amount of space associated with Disk 1 and Disk 2 is identical. In a striped volume, all member disks must be the same size.

5. On the Select Disks page, click Next.

6. On the Assign Drive Letter Or Path page, click Next.

7. On the Format Volume page, in the Volume Label text box, replace the text by typing **Striped Volume**.

8. On the Format Volume page, verify that the Perform A Quick Format check box is selected and then click Next.

9. On the Completing The New Striped Volume Wizard page, click Finish.

   After the creation and formatting complete, the new striped volume appears in Disk Management.

10. Spend a few moments browsing the information related to the new striped volume in Disk Management. Note, for example, the capacity of the volume and the fact that it is assigned a single drive letter.

11. Leave Disk Management open and proceed to Exercise 6.

EXERCISE 6   Shrinking and Extending a Volume

In this exercise, you shrink the spanned volume you created in Exercise 5. Then, after deleting the striped volume you created in the same exercise, you extend the spanned volume into the available space on Disk 1.

1. While you are still logged on to Contoso.com from Server2 as a domain administrator, in Disk Management, right-click the Spanned Volume on Disk 2 and then click Shrink Volume.

   The Querying Shrink Space box appears, and then the Shrink [Drive Letter] dialog box appears.

2. In the Shrink dialog box, read all the text.

   In the Enter The Amount Of Space To Shrink In MB text box, the default amount provided is equal to the maximum amount you can shrink the drive.

3. Click Shrink to shrink the volume the maximum allowable amount.

   After several moments, the spanned volume appears in its newer, smaller size. Now, the volume might or might not be limited to Disk 1.

4. In Disk Management, right-click the striped volume (not the spanned volume) and then click Delete Volume.

5. In the Delete Striped Volume dialog box, read all the text and then click Yes to confirm.

   After the volume is deleted, new unallocated space appears on Disk 1.

6. Right-click the spanned volume on Disk 1 and then click Extend Volume.

   The Extend Volume Wizard opens.

7. On the Welcome To The Extend Volume Wizard page, read all the text and then click Next.

8. On the Select Disk page, verify that only Disk 1 is shown in the Selected area.

9. On the Select Disk page, leave the default (full) amount of space to expand on Disk 1 and then click Next.

10. On the Completing the Extend Volume Wizard page, click Finish.

After a few moments, the volume appears in Disk Management, occupying all the space on Disk 1. If the volume is confined to Disk 1, it is now designated as a simple volume. If some portion remains on Disk 2, it is still designated as a spanned volume.

11. Right-click the volume on Disk 1, click Delete Volume, and then click Yes to confirm the deletion.

After a few moments, Disk Management shows that Disk 1 and Disk 2 have returned to their original state.

12. Log off Server2.

Lesson Summary

- In general, disk storage occurs in three varieties: direct-attached storage (DAS), network-attached storage (NAS), and storage-area networks (SANs). Both DAS and SANs provide block-based access to data storage, and NAS provides file-based access. SANs provide the additional benefit of shared storage that you can easily move from server to server.

- When vendor disk storage subsystems include a hardware provider for Virtual Disk Service (VDS), you can manage that hardware within Windows Server 2008 R2 by using tools such as Disk Management, Storage Manager for SANs (SMfS), Storage Explorer, iSCSI Initiator, or the DiskRAID.exe command-line tool.

- Disk Management is the main tool you can use for managing disks and volumes in Windows Server 2008 R2. Disk Management enables you to create simple, spanned, striped, mirrored, and RAID-5 volumes.

- By using Disk Management, you can extend or shrink a simple or spanned volume.

- By using Disk Management, you can configure a volume as a mount point in another volume.

Lesson Review

The following questions are intended to reinforce key information presented in this lesson. The questions are also available on the companion CD if you prefer to review them in electronic form.

> **NOTE ANSWERS**
>
> Answers to these questions and explanations of why each answer choice is correct or incorrect are located in the "Answers" section at the end of the book.

1. You work as a network administrator, and your responsibilities include managing server storage. You have been asked to purchase a new disk subsystem for your company's storage-area network (SAN). You are in the process of testing hardware solutions before making purchases, and you attach a new disk subsystem to the network. You

want to provision the new disks and create new logical unit numbers (LUNs) to assign to a server named Server1. You open Storage Manager for SANs, but you can't see the new hardware. However, you can connect to the new hardware by using the software provided by the vendor. You want to be able to manage the new disk subsystem you purchase by using Storage Manager for SANs. What should you do?

A. In Disk Management, choose the Rescan Disks option.

B. Choose a disk subsystem from a vendor that has a Virtual Disk Service hardware provider.

C. On Server1, configure iSCSI Initiator to specify the new hardware as a favorite target.

D. Use Storage Explorer to configure Server1 as an iSNS server.

2. You work as an IT support specialist. Your job responsibilities include managing server storage. You are designing storage for a new application server. The application makes heavy use of temporary storage, and you want to allocate three 20-GB disk drives to that storage. If excellent read and write performance is a high priority, and you also want to use as much available space as possible, which of the following volume types should you create?

A. Simple volume

B. Spanned volume

C. Mirrored volume

D. Striped volume

E. RAID-5 volume

3. Each client desktop in your company is configured with a K drive mapped to a network share on a file server running Windows Server 2008 R2. The shared folder on the file server is named Data, and it contains many personal folders and shared project data. The Data folder is stored on a nonsystem disk assigned the volume letter E, which is running low on storage space.

To address the problem of low storage space available through the K drive, you add another physical disk to the file server and create a new volume on it. Your goals are to maximize the space available through K and cause minimum disruption to users and their procedures for storing and sharing data. What should you do?

A. Mount the new volume as a folder within the Data folder.

B. Copy the Data folder to the new volume and re-create the Data share to point to the new location.

C. Extend the E drive onto the new volume.

D. Create a mirror consisting of the new volume and the E drive.

Lesson 2: Configuring Server Clusters

In enterprise networks, groups of independent servers are often used to provide a common set of services. Different physical computers, for example, can answer requests directed at a common website or database server. Although these server groups are often referred to generally as *clusters*, cluster types can serve very different purposes. This lesson describes the load balancing and high-availability server clusters you can configure in Windows Server 2008 R2.

After this lesson, you will be able to:

- Understand the features and limitations of DNS round-robin.
- Understand the main function and features of Network Load Balancing clusters.
- Know the basic steps to configure a Network Load Balancing cluster.
- Understand the main function and features of failover clusters.
- Understand the requirements for creating a failover cluster.

Estimated lesson time: 90 minutes

Server Cluster Fundamentals

In Windows Server 2008 R2, you can configure three types of server groups for load balancing, scalability, and high availability. First, a *round-robin distribution group* is a set of computers that uses DNS to provide basic load balancing with minimal configuration requirements. Next, a *Network Load Balancing (NLB) cluster* (also called an *NLB farm*) is a group of servers that not only provide load balancing but also increase scalability. Finally, a *failover cluster* can increase the availability of an application or service in the event of a server failure.

> **NOTE   WHAT IS LOAD BALANCING?**
>
> Load balancing is a means of distributing incoming connection requests to two or more servers in a manner that is transparent to users. Load balancing can be implemented with hardware, software, or a combination of both.

Round-Robin Distribution

Round-robin DNS is a simple method for distributing a workload among multiple servers. In round-robin, a DNS server is configured with more than one record to resolve another server's name to an IP address. When clients query the DNS server to resolve the name (find the address) of the other server, the DNS server responds by cycling through the records one at a time and by pointing each successive client to a different address and different machine.

For example, suppose that a DNS server that is authoritative for the contoso.com DNS domain is configured with two resource records, each resolving the name web.contoso.com by pointing to a different server, as shown in Figure 2-17. When the first client (Client1) queries the DNS server to resolve the web.contoso.com name, the DNS server answers by pointing the client to the server named websrv1 located at the 192.168.3.11 address. This is the information associated with the first DNS record matching "web." When the next client, Client2, queries the DNS server to resolve the same name (web.contoso.com), the DNS server answers the query with the information provided in the second record matching "web." This second record points to a server named websrv2, which is located at the 192.168.3.12 address. If a third client then queries the DNS server for the same name, the server will respond with information in the first record again.

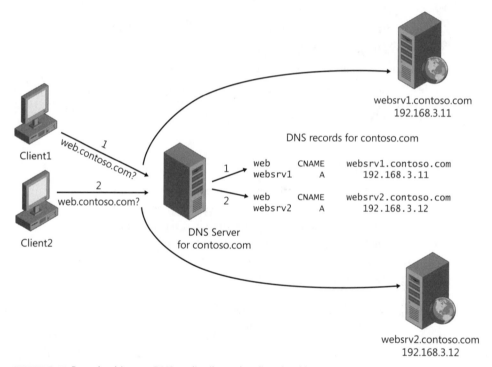

FIGURE 2-17 Round-robin uses DNS to distribute the client load between two or more servers.

The purpose of DNS round-robin is to load balance client requests among servers. Its main advantage is that it is very easy to configure. Round-robin DNS is enabled by default in most DNS servers, so to configure this simple sort of load balancing, you need only to create the appropriate DNS records on the DNS server.

However, there are serious limitations to round-robin as a load-balancing mechanism. The biggest drawback is that if one of the target servers goes down, the DNS server does not respond to this event, and it will keep directing clients to the inactive server until a network administrator removes the DNS record from the DNS server. Another drawback is that every record is given equal weight, regardless of whether one target server is more powerful than another or a given server is already busy. A final drawback is that round-robin does not always function as expected. Because DNS clients cache query responses from servers, a DNS client by default will keep connecting to the same target server as long as the cached response stays active.

Network Load Balancing

An installable feature of Windows Server 2008 R2, NLB transparently distributes client requests among servers in an NLB cluster by using virtual IP addresses and a shared name. From the perspective of the client, the NLB cluster appears to be a single server. NLB is a fully distributed solution in that it does not use a centralized dispatcher.

In a common scenario, NLB is used to create a *web farm*—a group of computers working to support a website or set of websites. However, NLB can also be used to create a terminal server farm, a VPN server farm, or a Forefront Threat Management Gateway (TMG) firewall cluster. Figure 2-18 shows a basic configuration of an NLB web farm located behind an NLB firewall cluster.

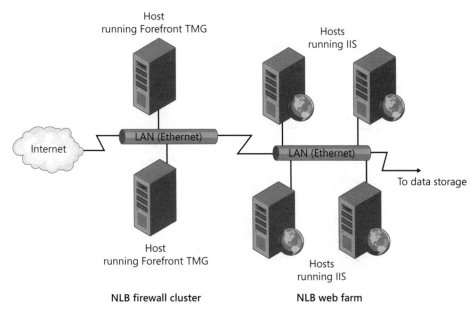

FIGURE 2-18 Basic diagram for two connected NLB clusters.

As a load-balancing mechanism, NLB provides significant advantages over round-robin DNS. First of all, in contrast to round-robin DNS, NLB automatically detects servers that have been disconnected from the NLB cluster and then redistributes client requests to the remaining live hosts. This feature prevents clients from sending requests to the failed servers. Another difference between NLB and round-robin DNS is that in NLB, you have the option to specify a load percentage that each host will handle. Clients are then distributed among hosts so that each server receives its percentage of incoming requests.

Beyond load balancing, NLB also supports scalability. As the demand for a network service such as a website grows, more servers can be added to the farm with only a minimal increase in administrative overhead.

Failover Clustering

A failover cluster is a group of two or more computers used to prevent downtime for selected applications and services. The clustered servers (called nodes) are connected by physical cables to each other and to shared disk storage. If one of the cluster nodes fails, another node begins to take over service for the lost node in a process known as failover. As a result of failover, users connecting to the server experience minimal disruption in service.

Servers in a failover cluster can function in a variety of roles, including the roles of file server, print server, mail server, and database server, and they can provide high availability for a variety of other services and applications.

In most cases, the failover cluster includes a shared storage unit that is physically connected to all the servers in the cluster, although any given volume in the storage is accessed by only one server at a time. In some cases, a separate shared volume called a *disk witness* is used (also called a *witness disk* or a *quorum disk*), which contains a copy of the cluster configuration database. A disk witness often improves the fault tolerance of the cluster.

Figure 2-19 illustrates the process of failover in a basic, two-node failover cluster.

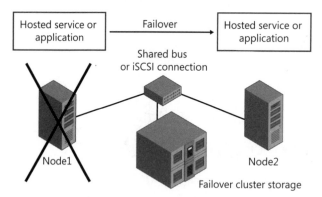

FIGURE 2-19 In a failover cluster, when one server fails, another takes over and uses the same storage.

In a failover cluster, storage volumes or LUNs that are exposed to the nodes in a cluster must not be exposed to other servers, including servers in another cluster. Figure 2-20 illustrates this concept by showing two two-node failover clusters dividing up storage on a SAN.

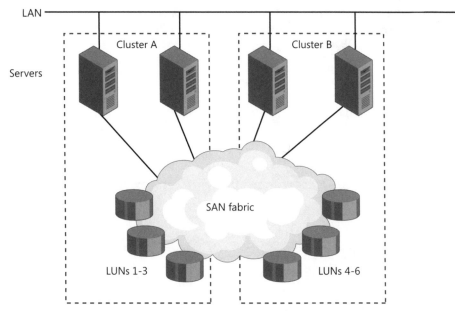

FIGURE 2-20 Each failover cluster must isolate storage from other servers.

Configuring an NLB Cluster

Creating an NLB cluster is a relatively simple process. To begin, install Windows Server 2008 R2 on two servers and then, on both servers, configure the service or application (such as IIS) that you want to provide to clients. Be sure to create identical configurations because you want the client experience to be identical, regardless of the server to which users are connected.

The next step in configuring an NLB cluster is to install the Network Load Balancing feature on all servers that you want to join the NLB cluster. For this step, simply open Server Manager and click Add Features. In the Add Features Wizard, select Network Load Balancing, click Next, and then follow the prompts to install.

The final step in creating an NLB cluster is to use Network Load Balancing Manager to configure the cluster. This procedure is outlined in the following section.

To create an NLB cluster, perform the following steps:

1. Launch Network Load Balancing Manager from Administrative Tools. (You can also open Network Load Balancing Manager by typing **Nlbmgr.exe** from a command prompt.)

   Network Load Balancing Manager is shown in Figure 2-21.

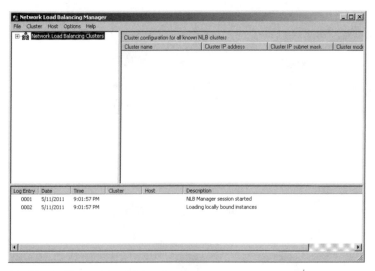

FIGURE 2-21 Network Load Balancing Manager.

2. In the Network Load Balancing Manager console tree, right-click Network Load Balancing Clusters and then click New Cluster. This step opens the New Cluster: Connect page, which is shown in Figure 2-22.

FIGURE 2-22 Connecting to the first host in a new NLB cluster.

3. Connect to the host that is to be part of the new cluster. In Host, enter the name of the host and then click Connect.

4. Select the interface you want to use with the cluster and then click Next. (The interface hosts the virtual IP address and receives the client traffic to load balance.)

5. On the New Cluster: Host Parameters page, shown in Figure 2-23, select a value in the Priority (Unique host identifier) drop-down list. This parameter specifies a unique ID for each host. The host with the lowest numerical priority among the current members of the cluster handles all the cluster's network traffic not covered by a port rule. You can override these priorities or provide load balancing for specific ranges of ports by specifying rules on the Port rules tab of the Network Load Balancing Properties dialog box.

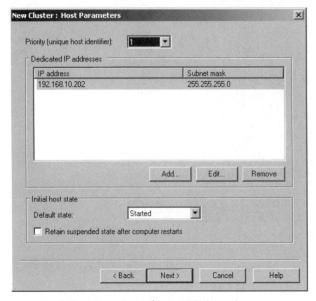

FIGURE 2-23 Setting a priority for an NLB cluster host.

6. On the New Cluster: Host Parameters page, verify that the dedicated IP address from the chosen interface is visible in the list. If not, click Add to add the address and then click Next to continue.

7. On the New Cluster: Cluster IP Addresses page, click Add to enter the cluster IP address shared by every host in the cluster. NLB adds this IP address to the TCP/IP stack on the selected interface of all hosts chosen to be part of the cluster. Click Next to continue.

NOTE **USE ONLY STATIC ADDRESSES**

NLB doesn't support Dynamic Host Configuration Protocol (DHCP). NLB disables DHCP on each interface it configures, so the IP addresses must be static.

8. On the New Cluster: Cluster Parameters page, shown in Figure 2-24, in the Cluster IP Configuration area, verify appropriate values for IP address and subnet mask and then type a full Internet name (Fully Qualified Domain Name) for the cluster.

   For IPv6 addresses, a subnet mask is not needed, and a full Internet name is not needed when using NLB with Terminal Services.

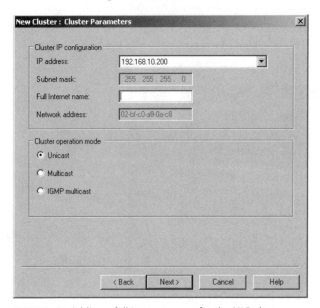

FIGURE 2-24 Adding a full Internet name for the NLB cluster.

9. On the New Cluster: Cluster Parameters page, in the Cluster Operation Mode area, click Unicast to specify that a unicast media access control (MAC) address should be used for cluster operations. In unicast mode, the MAC address of the cluster is assigned to the network adapter of the computer, and the built-in MAC address of the network adapter is not used. It is recommended that you accept the unicast default settings. Click Next to continue.

10. On the New Cluster: Port Rules page, shown in Figure 2-25, click Edit to open the Add/ Edit Port Rule dialog box, shown in Figure 2-26. Port rules define which incoming TCP/ IP requests are balanced among the hosts in the NLB cluster. Configure the NLB port rules as follows:

    ■ In the Port Range area, specify a range corresponding to the service you want to provide in the NLB cluster. For example, for web services, type **80** in the From and To fields so that the new rule applies only to HTTP traffic. For HTTPS traffic, type **443**. For Remote Desktop Services, type **3389**.

    ■ In the Protocols area, select TCP or UDP, as needed, to specify the transport-layer protocol the port rule should cover. Only the network traffic for the specified protocol is affected by the rule. Traffic not affected by the port rule is handled by the default host.

- In the Filtering Mode area, select Multiple Host if you want multiple hosts in the cluster to handle network traffic for the port rule. Choose Single Host if you want a single host to handle the network traffic for the port rule. If you choose Single Host, the port rule will direct matching traffic to the active cluster host with the lowest handling priority.

- In Affinity (which applies only for the Multiple host-filtering mode), select None if you want multiple connections from the same client IP address to be handled by different cluster hosts (no client affinity). Leave the Single option if you want NLB to direct multiple requests from the same client IP address to the same cluster host. Select Network if you want NLB to direct multiple requests from the local subnet to the same cluster host.

FIGURE 2-25 NLB port rules.

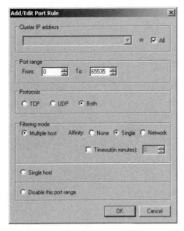

FIGURE 2-26 Configuring NLB port rules.

EXAM TIP

Understand all the configuration options for NLB port rules for the 70-643 exam.

11. After you add the port rules, click Finish to create the cluster.

    To add more hosts to the cluster, right-click the new cluster and then click Add Host To Cluster. Configure the host parameters (including host priority and dedicated IP addresses) for the additional hosts by following the same instructions you used to configure the initial host. Because you are adding hosts to an already-configured cluster, all the cluster-wide parameters remain the same.

Creating a Failover Cluster

Creating a failover cluster is a multistep process. The first step is to configure the physical hardware and shared storage for the cluster. Then, you must install the Failover Clustering feature and, optionally, run the Failover Cluster Validation tool, which ensures that the hardware and software prerequisites for the cluster are met. After the configuration has been validated by the tool, create the cluster by running the Create Cluster Wizard. Next, configure the cluster quorum settings by using the Configure Cluster Quorum Wizard. Finally, to configure the behavior of the cluster and to define the availability of selected services, install the desired application or service on cluster nodes and then run the High Availability Wizard.

Each of these steps is described in the following sections.

Preparing Failover Cluster Hardware

Failover clusters have fairly elaborate hardware requirements. To configure the hardware, review the following list of requirements for the servers, network adapters, cabling, controllers, and storage:

- **Servers** Use a set of matching computers that consist of the same or similar components (recommended).

- **Network adapters and cabling** The network hardware, like other components in the failover cluster solution, must be compatible with Windows Server 2008 R2. If you use iSCSI, each network adapter must be dedicated to either network communication or iSCSI, not both.

  In the network infrastructure that connects your cluster nodes, avoid having single points of failure. There are multiple ways of accomplishing this. You can connect your cluster nodes by multiple, distinct networks. Alternatively, you can connect your cluster nodes with one network constructed with teamed network adapters, redundant switches, redundant routers, or similar hardware that removes single points of failure.

- **Device controllers or appropriate adapters for the storage** If you are using serial attached SCSI or FC in all clustered servers, the mass-storage device controllers dedicated to the cluster storage should be identical. They should also use the same firmware version. If you are using iSCSI, each clustered server must have one or more network adapters or HBAs that are dedicated to the cluster storage. The network you use for iSCSI cannot be used for network communication. In all clustered servers, the network adapters you use to connect to the iSCSI storage target should be identical. It is also recommended that you use Gigabit Ethernet or higher. (Note also that for iSCSI, you cannot use teamed network adapters.)

- **Shared storage compatible with Windows Server 2008 R2** To configure storage for a failover cluster, you must first prepare each server node for shared storage. For example, if your servers have access to an iSCSI SAN, you must configure an iSCSI target and disks that will be shared by all nodes, and you must then use iSCSI Initiator to provision the disks on each of these nodes.

  For a two-node failover cluster, the storage should contain at least two volumes (LUNs). The first volume functions as the disk witness, witness disk, or quorum witness, a volume that holds a copy of the cluster configuration database. Disk witnesses, known only as quorum disks in Windows Server 2003, are used in many, but not all, cluster configurations.

  The second volume contains the files being shared to users. Storage requirements include the following:

  - To use the native disk support included in failover clustering, use basic disks, not dynamic disks.

  - It is recommended that you format the storage partitions with NTFS. (For the disk witness, NTFS is required.)

  After you have provisioned the disks on each node, use Disk Management on the server on which you will configure the failover cluster to bring these new disks online, initialize them, and create the desired volumes on them. (You should bring the disks online *on the one server node only* before adding them to the cluster.)

After you have met the hardware requirements and configured the storage on the cluster server, you can then install the Failover Cluster feature.

Installing the Failover Clustering Feature

Before creating a failover cluster, you have to install the Failover Clustering feature on all nodes in the cluster.

To install the Failover Clustering feature, begin by clicking Add Features in Server Manager. In the Add Features Wizard, select the Failover Clustering check box. Click Next and then follow the prompts to install the feature.

After the feature is installed on all nodes, you are ready to validate the hardware and software configuration.

Validating the Cluster Configuration

Before you create a new cluster, you can use the Validate A Configuration Wizard to ensure that your nodes meet the hardware and software prerequisites for a failover cluster.

To run the Validate A Configuration Wizard, first open Failover Cluster Manager in the Administrative Tools program group. In Failover Cluster Manager, click Validate A Configuration in the Management area or in the Actions pane, as shown in Figure 2-27.

After the wizard completes, make any configuration changes, if necessary, and then rerun the test until the configuration is successfully validated. After the cluster prerequisites have been validated, use the Create Cluster Wizard to create the cluster.

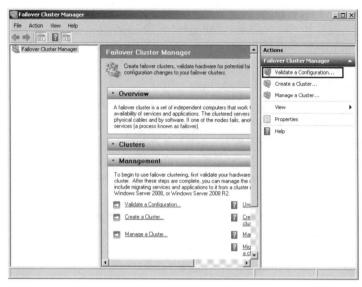

FIGURE 2-27 Validating failover server prerequisites.

Running the Create Cluster Wizard

The next step in creating a cluster is to run the Create Cluster Wizard, which installs the software foundation for the cluster, converts the attached storage into cluster disks, and creates a computer account in Active Directory for the cluster. To launch this tool, in Failover Cluster Manager, click Create A Cluster in the Actions pane, as shown in Figure 2-28.

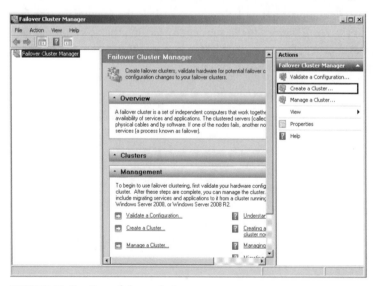

FIGURE 2-28 Creating a failover cluster.

During the wizard, you add nodes to the cluster and give the cluster a name. If you have already configured storage for the cluster, it will be detected automatically and added to the cluster. At this point, configure the quorum settings.

Configuring Quorum Settings

The *quorum configuration* in a failover cluster determines the number of node failures the cluster can sustain before the cluster stops running. In Windows Server 2008 R2, you can choose from among the following four quorum configurations:

- **Node Majority quorum configuration** This quorum configuration is recommended for clusters with an odd number of nodes. In node majority, the failover cluster runs as long as a majority of the nodes are running.

- **Node and Disk Majority quorum configuration** This quorum configuration is recommended for clusters with an even number of nodes. In node and disk majority, the failover cluster uses a witness disk as a tiebreaker node, and the failover cluster then runs as long as a majority of these nodes are online and available.

- **Node And File Share Majority quorum configuration** This quorum configuration is recommended for clusters that have an even number of nodes and that lack access to a witness disk. In this configuration, a witness file share is used as a tiebreaker node, and the failover cluster then runs as long as a majority of these nodes are online and available.

- **No Majority: Disk Only quorum configuration** In this quorum configuration, which is recommended only for testing and not for production environments, the failover cluster remains available as long as a single node and its storage remain online.

To define the quorum configuration, right-click the *cluster* node in the Failover Cluster Manager console tree, point to More Actions in the shortcut menu, and then click Configure Cluster Quorum Settings, as shown in Figure 2-29. This step launches the Configure Cluster Quorum Wizard, the main page of which is shown in Figure 2-30.

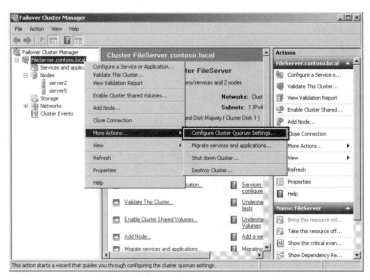

FIGURE 2-29 Configuring quorum settings.

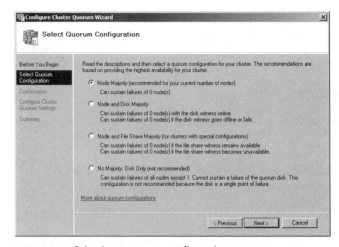

FIGURE 2-30 Selecting a quorum configuration.

If you select Node And Disk Majority, you must specify the volume you want to designate as the witness disk, as shown in Figure 2-31.

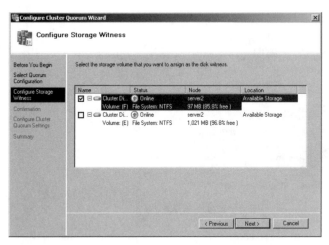

FIGURE 2-31 Selecting a disk for use as the quorum witness.

If you select Node And File Share Majority on the Select Quorum Configuration page, you use the wizard to specify a remotely hosted file share.

After you have defined the quorum configuration for the cluster, you are ready to configure the service or application for which you want to provide failover service.

 Quick Check

1. What is a witness disk?
2. What is the quorum configuration of a failover cluster?

Quick Check Answers

1. A witness disk is a shared volume used in many failover clusters that contains a copy of the cluster configuration database.
2. The quorum configuration is what determines the number of node failures a failover cluster can sustain before the cluster stops running.

 EXAM TIP

On the 70-643 exam, you might see basic questions about quorum configurations, witness disks, or witness file shares.

Configuring a Service for the Failover Cluster

The first step in configuring a service or application for failover service is to install the service or application on all the server nodes you want to host that service in the cluster. For example, if you want to configure high availability for a file server in a two-node cluster, you must add the File Services role on both server nodes in the cluster.

After you have added the desired service to the chosen server nodes in the cluster, you can run the the High Availability Wizard to configure failover for that service. To start the High Availability Wizard, in Failover Cluster Manager, right-click the *Services And Applications* node in the console tree and then select Configure A Service Or Application in the Action pane or the Configure area, as shown in Figure 2-32.

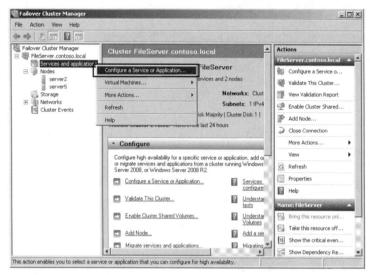

FIGURE 2-32 Configuring a service for failover.

To complete the High Availability Wizard, perform the following steps:

1. On the Before You Begin page, review the text and then click Next.

2. On the Select Service Or Application page (shown in Figure 2-33), select the service or application for which you want to provide failover service (high availability) and then click Next.

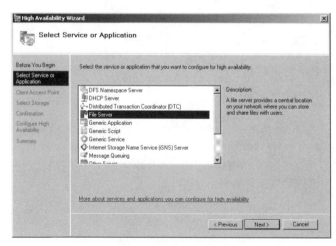

FIGURE 2-33 Selecting a service for high availability.

3. Follow the instructions in the wizard to specify required details about the chosen service. For example, for the File Server service, you would need to specify the following:

   ■ A name for the clustered file server

   ■ Any IP address information that is not automatically supplied by your DHCP settings—for example, a static IPv4 address for this clustered file server

   ■ The storage volume or volumes the clustered file server should use

4. After the wizard runs and the Summary page appears, to view a report of the tasks the wizard performed, click View Report.

5. To close the wizard, click Finish.

EXAM TIP

Be sure to understand the wizards used in failover clustering for the 70-643 exam. Understand what they are used for and how to start them.

After you run the wizard, the service you have specified appears in the Failover Cluster Manager console tree beneath the *Services And Applications* node, as shown in Figure 2-34.

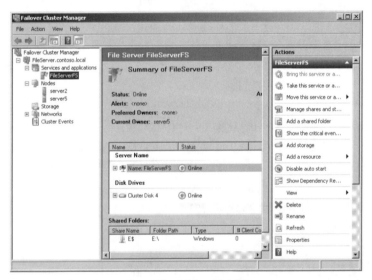

FIGURE 2-34 A service configured for high availability.

You can then configure preferred owner and failback behavior by right-clicking the service and then selecting Properties. The General tab, shown in Figure 2-35, enables you to designate one or more preferred owners of the service, in a specified order. These settings are used only if you enable failback on the Failover tab.

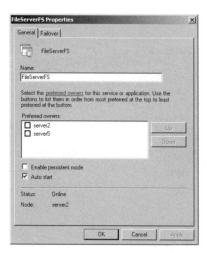

FIGURE 2-35 Configuring preferred owners for a service.

Selecting the Failover tab reveals the configuration options shown in Figure 2-36. In the Failover (top) area of this tab, you can specify the maximum number of failures that you want to allow the failover cluster to sustain within a given time period. When the maximum number is exceeded, the service is left in the failed state. By default, a service is allowed to fail over only once every six hours.

In the Failback (lower) area of this tab, you can choose whether you want a failed service to be moved (fail back) automatically to the most preferred owner or node available, according to the settings on the General tab. If you choose to allow failback, you must specify the hours during which failback is allowed according to a 24-hour clock. For example, if you want to allow failback only during business hours—9 A.M. to 5 P.M.—choose the Allow Failback option and then specify failback between 9 and 17 hours.

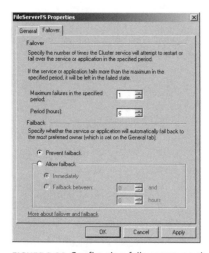

FIGURE 2-36 Configuring failover properties for a service.

EXAM TIP

You need to understand the failover and failback settings for the 70-643 exam.

Testing the Failover Cluster

After you complete the wizard, test the failover cluster in Failover Cluster Management. In the console tree, make sure the *Services And Applications* node is expanded and then select the service you have just added with the High Availability Wizard. Right-click the clustered service, click Move This Service Or Application To Another Node, and then click the available node, as shown in Figure 2-37.

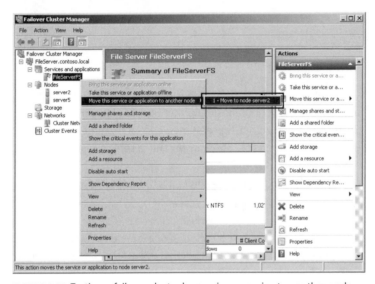

FIGURE 2-37 Testing a failover cluster by moving a service to another node.

You can observe the status changes in the center pane of the snap-in as the clustered service instance is moved, as shown in Figure 2-38. If the service moves successfully, the failover is functional.

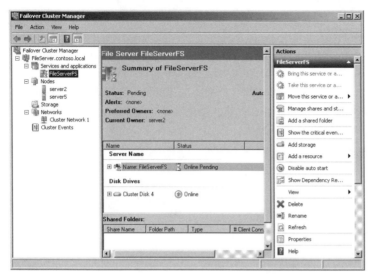

FIGURE 2-38 A service moving to another node.

Understanding Cluster Shared Volumes in Failover Clusters

In Windows Server 2008 and earlier, only one node could access a LUN or physical disk at any given time. If one application running on a LUN failed and needed to move to another node in the failover cluster, every single application on that LUN would also need to be failed over to the new node and potentially experience some downtime. To avoid this problem, applications were typically hosted on unique LUNs as a way to isolate failures. This strategy created another problem, however: a large number of LUNs that complicated setup and administration.

Windows Server 2008 R2 introduces *Cluster Shared Volumes* (CSVs), a new storage type intended for use with virtual machines. CSVs enable you to store on a single LUN the VHDs for multiple virtual machines. You can run the virtual machines on any node in the failover cluster, and when an application stored on a CSV fails, the application can be configured to fail over to a virtual machine on any other node in the cluster.

Aside from their use in failover clusters, CSVs also support live migration of virtual machines in Hyper-V. With live migration, a virtual machine is moved from one physical computer to another with almost no downtime. (Like CSVs, live migration is a new feature in Windows Server 2008 R2.)

> **NOTE** **WHERE ARE CSVs STORED?**
>
> On a Hyper-V host computer acting as a physical node in a failover cluster, CSVs appear as subfolders in the \ClusterStorage folder on the system drive. Example pathnames are C:\ClusterStorage\Volume1, C:\ClusterStorage\Volume2, and so on.

To enable Cluster Shared Volumes by using Failover Cluster Manager, perform the following steps:

1. In Failover Cluster Manager, select the failover cluster for which you want to enable CSVs.

2. Right-click the failover cluster and then click Enable Cluster Shared Volumes, as shown in Figure 2-39. The Enable Cluster Shared Volumes dialog box opens. Read and accept the terms and restrictions and click OK.

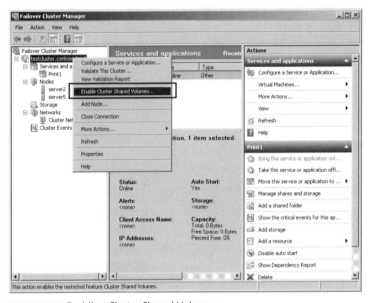

FIGURE 2-39 Enabling Cluster Shared Volumes.

To add a Cluster Shared Volume, perform the following steps:

1. In the Failover Cluster Manager snap-in, right-click the *Cluster Shared Volumes* node and then click Add Storage from the shortcut menu.

2. In Add Storage, select from the list of available disks and click OK. The disk or disks you selected appear in the Results pane for Cluster Shared Volumes.

MORE INFO **UNDERSTANDING CSVs**

For more information about the use of CSVs in a failover cluster, visit *http://technet.mi-crosoft.com/en-us/library/ff182346(WS.10).aspx* or search on TechNet for "Using Cluster Shared Volumes in a Failover Cluster in Windows Server 2008 R2."

In this practice, you perform an exercise to configure a Network Load Balancing cluster. Then, you complete a virtual lab assignment in which you configure various services for failover in a failover cluster.

EXERCISE 1   Creating a Network Load Balancing Cluster

In this exercise, you begin by taking a snapshot of both the Server2 and Core1 virtual machines in Hyper-V. Then, you configure a Network Load Balancing cluster by using these two computers. Finally, you revert the virtual machines to their previous states.

1. Log on to Contoso.local from Server2 as a domain administrator. In the Server2 On Localhost window that contains the Server2 virtual machine in Hyper-V, select Snapshot from the Action menu.

2. In the Snapshot Name dialog box, type **Before Chapter 2 Lesson 2 Exercise 1** and then click Yes.

3. Repeat steps 1 and 2 on Core1.

4. On Server2, change the IPv4 address configuration of the Local Area Connection to the following static configuration:

    ■ IP address: 192.168.10.202

    ■ Subnet mask: 255.255.255.0

    ■ Default gateway: 192.168.10.1

    ■ DNS server: 192.168.10.1

    You can complete this configuration step at an elevated command prompt by typing **netsh interface ipv4 set address "local area connection" static 192.168.10.202 255.255.255.0 192.168.10.1**, pressing Enter, and then typing **netsh interface ipv4 set dns "local area connection" static 192.168.10.1** and pressing Enter again.

5. On Core1, type **sconfig** at the command prompt to start the System Configuration utility and then select option 8 to open the network settings.

6. Use the System Configuration utility to change the IPv4 address configuration of the Core1 network adapter (NIC Index# = 0) to the following static configuration:

    ■ IP address: 192.168.10.204

    ■ Subnet mask: 255.255.255.0

    ■ Default gateway: 192.168.10.1

    ■ Preferred DNS server: 192.168.10.1 (do not set an alternate DNS server)

7. Shut down both Server2 and Core1. (To shut down Core1, select 4 in the System Configuration utility to return to the main menu and then choose option 12.)

    Leave the virtual machine windows open even after the virtual machines are turned off.

8. After Server2 shuts down, in the Server2 On Localhost – Virtual Machine Connection window, select Settings from the File menu.

9. In the Settings For Server2 window, select Legacy Network Adapter from the list of hardware.

10. In the Legacy Network Adapter configuration area on the top-right part of the Settings For Server2 window, select Enable Spoofing Of MAC Addresses and then click OK.

11. Perform steps 8 to 10 on Core1, selecting Network Adapter instead of Legacy Network Adapter.

    This step is currently required to configure an NLB cluster with virtual machines in Windows Server 2008 R2.

12. Start both Server2 and Core1 and log on to Contoso.local from both computers as a domain administrator.

13. In Server Manager on Server2, right-click the *Features* node in the console tree and then click Add Features.

14. Use the Add Features Wizard to add the Network Load Balancing feature. If prompted to do so, restart the computer and log on to Contoso.local again as a domain administrator to complete the installation. (You do not need to restart if you are not prompted to do so.)

15. On Core1, type the following and then press Enter:

    dism /online /enable-feature /featurename:NetworkLoadBalancingHeadlessSer ver

EXAM TIP

For the exam, remember that you can use the Dism command to add a feature.

16. After you receive a message on Core1 indicating that the operation has completed successfully, switch to Server2 and open Network Load Balancing Manager from the Administrative Tools menu.

17. In the console tree, right-click the *Network Load Balancing Clusters* node and select New Cluster.

18. On the New Cluster: Connect page, type Server2.contoso.local in the Host text box and then click Connect.

19. Verify that Local Area Connection is selected beneath Interface Name with an Interface IP of 192.168.10.202 and then click Next.

20. On the New Cluster: Host Parameters page, review the default settings and then click Next.

21. On the New Cluster: Cluster IP Addresses page, click Add.

22. In the Add IP Addresses dialog box, specify an IPv4 address of 192.168.10.200 and a subnet mask of 255.255.255.0. You do not need to add or generate an IPv6 address. Click OK.

23. On the New Cluster: Cluster IP Addresses page, click Next.

24. On the New Cluster: Cluster Parameters page, type **testNLB.contoso.local** in the Full Internet Name text box. Review the other default settings and click Next.

25. On the New Cluster: Port Rules page, review the default settings and then click Finish.

    The operation takes a minute to complete. After it completes, the *Server2* node appears surrounded by a green box in the Network Load Balancing Manager console tree.

26. In the Network Load Balancing Manager console tree, right-click the *testNLB.contoso.local* node and select Add Host To Cluster from the shortcut menu.

27. On the Add Host To Cluster: Connect page, type Core1.contoso.local in the Host text box and then click Connect.

28. Verify that Local Area Connection is selected beneath Interface Name with an interface IP of 192.168.10.204 and then click Next.

29. On the Add Host To Cluster: Host Parameters page, review the default settings and then click Next.

30. On the Add Host To Cluster: Port Rules page, review the default settings and then click Finish.

    The operation takes a minute to complete. After it completes, the *Core1* node appears surrounded by a green box in the Network Load Balancing Manager console tree. The green boxes indicate that the NLB hosts have successfully converged.

31. At a command prompt on Server2, type **ping 192.168.10.200**.

    The NLB cluster responds to the ping attempt. You can also ping the NLB cluster successfully from Server1 and Core1.

32. In the Server2 On Localhost – Virtual Machine Connection window, select Revert from the Action menu.

    The Server2 virtual machine is reverted to its state before Exercise 1.

33. In the Core1 On Localhost– Virtual Machine Connection window, select Core1 from the Action menu.

    The Core1 virtual machine is reverted to its state before Exercise 1.

EXERCISE 2   Configuring a Failover Cluster

Visit *http://msevents.microsoft.com* and search for event ID 1032380228. Perform the virtual lab titled, "TechNet Virtual Lab: Creating a Highly Available Infrastructure."

Lesson Summary

- You can configure groups of servers in Windows Server 2008 R2 to provide load balancing, scalability, or high availability for a particular service or application. These server groups are often called clusters and can be used for very different purposes. Typically, clusters are transparent and appear as a single server to clients.

- Round-robin DNS is a basic method of balancing requests for a single server between two or more servers. Round-robin is easy to configure but has significant limitations, such as the lack of awareness of server status.

- Network Load Balancing (NLB) is an installable feature of Windows Server 2008 and Windows Server 2008 R2. Like round-robin, NLB transparently distributes client requests for a single server between two or more servers. However, NLB overcomes the limitations of round-robin DNS by providing advanced features, such as the ability to redirect requests away from a downed or busy server automatically. NLB is often used to create web farms, which are NLB clusters that answer requests for a website or set of websites.

- Failover clustering is an installable feature of Windows Server 2008 R2 Enterprise Edition. A failover cluster is a group of computers that prevent downtime for selected applications and services. Servers (or nodes) in a failover cluster are connected to each other and to shared storage. Failover clusters have fairly elaborate hardware requirements, and you should be sure to review these requirements before making purchasing decisions.

Lesson Review

The following questions are intended to reinforce key information presented in this lesson. The questions are also available on the companion CD if you prefer to review them in electronic form.

NOTE ANSWERS

Answers to these questions and explanations of why each answer choice is correct or incorrect are located in the "Answers" section at the end of the book.

1. You work as a network administrator for Tailspintoys.com. Your job responsibilities include supporting company servers. The Tailspintoys.com network hosts a web server that runs on a single server named Websrv1. Recently, traffic to the website has been increasing, and the performance of the web server has been deteriorating. Traffic to the website is expected to continue to increase over the next five to eight years. You want a solution that can solve the performance problems of the web server and meet the increasing workload requirements for the website for the next five to eight years. What should you do?

A. Migrate the website to a more powerful server.

B. Use NLB to create a web farm to support the website.

C. Use failover clustering to support the website with multiple servers in a cluster.

D. Add a second web server and then use DNS round-robin to distribute web requests between the two servers. Add more servers as necessary.

2. You are configuring a failover cluster for a database server. You are assigning four nodes to the cluster. All nodes have access to a SAN, and adequate storage is available. Which of the following options should you choose for your quorum configuration?

   A. Node Majority

   B. Node And Disk Majority

   C. Node And File Share Majority

   D. No Majority: Disk Only

3. You work for a large company that uses an iSCSI-based storage area network (SAN) to provide storage for its 20 servers. You want to migrate four of your existing application servers to a failover cluster on Windows Server 2008 R2. Besides providing failover to the four applications servers, you also want to minimize the number of hardware components in the cluster, minimize the number of drives appearing in Disk Management on each physical cluster node, and prevent a single application server failure from triggering a failover on other application servers. Which of the following options will best help you achieve your goals? (Each answer presents part of the solution. Choose two.)

   A. Create and configure cluster shared volumes for the failover cluster.

   B. Create and configure pass-through disks for each application server.

   C. Run each application server as a virtual machine in Hyper-V.

   D. Run each application server on a separate LUN provisioned from the SAN.

Chapter Review

To further practice and reinforce the skills you learned in this chapter, you can perform the following tasks:

- Review the chapter summary.
- Review the list of key terms introduced in this chapter.
- Complete the case scenarios. These scenarios set up a real-world situation involving the topics of this chapter and ask you to create solutions.
- Complete the suggested practices.
- Take a practice test.

Chapter Summary

- Servers require block-based access to data to run operating systems and applications. Usually, direct-attached storage is used for this purpose. This type of storage includes all internally installed hard disks and externally attached storage.
- Windows Server 2008 and Windows Server 2008 R2 include the Virtual Disk Service (VDS) API, which exposes compatible storage subsystems to Windows Server 2008 administration tools such as Storage Manager for SANs.
- You can use Disk Management in Windows Server 2008 and Windows Server 2008 R2 to create simple volumes, spanned volumes, striped volumes, mirrored volumes, and RAID-5 volumes. You can also choose to extend or shrink existing volumes.
- Network Load Balancing (NLB) balances a workload among multiple servers. Clients connect to an NLB cluster by specifying a virtual computer name and virtual IP address. An available server in the NLB cluster then answers the request.
- Failover clustering is a solution that minimizes server downtime. In a failover cluster, cluster servers or nodes share the same storage. When one server fails, another server takes over for the failed server.

Key Terms

Do you know what these key terms mean? You can check your answers by looking up the terms in the glossary at the end of the book.

- block-based
- cluster
- Cluster Shared Volumes
- iSCSI initiator
- iSCSI target
- parity information

- partition style
- quorum configuration
- round-robin DNS
- SAN fabric
- web farm
- witness disk

Case Scenarios

In the following case scenarios, you apply what you've learned about storage and clusters in this chapter. You can find answers to these questions in the "Answers" section at the end of this book.

Case Scenario 1: Designing Storage

You are an IT support specialist for Woodgrove Bank. Your manager informs you that the bank has decided to create a SAN for shared storage among its servers, and you have been asked to research SAN technology options. Migration of chosen servers to SAN storage will occur in approximately one year.

The primary goal for the future SAN is to provide both flexible storage and extremely low latency for database servers. Other goals are to take advantage of the existing networking expertise of the IT staff as much as possible and to facilitate as much administration of the SAN as possible through the Windows Server 2008 R2 interface. No one currently employed on the IT staff has any expertise working with SANs.

1. Given the storage needs of the organization, which connection technology should you choose for the SAN?
2. Which element should you seek in vendor solutions that will enable you to meet the administrative goals of the SAN?

Case Scenario 2: Designing High Availability

You are a server administrator for Trey Research. Recently, Trey Research purchased a line-of-business application named App1 that is to be used heavily by all 500 employees throughout the day. App1 is a web-based application that connects to a back-end database.

You and other members of the IT staff are currently designing the servers to host App1 and its database. In general, the design team foresees two servers or clusters, one to host IIS and App1 and the second to host the database. All servers must run Windows Server 2008 R2. The goals for the server design are to minimize downtime and to provide the best possible performance for both the application and the database. In addition, the solution must use a single database that is always internally consistent. All tables must always be visible to App1.

Within the design team, you have been asked to research cluster solutions for the web application server and database server.

1. Which clustering technology built into Windows Server 2008 R2 is most suitable for the web application server, and why?

2. Which clustering technology built into Windows Server 2008 R2 is most suitable for the database server, and why?

Suggested Practices

To help you successfully master the exam objectives presented in this chapter, complete the following tasks.

Configure Storage

Perform the first practice on three reserved virtual machines running Windows Server 2008 R2. If you have access to a system with three extra disks, virtual or physical, you should perform the second practice.

- **Practice 1**   Visit the Microsoft Download Center at *http://download.microsoft.com* and search for "Microsoft iSCSI Software Target." Download the latest version of this software and install it on a server running Windows Server 2008 R2. Use the software to create an iSCSI target that specifies iSCSI initiators running on two other servers. Create two VHDs and attach them to the iSCSI target. Use the iSCSI Initiator tool on the other servers to connect to the target and provision the new disks.

- **Practice 2**   On a Windows Server 2008 system, create a RAID-5 volume. Save data to the volume. Bring one of the disks offline and then attempt to access the data.

Configure High Availability

Perform both practices. The second practice requires you to first complete Practice 1 under "Configure Storage."

- **Practice 1**   Watch the following sequence of four videos available on TechNet. These videos demonstrate how to configure a failover cluster that uses cluster shared volumes in Hyper-V Server 2008 R2.

  - "Hyper-V Server 2008 R2: Bare Metal to Live Migration," available at *http://technet. microsoft.com/en-us/edge/Ff955827.*

  - "Hyper-V R2: Building a Hyper-V R2 Cluster," available at *http://technet.microsoft. com/en-us/edge/video/ff955826.*

  - "Hyper-V R2: Making Highly Available VMs," available at *http://technet.microsoft. com/en-us/edge/video/ff955812.*

  - "Hyper-V R2: Introducing Cluster Shared Volumes," available at *http://technet.micro-soft.com/en-us/edge/Video/ff955813.*

- **Practice 2**   Add the Failover Clustering feature and the File Services role to two virtual machines running Windows Server 2008 R2 that have provisioned disks from an iSCSI target on a third server. Create a cluster with the two servers by using the New Cluster Wizard, and then use the High Availability Wizard to configure failover service for a file server.

Take a Practice Test

The practice tests on this book's companion CD offer many options. For example, you can test yourself on just one exam objective, or you can test yourself on all the 70-643 certification exam content. You can set up the test so that it closely simulates the experience of taking a certification exam, or you can set it up in study mode so that you can look at the correct answers and explanations after you answer each question.

> **MORE INFO**   **PRACTICE TESTS**
>
> For details about all the practice test options available, see the "How to Use the Practice Tests" section in this book's introduction.

CHAPTER 3

Installing and Configuring Remote Desktop Services

Remote Desktop Services (formerly named Terminal Services) is a server role that enables users to establish interactive sessions on a remote computer running Windows Server 2008 R2.

Remote Desktop Services holds an important role in a Windows applications infrastructure, and this position is reflected on the 70-643 exam. With the many features, tools, and functions associated with Remote Desktop Services, there's a fair amount to learn about this topic for both real-world administration and the test. For this reason, the content is divided into two chapters. This chapter covers the deployment and configuration of the core Remote Desktop Services role. The next chapter discusses the many complementary components that make up a Remote Desktop Services infrastructure.

Exam objectives in this chapter:

- Configure Remote Desktop Session Host.
- Configure Remote Desktop licensing.
- Configure Remote Desktop Connection Broker.

Lessons in this chapter:

Before You Begin

To complete the lessons in this chapter, you must have:

- A computer running Windows Server 2008 R2 named Server1 that is a domain controller in a domain named Contoso.local.

- A computer running Windows Server 2008 R2 named Server2 that is a member server in the Contoso.local domain.

- A Server Core installation of Windows Server 2008 R2 named Core1 that is a member server in the Contoso.local domain.

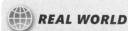

REAL WORLD

J.C. Mackin

Windows Server 2008 and Windows Server 2008 R2 introduce some radically new and important features beyond those offered by Remote Desktop or Terminal Services in any previous version of Windows Server. To begin, the RemoteApp feature enables you to run a remote program on another computer as if that program were installed locally. Another feature, Remote Desktop Web Access (Terminal Services Web Access in Windows Server 2008), provides a webpage from which you can launch these same remote applications. Remote Desktop Gateway (Terminal Services Gateway in Windows Server 2008), for its part, gives your organization an attractive alternative to VPNs by allowing authorized users to connect from the Internet to any desired desktop on your internal network. Finally, Windows Server 2008 R2 introduces a new feature called Remote Desktop Virtualization Host (RD Virtualization Host) that enables you to combine Remote Desktop Services with Hyper-V in deploying personal or shared virtual desktops to users.

In the past, such functionality was available only through third-party applications. Now that these powerful features are built into Windows Server, more organizations will start to take advantage of them. As a Windows support technician, you might have dismissed Remote Desktop/Terminal Services in the past as a feature you didn't really have to understand too well, but the role of Remote Desktop Services is now certain to grow.

Remote Desktop Services is moving closer to the core of essential, real-world support technologies you absolutely must know and understand. Given this, it's time to start looking very closely at this feature if you haven't already.

Lesson 1: Deploying a Remote Desktop Session Host

This lesson begins by introducing the name changes that accompany Remote Desktop Services and its components in Windows Server 2008 R2. It then describes the features of Remote Desktop Services and the steps necessary to deploy this server role.

> **After this lesson, you will be able to:**
> - Understand the name changes related to Remote Desktop Services.
> - Understand the basic features and functions of Remote Desktop Services and how they expand upon the built-in Remote Desktop feature in Windows.
> - Install the Remote Desktop Services role on a full installation and a server core installation of Windows Server 2008 R2.
> - Understand client licensing options for Remote Desktop Services.
> - Prepare a Remote Desktop Services Session Host for deployment.
>
> **Estimated lesson time: 60 minutes**

Understanding Remote Desktop Services Name Changes

Remote Desktop Services (RDS) is a server role in Windows Server 2008 R2 that corresponds to the Terminal Services server role in Windows Server 2008. Along with the new name for the server role, many component role services and management tools that accompany RDS have also been renamed. Before reading about the features of RDS, it's important to understand how its components align with those in previous versions of Windows. This is especially important if you are already familiar with the component names in Windows Server 2008.

Table 3-1 presents a summary of these name changes related to Terminal Services and Remote Desktop Services. The main component of RDS is called the Remote Desktop Session Host, formerly called the Terminal Server. The Remote Desktop Session Host provides the main functionality of RDS—that is, the ability to provide many users with a Remote Desktop session on the RDS server.

TABLE 3-1 Name Changes in Terminal Services/Remote Desktop Services

NAME IN WINDOWS SERVER 2008	NAME IN WINDOWS SERVER 2008 R2
Terminal Services	Remote Desktop Services
Terminal Server	Remote Desktop Session Host (RD Session Host)
Terminal Services Licensing (TS Licensing)	Remote Desktop Licensing (RD Licensing)
Terminal Services Gateway (TS Gateway)	Remote Desktop Gateway (RD Gateway)

Terminal Services Session Broker (TS Session Broker)	Remote Desktop Connection Broker (RD Connection Broker)
Terminal Services Web Access (TS Web Access)	Remote Desktop Web Access (RD Web Access)
Terminal Services Manager	Remote Desktop Services Manager
Terminal Services Configuration	Remote Desktop Session Host Configuration
TS Gateway Manager	Remote Desktop Gateway Manager
TS Licensing Manager	Remote Desktop Licensing Manager
TS RemoteApp Manager	RemoteApp Manager

Understanding Remote Desktop Services

RDS enables remote users to establish interactive desktops or application sessions on a computer running Windows Server 2008 R2. During an RDS session, Remote Desktop clients offload virtually the entire processing load for that session to the RD Session Host. This functionality enables an organization to distribute the resources of a central server among many users or clients. For example, Remote Desktop Services is often used to offer a single installation of an application to many users throughout an organization. This option can be especially useful for companies deploying line-of-business (LOB) applications and other programs responsible for tracking inventory.

Figure 3-1 illustrates how an RD Session Host server can make a central application available to remote clients.

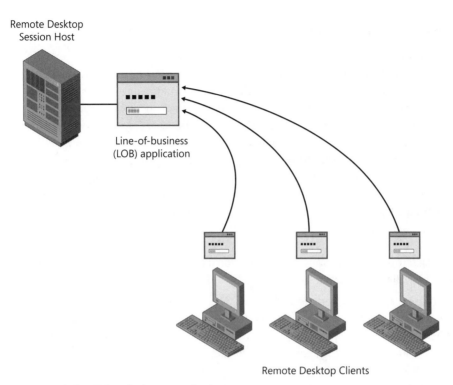

Remote Desktop
Session Host

Line-of-business
(LOB) application

Remote Desktop Clients

FIGURE 3-1 Using RDS to deploy an application.

Comparing Remote Desktop Services and the Remote Desktop Feature

All Windows operating systems since Windows XP include a feature called Remote Desktop, which, like RDS, enables users to establish an interactive desktop session on a remote computer. Both Remote Desktop and RDS use the same client software, Remote Desktop Connection (also called Mstsc.exe). Both rely on the same service, called Remote Desktop Services in Windows 7 and Windows Server 2008 R2, and called Terminal Services in earlier versions of Windows. Finally, both Remote Desktop and RDS establish sessions by means of the same protocol, *Remote Desktop Protocol* (RDP), which uses TCP port 3389.

RDS, however, offers much greater scalability than the built-in Remote Desktop feature. On a computer running Windows Server 2008 R2 on which Remote Desktop is enabled and the RDS server role is not installed, only two users can be connected concurrently to an active desktop session (including any active local user console session). However, no such limitation exists for a server on which the licensed version of Remote Desktop Services server role has been installed and configured.

> **NOTE CONNECTIONS VS. SESSIONS**
>
> Strictly speaking, what is the difference between a Remote Desktop Services connection and a Remote Desktop Services session? A Remote Desktop Services connection is merely an open Remote Desktop Connection window displaying a desktop on a remote computer. A Remote Desktop Services session, however, is a continuous period during which a user is logged on to a remote computer. If you close a Remote Desktop Connection window without logging off from a remote computer, the connection would end, but (provided that the server settings allow it) the session would continue. If you then reconnect to the remote server, you would find the same session in progress with the open programs and files exactly as you had left them. The console session, as you might guess from its name, is not a Remote Desktop Services session at all. Instead, it is the particular desktop session that is active at the physical computer.

Remote Desktop Services in Windows Server 2008 R2 also includes the following features beyond those available in Remote Desktop:

- **Multiuser capability**   Remote Desktop Services includes two modes: Execute mode (for the normal running of applications) and Install mode (for installing programs). When you install an application on a Remote Desktop Session Host in Install mode, settings are written to the Registry or to .ini files in a way that supports multiple users. Unlike Remote Desktop Services, the Remote Desktop feature in Windows does not include an Install mode or provide multiuser support for applications.

- **RemoteApp**   In Windows Server 2008 R2, the RemoteApp component of Remote Desktop Services enables you to deploy an application remotely to users as if the application were running on the end user's local computer. Instead of providing the entire desktop of the remote RD Session Host within a resizable window, RemoteApp enables a remote application to be integrated with the user's own desktop. The application deployed through Remote Desktop Services thus runs in its own resizable window with its own entry in the Start menu.

- **RD Web Access**   RD Web Access enables you to make applications hosted on a remote RD Session Host available to users through a web browser. When RD Web Access is configured, users visit a website (either from the Internet or from the organization's intranet) and view a list of all the applications available through RemoteApp. To start one of the listed applications, users simply click the program icon on the webpage.

- **RD Connection Broker**   By using Network Load Balancing (NLB) or DNS round-robin distribution, you can deploy a number of RDS servers in a farm that, from the perspective of remote users, emulates a single server. An RDS farm is the best way to support many users, and to enhance the functionality of such a farm, you can use the RD Connection Broker role service. The RD Connection Broker component ensures that clients connecting to an RDS farm can reconnect to disconnected sessions.

- **RD Virtualization Host**   With this feature, you can connect Remote Desktop sessions to virtual machines hosted in Hyper-V on the RDS server. Users can each connect to unique virtual machines, or you can use RD Connection Broker to create a pool of virtual machines and connect RD users to the pool.

- **RD Gateway**   RD Gateway enables authorized users on the Internet to connect to remote desktops and RD Session Hosts located on a private corporate network. RD Gateway provides security for these connections by tunneling each RDP session inside an encrypted Hypertext Transfer Protocol Secure (HTTPS) session. By providing authorized users broad access to internal computers over an encrypted connection, RD Gateway can eliminate the need for a virtual private network (VPN) in many cases.

- **RemoteFX**   New to Service Pack 1 of Windows Server 2008 R2, RemoteFX adds greatly enhanced graphical capabilities over RDP. For more information about RemoteFX, visit *http://technet.microsoft.com/en-us/library/ff817578(WS.10).aspx*.

Advantages of Remote Desktop

The main advantage of Remote Desktop, compared to Remote Desktop Services, is that its functionality is built into Windows Server 2008 R2 and does not require the purchase of any *Remote Desktop Services client access licenses* (RDS CALs). If you don't purchase any RDS CALs for Remote Desktop Services, the feature will stop working after 120 days. After this period, Remote Desktop Services functionality reverts to that of Remote Desktop.

Another advantage of Remote Desktop, compared to Remote Desktop Services, is that the feature is very easy to implement. Whereas enabling Remote Desktop Services requires installing and configuring a new server role, enabling Remote Desktop requires you only to select a single option in the System Properties dialog box.

Understanding Remote Desktop for Administration

The Remote Desktop feature in Windows Server 2003, Windows Server 2008, and Windows Server 2008 R2 is often called *Remote Desktop for Administration*. This special term is used because Remote Desktop for Administration differs slightly from the built-in Remote Desktop feature in Windows XP, Windows Vista, and Windows 7. With Remote Desktop for Administration, the server enables two active desktop sessions to the server: either two remote sessions or one remote session and one console session (session at the machine). Remote Desktop in Windows XP, Windows Vista, and Windows 7, however, does not allow concurrent sessions. Only one Remote Desktop user can connect at a time and, when a remote user does connect, any locally logged-on user must first be logged off.

Enabling Remote Desktop

Windows Server 2008 R2 does not accept connections from any Remote Desktop clients by default. To enable the Remote Desktop feature in Windows Server 2008 R2, use the Remote tab of the System Properties dialog box. You can access this tab by opening System in Control

Panel and then clicking the Remote Settings link. You can also access these settings by typing **systempropertiesremote** in the Search Programs And Files box of the Start menu.

On the Remote tab, if you want to require a high standard of security from RDP connections, select the option to require Network Level Authentication, as shown in Figure 3-2. This selection allows connections only from Remote Desktop Connection clients running Windows Vista or later. Alternatively, you can select the option to allow connections from computers running any version of Remote Desktop.

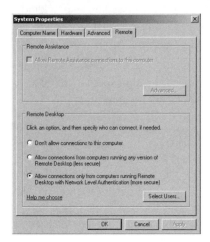

FIGURE 3-2 Enabling the Remote Desktop feature on Windows Server 2008 R2.

In Windows Server 2008 R2, when you use the System Properties dialog box to allow Remote Desktop connections, a Windows Firewall exception for RDP traffic is created automatically. Therefore, you do not have to create the exception manually to allow connections from Remote Desktop clients.

Understanding Network Level Authentication

Network-Level Authentication (NLA) is a feature of Remote Desktop Protocol 6.0 and later. NLA ensures that user authentication occurs before a Remote Desktop connection is fully established between two computers. With earlier versions of RDP, a user could enter a username and password for authentication only after a Log On To Windows screen from the remote computer appeared in the Remote Desktop session. Because every attempt to authenticate a session demanded relatively significant resources from the server, this behavior made Remote Desktop-enabled and RDS-enabled computers susceptible to denial-of-service attacks.

Also important to know is that, by default, NLA is supported only on Windows Vista, Windows 7, Windows Server 2008, and Windows Server 2008 R2. You can enable support for NLA in Windows XP SP3 by enabling the Credential Security Support Provider (CredSSP) in the Registry. You can do this automatically by applying the fix found at *http://support .microsoft.com/kb/951608*.

Enabling Remote Desktop for Administration on a Server Core Installation

The Server Core installations of Windows Server 2008 and Windows Server 2008 R2 do not support the full Remote Desktop Services server role. However, you can enable the Remote Desktop feature on a Server Core installation of Windows Server 2008 and Windows Server 2008 R2 by using the Server Core Registry Editor script, Scregedit.wsf. In addition, Windows Server 2008 R2 introduces the Sconfig tool, which you can use to enable Remote Desktop and configure other basic settings in a Server Core installation.

Enabling Remote Desktop for Administration with Scregedit.wsf

Scregedit.wsf provides a simplified way of configuring the most commonly used features in a Server Core installation of Windows Server 2008 and Windows Server 2008 R2.

> **IMPORTANT WHERE CAN YOU FIND SCREGEDIT.WSF?**
>
> Scregedit.wsf is located in the *%SystemRoot%*\System32 folder of every Server Core installation.

To use the Scregedit.wsf script to enable Remote Desktop, use Cscript.exe to invoke the script and then pass the */ar* switch a value of *0*, which allows Remote Desktop connections. (By default, the */ar* value is set to *1*, which disables Remote Desktop connections.) The full command to enable Remote Desktop is shown here:

```
Cscript.exe C:\Windows\System32\Scregedit.wsf /ar 0
```

By default, enabling Remote Desktop on the Server Core installation in this way configures the server to accept Remote Desktop connections only from clients running Windows Vista or later. To enable the server to accept Remote Desktop connections from earlier versions of Windows, you must relax the security requirements of the server by using the Scregedit.wsf script with the */cs* switch and a value of *0*, as shown here:

```
Cscript.exe C:\Windows\System32\Scregedit.wsf /cs 0
```

Enabling Remote Desktop for Administration with the Sconfig Tool

To use the Sconfig tool to enable Remote Desktop on a Server Core installation of Windows Server 2008 R2, you can type **sconfig** at the command prompt. The Server Configuration menu then appears, as shown in Figure 3-3.

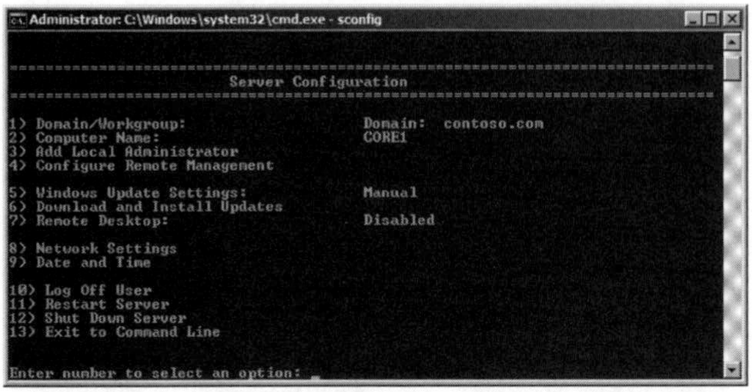

FIGURE 3-3 The Sconfig tool in the Server Core installation of Windows Server 2008 R2.

If you choose option 7, you are prompted to type **E** or **D** to enable or disable Remote Desktop. If you choose to enable Remote Desktop, you are then prompted to specify NLA settings for the server. Option 1 restricts Remote Desktop connections to clients that support NLA. Option 2 allows Remote Desktop connections from clients running any version of Remote Desktop Connection.

> **NOTE CONNECTING TO A SERVER CORE THROUGH REMOTE DESKTOP**
>
> When you connect to a Server Core installation by means of Remote Desktop, you receive the same interface you would receive if you were seated locally at the server. A Remote Desktop connection to a computer running Windows Server 2008 R2 Server Core, in other words, does not provide you with access to any additional graphical tools to manage the server.

Installing Remote Desktop Services

Unlike Remote Desktop for Administration, the full implementation of Remote Desktop Services requires you to add the Remote Desktop Services server role. As with any server role, the simplest way to install Remote Desktop Services on a full installation of Windows Server 2008 R2 is to click Add Roles in Server Manager or the Initial Configuration Tasks window.

Clicking Add Roles launches the Add Roles Wizard. On the Select Server Roles page, select the Remote Desktop Services check box, as shown in Figure 3-4.

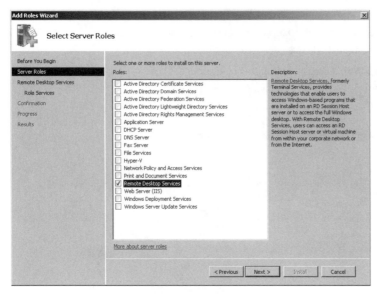

FIGURE 3-4 Adding the Remote Desktop Services role.

Click Next on the Add Roles Wizard page to open the Remote Desktop Services page. This page provides a brief description of the Remote Desktop Services role. Click Next on the Remote Desktop Services page to open the Select Role Services page.

Selecting Role Services

On the Select Role Services page of the Add Roles Wizard, you can select any of the following five role services associated with the Remote Desktop Services role:

- **Remote Desktop Session Host** This role service provides the basic functionality of Remote Desktop Services, including the RemoteApp feature.

- **Remote Desktop Virtualization Host** You should install this role service if you want to connect users to virtual machines hosted on the RDS server.

- **Remote Desktop Licensing** You must install this role service only if you have purchased Remote Desktop Services client access licenses (RDS CALs) and can activate a license server. Remote Desktop Services has a 120-day grace period; if you have not purchased any RDS CALs and installed them on a Remote Desktop licensing server by the end of this period, Remote Desktop Services stops functioning. (For information about how to install and configure Remote Desktop Services Licensing [RD Licensing], see Lesson 2, "Configuring a Remote Desktop Session Host," in this chapter.)

- **Remote Desktop Connection Broker** Install and configure this role service when you plan to implement Remote Desktop Services in a server farm. As mentioned earlier in this lesson, this role service enhances the functionality of the server farm by ensuring that clients are able to reconnect to disconnected sessions.

- **Remote Desktop Gateway**   Install this role service if you want to make a number of RDS servers accessible to authorized external clients beyond a firewall or Network Address Translation (NAT) device.

- **Remote Desktop Web Access**   Install this role service if you want to make applications deployed through RDS available to clients through a webpage.

The Select Role Services page is shown in Figure 3-5.

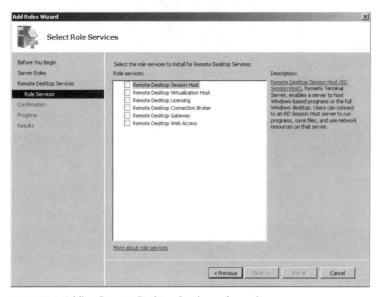

FIGURE 3-5 Adding Remote Desktop Services role services.

The following sections describe the tasks you must perform if you select only the Remote Desktop Session Host role service in the Add Roles Wizard.

Uninstalling Applications

After you select the RD Session Host role service, the Add Roles Wizard reminds you that any applications you want to deploy to users through RDS should be installed after you add the RDS role. If you have already installed any applications you want to deploy, you should uninstall and reinstall them later (in RDS Install mode) if you want them to be available to multiple users. This reminder is shown in Figure 3-6.

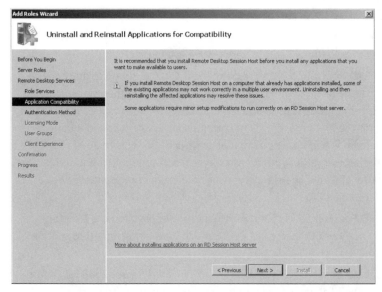

FIGURE 3-6 Reminder to reinstall applications on the RD Session Host server.

Specifying Network-Level Authentication Settings

Next, you must specify whether the Remote Desktop Session Host will accept connections only from clients that can perform Network-Level Authentication. When you select this requirement, as shown in Figure 3-7, Remote Desktop connections will be blocked from computers running operating systems earlier than Windows Vista (unless those computers have been configured to support NLA).

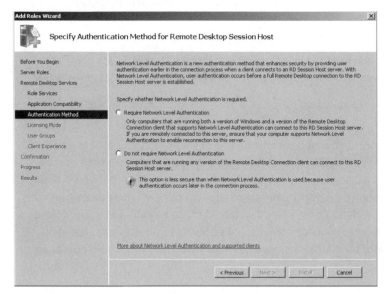

FIGURE 3-7 Setting NLA/client version requirements.

Specifying Client Access License Types

The Add Roles Wizard then gives you the option to specify the RDS CAL types you have purchased. Two types of CALs for Remote Desktop Services are available:

- **Per Device CALs** RD Per Device CALs are permanent CALs assigned to any computer or device that connects to an RD Session Host server more than once. When the Per Device licensing mode is used and a client computer or device connects to an RD Session Host for the first time, the client computer or device is issued a temporary license by default. When a client computer or device connects to an RD Session Host server for the second time, if the license server is activated and if enough RD Per Device CALs are available, the license server issues the client computer or device a permanent RD Per Device CAL.

- **Per User CALs** RD Per User CALs give users the right to access Remote Desktop Services from any number of devices. RD Per User CALs are not assigned to specific users.

  The ability to track RD Per User RDS CALs is new to Windows Server 2008 R2. Before Windows Server 2008 R2, if you opted for per user licensing, you simply needed to make sure that you had purchased enough licenses for all the users in your organization. If you install the Remote Desktop Licensing role service on a server running Windows Server 2008 R2, however, you can now use the Remote Desktop Licensing Manager tool to create reports to track per user CALs. Note that RDS Per User CAL tracking and reporting is supported only in domain-joined scenarios. In addition, for RDS Per User CAL tracking and reporting to work, the computer account for the license server must be a member of the Terminal Server License Servers group in AD DS. Finally, if the license server is installed on a domain controller, the Network Service account must also be a member of the Terminal Server License Servers group.

EXAM TIP

For the 70-643 exam, you need to know that you can track Per User RDS CALs only if the Remote Desktop Licensing role service is installed on a computer running Windows Server 2008 R2.

In deciding which of these two CALs to purchase for your organization, consider several factors. First, consider the number of devices and users in your organization. In general, it's financially preferable to choose per device CALs if you anticipate having fewer devices than users over the life of the RD Session Host server, but preferable to choose per user licensing if you anticipate fewer users than devices. Another factor to consider is how often your users travel and connect from different computers. Per user licensing is often preferable when a small number of users tend to connect from many sites, such as from customer networks. In general, if you prefer your users to be assigned permanent licenses, you should opt for per user CALs.

If you have not yet decided which RDS CALs to purchase, you can select the Configure Later option, as shown in Figure 3-8. You then have 120 days to purchase RDS CALs and to install these licenses on a locally activated license server. After this grace period, RDS stops functioning.

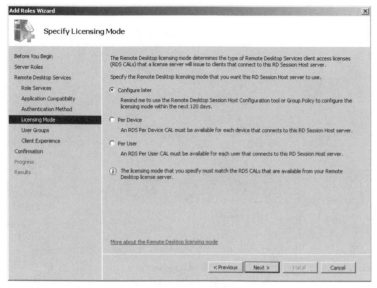

FIGURE 3-8 Specifying a licensing mode.

EXAM TIP

For the 70-643 exam, you need to know the difference between the client access license modes.

Authorizing Users

The next configuration step is to choose the users and groups to which you want to allow access through RDS. The Remote Desktop Users built-in local group is automatically granted the user right to connect to the local computer through RDS, and the Add Roles Wizard simply provides a fast way of adding accounts to this Remote Desktop Users group. By default, the local Administrators group is already allowed access to the RD Session Host server, as shown in Figure 3-9.

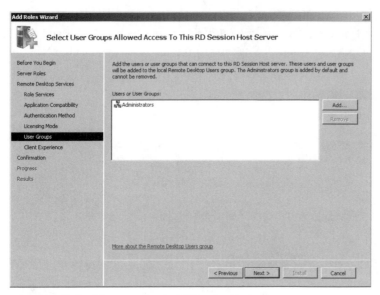

FIGURE 3-9 Authorizing users for the RD Session Host server.

Finally, the Add Roles Wizard enables you to configure the Remote Desktop client experience, as shown in Figure 3-10. You can configure the RD Session Host to provide audio and video playback, audio recording redirection from the client, or advanced desktop composition (Windows Aero features). If you choose the Audio And Video Playback or Desktop Composition, the Desktop Experience feature will be installed automatically on the RD Session Host server.

Be aware that these options are resource-intensive and add to the processing, memory, and bandwidth loads on the RD Session Host. Consequently, it is recommended that you only select these options in a production environment if they are truly needed.

After this last step, you simply confirm your selections in the Add Roles Wizard and begin the Remote Desktop Services installation. You must restart your server to complete the installation.

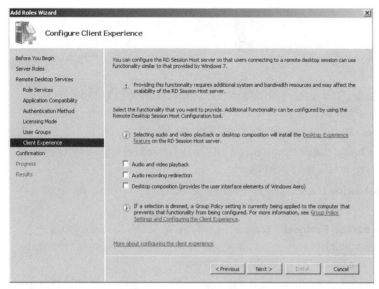

FIGURE 3-10 Configuring the Remote Desktop client experience.

Preparing an RD Session Host Server for Deployment

Before making an RD Session Host server available to receive Remote Desktop connections, you should install all the components on the server that you want to make available to Remote Desktop clients. At a minimum, this process includes installing appropriate server features.

Installing Windows Server 2008 R2 Features

You can use Server Manager to install Windows Server features before or after adding the Remote Desktop Services server role. Features are smaller Windows components that enable specific functionality in the operating system. To prepare an RD Session Host server for deployment, you must know which of these Windows Server 2008 R2 features you want to make available to clients connecting to RDS.

Because the only features available to remote users are those you install on the RD Session Host, you must review client needs and the functionality offered by each feature. For example, if you want Windows Media Player to be available to clients connecting to RDS, you should install the Desktop Experience feature on the computer running RDS.

Windows Server 2008 R2 includes 41 features that are available for deployment. Some of these features you might need to make available to RDS clients are in the following list. Successful deployment of RDS requires you to understand these features and to review them as you prepare the RD Session Host server.

- **Desktop Experience**   This feature installs Windows Media Player 12, desktop themes, and the photo gallery. It also makes the Windows Aero graphical features available, although these features must be enabled manually by each user.

- **Quality Windows Audio Video Experience**   This feature enables high-quality performance for streaming media over IP networks.

- **Network Load Balancing (NLB)**   The NLB feature enables you to join a server to an NLB cluster or NLB server farm.

- **Windows Server Backup Features**   You can install the Windows Server Backup Features to enable administrators to perform backups as part of remote maintenance of the computer running the Remote Desktop Services.

- **Group Policy Management**   Group Policy Management is a console that facilitates administration of Group Policy. You can install this feature if you anticipate that administrators will use the server to manage Group Policy remotely.

- **Windows System Resource Manager**   Windows System Resource Manager (WSRM) enables you to manage the resources of a server so that the workload is spread equitably among roles.

Installing RDS Applications

RDS is often used to deploy a single installation of an application to many users. Deploying an application in this way is frequently the best option for data-entry programs designed to run on a single server and for other programs tied to a locally installed database. However, you might also want to deploy an application through RDS to reduce associated licensing fees, to offload processing from client computers, or simply to improve user productivity within an RDS session.

Applications that you want to make available to RDS clients must be installed after you install the RD Session Host role service. You must then install these applications in a way that makes them available to multiple users by installing the applications while RDS is in Install mode. You can install programs in Install mode by using an MSI installer program, by using the Install Application On Remote Desktop program in Control Panel (shown in Figure 3-11), or by using the *Change user/install* or *Chgusr/install* command. For more information about using Install mode, see Chapter 4, "Configuring and Managing a Remote Desktop Infrastructure."

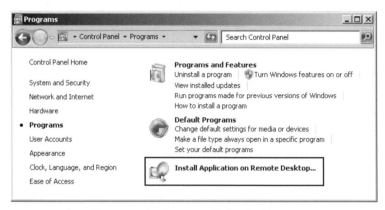

FIGURE 3-11 Installing an application on an RD Session Host.

✔ **Quick Check**

1. Which server feature is automatically installed on an RD Session Host server if you select the option to play audio and video in RDS sessions?

2. On a computer running Windows Server 2008 R2 that has the Remote Desktop for Administration feature enabled, what is the maximum number of concurrent active user sessions (including remote and console sessions) that can be hosted?

Quick Check Answers

1. Desktop Experience

2. Two

PRACTICE **Install Remote Desktop Services**

In this practice, you install Remote Desktop Services on a full installation of Windows Server 2008 R2 and then enable the Remote Desktop feature on a Server Core installation.

EXERCISE 1 Installing the Remote Desktop Services Server Role

In this exercise, you install the Remote Desktop Services server role on Server2.

1. As a domain administrator, log on to Contoso.local from Server2.

2. In Server Manager, select the *Roles* node in the console tree and then click Add Roles in the details pane.

   If the Before You Begin page is displayed, click Next.

3. On the Select Server Roles page of the Add Roles Wizard, select the Remote Desktop Services check box and then click Next.

4. On the Remote Desktop Services page, read all the text on the page and then click Next.

5. On the Select Role Services page, select the Remote Desktop Session Host check box and then click Next.

6. On the Uninstall And Reinstall Applications For Compatibility page, read all the text on the page and then click Next.

7. On the Specify Authentication Method For Remote Desktop Session Host page, read all the text on the page, select Require Network Level Authentication, and then click Next.

8. On the Specify Licensing Mode page, read all the text on the page, leave the default selection of Configure Later, and then click Next.

9. On the Select User Groups Allowed Access To This RD Session Host Server page, read all the text on the page and then click Next.

10. On the Configure Client Experience page, read all the text on the page and then click Next.

11. On the Confirm Installation Selections page, read all the text on the page and then click Install.

12. After the installation is complete, read all the text on the Installation Results page and then click Close.

13. In the Add Roles Wizard dialog box, click Yes to restart the server.

14. After the server restarts, log back on to Contoso.local from Server2 by using the same domain administrator account.

     After several moments, the Resume Configuration Wizard appears. When the Installation Results page appears, click Close.

15. In Control Panel, click System And Security and then click Windows Firewall.

16. Click Allow A Program Or Feature Through Windows Firewall.

17. On the Exceptions tab of the Windows Firewall Settings dialog box, verify that the Remote Desktop and Terminal Services check boxes are selected (along with the RemoteFX check box if Service Pack 1 is installed) and then click OK.

18. Close all open windows and then proceed to Exercise 2.

EXERCISE 2   **Testing the Remote Desktop Services Connection**

In this exercise, you test the Remote Desktop Services configuration on Server2 by connecting to it from a Remote Desktop Connection on Server1.

1. Log on to Contoso.local from Server1 as a domain administrator.

2. Click Start.

3. In the Search Programs And Files box, type **mstsc** and then press Enter.

The Remote Desktop Connection window opens.

EXAM TIP

You must know the function of the *mstsc* command for the 70-643 exam.

4. In the Computer text box of the Remote Desktop Connection window, type **server2**
   .contoso.local and then press Enter.

   The Windows Security window opens.

5. In the Windows Security window, enter the credentials of a domain administrator and
   then press Enter.

   After several moments, a Remote Desktop connection is established to Server2. Within
   the desktop of Server1, the remote Server2 desktop is designated with a blue banner
   labeled "server2.contoso.local."

6. Using the Start button within the Remote Desktop session to Server2, log off the
   Remote Desktop connection.

   The Remote Desktop window closes.

EXERCISE 3   Enabling Remote Desktop on a Server Core Installation of Windows Server
2008 R2

In this exercise, you enable Remote Desktop on the Core1 computer and then test the
configuration.

NOTE   **SERVER1 AND SERVER2**

Although Server1 is needed for this exercise, Server2 is not. If you are using virtual machines and do not have enough RAM to support all three computers, you can shut down
Server2 before beginning this exercise.

1. Log on to Contoso.local from Core1 as a domain administrator.
2. At the command prompt, type the following command: **cd C:\Windows\System32**.
3. At the command prompt, type the following command: **cscript scregedit.wsf /ar /v**.

   This command shows the current status of the fDenyTSConnections registry setting.
   When set to *1*, the local computer is configured to deny incoming Remote Desktop
   connections.

4. Type the following command: **cscript scregedit.wsf /ar 0**.
5. To verify the setting change, type the following command: **cscript scregedit**
   .wsf /ar /v.

   The output from the command reveals that the fDenyTSConnections registry setting is
   now set to *0*.

6. To ensure that the server accepts connections from RDP clients earlier than 6.0, or from clients native to Windows XP and earlier, type the following command: **cscript scregedit.wsf /cs 0**.

7. To verify the setting, type the following command: **cscript scregedit.wsf /cs /v**.

   The output from the command reveals that the RDP-Tcp UserAuthentication setting is now set to *0*. This setting enables connections from earlier versions of Remote Desktop.

8. Type the following command: **netsh advfirewall firewall show rule name="Remote Desktop (TCP-In)"**.

   This command states that the inbound rule for Remote Desktop has been enabled for the Domain and Private profiles but not for the Public profile.

9. Log on as a domain administrator to Contoso.local from Server1.

10. In the Search Programs And Files box, type **mstsc** and then press Enter.

    The Remote Desktop Connection window opens.

11. In the Computer text box, type **core1.contoso.local** and then click Connect.

12. In the Windows Security window, enter the credentials of a domain administrator.

13. In the Windows Security window, click OK.

    After a few moments, a Remote Desktop connection to Core1 is established. The Remote Desktop connection shows the same Server Core desktop that you can see when you log on to Core1 locally.

14. On Server1, within the Remote Desktop session to Core1, type **logoff** at the command prompt.

    On Server1, the Remote Desktop session closes.

15. On Core1, type **shutdown /p** at the command prompt to shut down the computer.

Lesson Summary

- In Windows Server 2008 R2, the Terminal Services server role in Windows Server 2008 has been renamed Remote Desktop Services. All the role services associated with the server role have also been renamed.

- Remote Desktop Services enables remote users to establish and interact with a desktop or application session on a server running Windows Server 2008 R2.

- Remote Desktop Services expands the functionality of the built-in Remote Desktop feature in Windows. The Remote Desktop feature allows two concurrent desktop sessions (including the console session) to a local computer running Windows Server 2008 R2. A server configured with the Remote Desktop Services server role does not include any such limits (although it does require licenses for remote connections).

- Remote Desktop Services includes many features that expand the basic functionality of Remote Desktop, such as RD Gateway, RemoteApp, RD Virtualization Host, and RD Web Access.

- Remote Desktop Services requires client access licenses (CALs) either for all connecting users or for all connecting devices. If you do not purchase and install Remote Desktop Services CALs, Remote Desktop Services stops working after 120 days.

Lesson Review

The following questions are intended to reinforce key information presented in this lesson. The questions are also available on the companion CD if you prefer to review them in electronic form.

> **NOTE ANSWERS**
>
> Answers to these questions and explanations of why each answer choice is correct or incorrect are located in the "Answers" section at the end of the book.

1. You want to enable Remote Desktop on a Server Core installation of Windows Server 2008 and then enable the server to accept connections from clients configured with RDP versions prior to 6.0. Which commands should you use? (Each correct answer presents part of a complete solution. Choose two.)

    A. *cscript scregedit.wsf /ar 0*

    B. *cscript scregedit.wsf /ar 1*

    C. *cscript scregedit.wsf /cs 0*

    D. *cscript scregedit.wsf /cs 1*

2. You are one of 75 consultants employed by an IT services company named Contoso .com. As part of your job, you and other team members provide network support for more than 150 businesses in your city. Your company is about to implement a business process in which consultants must connect to an application server on the Contoso .com network while working at customer premises. When connected to the application server, consultants provide critical information about each assignment in the field. To connect to the Contoso.com application server, consultants are expected to use Remote Desktop Connection on customer computers running Windows XP or Windows 7. You have been asked to determine whether your company needs to purchase client access licenses (CALs) for Remote Desktop Services. Which of the following options best suits the needs of your organization?

    A. Use Remote Desktop for Administration on the application server and purchase per user CALs.

    B. Use Remote Desktop for Administration on the application server and purchase per device CALs.

C. Install Remote Desktop Services on the application server and purchase per device CALs.

D. Install Remote Desktop Services on the application server and purchase per user CALs.

3. You work for a company whose network consists of ten servers running Windows Server 2008 R2 and 150 clients running Windows XP SP3 and Windows 7. You deploy Remote Desktop Services on an application server named App1. Users complain that they cannot connect to App1 from the computers running Windows XP. You want to fix the problem without compromising server security. You also want to reduce administrative overhead. What should you do?

A. Configure App1 to allow connections from computers running any version of Remote Desktop.

B. Enable CredSSP on the computers running Windows XP SP3.

C. Upgrade the computers running Windows XP to Windows 7.

D. Upgrade to Remote Desktop Connection 6.1 or later on the computers running Windows XP SP3.

Lesson 2: Configuring a Remote Desktop Session Host

The Remote Desktop (RD) Session Host Configuration console is the main tool used to config-ure the Remote Desktop Services role. The server options available in this tool primarily affect the user's environment when connecting to the local RD Session Host. Other options available in this tool, however, relate to server licensing and load-balancing features. After describ-ing all the options and features configurable in the RD Session Host Configuration console, this lesson describes supplementary configuration options available in Group Policy for one feature in particular: printer redirection.

> **After this lesson, you will be able to:**
> - Configure settings on the Remote Desktop Session Host.
> - Configure Remote Desktop load balancing.
> - Install and configure a Remote Desktop license server.
>
> **Estimated lesson time: 90 minutes**

Introducing the Remote Desktop Session Host Configuration Console

The RD Session Host Configuration console is designed to control settings that affect all users connecting to the local RD Session Host server or to control settings that affect users con-necting to the server through a particular connection type. For instance, you can use the RD Session Host Configuration console to set the encryption level of all Remote Desktop sessions, to configure the graphical resolution of sessions connecting through a particular adapter, or to set an idle session limit on users connecting through Citrix Systems software and the Independent Computing Architecture (ICA) protocol instead of RDP. The RD Session Host Configuration console is shown in Figure 3-12.

The RD Session Host Configuration console provides two general areas for configuration: the connection (RDP-Tcp) Properties dialog box and the Edit Settings area. The following sec-tions describe the options available through each of these configuration areas.

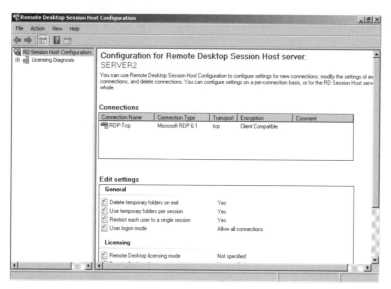

FIGURE 3-12 The RD Session Host Configuration console.

Configuring Connection (RDP-Tcp) Properties

Connection properties are used to customize the behavior of Remote Desktop sessions initiated through certain specific transport protocols (such as RDP) or through specific network adapters on the Remote Desktop Session Host server. By default, only one connection (named RDP-Tcp) is available for configuration; the properties configured for this connection apply to RDP sessions through all local network adapters. In addition to this default connection, you can also create new connections that apply to particular adapters. Also, if you are using third-party software, such as Citrix Systems software, that provides its own protocol to be used with Remote Desktop Services, you see an entry for that protocol here. (In general, it's preferable to use the third-party management tools to configure third-party protocols.)

For environments using only the built-in functionality offered by Windows Server 2008 R2, the RDP-Tcp connection normally serves as the only connection, and the RDP-Tcp Properties dialog box provides key configuration options for the entire server.

To open the properties of the RDP-Tcp connection, in the RD Session Host Configuration console Connections area, right-click RDP-Tcp and then click Properties. This procedure opens the RDP-Tcp Properties dialog box, as shown in Figure 3-13.

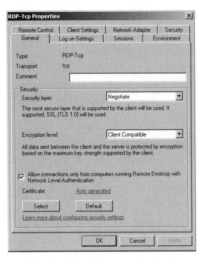

FIGURE 3-13 RDP-Tcp Properties General tab.

The following section explains the configurable options available through each of the eight tabs.

EXAM TIP

Learn all the settings on the eight RDP-Tcp Properties tabs, including which of these settings are configured by default for the 70-643 exam.

General Tab

The General tab enables you to modify security configuration settings relating to the security layer, the encryption level, and NLA. These settings are described in the following section.

SECURITY LAYER

All RDP connections are encrypted automatically. Security layer settings determine the type of encryption used for these Remote Desktop connections. Three options for the security level are available: RDP Security Layer, SSL (TLS 1.0), and Negotiate.

- The RDP Security Layer option limits encryption to the native encryption built into RDP. The advantages of this option are that it requires no additional configuration, that it is compatible with RDP clients earlier than version 6.0, and that it offers a high standard of performance. Its main disadvantages are that when it is used, clients cannot verify the identity of the RD Session Host, and NLA cannot be used. These features are available only in RDP 6.0 and later.

- The SSL (TLS 1.0) option offers two advantages over RDP encryption. First, it offers stronger encryption. Second, it offers the possibility of server authentication for RDP client versions earlier than 6.0. SSL is therefore a good option if you need to support RD Session Host authentication for Windows XP SP2 and earlier clients. However, this option does have some drawbacks. To begin, SSL requires a computer certificate for both encryption and authentication. By default, only a self-signed certificate is used, which provides only weak authentication. To improve security, you must obtain a valid computer certificate from a trusted certification authority (CA), and you must store this certificate in the computer account certificate store on the RD Session Host server. Another disadvantage of SSL is that its high encryption results in slower performance compared to that of other RDP connections.

- Negotiate is the default selection. When the Negotiate option is selected, the RD Session Host will use SSL security only when supported by both the client and the server. Otherwise, native RDP encryption is used.

ENCRYPTION LEVEL

The Encryption Level setting on the General tab enables you to define the strength of the en-cryption algorithm used in RDP connections. The default selection is Client Compatible, which chooses the maximum key strength supported by the client computer. The other available options are Low, High, and FIPS compliant. Low security uses 56-bit key encryption and does not support server authentication. High security uses 128-bit encryption, and clients that can-not negotiate this level of security are not permitted to connect. FIPS-compliant security uses a set of algorithms that are compatible with Federal Information Processing Standards. At the time of this writing, this option uses 3DES for encryption, RSA for public key exchange, and SHA-1 for TLS hashing.

NETWORK LEVEL AUTHENTICATION

When the Allow Connections Only From Computers Running Remote Desktop With Network Level Authentication setting is enabled, only clients that support NLA are allowed to connect to the RD Session Host.

To determine whether a computer is running a version of the Remote Desktop Connection (RDC) client that supports NLA, start the RDC client, click the icon in the upper-left corner of the Remote Desktop Connection dialog box, and then click About. Look for the phrase "Network Level Authentication Supported" in the About Remote Desktop Connection dialog box, shown in Figure 3-14.

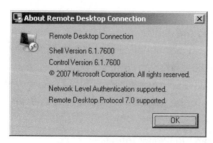

FIGURE 3-14 Verifying NLA support.

Log on Settings Tab

The Log on Settings tab, shown in Figure 3-15, enables you to configure all Remote Desktop clients to use a single predefined username and password. Sharing credentials in this way enables users to connect to the RD Session Host without having to supply any credentials. Choosing this option might be suitable for testing environments or for public terminals.

When you select the Always Prompt For Password option, the user must always supply at least a password (if not the username) before connecting.

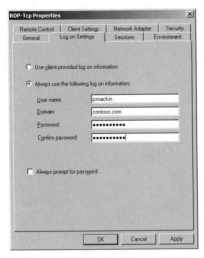

FIGURE 3-15 Configuring Remote Desktop log on settings.

Sessions Tab

You can use the Sessions tab to control session timeout settings for the RD Session Host. Specifically, this tab enables you to choose timeout settings for disconnected sessions, set time limits for active and idle sessions, and define the behavior for disconnections and session limits.

By default, these settings are defined not in this RDP-Tcp Properties dialog box, but in each user's domain account properties. To override these user-defined settings, you can click the Override User Settings check box, as shown in Figure 3-16, and then choose options for the following policies:

- **End A Disconnected Session** This setting determines when (if ever) a user is auto-matically logged off from a disconnected session.
- **Active Session Limit** This setting determines how long a user can stay active within a Remote Desktop session before automatically being disconnected.
- **Idle Session Limit** This setting determines how long a user can leave an inactive con-nection to a Remote Desktop session open before automatically being disconnected.

- **When Session Limit Is Reached Or Connection Is Broken**   This setting determines whether a user is logged off automatically when a connection is broken (manually or automatically).

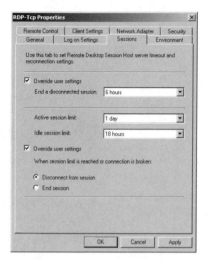

FIGURE 3-16 RD Session Host timeout and reconnection settings.

Environment Tab

This tab enables you to control whether initial programs defined in a user's profile should be allowed to run automatically at the start of a Remote Desktop session. It also enables you to specify a program to start for all users connecting to the local RD Session Host through RDP.

The Environment tab is shown in Figure 3-17.

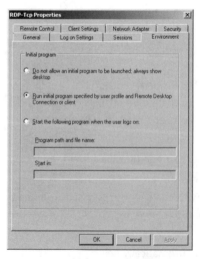

FIGURE 3-17 Initial program settings.

Remote Control Tab

The Remote Control feature of Remote Desktop Services enables an administrator to see or interact with another user's Remote Desktop session. By default, the properties that define the behavior of this feature are set on a per-user basis in each user account's properties dialog box. (These properties define how an administrator can view or control that user's Remote Desktop sessions.) The Remote Control tab enables you to control the settings of this feature on a per-server basis instead.

The default settings of a user account enable an administrator to interact with another user's Remote Desktop session only if the user provides consent. However, you can use the Remote Control tab of the RDP-Tcp Properties dialog box to enable administrators to interact with (or merely to view) all user sessions with or without consent. You can also completely prevent administrators from viewing or interacting with other users' sessions. The Remote Control feature is discussed in more detail in Lesson 1 of Chapter 4, "Configuring and Managing a Remote Desktop Infrastructure."

> **IMPORTANT   REMOTE CONTROL WORKS ONLY FROM REMOTE SESSION**
>
> You can use the Remote Control feature only from within an RDP session. If an administrator is logged on to an RD Session Host locally, the feature is disabled.

The Remote Control tab is shown in Figure 3-18.

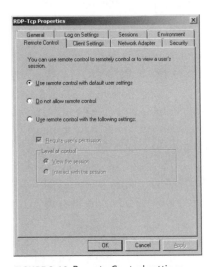

FIGURE 3-18 Remote Control settings.

Client Settings Tab

The Client Settings tab, shown in Figure 3-19, enables you to configure redirection of certain user interface features.

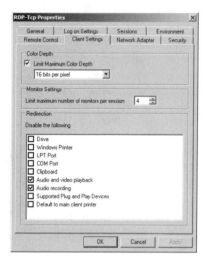

FIGURE 3-19 The Client Settings tab.

In the Color Depth area of the tab, you can define the amount of color detail sent from the RD Session Host to the client. The default setting is 16 bits per pixel, but you can adjust this to be higher or lower. In general, when you require more bit depth for RDP connections, appearance is improved at the expense of performance.

The Monitor Settings area of the tab controls a feature that is new to Windows Server 2008 R2 and Remote Desktop Client 7.0: support for multiple monitors in Remote Desktop sessions. The number you specify here sets a limit for the number of monitors through which users can view a Remote Desktop session. The default maximum number of monitors per session is four. Increasing this maximum can degrade the performance of the server.

In the Redirection—Disable The Following area of the tab, you can determine which features should not be redirected to the Remote Desktop session on the client. The advantage of disabling redirection is improved performance, but this improvement comes at the expense of the advantages offered by each particular feature you choose to disable.

- **Drive**   When you select this option, the drives local to the client cannot be included in the Remote Desktop session. (To include the drives, this check box must be cleared, and the Drives option must be selected on the Local Resources tab of the Remote Desktop Connection client.)

- **Windows Printer**   When you select this option, printers local to the client cannot be accessed in the Remote Desktop session. However, a user can still connect to the client printer at the command prompt by using LPT port mapping or COM port mapping.

- **LPT Port**   Selecting this option prevents users from mapping a connection to an LPT printer.

- **COM Port**   Selecting this option blocks a connection from the Remote Desktop session to COM devices on the client computer.

- **Clipboard** This option, when selected, prevents users from cutting or copying data from a Remote Desktop session and then pasting that data into the local session on the client computer. Over slow connections, disabling clipboard redirection can prevent screen freezes.

- **Audio And Video Playback** When enabled, this option prevents the transmission of audio and video data from the remote desktop to the local client computer. This option is selected if you have chosen the default selections when adding the Remote Desktop Services server role.

- **Audio Recording** This option prevents the remote user from recording audio through the Remote Desktop session. Along with Audio And Video Playback, the option is selected if you have chosen the default selections when adding the Remote Desktop Services server role.

- **Supported Plug And Play Devices** This option, when selected, prevents Plug and Play devices local to the client from being redirected to a Remote Desktop session.

- **Default To Main Client Printer** When you select this option, the default printer assigned to the Remote Desktop client is prevented from serving as the default printer for the Remote Desktop session.

Network Adapter Tab

This tab enables you to restrict the default RDP-Tcp connection to listen for RDP connection attempts on only one particular network adapter. The tab also enables you to set a limit on the number of connections allowed by the RD Session Host. By default, no limit is set, as shown in Figure 3-20.

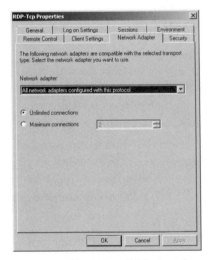

FIGURE 3-20 The Network Adapter tab.

Security Tab

This tab enables you to set user permissions for all RDP connections to the RD Session Host. It is recommended that you do not use this tab to configure user access to Remote Desktop Services; to do this, use the Remote Desktop Users group instead. You should use this tab to determine which users should have administrative control (Full Control) of Remote Desktop Services.

The Security tab is shown in Figure 3-21.

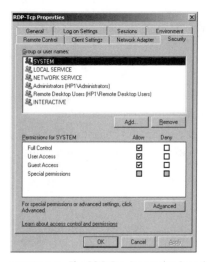

FIGURE 3-21 The RDP-Tcp Properties Security tab.

Configuring RD Session Host Server Settings

In addition to the RDP-Tcp Properties tabs, the RD Session Host Configuration console offers a second important set of configuration options for the RD Session Host that are available through the Edit Settings area. These settings apply to the entire RD Session Host server. Unlike the default RDP-Tcp connection settings or other connection settings, they cannot be configured to apply to only one transport protocol or to only one particular network adapter.

The Edit Settings area provides a summary of eight RD Session Host options organized under four categories: General, Licensing, RD Connection Broker, and RD IP Virtualization. To change these server options, double-click any one of them. This step opens a Properties dialog box whose four tabs are also named General, Licensing, RD Connection Broker, and RD IP Virtualization.

The options available in these four tabs are explained in the following section.

General Tab

The General tab enables you to configure the following features related to user logon sessions:

- **Delete Temporary Folders On Exit** When this option is enabled, as it is by default, all temporary data is deleted when a user logs off from a Remote Desktop session. Deleting temporary data in this way decreases performance but improves privacy because it prevents users from potentially accessing other users' data.

  This setting functions only when the next option, Use Temporary Folders Per Session, is also enabled.

- **Use Temporary Folders Per Session** Enabled by default, this option ensures that a new folder to store temporary data is created for each user session. When this option is disabled, temporary data is shared among all active sessions. Sharing temporary data among users can improve performance at the expense of user privacy.

- **Restrict Each User To A Single Session** This option is enabled by default. When enabled, it allows only one logon session to the RD Session Host per user. For instance, if you are logged on to a server locally with the built-in Administrator account, you cannot log on to the same computer through a Remote Desktop connection by using the same Administrator account until you first log off the server locally.

  By ensuring that you log off one session before beginning another, this default setting prevents possible data loss in the user profile. It also prevents stranded user sessions and, therefore, conserves server resources.

- **User Logon Mode** The settings in the User Logon Mode area enable you to prevent new users from logging on to the RD Session Host, for instance, in advance of a maintenance shutdown. The Allow All Connections option is the default setting. To prevent new users from connecting to the RD Session Host indefinitely, you can select Allow Reconnections, But Prevent New Logons. To prevent users from connecting to the server only until you restart the server, you can select Allow Reconnections, But Prevent New Logons Until The Server Is Restarted. Note that none of these options forces a session termination. If you must restart a server, you might need to end these sessions manually, as described in Chapter 4.

The General tab is shown in Figure 3-22.

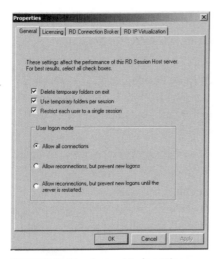

FIGURE 3-22 User Logon Mode settings.

EXAM TIP

The three settings available in the User Logon Mode area are new to Windows Server 2008 and Windows Server 2008 R2. For this reason, you should expect to see at least one question about these options on the 70-643 exam. Also note that the feature to prevent new logons is sometimes called Drain Mode.

Licensing Tab

The Licensing tab, shown in Figure 3-23, enables you to configure two features related to Remote Desktop licensing: the licensing mode and the license server discovery mode.

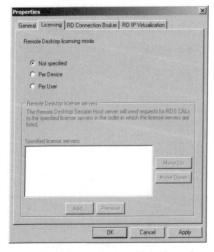

FIGURE 3-23 Server Options Licensing tab.

- **Remote Desktop Licensing Mode**   During the installation of the Remote Desktop Services server role, you can specify the licensing mode of the RD Session Host or select the option to configure the licensing mode later. To set or reset the licensing mode after installation, select the Licensing tab in this Properties dialog box and then choose the Per Device or Per User option in the Remote Desktop Licensing Mode area.

- **Remote Desktop License Servers**   By default, an RD Session Host attempts to contact any license servers published in Active Directory services or installed on domain controllers in the local domain. You can use this section to override the automatic selection of a license server and to specify a particular order in which license servers should be contacted. For example, you might choose this option if you have a preferred license server for use in your department and a secondary license server in your corporate division.

RD Connection Broker Settings Tab

The RD Connection Broker Settings tab, shown in Figure 3-24, is used to configure settings for an RD Session Host in an RD Connection Broker farm. RD Connection Broker can balance the session load among servers in a farm by directing new user sessions to the server in the farm with the fewest sessions. RD Connection Broker also ensures that users can reconnect automatically to disconnected sessions on the appropriate farm member server.

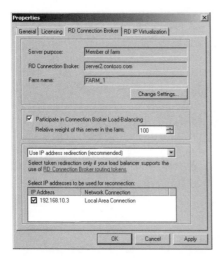

FIGURE 3-24 Configuring Remote Desktop Services load balancing.

Within an RD Connection Broker farm, there are two types of servers. First is the server on which the RD Connection Broker role service is installed. This server contains the configuration and user session data for the farm. Second is the group of RD Session Host servers that are members of the farm. The RD Connection Broker Settings tab is used to configure this second type of server, the farm member. For configuration of the member server to work, you must be able to specify a domain server on which RD Connection Broker has been installed. Otherwise, the configuration will fail.

To configure a Remote Desktop Services farm, the first step is to install the RD Connection Broker role service on a server that you want to use to track user sessions for the entire farm. This server becomes the RD Connection Broker server. You also perform the second step on the RD Connection Broker server. For each server you want to be a member of the farm, add that server's computer account to the Session Directory Computers local group on the RD Connection Broker server.

EXAM TIP

For the exam, remember that you need to add each farm member to the Session Directory Computers local group on the RD Connection Broker server.

You perform the third and final step on each server you want to be a farm member. In this step, you add each RD Session Host server to the farm by configuring the settings on the RD Connection Broker tab.

Perform the following steps to join an RD Session Host server to an RD Connection Broker farm:

1. Open the RD Session Host Configuration console by clicking Start, pointing to Administrative Tools, pointing to Remote Desktop Services, and then clicking Remote Desktop Session Host Configuration.

2. In the Edit Settings area, beneath RD Connection Broker, double-click Member Of Farm In RD Connection Broker.

    This step opens the RD Connection Broker tab of the Properties dialog box, as shown in Figure 3-24.

3. On the RD Connection Broker tab of the Properties dialog box, click Change Settings.

    This step opens the RD Connection Broker Settings dialog box, as shown in Figure 3-25.

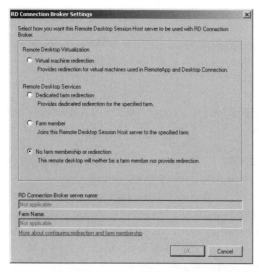

FIGURE 3-25 Configuring an RD Connection Broker farm member.

4. In the RD Connection Broker Settings dialog box, click Farm Member.

5. In the RD Connection Broker Server Name box, type the name of the RD Connection Broker server for the farm.

6. In the Farm Name box, type the name of the farm you want to join in RD Connection Broker.

> ***IMPORTANT* CONFIGURING THE FARM NAME**
>
> **You have to specify the same farm name on all RD Session Hosts joining the farm.**

7. Click OK to close the RD Connection Broker Settings dialog box.

8. To participate in RD Connection Broker Load Balancing, select the Participate In Connection Broker Load-Balancing check box.

9. Optionally, in the Relative Weight Of This Server In The Farm box, modify the server weight. By default, the value is 100. The server weight is relative. Therefore, if you assign one server a value of 50, and one a value of 100, the server with a weight of 50 will receive half the number of sessions that the server with the weight of 100 will.

10. Verify that you want to use IP address redirection. By default, the Use IP Address Redirection setting is enabled. If you want to use token redirection mode, select Use Token Redirection.

EXAM TIP

For the 70-643 exam, remember that you have to disable IP address redirection when your network includes a load balancer (usually a hardware load balancer) that supports routing tokens.

11. In the Select IP Addresses To Be Used For Reconnection box, select the check box next to each IP address you want to use.

LOAD BALANCING INITIAL CLIENT REQUESTS

To distribute the initial connections evenly to the server farm, RD Connection Broker must rely on a load balancing solution such as DNS round-robin, Network Load Balancing, or a hardware load balancer. These technologies distribute the initial Remote Desktop client requests to one of the farm members, which then immediately redirects the client request to the RD Connection Broker. The RD Connection Broker then directs the client back to one of the RD Session Hosts in the farm. If a user already has an open session on one of the servers, the client is redirected to that RD Session Host. Otherwise, the RD Connection Broker directs the client to an RD Session Host in a manner that reflects the relative weight value you have specified for it (in step 9 in the preceding procedure). For example, if you have assigned a weight of 50 to a particular farm member, the RD Connection Broker directs approximately half of the requests to that server that it directs to a server weighted at 100.

Of the three options for load balancing initial client requests, DNS round-robin is the easiest to implement. To configure round-robin load balancing in DNS, create a Host record in the local zone for each farm member. Each Host record should specify the farm name and point to one of the farm members, and a record should appear for each zone member. For example, if you have three RD Session Host servers in a farm named FARM1, with IP addresses of 10.0.1.10, 10.0.1.11, and 10.0.1.12, the DNS entries would resemble the following:

```
Farm1    Host(A)    10.0.1.10
Farm1    Host(A)    10.0.1.11
Farm1    Host(A)    10.0.1.12
```

By default, round-robin is enabled on DNS servers, but you should check to make sure that it has not been disabled. To check the status of round-robin, open the properties of the DNS server, click the Advanced tab, and verify that the Enable Round Robin check box is selected.

DEDICATED FARM REDIRECTION

In the RD Connection Broker Settings dialog box, as shown in Figure 3-25, you can select Dedicated Farm Redirection instead of Farm Member. This option enables you to configure the local RD Session Host as a dedicated redirector—a server in the farm that does not accept user sessions and serves only to redirect initial client requests to the RD Connection Broker. In a large farm with many concurrent client requests, this solution helps maintain good performance on farm members that host user sessions.

When you configure one or more dedicated redirectors for your RD Connection Broker farm, you should configure DNS so that the records for the farm point only to the redirectors. Delete any DNS entries that point DNS requests for the farm name toward other members servers. The purpose of these redirectors is to handle 100% of the initial Remote Desktop client requests and direct these initial requests to the RD Connection Broker. The RD Connection Broker will then direct the client to one of the farm members.

For example, suppose you have a farm named Farm2 with 15 members assigned the 10.0.2.1–10.0.2.15 addresses. If you have two additional RD Session Hosts configured as dedicated farm redirectors with the 10.0.2.21 and 10.0.2.22 addresses, the DNS entries for Farm2 should resemble the following:

```
Farm2     Host(A)     10.0.2.21
Farm2     Host(A)     10.0.2.22
```

RD IP Virtualization Tab

The RD IP Virtualization tab, shown in Figure 3-26, enables you to assign a unique IP address either to each active user session on an RD Session Host (Per Session mode) or to particular applications within a user session on an RD Session Host (Per Program mode). You might need to configure either of these IP Virtualization modes on an RD Session Host to provide compatibility with older applications, to enable per-user logging related to ISP regulatory requirements, or to help support network filtering and resource access control.

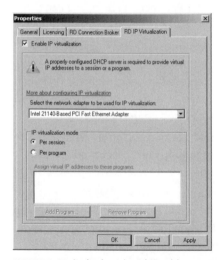

FIGURE 3-26 Assigning virtual IP addresses to each Remote Desktop user session.

To configure an RD Session Host for IP virtualization, perform the following steps:

1. Ensure that a local DHCP server is available and can provide enough addresses to support your needs.

2. In the RD Session Host Configuration console, in the Edit Settings area below RD IP Virtualization, double-click IP Virtualization.

3. On the RD IP Virtualization tab, select Enable IP Virtualization.

4. In the drop-down list box, select the network adapter you want to associate with the session or program.

5. In the IP Virtualization Mode area, choose Per Session or Per Program.

6. If you choose Per Program mode, click Add Program to add the programs to which you want to assign unique IP addresses.

    If you select Per Session mode, the user session in general is assigned the same IP address as the RD Session Host server. Only sessions within the specified programs are assigned unique IP addresses.

Configuring Remote Desktop Printer Redirection

Printer redirection enables the client's printers to be used as printers for a Remote Desktop session. Although you can easily modify basic options regarding printer redirection in the Client Settings tab of the RDP-Tcp Properties dialog box, Group Policy contains important additional options concerning this feature.

You can disable or customize the behavior of printer redirection by using Group Policy and the Group Policy Management console. To find printer redirection configuration options in Group Policy, open a Group Policy object (GPO) and navigate to Computer Configuration \Policies\Administrative Templates\Windows Components\Remote Desktop Services\Remote Desktop Session Host\Printer Redirection. Within the Printer Redirection folder, you can configure the following five policy settings:

- **Do Not Set Default Client Printer To Be Default Printer In A Session**   By default, Remote Desktop Services automatically designates the client default printer as the default printer in a Remote Desktop session. You can use this policy setting to override this behavior. If you enable this policy setting, the default printer in the Remote Desktop session will be designated as the printer specified on the remote computer.

- **Do Not Allow Client Printer Redirection**   This policy setting essentially disables printer redirection completely. If you enable this policy setting, users cannot redirect print jobs from the remote computer to a local client printer in Remote Desktop sessions.

- **Specify RD Session Host Server Fallback Printer Driver Behavior**   This policy setting determines the behavior that occurs when the RD Session Host does not have a printer driver that matches the client's printer. By default, when this occurs, no printer is made available within the Remote Desktop session. However, you can use this policy setting to fall back to a Printer Control Language (PCL) printer driver, to a PostScript (PS) printer driver, or to both printer drivers.

- **Use Remote Desktop Easy Print Printer Driver First**   The Remote Desktop Easy Print printer driver enables users to print reliably from a Remote Desktop session to the correct printer on their client computer. It also enables users to have a more consistent printing experience between local and remote sessions. By default, the RD Session Host first tries to use the Remote Desktop Easy Print printer driver to install all client printers. However, you can use this policy setting to disable the use of the Remote Desktop Easy Print printer driver.

- **Redirect Only The Default Client Printer** By default, all client printers are redirected to Remote Desktop sessions. However, if you enable this policy setting, only the default client printer is redirected in Remote Desktop sessions.

EXAM TIP

Be sure to understand these Group Policy settings for the 70-643 exam.

Configuring Display Data Prioritization

In Windows Server 2008 and Windows Server 2008 R2, you can control the flow of traffic between the Remote Desktop Session Host and Remote Desktop clients so that display, keyboard, and mouse data is given a higher priority than other traffic, such as printing or file transfers. This feature ensures that screen performance for users is not degraded by actions, such as large print jobs, that consume a lot of bandwidth.

By default, the Remote Desktop Session Host reserves 70 percent of bandwith for display and input data. All other traffic, such as clipboard, file transfers, and print jobs, is allocated 30 percent of available bandwidth by default.

You can modify these default settings by making changes to the registry of the Remote Desktop Session Host. Change the value of the following entries under the HKEY_LOCAL _MACHINE\SYSTEM\CurrentControlSet\Services\TermDD subkey:

- **FlowControlDisable** By default, this value is set to *0*. You can set this value to *1* to disable display data prioritization. When you disable display data prioritization, all data is given equal priority to and from the Remote Desktop Sesssion Host.

- **FlowControlDisplayBandwidth** This registry entry sets the relative priority of display and input data to and from the Remote Desktop Session Host. By default, this value is set to 70. The highest value you can assign is 255.

- **FlowControlChannelBandwidth** This registry entry sets the relative priority of all data other than display and input data that is sent to and from the Remote Desktop Session Host. This data includes clipboard, file transfers, and print jobs. By default, this entry is set to 30. The highest value you can assign is 255.

    Note that the bandwidth ratio used for display data prioritization is calculated based on the values of FlowControlDisplayBandwidth and FlowControlChannelBandwidth entries. For example, if FlowControlDisplayBandwidth is set to 200 and FlowControlChannelBandwidth is set to 50, the ratio is 200:50, so display and input data will be allocated 80 percent of the bandwidth.

- **FlowControlChargePostCompression** The value of this entry determines whether data prioritization ratios should be considered before or after data compression. By default, this entry is set to *0*, which means the ratios are determined before data compression. To configure the Remote Desktop Session Host to determine data prioritization ratios after data is compressed, set this entry to *1*.

If these entries do not appear, you can add them. To do this, right-click the TermDD subkey, point to New, and then click DWORD (32-bit) Value. Note also that if you make any changes to the registry values, you must restart the terminal server for the changes to take effect.

EXAM TIP

For the 70-643 exam, you need to understand the four registry settings used for display data prioritization. Also remember that these settings are configured on the Remote Desktop Session Host server, not the Remote Desktop clients.

 Quick Check

1. You want to prepare to take a server in a server farm offline. You do not want to force any users off. What should you do?

2. You want to enable audio in Remote Desktop connections to a server named RD1. What should you do?

Quick Check Answers

1. In the RD Session Host Configuration console, on the General tab of the server properties, choose the option to allow reconnections but prevent new logons.

2. Clear the Audio check box on the Client Settings tab in RDP-Tcp properties on RD1.

PRACTICE **Install and Configure a Remote Desktop License Server**

Even if you have not purchased any RDS CALs from Microsoft or a third party, it is a good idea to walk through the process of installing and configuring a Remote Desktop license server. In Exercises 1 through 4, you walk through those steps. If you do have RDS CALs available, you can perform the optional Exercise 5, in which you install the client licenses.

EXERCISE 1 Installing the Remote Desktop Licensing Server Role

In this exercise, you use the Add Roles Wizard to install a Remote Desktop license server on Server1.

1. Log on to Server1 as a domain administrator.

2. Open Server Manager.

3. In the Server Manager console tree, select the *Roles* node and then click Add Roles in the details pane.

The Add Roles Wizard opens.

4. On the Before You Begin page, click Next.

5. On the Select Server Roles page, select the Remote Desktop Services check box and then click Next.

6. On the Remote Desktop Services page, click Next.

7. On the Select Role Services page, select the Remote Desktop Licensing check box and then click Next.

8. On the Configure Discovery Scope For RD Licensing page, read all the text on the page.

9. Verify that the Configure A Discovery Scope For This License Server check box is cleared and then click Next.

10. On the Confirm Installation Selections page, read all the text on the page and then click Install.

    When the installation completes, the Installation Results page appears.

11. On the Installation Results page, click Close.

EXERCISE 2   Activating a Remote Desktop License Server

In this exercise, you activate the license server. This process requires Server1 to be connected to the Internet.

1. While you are logged on to Server1 as a domain administrator, open the RD Licensing Manager console by clicking Start, pointing to Administrative Tools, pointing to Remote Desktop Services, and then clicking Remote Desktop Licensing Manager.

   RD Licensing Manager opens.

   Although RD Licensing Manager is installed automatically on any server on which you have installed the Remote Desktop Licensing role service, you do not need to manage the licensing server from the server itself. You can also install RD Licensing Manager on any server and connect to the license server remotely.

2. In the RD Licensing Manager console tree, expand the *All Servers* node and then select the *SERVER1* node. (The node should be marked by a red X at this point because it has not been activated.)

3. Right-click the *SERVER1* node and then click Activate Server.

   The Activate Server Wizard appears.

4. On the Welcome To The Activate Server Wizard page, read all the text on the page and then click Next.

5. On the Connection Method page, read all the text on the page and then answer the following question: By default, which is the Connection Method assigned to the license server?

   Answer: Automatic Connection (Recommended)

6. On the Connection Method page, in the Connection Method drop-down list, select Web Browser.

7. Read the new associated Description and Requirements sections that have been refreshed on the page. The Web Browser connection method is useful when the licensing server does not connect to the Internet. With this option, you only need to be able to connect from another server to both the licensing server and the Internet.

8. On the Connection Method page, in the Connection Method drop-down list, select Telephone.

9. Read the new associated Description and Requirements sections that have been refreshed on the page. The Telephone connection method is useful when your network is not connected to the Internet.

10. On the Connection Method page, in the Connection Method drop-down list, select Automatic Connection and then click Next.

    The Activate Server Wizard dialog box briefly appears while Server1 contacts the activation server at the Microsoft Clearinghouse. After a moment, the Company Information page appears.

11. On the Company Information page, enter appropriate information in the First Name, Last Name, and Company text boxes and then choose your country from the Country Or Region drop-down list.

12. Click Next.

13. Another Company Information page appears. Providing the requested information is optional. Click Next.

    The Activate Server Wizard dialog box appears briefly, and then the Completing The Activate Server Wizard page appears. The Start Install Licenses Wizard Now check box is selected.

14. On the Completing The Activate Server Wizard page, read all the text and then click Next.

    The Welcome To The Install Licenses Wizard page appears.

15. Leave all windows open, switch to Server2, and proceed to Exercise 3.

EXERCISE 3   Specifying a License Server for the RD Session Host

In this exercise, you configure the RD Session Host on Server2 to point to the new license server on Server1.

1. Log on to Contoso.local from Server2 as a domain administrator.

2. Open the Remote Desktop Session Host Configuration console.

3. In the Edit Settings area, below Licensing, double-click Remote Desktop License Servers.

4. On the Licensing Tab of the Properties dialog box, click Per User.

5. Click Add.

6. In the Add License Server dialog box, select Server1.contoso.local from the list of known license servers and then click Add.

7. Click OK.

8. In the Properties dialog box, click OK.

9. Note that in the Licensing area beneath Edit Settings, the Remote Desktop Licensing mode is designated as "Per User," and the Remote Desktop License Servers is shown as "Specified."

10. Close the Remote Desktop Session Host Configuration console.

11. Return to Server1 and proceed to the next exercise.

EXERCISE 4 Installing RDS CALs

Installing client licenses is the last stage of deploying a license server. Even if you do not have any RDS CALs to install at this point, it is a good idea to review the pages of the Install Licenses Wizard to gain a better understanding of this deployment process in its entirety.

In this exercise, you review the process of installing RDS CALs in your newly activated server. The Welcome page of the Install Licenses Wizard page should still be open from Exercise 2.

1. On the Welcome To The Install Licenses Wizard page, read all the text on the page and then click Next.

   The Install Licenses Wizard briefly appears, and then the License Program page appears.

2. Read all the text on the License Program page.

3. Review the options from the License Program drop-down list.

4. Take a few moments to explore the various license program options by selecting each option and reading all the associated text on the page.

5. In the License Program drop-down list, ensure that the default option of License Pack (Retail Purchase) is selected and then click Next.

   The License Code page appears.

6. Read all the text on the page.

   If you have obtained a valid license code, you can perform Exercise 5. Otherwise, you can click Cancel to close the wizard and then simply read the next exercise.

EXERCISE 5 Finishing the Installation of RDS CALs (Optional)

1. In the License Code text boxes, type a valid license code and then click Add.

2. On the License Code page, click Next.

   The Install Licenses Wizard dialog box briefly appears, and then the Completing The Install Licenses Wizard page appears.

3. On the Completing The Install Licenses Wizard page, click Finish.

In the RD Licensing Manager console tree, the *Server1* node is now designated with a green check mark. The licensing server is now configured.

4. Close all open windows and then log off both Server1 and Server2.

Lesson Summary

- The main tool used for configuring Remote Desktop Services is the RD Session Host Configuration console.
- You can edit RDP-Tcp properties in the RD Session Host Configuration console to configure Remote Desktop session features such as encryption strength, timeout settings, and printer availability.
- The Edit Settings area in the RD Session Host Configuration console enables you to configure options related to load balancing, license server discovery, new logon prevention, and IP virtualization.
- Group Policy offers additional control for Remote Desktop printer redirection, most notably the option to fall back to a generic printer driver and to redirect only the default client printer.

Lesson Review

The following questions are intended to reinforce key information presented in this lesson. The questions are also available on the companion CD if you prefer to review them in electronic form.

> **NOTE ANSWERS**
>
> Answers to these questions and explanations of why each answer choice is correct or incorrect are located in the "Answers" section at the end of the book.

1. Your company network has implemented a Remote Desktop server farm named RDFARM1. The farm consists of five computers running Windows Server 2008 R2, including a server named RDCB1 on which the RD Connection Broker role service is installed. You want to add a sixth computer running Windows Server 2008 R2, named RDS6, to the farm. After configuring the server with the same hardware and software options as those of the other farm members, you join RDS6 to the farm by specifying RDCB1 as the RD Connection Broker server and RDFARM1 as the farm name in the RD Connection Broker properties on RDS6. You verify that some users who attempt to connect to the server name RDFARM1 are able to establish Remote Desktop sessions on RDS6, but these users are not able to reconnect to disconnected sessions. You want users connecting to RDS6 through RDFARM1 to be able to reconnect to disconnected RDP sessions. What should you do?

A. Add RDS6 to the Session Directory Computers local group on RDS6.

B. Add RDS6 to the Session Directory Computers local group on RDCB1.

C. In the DNS server, add a Host (A) record named RDFARM1 that maps to the IP address of RDS6.

D. In the DNS server, add a Host (A) record named RDS6 that maps to the IP address of RDS6.

2. Your company network consists of a single Active Directory domain named Contoso .com. In the company network, you have deployed Remote Desktop Services on a computer named RDS1 that is running Windows Server 2008 R2. Some users who connect to RDS1 through RDP complain that they cannot print successfully to their local printers. You want to ensure that RDS1 uses a generic PostScript printer driver whenever Remote Desktop Services cannot find an adequate driver for Remote Desktop client printers. What should you do?

A. On the Client Session tab of RDP-Tcp properties on RDS1, select the Windows Printer option.

B. On the Client Session tab of RDP-Tcp properties on RDS1, select the Default To Main Client Printer option.

C. In a Group Policy object (GPO), configure the Use Remote Desktop Easy Print Printer Driver First policy setting and then apply the GPO so that RDS1 falls within the scope of the policy.

D. In a Group Policy object (GPO), configure the Specify RD Session Host Fallback Printer Driver policy setting to default to PS and then apply the GPO so that RDS1 falls within the scope of the policy.

3. You work for a company with 500 employees. Your IT department has deployed a Remote Desktop server farm with 10 servers running Windows Server 2008 R2, and users connect to the farm very frequently for periods of five minutes or less. You are using DNS round-robin to distribute the Remote Desktop client requests among all 10 servers. Users complain that the server response time is occasionally slow during Remote Desktop sessions. You want to improve Remote Desktop performance by reducing the processing overhead resulting from initial client requests. What should you do?

A. Configure Network Load Balancing for the server farm.

B. Add Host records for all farm member servers in DNS.

C. Add another server to the farm and configure it for dedicated farm redirection.

D. Add another server to the farm and configure it as a farm member.

Chapter Review

To further practice and reinforce the skills you learned in this chapter, you can:

- Review the chapter summary.
- Review the list of key terms introduced in this chapter.
- Complete the case scenarios. These scenarios set up real-world situations involving the topics of this chapter and ask you to create solutions.
- Complete the suggested practices.
- Take a practice test.

Chapter Summary

- Remote Desktop Services is a server role in Windows Server 2008 R2. This server role is a renamed version of Terminal Services in Windows Server 2008 and earlier versions of Windows Server. The main role service of Remote Desktop Services—what was called Terminal Server in Windows Server 2008—is now called Remote Desktop Session Host. The other role services and management tools have also been renamed.

- Remote Desktop Services enables users to establish a desktop or application session on a remote computer. In Windows Server 2008 and Windows Server 2008 R2, this server role includes many new and important features, such as RD Gateway, RemoteApp, RD Virtualization Host, and RD Web Access.

- Remote Desktop Services requires client access licenses (CALs) either for all connecting users or for all connecting devices. If you do not purchase and install Remote Desktop Services CALs, the feature will stop working after 120 days.

- The main tool used for configuring Remote Desktop Services is the Remote Desktop Session Host Configuration console. In the RD Session Host Configuration console, you can edit RDP-Tcp properties to configure Remote Desktop user session features, such as encryption strength, timeout settings, and printer availability. You can also edit server properties to configure settings related to load balancing, license server discovery, new logon prevention, and IP virtualization.

Key Terms

Do you know what these key terms mean? You can check your answers by looking up the terms in the glossary at the end of the book.

- Network-Level Authentication (NLA)
- RD Connection Broker
- Remote Desktop for Administration (RDA)
- Remote Desktop Protocol (RDP)
- Remote Desktop Services client access licenses (RDS CALs)

Case Scenarios

In the following case scenarios, you apply what you've learned about Remote Desktop Services in this chapter. You can find answers to these questions in the "Answers" section at the end of this book.

Case Scenario 1: Choosing an RD Licensing Strategy

You work as a network administrator in a large company. Your department has recently implemented two servers, named App1 and NS2, and you have been tasked with making Remote Desktop licensing recommendations for each server.

App1 is an application server. Although the application is not considered mission critical, as many as five users tend to be connected to it through Remote Desktop simultaneously. Overall, 20 users need to connect to App1 through Remote Desktop at some point during the day. They can connect from any of 50 computers.

NS2 is a DNS server that occasionally requires remote maintenance and administration through Remote Desktop. Only administrators connect to NS2.

1. Do you need to install Remote Desktop Services on App1? Which type of client access licenses would you purchase, if any?

2. Do you need to install Remote Desktop Services on NS2? Which type of client access licenses would you purchase, if any?

Case Scenario 2: Troubleshooting a Remote Desktop Services Installation

You work in IT support for a large company whose network consists of a single Active Directory domain. One of your responsibilities is supporting Remote Desktop Session Host servers in the Advertising department. Over the course of a week, you encounter the following two problems:

1. You deploy Remote Desktop Services on a new computer running Windows Server 2008 R2 named App3, but you discover that no users running Windows XP can connect to it. What should you do?

2. Users who connect to a Remote Desktop Session Host named App2 complain that they cannot always reconnect to a disconnected session. What should you do?

Suggested Practices

To help you successfully master the exam objectives presented in this chapter, complete the following tasks.

Deploy a Remote Desktop Server Farm

In this practice, you create a load-balanced Remote Desktop server farm.

- **Practice** Using either virtual or physical computers, join two identical installations of Windows Server 2008 R2 to a domain. Install the RD Session Host role service on both computers but install the RD Connection Broker role service on just one. Add both computer names to the Session Directory Computers local group on the RD Connection Broker server. Use the RD Connection Broker tab in the Remote Desktop Session Host Configuration console on both computers to configure the Remote Desktop server farm. Create Host (A) records for the farm name in DNS, one record for each server IP address. Then, connect to the server farm through from a remote RDP client.

Watch a Webcast

In this practice, you watch a series of webcasts about Remote Desktop Services in Windows Server 2008 R2.

- **Practice** Watch "Windows Server 2008 R2: Remote Desktop Services—The Series" by Matt McSpirit.

  - Part 1 is called "RDS Session Host—Initial Installation & Configuration" and is available at *http://technet.microsoft.com/en-us/edge/Ff955824*.

  - Part 2 is called "RDS Web Portal—Initial Installation & Configuration" and is available at *http://technet.microsoft.com/en-us/edge/video/ff955820*.

  - Part 3 is called "RDS Connection Broker—Initial Installation & Configuration" and is available at *http://technet.microsoft.com/en-us/edge/video/ff955821*.

  - Part 4 is called "RDS Gateway—Initial Installation & Configuration" and is available at *http://technet.microsoft.com/en-us/edge/video/ff955822*.

  - Part 5 is called "RDP7 Deep Dive & User Experience" and is available at *http://technet.microsoft.com/en-us/edge/video/ff955823*.

Take a Practice Test

The practice tests on this book's companion CD offer many options. For example, you can test yourself on just one exam objective, or you can test yourself on all the 70-643 certification exam content. You can set up the test so that it closely simulates the experience of taking a certification exam, or you can set it up in study mode so that you can look at the correct answers and explanations after you answer each question.

> *MORE INFO* **PRACTICE TESTS**
>
> For details about all the practice test options available, see the "How to Use the Practice Tests" section in this book's introduction.

CHAPTER 4

Configuring and Managing a Remote Desktop Infrastructure

This chapter moves beyond the topic of deploying a Remote Desktop Session Host and discusses how to configure the components that comprise an entire Remote Desktop infrastructure—clients, servers, gateways, and applications.

Even more than with other Windows Server technologies, the components of Remote Desktop Services are best understood by working with them directly. With this idea in mind, be sure to perform the extensive practices at the end of each lesson to develop the skills you need for both the exam and the real world.

Exam objectives in this chapter:

- Configure Remote Desktop Session Host.
- Configure Remote Desktop Gateway (RD Gateway).
- Configure RemoteApp and Remote Desktop Web Access.
- Configure and monitor Remote Desktop resources.

Lessons in this chapter:

Before You Begin

To complete the lessons in this chapter, you must have:

- A computer running Windows Server 2008 R2 named Server1 that is a domain controller in a domain named Contoso.local.

- A computer running Windows Server 2008 R2 named Server2 that is a member server in the Contoso.local domain. On Server2, the Remote Desktop Services server role is installed, along with the Remote Desktop Session Host role service. No other role services or server roles are installed.

- Three domain administrator accounts, named ContosoAdmin1, ContosoAdmin2, and ContosoAdmin3.

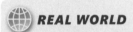

REAL WORLD

J.C. Mackin

Remote Desktop Session Host servers need a good amount of RAM, and the extra RAM you can install in a 64-bit system compared to a 32-bit system makes a big difference in terms of scalability and performance. In the 32-bit versions of Windows Server older than Windows Server 2008 R2, you can expect to host about 50 user sessions to a terminal server before the performance degrades noticeably, and that's assuming the server is maxed out with 4 GB of RAM. For a 64-bit server running Windows Server 2008 R2 configured with double the RAM, however, you can host almost *triple* the user sessions. Of course, by adding more RAM, you could support even more simultaneous users.

If you currently have a production terminal server running Windows Server 2008 or Windows Server 2003 on a 32-bit system, upgrading to the 64-bit-only Windows Server 2008 R2 and adding more RAM will give you a surprisingly large boost in performance.

Lesson 1: Configuring and Managing Remote Desktop Clients

A Remote Desktop Services (RDS) infrastructure includes many areas for client configuration, such as user profiles, client session options, resource allocation, and the Remote Desktop Connection client program (Mstsc.exe) itself.

This lesson introduces you to tools you can use to administer these and other aspects of Remote Desktop clients connections.

After this lesson, you will be able to:

- Understand the configuration options available in Remote Desktop Connection.
- Manage connections to Remote Desktop Services.

Estimated lesson time: 75 minutes

Configuring Remote Desktop Client Settings

Remote Desktop Client (RDC), also known as Mstsc.exe, is the primary client program that connects to Remote Desktop Services. RDC is highly configurable, both directly through its application interface and through Group Policy.

To explore the configuration options available through RDC, open RDC by clicking Start, All Programs, Accessories, and Remote Desktop Connection. In the Remote Desktop Connection window, click Options, as shown in Figure 4-1.

FIGURE 4-1 Accessing RDC options tabs.

This step reveals the six RDC options tabs. The following list describes the features you can configure on these RDC options tabs.

- **General** The General tab, shown in Figure 4-2, enables you to define a target computer and a set of authentication credentials for the connection. It also enables you to save the options defined for the connection in an RDP (Remote Desktop) file.

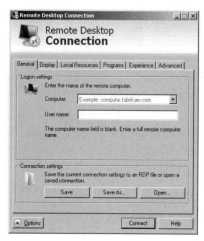

FIGURE 4-2 RDC General tab.

- **Display** The Display tab, shown in Figure 4-3, enables you to define the screen resolution and color bit depth for the Remote Desktop client window.

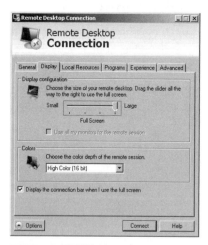

FIGURE 4-3 RDC Display tab.

- **Local Resources** The Local Resources tab enables you to choose which local resources (such as the Clipboard, any locally defined printers, and any local drives) should
  be made available within the Remote Desktop session. This tab also enables you to
  determine the remote audio settings through the *Settings* button. For audio playback,
  you can configure RDC to play audio on the local computer, the remote computer,
  or to play no audio at all. For remote audio recording, you can configure the RDC to
  either record audio captured through local input devices or not. (Although local audio
  playback in RDC is enabled and remote audio recording is disabled, both of these features are disabled by default in the RDP-Tcp properties of the Remote Desktop Session

Host.) Finally, the Local Resources tab enables you to determine how keystrokes, such as Alt+Tab, are used in the Remote Desktop session.

The Local Resources tab is shown in Figure 4-4.

FIGURE 4-4 RDC Local Resources tab.

- **Programs**   This tab enables you to define any program you want to start automatically when the Remote Desktop connection begins.

The Programs tab is shown in Figure 4-5.

FIGURE 4-5 RDC Programs tab.

- **Experience**   The Experience tab, shown in Figure 4-6, enables you to choose which optional graphical user interface (GUI) effects you want to display from the Remote Desktop Session Host. For example, the Desktop background and font-smoothing features visually enhance the Remote Desktop session, but can also strain network resources and slow Remote Desktop client performance. Performance settings will be selected automatically, as a suggestion, when you choose a connection speed.

FIGURE 4-6 RDC Experience tab.

- **Advanced** The Advanced tab, shown in Figure 4-7, enables you to configure client behavior for the Server Authentication and Remote Desktop Gateway (RD Gateway) features. Server Authentication is a feature, native to Remote Desktop Protocol 6.0 and later, through which a Remote Desktop Session Host can confirm its identity to Remote Desktop clients. On the Advanced tab, you can configure the Remote Desktop Connection client software either to provide a warning, to connect without warning, or not to connect to a Remote Desktop Session Host on which Server Authentication is unavailable or has failed.

  The RD Gateway feature enables a Remote Desktop client to traverse a corporate firewall and connect to any number of Remote Desktop Session Host servers in an organization. This feature and its configuration are described in detail in Lesson 2, "Deploying Remote Desktop Gateway."

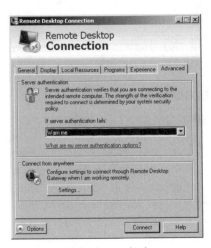

FIGURE 4-7 RDC Advanced tab.

Saving RDP Files

After you have defined the desired options for a Remote Desktop client in RDC, these settings are saved automatically in the Documents folder to a hidden file named Default.rdp. This file contains the settings used for RDC when you open the program from the Start menu. However, you can also save Remote Desktop client configuration settings in custom .rdp files by clicking Save As on the General tab. These .rdp files can then initiate Remote Desktop sessions with specific client options (such as server name and authentication information).

EXAM TIP

On the 70-643 exam, you might see a question about saving RDC settings in an .rdp file. Be sure to review the settings on all the RDC options tabs so that you understand the kind of configuration details that can be saved in such a file.

Configuring Remote Desktop Clients Through Group Policy

Group Policy enables you to enforce settings centrally on users or computers in an Active Directory Domain Services (AD DS) environment. As a way to manage many Remote Desktop clients, you can use a GPO to ensure that Remote Desktop Connection is always configured with the settings you choose. In many cases, this is the most efficient and effective way to manage Remote Desktop clients.

In both the Computer Configuration and User Configuration sections of a GPO, you can find settings for Remote Desktop Services in the \Policies\Administrative Templates\Windows Components\Remote Desktop Services section. Use the Remote Desktop Connection Client subfolder within this section to configure client settings that affect how the passwords should be saved in RDC, whether the client should always be prompted for credentials, and how clients should respond to server authentication failure. You can use other subfolders, such as Device and Resource Redirection, Remote Session Environment, and Session Time Limits, to configure settings related to other aspects of RDC client sessions.

Configuring User Profiles for Remote Desktop

A *user profile* refers to the collection of data that comprises a user's individual environment—including a user's individual files, application settings, and desktop configuration. In more specific terms, a user profile also refers to the contents of the personal folder that bears the name of an individual user. By default, this personal folder is created in the C:\Users folder when a user logs on for the first time. It contains subfolders, such as Documents, Desktop, and Downloads, as well as a personal data file named Ntuser.dat. For example, by default, a user named StefanR will store the data that makes up his personal environment in a folder named C:\Users\StefanR.

In a Remote Desktop Services environment, user profiles are stored on the Remote Desktop Session Host by default. This point is important because when many users access the Remote Desktop Session Host server, the profiles can consume a large amount of server disk space. If storage space on the Remote Desktop Session Host server is insufficient, plan to store user data and profiles on a disk that is separate from the operating system installation disk drive.

You can also use the Limit Profile Size policy setting in Group Policy to limit the size of a user profile. To find this setting, browse to User Configuration\Policies\Administrative Templates\System\User Profile. As an alternative, you can consider using disk quotas to limit the amount of space available to each user. (You can configure disk quotas through the properties of the drive on the Remote Desktop Session Host server where the profiles are stored.)

Roaming User Profiles and Remote Desktop

Another way to manage Remote Desktop user profiles is to configure users with a Remote Desktop Services user profile that is stored on a central network share. Such a profile is downloaded to the user's Remote Desktop session whenever and wherever such a session is initiated. This Remote Desktop Services profile can be defined on the Remote Desktop Services Profile tab of a user account's properties, as shown in Figure 4-8. Alternatively, you can use Group Policy to define these Remote Desktop roaming user profiles. (You can find Remote Desktop profile settings in a GPO in Computer Configuration\Policies\Administrative Templates\Windows Components\Remote Desktop Services\Remote Desktop Session Host\ Profiles. The specific policy setting used to configure Remote Desktop Services profiles is named Set Path For Remote Desktop Services Roaming User Profile.)

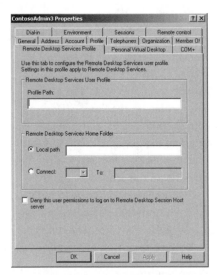

FIGURE 4-8 Configuring a Remote Desktop Services profile.

CAUTION ROAMING USER PROFILES AND REMOTE DESKTOP SERVICES

Ordinary roaming user profiles are those that follow a user as he or she logs on and off from various computers in a Windows domain. Ordinary roaming user profiles should not be used for Remote Desktop sessions because they can lead to unexpected data loss or corruption. If you have configured roaming user profiles in your organization, be sure to implement Remote Desktop Services profiles as well.

Roaming User Profile Cache Management

Through the profile caching feature, a copy of the Remote Desktop Services user profile is saved on a Remote Desktop Session Host server after a user logs on to that server. You can configure the maximum size of this user profile cache on a Remote Desktop Session Host server by applying the Limit The Size Of The Entire Roaming User Profile Cache Group Policy setting, which is new to Windows Server 2008 R2. If the size of the profile cache exceeds the size you configure, Remote Desktop Services deletes the least recently used profiles until the cache is reduced to a size below the designated limit. You can find this Group Policy setting in a GPO by browsing to Computer Configuration\Policies\Administrative Templates\Windows Components\Remote Desktop Services\Remote Desktop Session Host\Profiles.

Using Folder Redirection with Remote Desktop Services User Profiles

Large roaming user profiles can be slow to download from a network share. A good way to speed logon times is to use Folder Redirection, which you can apply through Group Policy. With Folder Redirection, folders in the user profile, such as Documents or Downloads, become simple pointers to locations on the network, so their contents are not downloaded at logon.

Configuring Remote Desktop Home Folders

When a user chooses to save a file, the default path points to a location known as the *home folder*. For Remote Desktop connections, the home folder is located on the Remote Desktop Session Host server by default. However, it is usually helpful to configure the home folder either on the local disk drive or on a network share. Configuring the home folder in this way ensures that users can locate their saved files easily. As with Remote Desktop Services profiles, you can define home folder locations for Remote Desktop either in the properties of the user account or in Group Policy. (Home folder settings for Remote Desktop can be found in a Group Policy object in Computer Configuration \Policies\Administrative Templates\Windows Components\Remote Desktop Services\Remote Desktop Session Host\Profiles. The policy setting used to configure home folders is named Set Remote Desktop User Home Directory.)

 Quick Check

1. Where is the default location of the user profile for a Remote Desktop user?
2. What is the most efficient way to configure RDC options for many users in your organization?

Quick Check Answers

1. On the Remote Desktop Session Host server
2. Group Policy

Managing Remote Desktop User Connections

Remote Desktop Services Manager (RDSM) is the main administrative tool used to manage connections to a Remote Desktop Session Host. You can use RDSM to view information about users connected to a Remote Desktop Session Host, to monitor user sessions, or to perform administrative tasks such as logging off users or disconnecting user sessions.

To open RDSM from the Start menu, point to Administrative Tools, point to Remote Desktop Services, and then click Remote Desktop Services Manager. You can also open RDSM by typing **tsadmin.msc** in the Search Programs And Files box or in the Run box on the Start menu.

The next section reviews the main management tasks you can perform in RDSM and provides many command-line alternatives for these management tasks. To learn more about using RDSM, be sure to perform the exercises at the end of this lesson.

EXAM TIP

Although RDSM is the main tool used to manage Remote Desktop user connections, most of the management functions provided also have command-line equivalents. Be sure to learn both the GUI functions and command-line commands described in this section for the 70-643 exam.

RDSM is shown in Figure 4-9.

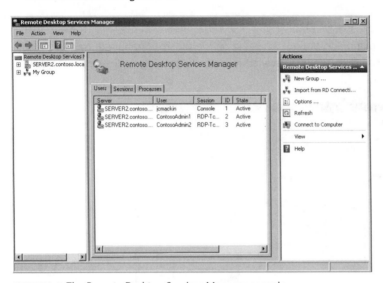

FIGURE 4-9 The Remote Desktop Services Manager console.

RDSM provides three tabs from which to view and manage Remote Desktop connections: Users, Sessions, and Processes.

- The Users tab displays information about users connected to the Remote Desktop Session Host, such as the currently logged on user accounts, the time of the user's logon to the server, and the session status.

  To display information about user sessions on a Remote Desktop Session Host, you can also use the *Query user* or *Quser* command-line commands.

> **MORE INFO   USE THE /? SWITCH FOR MORE INFO**
>
> To learn more about any of the command-line tools introduced in this section, simply type the command at the command prompt with the */?* switch. For example, to learn the syntax for *Quser*, type **quser /?**.

- The Sessions tab provides information about the sessions connected to the Remote Desktop Session Host. Because some sessions are initiated by services or by the operating system, sessions typically outnumber users.

To display information about sessions on a Remote Desktop Session Host, you can also use the *Query session* command.

- The Processes tab displays information about which programs each user is running on the terminal server.

To display information about processes that are running on the Remote Desktop Session Host, you can also use the *Query process* or *Qprocess* command.

Managing User Sessions

To manage user sessions in RDSM, simply right-click a user shown on the Users tab and then select any of the seven command options available on the shortcut menu. Alternatively, you can select a user and then click an action available on the Actions menu. Both of these options are shown in Figure 4-10.

FIGURE 4-10 The Remote Desktop Services Manager user-session commands.

The following list describes the seven management options available on the user session shortcut menu, along with their command-line tool equivalents.

- **Connect**   You can use the *Connect* command to reconnect to your own active or disconnected user session. In addition, if you have been granted the *Full Control* or *Connect* special access permission on the server's RDP-Tcp connection (configured in the Remote Desktop Session Host Configuration console), you can also use this command to connect to the active or disconnected session of another user.

As an alternative to using RDSM to connect to a Remote Desktop client session, you can use the *Tscon* command-line command.

- **Disconnect**   You can use the *Disconnect* command in the Actions pane or on the shortcut menu to disconnect a user from a session. When you disconnect a user from a session, all the programs and processes running in the session continue to run. Therefore, too many disconnected sessions can drain Remote Desktop Session Host server resources and slow server performance.

  As an alternative to using RDSM to disconnect a Remote Desktop client session, you can use the *Tsdiscon* command-line tool.

  Disconnecting another user from a session requires the *Full Control* or *Disconnect* special access permission on the server's RDP-Tcp connection.

- **Send Message**   The *Send Message* command enables you to send a simple console message to a user connected to a Remote Desktop Session Host. Use this command, for example, when you need to warn a user that he or she is about to be disconnected or logged off.

  To send a message to a user on a Remote Desktop Session Host, you can also use the *Msg* command-line tool.

  Sending a message to another user in Remote Desktop requires the *Full Control* or *Message* special access permission on the server's RDP-Tcp connection.

- **Remote Control**   The *Remote Control* command enables you to view or control another user's Remote Desktop client session. (You can configure the behavior of the Remote Control feature in the Remote Desktop Session Host Configuration console, on the Remote Control tab of a user account's properties, or in Group Policy.)

  You can also use the *Shadow* command-line tool to control an active session of another user on a Remote Desktop Session Host remotely.

  To control another user's session remotely, you must be assigned the *Full Control* or *Remote Control* special access permission on the server's RDP-Tcp connection.

- **Reset** Resetting a Remote Desktop session deletes that session immediately without saving any session data. Reset a session only when it appears to have stopped responding.

  You can also use the *Rwinsta* or *Reset session* command-line command to reset a user session on a Remote Desktop Session Host.

  Resetting another user's Remote Desktop session requires the *Full Control* access permission on the server's RDP-Tcp connection.

- **Status** When you right-click a user session shown on the Users tab and then select the *Status* command from the shortcut menu, the Status dialog box appears with additional status information about the session. This information includes the Remote Desktop client's IP address, computer name, and total bytes transmitted during the session. Figure 4-11 shows a status dialog box.

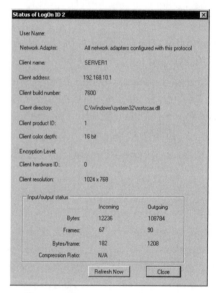

FIGURE 4-11 The Remote Desktop Services Manager Status dialog box.

To view the status of another user's session, you must be granted the *Full Control* or *Query Information* special access permission on the server's RDP-Tcp connection.

- **Log Off** Logging off a user ends all user processes and then deletes the session from the Remote Desktop Session Host. If you want to log off a user, send the user a message first. Otherwise, the user could lose unsaved session data.

  Besides using RDSM to log off a user, you can also use the *Logoff* command-line command.

  To log off another user from a session, you must have the *Full Control* permission on the server's RDP-Tcp connection.

Ending a Remote Desktop User Session Process

You can use the Processes tab in RDSM to force a particular process in a user session to close. This might be necessary, for example, if a certain application is hanging in a user session and is causing a screen freeze. To end a process for this or any other reason, simply right-click the process in question and then click End, as shown in Figure 4-12.

FIGURE 4-12 Ending a process in a Remote Desktop user session.

To end a process within a Remote Desktop user session, you can also use the *Tskill* command-line command.

✔ **Quick Check**
- On a Remote Desktop Session Host, what is a console session?

Quick Check Answer
- A console session is the session of the locally logged-on user.

Managing Resources in Client Sessions

Windows Server 2008 R2 introduces a new feature called Fair Share CPU Scheduling, which ensures that each user session connected to a Remote Desktop Session Host gets an equal share of processing time by default. For example, if five users are connected to a Remote Desktop Session Host, each user will be allocated 20 percent of the processor by default, regardless of the processes and applications each user might run.

In most circumstances, sharing the processor time equally is desirable. However, you might want to disable Fair Share CPU Scheduling and allow each user session to use as much processor time as needed. You can turn off Fair Share CPU Scheduling in Group Policy through the policy setting found at Computer Configuration\Policies\Administrative Templates\Windows Components\Remote Desktop Services\Remote Desktop Session Host\ Connections\Turn Off Fair Share CPU Scheduling.

If you want to override Fair Share CPU Scheduling and customize resource allocation, you can use the Windows System Resource Manager (WSRM) feature in Windows Server 2008 and Windows Server 2008 R2 to distribute processor time in a way that best suits your needs. To use WSRM, you must first install it by opening Server Manager, selecting the *Features* node, and then clicking Add Features. You can then use the Add Features Wizard to select the feature and proceed with the installation. After the tool is installed, you can access WSRM through Administrative Tools.

WSRM uses resource allocation policies to determine how computer resources are allocated to processes running on the computer. At any given time, only one resource allocation policy is considered the *managing policy*, or the policy in effect.

Five resource allocation policies are built into WSRM, and three are specifically designed for computers running Remote Desktop Services:

- **Equal_Per_User** When this policy is set as the managing policy, available CPU bandwidth is shared equally among users, not sessions. For example, if two users are running multiple applications that consume 100 percent of the allocated CPU bandwidth, WSRM will lower the priority of processes run by the user who exceeds 50 percent CPU usage. In this policy, the number of terminal services sessions owned by each user is not considered.

- **Equal_Per_Session** This resource allocation policy is equivalent to Fair Share CPU Scheduling. When you set this policy as the managing policy, each user session (and its associated processes) gets an equal share of the CPU resources on the computer.

- **Weighted_Remote_Sessions** New to Windows Server 2008 R2, this policy enables you to assign CPU priorities to user or group accounts. The three priority levels (in descending order of priority) are Premium, Standard, and Basic.

In addition to the built-in Resource Allocation Policies, you can also create custom policies. When you create custom Resource Allocation Policies, you define *Process Matching Criteria* that specify services, processes, or applications on the local server. Then, in the Resource Allocation Policy, you can allocate a certain amount of CPU or memory resources to those chosen services, processes, or applications.

In general, you can think of these built-in Resource Allocation Policies in WSRM as a way to override Fair Share CPU scheduling if you need to give priority to certain users or groups or if you need to allocate resources fairly among users who connect to the local Remote Desktop Session Host through multiple Remote Desktop sessions.

EXAM TIP

You must understand Fair Share CPU Scheduling and the predefined WSRM Resource Allocation Policies for the 70-643 exam. You also must understand the general role Process Matching criteria play in a custom Resource Allocation Policy.

PRACTICE **Manage Client Connections**

In this practice, you use Remote Desktop Services Manager to view, control, and end Remote Desktop user sessions.

EXERCISE 1 Viewing Remote Desktop Sessions

In this exercise, you use the Remote Desktop Services Manager console to view Remote Desktop sessions from within a console (local logon) session. This practice requires the use of three domain administrator accounts. In the following steps, these accounts are named ContosoAdmin1, ContosoAdmin2, and ContosoAdmin3, respectively.

1. Log on to Contoso.local from Server2 as ContosoAdmin1.

2. Open Remote Desktop Services Manager by clicking Start, pointing to Administrative Tools, pointing to Remote Desktop Services, and then clicking Remote Desktop Services Manager.

3. If a Remote Desktop Services Manager message box appears, read all the text and then click OK.

4. In the console tree, select the *Server2.contoso.local* node.

   The details pane within the middle portion of the console is named Manage Remote Desktop Session Host Server: Server2.contoso.local. This area contains three tabs: Users, Sessions, and Processes.

5. Verify that the Users tab in the center pane is selected and then answer the following questions.

   How many users are currently connected?

   Answer: One

   What is the session type associated with the listed user(s)?

   Answer: Console

   Is this session type associated with a local or remote user?

   Answer: Local

6. Right-click the user displayed on the Users tab and then answer the following questions.

   Which commands are available from the shortcut menu?

   Answer: *Disconnect*, *Send Message*, and *Log Off*

Which commands listed on the shortcut menu are not available?

Answer: *Connect*, *Remote Control*, *Reset*, and *Status*

Why are these commands unavailable?

Answer: *Connect* and *Remote Control* cannot be performed from within a console session. *Reset* and *Status* can only be performed on another user session.

7. Log on to Contoso.local from Server1 as ContosoAdmin2.

8. On Server1, open Remote Desktop Connection by clicking Start, typing **mstsc** in the Search Programs And Files box, and then pressing Enter.

9. In the Computer text box of Remote Desktop Connection, type **server2.contoso.local** and then click Connect.

10. In the Windows Security dialog box, enter the credentials of ContosoAdmin2 and then click OK.

11. On Server1, minimize the Remote Desktop window.

12. On Server1, open another instance of Remote Desktop Connection.

13. In the Computer text box in Remote Desktop Connection, type **server2.contoso.local** and then click Connect.

14. In the Windows Security dialog box, click Use Another Account.

15. Use the text boxes to enter the credentials of ContosoAdmin3 and then click OK.

16. Return to the Remote Desktop Services Manager console on Server2. Refresh the Users tab by clicking Refresh in the Actions pane.

17. Answer the following questions:

How many user sessions are now visible on the Users tab?

Answer: Three

What is the session type associated with the ContosoAdmin2 and ContosoAdmin3 sessions?

Answer: RDP-Tcp

Which two commands are available for the RDP-Tcp sessions that are not available for the console session?

Answer: *Reset* and *Status*

What is the difference between the *Reset* and *Log Off* commands?

Answer: Both commands disconnect and end a session. However, the *Reset* command deletes a session immediately without logging off the user.

18. Leave all windows open and proceed to Exercise 2.

EXERCISE 2   Managing Remote Desktop Sessions

In this exercise, you manage one Remote Desktop session from within another. This practice assumes that you have two active Remote Desktop sessions from Server1 to Server2.

1. Return to Server1.

2. In the ContosoAdmin2 Remote Desktop session, open Remote Desktop Services Manager. (You can use the Start menu to help you distinguish between the two Remote Desktop sessions.)

3. Answer the following question: Which is the only user session on the Users tab that is designated by a green arrow pointing upward?

   Answer: The ContosoAdmin2 user session

4. On Server1, switch to the ContosoAdmin3 Remote Desktop window. If the screen is locked, provide credentials so that you can see the remote desktop session on Server2 again.

5. Mark the ContosoAdmin3 desktop in some way so that you can recognize it as belonging to ContosoAdmin3. For example, you can save a Notepad file named ADMIN3 on the desktop.

6. Switch back to the ContosoAdmin2 Remote Desktop window. In Remote Desktop Services Manager, right-click the ContosoAdmin3 user session and then click Remote Control.

7. In the Remote Control dialog box, read the entire text and then click OK.

8. Switch to the ContosoAdmin3 Remote Desktop window.

   The Remote Control Request dialog box appears. The dialog box informs you that ContosoAdmin2 is requesting to control your session remotely and asks you whether you accept the request.

9. In the Remote Control Request box, click Yes.

10. Switch back to the ContosoAdmin2 remote desktop session.

    The ContosoAdmin3 desktop is now visible in the ContosoAdmin2 session.

11. From the remote control window, perform any action, such as opening Notepad.

    ContosoAdmin2 is now able to control the ContosoAdmin3 desktop.

12. Switch to Server2.

13. On the Users tab in Remote Desktop Services Manager, right-click the ContosoAdmin3 session and then click Log Off.

14. In the Remote Desktop Services Manager dialog box, click OK to confirm the choice.

    The ContosoAdmin3 session is ended. (To see the user session disappear from the list, you might need to click Refresh.)

15. On the Users tab in Remote Desktop Services Manager, right-click the ContosoAdmin2 session and then click Disconnect.

16. In the Remote Desktop Services Manager dialog box, click OK to confirm the choice.

    The ContosoAdmin2 session state changes from *Active* to *Disconnected*. (To see this change, you might need to click Refresh.)

17. Leave all windows open and proceed to Exercise 3.

EXERCISE 3 Reconnecting to a Disconnected Session

In this exercise, you reconnect to a disconnected session. You then attempt a second connection to the Remote Desktop Session Host with the same username and observe the effects.

1. In Remote Desktop Services Manager on Server2, click the Sessions tab.

   The Sessions tab shows that the ContosoAdmin2 session is disconnected.

2. Click the Processes tab.

   The Processes tab shows that many processes from the ContosoAdmin2 session are still running.

3. Right-click any of the processes listed.

   The shortcut menu that appears provides the option to end the process. You can perform the same function with the End Process option in the Actions pane on the right side of the Remote Desktop Services Manager console. You can also perform this function with the *Tskill* command-line command.

4. Without choosing to end the process you have selected, switch to Server1.

   A Remote Desktop Connection message box has appeared with an error symbol, informing you that the remote desktop session has ended.

5. Click OK to close the Remote Desktop Connection message box. When a desktop appears, close the second message box with an error symbol.

6. Use the Remote Desktop Connection client and the credentials for ContosoAdmin2 to establish a new connection to Server2 from Server1.

7. Switch to Server2.

8. In the Remote Desktop Services Manager console on Server2, click the Users tab.

   The ContosoAdmin2 session is listed as Active again.

9. Switch to Server1.

10. Minimize the current Remote Desktop window on Server1.

11. Open Remote Desktop Connection by using the *Mstsc* command.

12. Use the ContosoAdmin2 credentials to attempt to create a second Remote Desktop session to Server2.

13. Investigate all open windows on Server1 and Server2 and then answer the following question: Were you able to establish a second simultaneous Remote Desktop session to Server2?

    Answer: No. The second connection attempt merely took over the active user session, and the first connection was deleted.

14. Switch to Server2.

15. Open the Remote Desktop Session Host Configuration console by clicking Start, pointing to Administrative Tools, pointing to Remote Desktop Services, and then clicking Remote Desktop Session Host Configuration.

16. In the center pane of the Remote Desktop Session Host Configuration console, under Edit Settings—General, double-click the Restrict Each User To A Single Session option.

17. In the Properties dialog box, clear the Restrict Each User To A Single Session check box and then click OK.

18. If a Remote Desktop Session Host Configuration error message appears, read the message and then click OK.

19. Return to Server1 and once again attempt to establish a second Remote Desktop connection to Server2 by using the ContosoAdmin2 credentials.

    The second Remote Desktop connection is established. In the Remote Desktop Services Manager console on Server2, if you click Refresh, you can see that two sessions from ContosoAdmin2 are now listed as Active.

    When you enable simultaneous sessions to a Remote Desktop Session Host, you leave open the possibility of orphaned sessions.

20. On Server2, use Remote Desktop Session Manager to log off the first ContosoAdmin2 session and to reset the second.

21. On Server2, use the Remote Desktop Session Host Configuration console to re-enable the option to restrict each user to a single session.

22. On both Server1 and Server2, close all open windows and log off all users.

Lesson Summary

- You can configure Remote Desktop client settings at the client level by using Remote Desktop Connection options, or at the domain level by using a Group Policy object (GPO).

- When users connect to a Remote Desktop Session Host, their profiles are stored on the remote server by default. As a result, when many users access the Remote Desktop Session Host, profiles can consume a large amount of disk space. To remedy this, you can use disk quotas.

- You can manage a Remote Desktop user profile by configuring a Remote Desktop–specific roaming user profile that is stored on a central network share. This Remote Desktop Services profile can be defined on the Remote Desktop Services Profile tab of a user account's properties or in Group Policy.

- Remote Desktop Services Manager (RDSM) is the main administrative tool used to manage connections to a Remote Desktop Session Host. You can use RDSM to view information about users connected to a Remote Desktop Session Host, to monitor user sessions, or to perform administrative tasks such as logging off users or disconnecting user sessions.

- Windows Server 2008 R2 includes Fair Share CPU Scheduling, which automatically distributes processor time equally among active user sessions. If you want to adjust this default CPU resource allocation, you can either disable Fair Share CPU Scheduling or use Windows System Resource Manager (WSRM) to assign CPU time to Remote Desktop users in a way that best suits the needs of your organization.

Lesson Review

The following questions are intended to reinforce key information presented in this lesson. The questions are also available on the companion CD if you prefer to review them in electronic form.

> **NOTE   ANSWERS**
>
> Answers to these questions and explanations of why each answer choice is correct or incorrect are located in the "Answers" section at the end of the book.

1. RDS1 is a server running Windows Server 2008 R2 and Remote Desktop Services. Users in your organization connect to the RDS1 server to run a line-of-business application. Recently, you have noticed that user profiles are threatening to consume the total disk capacity on RDS1. You want users to be able to save their own data, but you also want to prevent profiles from exhausting the total storage capacity of the disk on RDS1. What should you do?

   A. Use Group Policy to assign mandatory profiles to users who connect to RDS1.

   B. Configure disk quotas for the disk on RDS1 on which user profiles are stored.

   C. Use Group Policy to assign Remote Desktop Services roaming user profiles to users who connect to RDS1.

   D. Configure disk quotas for the local disk of each user who connects to RDS1.

2. RDS3 is a server running Windows Server 2008 R2 and Remote Desktop Services. You have the responsibility of supporting users who connect to RDS3 to run various applications. Users complain that performance is slow inside Remote Desktop Sessions. You use the *quser* command on RDS3 and discover that many users have multiple disconnected sessions on the server with idle times of two days or more. You want to reduce the strain on RDS3 by eliminating disconnected sessions that have been idle for more than two days. What should you do?

   A. Use the *Rwinsta* command.

   B. Use the *Tsdicon* command.

   C. Use the *Tskill* command.

   D. Use the *Tscon* command.

3. Users in your organization connect to a server named App1 to run various financial and line-of-business applications through RemoteApp. Members of the Finance department claim that their RemoteApp applications run too slowly during high-usage periods before financial deadlines. You want to improve the performance of the RemoteApp applications that members of the Finance department use. You begin by installing Windows System Resource Manager on App1. Which of the following resource allocation policies will help you achieve your goal?

A. Equal_Per_Process

B. Equal_Per_User

C. Equal_Per_Session

D. Weighted_Remote_Sessions

Lesson 2: Deploying Remote Desktop Gateway

Remote Desktop Gateway (RD Gateway) enables authorized users to establish connections to Remote Desktop Session Hosts located behind a firewall. Connections to the RD Gateway are secured and encrypted through an HTTPS tunnel. By providing secure access from the Internet to a network's internal resources, RD Gateway provides an alternative to a virtual private network (VPN) for authorized users.

This lesson introduces you to RD Gateway and then describes how to install, configure, and use this feature.

After this lesson, you will be able to:

- Understand the function of RD Gateway.
- Install RD Gateway.
- Configure RD Gateway.
- Configure Remote Desktop Connection to use RD Gateway.

Estimated lesson time: 60 minutes

Overview of Remote Desktop Gateway

RD Gateway is an optional Remote Desktop Services role service that enables authorized Remote Desktop clients to establish Remote Desktop Protocol (RDP) sessions between the Internet and Remote Desktop resources found behind a firewall on a private network. ("Remote Desktop resources," in this case, refers to Remote Desktop Session Hosts, computers with Remote Desktop enabled, virtual desktops, and RemoteApp programs.) As they pass over the Internet, RDP connections to an RD Gateway server are secured and encrypted by the Secure Sockets Layer (SSL) protocol. A key feature of RD Gateway is that it enables RDP traffic to stream through corporate firewalls at TCP port 443, which is normally open for SSL traffic. (By default, RDP traffic communicates over TCP port 3389.)

In a basic RD Gateway deployment, shown in Figure 4-13, a user on a home computer (point 1) connects over the Internet to RD Gateway (point 2), which is located behind an external corporate firewall.

As an alternative to the basic scenario illustrated in Figure 4-13, you can use Microsoft Forefront Threat Management Gateway (TMG) instead of an RD Gateway server to serve as the SSL/HTTPS endpoint for the incoming Remote Desktop client connection. In this scenario, illustrated in Figure 4-14, Forefront TMG (point 2) serves as either an HTTPS-to-HTTPS or an HTTPS-to-HTTP bridge to the RD Gateway server (point 3), and the RD Gateway server then directs the RDP connection to the appropriate internal resource (point 4). This method provides the advantage of protecting Active Directory information within the corporate network.

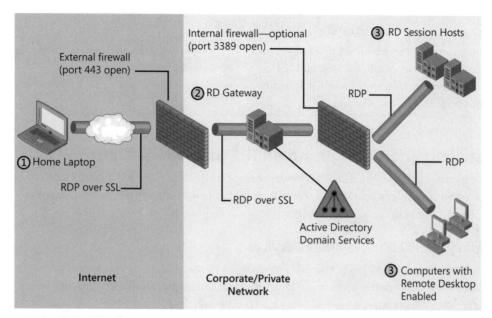

FIGURE 4-13 Basic RD Gateway scenario.

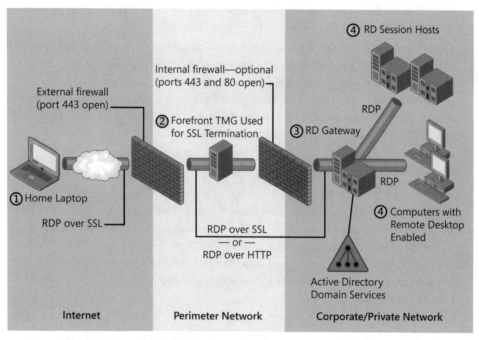

FIGURE 4-14 RD Gateway used with Forefront TMG for SSL termination.

EXAM TIP

When you use Forefront TMG as an HTTPS-to-HTTPS bridge to RD Gateway, remember to export the server certificate used for SSL from the RD Gateway server to the computer running Forefront TMG and to install that certificate on the latter server. Be sure to remember this point for the 70-643 exam.

Installing and Configuring an RD Gateway Server

You can install and configure an RD Gateway server first by adding the RD Gateway role service and then by configuring the clients to point to the RD Gateway server. These steps are described in detail in the following section.

Adding the RD Gateway Role Service

When you choose to add the RD Gateway role service by using Server Manager, the Add Role Services Wizard launches and then performs two main tasks. First, it automatically installs (if necessary) the prerequisite role services for RD Gateway: the IIS Web server and Network Policy Server (NPS). Second, it guides you through the process of configuring the three component features of RD Gateway that are required for the role service to function: a server certificate for SSL encryption, an *RD Connection Authorization Policy* (RD CAP), and an *RD Resource Authorization Policy* (RD RAP).

- **Server Certificate for SSL** Remote Desktop clients' connections to RD Gateway are encrypted by using SSL (also known as Transport Layer Security [TLS]), which requires a *server certificate*. This server certificate can originate from a trusted third-party *certificate authority* (CA) or from a trusted local CA (such as Certificate Services). As a less secure alternative suitable for testing environments, the Add Role Services Wizard can also generate a *self-signed server certificate* for use with RD Gateway.

> **IMPORTANT** **THE CLIENT MUST TRUST THE SERVER'S ROOT CERTIFICATE**
>
> Every Remote Desktop client that connects to the RD Gateway server must trust the CA that issued the RD Gateway server's certificate. If neither a trusted third-party CA nor a CA integrated in the client's own Active Directory domain has issued the certificate, you must export and install RD Gateway Server Root Certificate in the Trusted Root Certification Authorities store on the Remote Desktop client. You can view this store by using the Certificates snap-in. For a demonstration of this procedure, see the practice section at the end of this lesson.

Figure 4-15 shows the page in the Add Role Services Wizard on which you can specify or create a server certificate for SSL encryption.

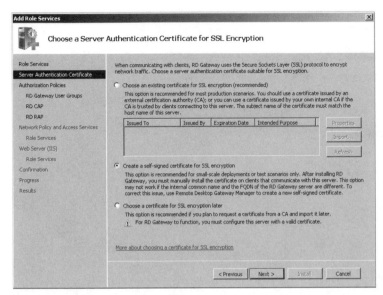

FIGURE 4-15 Choosing a server certificate for SSL encryption.

- **RD CAP** An *RD CAP* is essentially a policy that specifies which external users or computers can connect to the local RD Gateway. The Add Role Services Wizard only enables you to create the first and primary RD CAP, but you can create others later by using RD Gateway Manager, which is available in Administrative Tools program group of the Start menu, in the Remote Desktop Services folder, after you install the RD Gateway role service.

> **NOTE   CREATING AN RD CAP IN RD GATEWAY MANAGER**
>
> To open RD Gateway Manager, click Start, point to Administrative Tools, point to Remote Desktop Services, and then click RD Gateway Manager.
>
> To create a new RD CAP in RD Gateway Manager, right-click the Connection Authorization Policies folder in the console tree, select Create New Policy in the shortcut menu, and then point to Wizard or Custom, as desired. To modify the properties of an existing RD CAP, right-click an existing RD CAP in the Connection Authorization Policies pane and then click Properties.

On the Select User Groups That Can Connect Through RD Gateway page of the Add Role Services Wizard, the process of creating the first RD CAP is simplified, and enables you to specify users (typically, Active Directory security groups) that are permitted to connect. These same user groups are then made available to the main RD RAP created next by the wizard.

An RD CAP also enables you to choose an authentication method for remote users: Password, Smart Card, or both.

The Select User Groups page is shown in Figure 4-16.

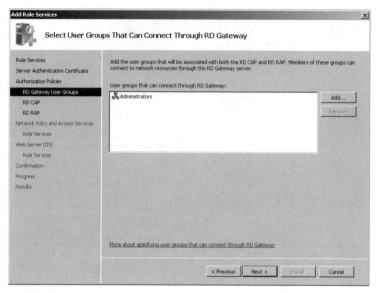

FIGURE 4-16 Defining groups for an RD CAP and RD RAP.

Certain additional configuration options for an RD CAP are available only in the RD Gateway Manager tool, after you have added the RD Gateway role. For example, you can use RD Gateway Manager to specify the external client computers (as opposed to users) for which you want to enable access to the RD Gateway. Another configuration choice for an RD CAP, available only in the RD Gateway Manager console, is the option to restrict device redirection. In other words, you can use an RD CAP to prevent certain client devices, such as a USB drive, from being redirected to the RD user session through RD Gateway. Finally, you can use the RD CAP properties dialog box in RD Gateway Manager to specify idle timeouts and session limit timeouts for all remote sessions connecting through the RD Gateway server.

The Properties sheet of an RD CAP, available in the RD Gateway Manager console, is shown in Figure 4-17.

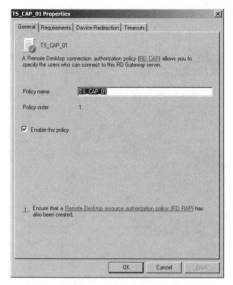

FIGURE 4-17 Modifying an RD CAP.

- **RD RAP** An *RD RAP* is an RD Gateway policy that specifies which users can connect to which Remote Desktop resources in an organization. The Add Role Services Wizard enables you to create the first and primary RD RAP, but you can create others later by using the RD Gateway Manager console.

> **NOTE RD GATEWAY MANAGER AND RD RAPs**
>
> To create a new RD RAP in RD Gateway Manager, right-click the Resource Authorization Policies folder in the console tree, select Create New Policy in the shortcut menu, and then click Wizard or Custom, as desired. To modify the properties of an existing RD RAP, simply right-click an existing RD RAP in the Resource Authorization Policies pane and then click Properties.

In the simplified policy created by the Add Role Services Wizard, you determine whether the user group you have selected on the Select User Groups That Can Connect Through RD Gateway page should be granted access to all terminal servers on the network or to only a subset, defined by an Active Directory security group.

The Create An RD RAP For RD Gateway page of the Add Role Services Wizard is shown in Figure 4-18.

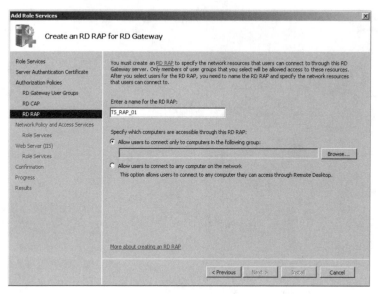

FIGURE 4-18 Creating an RD RAP in the Add Role Services Wizard.

As with an RD CAP, using the RD Gateway Manager console to create or modify an RD RAP presents additional configuration options. For example, when you use the RD Gateway Manager console to create an RD RAP, the computer group to which you enable access can be an Active Directory security group or a network resource group, as shown in Figure 4-19. Network resource groups might include a security group containing computer accounts in AD DS or a group created in RD Gateway (called an RD Gateway-managed group) that includes servers in an RDS farm. Another RD RAP configuration choice only available in the RD Gateway Manager console is the option to control the TCP ports through which a Remote Desktop client can connect to a resource. For example, you can restrict all RDP connections to TCP port 3389 (the standard port for RDP), or you can specify a nonstandard port or set of ports on which the computer group will listen for connections.

> **NOTE** **VIEWING CONNECTED SESSIONS**
>
> You can use the *Monitoring* node in RD Gateway Manager to view the user sessions currently connecting through the RD Gateway.

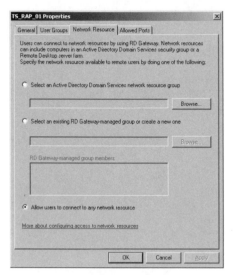

FIGURE 4-19 Specifying a network resource group for an RD RAP.

Configuring Remote Desktop Connection to Use RD Gateway

To use Remote Desktop Connection to initiate connections through RD Gateway, you must first configure RDC to use the gateway. To do this, first open RDC, click Options if necessary, and then select the Advanced tab. On the Advanced tab, click Settings in the Connect From Anywhere section, as shown in Figure 4-20.

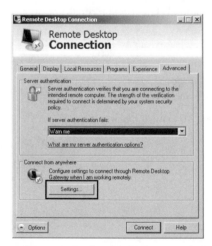

FIGURE 4-20 Configuring RDC to use RD Gateway, step 1.

This procedure opens the RD Gateway Server Settings dialog box, as shown in Figure 4-21.

FIGURE 4-21 Configuring RDC to use RD Gateway, step 2.

In the RD Gateway Server Settings dialog box, select Use These RD Gateway Server Settings. Specify the RD Gateway server in the Server Name box and an appropriate logon method (password or smart card) in the Logon Method box. To force RDC to use RD Gateway even for computers on your LAN, clear the option to bypass RD Gateway for local addresses.

In the Logon Settings area of the dialog box, you can specify whether the RD Gateway server should pass your credentials along to the remote computer. By default, this option is enabled and not configurable. However, if you need to enter a different username or password at the remote computer, select Use These RD Gateway Server Settings in the Connection Settings area and then clear the Use My RD Gateway Credentials For The Remote Computer option.

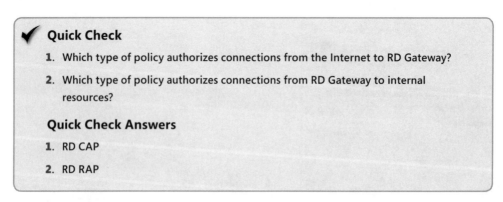

✔ **Quick Check**

1. Which type of policy authorizes connections from the Internet to RD Gateway?
2. Which type of policy authorizes connections from RD Gateway to internal resources?

Quick Check Answers

1. RD CAP
2. RD RAP

PRACTICE **Install and Configure RD Gateway**

In this series of exercises, you install RD Gateway on Server2 and then configure RDC on Server1 to connect to a Remote Desktop Session Host through the gateway. Before you can achieve this, you must install Server2's server certificate on Server1.

EXERCISE 1   Adding the RD Gateway Role Service

In this exercise, you install the RD Gateway role service on Server2.

1. Log on to Contoso.local from Server2 as a domain administrator.

2. Open Server Manager.

3. In the Server Manager console tree, expand the *Roles* node, right-click the *Remote Desktop Services* node, and then click Add Role Services.

   The Add Role Services wizard opens.

4. On the Select Role Services page of the Add Role Services Wizard, select the Remote Desktop Gateway check box.

   At this point, the Add Role Services dialog box might appear and ask whether you want to add the role services required for RD Gateway.

5. If the Add Role Services dialog box appears, click Add Required Role Services.

6. On the Select Role Services page of the Add Role Services Wizard, click Next.

7. On the Choose A Server Authentication Certificate For SSL Encryption page, read all the text on the page.

   At this point, in a production environment, you would designate a server authentication certificate obtained from a trusted CA. In this test environment, you specify a self-signed certificate.

8. Select Create A Self-Signed Certificate For SSL Encryption and then click Next.

9. On the Create Authorization Policies For RD Gateway page, read all the text on the page and then, leaving the default option to create authorization policies now, click Next.

10. On the Select User Groups That Can Communicate Through RD Gateway page, read all the text on the page and then click Next.

11. On the Create An RD CAP For RD Gateway page, read all the text on the page and then, leaving the Password box checked, click Next.

12. On the Create An RD RAP For RD Gateway page, read all the text on the page and then select the option to allow users to connect to any computer on the network.

13. Click Next.

14. On the Network Policy And Access Services page, read all the text on the page and then click Next.

15. On the Select Role Services page, read all the text on the page and then click Next.

16. On the Web Server (IIS) page, read all the text on the page and then click Next.

17. On the Select Role Services page, click Next.

18. On the Confirm Installation Selections page, review your installation selections and then click Install.

The Installation Progress page appears while the selected role services are installed. After installation, the Installation Results page appears.

19. On the Installation Results page, click Close.

EXERCISE 2   Creating a Certificates Console to Manage Certificates

In this exercise, you create consoles on Server1 and Server2 from which to manage certificates.

1. Log on to Contoso.local from Server1 as a domain administrator.

2. In the Search Programs And Files box of the Start menu, type **mmc** and then press Enter.

3. From the File menu, click Add/Remove Snap-In.

4. In the Add Or Remove Snap-Ins window, click Certificates from the list of available snap-ins and then click Add.

5. On the Certificates Snap-In page, select Computer Account and then click Next.

6. On the Select Computer page, click Finish.

7. In the Add Or Remove Snap-Ins window, click OK.

8. Use the File menu to save the menu with the name **Certificates MMC**. Save the console in the default location, the Administrative Tools folder.

9. Repeat steps 1 through 8 on Server2.

EXERCISE 3   Exporting a Server Certificate

In this exercise, you export a self-signed certificate to the Documents folder on Server2. You then copy the exported certificate to Server1.

1. Open the Certificates MMC console on Server2. If you have saved this console in the Administrative Tools folder, you can find it by clicking Start, All Programs, Administrative Tools, and then Certificates MMC.

2. In the Certificates MMC console tree on Server2, navigate to Certificates (Local Computer)\Personal\Certificates.

   When the Certificates folder is selected, the details pane displays a certificate named Server2.contoso.local. This certificate has been issued by the local computer. It is the self-signed certificate that you created in Exercise 1.

3. Right-click the Server2.contoso.local certificate, point to All Tasks on the shortcut menu, and then click Export.

   The Certificate Export Wizard appears.

4. On the Welcome page of the wizard, read all the text on the page and then click Next.

5. On the Export Private Key page, leave the default option not to export the private key and then click Next.

6. On the Export File Format page, leave the default selection and then click Next.

7. On the File To Export page, click Browse.

8. In the Save As dialog box, give the file the name **Server2Cert** and save the file in the Documents folder.

9. On the File To Export page, click Next.

10. On the Completing The Certificate Export Wizard page, review the name and location of the exported certificate and then click Finish.

11. The Certificate Export Wizard message box appears, informing you that the export was successful. Click OK.

12. Using any method you choose, copy the Server2Cert.cer file from Server2 to Server1 and then proceed to Exercise 4. For instance, you can connect to the Internet on both servers and send and retrieve the certificate through a web mail account, or you can share the Documents folder on Server2 and copy the file over the local network to Server1.

EXERCISE 4 Importing a Server Certificate

In this exercise, you import the certificate you exported from Server2 into the Trusted Root Certification Authorities store on Server1.

1. Open the Certificates MMC console on Server1. If you have saved this console in the Administrative Tools folder, you can find it by clicking Start, All Programs, Administrative Tools, and then Certificates MMC.

2. In the Certificates MMC console tree on Server1, navigate to Certificates (Local Computer)\Trusted Root Certification Authorities\Certificates.

3. Right-click the Certificates folder, point to All Tasks on the shortcut menu, and then click Import.

   The Certificate Import Wizard appears.

4. On the Welcome page of the wizard, read all the text on the page and then click Next.

5. On the File To Import page, click Browse.

   The Open window appears.

6. Using the navigation tree in the window, browse for and select the local copy of Server2Cert.cer file that you saved in Exercise 3 and then click Open.

7. On the File To Import page, click Next.

8. On the Certificate Store page, leave the default selection and then click Next.

9. On the Completing The Certificate Import Wizard page, click Finish.

10. The Certificate Import Wizard message box appears. Click OK.

EXERCISE 5 Connecting to RD Gateway through Remote Desktop Connection

In this exercise, you configure RDC to connect to the Remote Desktop Session Host on Server2 through the RD Gateway component on Server2. You then test the connection.

1. While you are logged on to Server1 as a domain administrator, open Remote Desktop Connection.

2. In the Remote Desktop Connection window, click Options to expand the window.

3. Click the Advanced tab.

4. In the Connect From Anywhere area, click Settings.

   The RD Gateway Server Settings dialog box appears.

5. In the Connection Settings area, select Use These RD Gateway Server Settings.

   (The option to detect RD Gateway server settings automatically queries Group Policy for the appropriate setting.)

6. In the Server Name text box, type **server2.contoso.local**.

7. In the Logon Method drop-down list box, select Ask For Password (NTLM).

8. Clear the Bypass RD Gateway Server For Local Addresses check box.

9. In the RD Gateway Server Settings dialog box, click OK.

10. In the Remote Desktop Connection window, click the General tab.

11. In the Computer text box, type or select **server2.contoso.local**.

12. In the User Name text box, enter the credentials of a domain administrator.

13. Click Connect.

    The Windows Security dialog box appears.

14. Read all the text in the Windows Security dialog box. The credentials you supply will be used for the RD Gateway server and for the Remote Desktop Session Host.

15. Type the credentials of a domain administrator and then click OK.

    A Terminal Services connection to Server2 is established through RD Gateway.

16. Log on to Contoso.local from Server2 with a different domain administrator account than the one you just used to connect through RDC on Server1.

17. On Server2, open Remote Desktop Gateway Manager by clicking Start, pointing to Administrative Tools, pointing to Remote Desktop Services, and then clicking Remote Desktop Gateway Manager.

    RD Gateway Manager opens.

18. In the RD Gateway Manager console tree, select SERVER2 (Local)\Monitoring.

    In the center (Monitoring) pane, you can see the connection from Server1 is listed, specified by the client IP address of 192.168.10.1. The connection has been successfully relayed by RD Gateway.

19. On Server1, from the Remote Desktop window, log off Server2.

20. On both Server1 and Server 2, close all open windows and log off.

Lesson Summary

- RD Gateway is a role service that enables authorized remote users to establish RDP connections to terminal servers located behind a corporate firewall.

- Remote Desktop client communications with RD Gateway are encrypted with SSL and use SSL port 443.

- Typically, the RD Gateway server is located in a perimeter network, and Remote Desktop clients communicate with it directly. However, you can also use Forefront TMG to forward client requests to RD Gateway.

- Three components are required for RD Gateway to function: a server certificate for SSL, an RD CAP (which authorizes connections to the gateway), and an RD RAP (which authorizes connections to internal resources).

- The main tool used to manage RD Gateway is RD Gateway Manager.

Lesson Review

The following questions are intended to reinforce key information presented in this lesson. The questions are also available on the companion CD if you prefer to review them in electronic form.

> **NOTE ANSWERS**
>
> Answers to these questions and explanations of why each answer choice is correct or incorrect are located in the "Answers" section at the end of the book.

1. Which TCP port must you leave open in your company's firewall if you want clients to be able to initiate RDP connections to terminal servers through Remote Desktop Gateway?

   A. 25

   B. 3389

   C. 443

   D. 80

2. Your network includes a Remote Desktop (RD) Gateway server named RDG1. RDG1 has installed a self-signed server certificate that it uses for SSL communications. You want to use a computer running Forefront Threat Management Gateway (TMG) as an SSL endpoint for RD Gateway connections. Which of the following steps must you take to ensure that Forefront TMG can communicate with RD Gateway?

   A. Enable HTTPS–HTTP bridging between Forefront TMG and RD Gateway.

   B. Open TCP port 443 on the computer running Forefront TMG.

   C. Export the SSL certificate of the Forefront TMG server to the RD Gateway server.

   D. Export the SSL certificate of the RD Gateway server to the Forefront TMG server.

3. Employees in your organization use Remote Desktop to connect to a line-of-business application running on a server named App1. Some of these users connect to App1 from home through a Remote Desktop Gateway named RDG1. No other internal resources have been made available through RDG1.

   You have noticed that many users who connect to App1 from home tend to leave the Remote Desktop sessions open after they have finished working. You want to automatically disconnect users connecting to App1 from outside the network after five hours. What should you do?

   A. On RDG1, configure a session timeout value of 300.

   B. On RDG1, configure an idle timeout value of 300.

   C. On App1, configure a session timeout value of 300.

   D. On App1, configure an idle timeout value of 300.

Lesson 3: Deploying RemoteApp Programs and Virtual Desktops

Previously, you saw how Remote Desktop Services enables users to connect remotely to the desktop of a Remote Desktop Session Host. However, Remote Desktop Services can also enable users to connect remotely to individual applications or to virtual machines. For remote connections to applications, you can use the Remote Desktop Session Host role service alone, but this functionality is best used with the Remote Desktop Web Access role service. For remote connections to virtual machines, you use the Remote Desktop Virtualization Host role service with the Hyper-V server role.

After this lesson, you will be able to:

- Understand the RemoteApp feature of Remote Desktop Services and the scenarios in which it can be used.
- Install an application on a Remote Desktop Session Host so that the application can support multiple users.
- Make an application installed on a Remote Desktop Session Host available to remote users through a web browser.
- Create an RDP file that launches an application installed on a Remote Desktop Session Host.
- Create a Windows Installer package that creates shortcuts to a RemoteApp application in the user's Start menu and desktop.
- Configure a virtual desktop infrastructure to deploy virtual desktops by using Remote Desktop Virtualization Host and other network components.
- Use RemoteApp and Desktop Connections to subscribe to a feed of RemoteApp programs and virtual desktops.

Estimated lesson time: 90 minutes

Overview of RemoteApp

RemoteApp enables programs to run through Remote Desktop Services and appear as if they were running on a user's local computer. Before Windows Server 2008, Remote Desktop users who needed to run an application on a remote terminal server first needed to establish a desktop session on the server and then launch the application within that desktop session. With RemoteApp, the application alone is streamed through RDP to a resizable window on the user's local desktop.

You can deploy a RemoteApp program to users in any of the following ways:

- You can make RemoteApp programs available on a website by distributing the RemoteApp programs through the *RD Web Access* page. This page is located at *http://servername/rdweb* or *https://servername/rdweb* (if the web server can accept SSL connections). In this scenario, you configure the Remote Desktop Web Access page to display icons of available RemoteApp programs. Clicking any of these icons launches the RemoteApp program on the user's computer.

- You can distribute RemoteApp programs as RDP files or Windows Installer packages through a file share or through another distribution mechanism, such as Microsoft System Center Configuration Manager or Active Directory software distribution. After obtaining the RDP file or installing it through a Windows Installer package, a user launches the program by double-clicking that RDP file, by accessing the program from the Start menu, or by opening a file whose extension is associated with the RemoteApp program.

- RemoteApp and Desktop Connections is a Control Panel feature new to Windows 7 and Windows Server 2008 R2. Through *RemoteApp and Desktop Connections*, clients can subscribe to a feed of all the RemoteApp programs on a Remote Desktop Session Host or virtual desktops on a Remote Desktop Virtualization Host. By default, the URL of the feed is *https://servername/rdweb/feed/webfeed.aspx*. After using RemoteApp and Desktop Connections to connect to an RDS server feed, RemoteApp programs and virtual desktop become available to the client through the Start menu.

After launching the RemoteApp program by using one of these methods, a user is able to run the program as if it were installed locally. As with any Remote Desktop session, the Remote Desktop Session Host provides virtually all the resources needed to run the RemoteApp program.

> **NOTE REMOTEAPP AND USER SESSIONS**
>
> When a user runs two RemoteApp programs hosted on the same Remote Desktop Session Host, the programs belong to the same Remote Desktop user session.

RemoteApp enables you to take advantage of the resources of a central server and to reduce management complexity in the following situations:

- Users need to access programs hosted on your network from remote locations. In this case, you can deploy RemoteApp together with RD Gateway so that the remote users can access the programs from the Internet.

- Your network includes old computers that lack the hardware or software resources needed to run a required application.

- Your company has a branch office that lacks the IT personnel needed to support a given application on site.

- Your network includes user desktops with operating system or software conflicts that prevent the installation of a required application.

- You need to support users who do not have assigned computers but who do need to use a particular application consistently.

- You want to reduce costs associated with an application by installing it on only one computer.

Configuring a Server to Host RemoteApp Programs

To prepare a server to host RemoteApp programs, you first must install the Remote Desktop Session Host role service on that server.

The next step in configuring a server to host RemoteApp programs is to install the desired applications in a way that makes them available to multiple users. You can achieve this only by installing the program while the Remote Desktop Session Host is in *Install mode*. When the Remote Desktop Session Host is in Install mode, installing an application creates only master copies of the Registry entries or .ini files that store user-specific application data. Only when users later launch the application are these master entries copied into the users' profiles to store personal settings.

To install an application in Install mode, you have three options:

- You can use a Windows Installer package (MSI) file to install the program. When you install a program by using a Windows Installer package, the program installs in Remote Desktop Services Install mode.
- You can use Install Application On Remote Desktop Server in Control Panel to install the program. This option is shown in Figure 4-22.

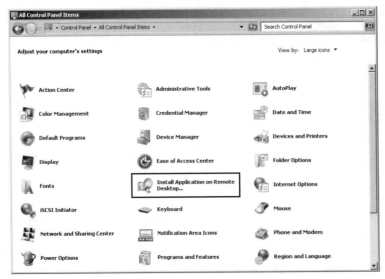

FIGURE 4-22 Use the Control Panel option to install a program for multiple Remote Desktop users.

- Before you install a program, you can run the *Change user/install* command from the command line. After the program is installed, run the *Change user/execute* command to exit Install mode.

EXAM TIP

For the 70-643 exam, know the significance of Remote Desktop Services Install mode and all the ways you can install an application in this mode.

Adding Programs for Publication in RemoteApp Manager

After you install the required applications in Install mode, you must add these programs to the RemoteApp Programs list in RemoteApp Manager.

To perform this step, open RemoteApp Manager and then click Add RemoteApp Program in the Actions pane. After you select the program in a simple wizard, the application appears in the RemoteApp Programs list, as shown in Figure 4-23. (You can open RemoteApp Manager by clicking Start, Administrative Tools, Remote Desktop Services, and then RemoteApp Manager.)

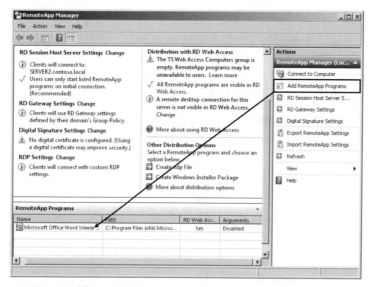

FIGURE 4-23 Adding a RemoteApp program.

After programs are added to this list, they automatically appear in RD Web Access to all users by default if the Remote Desktop Web Access role service is installed on the local server. However, in a feature called per-user filtering that is new to Windows Server 2008 R2, you can now configure the permissions of each RemoteApp icon individually so that only certain users will be able to see it. To restrict the read permissions of a RemoteApp program icon, open the properties of the RemoteApp program in RemoteApp Manager and click the User Assignment tab, shown in Figure 4-24. Click Specified Domain Users And Domain Groups and then click Add to select the domain users and groups to which you want to make the RemoteApp program available. No other accounts will then see the RemoteApp program icon if Remote Desktop Web Access is later installed.

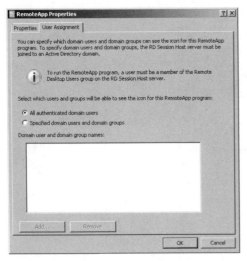

FIGURE 4-24 Per-user filtering of RemoteApp programs in RD Web Access.

In general, you can use RemoteApp Manager to make RemoteApp programs available to users in any of three ways: by publishing the RemoteApp program in RD Web Access, by distributing RDP files of RemoteApp programs, or by distributing or publishing Windows Installer packages of RemoteApp programs.

All three of these publishing options are described in more detail in the following sections.

Deploying a RemoteApp Program through Remote Desktop Web Access

To make the Remote Desktop Web Access feature available, you must install the Remote Desktop Web Access role service. If you install Remote Desktop Web Access on the same server as the Remote Desktop Session Host hosting the RemoteApp programs, all the programs listed in the RemoteApp Programs list in RemoteApp Manager appear on the RD Web Access page by default.

To access the RD Web Access page, users open Internet Explorer and browse to *https://servername/rdweb*. RD Web Access in Windows Server 2008 R2 now uses forms-based authentication (FBA), which means that to connect to the RD Web Access page, a logon page first appears requiring users to enter valid credentials, as shown in Figure 4-25.

FIGURE 4-25 Forms-based authentication for RD Web Access in Windows Server 2008 R2.

NOTE **CONFIGURING SINGLE SIGN-ON (SSO)**

SSO is a new feature in Windows Server 2008 R2 that enables users to sign on once to all RemoteApp programs when connecting through RD Web Access. SSO requires configuration on the server side and client side. On the server side, the RemoteApp programs must be signed with the same SSL or code signing certificate. On the client side, SSO requires Remote Desktop Connection 7.0 or later, and each client must be configured to trust the publisher of the certificate used to sign the RemoteApp programs. For more information about how to configure SSO, visit *http://blogs.msdn.com/b/rds/* and search for "Introducing Web Single Sign-On for RemoteApp and Desktop Connections."

After the user provides credentials and signs in, the RD Web Access page appears, as shown in Figure 4-26.

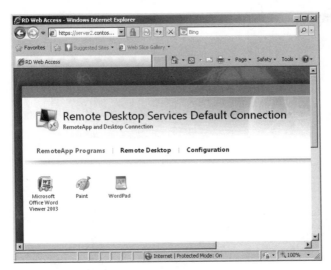

FIGURE 4-26 The RD Web Access page.

On the RD Web Access page, users can launch any of the RemoteApp programs by clicking the appropriate icon. In a two-server scenario, RD Web Access and the RD Session Host run on separate servers. In this case, you need to take two additional steps to ensure that the RD Web Access page displays RemoteApp programs hosted on the Remote Desktop Session Host.

1. After clicking the Configuration link on the menu of the RD Web Access page, type the name of an RD Connection Broker server or of one or more RemoteApp sources, as shown in Figure 4-27. (To see the Configuration link, you must connect to the RD Web Access server with the credentials of a user account that is a member of the TS Web Access Administrators local group on the RD Web Access server.)

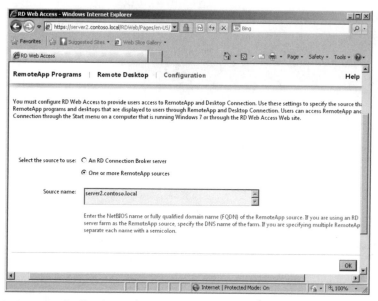

FIGURE 4-27 Configuring RemoteApp sources for RD Web Access.

2. Note that to allow the RD Web Access server to access RemoteApp information from another server, you must add the computer account of the RD Web Access server to the TS Web Access Computers security group on the other server.

Creating an RDP File of a RemoteApp Program for Distribution

You can create an RDP file of any program listed in the RemoteApp Programs list in RemoteApp Manager. To do so, simply select the program from the list and then click Create .RDP File under Other Distribution Options, as shown in Figure 4-28.

This procedure launches the RemoteApp Wizard. Before creating an RDP file that points to a remote program, the RemoteApp Wizard enables you to configure certain settings for that RDP file on the Specify Package Settings page. For example, you can specify the name and TCP port for the connection to the RD Session Host. (The standard port is 3389.) The wizard also enables you to require user connections to proceed through a specified RD Gateway server before launching the RemoteApp program. Finally, the wizard enables you to sign the RDP file digitally with a certificate. This signature assures clients that the RDP files have been issued by a trusted publisher.

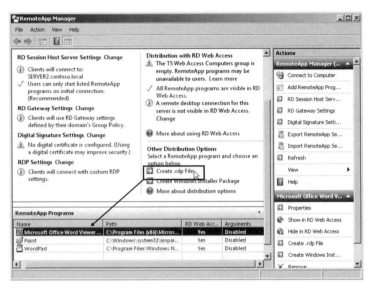

FIGURE 4-28 Creating an RDP file that points to a RemoteApp program.

The Specify Package Settings page is shown in Figure 4-29.

FIGURE 4-29 Specifying settings for an RDP file.

After you create the RDP file by using the RemoteApp Wizard, you can distribute the file to client computers by using your existing software distribution process, such as Microsoft System Center Configuration Manager or Group Policy. Alternatively, you can distribute the file through email or a network share.

Creating a Windows Installer Package of a RemoteApp Program for Distribution

As an alternative to creating RDP files for distribution, you can create and distribute MSI files instead. To perform this task, select the desired RemoteApp program in the RemoteApp program list in RemoteApp Manager and then click Create Windows Installer Package under Other Distribution Options, as shown in Figure 4-30.

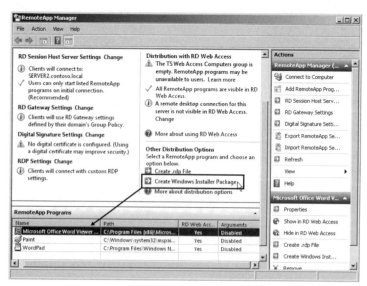

FIGURE 4-30 Creating a Windows Installer for a RemoteApp program.

This step opens the RemoteApp Wizard. As with RDP files, the RemoteApp Wizard includes a Specify Package Settings page on which you can specify an RD Session Host, an RD Gateway setting, and a digital certificate whenever you create a Windows Installer package.

However, when you create a Windows Installer package, the RemoteApp Wizard also displays a Configure Distribution Package page with a second set of options. First, you can use this page to specify the location of the shortcuts to the RemoteApp program that will be installed. The optional locations are the user's desktop and a Start menu folder with a name of your choice. Second, you can also use the Configure Distribution Package page to configure the RemoteApp program to open every time a file with the associated file extension is opened. (Use this option only when clients do not have locally installed versions of the program.)

The Configure Distribution Package page of the RemoteApp Wizard is shown in Figure 4-31.

FIGURE 4-31 Configuring installation options for a Windows Installer package.

As with RDP files, you can distribute Windows Installer packages to clients by using System Center Configuration Manager or Group Policy. Alternatively, you can distribute the files through email or a network share.

> **NOTE RD WEB ACCESS AND EASE OF MANAGEMENT**
>
> One advantage of publishing applications through RD Web Access is that the changes you make to the properties of RemoteApp programs are immediately registered by clients. In contrast, if you have made a RemoteApp program available through RDP or MSI files and want to change its properties so that (for example) clients would now be required to connect to it through RD Gateway, you would need to re-create those files and then redistribute them to users.

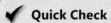
Using RemoteApp and Desktop Connections

Windows 7 and Windows Server 2008 R2 include a new Control Panel item called RemoteApp And Desktop Connections, as shown in Figure 4-32. RemoteApp And Desktop Connections enables you to subscribe to one or more RD Web Access feeds that display available RemoteApp programs and virtual desktops. After you subscribe to a feed, these programs and desktops are made available to you through the Start menu or through this Control Panel program. The list of programs and virtual desktops is updated automatically once a day as the availability of these resources changes.

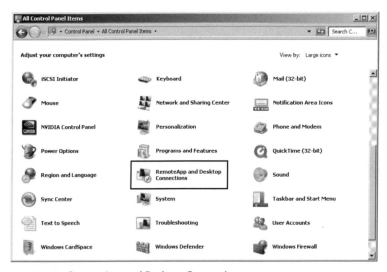

FIGURE 4-32 RemoteApp and Desktop Connections.

To subscribe to an RD Web Access feed on an individual machine, first open RemoteApp And Desktop Connections by typing **RemoteApp and Desktop Connections** in the Search Programs And Files box of the Start menu. Click the option to set up a new connection with RemoteApp And Desktop Connections, which is shown in Figure 4-33.

FIGURE 4-33 Subscribing to a feed from an RD Web Access server.

This step opens the first page of a wizard in which you can enter the address of the Web feed of an available RD Web Access server. For any RD Web Access server with the *servername* name, by default the address of the RD Web Access feed is *https://servername/rdweb/feed/ webfeed.aspx*, as shown in Figure 4-34.

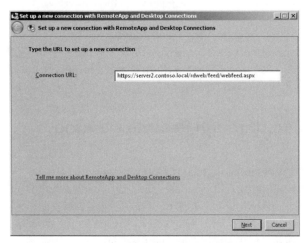

FIGURE 4-34 Specifying the URL of the RD Web Access feed.

After you complete the wizard, RemoteApp programs and virtual desktops from that RD Web Access source appear in the Start menu, as shown in Figure 4-35.

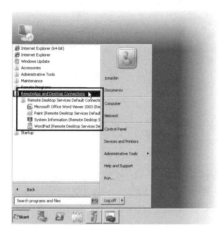

FIGURE 4-35 RemoteApp and Desktops automatically installs remote resources in the Start menu.

You can use a script and Group Policy to configure many clients to subscribe to an RD Web Access feed. To find such a script, visit *http://gallery.technet.microsoft.com/ ScriptCenter/313a95b3-a698-4bb0-9ed6-d89a47eacc72/* or perform a search for "Configure RemoteApp and Desktop Connection on Windows 7 Clients."

Deploying Virtual Machines through Remote Desktop Services

Remote Desktop Virtualization Host (RD Virtualization Host) is a Remote Desktop Services role service that is new to Windows Server 2008 R2. RD Virtualization Host enables you to provide users with *virtual desktops*, or virtual machines (VMs), through Remote Desktop connections. You can configure virtual desktops in two ways. First, you can assign a user a unique virtual machine (called a *personal virtual desktop*). Alternatively, you can direct users to a pool of virtual machines (called a *virtual desktop pool*) that are shared by many users.

Virtual Desktop Infrastructure Components

The RD Virtualization Host role service does not work alone. To make virtual machines available through Remote Desktop Services, you must create and configure an entire virtual desktop infrastructure (VDI). The Microsoft VDI solution includes the following components:

■ An RD Virtualization Host server with Hyper-V installed

This component is the only VDI component that must be a physical server. An RD Virtualization Host monitors and interacts with the VM guest sessions running in Hyper-V on the local machine. The RD Virtualization Host also prepares VMs for an imminent remote desktop connection (for example, by starting the VM). For the RD Virtualization Host to perform these functions, the guest operating systems must be configured to give appropriate permissions to the RD Virtualization Host.

Note that a VDI implementation can include multiple RD Virtualization Host servers. The VMs available in VDI are therefore not limited to the capacity of a single RD Virtualization Host. To be integrated into a single VDI implementation, each RD Virtualization Host must be registered with the RD Connection Broker.

> **NOTE** **DYNAMIC MEMORY AND VDI**
>
> Service Pack 1 of Windows Server 2008 R2 introduces dynamic memory to Hyper-V. This feature significantly improves the scalability of Microsoft VDI.

- An RD Session Host server (running in redirection mode)

  This component acts as a dedicated redirector for virtual desktops. It receives original RDP connection requests from remote clients and, upon receiving an IP address from the RD Connection Broker, directs the requests to a destination VM. (It is recommended that you install this role service on the same server as the RD Connection Broker server.)

- An RD Connection Broker server

  This component registers all the components of VDI and performs a number of important functions. For example, it identifies an appropriate target VM for a user by connecting a user to a personal virtual desktop, by reconnecting a user to an open session in a virtual desktop pool, or by connecting a user to a new desktop session in a virtual desktop pool. It also determines the IP address of the target VM by communicating with the RD Virtualization Host. This IP address is then returned to the Remote Desktop Session Host server running in redirection mode. The RD Connection Broker in VDI also prepares the target VM for remote connections by turning on the VM if necessary.

- An RD Web Access server

  This component enables users to discover and initiate connections to virtual machines.

- One or more remote clients that will connect to the virtual machines

- One or more virtual machines running Windows client operating systems as guests on the RD Virtualization Host server(s)

- An available AD DS domain controller

Aside from these necessary components, note the following requirements for implementing VDI:

- All servers, virtual machines, and user accounts must be members of a single AD DS domain.

- Microsoft VDI supports only Windows client operating systems, specifically Windows XP SP3, Windows Vista SP1, and Windows 7. You cannot assign a virtual machine running Windows Server 2008 R2 as a virtual desktop in VDI.

- For personal virtual desktops, the name of the virtual machine in the Hyper-V Manager tool must match the fully qualified domain name (FQDN) of the computer.
- The virtual machines in a virtual desktop pool must be identically configured, including the programs installed.

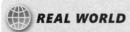 **REAL WORLD**

J.C. Mackin

Although RD Virtualization Host and RD Connection Broker are tested on the 70-643 exam, it is important to understand that they are suitable primarily for small-scale VDI solutions intended for prototyping and testing. Real-world VDI solutions typically include a third-party connection broker, such as one from Citrix XenDesktop, and draw upon Microsoft System Center products, including System Center Virtual Machine Manager, to make them more scalable and manageable.

Connecting to Virtual Desktops

When properly configured, the components in a VDI implementation work together to provide connections to personal virtual desktops or virtual desktop pools through the following procedure:

1. A user initiates the connection to the personal virtual desktop by using RD Web Access or by using RemoteApp and Desktop Connection.
2. The request is sent to the RD Session Host server running in redirection mode.
3. The RD Session Host server running in redirection mode forwards the request to the RD Connection Broker server.
4. For a connection to a personal virtual desktop, the RD Connection Broker server then queries Active Directory Domain Services and retrieves the name of the virtual machine assigned to the requesting user account.

   For a connection to a virtual desktop pool, the RD Connection Broker checks to see whether an existing session exists for the requesting user account. If no such session already exists, the procedure continues in step 5. Otherwise, the next step is skipped, and the procedure continues in step 6.
5. The RD Connection Broker server sends a request to the RD Virtualization Host server to locate and start the virtual machine.
6. The RD Virtualization Host server returns the address of the virtual machine to the RD Connection Broker server. The RD Connection Broker server then sends this information to the RD Session Host server running in redirection mode.

7. The RD Session Host server running in redirection mode redirects the request to the client computer that initiated the connection.

8. The client computer connects to the personal virtual desktop or virtual desktop pool.

This eight-step procedure is illustrated in Figure 4-36. (In the figure, step 4 is performed only if the user is connecting to a personal virtual desktop.)

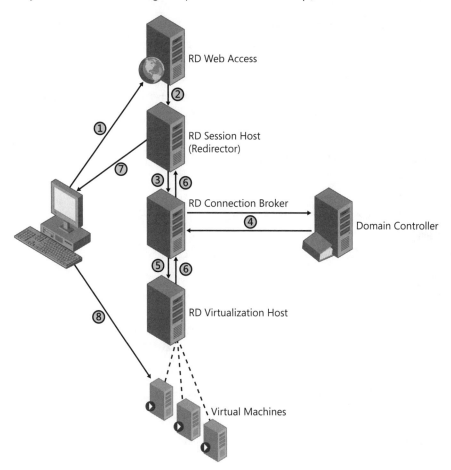

FIGURE 4-36 Connecting to a virtual machine in a VDI.

Configuring a Virtual Desktop Infrastructure

To configure a VDI implementation on your network, perform the following steps:

- Install the RD Virtualization Host on a physical server running Windows Server 2008 R2.

- Install and configure RD Web Access on a server running Windows Server 2008 R2.

- Install an RD Session Host to act as a redirector for VDI.

- Install and configure the RD Connection Broker.

- Assign personal virtual desktops as needed.

- Create virtual desktop pools as needed.

- Configure the virtual machines on the RD Virtualization Host so that they can work in the virtual desktop infrastructure.

INSTALLING THE RD VIRTUALIZATION HOST

The RD Virtualization Host server is a role service of Remote Desktop Services. This component is the physical server hosting virtual machines that are eventual destinations of client requests. To install this component, use the Add Roles Wizard to add the Remote Desktop Services role, but select only the Remote Desktop Virtualization Host role service, as shown in Figure 4-37. When you install the RD Virtualization Host role service, the Hyper-V role is also installed automatically if it is not already installed.

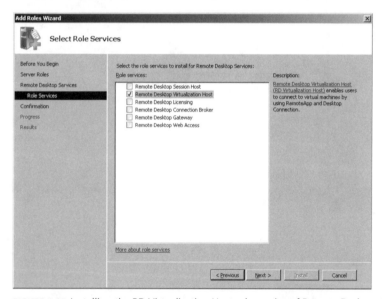

FIGURE 4-37 Installing the RD Virtualization Host role service of Remote Desktop Services.

After you install the RD Virtualization Host, perform the following configuration steps in Hyper-V on the RD Virtualization Host server:

- Rename each VM that will act as a personal virtual desktop to match its full computer name (FQDN) within the operating system.

- Take a snapshot of each VM that will act as a member of a virtual desktop pool and rename each snapshot **RDV_Rollback**. Virtual machines will roll back to this snapshot after user sessions have ended. (Perform this step only after you have configured the VMs for virtual desktops, as described in the "Configuring the Guest Operating Systems for a VDI" section later in this lesson.)

EXAM TIP

Be sure you understand the significance of the RDV_Rollback snapshot for the 70-643 exam.

CONFIGURING THE RD WEB ACCESS SERVER FOR THE PERSONAL VIRTUAL DESKTOP

Configuring the RD Web Access server requires two steps. First, you should add administrators to the TS Web Access Administrators local group. Members of this group can manage the RD Web Access website. (By default, local administrators already have this right.)

Next, you have to configure the RD Web Access website so that it specifies the RD Connection Broker server as a source. Specify this source for personal and pooled VMs because the RD Connection Broker is the only source that is aware of personal and pooled VM assignments. To perform this procedure, follow these steps:

1. Log on to the RD Web Access server as a domain administrator.

2. Open the Remote Desktop Web Access page by clicking Start, pointing to Administrative Tools, pointing to Remote Desktop Services, and then clicking Remote Desktop Web Access Configuration.

3. Click Continue To This Website (Not Recommended).

> ***IMPORTANT*** **SELF-SIGNED CERTIFICATES IN A PRODUCTION ENVIRONMENT**
>
> These instructions use a self-signed certificate for the RD Web Access server. Self-signed certificates are not recommended in a production environment. You should use a certificate that is trusted from a certification provider when deploying RD Web Access in a production environment.

4. In the Domain\User Name box, type domain administrator credentials.

5. In the Password box, type the appropriate password and then click Sign In.

6. On the Configuration page, click An RD Connection Broker Server.

7. In the Source name box, type the name of the RD Connection Broker server and then click OK.

CONFIGURING THE RD CONNECTION BROKER AND RD SESSION HOST REDIRECTOR

For these instructions, it is assumed that you have installed the Remote Desktop Connection Broker and Remote Desktop Session Host role services on the same server. These two components can therefore be configured together. (This is the recommended configuration.)

To configure the RD Connection Broker/RD Session Host redirector server, you must perform a number of procedures.

- Add the RD Web Access server to the TS Web Access Computers local group.

This procedure enables the RD Web Access server to determine which virtual desktops are available to users. To add the RD Web Access server to the TS Web Access Computers local group, type **Edit Local Users And Groups** in the Search Programs And Files box of the Start menu and then press Enter. Use the Local Users And Groups console to locate and open the TS Web Access Computers group and then click Add to add the computer name of the RD Web Access server. To specify a computer name, you first must click Object Types and then select Computers so that computer names are the objects of the search in the AD DS database.

- Run the Configure Virtual Desktops Wizard. This wizard enables you to define a VDI by specifying an RD Virtualization Host, an RD Session Host redirector, and an RD Web Access server. Before you run the wizard, make sure that all the appropriate role services are installed on the various servers.

- Run the Assign Personal Virtual Desktop Wizard (if you are configuring personal virtual desktops).

- Run the Create Virtual Desktop Pool Wizard (if you are configuring virtual desktop pools).

The instructions to complete these three wizards follow. The first wizard to complete is the Configure Virtual Desktops Wizard. To run the Configure Virtual Desktops Wizard, perform the following steps:

1. On the RD Connection Broker server, open Remote Desktop Connection Manager by clicking Start, pointing to Administrative Tools, pointing to Remote Desktop Services, and then clicking Remote Desktop Connection Manager.

   Remote Desktop Connection Manager is shown in Figure 4-38.

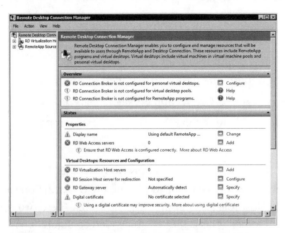

FIGURE 4-38 You use Remote Desktop Connection Manager to configure a VDI.

2. In the left pane, click RD Virtualization Host Servers and then, on the Action menu, click Configure Virtual Desktops, as shown in Figure 4-39.

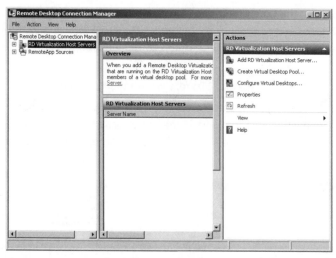

FIGURE 4-39 Starting the Configure Virtual Desktops Wizard.

3. On the Before You Begin page, review the information and then click Next.

4. On the Specify An RD Virtualization Host Server page, add or remove RD Virtualization Host servers and then click Next.

5. On the Configure Redirection Settings page, type the name of the RD Session Host server that will perform redirection. It is recommended that you specify the local server for this function. This step automatically configures the specified RD Session Host to perform redirection.

6. Click Next.

7. On the Specify An RD Web Access Server page, if an RD Web Access server has already been specified, type the name of the RD Web Access server you want to display RemoteApp and Desktop Connection from the RD Connection Broker server to users and then click Next.

8. On the Confirm Changes page, review your selections and then click Apply.

9. On the Summary Information page, review the information.

10. If you do not want to assign personal virtual desktops to users, clear the Assign Personal Virtual Desktop check box and click Finish. Otherwise, leave the option enabled and click Finish to start the Assign Personal Virtual Desktop Wizard.

> *NOTE* **ADJUSTING REDIRECTION SETTINGS**
>
> After you complete the Configure Virtual Desktops Wizard, you can adjust the Redirection Settings at any time by right-clicking the *RD Virtualization Host Servers* node in Remote Desktop Connection Manager and then clicking Properties.

When you have completed the Configure Virtual Desktops Wizard, you are ready to assign any personal virtual desktops to users if that is part of your VDI design. You do this through the Assign Personal Virtual Desktop Wizard, which opens by default after the Configure Virtual Desktops Wizard.

To run the Assign Personal Virtual Desktop Wizard, perform the following steps:

1. If you need to open the Assign Personal Virtual Desktop Wizard manually, open Remote Desktop Connection Manager and, in the center pane beneath Virtual Desktop Resource: Personal Virtual Desktop, click Assign. This option is shown in Figure 40.

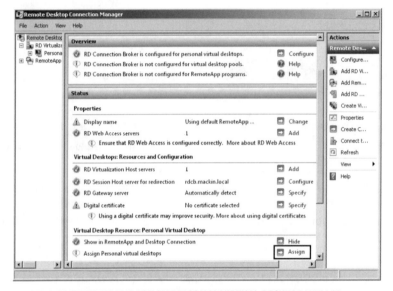

FIGURE 4-40 STARTING THE ASSIGN PERSONAL VIRTUAL DESKTOP WIZARD.

2. On the Assign Personal Virtual Desktop page, click Select User.

3. In the Select User dialog box, in the Enter The Object Names To Select box, specify the user to whom you want to assign a personal virtual desktop and then click OK.

4. In the Virtual Machine box, select the virtual machine you want to assign to the user and then click Next.

5. On the Confirm Assignment page, review your selections and then click Assign.

6. On the Assignment Summary page, confirm that the assignment succeeded. If you want to assign another virtual machine to another user, click Continue, and you are taken back to the Assign Personal Virtual Desktop page. If you are finished, clear the Assign Another Virtual Machine To Another User check box and then click Finish.

If your VDI design includes virtual desktop pools, you can use the Create Virtual Desktop Pool Wizard at this time. To start the Create Virtual Desktop Pool Wizard, in the Remote

Desktop Connection Manager console tree, right-click the *RD Virtualization Host Servers* node and then click Create Virtual Desktop Pool, as shown in Figure 4-41.

FIGURE 4-41 Starting the Create Virtual Desktop Pool Wizard.

To complete the Create Virtual Desktop Pool Wizard, perform the following steps:

1. On the Welcome to the Create Virtual Desktop Pool Wizard page, review the information and then click Next.

2. On the Select Virtual Machines page, select the virtual machines you want to include as part of the virtual desktop pool. To select a virtual machine, click the name of the virtual machine. To select multiple virtual machines, press Ctrl and click or press Shift and click.

3. After you have selected the virtual machines, click Next.

4. On the Set Pool Properties page, enter a display name and a pool ID. Users see the display name when the virtual desktop pool is displayed in RemoteApp and Desktop Connection. They do not see the pool ID.

> **NOTE   RD CONNECTION BROKER CLUSTERS**
>
> If you are creating a virtual desktop pool on an RD Connection Broker cluster, ensure that the display name and the pool ID are the same on all nodes of the cluster.

5. After you enter a display name and a pool ID, click Next.

6. On the Results page, click Finish.

The virtual desktop pool appears in the left pane under the *RD Virtualization Host Servers* node.

> **NOTE   CHANGING NODE PROPERTIES**
>
> The new virtual desktop pool appears as a node in the Remote Desktop Connection Manager console tree beneath the *RD Virtualization Host Servers* node. To change the properties of the virtual desktop pool, right-click its node and select Properties.

CONFIGURING THE GUEST OPERATING SYSTEMS FOR A VDI

The guest machines running in Hyper-V on the RD Virtualization Host need to be specially configured for the VDI implementation. On each machine, you can either run a special PowerShell script or configure the machine manually.

To configure a virtual machine by using a Windows PowerShell script, perform the following steps:

1. Log on to the guest operating system as an administrator.

2. Within the guest operating system, visit *http://go.microsoft.com/FWLink/?Linkid =184804*.

3. Above the script, click Copy Code. If a message box appears, click Allow Access to allow the webpage access to your clipboard.

4. Paste the script into Notepad.

5. Save the file as Configure-VirtualMachine.ps1 in the default location. (The default location is the Documents folder.)

   To save the file with a .ps1 extension, change Save As Type from Text Documents to All Files and then specify a name of Configure-VirtualMachine.ps1.

6. Open an elevated Windows PowerShell prompt by clicking Start, clicking All Programs, clicking Accessories, clicking the Windows PowerShell folder, right-clicking Windows PowerShell, and then clicking Run As Administrator.

7. At the Windows PowerShell prompt, type **Set-ExecutionPolicy remotesigned –force** and then press Enter.

8. At the PowerShell prompt, type the following command: **C:\Users\<Username>\ Documents\Configure-VirtualMachine.ps1**

   –RDVHost <Domain>\<Server> -RDUsers <Remote Desktop Users>

   where <Username> is the name of the profile folder of your currently logged-on account, <Domain> is the name of the AD DS domain, <Server> is the FQDN of the RD Virtualization Host server on which the virtual machine is running, and <Remote Desktop Users> are the user accounts of any users you want to add to the Remote Desktop Users local group. (You can open the script before running it to see usage examples in the comments section.) Next, press Enter.

As an alternative to using the Windows PowerShell script, you can configure each virtual machine manually. To do this, perform the following configuration tasks within each guest operating system. Be sure to log on to each computer as an administrator.

1. Enable Remote Desktop.

   a. In the Search Programs And Files box, type **Allow Remote Access To Your Computer**.

   b. On the Remote tab of the System Properties dialog box, if you need to support RDP clients 6.0 and earlier, select Allow Connections From Computers Running

Any Version Of Remote Desktop. Otherwise, select Allow Connections Only From Computers Running Remote Desktop With Network Level Authentication.

   c. Click Select Users.

   d. In the Remote Desktop Users dialog box, click Add and then add the users and groups to whom you want to grant access to the local computer. (Administrators already have access.)

   e. Click OK in all open dialog boxes.

2. Allow Remote RPC for Remote Desktop Services.

   a. While you are logged on to the client as an administrator, in the Search Programs And Files box of the Start menu, type **regedit.exe** and then press ENTER.

   b. Navigate to HKEY_LOCAL_MACHINE\SYSTEM\CurrentControlSet\Control\ TerminalServer.

   c. Double-click the AllowRemoteRPC registry entry. In the Value data box, type **1** and then click OK.

   d. Close Registry Editor.

3. Create a firewall exception to allow Remote Service Management.

   a. In the Search Programs And Files box of the Start menu, type **Allow A Program Through Windows Firewall** and then press Enter.

   b. In the Allow Programs To Communicate Through Windows Firewall window, click Change.

   c. In the list of allowed programs and features, select Remote Service Management for the Domain profile and then click OK.

4. Add permissions to the RDP protocol. You must add the WINSTATION_QUERY, WINSTATION_LOGOFF, and WINSTATION_DISCONNECT permissions to the RD Virtualization Host computer.

   a. At an elevated command prompt within the guest operating system, type the following six commands, where <Domain> is the name of the AD DS domain and <Server_Name> is the host name of the RD Virtualization Host server. Press Enter after each command.

```
wmic /node:localhost RDPERMISSIONS where TerminalName="RDP-Tcp" CALL AddAccount
"<Domain>\<Server_Name>$",1

wmic /node:localhost RDACCOUNT where "(TerminalName='RDP-Tcp' or
TerminalName='Console') and AccountName='<Domain>\\<Server_Name>$'" CALL
ModifyPermissions 0,1

wmic /node:localhost RDACCOUNT where "(TerminalName='RDP-Tcp' or
TerminalName='Console') and AccountName='<Domain>\\<Server_Name>$'" CALL
ModifyPermissions 2,1

wmic /node:localhost RDACCOUNT where "(TerminalName='RDP-Tcp' or
```

```
TerminalName='Console') and AccountName='<Domain>\\<Server_Name>$'" CALL
ModifyPermissions 9,1

Net stop termservice

Net start termservice
```

b. Log off the virtual machine.

CONNECTING TO VIRTUAL DESKTOPS

Users are able to connect to virtual desktops within a configured VDI by using the RD Web Access page at *http://RDWebAccessServerName/rdweb*. When users connect to the page, virtual desktops appear as RemoteApp programs, as shown in Figure 4-42.

FIGURE 4-42 Virtual Desktops appear on the RD Web Access page.

When you click a virtual desktop icon, the RD Connection Broker sends a request to the RD Virtualization Host, which prepares the virtual machine for the connection. If the virtual machine is not already started, you see the message shown in Figure 4-43 for a minute or two before a Remote Desktop connection on the virtual desktop is established.

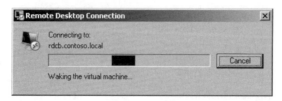

FIGURE 4-43 You can start an RD connection to a virtual desktop even when the machine is shut down.

Publish Applications with RemoteApp Manager

In this series of exercises, you *publish* an application in three ways. First, you enable users to launch a remote application by means of a Web page. Second, you create and distribute an RDP file for the remote application. Finally, you create and distribute an installer package to enable users to install an RDP file to the remote application.

EXERCISE 1   Installing the Remote Desktop Web Access Role Service

The simplest way to publish a RemoteApp program is through RD Web Access. In this exercise, you prepare the Remote Desktop Session Host for publishing applications by installing the Remote Desktop Web Access Role Service.

1. Log on to Contoso.local from Server2 as a domain administrator.
2. Open Server Manager.
3. In the Server Manager console tree, expand the *Roles* node and then select Remote Desktop Services.
4. Right-click the *Remote Desktop Services* node and then click Add Role Services.

    The Select Role Services page of the Add Role Services Wizard appears.
5. In the list of available role services, select the Remote Desktop Web Access check box.

    At this point, the Add Role Services dialog box might appear and ask whether you want to add the role services required for Remote Desktop Web Access.
6. If the Add Role Services dialog box appears, click Add Required Role Services.
7. On the Select Role Services page, click Next.
8. If the Web Server (IIS) page appears, read all the text on the page and then click Next.
9. If the Select Role Services page appears, read all the text on the page and then click Next.
10. On the Confirm Installation Selections page, click Install.

    The Installation Progress page appears while the components are being installed. When the installation completes, the Installation Results page appears.
11. On the Installation Results page, click Close.

EXERCISE 2   Publishing an Application for RD Web Access

In this exercise, you add MS Paint to the list of RemoteApp programs in RemoteApp Manager.

1. If you have not already done so, log on to Contoso.local from Server2 as a domain administrator.
2. Open RemoteApp Manager by clicking Start, Administrative Tools, Remote Desktop Services, and then RemoteApp Manager.
3. In RemoteApp Manager, in the Actions pane on the right side of the console, click Add RemoteApp Programs.

4. On the Welcome page of the RemoteApp Wizard, click Next.

5. On the Choose Programs To Add To The RemoteApp Programs List page, select Paint from the list and then click Next.

6. On the Review Settings page, click Finish.

   In RemoteApp Manager, Paint is now listed in the RemoteApp Programs area. Note that its RD Web Access status is set to Yes.

7. Proceed to Exercise 3.

EXERCISE 3   Launching a Remote Application through RD Web Access

In this exercise, you run Paint through RD Web Access.

1. Log on to Contoso.local from Server1 as a domain administrator.

2. Open Internet Explorer.

3. In the Internet Explorer address box, type **https://server2.contoso.local/rdweb** and then press Enter.

   The Remote Desktop Services Default Connection Web page appears. At the top of the window, a yellow security banner appears, informing you that the website wants to run an add-on.

4. Click the yellow security banner on the Web page and then click Run Add-on from the menu that appears.

5. In the Internet Explorer—Security Warning dialog box, click Run to run the ActiveX control.

6. In the Remote Desktop Services Default Connection page, type the credentials of a domain administrator and then click Sign In.

   After the logon procedure, the RemoteApp Programs tab is selected in the Remote Desktop Services Default Connection window, and a Paint icon appears in the main area of the Web page.

7. Click the Paint icon.

   A RemoteApp Starting window briefly appears, and then a RemoteApp warning message appears.

8. Read all the text in the warning message and then click Connect.

9. In the Windows Security window, enter the credentials of a domain administrator and then click OK.

   After a minute, a Paint window opens.

10. From the File menu, click Save.

    The Save As window appears.

    Answer the following question:

    Is the default location for a saved file found on Server1 or Server2? Why?

Answer: Server2, because the program is actually running on Server2

In the Save As window, click Cancel and then close the Paint window.

EXERCISE 4 Creating a Distribution Share

In this exercise, you create a distribution share with read access for all domain users. The share will distribute RDP files and RD-enabled installer packages.

1. Log on to Contoso.local from Server2 as a domain administrator.
2. Create a folder named **RD Apps** at the root of the C drive.
3. Right-click the RD Apps folder, point to Share With from the shortcut menu, and then click Specific People.
4. The File Sharing window opens.
5. In the text box provided, type **Domain Users** and then click Add.
6. Domain Users now appears in the Name list with an associated Permission Level of *Read*.
7. Click Share.

   The File Sharing window displays the message that your folder is shared.
8. Click Done.

EXERCISE 5 Creating an RDP File for a Published Application

In this exercise, you create an RDP file for WordPad and save it to the RD Apps distribution share.

1. While you are logged on to Contoso.local from Server2 as a domain administrator, open RemoteApp Manager if it is not already open.
2. In RemoteApp Manager, in the Actions pane, click Add RemoteApp Programs.
3. Use the RemoteApp Wizard to add WordPad to the RemoteApp Programs list, as described in Exercise 2.

   When you have completed the wizard, WordPad appears in the RemoteApp Programs list in RemoteApp Manager.
4. Select WordPad in the RemoteApp Programs list and then, in the Other Distribution Options area in RemoteApp Manager, click Create .Rdp File.

   The RemoteApp Wizard opens.
5. On the Welcome page of the RemoteApp Wizard, click Next.
6. On the Specify Package Settings Page, read all the text on the page and then click Browse.
7. In the Browse For Folder dialog box, locate and select the RD Apps folder in the root of the C drive. Click OK.
8. On the Specify Package Settings page of the RemoteApp Wizard, click Next.

9. On the Review Settings page, click Finish.

10. Proceed to Exercise 6.

EXERCISE 6 Launching a Remote Application with a Local RDP File

In this exercise, you copy an RDP file from a distribution share to Server1 and then use that RDP file to launch a remote application.

1. If you have not already done so, log on to Contoso.local from Server1 as a domain administrator.

2. In the Search Programs And Files box of the Start menu, type **\\Server2** and then press Enter.

   A Server2 window opens in Windows Explorer.

3. In the Server2 window, double-click the network share named RD Apps.

4. In the RD Apps share, copy the Wordpad.rdp to your desktop on Server1.

5. Close all open windows on Server1 and then double-click the WordPad file on the Server1 desktop.

   The RemoteApp Starting window appears, and then a RemoteApp warning message appears.

6. Read all the text in the warning message and then click Connect.

7. If a Windows Security prompt appears, provide the credentials of a domain administrator and then click OK.

8. After a minute, WordPad opens on Server1.

9. Close all open windows.

EXERCISE 7 Creating a RemoteApp Installer Package for Distribution

In this exercise, which requires an Internet connection, you download and install Microsoft Word Viewer from the Microsoft Download Center and then add it to the RemoteApp Programs list. You then create an installer package to distribute to users over the network.

> **NOTE** **USE AN ALTERNATE PROGRAM IF DESIRED**
>
> In this exercise, Word Viewer is simply used as an example. You can substitute any installable program for Word Viewer.

1. Log on to Contoso.local from Server2 as a domain administrator.

2. Use Internet Explorer to connect to the Microsoft Download Center at *http://www .microsoft.com/downloads*. On the Microsoft Download Center website, locate and download Word Viewer.

3. Install Word Viewer on Server2.

4. After the installation has completed, open RemoteApp Manager.

5. In RemoteApp Manager, in the Actions pane on the right side of the console, click Add RemoteApp Programs.

6. Use the RemoteApp Wizard to add Microsoft Office Word Viewer to the RemoteApp Programs list, as described in Exercise 2.

   After you have completed the wizard, Microsoft Office Word Viewer 2003 appears listed in the RemoteApp Programs area of the RemoteApp Manager.

7. Select Microsoft Office Word Viewer 2003 in the list and then, in the Other Distribution Options area of RemoteApp Manager, click Create Windows Installer Package.

8. On the Welcome page of the RemoteApp Wizard, click Next.

9. On the Specify Package Settings page, read all the text on the page and then click Browse.

10. In the Browse For Folder dialog box, select the RD Apps folder in the root of the C drive and then click OK.

11. On the Specify Package Settings page, click Next.

12. On the Configure Distribution Package page, read all the text on the page, select the Desktop check box, and then click Next.

13. On the Review Settings page, click Finish.

14. Proceed to Exercise 8.

EXERCISE 8   Installing a Remote Program

In this exercise, you use the installer package created in the previous exercise to install Word Viewer as a remote application.

1. If you have not already done so, log on to Contoso.local from Server1 as a domain administrator.

2. In the Search Programs And Files box of the Start menu, type **\\Server2** and then press Enter.

   A Server2 window opens in Windows Explorer.

3. In the Server2 window, double-click the network share named RD Apps.

4. In the RD Apps share, copy the Windows Installer Package (.MSI file) named WORDVIEW to your desktop on Server1.

5. Close all open windows on Server1 and then double-click the WORDVIEW file on the Server1 desktop.

   When the program finishes installing, a new shortcut to an RDP file appears on the desktop. The shortcut is named Microsoft Office Word Viewer 2003.

6. Double-click the Microsoft Office Word Viewer 2003 shortcut.

   A RemoteApp warning message appears.

7. Read all the text in the warning message and then click Connect.

8. If the Windows Security window appears, enter the credentials of a domain administrator.

   After several moments, Word Viewer opens along with an Open dialog box that prompts you to specify a Word file to open.

9. Close all open windows and then log off both Server1 and Server2.

Lesson Summary

- RemoteApp enables programs to run through Remote Desktop Services and appear as if they were running on a user's local computer. RemoteApp is useful when users need to access applications remotely or simply lack the hardware or software required to run the application in question.

- A program that is published through RemoteApp is known as a RemoteApp Program. There are three ways to publish RemoteApp Programs: through the RD Web Access page, through RDP files, and through Windows Installer packages.

- When you install an application to be published on a Remote Desktop Session Host, you have to make sure that the Remote Desktop Session Host is in Install mode. Installing the application while the server is in this mode enables the application to support multiple users.

- The main tool used to configure and manage RemoteApp programs is RemoteApp Manager.

- Configuring a virtual desktop infrastructure to deploy virtual desktops requires you to configure several components, including an RD Connection Broker, an RD Web Access Server, and virtual machines running as guests on a computer running RD Virtualization Host.

- Windows 7 and Windows Server 2008 R2 include RemoteApp and Desktop Connection in Control Panel. You can use this program to subscribe to a network feed of RemoteApp programs and virtual desktops that appear in the Start menu and update automatically.

Lesson Review

The following questions are intended to reinforce key information presented in this lesson. The questions are also available on the companion CD if you prefer to review them in electronic form.

> **NOTE ANSWERS**
>
> Answers to these questions and explanations of why each answer choice is correct or incorrect are located in the "Answers" section at the end of the book.

1. How can you ensure that an application installed on a Remote Desktop Session Host server can support multiple users?

   A. Use the *Chglogon* command.

   B. Use the *Change user/install* command.

   C. Use the *Qappsrv* command.

   D. Use the *Mstsc* command.

2. You have recently created and distributed RDP files for a certain RemoteApp program. However, you find that the application performs poorly and needs to be migrated to a more powerful server. What should you do to ensure that users can connect to the RemoteApp program after it is migrated? (Each correct answer presents a complete solution. Choose two.)

   A. Create a new RD Web Access site for the new Remote Desktop Session Host and publish the application to the new site.

   B. Re-create an RDP file for the RemoteApp program after the migration and distribute the file to users.

   C. Modify the properties of the existing RDP file and redistribute the file to users.

   D. In RemoteApp Manager on the old Remote Desktop Session Host, change the Remote Desktop Session Host server settings so that the server name listed is the new Remote Desktop Session Host.

3. You want both RemoteApp programs and virtual desktops to appear automatically in users' Start menus. Which of the following actions enables you to achieve this goal?

   A. Publishing resources in Remote Desktop Web Access

   B. Creating .rdp files for distribution

   C. Creating a Windows Installer package for distribution

   D. Subscribing to feeds through RemoteApp and Desktop Connections

Chapter Review

To further practice and reinforce the skills you learned in this chapter, you can perform the following tasks:

- Review the chapter summary.
- Review the list of key terms introduced in this chapter.
- Complete the case scenarios. These scenarios set up real-world situations involving the topics of this chapter and ask you to create solutions.
- Complete the suggested practices.
- Take a practice test.

Chapter Summary

- You can configure Remote Desktop client properties by choosing options directly in Remote Desktop Connection or by enforcing settings in Group Policy objects (GPOs).
- To manage user sessions on a Remote Desktop Session Host, use Remote Desktop Services Manager (RDSM). You can use RDSM to display information about users connected to a Remote Desktop Session Host, to monitor user sessions, or to perform administrative tasks, such as logging off users or disconnecting user sessions.
- An RD Gateway server enables authorized users to connect to Remote Desktop Session Hosts located behind a firewall. An RD Gateway server provides confidentiality to Remote Desktop client sessions by encrypting them with SSL. To configure and manage an RD Gateway server, use RD Gateway Manager.
- The RemoteApp feature enables you to publish programs running on a Remote Desktop Session Host so that they appear to be running on the client instead. You can use RemoteApp when users need to access applications remotely or lack the requirements to install the program locally. To configure and manage RemoteApp, use RemoteApp Manager.
- You can make RemoteApp programs available to users through RD Web Access, RDP files, Windows Installer packages, or the RemoteApp and Desktop Connections program in Control Panel.
- You can enable users to use Remote Desktop Web Access to connect to virtual machines running on a Remote Desktop Virtualization Host server. Providing this functionality requires you to configure a virtual desktop infrastructure made up of several components of Remote Desktop Services.

Key Terms

Do you know what these key terms mean? You can check your answers by looking up the terms in the glossary at the end of the book.

- certification authority (CA)
- console session
- home folder
- HTTPS
- Install mode
- personal virtual desktop
- publish (an application)
- RD CAP
- RD Gateway
- RD RAP
- RD Web Access
- RemoteApp
- RemoteApp and Desktop Connection
- self-signed server certificate
- server certificate
- SSL
- user profile
- virtual desktop pool

Case Scenarios

In the following case scenarios, you apply what you've learned about Remote Desktop Services in this chapter. You can find answers to these questions in the "Answers" section at the end of this book.

Case Scenario 1: Managing Remote Desktop Sessions

You are the administrator of a computer named RDS1 that is running Windows Server 2008 R2. RDS1 is running Remote Desktop Services and is hosting several applications. Throughout the day, many users are connected to RDS1, and you are responsible for managing the user sessions to the server.

1. A user informs you that his Remote Desktop session on RDS1 is frozen. What commands can you use to find his session ID and then end his session?

2. A new user calls to inform you that she is having trouble using an application on RDS1. Because she works in another building, you want to be able to show her how to use the application without having to visit her desk. How can you achieve this?

Case Scenario 2: Publishing Applications

Your company has recently configured a server named Server1 to host a line-of-business application named App1. Server1 is running Windows Server 2008 R2 and Remote Desktop Services. You are part of the team testing and publishing the application in Windows Server 2008 R2. Your first goal is to publish the App1 application to all users in the Contoso.local domain.

1. After installing App1 on Server1, your team wants to publish App1 to users' desktops. You do not want to have the users copy files from a share to run the remote application. Which deployment method or methods would you recommend?

2. You want users to see the application listed in the Start menu and, if users open a file associated with App1, you want the remote program to start automatically. How can you achieve this most efficiently?

3. You want to make App1 available to users as a RemoteApp program in remote locations outside of the corporate network. How can you accomplish this? (Assume that your company has a firewall and perimeter network that hosts public servers.)

Suggested Practices

To help you successfully master the exam objectives presented in this chapter, complete the following tasks.

Deploy a Remote Desktop Services Infrastructure

In this practice, you deploy an RD Session Host, an RD Gateway server, and a RemoteApp program.

- **Practice 1** Install Windows Server 2008 R2 and Remote Desktop Services on a server in your organization. Install an application on the server while the server is in Install mode and then add the application to the list of RemoteApp Programs in RemoteApp Manager. Install RD Web Access on the same server and then connect to the RD Web Access page from another computer. Launch the RemoteApp program from the RD Web Access page.

- **Practice 2** Deploy RD Gateway on a second server in your organization. Use RemoteApp Manager on the first server to create an RDP file for the same application. Configure the RDP file to specify the new RD Gateway address. Export the RD Gateway server's certificate to a client computer (if necessary) and then use the RDP file on the client computer to launch the RemoteApp program through the gateway.

Perform a Virtual Lab

In this practice, you configure and manage a Remote Desktop Services infrastructure online.

- **Practice**   Visit *http://go.microsoft.com/?Linkid=9694259*. Register for and perform the virtual lab named "TechNet Virtual Lab Express: Windows Server 2008 R2: Remote Desktop Services."

Take a Practice Test

The practice tests on this book's companion CD offer many options. For example, you can test yourself on just one exam objective, or you can test yourself on all the 70-643 certification exam content. You can set up the test so that it closely simulates the experience of taking a certification exam, or you can set it up in study mode so that you can look at the correct answers and explanations after you answer each question.

> **MORE INFO**   **PRACTICE TESTS**
>
> For details about all the practice test options available, see the "How to Use the Practice Tests" section in this book's introduction.

CHAPTER 5

Installing and Configuring Web Applications

M odern websites provide functionality on par with the experience found in many lo-cally installed client applications. They provide access to databases in both public and intranet environments and enable users to customize their experience based on specific needs. Web applications or web services rely upon a variety of standards, protocols, and development technologies.

The Windows Server 2008 R2 operating system includes *Internet Information Services (IIS) 7.5*, a complete web services platform capable of supporting various types of web content and applications. IIS 7.5 and IIS 7.0, which were released with Windows Server 2008, are known collectively as IIS 7. IIS 7 provides significant enhancements in manageability, scalability, and reliability. It also provides backward compatibility to support the millions of websites already hosted on previous versions of IIS.

In this chapter, you learn how to install and configure the Web Server (IIS) and Application Server roles in Windows Server 2008 R2. You can enable numerous features and services based on the needs of your environment. This information will help you deploy and configure IIS and its related features in production environments.

Exam objectives in this chapter:

- Configure Web applications.
- Manage Web sites.
- Manage the Web Server (IIS) role.

Lessons in this chapter:

Before You Begin

To complete the lessons in this chapter, you must have:

- A computer running Windows Server 2008 R2 named Server1 that is a domain controller in a domain named Contoso.local.
- A computer running Windows Server 2008 R2 named Server2 that is a member server in the Contoso.local domain. On Server2, no server roles are installed. (If you have roles installed from exercises in previous chapters, you can remove them by using Server Manager and the Remove Roles Wizard.)

 REAL WORLD

Anil Desai

The success of a server installation is often based on how well its configuration matches the needs of users and developers. If some features are missing, applications will not run as expected. If too many features are enabled, there could be security, compatibility, or performance implications. The goal is to "get it right." This is one area in which communication is important.

In many IT departments, I've seen a significant disconnect between development teams (such as groups of web developers) and the systems administrators responsible for deploying and supporting the applications the developers create. Often, the responsibilities of each part of the organization are not clearly defined, and it can become difficult to figure out who is ultimately responsible for the final configuration.

Fortunately, these types of problems can be avoided. On the systems administration side, IT staff should try to determine the specific business and technical needs of the web applications they support. Web developers can do their part by proactively communicating upcoming requirements and potential implications for the configuration of production servers. Writing documentation is helpful for thinking through and communicating the most important points. Finally, it's important to remember end users. Whether these are people who are part of your organization or members of the public at large, it's important to understand their specific reasons for visiting your websites. Marketing input can often help in this area.

Lesson 1: Installing the Web Server (IIS) Role

Although enabling IIS and its related components is usually a simple procedure, the primary challenge lies in understanding the architecture, components, and available features of the platform. In this lesson, you learn about the modular architecture of IIS and how to configure a computer running Windows Server 2008 R2 as a web server.

> **After this lesson, you will be able to:**
> - Describe the architecture of IIS 7, including new features.
> - Define the purpose of the Application Server role.
> - Describe the purpose of role services related to the Web Server (IIS) role.
> - Install the Web Server (IIS) role and add and remove role services.
> - Perform command-line installations and automated installations of the Web Server (IIS) role.
>
> **Estimated lesson time: 50 minutes**

Understanding Web Server Security

IIS 7 includes an array of features and options to support different types of web services and applications. Using the Server Manager utility simplifies the process of installing IIS and its related features and options. As a systems administrator, you will be responsible for deploying IIS based on different needs and requirements. Therefore, it is important to understand the design of IIS before learning methods for installing the Web Server and Application Server roles. This section provides details about deployment options for the IIS platform.

> **MORE INFO**   **OTHER FEATURES OF IIS**
>
> In addition to supporting web applications, the IIS platform also provides server components for the File Transfer Protocol (FTP) and the Simple Mail Transfer Protocol (SMTP). This chapter focuses on web-based applications. For more information about these other features, see Chapter 7, "Configuring FTP and SMTP Services."

Web Standards and Protocols

To understand the purpose and function of the IIS platform, you must first understand the protocols and standards web applications use. *Hypertext Transfer Protocol* (HTTP) is the primary protocol that communicates with web services. HTTP is designed to provide a request–response model for communicating among computers across a network. HTTP traffic is accessed by using Transmission Control Protocol/Internet Protocol (TCP/IP)–based network connections. Due to the importance of web-based traffic, most organizations allow their users to access the Internet by using TCP port 80, the default HTTP port. The HTTP protocol is stateless; that is, it provides no built-in mechanism to keep track of conversations between clients and servers. Each request must include details that identify the requester and any other data that might be required to complete a transaction.

Web standards and protocols also include methods for securing data as it is passed among computers. By default, HTTP traffic is transmitted using a plaintext stream that can be decoded easily. Although this is acceptable when users are accessing public content, many websites and applications need to transmit information securely between clients and servers. The most common example is that of a payment-processing site that accepts credit card information over the Internet. The *HTTP Secure* (HTTPS) *protocol* is designed to provide support for encryption of HTTP-based traffic. By default, HTTPS connections use TCP port 443 for communications, although any other port can be used as well. The most commonly used encryption mechanisms are *Secure Sockets Layer (SSL)* and Transport Layer Security (TLS). Other encryption mechanisms can also be used, especially in intranet environments.

Web standards and protocols provide a consistent method of exchanging information among computers. The Hypertext Markup Language (HTML) is the primary specification for webpages. The tag-based format of HTML pages enables developers to use a variety of technologies to create their content in a way that is accessible by different web browsers. The development tools can range from text editors, such as Windows Notepad, to full-featured development environments, such as the Microsoft Visual Studio platform.

The HTTP and HTML specifications were designed to provide basic communication and presentation services. Modern web applications include features that enable complex application functionality to be presented by using these standards. Web developers can use development platforms such as ASP.NET (a component of the Microsoft .NET Framework) to build active websites. These sites can keep track of user sessions and can provide access to databases and other information stored within the environment.

> **MORE INFO**   **FURTHER DETAILS ABOUT INTERNET STANDARDS**
>
> For more information about specific Internet and web-based standards, see the World Wide Web Consortium (W3C) website at *http://www.w3.org* and the Internet Engineering Task Force (IETF) website at *http://www.ietf.org*. Both sites include the official specifications and descriptions for basic Internet protocols.

Web Server Usage Scenarios

The primary advantage of using web-based content and applications is accessibility from a broad range of client computers. Unlike standard applications, there is generally no need to install or configure any software on users' computers. Because modern operating systems include or support standards-based web browsers, such as Internet Explorer, most users already have the basic client tools they need to access content. IT staff and software developers can use various technologies to present content and deploy applications to both internal and external users.

The IIS platform has been designed to support a variety of scenarios. Some examples include:

- **Public websites** Many businesses have relatively simple needs for communicating information on the Internet. For example, a small business might want to provide contact information and details about its services on a simple website.

- **Online shopping** The Internet has become a commercial marketplace that enables vendors to display and sell a wide variety of products. Online sites include shopping-cart functionality, order processing, and customer support features.

- **Intranet scenarios** The web provides a simple method for all users within an organization to access and present content. Company tasks, such as creating expense reports or verifying benefits, can often be performed online without the need to contact internal staff.

- **Enterprise applications** A common challenge with enterprise line-of-business applications is the need to deploy and manage client-side installations. To alleviate some of these problems, many organizations have created internal applications designed to be accessed through a web browser. The applications can range from basic single-function sites to distributed, enterprise-wide systems.

- **Internet applications** Users can access their email and create documents, for example, without installing applications on their computers. Distributed organizations and teams can also take advantage of secure access to corporate applications by using the Internet while traveling or working from remote locations.

- **Extranet scenarios** Businesses commonly partner with other organizations to obtain services. An extranet scenario is one in which users from outside the organization are able to access information. Security is an important concern, but web-based applications are a good choice because they provide a standard method by which users can access the information they need.

- **Web hosting** Many companies have focused on offering the service of hosting websites for their customers. These hosting companies tend to run large numbers of websites on a single physical server, so ensuring security, performance, and reliability are key concerns.

Most organizations deploy IIS in several roles within the organization. It is important to note that requirements related to features and options vary based on the specific needs of each deployment.

You learn more about the specific features and services the IIS platform supports later in this lesson.

New Features in IIS 7

The IIS platform is one of the most popular web servers in use for both public and private websites. IIS 7 in Windows Server 2008 and Windows Server 2008 R2 includes numerous new features that provide increased performance and functionality in a broad range of areas. The major areas of improvement include:

- **Administration**   One of the primary challenges of working with previous versions of IIS was dealing with a large number of property pages and dialog boxes. IIS 7 includes new administration tools designed to manage the many available options and settings more effectively. The user interface has been designed to be both powerful and accessible for both web developers and systems administrators.

- **Security**   By default, the Web Server (IIS) server role is enabled with only a basic set of functionalities. Even the binary files for unused features are not available for access in the standard operating system locations. Systems administrators must enable additional services and features explicitly. This helps reduce the attack surface of IIS while also simplifying manageability. In addition, functionality for automatically detecting common unauthorized access attempts is included with the product itself. (This feature was commonly enabled in the past by installing the URLScan utility.)

- **Diagnostics and troubleshooting**   Because organizations depend on web services as a mission-critical component of their infrastructure, it's important to detect and resolve any web-based errors quickly. IIS 7 includes new features that make it easier to pinpoint problems and obtain the details necessary to address them.

- **Centralized configuration management**   Many organizations support dozens or even hundreds of IIS installations. To meet scalability and performance requirements, it is often necessary to deploy numerous web servers that have essentially the same configuration settings. In previous versions of IIS, it was difficult to manage these configurations without connecting to each server. IIS 7 provides a simplified method by which administrators can share configuration information across server farms. Further, a consistent set of user accounts, including globally unique identifiers (GUIDs) and permissions, is used for IIS security accounts. This means administrators can depend on specific account names and settings when scripting and automating common processes. IIS 7 also includes greatly improved command-line support.

- **Support for delegation**   It is often necessary to divide web server administration tasks for security or management reasons. IIS 7 provides the ability to implement granular security configuration permissions to support web-hosting environments and enterprise-level configurations.

- **Backward compatibility**   The vast majority of websites and applications that were created for previous versions of IIS will remain compatible with IIS 7. In addition, IIS 6.0 management tools are provided for those applications that depend on them.

- **Request filtering**   This is a feature by which you can restrict or block specific HTTP requests. It is available as an extension in IIS 7.0 and is built into IIS 7.5.

- **IIS module for Windows PowerShell**   New to Windows Server 2008 R2, this Windows PowerShell module contains many new cmdlets for IIS administration.

- **Configuration logging and tracing**   New to IIS 7.5, this feature enables you to audit access to the IIS configuration.

Overall, IIS 7 has been designed to address the most common issues encountered with previous versions of IIS. There are numerous additional improvements in IIS that you learn about as this chapter discusses the various features in depth.

Understanding IIS Components and Options

The IIS platform has been designed with a modular, component-based architecture. In its simplest configuration, the web server component provides basic HTTP functionality. IIS includes many components and features that support different types of content and applications. Most deployments need only a subset of these features. Therefore, administrators can choose to enable only the components their web applications require.

Although the modular approach requires systems administrators to explicitly enable the features they require, this architecture provides numerous advantages:

- **Enhanced security**   Each enabled service or feature can increase the security attack surface on an IIS server. This is a significant concern for publicly accessible servers that might be the targets of unauthorized access attempts. For example, a defect or vulnerability in a specific type of IIS extension might be used to perform unauthorized actions on the server. Administrators can reduce these risks greatly by enabling only those features and services that are required by their content and applications.

- **Improved performance**   Installing and enabling unnecessary components can use up system resources on the server running IIS. By enabling only those features that are specifically required, server resources can be retained for use by other applications. The result is better performance and scalability.

- **Ability to customize server configurations**   As mentioned earlier in this lesson, organizations tend to use IIS in a variety of deployment scenarios. The security and functionality requirements can vary significantly, and a modular architecture enables systems administrators to customize each deployment based on its specific needs. For example, the authentication and security requirements of internal web servers and Internet-accessible servers often differ. Administrators can enable the required features for each type of server independently.

In this section, you learn about components and options related to the IIS platform.

MORE INFO   **INFORMATION FROM THE IIS TEAM**

The IIS team at Microsoft has created a website that includes tutorials, technical articles, and other details about working with the IIS platform. This is a great resource for in-depth information about the many available features and components. The site includes links to

---

downloads and information about products that work with (or on) the IIS platform. Team members have their own blogs, too, which focus on their specific areas of expertise. The main page is located at *http://www.iis.net*.

Understanding the Application Server Role

One of the primary strengths of the Windows platform is its ability to support a range of application development technologies. Modern applications often rely on extensive communications features. For example, a distributed application might need to create and manage transactions across several sites and services by using a distributed network. Building this type of functionality can be difficult and complicated. Applications developers can save significant time and effort by taking advantage of the features that are already available on their operating system platform.

Windows Server 2008 and Windows Server 2008 R2 include the Application Server role to provide support for a variety of application development technologies. The Application Server role is based on .NET Framework 3.0 technology and includes support for other communications and presentation features. Although the Application Server role does not specifically depend on the Web Server (IIS) role, distributed applications built by using ASP.NET or Windows Communication Foundation (WCF) require both roles.

You can install the Application Server role by using the Add Roles Wizard in Server Manager. When you add the role, you can determine which additional role services you plan to enable. The specific features include:

- **.NET Framework 3.5.1** This is a required feature of the Application Server role. It includes WCF, Windows Presentation Foundation (WPF), and Windows Workflow Foundation (WF).

- **Web Server (IIS) Support** The Application Server role can be integrated with the Web Server (IIS) role to enable web applications to access advanced features. When you select this option, the Add Roles Wizard prompts you to install IIS automatically if it is not already installed.

- **COM+ Network Access** The Component Object Model (COM) standard provides applications developers with a method for accessing different pieces of application code. COM+ provides the ability to invoke (or access) application code remotely across a network. Distributed applications, such as those that require multiple tiers of functionality, might require this feature.

- **TCP Port Sharing** A potential management challenge of working in distributed environments is supporting many server applications on a single computer. Generally, each application requires its own TCP port for responding to inbound requests. The TCP Port Sharing feature enables multiple applications to share the same port to simplify server and firewall configuration.

- **Windows Process Activation Service Support** The Windows Process Activation Service (WAS) provides the ability to access application services over the network by using different types of protocols and services. IIS itself can use this feature to support additional protocols and communications methods.

- **Distributed Transactions** Applications that involve distributed transactions require multiple servers and applications to coordinate their activities before changes are made permanent. By using this section, you enable incoming and outgoing remote transactions and support the WS-Atomic Transactions standard for Web Services.

Generally, you should verify requirements with web application developers to determine which Application Server components (if any) are required.

When done correctly, collecting and communicating web server requirements can help ensure that systems administrators are aligned with the developers and users they support. From an IT standpoint, IIS is one of those technology areas that can benefit from input and expertise from all areas of your organization. If you do your homework before diving into the configuration process you're much more likely to end up with the right IIS configuration.

Understanding IIS 7 Role Services

Role services define which specific features and options of the IIS platform are available for use on the local web server. You can add these role services by using Server Manager. When you use Server Manager, you see a dialog box like the one shown in Figure 5-1.

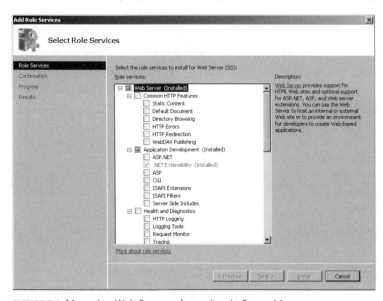

FIGURE 5-1 Managing Web Server role services in Server Manager.

IIS role services are organized into several major areas:

- Common HTTP Features

- Application Development
- Health and Diagnostics
- Security
- Performance
- Management Tools
- FTP Server

The top level of the hierarchy is the Web Server itself. This item represents the core IIS services required by the optional components that are also available for installation. Two other items, Management Tools and FTP Server, can be installed independently of the Web Server role service. Each area contains features and options that are related. Several of the items depend on other role services. If you select an item without first selecting its dependencies, you are given the option to add the required role services automatically. (See Figure 5-2.)

FIGURE 5-2 Including role dependencies when adding a role service.

Default IIS Role Services

As mentioned earlier, the default configuration includes a limited set of functionalities. It is appropriate for installations that serve only limited static content and do not need advanced security or development features. In many cases, you will want to enable additional options.

Table 5-1 lists the role services that are included when you add the Web Server (IIS) server role to the computer.

TABLE 5-1 Default Role Services in the Web Server (IIS) Server Role

GROUP/CATEGORY	FEATURE(S)
Common HTTP Features	Static Content
	Default Document
	Directory Browsing
	HTTP Errors
	HTTP Redirection
	WebDAV Publishing
Health and Diagnostics Features	HTTP Logging
	Request Monitor

Security	Request Filtering
Performance Features	Static Content Compression
Management Tools	IIS Management Console

In the following sections, you learn more about the purpose of these and the many optional role services.

Common HTTP Features

The most important function of the Web Server (IIS) role is to serve HTML web pages by using the HTTP protocol. The components of the Common HTTP Features group that are available to install are:

- **Static Content**   This functionality allows for serving static web pages to clients by using HTTP. The most common content types are static HTML pages and images. Static content files are usually sent directly to users without any server-side processing.

- **Default Document**   This feature allows IIS to return a specific file automatically for a website when one is not explicitly requested in the URL. For example, if a user attempts to connect to *http://www.contoso.local*, the web server can be configured to return the default.htm file as a response.

- **Directory Browsing**   IIS includes built-in functionality for providing basic directory listings to users. When enabled, directory browsing sends information about the files and folders on a website to the client's web browser. Because users can access and download any files to which they have the appropriate permissions, this feature is usually disabled for public websites. If the default document feature is enabled and a default document is found, users will not see the directory browsing screen.

- **HTTP Errors**   By default, most web browsers are designed to present an error message automatically to users whenever a problem occurs. For example, if a page cannot be found or if the server is too busy, the web browser displays this information to the user. To enhance the user experience, IIS can be configured to return custom error pages automatically when these problems occur. The content of the error pages can include contact information for the website's administrator or other details about resolving the problem.

- **HTTP Redirection**   The HTTP protocol supports a method of redirecting a request from one site to another. The web server can be configured to send an HTTP redirect request automatically to a web user when a specific site is accessed. Site redirection is useful for situations in which a website has been relocated to a different URL or when multiple URLs are designed to access the same content.

- **WebDAV Publishing**   Web Distributed Authoring and Versioning (WebDAV) Publishing enables you to publish files to and from a web server by using the HTTP protocol. Because WebDAV uses HTTP, it works through most firewalls without modification.

Although these common HTTP features can be added, the specific behavior of each IIS website will be based on its content and configuration settings.

Application Development Features

Although some basic websites can meet their requirements by using only static content, it's far more common for production sites to require dynamic web services and web application support. IIS has been designed to support a broad array of features and technologies to support these requirements. The list of Application Development role services includes:

- **ASP.NET** ASP.NET is the primary Microsoft web server development platform. It is based on the .NET Framework and provides a powerful and flexible development framework for handling common website design tasks. Features include built-in support for managing access to databases, security and authorization methods, and reliability and scalability features.

- **.NET extensibility** The Microsoft .NET Framework programming platform can be used to make modifications to IIS web server functionality. This role service enables developers to access the IIS management namespaces and objects for building logic that interacts with web server requests.

- **ASP** Active Server Pages (ASP) technology is the predecessor to the ASP.NET platform. ASP provided a simplified, script-based method of developing web-based applications. ASP scripts run on the web server and generate HTML content that is passed back to the user through IIS. Support for ASP is provided primarily for backward compatibility with applications that have not yet been moved to the ASP.NET platform.

- **CGI** The Common Gateway Interface (CGI) is a standard that defines how web servers can pass information to programmatic scripts. It is required by some server-side components, especially those that have been written to run on multiple web server platforms. Web development languages, such as PHP: Hypertext Preprocessor (PHP), rely on CGI support within the web server. IIS 7.0 includes features that can improve the performance of CGI processing significantly.

- **ISAPI extensions** IIS supports an extensibility standard known as the Internet Server Application Programming Interface (ISAPI). By building ISAPI extensions, web developers can create their own content handlers that can interact with every aspect of the web request pipeline. The ISAPI standard is designed to provide scalability for supporting many simultaneous requests.

- **ISAPI filters** ISAPI filters are custom code that developers can create to process specific web server requests. The logic can receive web request details and return the appropriate content based on server-side logic. IIS attempts to match web requests with the most appropriate ISAPI filter for handling that type of content. Enabling this role service enables developers to add custom ISAPI filters to IIS.

- **Server Side Includes** Web designers can often benefit from being able to embed certain common content on all their webpages. Examples include a site header, navigation elements, and site footers. The Server Side Includes role service enables the web server to include other pieces of content when generating a web server request. For security reasons, this feature is disabled by default. However, sites that do not rely on other web development technologies (such as ASP.NET) might require this capability.

When planning to deploy production websites, determine which additional features should be enabled. This information is usually available from the web application development team or organization.

Health and Diagnostics Features

Although basic web server functionality can appear simple, numerous steps must be performed during the processing of a typical web request. Organizations that depend on their web servers for access to critical information and systems need a method of isolating and troubleshooting any problems that might occur. Role services included in the Health and Diagnostics features section are designed to help administrators and developers collect and analyze information about web requests.

A common challenge of monitoring websites is managing the volume of information that is generated. The process of recording in-depth details about all requests can add a significant level of performance overhead to production systems. To help address this issue, IIS 7.0 includes enhanced features for collecting details on specific requests and for configuring which information should be collected. The specific role services are:

- **HTTP Logging** The most basic form of logging in IIS is to store HTTP request information within text files on the server's file system. HTTP logging enables this functionality along with a set of default settings for logging requests. Details can be customized by accessing the properties of each website. The default location for log files is *%SystemDrive%*\Inetpub\Logs\LogFiles. Figure 5-3 shows a list of fields that can be included in the log files.

FIGURE 5-3 Configuring logging options.

- **Logging Tools** Raw HTTP request logs are difficult to view and analyze manually. On busy web servers, the files can quickly become extremely large. Because the content typically is organized with a single row per request, administrators might need to search through thousands of rows to get the information they need. The Logging Tools role service provides simple utilities for accessing and analyzing log files.

- **Request Monitor**   A common difficulty with diagnosing performance-related issues on a web server is trying to determine which activity is occurring currently. The Request Monitor feature enables administrators to see which requests are executing within the web server process at a given moment. This can help isolate the potential source of slowdowns or loss of service due to long-running requests or other issues.

- **Tracing**   When an error or performance-related issue occurs on a web server, it is useful to collect as much information as possible about the problem. Unfortunately, due to performance requirements, it's usually impractical to store details about all requests. Tracing functionality enables IIS to store detailed information for any failed requests. This feature works by keeping information about an executing request in memory just long enough to determine whether it was successful. If it was not, the results can be stored on the web server for later analysis.

- **Custom Logging**   The HTTP Logging feature provides a default text-based format for storing web request information. Although this can meet the basic needs for most websites and services, organizations can also create their own COM-based modules by using the Custom Logging option. Developers must build the logging module and then register it with IIS for it to store data. This approach provides the greatest flexibility in determining which details are important to record.

- **ODBC Logging**   Although storing data in a text file is an efficient method of logging requests, it makes the process of analyzing and reporting on web server performance difficult. The ODBC Logging role service enables applications to store web request data in any format that is supported by an Open Database Connectivity (ODBC) connection. Examples include relational database servers, such as Microsoft SQL Server, and file-based formats, such as Microsoft Excel. However, logging to ODBC-based sources can cause significant processing and storage overhead, especially on busy web servers.

Web administrators often use log analyzer applications to process the text-based log files that store request information. Details can be examined to isolate problems (such as erroneous links or missing content) and analyze traffic and the popularity of specific webpages.

Security Features

Maintaining security for websites, web applications, and web services is an important concern with all web servers. Depending on the specific deployment and usage configuration, organizations can enable a wide variety of security mechanisms. The Security role services that are available for IIS include:

- Basic Authentication
- Windows Authentication
- Digest Authentication
- Client Certificate Mapping Authentication

- IIS Client Certificate Mapping Authentication
- URL Authorization
- Request Filtering
- IP and Domain Restrictions

Selecting and implementing these security mechanisms is covered in Chapter 6, "Managing Web Server Security."

Performance Features

Organizations often find that they receive a large volume of activity on their production web servers, so it is fundamental for all types of web servers to be able to service a large number of requests in a given amount of time. IIS includes numerous architectural features that help make the servicing of web requests as efficient as possible. In addition, the Performance role services section includes two additional options:

- **Static Content Compression** The HTTP protocol provides a method by which static webpages (such as HTML files) can be compressed before they are sent to clients' web browsers. The web browser expands the information and renders the webpage. This method can save significant bandwidth with a minimal cost to CPU performance on the client and the server. In addition, IIS can store frequently accessed static content in memory, further increasing performance and scalability. This feature is enabled by default and works automatically as long as users' web browsers support HTTP compression.

- **Dynamic Content Compression** Dynamic content usually results in different information being sent to different users. Because dynamic content often changes for each request made to the web server, the amount of processing overhead for compressing the data can be significant. Dynamic content compression is disabled by default, but it can be added to help reduce bandwidth consumption for web applications.

In general, bandwidth is more limited than processing power is on modern servers. Therefore, unless an organization has a specific reason to disable it, it is recommended that static content compression remain enabled.

Management Tools

The Management Tools section provides administrators with the ability to determine which programs will be available for working with IIS. By default, only the primary administration tool, the IIS Management Console, is installed along with the Web Server (IIS) role. This tool provides a graphical method of configuring and managing IIS Web services. You can choose to remove the IIS Management Console if you will be managing the server remotely or if your corporate security policy requires it.

The other two available Management Tools options are IIS Management Scripts and Tools, which allows for command-line administration of IIS, and the Management Service, which enables you to administer IIS remotely by using the IIS Management Console.

An important design goal for IIS 7 was to provide support for IIS 6.0–based web applications. Although many applications can be moved directly to IIS 7, several backward-compatibility features are included as role services:

- IIS 6.Management Compatibility
- IIS 6 Metabase Compatibility
- IIS 6 WMI Compatibility
- IIS 6 Scripting Tools
- IIS 6 Management Console

You'll learn more about these features and how you can use them in Lesson 2, "Configuring Internet Information Services."

Installing the Web Server (IIS) Role

Although numerous features and options are available for the Web Server (IIS) role, installing the appropriate options is a simple task. Adding this role is the basis for providing web server functionality. Components of IIS are also required by several other features and options that are part of Windows Server 2008 R2. You begin the server role process by using the Add Roles Wizard in Server Manager. (See Figure 5-4.)

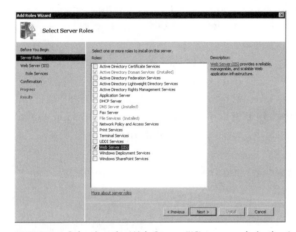

FIGURE 5-4 Selecting the Web Server (IIS) server role in the Add Roles Wizard.

The Add Roles Wizard evaluates the configuration of the local computer automatically and determines whether any additional role services are required. For example, if the Windows Process Activation Service has not yet been installed, you are prompted to add it.

The Web Services (IIS) step provides some introductory information about IIS. The note also provides information about installing Windows System Resource Manager (WSRM) to ensure performance if the computer will be servicing multiple roles.

The Select Role Services page enables you to decide which components of IIS will be installed as part of the role setup process, as shown in Figure 5-5. The default options provide a minimal set of features for the core web server role. As described later in this section, you can also add or remove role services after the Web Server (IIS) role has been enabled. Because some role features depend on other features, you might be prompted to add those dependencies when selecting an item.

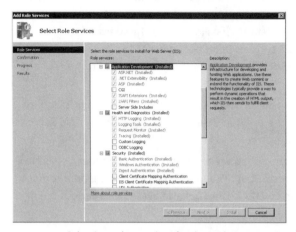

FIGURE 5-5 Selecting roles services for the Web Server (IIS) role.

The Confirm Installation Selections page provides you with a list of the configuration settings and role services you have chosen. After you review the list and click Finish, the installation process begins. Depending on which role services you've selected, the setup process might take significant time, require a restart of the computer, or both. If a restart is required, the Add Roles Wizard resumes from its previous ending point after you log on to the server again. Finally, on the Installation Results page (shown in Figure 5-6), you see a confirmation of which features have been installed and any additional information that should be noted.

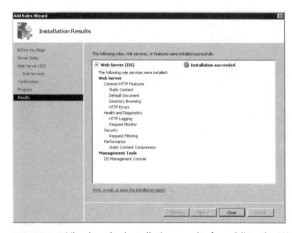

FIGURE 5-6 Viewing the installation results for adding the Web Server (IIS) server role.

Verifying the IIS Installation by Using Server Manager

After you have installed IIS, there are several ways in which you can verify that the web server processes are working properly. The first is by using the Server Manager tool. Expand the Roles section and then click Web Server (IIS) to view the relevant details. This page provides information on any event log items that need attention. In addition, it lists the services that have been installed, along with their current state. (See Figure 5-7.) The specific list of included items will vary based on which role services and dependencies you have installed. The World Wide Web Publishing Service (W3SVC) component is the main process responsible for responding to web requests.

Server Manager also shows information about which role services have been installed for the web server. (See Figure 5-8.) You can use the Add Role Services and Remove Role Services links to make changes to the configuration.

Finally, the Resources And Support section shows recommendations and other detailed information that can be helpful when you first set up IIS and the Web Server role on a computer. You learn more about these options in Lesson 2. Links are also available to various online resources for learning more about IIS.

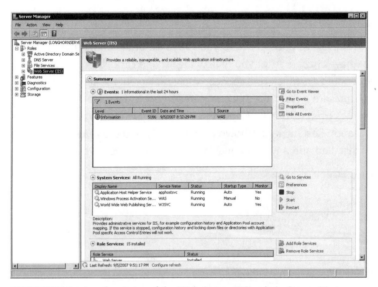

FIGURE 5-7 Viewing the status of the Web Server (IIS) role in Server Manager.

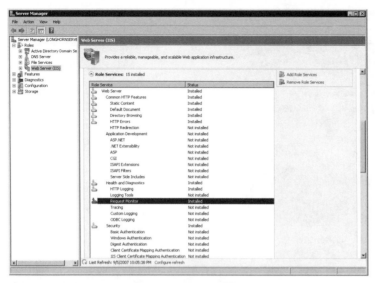

FIGURE 5-8 Viewing a list of installed role services in Server Manager.

Verifying the IIS Installation by Using Internet Explorer

When you add the Web Server (IIS) role to a computer running Windows Server 2008 R2, a default website that is configured to respond on HTTP port 80 is created automatically. The default location for this site is the *%SystemDrive%*\Inetpub\wwwroot folder. The default content includes only a simple static HTML page and an image file.

Because the purpose of IIS is to serve webpages, a good way to verify that it is working properly is to launch a web browser and connect to the local computer. You can use the built-in local alias by browsing to *http://localhost*, or you can use the local computer's fully qualified name (for example, *http://server1.contoso.local*). Using either method, you should see the default welcome page, as shown in Figure 5-9. When you click a language, the links take you automatically to the *http://www.iis.net* website (assuming that the server has access to the Internet).

It is also a good idea to attempt to access the IIS website from a remote computer. Just open any web browser and connect to the fully qualified address of the web server. If you are unable to connect, some of the likely causes are Domain Name System (DNS) name resolution issues or firewall configuration problems.

FIGURE 5-9 Viewing the default IIS website.

Managing Role Services

The modular architecture of IIS enables you to add or remove role services quickly and easily after the Web Server (IIS) role has been enabled on a computer running Windows Server 2008 or Windows Server 2008 R2. The most common reasons for changing the role service configuration are to support a new type of web application or web service. You can also remove services if they are no longer needed or if the technical requirements have changed. Because the removal or addition of a role service affects the configuration of the entire server, make sure to consider the potential effects on all the websites on the server.

To do this, open Server Manager, expand Roles, right-click Web Server (IIS), and choose either Add Role Services or Remove Role Services. The dialog box shows which components are installed. The check mark means that an item (or an item and all its children, if there are any) has been installed. A cleared check box indicates that the item has not been installed. A dimmed box means that some of the role services components have been installed.

When you add or remove role services, you receive a confirmation message, and then the process continues. If a restart of the computer is required, the configuration process resumes automatically whenever you next log on to the computer.

Using Command-Line and Automated Installation Options

Organizations that rely on IIS often need to deploy many installations of IIS. Although you can perform the process locally on each server, it is often more efficient to create scripts or commands for performing the necessary steps. There are several methods of performing automated and command-line-based installations.

The ServerManagerCmd.exe utility can be launched to install the Web Server (IIS) server role from the command line. For example, the *ServerManagerCmd.exe –install Web-Server* command attempts to install the default web server components. You can use the *ServerManagerCmd.exe –query* command to view which roles and features have been installed on the local computer, as shown in Figure 5-10. This can be helpful when you want to collect complete configuration information quickly to determine whether changes are required to support a new web application. For more information about using this command, type **ServerManagerCmd.exe -?** at a command prompt. You can also use this command to add or remove features such as WSRM.

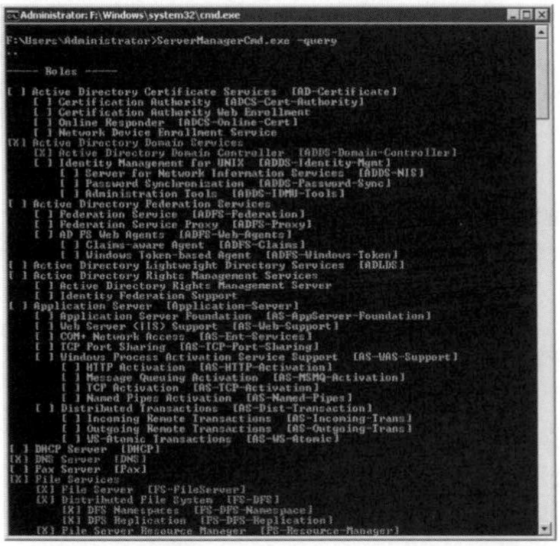

FIGURE 5-10 Viewing a list of installed role services and features by using *ServerManagerCmd.exe*.

> **NOTE** *SERVERMANAGERCMD.EXE* **IS DEPRECATED**
>
> Although *ServerManagerCmd.exe* will remain functional in both Windows Server 2008 and Windows Server 2008 R2, it might not be supported in future versions of Windows.

Another option for performing a command-line installation of the Web Server (IIS) server role is to use the Deployment Image Servicing and Management utility, Dism.exe. Dism enables you to install the Web Server (IIS) server role, its role services, and various features such as ASP.NET and the Management Service. To use Dism for this purpose, use the following syntax:

```
dism /online /enable-feature /featurename:name_of_feature
```

For example, to enable ASP.NET, type the following command:

```
dism /online /enable-feature /featurename:IIS-ASPNET
```

> **NOTE INSTALLING IIS ON SERVER CORE**
>
> You can use the Dism.exe utility to install IIS on a server core installation of Windows Server 2008 R2. For example, to perform a basic installation of IIS on a server core installation, type the following command at the command prompt:
>
> ```
> dism /online /enable-feature /featurename:IIS-WebServerRole
> ```
>
> For more information about installing, configuring, and managing IIS on a server core installation, visit *http://msdn.microsoft.com/en-us/gg981567*.

In Lesson 2, you learn how to use other commands to configure IIS further by using the command line or from within scripts.

Removing the Web Server (IIS) Role

If you no longer require an installation of Windows Server 2008 R2 to serve as a web server, you can remove IIS and all its related components by using the *Remove Roles* command in Server Manager. Keep in mind, however, that many components and features of the operating system might require the web server to be installed. If the Web Server (IIS) server role is removed, these features might become unavailable. Figure 5-11 shows the Confirm Removal Selections page.

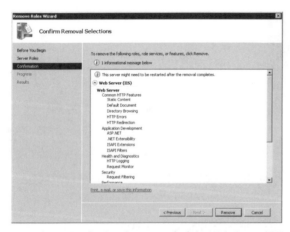

FIGURE 5-11 Confirming the removal of the Web Server (IIS) role.

Depending on which features were installed, it might be necessary to restart the computer during the removal process. If that is necessary, the process resumes automatically whenever a user next logs on to the computer.

Removing the Web Server (IIS) role removes all the binary files and role services associated with the web server. The basic server configuration, including the list of websites and their settings, is retained if you choose to reinstall the web server role. Actual website content is not deleted automatically. If you are planning to remove web services permanently from the server, manually delete any remaining webpages and data that are no longer required.

Using Windows System Resource Manager

An important consideration for any server is to ensure that critical services are not interrupted when the system is under load. By default, most services in Windows Server 2008 R2 run at an equal priority level. *Windows System Resource Manager* (WSRM) helps administrators assign priorities to various system processes such as IIS. Although WSRM is not a requirement for running IIS, on busy web servers or servers that are providing many important services, enabling this feature can be helpful. For example, administrators can create Resource Allocation policies to define CPU and memory limitations to ensure that the system continues to respond well even when under heavy load. (See Figure 5-12.)

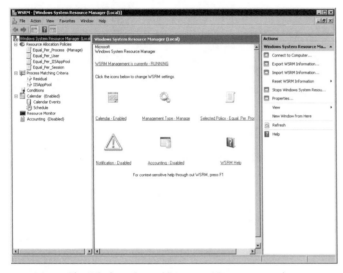

FIGURE 5-12 The Windows System Resource Manager console.

You can add WSRM to a computer running Windows Server 2008 R2 by using Server Manager. Right-click the Server Manager item and select Add Features to start the process. The Add Features Wizard includes an option to add WSRM. For more information about WSRM, in the Start menu Start Search box, type **system resource** and then press Enter. The help file includes details about creating and managing resource settings.

Quick Check

1. What are two methods by which you can verify a successful installation of the Web Server (IIS) role?

2. When can you add role services to the Web Server (IIS) server role?

Quick Check Answers

1. You can use Server Manager to verify that the proper services have been installed and started, and you can use Internet Explorer or another web browser to verify that the default website is responding.

2. You can add the role services when you initially add the server role, or you can add them after the Web Server (IIS) role has been enabled.

PRACTICE **Install and Verify the Web Server (IIS) Role**

In this practice, you perform the steps to install the Web Server (IIS) server role on the server2.contoso.local server. You must complete Exercise 1 before performing Exercise 2.

> **NOTE** **REMOVE ROLES ON SERVER2**
>
> Be sure to remove any roles installed on Server2 before beginning this exercise.

EXERCISE 1 Installing the Web Server Role

In this exercise, you perform the steps required to add the Web Server (IIS) server role. You install the service with only the basic role services enabled by default.

1. Log on to Contoso.local from Server2 as a domain administrator.

2. Open Server Manager. In the console tree, right-click Roles and then select Add Roles to open the Add Roles Wizard.

3. On the Before You Begin page, click Next.

4. On the Select Server Roles page, select the Web Server (IIS) server role and click Next.

5. On the Web Server (IIS) page, read the basic introductory information about IIS. You can use the Additional Information links to learn more about IIS and related components. Click Next.

6. On the Select Role Services page, the default selections include the components that are part of the basic Web Server (IIS) role. You can obtain more information about each item in the list by selecting it and reading the text on the right side of the page. Links to additional information in the help file are available for most items. For the purpose of this exercise, keep only the default options selected and then click Next. For a list of which options are selected by default, see Table 5-1.

7. On the Confirm Installation Selections page, verify the role service selections that will be included. Optionally, you can choose to print, email, or save the information to keep a record of which components were installed. When you are ready to begin the installation process, click Install.

8. When the installation process has completed, verify the installed roles and services on the Installation Results page. To complete the process, click Close.

EXERCISE 2   Verifying the IIS Installation

In this exercise, you verify the installation of the Web Server (IIS) role you added to server2. contoso.local in Exercise 1. Specifically, you use both Server Manager and Internet Explorer to ensure that IIS is working properly.

1. If you have not done so already, log on to Contoso.local from Server2 as a domain administrator.

2. In Server Manager, expand the *Roles* node and then click Web Server (IIS).

   You see a summary of information about the Web Server role. The Events section displays any important messages related to the Web Server (IIS) server role.

3. In the System Services section, verify that the World Wide Web Publishing Service (W3SVC) is started. You also see the Application Host Helper Service (apphostsvc) and the Windows Process Activation Service (WAS). If either of these services is stopped, click it and choose to start it.

4. In the Role Services section, view a list of the installed items and verify that all the default options have been installed. (The list of default role services is provided in Table 5-1 in Lesson 1, "Installing the Web Server (IIS) Role.")

5. Close Server Manager and open Internet Explorer. In the Address box, type **http://localhost** and then press Enter. You should see the default IIS welcome page.

6. In the Internet Explorer Address box, type **http://server2.contoso.local** and press Enter. You should again see the IIS welcome page. Close Internet Explorer.

7. When you are finished, close Server Manager.

Lesson Summary

- The Web Server (IIS) role is designed to provide access to website content by using the HTTP protocol.

- The Application Server role provides support to applications that require features of the .NET Framework 3.0, COM+, and distributed transactions.

- You can use Windows System Resource Manager (WSRM) to assign resource allocation rules to various workloads and services, such as IIS.

- IIS 7 role services include features for application development, health and diagnostics, security, performance, and management.

- You can use Server Manager to add the Web Server (IIS) server role and to manage role services.
- You can verify the installation of IIS by using Server Manager or by browsing to the default website by using Internet Explorer.

Lesson Review

You can use the following questions to test your knowledge of the information in Lesson 1, "Installing the Web Server (IIS) Role." The questions are also available on the companion CD if you prefer to review them in electronic form.

1. You are a systems administrator who is attempting to troubleshoot a problem with accessing a website on a computer running Windows Server 2008 R2. In the past, users have been able to access the website by using *http://hr.contoso.com*. However, when they attempt to access the site now, they receive the error message, "Internet Explorer Cannot Display The Web page." Which of the following steps should you take to resolve the error?

   A. Using Server Manager, add the HTTP Errors role service.

   B. Using Server Manager, verify that the World Wide Web Publishing Service has been started.

   C. Verify the configuration of the users' web browsers.

   D. Using Server Manager, add the HTTP Logging role service.

   E. Using Server Manager, click Web Server (IIS) in the list of roles and verify that the IIS Admin Service has been started.

2. Your network includes a Server Core installation of Windows Server 2008 R2 named Web-Core-01. Web-Core-01 has the Web Server (IIS) server role installed. Which utility can you use to install the ASP.NET feature on the server?

   A. Wdsutil.exe

   B. Wbadmin.exe

   C. Dism.exe

   D. Slmgr.vbs

3. Your network contains a web server named Web01 that is running Windows Server 2008 R2. Web01 has the Web Server (IIS) feature installed. Which role service do you need to install on Web01 to enable remote management of this server?

   A. Directory Browsing

   B. ASP.NET

   C. Management Server

   D. IIS Management Console

Lesson 2: Configuring Internet Information Services

After you have installed the Web Server (IIS) role, you will likely need to create and manage websites and enable specific features that are required by your applications. The details of these tasks will be based on the type of web services you require and the way IIS will be used. Considerations include migrating websites from previous versions of IIS and managing multiple sites and applications on the same server. IIS includes several useful management tools and methods for simplifying administration. In this lesson, you learn about how to manage websites and server settings for the Web Server (IIS) role in Windows Server 2008 and Windows Server 2008 R2.

> **MORE INFO** **SECURING IIS**
>
> One of the most important considerations for production web servers is managing security settings and permissions. This lesson focuses on configuring web applications and features other than security. For more information about authentication and authorization approaches, see Chapter 6.

After this lesson, you will be able to:

- Use the IIS Manager utility to connect to and manage server settings for the Web Server role.
- Create and configure settings for websites, including site bindings.
- Create and manage new web applications within websites.
- Describe the purpose of application pools and manage application pool settings for websites and web applications.
- Create and manage virtual directories.
- Use *AppCmd.exe* to perform common IIS web server administration tasks.
- Describe how IIS 7 manages configuration settings stored in the ApplicationHost. config and Web.config files.
- Provide support for migrating applications from IIS 6.0.

Estimated lesson time: 75 minutes

Working with IIS Management Tools

As you learned in Lesson 1, IIS includes many features and options that can be enabled to meet technical and business requirements. The Internet Information Services (IIS) Manager utility is the primary tool you use to configure and manage websites and their related settings. It is installed automatically when you add the Web Server (IIS) server role to a computer running Windows Server 2008 or Windows Server 2008 R2 using the default options. You can launch it by selecting Internet Information Services (IIS) Manager from the Administrative Tools program group. Figure 5-13 shows the user interface.

FIGURE 5-13 Using the IIS Manager console to connect to the local server.

By default, IIS Manager connects to the local server. This enables you to make configuration changes to the server and other settings for this computer. IIS Manager has been designed to provide a vast array of information by using simple and consistent user interface features. The left pane shows information about the server to which you are connected. You can expand these branches to view information about websites and other objects that are hosted on that server. Some items contain additional commands that are available by right-clicking the object name.

Using the Features Views

The center pane of the display provides details and options that are related to the selected item in the left pane. Two main views can be selected at the bottom of the screen. Features View shows a list of all the available settings that can be configured for the selected item. The specific list of items varies based on which role servers you have added to the server's configuration. The Group By drop-down list enables you to specify how you want the various items to be displayed. The options are:

- **No Grouping** All items are displayed alphabetically in a single list.
- **Category** Items are grouped based on their functional areas (for example, Performance and Security).
- **Area** Items are groups based on the configuration areas they will affect.

Figure 5-14 shows the items displayed when the server item is selected in the left pane and when the Category grouping is selected. In addition to these options, you can use the *View* command in the View menu to display the items by Details, Icons, Tiles, or List options. The overall layout is similar to that of Windows Explorer. It is designed to organize and display a large number of settings in a way that is easy for systems administrators to understand and manage.

FIGURE 5-14 Viewing IIS Manager configuration items grouped by category.

Double-clicking specific features loads a separate options page that enables you to modify those settings.

EXAM TIP

Learning about the many features and options that are part of the IIS platform can be daunting, especially if you're not already familiar with web development and management. There's no substitute for doing, so a good way to prepare for the exam is simply to access the various properties pages for the many features and role services that are available. Reviewing all available options can be helpful when deciding how best to meet specific requirements, both on the exam and in the real world.

Using the Content View

Content View is designed to show the files and folders that are part of a website. It displays details in a Windows Explorer format and offers the ability to filter and group the list of files. (See Figure 5-15.) Content View is most useful when you are managing site content rather than site settings. It is similar to default display in the management tools from previous versions of IIS.

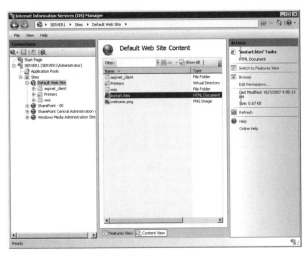

FIGURE 5-15 Using Content View in IIS Manager.

> **MORE INFO** **TRANSITIONING FROM IIS 6.0**
>
> If you're moving to IIS 7 after having worked with IIS 6, rest assured that all the functionality you're used to seeing is still here. Roughly speaking, the Features View is a replacement for the properties pages that were available for configuring an IIS 6 web server. Content View shows the information about the files and folders within each selected website and directory in a way that is similar to the right-side pane in IIS 6. The goal in IIS 7 is to organize the presentation of a wide range of options without overwhelming systems administrators.

Using the Actions Pane

The right side of the IIS Manager screen displays the Actions pane. The specific commands that appear here are context-sensitive. For example, when you select a website, you see actions for browsing to the website and for stopping, starting, or restarting the website. (See Figure 5-16.) Furthermore, when you are changing settings for specific features, you generally find Accept and Cancel links within the Actions pane.

FIGURE 5-16 Viewing commands for managing a website in the IIS Manager Actions pane.

Creating and Configuring Websites

Although some web servers might be responsible primarily for hosting only a single website, it is much more common for a single IIS server to host many web services and applications. Before you learn how to administer IIS, it is important to understand how the different web server components and objects fit together.

Understanding Sites and Site Bindings

Websites are the top-level containers that provide access to web content. Every website must map to a physical path on the server. Generally, this path contains the root folder for all content that will be available to users who access the site.

The configuration of the website specifies which protocols, ports, and other settings connect to the web server. This information is known collectively as a *site binding*. Each site can have multiple bindings, based on the needs of the server. The details that can be specified in a site binding include:

- **Type** Specifies the protocol that connects to the web server. The two default options are HTTP and HTTPS.

> **NOTE** **SUPPORTING OTHER PROTOCOLS**
>
> One of the benefits of the Windows Process Activation Service (WAS) is that it enables IIS 7 to create sites that respond to protocols other than HTTP and HTTPS. For the purpose of taking the exam (and the content in this chapter), you learn primarily about working with the two most common web server protocols. When supporting distributed applications, such as those that use the WCF, keep in mind that IIS sites can support direct TCP connections and other methods of communications.

- **IP Address** The list of IPv4 or IPv6 addresses on which the server responds. If the server is configured with more than one IP address, different websites can be configured to respond to each. In addition to selecting a specific IP address, administrators can also choose the (All Unassigned) option to allow the website to respond to a request on any interface that doesn't have an explicit port and protocol binding.

- **Port** Specifies the TCP port on which the server listens and responds. The default port for HTTP connections is port 80. Users who need to access websites on alternative ports must specify the port number in their URL. For example, the *http://Server1.contoso.local:5937* URL address will attempt to connect to the web server named Server1.contoso.local by using the HTTP protocol on TCP port 5937. The standard range for TCP ports is between 1 and 65535. Generally, many of the port numbers under 1024 are reserved for use by specific well-known applications, although there is no technical reason they cannot be used for hosting a website.

- **Host Name** This text setting allows multiple websites to share the same protocol type, IP address, and port number while still allowing users to connect to different websites. The method works by interpreting the host header information stored in an HTTP request. Site administrators can configure their DNS settings to allow multiple domain names to point to the same IP address. The web server then uses the domain name information to determine the website to which the user is attempting to connect and to generate the response from the appropriate site.

The combination of site binding settings must be unique for every website hosted on an installation of IIS. For example, no two websites can respond using the same protocol, IP address, port, and host name setting. Although it is possible to create multiple sites with the same site bindings, IIS will allow only one of these sites to be started at a time.

EXAM TIP

You need to understand bindings for the 70-643 exam.

Managing the Default Web Site

Initially, the Web Server (IIS) role includes a site called Default Web Site. In IIS 7.5, the Default Web Site is initially configured to respond to HTTP requests over port 80 at all local server IP addresses that are not assigned to other sites. To view a list of the bindings, right-click the Default Web Site in IIS Manager (see Figure 5-17) and select Edit Bindings. (You can also use the Bindings link in the Actions pane to open the same dialog box.)

When you launch a web browser and connect to a URL, such as *http://server2.contoso.local*, IIS receives the request on HTTP port 80 and returns the content from the appropriate website.

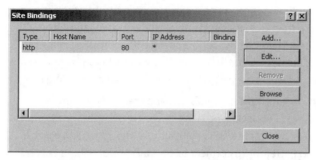

FIGURE 5-17 Viewing the site bindings for the Default Web Site.

To add a new site binding for the Default Web Site, click Add in the Site Bindings dialog box. As shown in Figure 5-18, you can specify the protocol type, IP address, and port information along with an optional host name. If you attempt to add a site binding that is already in use, you are reminded that you must configure a unique binding.

FIGURE 5-18 Adding a new site binding to the Default Web Site.

Adding Websites

Start the process of adding a new website to IIS by right-clicking the *Sites* container in IIS Manager and selecting Add Web Site. Figure 5-19 shows the available options for the new site.

FIGURE 5-19 Adding a new website by using IIS Manager.

In addition to specifying the default protocol binding for the site, you must provide the site name. This setting is simply a logical name that users of the site do not see. By default, IIS Manager creates a new application pool with the same name you provide for the website. You can also select an existing application pool by clicking Select. You learn more about application pools and their purpose later in this lesson.

The Content Directory section enables you to provide the full physical path to the folder that will be the root of the website. The default root location for IIS web content is *%SystemDrive%* \Inetpub\wwwroot. The initial files for the Default Web Site are located in this folder. You should create a new folder (either within this path or in another one) to store the content of the new website. The *Connect As* button enables you to specify the security credentials that IIS uses to access the content. The default setting is Pass-Through Authentication, which means that the security context of the requesting web user is used. You learn more about securing website content in Chapter 6.

The final check box enables you to specify whether you want the site to be started immediately after you click OK. Again, you are given a warning if the website binding information is already in use, as shown in Figure 5-20.

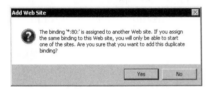

FIGURE 5-20 Attempting to create a new website by using duplicate binding information.

After you click OK to add the website, it appears within the left pane of IIS Manager. Websites can be started and stopped individually by selecting them and using the commands in the Actions pane or by right-clicking and selecting the Manage Web Site menu. Other details, such as site bindings, can also be modified at any time. This enables you to create, reconfigure, and stop sites individually without affecting other sites on the same server. In addition to the basic site-related settings, some configuration settings are defined at the site level.

Configuring Web Site Limits Settings

Web Site Limits settings place maximum limitations on the amount of bandwidth and the number of connections that can be supported by the website. These settings enable systems administrators to ensure that one or more sites on the server do not use excessive network bandwidth or consume too many resources. To configure website limits, select the appropriate website and click the *Limits* command in the Actions pane. Figure 5-21 shows the default settings for a new website.

FIGURE 5-21 Configuring bandwidth usage and user connection limits for a website.

The Limit Bandwidth Usage option (which is initially disabled) enables you to enter the maximum number of bytes per second that the web server will support. If this limit is exceeded, the web server throttles responses by adding a time delay.

The Connection Limits section refers to the maximum number of user connections that can be active on the site. Each user connection is timed out automatically if a new request is not received within the specified number of seconds. (The default is 120 seconds, or two minutes.) In addition, you can configure the maximum number of connections allowed for the site. If this number is exceeded, users who attempt to make a new connection receive an error message stating that the server is too busy to respond.

Configuring Site Logging Settings

Another site-level setting is Logging. You can access these properties by selecting the appropriate website and, in the Features View, double-clicking Logging. Figure 5-22 shows the default options for logging.

FIGURE 5-22 Configuring logging settings for a website.

The specific options that are available are based on which role services were installed for the web server. By default, each new site is configured to store text-based log files within the %SystemDrive%\Inetpub\Logs\LogFiles path on the local server. Each website will be assigned its own folder, and each folder will contain one or more log files. You can choose from different log file formats, but the default is the W3C format, which is a standard that can be used to compare log information from different web server platforms. The *Select Fields* button enables you to determine which information is stored in the log file. The default field settings are designed to provide a good balance between performance and useful information. Adding fields can affect web server performance adversely and increase log file size, so add only the information you plan to use in later analysis.

On busy web servers, log files grow quickly. Because the log files are text based, it can often be difficult to manage and analyze large files. The Log File Rollover section enables you to specify when IIS will create a new log file. By default, a new log file is created daily. You can choose a different time interval, or you can specify the maximum size of each log file. There is also an option to use only a single log file. Although it is possible to obtain information by opening the log files in a text viewer, such as Notepad, it is much more common to use log analysis utilities to parse the results.

> **NOTE   LOG PARSER**
>
> Log Parser is a free utility that you can use to view logs and other data sources. You can download Log Parser from the Microsoft Download Center at *http://download .microsoft.com*.

Understanding Web Applications

It is common in many web server usage scenarios for a single site to provide access to different types of content. Web applications are created within websites to point to the physical location of a set of content files. For example, an online news site might include two web applications: one for registered users and one for nonregistered users. Each web application can point to a separate physical folder on the computer so IIS can determine how to process the requests. Web applications can also use other methods to ensure that the same content (such as news stories) is available to both sites.

Creating Web Applications

You can create new web applications easily by using IIS Manager. Right-click the website within which you want to create a web application and then select Add Application. Figure 5-23 shows the available options. The first setting option is the alias that will be used for the site. This is the name that users will type as part of their URL to connect to the content. For example, if a new web application with the alias Engineering is created within the default website, visitors will use a URL such as *http://server1.contoso.local/Engineering* to access the content. You learn about application pool setting later in this lesson.

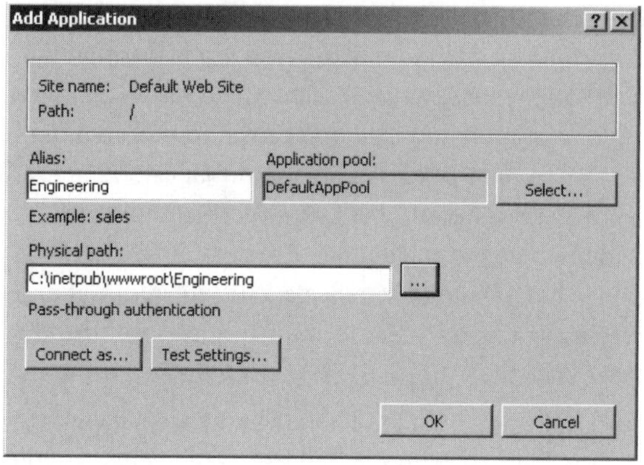

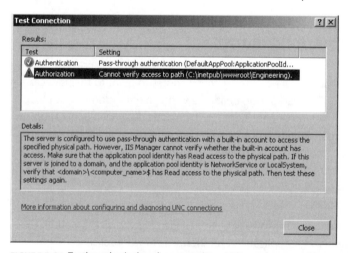

FIGURE 5-23 Adding a new web application to a website.

The Physical Path option enables you to specify the folder in which the content for the web application will be stored. Generally, the file system location should be unique and not shared with other web applications. As with the process of creating a site, you can keep the default setting of Pass-Through Authentication or click Connect As to specify a username and password to use. The *Test Settings* button enables you to verify the connection details you have entered (if any). The Test Connection dialog box, as shown in Figure 5-24, states that if you keep the default setting, IIS Manager will be unable to verify the authorization permissions. (You learn more about authentication and authorization in Chapter 6.) This is because the specific user context is not defined until a user attempts to access the content.

FIGURE 5-24 Testing physical path connection settings when creating a new web application.

To finish the creation of the web application, click OK. You now see a new web application under the site object in IIS Manager. You can now also modify other settings for the web application by using the Features View.

Managing Web Application Settings

By default, many of the settings for a new web application are inherited automatically from the website in which it was created. This enables you to use the same default settings easily for each new site. In most cases, you can also override the settings at the web application level based on specific needs of the application. To do this, double-click any of the items in the Features view and make the corresponding changes at the web application level. Most of these settings override those assigned for the parent site.

Working with Application Pools

One of the primary concerns with managing web servers is the potential for one website or application to affect operations of others on the same computer negatively. Issues such as memory leaks or application bugs can cause a loss of service or reduced performance for many web applications. *Application pools* are reserved sections of physical memory designed to isolate different sites from each other so that failures and other problems can be contained. Within each application pool, worker processes are actually responsible for completing web requests. Each application pool contains its own set of worker processes, so it is impossible for problems in one pool to affect processes in another. Application pools can also be started and stopped independently.

By default, IIS 7.5 includes the DefaultAppPool application pool. DefaultAppPool, as its name implies, supports the Default Web Site.

By default, IIS Manager creates a new application pool when you create a new website. The application pool will have the same name as the site. This is the recommended approach because it allows the processes within each website to run independently of others. When you create a new web application, you can select from any of the available application pools.

Creating Application Pools

The IIS Manager console tree includes an *Application Pools* container that enables you to manage application pools on the web server. The default display shows all the application pools that currently exist on the server, along with their current status and settings. (See Figure 5-25.)

To create a new application pool, right-click the *Application Pools* object and select Add Application Pool. Figure 5-26 shows the available options. Systems administrators use the name option to identify the purpose of the application pool. If you are creating this object to support a specific website, include identifying information in the name. The .NET Framework version options are based on the versions that are available on the local computer. By default, the .NET Framework 2.0.50727 and No Managed Code options are offered. The latter option specifies that .NET functionality will not be available for web applications that are part of the pool.

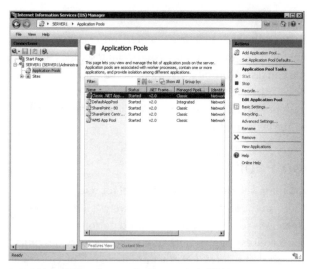

FIGURE 5-25 Managing application pools in IIS Manager.

FIGURE 5-26 Creating a new application pool.

Managed Pipeline Mode specifies the method that is supported for code that needs to intercept and modify web request processing. Two modes are available: Classic and Integrated. The Classic option supports ASP.NET applications that were written for previous versions of IIS and that depend on integrating with request pipeline events. The Integrated mode provides better performance and functionality for ASP.NET applications and is recommended for web applications that do not depend directly on the Classic Managed Pipeline Mode. Finally, you can choose whether you want to start the application pool immediately.

Managing Application Pools

Each application pool that is present on a web server can be started and stopped independently. Stopping an application pool prevents requests from being processed by any applications that are part of that pool. Users who attempt to access content from these sites receive an error message stating HTTP Error 503, "Service Unavailable." It is a good idea to verify which applications are using an application pool before you stop it. You can do this by right-clicking one of the application pool items in IIS Manager and selecting View Applications.

Configuring Recycling Settings

An alternative to stopping an application pool is to recycle it using the *Recycle* command in the Applications Pool Tasks menu in the Actions pane. This command instructs IIS to retire any current worker process automatically after it has executed existing requests. The benefit is that users will not see a disruption to service on their computers, but the worker process will be replaced by a new one as quickly as possible. Recycling application pools is generally done when issues such as memory leaks or resource usage tend to increase significantly over time. Often, the cause of this problem is a defect or other problem in the application code. The ideal solution is to correct the underlying application problem. However, it is possible at least to address the symptoms by using the *Recycle* command.

In some cases, you might automatically recycle worker processes based on resource usage or at specific times. You can access these options by clicking the *Recycling* command under Edit Application Pool in the Actions pane, as displayed in Figure 5-25. Doing this opens the Edit Application Pool Recycling Settings dialog box. (See Figure 5-27.)

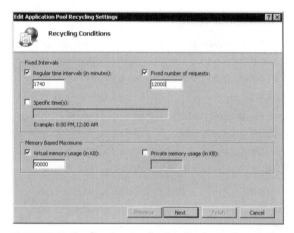

FIGURE 5-27 Configuring Application Pool recycling settings.

The primary options for recycling settings are either Fixed Intervals (which are based on specific times or after a fixed number of requests is processed) or Memory Based Maximums. The most appropriate options are based on the specific problems you are trying to trouble-shoot or avoid. In general, recycling application pools too quickly can reduce performance. However, if a web application has serious problems, it is preferable to address them through recycling worker processes before users see slowdowns or errors on the website.

Keeping track of application pool recycle events is also an important part of ensuring that your web server and its applications are running as expected. For example, if you set the maximum memory settings, you will likely want to know how often the application pool has been recycled. Figure 5-28 shows the Recycling Events To Log step that enables you to define which events are recorded. To view the Recycling Events To Log page, click Next.

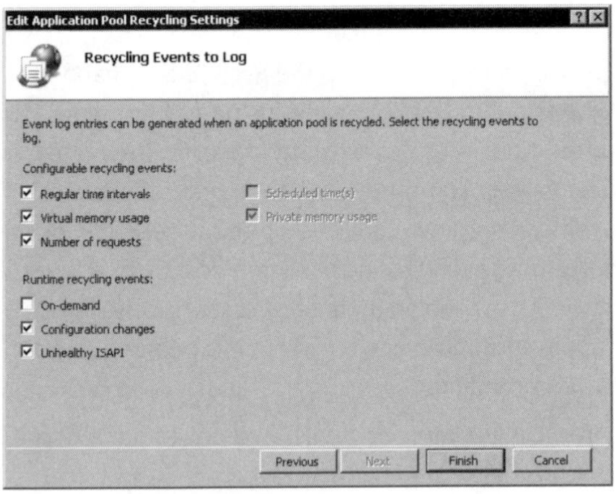

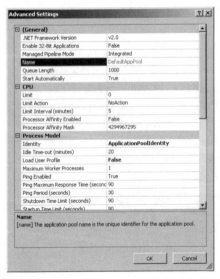

FIGURE 5-28 Choosing which recycling events should be logged.

Configuring Advanced Application Pool Settings

In addition to the basic configuration settings and recycling options for an application pool, systems administrators can configure additional details to control the behavior of worker processes. To access these settings, select an application pool in IIS Manager and click the Advanced Settings link in the Actions pane. (See Figure 5-29.)

The options allow for setting detailed parameters related to CPU and memory resource usage. In general, you should not change these parameters manually unless you are reasonably sure of their intended effects. Some modifications can result in reducing processing speed for the applications that are part of the pool. Others can result in reserving or using too many system resources for a particular pool.

FIGURE 5-29 Configuring Advanced Settings for an application pool.

Working with Virtual Directories

A common requirement within websites is to include content from folders located outside the websites' primary folder structures. For example, multiple websites that share the same set of images might need to access a pointer to a single path from which they can all access files. Virtual directories are designed to provide this capability and can be created either at the level of a website or within a specific web application. They include an alias name (which will be used in the requesting URL) and point to a physical file system location path.

Creating a Virtual Directory

The process of creating a virtual directory is similar to that of creating a web application. In IIS Manager, right-click the appropriate parent website or web application and then select Add Virtual Directory. You will be able to provide an alias for the virtual directory (such as Images) along with security credentials and the physical path to the virtual directory. When a request is received for this alias, IIS will look in the appropriate file system location automatically for the requested content.

Comparing Virtual Directories and Web Applications

Although the settings for a virtual directory are similar to those of a web application, there are some differences in their usage. Web applications are generally designed to support executable web code, such as applications built using ASP.NET. They run within an isolated process space by using WAS. The reliance on WAS also enables web applications to respond by using protocols other than HTTP and HTTPS (assuming that other protocols have been installed and configured on the local server).

Virtual directories, however, primarily point to static content stored in an alternate file system location. Both web applications and virtual directories form a portion of the complete URL that accesses a website. They can also both be nested to provide access to multiple levels of site content. The more appropriate choice will be based on the requirements of the web application you plan to support.

> **MORE INFO**   **KEEPING THE CONFIGURATION SIMPLE**
>
> Web applications and virtual directories offer a lot of power and flexibility for both web server administrators and web developers. In general, try to keep your configurations as simple and intuitive as possible. For example, although both types of objects can be nested within each other, complex nesting can be confusing (especially if some of the objects share the same names). Overall, keep management of the website in mind when creating and designing the site structure.

Using Command-Line Management

Performing simple administrator tasks on a few IIS servers is a relatively simple process on the IIS Manager console. However, when you want to commit the same changes on many servers, or you want to automate the configuration process by using scripting, command-line utilities can make these tasks more efficient. IIS includes an executable command, *AppCmd.exe*, which provides a simple way for systems administrators to perform common operational tasks. The actual parameters are designed to map to the structure of IIS websites, web applications, and virtual directories.

The AppCmd.exe file is located within the *%SystemRoot%*\System32\Inetsrv folder. You can get initial help for the utility by running the command with the *-/?* switch. (See Figure 5-30.) You can use the same switch to get additional details about other commands. The general syntax for the command is:

```
AppCmd.exe Command Object "ObjectName" /parameter:value
```

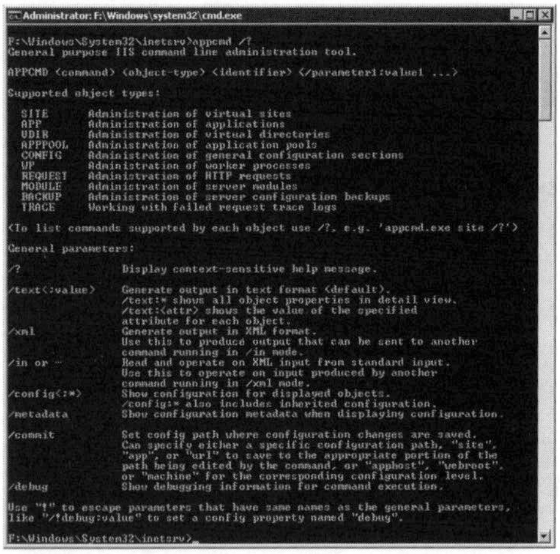

FIGURE 5-30 Viewing help for the AppCmd.exe utility.

Understanding Command Options

AppCmd has been designed to use a simple set of six commands for performing tasks on objects. The list of commands includes:

- **List**   Returns information about the specified object.
- **Add**   Creates a new object of the type that is specified. Details can be added by using parameters and values.
- **Delete**   Deletes the specified object (such as a website or web application).
- **Set**   Changes settings for the object, as specified by the parameters and values.
- **Start/Stop**   Available for objects that support these actions (such as a website).

If you want to perform multiple operations (either from a script file or from the command line), you must call *AppCmd.exe* for each operation. This helps keep the syntax of the statements simple and easy to read.

Understanding Objects

In a standard *AppCmd* statement, you must provide an object type and the name of the object you plan to use. The types of objects supported by *AppCmd.exe* include the following:

- *App (Web Application)*
- *AppPool (Application Pool)*
- *Backup (Server configuration backups)*
- *Config (Server configuration information)*
- *Module*
- *Request*
- *Site (Web Site)*
- *Trace*
- *VDir (Virtual Directory)*
- *WP (Worker Process)*

You can get more information about the parameters and values that apply to an object by typing **-?** after the command.

```
Appcmd site -?
```

Examples of Commands

The process of listing, creating, and managing IIS configuration settings by using *AppCmd* is generally fairly simple. Table 5-2 provides some examples of common commands and their purposes.

TABLE 5-2 Sample Commands for AppCmd.exe

COMMAND	PURPOSE
AppCmd list site	Returns a list of websites on the local server
AppCmd add site /name:TestSite01	Adds a new website called TestSite01
AppCmd add app /site.name Contoso /path: /Marketing/physicalPath:c:\Application	Adds an application named Marketing to a site named Contoso, with content at c:\Application
AppCmd add vdir /app.name:"Default Web Site/" /path:/Images /physicalPath:"C:\Inetpub \wwwroot\images"	Adds a new virtual directory with the alias images, and points to the specified physical file system location

AppCmd list request	Returns a list of currently running web server requests
AppCmd list config	Returns the entire contents of the current web server configuration in XML format
AppCmd set config-section: SampleConfigurationSection/enabled:true	Sets the enabled property on a section of the XML configuration file for the entire server
AppCmd set app /site.name Contoso /path: /Accounting/physicalPath:d:\Accounting	Sets the location of an existing web application named Accounting, in a site named Contoso, to the d:\Accounting path

Using Windows PowerShell

In addition to using the AppCmd utility, web server administrators can use the command shell and scripting language, Windows PowerShell. In Windows Server 2008 R2, Windows PowerShell 2.0 is installed and enabled by default. *Windows PowerShell* enables you to write and create powerful scripts for performing many common administration operations.

Windows Server 2008 R2 includes a module that contains many new cmdlets for IIS administration. You can add this IIS Module manually by typing **add-pssnapin WebAdministration** at a Windows PowerShell prompt.

The following Windows PowerShell cmdlets are useful for IIS administration.

- **Get-PSProvider**   Verifies that the WebAdministration PowerShell module is installed.
- **Get-ChildItem IIS:**   Displays a list of items in the root of the IIS namespace.
- **Get-ChildItem IIS:\Site**   Displays a list of websites on the server.
- **Install-ADServiceAccount**   This cmdlet is not specific to the IIS module, but it is useful for IIS administration. It installs an existing Active Directory managed service account on the computer on which the cmdlet is run. The password of the service account is then periodically reset without user interaction.

Configuring Managed Service Accounts

Managed service accounts (MSAs) are a new feature in Windows Server 2008 R2. MSAs are AD DS accounts tied to a particular computer whose passwords are generated and updated automatically. These accounts are useful to run services in an isolated security context, as an alternative to running services within the shared context of the Local System account. To use MSAs, your Active Directory schema must be extended to Windows Server 2008 R2. In addition, to receive the benefit of full automated management from an MSA, the local AD DS domain must operate at the Windows Server 2008 R2 functional level.

MSAs are created and configured by using Windows PowerShell. To begin the process of creating an MSA, first install the Windows feature named "Active Directory module for Windows PowerShell" on the computer running Windows Server 2008 R2 on which you want to install the managed service account. (You can find this feature in the Add Features Wizard in the Remote Server Administration Tools feature group, beneath the Role Administration Tools and AD DS and AD LDS Tools subgroups.) After you install this feature, access Active Directory Module For Windows PowerShell in Administrative Tools and choose to run it as Administrator. When the prompt appears, type the following to create a new MSA: **New-ADServiceAccount -Name <MSA account name> -Enabled $true**, where <MSA account name> is the unique name you want to assign the managed service account. Then, type the following to install the MSA on the local computer: **Install-ADServiceAccount -Identity <MSA account name>**, where <MSA account name> is the name of the account you just created in the previous step. Finally, use the Services console to specify the account on the Log On tab for the desired service or services. When typing the name of the account, be sure to add a "$" after the name. For example, if you created an account named IISaccount in the domain Contoso, type **contoso\ IISaccount$** in the This Account text box on the Log On tab for the desired services. (For IIS, those services are typically Application Host Helper Service and the World Wide Web Publishing Service.)

MORE INFO **LEARNING WINDOWS POWERSHELL**

Although a complete description of how to use PowerShell is beyond the scope of this book (and the 70-643 exam), you can find more information about using it to manage IIS by searching for PowerShell at *http://www.iis.net*. The Microsoft TechNet Scripting with Windows PowerShell website offers tutorials and examples for creating new scripts at *http://www.microsoft.com/technet/scriptcenter/hubs/msh.mspx*.

EXAM TIP

Know at least the AppCmd commands and Windows PowerShell cmdlets covered in this section for the exam. You should also review others found at *http://support.microsoft.com/ kb/930909* and *http://technet.microsoft.com/en-us/library/ee790599.aspx*.

Automation Using .NET Framework

Many web developers already have a significant amount of knowledge about working with the .NET Framework. Therefore, it can be helpful for them to manage IIS by using standard .NET code. IIS 7 provides two .NET namespaces you can use to manage IIS configuration settings programmatically. They are:

- **Microsoft.Web.Administration** This namespace provides objects and methods that are useful for managing and changing web server settings. It is focused primarily on performing configuration changes for an IIS web server.

- **Microsoft.Web.Management** Although the default IIS Manager user interface has been designed to provide simple access to the majority of commonly used functionality, some environments might want to create their own management extensions for performing specific tasks. The *Microsoft.Web.Management* namespace includes objects and methods that enable developers to extend the user interface functionality of IIS management tools. These additions can then be configured to run in a stand-alone environment, or they can be integrated with the built-in IIS Manager utility for easy access.

Understanding how to write applications by using the .NET Framework is beyond the scope of the 70-643 exam, but it can be helpful to know that these options are available for automating configuration and management tasks. Additional information about the namespaces mentioned here and others can be found at *http://msdn2.microsoft.com/en-us /library/aa388745.aspx*.

Managing Web Server Configuration Files

Although it is easiest to make configuration settings on one or a few servers by using graphical tools, systems administrators often need to configure many web servers. In addition to using IIS Manager and related tools for configuring settings, you can also configure your web server by using XML configuration files. Moreover, by storing settings in a single file, you can back up and restore settings to other IIS installations easily. In this section, you'll learn about where web server and website settings are stored.

Understanding ApplicationHost.config

All the configuration settings that have been defined for the local IIS web server are stored in an XML text file named ApplicationHost.config. The default file system location for these files is *%SystemDrive%*\Inetpub\History. Within this base folder is a series of folders, each of which contains a copy of the ApplicationHost.config file. The ApplicationHost Helper Service, a default component included when you install the Web Server (IIS) role, automatically makes periodic backups of the configuration of the local web server. This process automatically creates a new folder and a copy of the ApplicationHost.config file. The schema subfolder contains a file that describes and interprets the specific settings that can be used in the configuration files.

An *ApplicationHost.config file* can be opened and modified by using a standard text editor (such as Notepad) or by using an XML-aware application (such as Visual Studio). The contents are arranged in a hierarchy that defines the various settings and options that can be configured within IIS. (See Figure 5-31.) Before you make changes directly to a configuration file, be sure to make a backup copy of it. It is fairly easy to introduce changes that can cause errors in IIS.

FIGURE 5-31 Using Internet Explorer to view a backed-up version of the ApplicationHost.config file.

Restoring the ApplicationHost.config File

If you need to revert the configuration of IIS to an earlier state by using the automatic backup files, you can copy over the working config file manually. The active version of the ApplicationHost.config file is in the *%SystemRoot%*\System32\Inetsrv\Config folder. To roll back the configuration of IIS, find the ApplicationHost.config version you want to use and then copy it over the current file. Note that for the changes to be reflected, it might be necessary to restart the web server and IIS Manager. It is also highly recommended to copy the current configuration file to a backup location in case you need to refer to it later.

Understanding Web.config Files

A common problem related to managing web applications and websites is retaining settings as sites are moved between servers. In previous versions of IIS, it was often necessary to re-create settings manually to ensure that the site would run properly. IIS 7 uses a hierarchical approach to create and manage configuration settings. In addition to the server-level settings that are defined in the ApplicationHost.config file, systems administrators and web developers can include other settings in Web.config files.

Web.config files can be located within the root folder for a website or web application. These files can contain settings that override the default server-level settings included in the ApplicationHost.config file. The formats of the files and options are similar. By default, a new Web.config file is created automatically whenever you add a new website or a new web application. The default settings are inherited from the server-level settings unless you specifically change them.

Overall, the hierarchy for configuration files is:

1. Host (ApplicationHost.config)

2. Site (Web.config)

3. Application (Web.config)

Settings in lower-level files can override settings defined in the parent. A benefit of this approach is that the configuration information is included automatically when you choose to copy an entire folder of web content to another server or to another location on the same server.

> **NOTE CONFIGURATION EDITOR**
>
> Windows Server 2008 R2 introduces a new tool in IIS Manager called Configuration Editor, which simplifies the process of editing the IIS configuration files. Configuration Editor appears in Features view in the Management group.
>
> Using Configuration Editor is beyond the scope of the 70-643 exam, but you can find out more about this new feature by watching the screencast at *http://technet.microsoft.com /en-us/edge/Video/ff710902*.

Migrating Websites and Web Applications

The presence of Web.config files within web application and website folders helps make the process of migrating websites to different servers or physical locations simpler. For most applications, all that is required is for all the files within the appropriate folders to be moved or copied to the new location by using, for example, the xcopy utility. Then, within IIS Manager, you can re-create any additional websites, web applications, and virtual directories that are required. It is important, however, to test any migrated web application thoroughly. In some cases, incompatibilities or other issues between server-level and application-level settings can have unintended consequences. Overall, however, the process of moving and copying websites is usually fairly simple and straightforward.

> **MORE INFO   XCOPY DEPLOYMENT**
>
> New in IIS 7 is the ability to use Windows Explorer, the File Transfer Protocol (FTP), or the *Xcopy* command to copy configuration settings for ASP.NET web applications from one location to another. Previous versions of IIS stored some web application settings in the registry. By contrast, IIS 7 stores all web applications as XML in Web.config files. This makes

Backing Up and Restoring Configuration Data by Using *AppCmd.exe*

An important aspect of web server administration is ensuring that the configuration of the server is protected against data loss. Because IIS configuration settings are stored automatically in the *%SystemDrive%*\Inetpub\History folder, ensure that this folder is included in file system backup policies. In addition, it's important to back up websites and web applications to ensure that they can be restored quickly in the case of a failure. Often, however, you'll need to create your own configuration backups manually. For example, if you want to transfer configuration data to another IIS installation, or if you want to protect against unwanted changes, it is a good idea to make an on-demand configuration backup.

You can use *AppCmd.exe* to create a backup of the configuration of IIS and store it to a text file. The utility offers simple capabilities for creating a backup and for restoring from it. The standard command for adding a new backup is:

```
AppCmd add backup "BackupName"
```

BackupName specifies the name of the file you want to create. You can leave off the name, and an automatic filename that includes a timestamp will be generated. The file will be created in the location in which *AppCmd.exe* was run, but you can always move or copy the file manually to another location.

You can restore the configuration information from the backup by using the following command:

```
AppCmd restore backup "BackupName"
```

This process restores the configuration of the IIS web server to the settings that were included in the backup file. If you want to view a list of backups that have been made, you can use the following command:

```
AppCmd list backups
```

You will see a list of all the backup files you have created. Figure 5-32 shows an example of all these backup-related commands at work.

FIGURE 5-32 Performing IIS configuration backup and restore operations by using *AppCmd.exe*.

Using Centralized Configuration for Server Farms

As organizations place a greater reliance on their websites and web-based applications, the ability to improve performance, scalability, and reliability has become an important goal. For web servers, a common configuration is known as a *web server farm*. In this approach, many web servers are configured to provide access to the same content. Generally, they have the same configuration settings and either store local copies of websites and applications or access them from a shared location.

From a systems administration standpoint, managing large groups of web servers can be challenging. When configuration changes are required, they often have to be committed manually to many computers. Even with the use of automation or scripting, it is possible to overlook one or a few servers. To support the server farm usage scenario better, IIS 7 enables you to share centrally stored configuration data with multiple web servers.

The first step in the process of creating a shared configuration is to export the configuration of a single IIS server. Generally, you configure this server with all the settings you want to use on the other servers. Then, using IIS Manager, click the server name and double-click Shared Configuration in Features View. To generate an export, click the *Export Configuration* command in the Actions pane. (See Figure 5-33.) You will be able to provide a path into which the configuration files will be stored. To protect sensitive information in the configuration files, you must type and confirm an encryption key password. This password will be required to view the settings in the file. You can also use the Connect As option to provide security credentials if you are planning to store the configuration in a network location.

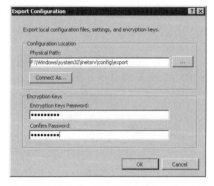

FIGURE 5-33 Exporting IIS configuration information.

The second step of the process is to place the shared configuration file in a location that is accessible to all the web servers. Usually, the best choice is a shared network folder on a reliable server. When you know the path to the files, you can use the Shared Configuration feature to enter the details. First, select the Enable Shared Configuration check box. (See Figure 5-34.) This enables you to specify the Physical Path setting. You can use a local file system location or a Universal Naming Convention (UNC)–based network path (for example, \\Server1\WebConfig). The User Name and Password fields enable you to enter the security credentials IIS uses to connect to the physical path you have specified.

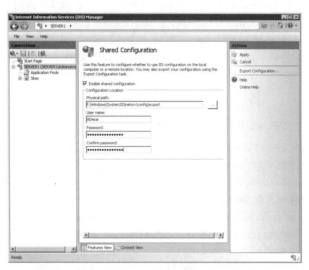

FIGURE 5-34 Enabling Shared Configuration for an IIS web server.

To save the settings, click Apply in the Actions pane. You will be prompted to enter the encryption key password for the configuration files. After the configuration import is complete, you will be notified that you must restart IIS Manager for it to recognize the configuration changes. You can disable the shared configuration settings later by clearing the Enable Shared Configuration check box. This returns the web server to using locally defined configuration settings.

MORE INFO **CREATING PRODUCTION SERVER FARMS**

The ability to share settings easily among web servers is helpful for setting up IIS-based web server farms. However, sharing configuration data is only one part of an overall web server farm configuration. Other considerations include deploying and synchronizing content updates, handling session state, managing security, implementing load balancing, and responding to fail-over events. Rest assured, there are many good ways of addressing these challenges. However, always be sure to involve web developers and systems administrators when designing a scale-out strategy.

Migrating from IIS 6.0

A large number of web developers have depended on previous versions of IIS to support their web applications and websites. IIS 6.0, the version included with Windows Server 2003, provided several enhancement features and capabilities over previous versions. IIS 7 provides even more improvements in functionality, performance, reliability, and management capabilities. However, with these new improvements, preserving backward compatibility with existing applications built for IIS 6.0 was an important goal.

For websites and web applications that rely primarily on static content, the migration process to IIS 7 should be fairly easy. Generally, all that is required is for the content to be moved and any associated site-level or application-level settings to be re-created. However, there are additional options and considerations for other types of applications, such as those that were built using ASP.NET or that rely on IIS 6.0 architectural features. In this section, you learn about how to migrate web applications to IIS 7.

Upgrading from Windows Server 2003 and IIS 6.0

One approach to moving web applications to Windows Server 2008 or Windows Server 2008 R2 is to perform an in-place upgrade of a computer running Windows Server 2003. The upgrade process automatically makes decisions that help preserve compatibility with earlier applications. For example, the majority of role services that are optional with a standard Web Server (IIS) role installation are included automatically. Furthermore, IIS 6.0 management tools and features are available for use. Following an upgrade to Windows Server 2008 or Windows Server 2008 R2 and IIS 7, verify which installed components are required and remove those that are not. And, as with any migration, thoroughly test the functionality of your websites before redeploying them into production.

Another option for upgrading to IIS 7 is to migrate websites manually by copying the relevant content to a new Windows Server 2008 or Windows Server 2008 R2 installation. In this approach, the existing content is transferred to a new server, and websites and web applications must be reconfigured.

Installing IIS 6 Management Compatibility

Some websites and web applications might include application code that relies on the architecture of IIS 6.0 for handling requests. Examples include web applications that need access to the IIS 6.0 configuration database and compatibility with earlier scripting methods. In addition, some applications might require access to an earlier version of the management console.

By default, backward-compatibility features are not installed automatically for new web server installations in Windows Server 2008 or Windows Server 2008 R2. To provide backward compatibility, you can use Server Manager to add role services to the Web Server (IIS) role. The available options are:

- **IIS 6 Management Compatibility** This role service contains the following four subcomponents: IIS 6 Metabase Compatibility, IIS 6 WMI Compatibility, IIS 6 Scripting tools, and IIS 6 Management Console. Aside from these four subcomponents, IIS 6 Management Compatibility provides support for two scripting and administration features that were included with IIS 6.0: Admin Base Object (ABO) and Active Directory Services Interface (ADSI). Web applications that relied on these technologies need these features to operate correctly.

- **IIS 6 Metabase Compatibility**   IIS 6.0 used a configuration database known as the metabase for storing server settings and other details. In IIS 7, this has been replaced by new types of XML-based configuration files, such as ApplicationHost.config and Web.config files. IIS 6.0 web applications could use the ability to query the metabase to manage IIS settings. To support these applications, you must enable the IIS 6 Metabase Compatibility role service.

- **IIS 6 WMI Compatibility**   Windows Management Instrumentation (WMI) is a programming interface that enables application code to query and manage IIS settings by using scripts or WMI-capable tools. This role service adds compatibility that enables IIS 6.0 WMI–based commands to apply to IIS 7 web servers.

- **IIS 6 Scripting Tools**   Web developers and systems administrators can transition IIS 6.0 management scripts to IIS 7 by enabling this role service. The IIS 6 Scripting Tools option adds support for using ActiveX Data Objects (ADO) and ADSI.

- **IIS 6 Management Console**   For systems administrators who want to manage IIS 6.0 installations remotely, it is possible to install IIS 6 Management Console on Windows Server 2008 and Windows Server 2008 R2. This console is capable only of connecting to IIS 6.0 servers, however, and cannot connect to a Windows Server 2008 or Windows Server 2008 R2 web server.

Overall, these tools and features can help ensure that previous versions of applications that relied on IIS 6.0 continue to function in Windows Server 2008 and Windows Server 2008 R2.

Understanding ASP.NET Integration Modes

IIS 7 provides enhancements for the ASP.NET development platform. In previous versions of IIS, ASP.NET processing was performed through an ISAPI code module. Although this approach worked well, there were some important limitations. In IIS 7, ASP.NET integration has been enhanced by more closely incorporating the process of ASP.NET webpages with the web server request pipeline. This new architecture offers several benefits, including greater control over request processing and the ability to use ASP.NET features for types of content other than dynamic webpages.

All ASP.NET applications can take advantage of the new Integrated Pipeline mode when they are running on IIS 7. However, applications that relied on IIS 6.0 architecture for intercepting and modifying requests will need support for the Classic Pipeline mode. You can configure the processing mode by changing application pool settings or by modifying the configuration of existing application pools. (Both topics were covered earlier in this lesson.)

PRACTICE Configure and Manage IIS Settings

In this practice, you create websites and web applications on Server2.contoso.local and test the backup and recovery process for configuration settings. The steps in the exercise assume that you have already installed the Web Server (IIS) role by using the default role services on this computer. (For more information about adding the role, see Lesson 1, Exercise 1.) The steps in Exercise 2 require you to complete the steps in Exercise 1, because the new website you created will be used for testing the backup and restore processes.

EXERCISE 1 Creating Websites and Web Applications

In this exercise, you use IIS Manager to create a new website on the local server. Because the default website is already configured to use the standard HTTP port, you specify alternate site-binding information. You also create a new web application that includes a test webpage to ensure that the server is responding properly.

1. Log on to Server2.contoso.local as a local administrator.

2. Before you create a new website, you create content folders within the file system. Using Windows Explorer, navigate to the *%SystemDrive%*\Inetpub\wwwroot path on the computer's system drive.

3. Within the Wwwroot folder, create a new folder called **Contoso**. Within the Contoso folder, create another new folder called **WebApp01**.

   You use these folders as the physical paths for the website and web application you create in later steps.

4. Copy the Iisstart.htm and Welcome.png files from the Wwwroot folder to the Contoso folder. Rename the Iisstart.htm file to **Default.htm**. If a message box appears, informing you that you'll need to provide administrator permission to move the folder, click Continue.

5. Within the *%SystemDrive%*\Inetpub\wwwroot\Contoso\WebApp01 folder, create a new text file named **Default.htm**. Within the text file, enter the following text and then save the file:

```
<html>
<head>
<title>Web Application 01</title>
</head>
<body>
<h1>Welcome to Web Application 01.<h1>
</body>
</html>
```

6. Launch Internet Information Services (IIS) Manager from the Administrative Tools program group.

7. If prompted to connect to a server, choose to connect to the local computer.

8. Expand the *local computer* object and the *Sites* container to view a list of existing websites.

   You see the default website (which is named Default Web Site) that was installed when the Web Server (IIS) role was added to the computer.

9. To create a new website, right-click the *Sites* container and click Add Web Site.

   This will open the Add Web Site dialog box.

10. For the name of the new website, type **Contoso Test Site**. Note that, by default, a new application pool of the same name is created and selected automatically. For this practice exercise, use this new application pool; however, you can choose an existing pool by clicking Select.

11. For Physical Path, browse to the *%SystemDrive%*\Inetpub\wwwroot\Contoso folder you created earlier. Accept the default security setting of Pass-Through Authentication and then click Test Settings. Note that IIS is able to verify authentication but not authorization because this information will not be known until a user attempts to access the site.

12. Click Close to return to the Add Web Site dialog box.

13. In the Binding section, choose the following settings:

   - Protocol: **HTTP**
   - IP Address: **All Unassigned**
   - Port: **8000** .
   - Host Name: (blank)

14. Verify that the Start Web Site Immediately option is selected and then click OK to create and start the new website automatically.

15. Click the newly created *Contoso Test Site* object in the left pane of IIS Manager. Note that the Actions pane provides commands for working with the website. To verify that the site is configured properly, click the *Browse *:8000 (http)* command. This will launch Internet Explorer automatically and connect to *http://localhost:8000*. You should see

the default IIS start page content in the web browser. When you are finished, close Internet Explorer.

16. To create a new web application, right-click Contoso Test Site in IIS Manager and select Add Application.

17. For the Alias of the application, type **TestApp**. For the physical path, type or browse to the *%SystemDrive%*\Inetpub\wwwroot\Contoso\WebApp01 physical path. The Contoso Test Site option is selected for the application pool.

18. Click OK to create the new web application.

19. In the left pane of IIS Manager, you see a new web application called TestApp under the *Contoso Test Site* object. To verify the content of this application, select the TestApp item and then click Content View at the bottom of the center pane in IIS Manager. You see the default.htm file you created earlier.

20. To test the web application, click Browse in the Manage Application section of the Actions pane. This launches Internet Explorer and connects to *http://localhost:8000/TestApp/*. The title bar for the web browser reads Web Application 01, and the text displays the welcome message you specified in the HTML file. When finished, close Internet Explorer.

21. Close IIS Manager.

EXERCISE 2   Backing Up and Restoring the IIS Configuration

In this exercise, you perform the steps required to make a backup of the IIS configuration by using the AppCmd.exe utility. You then delete the *Contoso Web Site* object that you created in Exercise 1 by using IIS Manager. To restore the website configuration, you again use the AppCmd.exe utility.

1. Log on to Server2.contoso.local with local administrative credentials.

2. Open an elevated command prompt.

3. Change the current working directory to the location of AppCmd.exe by typing **cd %SystemRoot%\System32\Inetsrv**.

4. To create a new backup of the IIS configuration, type the following command at the command prompt:

   ```
   AppCmd add backup "IISBackup01"
   ```

5. To verify that the backup has been created, type the following command:

   ```
   AppCmd list backups
   ```

6. You should see the IISBackup01 item in the list. (If other backups of the configuration have been made, they will also appear in the list.)

7. Leave the command prompt window open and then launch the Internet Information Services (IIS) Manager console.

   In the next step, you remove a website from the configuration of IIS.

8. Connect to the local server and expand the *Sites* object. Right-click the *Contoso Test Site* object and select Remove. When prompted, select Yes to confirm the removal. Note that the site and its web application have been deleted.

9. Return to the command prompt window and type the following command to restore the IIS configuration from the backup you created earlier:

```
AppCmd restore backup "IISBackup01"
```

10. When the command finishes, close the command prompt and return to the IIS Manager console.

11. To refresh the display, press F5.

    You now see the *Contoso Test Site* object. Note that removing the website did not delete any of the content that was stored in the file system, so the site should be available for use. In some cases, it might be necessary to close the IIS Manager console and reload it after the restore process has been performed.

12. When you are finished, close IIS Manager.

Lesson Summary

- IIS Manager provides an integrated graphical user interface for managing IIS-related settings, features, and web content.

- Websites have associated site bindings that specify the protocol, IP address, port, and host headers to which a site will respond. Systems administrators can configure bandwidth limitations, user connection limits, and logging settings for each website.

- Application pools are sections of physical memory that provide independence and isolation for multiple websites and web applications that are running on the same IIS installation.

- Systems administrators and web developers can use *AppCmd.exe* to perform common IIS management tasks from the command line.

- IIS server configuration settings are stored in the ApplicationHost.config file. These settings can be overridden by Web.config files that are located in content folders.

- Windows Server 2008 and Windows Server 2008 R2 provide numerous backward-compatibility features for supporting applications built for IIS 6.0 and for managing IIS 6.0 servers.

Lesson Review

You can use the following questions to test your knowledge of the information in Lesson 2, "Configuring Internet Information Services." The questions are also available on the companion CD if you prefer to review them in electronic form.

1. You are a systems administrator responsible for managing a Windows Server 2008 R2 web server. Currently, no websites are configured on the server. You need to configure the server to host two web applications: EngineeringApp and SalesApp. Both web applications must be accessible by using HTTP port 80 without the use of host headers. Also, you must protect against problems in one web application affecting the performance or reliability of the other web application. Which two steps should you take to meet these requirements? (Each correct answer presents part of a complete solution. Choose two.)

   A. Create a single website that contains both web applications.

   B. Create two websites, one for each web application.

   C. Assign both web applications to the same application pool.

   D. Assign each web application to its own application pool.

2. You have installed the Web Server (IIS) server role on a server running Windows Server 2008 R2. You create a new website named Contoso.com and then copy an application named Engineering to the server. How can you use IIS Manager to enable the Engineering application on the Contoso.com website?

   A. Select the option to add an application.

   B. Select the option to add a virtual directory.

   C. Select the option to add an application pool.

   D. Select the option to add a website.

3. You are a systems administrator responsible for managing a Windows Server 2008 R2 web server. You have not created any manual backups of the IIS configuration. Recently, a web developer reported that he had accidentally removed two websites from the IIS configuration. Both websites contained several web applications. You have verified that the two sites do not appear when you open the IIS Manager console and expand the *Sites* object. You have also verified that the content for the two websites is still present in the C:\WebSites folder. By interviewing other members of the web development team, you have also ensured that no other changes have been made to the IIS configuration. Which of the following steps should you take to restore the two missing websites with their associated settings as quickly as possible?

   A. Manually re-create the two websites and then re-create the associated web applications.

   B. Manually modify the web server's ApplicationHost.config file and add the website and web application settings.

C. Restore the IIS configuration by using the AppCmd utility.

D. Copy an earlier version of the ApplicationHost.config file from the *%SystemDrive%* \Inetpub\wwwroot\History folder over the current active version of ApplicationHost.config.

Chapter Review

To further practice and reinforce the skills you learned in this chapter, you can perform the following tasks:

- Review the chapter summary.
- Review the list of key terms introduced in this chapter.
- Complete the case scenarios. These scenarios set up real-world situations involving the topics of this chapter and ask you to create a solution.
- Complete the suggested practices.
- Take a practice test.

Chapter Summary

- The Web Server (IIS) role in Windows Server 2008 and Windows Server 2008 R2 is designed to support websites and web applications.
- The Web Server (IIS) role offers numerous role services related to security, performance, diagnostics, and backward compatibility.
- The IIS Manager console is the primary method for creating and managing websites, web applications, application pools, and virtual directories.
- IIS can be managed by using the AppCmd.exe command-line utility, Windows PowerShell, and the .NET Framework.
- Windows Server 2008 and Windows Server 2008 R2 provide several methods for maintaining backward compatibility with applications built for previous versions of IIS.

Key Terms

Do you know what these key terms mean? You can check your answers by looking up the terms in the glossary at the end of the book.

- AppCmd.exe
- application pools (IIS)
- ApplicationHost.config file
- ASP.NET
- Hypertext Transfer Protocol (HTTP)
- Hypertext Transfer Protocol Secure (HTTPS
- IIS Manager
- Internet Information Services (IIS)
- Secure Sockets Layer (SSL)
- site bindings

- Web Server (IIS) server role
- web server farms
- Web.config files
- Windows PowerShell
- Windows System Resource Manager (WSRM)

Case Scenarios

In these case scenarios, you apply the information you have learned about websites and web applications to meet business and technical requirements.

Case Scenario 1: IIS Web Server Administration

You are a systems administrator responsible for managing five web servers for your organization. Each web server supports multiple web applications. Your general requirements include ensuring reliability and performance for all web applications. In addition, you must simplify administration tasks for the servers. The organization requires that no more than four hours of configuration or site content changes can be lost in the event of a hardware failure. A web developer has stated that she needs to make multiple changes to the IIS settings on one test web server.

1. How can you simplify the configuration of all the servers, assuming that the settings must be the same for all of them?
2. Which content should you include in the backup process?
3. What are two ways in which you can roll back the server configuration on a test server if an accidental or unwanted modification is made?

Case Scenario 2: Managing Multiple Websites

You are a server administrator responsible for managing 15 websites on a single Windows Server 2008 R2 web server. For security, reliability, and performance reasons, you need to prevent problems in one web application from causing issues with others. In addition, several web applications must be configured to respond on HTTP port 80 and HTTP port 443 by using the same public IP address. One of the ASP.NET web applications was originally designed for IIS 6.0 and takes advantage of advanced request processing features.

1. How can you minimize the risks associated with web application defects affecting other web applications on the same server?
2. Which configuration settings enable you to meet the default HTTP and HTTPS connection requirements?
3. What are some methods by which you can support the IIS 6.0 web application on Windows Server 2008 R2?

Suggested Practices

To help you successfully master the exam objectives presented in this chapter, complete the following tasks.

Perform the following exercises to practice the process of creating and managing web applications by using IIS Manager and command-line utilities.

- **Practice 1**   Web applications often have numerous requirements and features that must be enabled to function properly in IIS. If possible, download sample web applications and deploy them in IIS. Use various settings for application pools and other options. A good starting point for downloading applications based on ASP.NET is the Microsoft ASP.NET Starter Kit site at *http://www.asp.net/community/projects*. In addition, if your organization has any existing websites or applications, attempt to install them in a test environment.

- **Practice 2**   When you are familiar with the concepts of using IIS Manager to create and manage websites, try performing the same actions by using the command line. Use the AppCmd.exe utility to perform operations such as:
  - Creating a new website, including unique site-binding parameters.
  - Creating multiple web applications within the new website.
  - Adding virtual directories that point to file system locations outside the folder for the default site or web application.
  - Backing up and restoring the IIS configuration.
  - Deleting the test sites and other objects you have created.

- **Practice 3**   Watch a screencast about running IIS on a Server Core installation of Windows Server 2008 R2. The screencast is titled "IIS 7.5 on Server Core: Windows Server 2008 R2 Demo Screencast 1 of 5" and can be found at *http://technet.microsoft.com/en-us/edge/Video/ff710901*.

- **Practice 4**   Watch a screencast about using the new IIS Configuration Editor in Windows Server 2008 R2. The screencast is titled "IIS 7.5 Configuration Editor: Windows Server 2008 R2 Demo Screencast 2 of 5" and can be found at *http://technet.microsoft.com/en-us/edge/video/iis-75-configuration-editor-windows-server-2008-r2-demo-screencast-2-of-5*.

- **Practice 5**   Watch a screencast about administering IIS by using Windows PowerShell. The screencast is titled "PowerShell and IIS 7.5: Windows Server 2008 R2 Demo Screencast 3 of 5" and can be found at *http://technet.microsoft.com/en-us/edge/powershell-and-iis-75-windows-server-2008-r2-demo-screencast-3-of-5.aspx*.

If you need to create many sites on several web servers, you can also combine multiple commands in a batch file to automate the process.

Take a Practice Test

The practice tests on this book's companion CD offer many options. For example, you can test yourself on just one exam objective, or you can test yourself on all the 70-643 certification exam content. You can set up the test so that it closely simulates the experience of taking a certification exam, or you can set it up in study mode so that you can look at the correct answers and explanations after you answer each question.

> **MORE INFO PRACTICE TESTS**
>
> For details about all the practice test options available, see the "How to Use the Practice Tests" section in this book's introduction.

CHAPTER 6

Managing Web Server Security

From a systems administration standpoint, one of the main goals for managing web servers is to maintain a high standard of security. Security is an important concern in all areas of IT, but it's especially important for information and applications that are readily accessible to large numbers of users. In this chapter, you learn how to configure security for a Windows Server 2008 R2 web server.

Lesson 1, "Configuring IIS Security," focuses on securing access to Internet Information Services 7 (IIS 7) and the content it contains. You learn how to configure permissions for remote management and how to increase the security of the server by disabling or removing unneeded features and options. In Lesson 2, "Controlling Access to Web Services," you learn about ways in which you use authentication and authorization. You also learn how to increase security through server certificates and IP address restrictions.

Exam objectives in this chapter:

- Configure Web applications.
- Manage Web sites.
- Manage the Web Server (IIS) role.
- Configure SSL security.
- Configure Web site authentication and permissions.

Lessons in this chapter:

Before You Begin

To complete the lessons in this chapter, you should have:

- Installed the Web Server (IIS) server role on Server2.contoso.local by using the default installation options for this server role. If you have created additional websites or web applications in previous exercises, you may leave them configured on this server.
- The ability to create and manage websites and web applications. These topics are covered in Chapter 5, "Installing and Configuring Web Applications."

REAL WORLD

Anil Desai

The primary goal for systems administrators who are responsible for managing access to Web Services is to minimize the potential for unauthorized access to and misuse of applications or data. One of the primary ways to secure a server is by reducing its attack surface. If certain web applications do not require a particular technology (for example, support for the Microsoft .NET Framework), you can reduce potential unauthorized access to the system by disabling that feature.

Another major strategy related to web server security is *defense in depth*. This technique involves a multilayered security approach. Security options include authentication, authorization, file system permissions, and other settings that provide multiple barriers to access. These security mechanisms work together to ensure that only authorized users have access to the system. In addition, if one layer of security is incorrectly configured or is compromised, other security settings can help restrict or prevent unauthorized access.

Security settings can often be difficult and complicated to manage, and this complexity reduces security because many systems administrators find it challenging to set up the appropriate permissions. IIS simplifies security management through a hierarchical arrangement that helps organize settings and content. For example, you can apply security-related settings at the server level, for specific websites, for specific web applications, or directly on virtual directories, physical files, and folders.

In general, applying permissions at higher levels in the hierarchy simplifies administration. Figure 6-1 shows how objects, such as the web server, websites, web applications, and other items, are arranged into nested parent–child relationships. In general, settings placed on higher-level objects (such as a website) apply automatically to all the lower-level objects (such as multiple web applications). Administrators can then override settings for specific web applications by using whatever method is dictated by business or technical requirements. The result of this configuration strategy is a high level of security with minimal administrative effort.

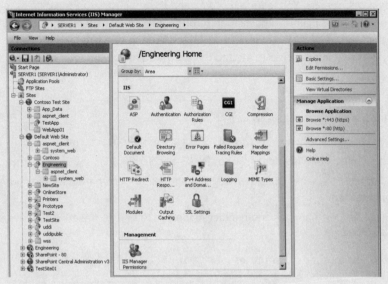

FIGURE 6-1 Viewing a hierarchy of objects in IIS Manager.

Lesson 1: Configuring IIS Security

In this lesson, you learn how to configure and manage security for the Web Server (IIS) server role and its associated components. You first learn how to determine the permissions administrators have on web servers. You learn ways to extend IIS administration capabilities to other users and web developers in your organization through remote management and delegation settings. You then learn how to increase security by configuring request handlers and their associated settings to minimize risks related to the execution of unwanted or malicious code or content.

> **After this lesson, you will be able to:**
> - Describe the security architecture of IIS, including built-in accounts.
> - Enable remote management features for IIS web servers.
> - Configure IIS Manager users, permissions, and feature delegation for distributed administration.
> - Manage request handlers and handler mappings to reduce the attack surface of the web server.
>
> **Estimated lesson time: 75 minutes**

Understanding IIS 7 Security Accounts

When you add the Web Server (IIS) role to a computer running Windows Server 2008 or Windows Server 2008 R2, as discussed in Chapter 5, the process makes numerous changes and additions to the configuration of the server. In earlier versions of IIS, each installation used service accounts that were based on the name of the server. Because the accounts and their security identifiers (SIDs) were different, copying web content and settings between web servers required multiple steps.

In IIS 7, a built-in, internal account named IUSR and a local security group called IIS_IUSRS are used on each computer running Windows Server 2008 and Windows Server 2008 R2 web server. Passwords for the accounts are managed internally, so administrators do not need to keep track of them.

Managing File System Permissions

To implement security, web server administrators must be able to define which content should be protected. They must also be able to specify which users or groups of users have access to protected content. Permissions settings for web content are managed through NTFS file system permissions. These permissions can be administered directly by using Windows Explorer or by right-clicking a specific object in the IIS Manager hierarchy and then clicking Edit Permissions. As shown in Figure 6-2, the permissions settings display which users or groups of users have access to the content and which permissions they have. IIS uses these permissions to determine whether credentials are required when attempting to complete a request from a web client.

FIGURE 6-2 Viewing permissions for a folder within the Engineering website.

Configuring IIS Administration Features

When you add the Web Server (IIS) role to a computer running Windows Server 2008 or Windows Server 2008 R2, the default configuration enables only local administration of the server. This enhances security because users of other computers are unable to use IIS Manager to make changes to the server's configuration. Although this is appropriate for small, simple installations, often systems administrators benefit from the ability to use IIS Manager to configure the server remotely.

In many environments, multiple systems administrators manage websites and web applications. In large deployments, it is common for several administrators to be responsible for the same web server. For example, a single IIS server might host several important web applications, each of which is administered by a different individual or group. In hosting situations—when an organization provides IIS server access to subscribers—you must enable subscribers to control certain web content and features. In this case, subscribers act as remote administrators for certain portions of the servers. Remote administration is helpful for both multiple administrators and management performance from multiple locations.

To enable remote administrators to manage IIS, you must first enable remote management on the server. You can then define and configure IIS Manager users. *Feature delegation* enables you to specify which actions remote administrators can perform.

Enabling Remote Management

To enable remote management functionality, you first add the Management Service role service to the local server. You can do this by using Server Manager. Right-click the Web Server (IIS) role in the Roles folder and then select Add Role Services. Add Management Service, which is located in the Management Tools section of the available role services.

The Management Service role service is associated with the Web Management Service (WMSVC), which works by using a standard HTTP or HTTPS connection. Communications are configured to transmit over port 8172 by default. Assuming that traffic is allowed on this port through any firewalls or network security devices, this enables remote administrators to manage their IIS servers over a local network connection or over the Internet.

After you have added the Management Service role service to the Web Server (IIS) role, you can use IIS Manager to enable remote management. To do this, open IIS Manager and select the server object in the left pane. Double-click Management Service from the Management section in the Features view. (See Figure 6-3.)

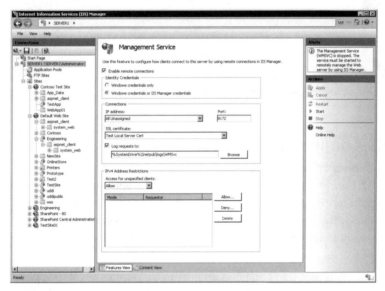

FIGURE 6-3 Configuring Management Service using IIS Manager.

Initially, the Enable Remote Connections option will be cleared. To enable authorized users to connect to IIS over the network, select Enable Remote Connections. The Identity Credentials section enables you to specify whether you will allow authentication by using Windows credentials only (the default setting) or by using IIS Manager credentials as well.

The Connections portion of the settings enables you to specify the IP addresses and ports on which the management service will respond. The default setting is for the service to respond to all available IP addresses on port 8172. If your web server is configured with multiple network connections or IP addresses, you can increase security by restricting remote access connections to a specific address. The SSL Certificate section enables you to select one of the SSL certificates that has been configured on the local server. You can also configure the path into which remote management requests are logged. The default is *%SystemDrive%* \Inetpub\Logs\WMSvc.

Finally, the IPv4 Address Restrictions section enables you to increase security by restricting which computers can connect to IIS remotely. As shown in Figure 6-4, you can configure rules based on a specific IPv4 address or on an address range (which is defined by a combination of an IP address and subnet mask). The Access For Unspecified Clients drop-down list in the Management Service feature defines whether IP addresses without entries are allowed or denied. You can then create Allow or Deny entries to define which IP addresses can connect. These options are most useful when you have control over the groups of computers that will be used for administering web services.

FIGURE 6-4 Configuring IPv4 address restrictions for Management Service in IIS Manager.

Because WMSVC is stopped by default, you must click the *Start* command in the Actions pane to start allowing remote connections. You must stop the service to make changes to the configuration.

Understanding IIS Manager Users

To connect to a Windows Server 2008 or Windows Server 2008 R2 web server by using IIS Manager, users must have the necessary permissions. Users who are logged on to a computer running Windows Server 2008 or Windows Server 2008 R2 with administrator credentials have the necessary permissions to complete all the available tasks on the server. For other types of users, such as remote systems administrators, you must decide how you want to manage permissions.

By default, the Web Server (IIS) role enables permissions to be assigned using Windows authentication only. This means that all administrators who attempt to manage IIS must have Windows-based credentials and permissions. Windows authentication is most appropriate for environments in which all the web server administrators belong to the same domain. Users who are logged on to the domain will not have to supply credentials manually when they connect to a server using IIS Manager, assuming they have the necessary permissions. Windows authentication is also useful when you plan to create either local or domain accounts for all the administrators who need access to IIS Manager.

In some cases, it might be impractical to create local or domain accounts for each of the potential IIS administrators. For example, web service hosting companies can have hundreds of users who require the ability to manage their servers. In these environments, each user can generally modify specific settings for his or her own website. These users should not have access to other users' websites and often will be restricted to changing only certain settings. To support these scenarios, you must enable the Windows Credentials Or *IIS Manager*

Credentials option. When this option is enabled by using the Management Service described in the previous section, you can create username and password combinations solely for the purpose of managing IIS. These credentials can then be given to other users and administrators so they can connect to the web server without requiring individual Windows accounts for each of the users.

Creating IIS Manager Users

The IIS Manager utility enables you to define which users can connect to and administer websites and web services. To configure these settings:

1. Open IIS Manager and select a server in the left pane.

2. Click IIS Manager Users in the Management section of the features view. By default, the IIS installation will not contain any locally defined users.

3. To create a new user, first click Open Feature in the Actions pane and then click the *Add User* command in the Actions pane. You will be prompted to provide a username and to type and confirm a password. (See Figure 6-5.) These settings are defined locally in IIS, so it is not necessary to use a fully qualified username that is compatible with your domain design.

FIGURE 6-5 Adding an IIS Manager user.

In addition to configuring permission through IIS Manager users, you can use group membership settings to determine which users can connect remotely. Users who have permission to log on to the local computer and to use IIS Manager will be able to do so from a remote computer.

Defining IIS Management Permissions

So far, you have learned how to enable remote management and how to specify which users can use IIS Manager to administer a web server. Next, you must decide which permissions remote administrators will have after they connect. In some cases, you might want to enable a remote administrator to have full administrative access to the web server. In other cases, you will want to restrict access to only specific websites or web applications. You can configure IIS Manager Permissions at the website and application levels. However, you cannot configure permissions directly at the server level. This helps ensure that users are given permissions to modify the settings for only the specific websites and web applications to which they need access.

To manage permissions, select a website or web application and then click IIS Manager Permissions in the Management section of the Features View. By default, new IIS Manager users are not given permissions to connect to a specific website or web application. To enable a new user to connect at the selected level, first click Open Feature in the Actions pane and then click the *Allow User* command in the Actions pane. You are given the opportunity to specify a Windows user or an IIS Manager user (if IIS Manager credentials are accepted), as shown in Figure 6-6. If you are using the Windows option, you can select an existing user or group that is defined either in the domain (if the server is a member of a domain) or locally.

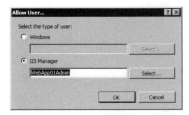

FIGURE 6-6 Allowing a user to administer a website.

When users connect to IIS remotely, they can access only those websites and web applications on which they have been allowed. By default, permissions from higher-level objects are inherited automatically by lower-level objects.

To simplify administration of many users, two commands are available when managing permissions for a website. *Show All Users* provides a list of all the users available on the IIS installation. *Show Only Site Users* restricts the display to only the users who have access to the site.

Configuring Feature Delegation

The ability to define users and permissions enables you to manage administration based on site content structure. However, it is also important to determine which features users can view and configure. For example, you might want a web server administrator to connect to the Default Web Site, but you do not want her to be able to change authentication settings. Delegation is the process by which an administrator can determine which features of IIS a user can view and change.

Default settings for feature delegation are defined initially at the server level in IIS. To access these settings by using IIS Manager, select the *server* object in the left pane and then double-click Feature Delegation in the Management section of Features View, as shown in Figure 6-7.

The list of items available for delegation includes all the features that have been added through the Web Server (IIS) server role and enabled role services. To change the setting for a feature, select it from the list and use the commands in the Set Feature Delegation section of the Actions pane. Most features have options of Read Only or Read/Write. In addition, some items have a Configuration Read/Write or Configuration Read Only setting. These settings enable web developers to specify settings in their configuration files or to manage them based on database settings. The Not Delegated setting means that the feature has not been enabled for delegation at lower levels and is not available for configuration. You can also use the Delegation option in the Group By drop-down list to determine quickly how all the settings have been configured, as shown in Figure 6-8.

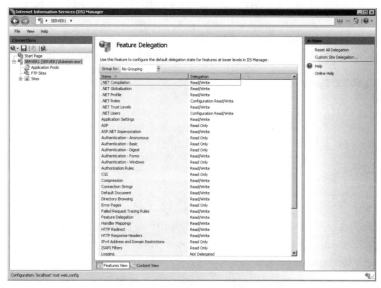

FIGURE 6-7 Viewing Feature Delegation settings for an IIS web server.

FIGURE 6-8 Viewing Feature Delegation configuration grouped by the delegation setting.

The settings you define at the server level automatically apply to all child websites and applications by default. In some cases, you will want to restrict feature delegation at the site level. To do this, click the *Custom Site Delegation* command in the Actions pane. This brings up the Custom Site Delegation screen, as shown in Figure 6-9, and enables you to select specific sites to which you want delegation settings to apply.

FIGURE 6-9 Specifying Custom Site Delegation settings.

The *Copy Delegation* button enables you to copy the currently selected settings to one or more websites on the server. You can also use the *Reset To Inherited* and *Reset All Delegation* commands in the Actions pane to change groups of settings quickly to earlier values. (*Reset To Inherited* appears in the Actions pane only when you select a particular item or group of items for configuration within a site.) You use feature delegation settings to determine which parts of the system configuration will be available when remote users connect to the server by using IIS Manager.

> **NOTE**   **IMPLEMENTING REMOTE MANAGEMENT SECURITY**
>
> When implementing remote management security, keep in mind the specific administration requirements. Some settings, such as IIS Manager Users and Feature Delegation, can be configured only at the level of the web server. That makes these settings applicable to all the lower-level objects. Alternatively, IIS Manager Permissions can be configured for specific websites and web applications to enable you to implement granular security for those users who should have access to only limited portions of the web server.

Connecting to a Remote Server by Using IIS Manager

After you have enabled remote management and configured the appropriate permissions and settings, remote users will be able to connect to the server by using the IIS Manager console. To verify the configuration from either the local computer or from a remote computer that has the IIS Manager console installed, use Start Page in IIS Manager or the File menu to connect to IIS. As shown in Figure 6-10, remote users will be able to connect to the server at one of several levels. The available commands include:

- *Connect To A Server*
- *Connect To A Site*
- *Connect To An Application*

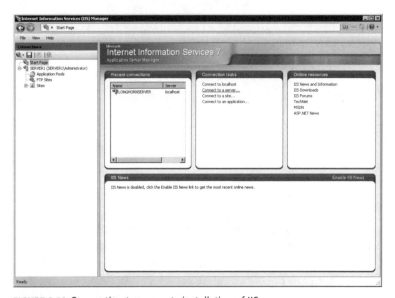

FIGURE 6-10 Connecting to a remote installation of IIS.

> **MORE INFO**   **DOWNLOADING THE IIS MANAGER CONSOLE**
>
> Users of Windows Server 2003, Windows XP, Vista, and Windows 7 can download a copy of the IIS Manager console to install on their own computers. To find the download, visit *http://www.iis.net/download/IISManager*. After remote users install the program, they can connect to installations of Windows Server 2008 and Windows Server 2008 R2 that include the Web Server (IIS) server role and for which remote management is enabled.

Figure 6-11 shows the options available for connecting directly to a web application. Remote administrators will be prompted to provide credentials (including a username and password) to make the connection. If the connection is successful, remote administrators see a new object in the left pane of the IIS Manager. These administrators also can name or rename these connections to keep track of multiple connections.

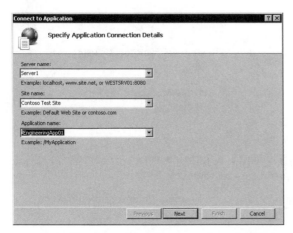

FIGURE 6-11 Creating a connection to a web application.

The specific items available for management are based on feature delegation settings. Although the same icons might appear, remote administrators will be unable to make or save configuration changes for particular items. For most settings, they can access the configuration page that shows the details, but the controls themselves will be disabled. Figure 6-12 shows an example.

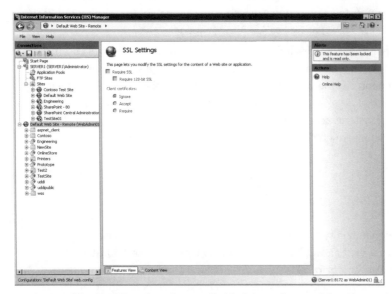

FIGURE 6-12 Viewing SSL options that are disabled due to feature delegation settings.

Managing Request Handlers

To provide support for various web application technologies, the architecture of IIS allows for enabling and disabling request handlers. *Request handlers* are programs that can process web requests and generate responses that are then returned to clients. Web servers and web applications can be configured with their own sets of request handlers, based on the types of content that must be supported. For example, a web application might be configured to support static content (such as HTML) as well as ASP.NET webpages.

The primary benefit is that web developers can choose the technologies most useful for their tasks. However, there is a drawback from a security standpoint. When IIS is configured with multiple request handlers, the security *attack surface* is increased. A vulnerability in any of the enabled request handlers can result in unauthorized access or related issues. Therefore, it is recommended that systems administrators enable only those request handlers they plan to use. In this section, you learn how to enable and disable request handlers.

 REAL WORLD

Anil Desai

Web developers and systems administrators tend to grant far too many permissions on their web servers. Their motivation is simple: it's just easier to provide complete access for all features and settings. That way, it's unlikely that you'll miss some strange requirement. Often, systems administrators don't understand the complexities of web application security, and web developers don't appreciate the importance of minimizing the attack surface of production web servers. The result is less than ideal security and increased risk of unauthorized access. So what's the solution?

The most important aspect of determining ideal security settings is communication. Server administrators should ask web application developers for a list of specific requirements for applications running in production. A preproduction checklist that includes details about intended users, required IIS handlers, authentication requirements, and code access security requirements is a good start. Web developers should understand the importance of minimizing exposure of services and of reducing execution permissions for their applications. To ensure that these goals are being met, both teams can develop tests that validate the configuration from functional and security standpoints.

Overall, web developers and web server administrators tend to have different technical backgrounds and areas of expertise. This is a positive difference as long as both groups understand the benefits of implementing production server security.

Understanding Handler Mappings

When the web server receives a request, IIS uses the definition of handler mappings to determine which request handler to use. A *handler mapping* includes the following information:

- **Verb** HTTP requests include verbs that define the type of request being made. The two most common verbs are GET, which obtains information from the web server, and POST, which can also include information sent from the client browser to the web server.

- **Request extension** Web servers commonly return a wide array of content types. The most common types of information are standard HTML pages and images such as .jpg and .gif files. IIS can use the file extension information from the HTTP request to determine which type of content must be processed. For example, the default file extension for ASP.NET webpages is .aspx. Requests for .aspx pages are mapped automatically to the ASP.NET request handler. Most web development platforms have their own conventions for extensions. It is also possible to create new extensions and provide the appropriate mappings for them.

- **Handler information** The handler mapping includes details related to the specific request handler IIS should call based on the verb and request extension. This information can be provided in different ways, including as a full path to an executable or as the name of a program designed to handle the request.

In addition to specific handler mappings based on these settings, IIS provides the ability to return content by using a default handler. The StaticFile handler mapping is configured to respond to requests that do not map to an existing file. The specific response is based on the settings for the web application. If a default document is specified for the web application or virtual directory, that document is returned if a file is not specified in the URL. For example, a request to *http://Server1.contoso.local/TestSite* results automatically in the return of the default.htm document (if one exists).

If a default document does not exist or the feature is disabled, the StaticFile handler checks whether directory browsing is enabled. If it is, a listing of the contents of the folder is returned to the requester. Finally, if neither of these methods is able to complete the request, the user receives an error stating that the request is forbidden. The complete error message is HTTP Error 403.14, The Web Server Is Configured To Not List The Contents Of This Directory. (See Figure 6-13.)

> **NOTE LOCAL VS. REMOTE ERROR MESSAGES**
>
> For security purposes, IIS is configured to provide one type of error message to web users who access the server from the local computer and another type of error message to users who access it remotely. This is done to maintain security; potentially sensitive information is not exposed to remote web browser users, but useful troubleshooting information is still provided to systems administrators and web developers.

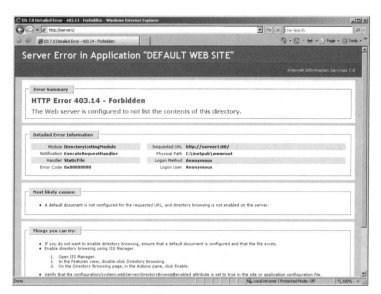

FIGURE 6-13 A detailed Request Not Found error page.

Configuring Handler Mappings

When you add the Web Server (IIS) role to Windows Server 2008 or Windows Server 2008 R2, a default set of handler mappings is defined for the web server and for the default website. New websites and web applications are also configured with a default set of handler mappings. In addition, when you add role services to the Web Server (IIS) role, additional handler mappings might be added automatically to the configuration.

You can use IIS Manager to configure handler mappings. After you have connected to an installation of IIS, you must choose the level at which you want to configure mappings. You can configure mappings at the following levels:

- Web Server
- Web Sites
- Web Applications
- Virtual Directories
- Web Folders

Child items in the hierarchy automatically inherit handler mappings. For example, a child item automatically inherits the default handler mappings for a new web application from the configuration of the parent website. Settings made at lower levels override the settings from higher levels. This enables a specific web application to support a certain type of file content, such as ASP.NET pages, whereas other applications and the parent website might support only static content.

To view the handler mappings that are configured at a specific level, click the relevant object in the left pane of IIS Manager. Then, double-click Handler Mappings from the Features View in the center pane. Figure 6-14 shows the handler mappings that are defined for a website.

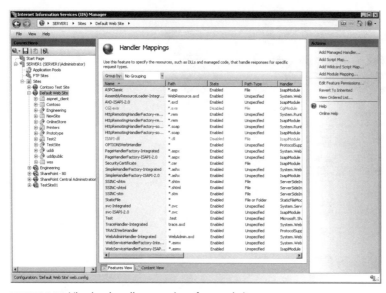

FIGURE 6-14 Viewing handler mappings for a website.

The display includes information about all the handler mappings defined at the selected level. The name specifies information about the request handler itself. Examples include StaticFile and ASPClassic. Built-in handler mappings have default names, but administrators can provide names for new mappings when they are created. The Path column shows the specific request extensions for which the handler will be used.

The State column specifies whether the handler is enabled or disabled. If the handler is disabled, requests that match the mapping will not be processed. The Handler column specifies details about the program to be called. Finally, the Entry Type specifies whether the handler mapping is inherited from a parent object or is Local (defined directly for this object).

You can use the Group By drop-down list to view handler mappings based on different criteria. These view options make it easy to determine the security attack surface for each component of the web server.

Removing Handler Mappings

To secure your web content, it is a good idea to remove any request handlers that you know will not be required when running in production. To remove a handler mapping, click it and then select the *Remove* command from the Actions pane. After a handler is removed, requests for the types of content that it handled will not be processed. For example, Figure 6-15 shows the result returned to a local web browser when the StaticFile request handler for the web application has been removed. In this case, the request file (default.htm) is present in the web application folder. However, because no request handler is available for the .htm file extension, the request cannot be processed. To the requester, it appears that the file does not exist.

FIGURE 6-15 A detailed request handler error page.

Managing Handler Inheritance

The inheritance feature of handler mapping settings can significantly simplify the administration of servers that host many websites and web applications. In general, configure handler mappings at the highest applicable level. For example, if you are sure that none of the web applications in a specific website must respond to the .soap file extension, you can remove this handler mapping at the level of the website. As mentioned earlier, to increase security, minimize the numbers and types of handlers that are enabled.

By default, it is possible for lower-level objects on the web server to override handler mapping settings from parent objects. In some cases, you might want to prevent some types of requests from being processed on the entire server, regardless of settings for websites and web applications. You do this by locking the configuration of the request handler. To lock the configuration, click the web server object in IIS Manager and then double-click Handler Mappings. Select the handler mapping you wish to lock and then click the *Lock* command in the Actions pane.

It is also possible to restore the handler mappings settings to their default values. To do this, click the *Revert To Parent* command in the Actions pane in IIS Manager. Performing this action restores mappings from the parent object, but it also results in the loss of any locally defined handler mappings.

Adding Handler Mappings

The architecture of IIS enables systems administrators to add new handler mappings based on specific needs. For example, if you want to provide support for a type of file that has a .mypage extension, you can add a handler for this path type. In addition, web developers can create their own programs to manage new types of requests.

To add a handler mapping, select the appropriate object and then double-click Handler Mappings in the Features View in IIS Manager. The Actions pane contains several options for adding new types of request handlers. They are:

- **Add Managed Handler**   A managed handler processes requests based on a .NET-based code library. The Type setting enables you to choose from the existing .NET code modules registered on the local server, as shown in Figure 6-16. These types of options all belong to the *System.Web* namespace.

FIGURE 6-16 Adding a managed handler for a website.

- **Add Script Map**   Scripting mappings send request processing to a dynamic link library (DLL) or executable (.exe) file type. These types of programs are designed to process request information and generate a response for IIS to send back to the end user.

- **Add Wildcard Script Map**   Wildcard script mappings specify a default handler for types of documents that are not managed by other handlers. The Executable path option points to either a .dll or an .exe file designed to handle requests.

- **Add Module Mapping**   *Modules* are programs designed to integrate with the IIS request processing pipeline. They can provide a wide range of functions and are included with the default and optional role services that are part of the Web Server (IIS) role. Examples include *FastCGIModule*, for processing scripts based on the Common Gateway Interface (CGI) specification, and *StaticCompressionModule*, which compresses static HTML content to reduce bandwidth usage. In addition to specifying the module to be used for processing, administrators can define an optional executable or .dll file to be used when processing requests, as shown in Figure 6-17.

FIGURE 6-17 Adding a module mapping to a web application.

When you add a new request handler, you are prompted to provide information about the request path. You can use wildcards, or you can specify a list of specific files. Examples include *.mypage (for responding to a request for any file with this extension) and Config.mypage (for responding to requests for this specific file name). You use the Name setting to help other developers and administrators identify the purpose of the handler mapping.

Configuring Request Restrictions

Besides specifying the paths and file names to which specific request handlers will be mapped, you can further secure IIS through request restrictions. To see the available options, click Request Restrictions in the dialog box when you are adding a mapping. Three tabs organize the request restrictions options: Mapping, Verbs, and Access.

You can use the Mapping tab to specify additional details related to whether files, folders, or both will be included in the mapping. The default setting is for the handler to handle requests automatically for both files and folders. You can choose either files or folders to limit whether the handler will respond to default documents or explicit file requests.

You can use the Verbs tab, shown in Figure 6-18, to specify the HTTP request verbs to which the handler will respond. Although the most common types of verbs are GET and POST, some applications might use other verbs (such as HEAD) to request other details from the web server. By default, all verb types are sent to the request handler. If you want to use different handlers for different verbs, or if you want the handler mapping to apply only to specific types of requests, you can specify this by using the One Of The Following Verbs option.

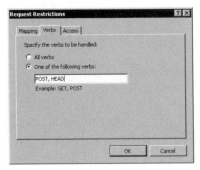

FIGURE 6-18 Viewing Verb Request Restrictions options for a handler mapping.

Finally, the Access tab specifies the access permissions that will be granted to the request handler. To improve security, minimize the types of access the handler will have. The default setting is *Script*, which is acceptable for most types of executable handlers. Other options include *None*, *Read*, *Write*, and *Execute*.

Configuring Feature Permissions

Feature permissions specify which types of actions a request handler can take. You can configure these options by double-clicking Handler Mappings and clicking Edit Feature Permissions in the Actions pane, as shown in Figure 6-19.

FIGURE 6-19 Configuring Feature Permissions for a request handler.

The three permission options are:

- **Read** Enables the handler to read files stored within the file system.
- **Script** Enables the handler to perform basic scripting-related tasks on the server.
- **Execute** Enables the handler to run executable program code (such as .dll or .exe) files on the computer when processing a request. For *Execute* to be enabled, *Script* permissions must also be assigned.

By default, the *Read* and *Script* feature permissions are enabled for new handler mappings.

Understanding Request Filtering

In Windows Server 2008 R2, you can use the Request Filtering item in Features View of IIS Manager to restrict the kinds of HTTP requests your web server will process. Request Filtering is a security feature that helps you limit the attack surface of your web server.

> **NOTE   REQUEST FILTERING IN WINDOWS SERVER 2008**
>
> In the RTM version of Windows Server 2008, the Request Filtering item is available in IIS Manager only if you install the Administration Pack for IIS 7.0, which is available on the Microsoft website. However, the full capabilities of this administration feature are still available. You can filter requests in Windows Server 2008 by running Appcmd.exe commands in a command-line window, by editing configuration files directly, or by writing WMI scripts. For more information about Request Filtering in IIS 7.0, visit *http://www.iis .net/ConfigReference/system.webServer/security/requestFiltering*.

The Request Filtering item in IIS 7.5 provides the following tabs to help you restrict HTTP requests.

- File Name Extensions

    With this tab, you can allow or deny access to web services according to a list of file name extensions specified in HTTP requests.

- Rules

    You can use the Rules tab to configure rules for allowing or denying web access according to various parameters, such as headers and deny strings.

- Hidden Segments

    This tab enables you to define a list of URL segments for which web access will be denied access and excluded from directory listings. (A segment is any part of a URL path between two slash [/] marks.)

- URL

    This tab enables you to allow specific URLs or to deny access to specific sequences within an URL. For example, if you specify "admin/config.xml" as a URL sequence, requests to *http://contoso.com/application/admin/config.xml* will be denied.

- HTTP Verbs

    Use this tab to create a list of HTTP verbs (such as GET, POST, or HEAD) whose access will be specifically allowed or denied.

- Headers

    Use this tab to create a list of HTTP headers whose access will be denied if a specified size limit is surpassed.

- Query Strings

  With this tab, you can create a list of query strings for which web access will be explicitly allowed or denied. An example of a query string is "%3b", which represents HTTP URL encoding for the apostrophe character and is used in some SQL injection attacks.

PRACTICE   Manage IIS Security Settings

This practice walks you through the steps required to manage security for a computer running Windows Server 2008 R2 that has the Web Server (IIS) role installed. Specifically, you learn how to enable remote administration and the effects of configuring handler mappings to increase security. The steps assume that you have already installed the Web Server (IIS) role by using the default options on Server2.contoso.local, and that you are familiar with the process of adding role services.

EXERCISE 1   Configuring and Managing Remote Administration

In this exercise, you use the *IIS Management Service* features to enable a user to connect to the computer. First, you must install the IIS Management Service role service, and then you create a new user based on IIS Manager credentials and configure permissions to access the Default Web Site. Finally, you connect to IIS, using the new user account to verify that the permissions and feature delegation settings are in effect. The final steps can be performed locally on Server2, or you can use another computer, running either Windows 7 or Windows Server 2008 R2, that has the IIS 7 Manager console installed. The steps assume that you perform the tasks locally on Server2.

1. Log on to Server2 as a user who has Administrator permissions.

2. Using Server Manager, add the Management Service role service to the web Server (IIS) server role. You can begin this process by right-clicking the *Web Server (IIS)* node and then selecting Add Role Services. On the Select Role Services page of the Add Role Services Wizard, you can find the Management Service role service within the Management Tools group.

3. After you have added the Management Service role service, open IIS Manager and connect to the local server (Server 2).

4. Click the server object in the left pane and then double-click the Management Service icon in Features View.

5. On the Management Service page, you should see a message stating that the Management Service (WMSVC) is stopped. This is necessary to make configuration changes. Select the Enable Remote Connections option.

6. In the Identity Credentials section, choose Windows Credentials Or IIS Manager Credentials. This enables you to create IIS Manager users later. Leave all other settings at their default values. Note that Management Service responds on port 8172 by default.

7. Start Management Service by clicking Start in the Actions pane. Note that you are unable to modify settings while the service is running.

8. If the Management Service message box appears, click Yes to save the settings before starting the service.

9. Return to Features View by clicking Back in the top toolbar.

10. Double-click IIS Manager Users to view a list of users who have been allowed to access the system. Note that, by default, there are no users in the list.

11. Click Add User in the Actions pane to create a new IIS Manager user. Use the WebAdmin01 username and the 1w3b!admin password. (Always use strong passwords.) Click OK to create the new user and verify that it appears in the list of IIS Manager Users.

12. In the left pane of IIS Manager, expand the *Sites* container and then click the *Default Web Site* object. Next, double-click IIS Manager Permissions in the Management section of Features View.

13. Click Allow User in the Actions pane. For the type of user, select IIS Manager and then type **WebAdmin01** in the text box.

    You can also click Select to select from all the users who have been defined on the server.

14. Click OK.

15. In IIS Manager, click the *Server2* object and then double-click Feature Delegation in the Management section of Features View. In the Group By drop-down list, select Delegation. Note which features in the list are set to Read Only. In later steps, you attempt to change SSL Settings to verify that feature delegation is working.

16. In IIS Manager, click Start Page in the left pane. In the center pane, click the Connect To A Site link.

17. For Server Name, type **server2.contoso.local**. For Site Name, type **Default Web Site**. Click Next.

18. For Username, type **WebAdmin01** and type **1w3b!admin** for Password. Click Next.

19. For the name of the connection, change the name to **Default Web Site – Test** to specify that this is a test connection. Click Finish.

    When the connection is complete, you see a new item called Default Web Site – Test in the left pane of IIS Manager. You can click this connection to administer the site, just as you would with the default local connection. However, note that the new connection shows only the contents of Default Web Site. You will have only the permissions that have been assigned to the WebAdmin01 user.

20. To verify the feature delegation settings, double-click SSL Settings in the IIS section of Features View.

    Note the message in the Actions pane stating that the feature has been locked and set to read only. Verify that you are unable to make changes to these settings.

21. Remove the new connection in IIS Manager by right-clicking it and selecting Remove Connection.

22. When you are finished, close IIS Manager. You can click Yes to save the changes.

EXERCISE 2 Managing Handler Mappings

In this exercise, you learn how to configure and manage handler mappings for a web application. Initially, you verify that content is being presented correctly to web users. You then disable a request handler mapping and verify that the content is no longer accessible. Finally, you revert the handler mappings to their inherited settings to restore access to the content.

1. If you have not done so already, log on to Server2 as a user who has Administrator permissions.

2. Using Windows Explorer, navigate to the *%SystemDrive%*\Inetpub\Wwwroot folder.

3. From the Organize menu in Windows Explorer, select Folder And Search Options.

4. On the View tab of the Folder Options dialog box, clear the Hide Extensions For Known File Types check box and then click OK.

5. Make a copy of the Iisstart.htm file and name it **Iisstart.test**.

6. When you are finished, close Windows Explorer.

7. Open IIS Manager and connect to the local server.

8. In the left pane of IIS Manager, expand the *Sites* node and select Default Web Site. In the Actions pane, click *Browse *:80 (http)*.

   This launches Internet Explorer and connects to the default content for the site. Note that the default document (in this case, Iisstart.htm) is displayed and that the page contains a .png image type.

9. In Internet Explorer, modify the URL to request the iisstart.test page. An example of the full URL would be *http://Server2/iisstart.test*.

   Although the file exists, you receive an HTTP Error 404.3. The error states that no handler is available to process the request.

10. When you are finished, close Internet Explorer.

11. In IIS Manager, with the Default Web Site still selected, double-click Handler Mappings in Features View.

    You see a list of all the default handlers that have been registered on the system.

12. Click the Add Module Mapping link to create a new mapping. For Request Path, type ***.test**. For Module, select StaticFileModule. For Name, type **Test Page Handler**. Leave the other settings at their default values and then click OK to create the mappings.

    This enables the web server to process files that have the .test extension.

13. Open Internet Explorer and navigate to the Iisstart.test page by using the same URL you used in step 9.

This time, you see a blank page, and no error message appears. This indicates that the new handler mapping you created is functioning properly. (By default, the HTML in the file with the .test extension cannot be read without coding a new custom handler. The default.png image does not appear in lisstart.test for this reason.)

14. Close Internet Explorer.

15. In IIS Manager, return to the Handler Mappings section for Default Web Site and then click Revert To Parent in the Actions pane. Click Yes to confirm the changes.

    This restores the default handler mappings and removes the Test Handler Mapping you created in a previous step.

16. When you are finished, close IIS Manager.

Lesson Summary

- When implementing IIS security, consider the overall goals of implementing defense-in-depth best practices and reducing the server's attack surface.

- IIS 7 uses consistent built-in user and group accounts for managing security.

- You can enable remote management of IIS by adding the Management Service role service.

- You can manage remote management capabilities by creating users, assigning permissions, and configuring feature delegation.

- Request handler mappings determine which types of content IIS will allow for a particular component in the hierarchy.

Lesson Review

You can use the following questions to test your knowledge of the information in Lesson 1, "Configuring IIS Security." The questions are also available on the companion CD if you prefer to review them in electronic form.

1. You are a systems administrator responsible for securing a Windows Server 2008 R2 web server. You have created a new website called Contoso Intranet that will contain seven web applications. One of the application developers has told you that her web application requires a new request handler that is processed by using a .NET library her team created. How can you meet these requirements while also maximizing security for the server?

A. Add a new managed handler to the Contoso Intranet website.

B. Add a new managed handler for the specific web application that requires it.

C. Add a new module mapping to the Contoso Intranet website.

D. Add a new module mapping for the specific web application that requires it.

2. You are a systems administrator responsible for managing a Windows Server 2008 R2 web server. Recently, your organization set up a new IIS website that users outside your organization will access. Consultants should be able to connect to this website by using IIS Manager. Your organization's security policy prevents you from creating domain accounts or local user accounts for these users. You attempt to use the IIS Manager Permissions feature for the website. However, when you click Allow User, you are able to select only Windows users. How can you resolve this problem?

A. Verify that Management Service has been started.

B. Reconfigure the file system permissions for the root folder of the website.

C. Reconfigure Management Service to enable Windows and IIS Manager credentials.

D. Verify the authentication settings for the website.

Lesson 2: Controlling Access to Web Services

Web servers are deployed in many configurations. Some servers provide content intended for the general public through the Internet. Others contain web application content intended only for a limited set of users. Web server administration must be able to define which users can connect to a web service and, after users have proven their identities, rules must be in place for determining which content is available to them.

In this lesson, you learn about how you can configure authentication and authorization for protecting web content in IIS. Due to the many security standards and approaches for web services, it is important to understand how to select the most appropriate one for a given scenario. You also learn how you can use features such as IP Address And Domain Restrictions and .NET trust levels to secure your web services further.

After this lesson, you will be able to:

- Describe the authentication options available for IIS web services.
- Configure authentication options for a web server, website, or web application.
- Implement and manage authorization rules to limit access to specific web content.
- Configure server certificates and enable Secure Sockets Layer (SSL) functionality for an IIS server.
- Create and manage IP Address And Domain Restrictions settings to limit access to an IIS web server.
- Configure .NET trust levels based on the needs of specific web applications.

Estimated lesson time: 75 minutes

Managing IIS Authentication

Authentication refers to the process by which a user or computer proves its identity for security purposes. The most familiar method is through a logon or username and an associated password. When working with web servers such as IIS, authentication settings and options determine how users will provide their credentials to access content stored on the web server. IIS provides numerous methods for securing content. By default, content stored in new websites, web applications, and virtual directories will allow access to anonymous users. This means that users are not required to provide any authentication information to retrieve the data. In this section, you learn about the authentication modes supported by IIS and how you can configure them.

Understanding Anonymous Authentication

For many types of web servers, users should be able to access at least a default page or some content without being required to provide authentication information. When you enable the Web Server (IIS) role by using default options, anonymous authentication is enabled for the Default Web Site and its associated web content. Anonymous authentication is designed to provide access to content that should be available to all users who can connect to the web server. An example is the default IIS webpage for Default Web Site. When IIS receives a request for content, it automatically uses a specific identity to attempt to complete the request. By default, anonymous authentication uses the IUSR built-in account. (See Figure 6-20.) As long as this user account has permission to access the content (based on NTFS permissions), the request is processed automatically.

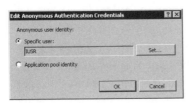

FIGURE 6-20 Editing settings for anonymous authentication credentials.

It is also possible to use the Set option to provide a username and password for a different account. This is useful when you plan to use different NTFS permissions for different web content. Finally, there is an option to use Application Pool Identity. This setting instructs IIS to use the same credentials that are applied to the application pool used by the website or web application.

If all the content on the web server should be available to all users, then no further authentication configuration is required. More commonly, however, you want to restrict access to at least some content on the server. For example, an intranet server might include a web application or virtual directory that is intended for only members of the Human Resources department. To restrict access to content, you can use NTFS permissions. If the credentials configured for the anonymous authentication option are insufficient to access the content, it will not be returned to the user automatically. Generally, you enable one of the other available authentication methods so that authorized users can access the content.

> **NOTE SIMPLIFYING CONTENT PROTECTION**
>
> On all web servers, some content exists that should not be accessible to any users. Examples include contents of system folders (such as the Windows system folder) and application source code stored within web content folders. You can use *Deny* NTFS permissions to ensure that users cannot use anonymous credentials to access this content. If you are using multiple accounts for anonymous authentication of different content, it is best to create a group that contains these accounts. You can then deny permission to the group to simplify administration.

Understanding Forms Authentication

A common security approach web developers use is to use standard HTTP forms to transmit logon information. Forms authentication uses an HTTP 302 (Login/Redirect) response to redirect users to a logon page. Generally, the logon page provides users with locations to enter a logon name and password. When this information is submitted back to the logon page, it is validated. Assuming that the credentials are accepted, users are redirected to the content they originally requested. By default, form submissions send data in an unencrypted format. To secure the transmission of logon information, enable encryption through SSL or TLS.

Forms authentication is the most common approach used on the Internet because it does not have any specific web browser requirements. Web developers typically build their own logon pages. Logons are often validated against user account information stored in a relational database (for Internet sites) or against an Active Directory Domain Services (AD DS) domain.

The default settings for forms authentication are designed for use by ASP.NET web applications, and the Forms Authentication option appears only when you have added the ASP.NET role service to the Web Server (IIS) role. You can edit the settings of forms authentication to manage several settings. (See Figure 6-21.) The primary setting is the Login URL. This specifies the name of the webpage to which users are sent when they attempt to access protected content.

After the user has provided authentication information, cookies are sent from the web browser to the web server during each request. This enables the client to prove that it has authenticated with the web server, which is necessary because HTTP is a stateless protocol. The Cookie Settings section enables you to configure how cookies will be used by the site. The Mode options include:

- Do Not Use Cookies
- Use Cookies
- Auto Detect
- Use Device Profile

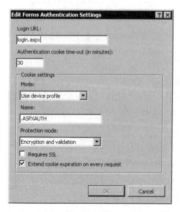

FIGURE 6-21 Configuring settings for forms authentication.

The most appropriate option will be based on web browser requirements (for example, whether your website requires users to enable support for cookies) and the requirements of the web application or web content.

Understanding Challenge-Based Authentication

Users who access secure websites on the Internet are familiar with the process of providing a username and password to access secured content or to perform actions such as placing on-line orders. IIS supports three methods of presenting a security challenge to users who are attempting to access web content that has been secured using file system permissions. Each of these methods relies on sending an HTTP 401 Challenge—a standard method that prompts users to provide logon information. These three authentication methods are:

- **Basic authentication**   Presents an authentication challenge to web users through a standard method that is supported by all web browsers. The main drawback to this method is that information users provide is encoded but not encrypted. This means that, if the information is intercepted, the logon and password details can be obtained easily. To transfer basic authentication information securely, either ensure that your network connections are secure (for example, in a data center environment) or enable encryption using SSL or TLS.

- **Digest authentication**   Relies on the HTTP 1.1 protocol to provide a secure method of transmitting logon credentials. It does this by using a Windows domain controller to authenticate the user. A potential drawback is that it requires clients' web browsers to support HTTP 1.1. Current versions of most popular browsers support this method, so it is possible to use digest authentication for both Internet and intranet environments.

- **Windows authentication**   Provides a secure and easy-to-administer authentication option. It relies on the use of either the NTLM or Kerberos authentication protocol to validate users' credentials against a Windows domain or local security database. This method is designed primarily for use in intranet environments, where clients and web servers are members of the same domain. To simplify administration, administrators can use AD DS domain accounts to control access to content.

One important consideration about these challenge-based authentication methods is their interaction with anonymous authentication. If you want to require users to provide logon information before accessing web content, you must disable anonymous authentication. If anonymous authentication remains enabled, content that is not protected by using file system permissions is automatically made available to users without requiring authentication. Another requirement to note is that you cannot enable both forms authentication and challenge-based authentication for the same content.

Understanding ASP.NET Impersonation

Like form authentication, *ASP.NET impersonation* appears as an authentication option when you add the ASP.NET role service. Impersonation is a security method by which an IIS web request is processed by using the security information provided by a specific user account or by the user who is accessing the site. When ASP.NET impersonation is disabled (the default setting), the security context for processing requests is based on the account the web application uses. When you enable impersonation, you can specify a user account for determining the security context. (See Figure 6-22.) To provide the username and password information, click Set.

FIGURE 6-22 Configuring ASP.NET impersonation settings.

Another option is to configure ASP.NET impersonation to the Authenticated User option. This setting specifies that the security permissions of a user who has been authenticated (using one of the other authentication options) will be used to provide access to content. This setting is useful when you want to use file system permissions that use specific users and groups to decide which content should be protected. When used in this way, it is most appropriate for environments that support relatively small numbers of users, such as department-level intranet web servers.

Understanding Client Certificate Authentication

In addition to the other available authentication options, IIS provides support for using client certificates to validate the identity of a web user. This method requires users to have security certificates installed on their computers. When a request is made for protected content, IIS automatically validates the identity of the client by querying the certificate information. There are three main modes by which client certificates can be used:

- **One-To-One mappings** In this configuration, the web server must contain a copy of the client certificate used by every computer that will access restricted content. The server compares its copy of the certificate with the one presented by the client to validate requests.

- **Many-To-One mappings** It is often impractical to manage certificates for all possible web users on the server. Although this method is slightly less secure, many-to-one mappings are based on the web server performing authentication by using certain information found in the client certificate. A common example is validating the organization information in the certificate to ensure that the user is coming from a trusted company.

- **Active Directory mappings** Active Directory Certificate Services can simplify the creation and management of client certificates. To enable this method, organizations must first set up their own certificate-based infrastructure.

Because of the certificate requirements for client certificate authentication, this method is most often used in environments in which systems administrators have control over end users' computers. It is impractical to require certificates for publicly accessible Internet websites and applications.

Understanding Authentication Requirements

Handlers and modules manage IIS authentication. The specific authentication options available for a web server are based on the Web Server (IIS) role services installed. The list of available role services includes:

- Basic Authentication
- Windows Authentication
- Digest Authentication
- Client Certificate Mapping Authentication
- IIS Client Certificate Mapping Authentication
- ASP.NET (for forms authentication and ASP.NET impersonation)

To add or remove a security-related role service, open Server Manager, expand the Roles section, right-click Web Server (IIS), and then select either Add Role Services or Remove Role Services. (See Figure 6-23.) Because role services affect the available authentication options for the entire web server, determine the requirements of all the web applications and web content on your server.

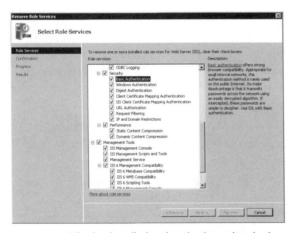

FIGURE 6-23 Viewing installed authentication-related role services.

In addition to role service settings, each of the authentication methods has specific module requirements, as shown in Table 6-1. For more information about managing modules, see the "Managing Request Handlers" section earlier in this chapter.

TABLE 6-1 IIS Authentication Methods and Their Requirements

AUTHENTICATION METHODS	REQUIRED MODULE(S)
Anonymous	AnonymousAuthModule
ASP.NET Impersonation	ManagedEngine
Basic	BasicAuthModule
	TokenCacheModule
Client Certificates	iisClientCertificateMappingModule
Client Certificates (Active Directory Mapping)	CertificateMappingAuthenticationModule
Digest	DigestAuthModule
Forms	FormsAuthenticationModule
Windows	WindowsAuthenticationModule

Configuring Authentication Settings

IIS enables you to define configuration settings by using the web object hierarchy. Authentication settings can be configured for objects at the following levels:

- Web server
- Websites
- Web applications
- Virtual directories
- Physical folders and individual files

Authentication settings that are defined at higher levels (such as for a web application) apply automatically to lower-level objects. This method makes it easier to manage settings for multiple websites, web applications, and their related content.

To configure authentication settings by using IIS Manager, select the appropriate object in the left pane and then double-click Authentication in Features View. Figure 6-24 shows the default authentication options for the Default Web Site object.

The default display shows a complete list of the available authentication options, grouped by the response type used. Each method can be enabled or disabled by selecting the item and using the *Enable* or *Disable* commands in the Actions pane. In addition, some authentication options provide additional commands for managing settings. By default, when you enable or disable an authentication option, the setting applies to all lower-level objects and content in the IIS hierarchy. You can override this behavior by explicitly enabling or disabling authentication methods at lower levels.

To verify your authentication-related settings, you should always test access to content by using a web browser. In some cases, it might be necessary to use a second computer to ensure that authentication is working properly. For example, if you are already connected to a computer running Windows Server 2008 R2 as a member of the administrators group and you want to test Windows Authentication, you should attempt to connect from another computer in the environment to help prevent automatic authentication from affecting your test results.

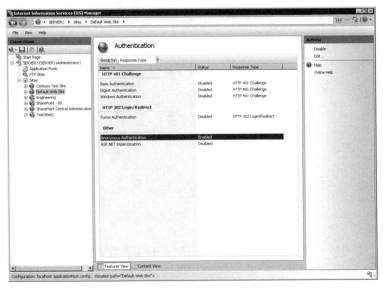

FIGURE 6-24 Viewing authentication options for Default Web Site by using IIS Manager.

Managing URL Authorization Rules

Authorization is a method by which systems administrators can determine which resources and content are available to specific users. Authorization relies on authentication to validate the identity of a user. After the identity has been proven, authorization rules determine which actions a user or computer can perform. IIS provides methods of securing different types of content by using URL-based authorization. Because web content is generally requested by using a URL that includes a full path to the content being requested, you can configure authorization settings easily by using IIS Manager.

Creating URL Authorization Rules

To enable URL authorization, the UrlAuthorizationModule must be enabled. Authorization rules can be configured at the level of the web server for specific websites, for specific web applications, and for specific files (based on a complete URL path). *URL authorization rules* use inheritance so that lower-level objects inherit authorization settings from their parent objects (unless they are specifically overridden).

To configure authorization settings, select the appropriate object in the left pane of IIS Manager and then select Authorization Rules in Features View. Figure 6-25 shows an example of multiple rules configured for a website.

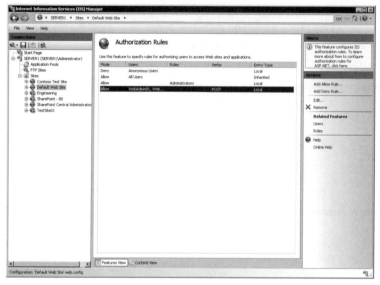

FIGURE 6-25 Viewing authorization rules for a website.

There are two types of rules: Allow and Deny. You can create new rules by using the *Add Allow Rule* and *Add Deny Rule* commands in the Actions pane. The available options for both types of rules are the same, as shown in Figure 6-26. When creating a new rule, the main setting is determining the users to which the rule applies. The options are:

- All Users
- All Anonymous Users
- Specific Roles Or User Groups
- Specific Users

FIGURE 6-26 Creating a new Allow Rule for a web application.

When you choose to specify users or groups to which the rule applies, you can type the appropriate names in a comma-separated list. The specific users and groups are defined using .NET role providers. This is a standard feature that is available to ASP.NET web developers. Developers can create their own roles and user accounts and can define permissions within their applications. Generally, information about users and roles is stored in a relational database or relies on a directory service such as Active Directory.

In addition to user and role selections, you can further configure an authorization rule based on specific HTTP verbs. For example, if you want to apply a rule only for *POST* commands (which typically send information from a web browser to a web server), add only the POST verb to the rule.

Managing Rule Inheritance

As mentioned earlier in this section, authorization rules are inherited automatically by lower-level objects. This is useful when your website and web content is organized hierarchically based on intended users or groups. The Entry Type column shows whether a rule has been inherited from a higher level or has been defined locally. IIS Manager automatically prevents you from creating duplicate rules. You can remove rules at any level, including both *Inherited* and *Local* entry types.

Configuring Server Certificates

One of the many challenges related to security is verifying the identity of a web server, and, after you are reasonably sure that the server can be trusted, you must protect communications between the web client and the web server. On many networks, and especially on the Internet, providing secure communications for sensitive data is a key concern. Server certificates are designed to provide added security for web services. IIS provides built-in support for creating and managing server certificates and for enabling encrypted communications. In this section, you learn how to configure and enable these options.

Understanding Server Certificates

Server certificates are a method by which a web server can prove its identity to the clients attempting to access it. The general approach to providing this functionality is by a hierarchy of trust authorities. The party that issues a server certificate is known as a *certificate authority (CA)*. On the Internet, numerous third-party organizations are available for validating servers and generating certificates. Assuming that users trust these third parties, they should be able to extend the trust to validated websites. Organizations can also serve as their own CA for internal servers. This enables systems administrators to validate and approve new server deployments by using a secure mechanism.

The general process for obtaining a server certificate involves three major steps:

- **Generating a certificate request** The request is created on a web server, which produces a text file containing the information about the request in an encrypted format. The certificate request identifies the web server uniquely.

- **Submitting the certificate request to a CA**   The certificate request is submitted to a CA (generally by using a secure website or email). The CA then verifies the information in the request and creates a trusted server certificate.

- **Obtaining and installing a certificate on the web server**   The CA returns a certificate to the requester, usually in the form of a small text file. This file can then be imported into the web server configuration to enable secure communications.

> *NOTE* **CLIENT CERTIFICATES VS. SERVER CERTIFICATES**
>
> Certificate-based technology can be used with a web server by several methods. Use client-based certificates to verify access to a web server by validating clients. In this case, the client holds a certificate the server can validate. You learned about this method earlier in this lesson. Server-side certificates are installed on web server computers to prove their identity to web clients and to enable encrypted communications. Client-side certificates are generally used in intranet or extranet environments, whereas server-side certificates are common for securing all types of web servers.

Creating an Internet Certificate Request

Use IIS Manager to obtain a certificate for use on an IIS web server. To begin the process, connect to a web server running Windows Server 2008 or Windows Server 2008 R2 and double-click Server Certificates in Features View, as shown in Figure 6-27. Note that certificate requests are generated at the level of the web server and not for other objects, such as websites or web applications.

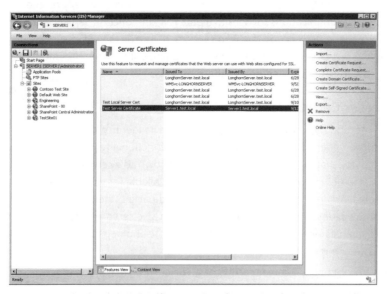

FIGURE 6-27 Viewing Server Certificate options for an IIS web server.

Depending on the configuration of the local server, some certificates might already be included in the default configuration. The Actions pane provides commands for creating new certificates.

To begin the certificate request process, click Create Certificate Request. As shown in Figure 6-28, you will be required to provide information about the requesting organization. The CA uses this information to determine whether to issue the certificate. Therefore, it is important for information to be exact. For example, the Organization field should include the complete legal name of the requesting company. The Common Name field generally defines the domain name that will be used with the certificate.

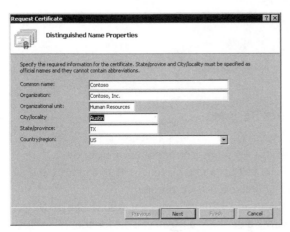

FIGURE 6-28 The Distinguished Name Properties page.

The second step of the certificate request process requires you to choose the cryptographic method to secure the certificate request. (See Figure 6-29.) The Cryptographic Service Provider setting should use a method accepted by the certificate authority. (The default option, Microsoft RSA SChannel Cryptographic Provider, is accepted by most third-party CAs.) The Bit Length setting indicates the strength of the encryption. Larger values take more time to process (due to computational overhead) but provide added security.

The final step of the process involves storing the certificate request to a file. Here you can provide a fully qualified path and file name into which the request will be stored. The request itself will be stored in a text file that contains encrypted information.

The next step of the process involves submitting the certificate request to a CA. Generally, the issuer's website will request that you either upload the certificate request or copy and paste the contents into a secure website. The issuer will also require additional information, such as details about your organization and payment information.

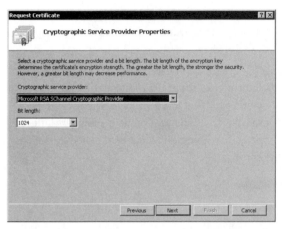

FIGURE 6-29 The Cryptographic Service Provider Properties page.

Completing an Internet Certificate Request

The amount of time a public third-party CA can take to process a request varies. After the request has been processed and approved, the CA sends a response by email or through its website. You can then store this response in a text file and provide it to IIS to complete the process by selecting the appropriate request in the Server Certificates feature view and then clicking the *Complete Certificate Request* command in the Actions pane. You will be asked to specify the path and file name of the response along with a friendly name for administration purposes, as shown in Figure 6-30. The convention is to use a file name with a .cer extension for the response; however, any type of standard text file will work.

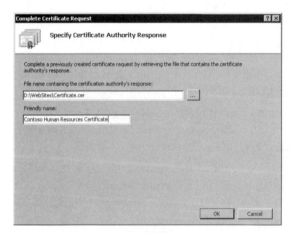

FIGURE 6-30 Completing the certificate request process.

Assuming that the certificate request matches the response, the certificate is imported into the configuration of IIS and is ready for use.

Creating Other Certificate Types

In addition to the standard certificate request process, you can use two other commands to create certificates. These commands are also available in the Actions pane in the properties of the Server Certificates feature. The *Create Domain Certificate* option generates a request to an internal certificate authority. This is commonly used in organizations that have their own certificate services infrastructure. Instead of sending the request to a third-party CA, the request is designed to be sent to an internal server. Figure 6-31 shows the available options. The Specify Online Certificate Authority text box accepts the path and name of an internal CA server. The Friendly Name can identify the purpose of the certificate.

> **MORE INFO   ACTIVE DIRECTORY CERTIFICATE SERVICES**
>
> Windows Server 2008 and Windows Server 2008 R2 include the Active Directory Certificate Services server role, which enables administrators to create their own certificate-based security infrastructure. The details of implementing these services are outside the scope of this book and the scope of the 70-643 exam. For more information about configuring certificate services, see *http://technet.microsoft.com/en-us/windowsserver/dd448615.aspx*.

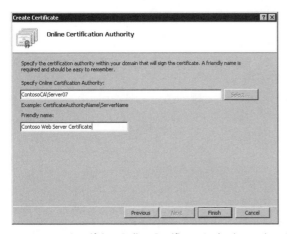

FIGURE 6-31 Specifying Online Certificate Authority settings for a Domain Certificate.

Creating a Self-Signed Certificate

The certificate creation and management process can require several steps, and usually requires an added cost for obtaining a certificate from a trusted third-party CA. Although these steps are necessary to ensure security in a production environment, an easier method is preferable for development and test environments. *Self-signed certificates* can test certificate functionality by creating a local certificate. By avoiding the CA process, it is easy to create these certificates by using the *Create Self-Signed Certificate* command in the Actions pane. Figure 6-32 shows the dialog box.

Unlike other certificate types, it is not necessary to provide organizational information for the certificate because the certificate itself is created immediately on the local computer. The primary drawback of self-signed certificates is that users who access the web server using a secure connection receive a warning that the certificate has not been issued by a third party. (See Figure 6-33.) Whereas this is generally not a problem in test environments, it prevents the use of self-signed certificates for production web servers.

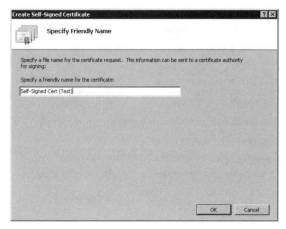

FIGURE 6-32 Creating a self-signed certificate.

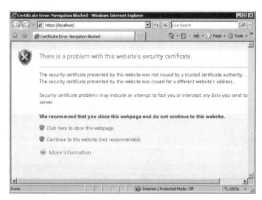

FIGURE 6-33 Viewing a certificate-related error when accessing a server that is using a self-signed certificate.

Viewing Certificate Details

The contents of a server certificate include several details and properties. To view this information, double-click an item in the Server Certificates list for a web server. The Certificate dialog box, shown in Figure 6-34, provides information about the server certificate. The General tab displays details about the issuer of the certificate. For an Internet-based certificate, this is the name of the trusted third party that issued it. Additionally, certificates have a range of valid dates.

FIGURE 6-34 Viewing general information for a server certificate.

The Details tab displays additional properties of the certificate, including the encryption method. The Certification Path tab shows the entire trust hierarchy for the certificate. In environments that have multiple levels of CAs, this is useful for tracking all the trust relationships that are used. For the certificate to be considered valid, all the levels must be trusted. (See Figure 6-35.)

FIGURE 6-35 Viewing certificate information for a public website by using Internet Explorer.

Importing and Exporting Certificates

After a certificate has been installed on a web server, you might need to export it to a file. You can use IIS Manager to do this by right-clicking the certificate and choosing the *Export* command. You can then provide an export location and file name for the file along with a password to protect the certificate from being installed by unauthorized users. (See Figure 6-36.) By default, exported certificate files use the .pfx extension. However, you can use any other extension. The contents of the exported certificate are encrypted and protected with the password you provide.

FIGURE 6-36 Exporting a server certificate by using IIS Manager.

To import a certificate, click the *Import* command in the Actions pane. You are prompted to provide the file system location of the exported certificate file along with the password to open it. In addition, you can choose whether you want to allow the certificate to be exported in the future.

Enabling Secure Sockets Layer

After you have added a server certificate to an IIS web server, you can enable SSL-based connections. SSL-based connections rely on certificates to validate the identity of the web server. After the identity has been proven, users can create a secure connection by using the HTTP Secure (HTTPS) protocol. By default, HTTPS connections use TCP port 443 for communications. To modify the details or to enable HTTPS for a website, you must configure the site bindings for a website. (For complete details about configuring site bindings, see Chapter 5.)

You can also require SSL-enabled connections for specific websites by using IIS Manager. To do this, select a website, a web application, or a folder and then double-click SSL Settings in the Features view. In Windows Server 2008 R2, websites have only an HTTP binding by default, so you first must add an HTTPS binding before you can configure SSL. (Adding an HTTPS binding requires you to specify a server SSL certificate.) Figure 6-37 shows the available SSL settings after you have added an HTTPS binding to a website. The check boxes enable you to specify whether SSL is required to access this content. If the option is enabled, standard HTTP connections are not enabled. Optionally, you can specify whether client certificates will be ignored, accepted, or required.

Overall, server certificates and SSL provide a standard method of protecting web-based connections and web server content. Support for server certificates and SSL is often expected for all types of web servers that contain sensitive information.

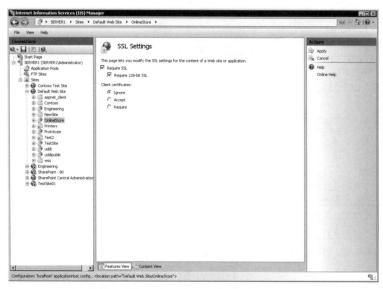

FIGURE 6-37 Configuring SSL settings for a web application.

Configuring IP Address and Domain Restrictions

Although some web servers are configured to provide public access to all content, it's also common to need to restrict access to only specific groups of users. By default, IIS is configured to accept requests on all connections based on site binding settings such as IP address and TCP port. Systems administrators can further restrict access to websites by responding only to requests that originate from specific IP addresses or domains using IIS Manager.

The first step is to select the level at which you want to assign the restrictions. The IP Address and Domain Restrictions feature is available at the server, site, web application, virtual directory, and folder levels. In general, assign restrictions at the highest level for which the settings will apply. For example, if all the web applications in a particular site should respond to requests from a single domain only, configure the request settings at the site level. By default, IIS does not include any restrictions. To configure request settings, select the appropriate object in the left pane of IIS Manager and then double-click IP Address and Domain Restrictions in Features View. (This feature becomes available when you add the IP and Domain Restrictions component of the Security role service.) Figure 6-38 provides an example of the settings.

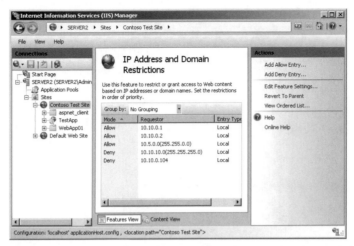

FIGURE 6-38 Configuring IPv4 Address and Domain Restrictions for a website.

Adding Allow and Deny Entries

You can add two main types of entries to the IP Address and Domain Restrictions configuration. Allow entries specify which IP addresses can access web content; Deny entries define which addresses cannot access the content. When configuring *IP address restrictions*, you can specify either a single IP address or a range of IP addresses. (See Figure 6-39.) When specifying a range, you can enter the initial IP address and the subnet mask. This determines the range of addresses that will be allowed or denied. It is possible to exclude specific addresses or ranges by using additional allow or deny rules. Overall, however, try to keep the configuration simple to make administration and management as easy as possible.

FIGURE 6-39 Adding a Deny entry IP address restriction for a website.

The single address option is useful if only a few users require access to the site or if only a few other servers require access to the content. This is common in environments that support distributed server-side web applications that are not designed for direct user access. IP address ranges are more appropriate when groups of users and computers should have access to the environment. For example, if all the users in the Human Resources department are located on the same subnet, that subnet can be allowed while other subnets are denied.

When evaluating connection rules, IIS evaluates all allow and deny rules to determine whether an address has access. Deny rules take precedence over allow rules. If users are denied access to a site, they see a screen similar to the one shown in Figure 6-40.

An additional setting defines the default behavior for any IP addresses that are not explicitly added to either the Allow or Deny list. By default, IIS allows access automatically from these addresses. To change the setting, click Edit Feature Settings in the Actions pane and choose Deny for the Access For Unspecified Clients setting. (See Figure 6-41.)

FIGURE 6-40 An error message returned to a user, based on site restriction settings.

FIGURE 6-41 Configuring feature settings for IPv4 Address and Domain Restrictions.

Adding Domain Restrictions

Managing access to web services by using IP addresses is useful when the list of incoming clients is well known. This is typical of intranet and internal network environments in which network administrators can configure and manage IP address ranges. In other types of web server scenarios—such as public web servers or extranets—managing IP address ranges can be time consuming and impractical.

An alternative to using IP address-based restrictions is specifying allow and deny settings by using domain name restrictions. This method depends on a Domain Name System (DNS) reverse lookup operation. Whenever a user attempts to connect to IIS, the web server performs a reverse DNS lookup to resolve the requester's IP address to a domain name. IIS then uses the domain name to determine whether the user should have access. Domain-based restrictions are disabled by default because this feature can decrease server performance significantly. Every incoming request must be resolved, adding overhead to request processing. In addition, this can place significant load on the DNS server infrastructure. From a management standpoint, however, this feature can sometimes be useful (especially in low-volume scenarios).

To enable domain name restrictions, double-click the IP Address And Domain Restrictions feature for a portion of the website and then click Edit Feature Settings in the Actions pane. As shown in Figure 6-41, you can select the Enable Domain Name Restrictions check box to enable this feature. Figure 6-42 shows the confirmation warning when you enable this feature.

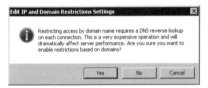

FIGURE 6-42 Viewing a warning when enabling domain name restrictions.

After you have enabled domain name restrictions, you can use the *Add Allow Entry* and *Add Deny Entry* commands to configure the rules. As shown in Figure 6-43, the dialog boxes include a setting for Domain Name.

FIGURE 6-43 Adding a domain name restriction to a website.

As mentioned earlier, the default behavior for allow and deny entries is for these restrictions to flow from parent objects to child objects. If you have made explicit changes to the settings for an object such as a web application, you can use the *Revert To Parent* command in the Actions pane to remove settings at that level. The effective settings are then based on the parent hierarchy.

Configuring .NET Trust Levels

The .NET Framework technology provides web developers with a strong set of features for implementing applications. The functionality includes web applications (based on the ASP. NET platform) and other managed code features. It is relatively simple to create .NET applications that can perform a wide array of operations on a computer. From a security standpoint, however, it is important to restrict the permissions that are granted to a .NET application. Malicious or defective code can cause problems ranging from unauthorized access to data to the accidental deletion of content.

To help systems administrators manage permissions on production servers better, IIS supports Code Access Security (CAS) policy. CAS policies can determine which operations are available to .NET-based application code. There are two main types of configuration. The full trust option provides ASP.NET application code with all permissions on the computer. For compatibility reasons, this is the default setting for applications that are based on.NET Framework 1.0, 1.1, and 2.0.

Understanding Partial Trust Levels

The other CAS policy option is partial trust, which limits the actions .NET applications can perform. These options are available to applications that are built using .NET Framework 1.1 and .NET Framework 2.0. The goal of partial trust is to enable only the permissions that are necessary for a specific web application.

Trust levels can be configured at different levels in the web server object hierarchy. These levels include:

- Web server
- Websites
- Web applications
- Virtual directories and physical folders

As with other security-related settings, trust levels that are defined at parent levels automatically apply to child objects unless they are specifically overridden. In general, define *.NET trust level* settings at the highest relevant setting. For example, if none of the web applications in a website should have full permissions, you can configure these settings at the site level. You can then manage exceptions by assigning the necessary .NET trust level settings for specific web applications or folders.

Understanding .NET Trust Levels

The .NET Framework contains many features and operations that can cause security issues on a web server. To provide a simpler method of configuring and applying trust settings, IIS includes five built-in levels that can be applied to IIS objects. The specific settings for each level are defined within various .config files. (For more information about using configuration files, see Chapter 5.) It is also possible to view and modify the settings in these files by using an XML editor or text editor. Table 6-2 lists the levels and their effects.

TABLE 6-2 .NET Trust Levels and Their Descriptions

.NET TRUST LEVEL	CONFIG FILE NAME	DESCRIPTION	RESTRICTED ACTIONS
Full (internal)	N/A	Provides full permissions to an ASP.NET application	N/A
High	Web_hightrust.config	Provides access to most actions on the server and is designed for well-trusted and well-tested web applications	<ul><li>Calling unmanaged code</li><li>Calling serviced components</li><li>Writing to the event log</li><li>Accessing message queuing services</li><li>Accessing ODBC, OLEDB, and Oracle data sources</li></ul>
Medium	Web_medium trust. config	Provides additional restrictions for web applications that should not need to access the file system or registry	<ul><li>Accessing files outside of the application's directory</li><li>Accessing the registry</li><li>Making network or web service calls</li></ul>
Low	Web_lowtrust.config	Further restricts application capabilities	<ul><li>Writing to the file system</li><li>Calling the Assert method (a method that is often used for testing application code)</li></ul>
Minimal	Web_minimal trust. config	Allows only *Execute* permissions and prevents access to other resources on the computer	Performing actions that require permissions greater than *Execute*

EXAM TIP

Expect to see questions on .NET trust levels. Familiarize yourself with the purpose of each .NET trust level and keep in mind which types of operations are considered the most risky. The levels are cumulative, from a standpoint of restrictions. For example, the Low level adds further restrictions to the Medium level and the levels above it. On the exam, be sure to understand a web application's requirements before deciding which trust level is most appropriate.

The default setting is Full (internal), which provides the best compatibility but also the greatest security risk. Whenever possible, lower the .NET trust levels to ensure that application code is being run with minimal permissions. Often, this involves interactions with web developers to determine requirements and perform complete testing at various security levels.

Configuring .NET Trust Levels

To configure .NET trust levels by using IIS Manager, select the object for which you want to assign the settings and then double-click .NET Trust Levels from Features View, as shown in Figure 6-44. To change the setting, select the appropriate level from the drop-down list and click Apply. After the trust level is set, it will apply to all ASP.NET applications running at the selected level and to any child objects unless the settings are explicitly overridden.

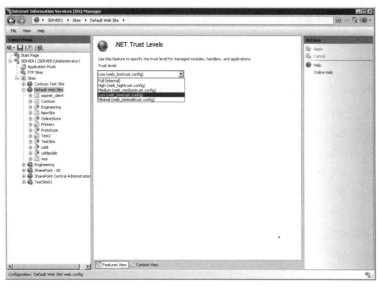

FIGURE 6-44 Viewing .NET Trust Levels options for a website.

✔ Quick Check

1. How can you manage which content is available to users without requiring any authentication?

2. What are the requirements for enabling SSL on an IIS web server that will be accessible from the Internet?

3. How can you restrict access to an IIS web application to only a limited set of computers?

Quick Check Answers

1. Assuming that anonymous authentication is enabled, IIS will use NTFS file system permissions settings to determine which content requires credentials to access.

2. To provide SSL security for Internet-based connections, obtain a security certificate from a trusted third-party issuer and install the certificate on the web server. You can then enable SSL through an HTTPS site binding.

3. You can use IP address restrictions to specify which computers should have access to an IIS web server. Other options are also possible, including the use of client certificates.

PRACTICE   **Secure Web Servers and Web Content**

In these exercises, you apply the information you learned about ways to add security to specific web content. The steps assume that you have installed the Web Server (IIS) role using the default settings and that you are familiar with the process of adding role services.

EXERCISE 1   Managing and Testing Authentication Settings

In this exercise, you configure and verify the effects of various authentication settings.

1. Log on to Contoso.local from Server2 as a domain administrator.

2. Using Server Manager, add the following role services to the Web Server (IIS) role. You can find these role services in the Security group.

   ■ Basic Authentication

   ■ Windows Authentication

   ■ Digest Authentication

   ■ URL Authorization

   ■ IP and Domain Restrictions

3. When you are finished, close Server Manager.

4. Open IIS Manager, browse to the *Sites* container, and select Default Web Site in the left pane. Double-click Authentication in Features View.

   The default settings specify that only anonymous authentication is enabled.

5. Click Default Web Site again and then click Browse *:80 (http) in the Actions pane. Verify that the default IIS start page is displayed. Keep the web browser open, but return to IIS Manager.

6. Again, double-click Authentication in Features View. Select Digest Authentication and then click Enable in the Actions pane.

7. Return to Internet Explorer and type **http://server2** in the address box.

   Note that you are not prompted to provide authentication information. This is because anonymous authentication is still enabled for the site.

8. Return to IIS Manager, select anonymous authentication, and then click Disable in the Actions pane.

9. Return to Internet Explorer and refresh the page. This time, you are prompted to provide logon information to access the site. Enter your username and password and then click OK to verify that the site loads. Optionally, you can provide invalid logon

information (such as a user account that does not exist) to see that you cannot access the site. When you are finished, close Internet Explorer.

10. To restore the original authentication settings, return to IIS Manager. Disable Digest Authentication and enable anonymous authentication.

11. When you are finished, close IIS Manager and log off Server2.

EXERCISE 2 Configuring Server Certificates

In this exercise, you create a self-signed security certificate for Server2.contoso.local and then require SSL to access Default Web Site and test the settings by using Internet Explorer.

1. Log on to Server2 as a user with *Administrator* permissions on the computer.

2. Open IIS Manager and select the server object in the left pane.

3. Double-click Server Certificates in the IIS section of Features View.

   Depending on which roles and role services have been installed on the local server, some certificates might already be available on the server.

4. Click Create Self-Signed Certificate in the Actions pane.

5. For the name of the certificate, type **Test Local SSL Certificate** and then click OK.

   You should now see the new certificate in the Server Certificates view of IIS Manager.

6. To view the properties of the new certificate, right-click it and select View.

   Note details such as the issuer (which is the name of the server) and the dates for which the certificate is valid. (New certificates expire in one year.) The Certification Path tab shows only the certificate itself and not a chain of trust, which signifies that it has not been issued by a trusted certificate authority (CA). For this reason, the certificate is not suited for access by users on public networks such as the Internet.

7. Click OK when you are finished.

8. In IIS Manager, right-click the *Default Web Site* object and select Edit Bindings.

9. In the Site Bindings dialog box, Click Add.

10. In the Add Site Bindings dialog box, in the Type drop-down list, select HTTPS.

11. In the SSL Certificate list, select Test Local SSL Certificate. Click OK to save the settings and then click Close. (If, after you click OK, a message box informs you that the binding is already being used, first click Yes and then click Close.)

12. In IIS Manager, ensure that the *Default Web Site* object is selected and then double-click SSL Settings in Features View. Enable the Require SSL option and then click Apply in the Actions pane.

13. Click Back to return to Features View for Default Web Site. In the Actions pane, choose Browse *:80 (http). This launches Internet Explorer and attempts to connect to the site by using a non-SSL (HTTP) connection. You receive an error stating, "The Page You Are Trying To Access Is Secure With Secure Sockets Layer (SSL)." Close Internet Explorer.

14. In IIS Manager, click Browse *:443 (https) in the Actions pane.

This time, you receive a warning stating that there is a problem with the website's security certificate. This is because a self-signed certificate was not issued by a trusted CA.

15. To access the site anyway, click Continue To This Website. In the Security Alert message box, click OK.

    The address bar turns red, and a Certificate Error message appears. The site content is, however, accessible.

16. When you are finished, close Internet Explorer.

17. In IIS Manager, double-click the SSL Settings feature for Default Web Site and disable the Require SSL option. Click Apply in the Actions pane to save the setting.

18. When you are finished, close IIS Manager.

Lesson Summary

- Anonymous authentication provides access to site content without requiring users to provide credentials.
- Forms authentication is useful for public websites and applications that manage their own security.
- URL authorization rules can determine which users or groups have access to which website content.
- Web server administrators can use Internet server certificates to enable encrypted connections through SSL over the Internet.
- Administrators can create self-signed server certificates for testing and development purposes.
- You can use IP Address And Domain Restrictions to restrict access to web content.
- .NET trust levels restrict the permissions that managed code has on a web server.

Lesson Review

You can use the following questions to test your knowledge of the information in Lesson 2, "Controlling Access to Web Services." The questions are also available on the companion CD if you prefer to review them in electronic form.

> **NOTE ANSWERS**
>
> Answers to these questions and explanations of why each answer choice is correct or incorrect are located in the "Answers" section at the end of the book.

1. You are an IIS web server administrator implementing authentication settings for a new Human Resources website. According to the requirements for the website, users should be prompted for authentication information when they attempt to access the site. The site will be accessed only by users who have accounts in your organization's

Active Directory domain. You have already configured the file system permissions for the content based on the appropriate settings. You also want to maximize security of the site. Which two actions should you take to meet these requirements? (Each correct answer presents part of a complete solution. Choose two.)

A. Enable Windows authentication.

B. Enable basic authentication.

C. Disable anonymous authentication.

D. Enable anonymous authentication.

2. You are a systems administrator troubleshooting a problem with accessing a web server running Windows Server 2008 R2. Previously, another administrator created and installed a server certificate on the computer. Users report that they are able to connect to the site using HTTP, but that they receive a warning in Internet Explorer when trying to connect by HTTPS. You want to enable users to connect using both HTTP and HTTPS. You attempt to access the site by using an instance of Internet Explorer on the server itself, and you receive the same warning message for HTTPS connections. How can you resolve this issue?

A. Change the site binding for the website to enable connections on port 443.

B. Change the SSL settings for the website to enable the Require SSL option.

C. Obtain and install an Internet certificate on the web server.

D. Export and reimport the existing security certificate.

E. Reconfigure clients' firewall settings to enable traffic on port 443.

Chapter Review

To further practice and reinforce the skills you learned in this chapter, you can perform the following tasks:

- Review the chapter summary.
- Review the list of key terms introduced in this chapter.
- Complete the case scenarios. These scenarios set up real-world situations involving the topics of this chapter and ask you to create a solution.
- Complete the suggested practices.
- Take a practice test.

Chapter Summary

- Web server administrators should focus on implementing defense in depth and reducing the attack surface of IIS by using features such as request handler mappings.
- IIS allows for managing remote administration by configuring users, permissions, and feature delegation for the management service.
- Server administrators can control access to the web server by using authentication settings, URL authorization rules, server certificates, and IP Address And Domain Restrictions.

Key Terms

Do you know what these key terms mean? You can check your answers by looking up the terms in the glossary at the end of the book.

- ASP.NET impersonation
- attack surface
- certificate authority (CA)
- Client Certificate Authentication
- defense in depth
- domain restrictions (IIS)
- feature delegation (IIS)
- handler mappings (IIS)
- IIS Management Service
- IIS Manager credentials
- Internet certificate request (IIS)
- IP address restrictions (IIS)
- modules (IIS)

- .NET trust levels
- request handlers
- self-signed certificate
- server certificates
- URL authorization rules

Case Scenarios

In these case scenarios, you apply the information that you have learned about securing IIS.

Case Scenario 1: Configuring Remote Management for IIS

You are a systems administrator responsible for managing four web servers running Windows Server 2008 R2. You would like to use a single instance of IIS Manager to connect to all the servers. In addition, three other systems administrators need to manage the servers. One of these administrators is a consultant, and she does not have a Windows domain or local user account. You would like to create a username and password for her that is limited to managing IIS. You want all administrators other than you to be able to view but not change settings for the Default Document and Directory Browsing features.

1. What is the easiest method of managing settings for all the web servers by using IIS Manager?

2. How can you set up a username and password for a remote systems administrator?

3. How can you prevent the other users from modifying the Default Document and Directory Browsing features when using IIS Manager?

Case Scenario 2: Increasing Website Security

You are a systems administrator responsible for implementing and managing security for a production web server running Windows Server 2008 R2. The server is accessible from the Internet and contains eight websites. Each site contains at least one web application. A web application named Customer Database contains an ASP.NET 2.0 web application that needs to access a remote database server. Another website, named Service Desk, contains static content, most of which should be available to all users. However, a folder called Admin should be available only to specific users. Finally, you have a new requirement for an application named Contoso Central that specifies that all connections should use an encrypted connection.

1. Which .NET trust level should you configure for the Customer Database application?

2. How can you configure security for the Admin folder within the Service Desk application?

3. How can you require encryption security for connections to the Contoso Central application?

Suggested Practices

To help you successfully master the exam objectives presented in this chapter, complete the following tasks. The practices in this section enable you to apply the methods you have learned to secure IIS-based web servers, websites, and web applications.

- **Practice 1**   Create a new website by using IIS Manager. The content of the website can contain copies of the lisstart.htm file or other HTML files you have available. Place some of the files within folders and create scenarios in which you want to protect content. Apply file system permissions, authentication settings, and URL authorization rules to ensure that only certain users can access the site. For example, create a new subfolder within a web application called SecureDocuments. Place the appropriate limitations to ensure that users must provide credentials to access the content. Also, test the effects of changing handler mappings. For example, remove the StaticFile handler mapping for a website and test the effects by using Internet Explorer. You can also add your own custom handler mappings for new file types (such as files that have a .secure extension).

- **Practice 2**   Add the Management Service role service to a web server running Windows Server 2008 R2. Practice using a variety of security features to support web server administrators with different levels of restrictions. Options to test include:

  - Creating IIS Manager users.

  - Assigning IIS Manager Permissions settings to control which websites and web applications administrators can access.

  - Assigning permissions to non-administrator users who have Windows accounts.

  - Creating IP address restrictions to control which computers can administer IIS.

  - Using feature delegation to control which settings can be modified by using IIS Manager.

  To test settings most efficiently, it is recommended that you use a remote computer running Windows 7 or Windows Server 2008 R2 that has IIS 7 Manager installed.

- **Practice 3**   View the following webcasts and resources for more information about IIS:

  - The webcast entitled, "Secure, Simplified Web Publishing Using Internet Information Services 7.0 (Level 300)," by Robert McMurray, available on the companion CD in the Webcasts folder. Alternatively, you can find this webcast by visiting *http://msevents.microsoft.com* and searching for event ID 1032352159.

  - The webcast entitled, "Securing and Tuning Internet Information Services 7.0 (Level 300)," by Nazim Lala, available on the companion CD in the Webcasts folder. Alternatively, you can find this webcast by visiting *http://msevents.microsoft.com* and searching for event ID 1032352141.

  - The Microsoft Internet Information Services website at *http://www.microsoft.com/iis*.

  - The IIS.NET website at *http://www.iis.net*.

- IIS 7 webcasts at *http://learn.iis.net/Videos.*
- IIS 7 virtual labs at *http://technet.microsoft.com/en-us/virtuallabs/bb499672.*

Take a Practice Test

The practice tests on this book's companion CD offer many options. For example, you can test yourself on just one exam objective, or you can test yourself on all the 70-643 certification exam content. You can set up the test so that it closely simulates the experience of taking a certification exam, or you can set it up in study mode so that you can look at the correct answers and explanations after you answer each question.

> **MORE INFO** **PRACTICE TESTS**
>
> For details about all the practice test options available, see the "How to Use the Practice Tests" section in this book's introduction.

CHAPTER 7

Configuring FTP and SMTP Services

The Internet Information Services (IIS) platform includes capabilities for sharing information by using several protocols. The *File Transfer Protocol (FTP)* provides a standard method by which computers can transfer files and other types of data to each other. It is commonly used on both internal networks and the Internet to upload and download content. The *Simple Mail Transfer Protocol (SMTP)* is a standard method for transmitting email messages. It is often used by web applications to send notifications and communications to users' email addresses.

In this chapter, you learn how to configure these services in Windows Server 2008 R2. In Lesson 1, "Configuring FTP," you learn how to install and configure FTP functionality. In Lesson 2, "Configuring SMTP," you learn how to install and configure the SMTP service.

Exam objectives in this chapter:
- Configure a File Transfer Protocol (FTP) server.
- Configure Simple Mail Transfer Protocol (SMTP).

Lessons in this chapter:

Before You Begin

To complete the lessons in this chapter, you should have:

- A solid understanding of IIS configuration basics, including how to add the Web Server (IIS) server role and optional role services. This information is covered in Chapter 5, "Installing and Configuring Web Applications."
- Installed the Web Server (IIS) server role on Server2.contoso.local, using the default installation options for this server role. If you have created additional websites or web applications in previous exercises, you may leave them configured on this server.

Lesson 1: Configuring FTP

Windows Server 2008 R2 introduces a new FTP server, known as FTP 7. In Windows Server 2008, FTP 7 was available only as an installable download from the Microsoft website. In Windows Server 2008 R2, this latest version of the FTP server is available as a role service within the Web Server (IIS) server role. In this lesson, you learn about how to set up and manage the FTP Server role service on a computer running Windows Server 2008 R2.

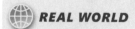 **REAL WORLD**

Anil Desai

In working as an IT consultant, I often see server and service configurations that seem to be set up haphazardly and without an understanding of security or other best practices. In some cases, systems administrators are faced with numerous priorities and don't have enough time to set up these services correctly. In other cases, they lack the knowledge to understand the implications. Regardless of the cause, the issue is the same: services are often deployed insecurely.

When you're responsible for deploying new features and services that provide additional functionality, it's important to consider the possible security ramifications of the changes. Implementing an FTP server is a good example. FTP sites provide a method by which users can upload and download data from your network. Especially when providing access through the Internet or external networks, it's important to ensure that only authorized users have access to the server. Configuration options such as authentication methods, encrypted connections, authorization settings, and user home directories can help ensure that a new FTP site does not lead to security breaches. (You'll learn about these features in Lesson 1.)

Be sure to take the time to understand the security implications of setting up network services such as FTP servers. A good rule of thumb is that if you don't have the time or experience to deploy the server securely, it's probably better not to deploy it at all.

After this lesson, you will be able to:

- Install and configure the FTP Publishing Service in Windows Server 2008 R2.
- Create and configure a new FTP site.
- Administer FTP using IIS Manager.
- Configure FTP site bindings for an IIS 7 website.
- Manage FTP settings, including SSL settings, authentication, authorization, and user isolation.
- Use FTP client software to connect to and test an FTP site.

Estimated lesson time: 75 minutes

Installing the FTP Server

Windows Server 2008 R2 includes an FTP server as an optional role service for the Web Server (IIS) server role. You can add the role to the server by using Server Manager. If you have already installed the Web Server (IIS) server role, you can use the *Add Role Services* command to add the necessary item, as shown in Figure 7-1.

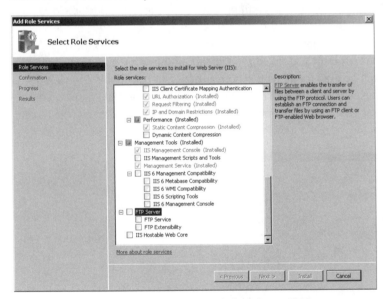

FIGURE 7-1 Installing FTP 7 functionality in Windows Server 2008.

The FTP Server role service includes two component role services, FTP Service and FTP Extensibility.

Removing the FTP Server

If you no longer require the server to provide access through FTP, you should remove the FTP Server role service. To do so, open Server Manager, expand Roles, right-click Web Server (IIS), and then select Remove Role Services. Remove the FTP Server and its optional components to disable FTP publishing functionality on the server. The contents of your FTP file system folders will not be deleted or modified during this process.

Managing FTP

In Windows Server 2008 R2, the primary administration tool for FTP is IIS Manager. Systems administrators, in other words, use the same administration interface to configure both HTTP and FTP services. After you have installed the FTP Server role service, you can launch IIS Manager to configure server settings. Note that FTP is not available by default when you install the Web Server (IIS) server role. You add FTP service to your server either by creating a new FTP-only site or by adding FTP binding to an existing website. In this section, you learn how to create new FTP sites and how to add FTP functionality to an existing website.

Creating a New FTP Site

You can create new FTP sites to support different groups of users or to provide access to different sets of files. To create a new FTP site, right-click either the *server* node or the Sites folder in the left pane of IIS Manager and then select Add FTP Site. This starts the Add FTP Site Wizard. The first page prompts you for information about the name of the site. (See Figure 7-2.) This name will be used for administration purposes, so you should choose a descriptive name if you plan to host multiple FTP sites on the same server. The Physical Path setting enables you to specify the root folder for the FTP site. You can choose any existing folder path, but many installations will use a subfolder within the *%SystemDrive%*\Inetpub folder.

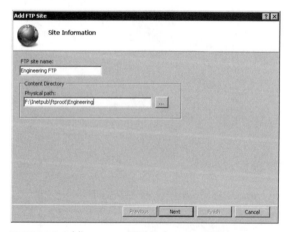

FIGURE 7-2 Adding a new FTP site by using IIS Manager.

On the second page of the wizard, you can specify the binding and SSL settings for the new FTP site. (See Figure 7-3.) The binding settings include the following options:

- **IP Address** The default setting (All Unassigned) is for the FTP site to respond to all incoming requests on any network adapter or IP address on the server. If the computer is configured with multiple network adapters or multiple IP addresses on the same adapter, you can choose a specific address by using the drop-down list.

- **Port** This is the TCP port on which the FTP site will respond. By convention, the default port for FTP communications is port 21. If you choose a different port, FTP users will be required to configure their FTP client software to connect by using the server's port number.

- **Enable Virtual Host Names And Virtual Host** Administrators can create multiple websites that respond on the same IP address and port through virtual host names. These names rely on Domain Name System (DNS) entries to determine the site to which users will connect. Users can also include the virtual host name as part of their logon name to specify the site to which they want to log on.

- **Start FTP Site Automatically** When this option is enabled, the FTP site starts automatically and whenever the computer or the FTP service is restarted. If you plan to start the FTP site manually whenever it is required, disable this option.

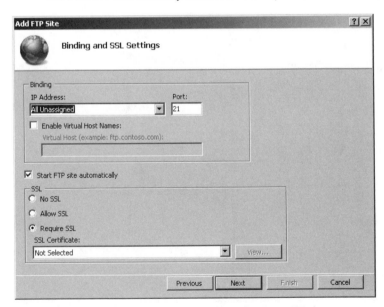

FIGURE 7-3 Configuring Binding And SSL Settings for a new FTP site.

You can also select an SSL certificate and whether to allow or require Secure Socket Layer (SSL) connections for this FTP site. You learn more about these options later in this lesson.

On the Authentication And Authorization Information page, you specify how security will be managed for the new FTP site, as shown in Figure 7-4.

When you click Finish, the new FTP site will be created and added to the left pane of IIS Manager. When you select the *FTP Site* node, you can use the commands in the Actions pane to start, restart, or stop the FTP site. You will also see a list of all the configuration options for the FTP site in the center pane of IIS Manager. (See Figure 7-5.)

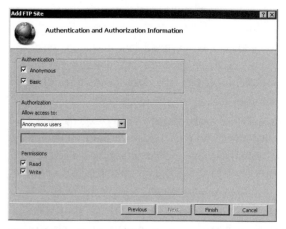

FIGURE 7-4 Configuring Authentication and Authorization Information settings for a new FTP site.

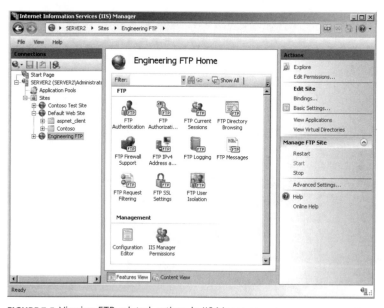

FIGURE 7-5 Viewing FTP-related options in IIS Manager.

Understanding FTP Configuration Files

All configuration settings for FTP sites are stored in the XML-based .config files. You can view and edit these settings by using a text editor. Server-level settings for both websites and FTP sites are stored within the ApplicationHost.config file. For more information about using these configuration files and for performing configuration backups, see Chapter 5, "Installing and Configuring Web Applications."

Creating Virtual Directories

You can easily organize content through physical folders within an FTP site. For example, you can create a folder hierarchy for different types of applications and data. In some cases, however, you will want to provide access to content that is not located within the FTP root folder. To do this, you can create virtual directories. Virtual directories are pointers to folder locations and can be nested within other virtual directories or physical folders. Assuming that users have the appropriate permissions, they will see the virtual directory as if it were a physical folder. All upload and download operations, however, are directed to the physical folder. Virtual directories are useful when you want some content to be shared among multiple physical sites or when you do not want to move or copy the data to the FTP root folder.

To create a new virtual directory, right-click the *parent* node in the left pane of IIS Manager and select Add Virtual Directory. This launches the Add Virtual Directory dialog box, as shown in Figure 7-6. Site Name and Path information shows you details about the location in which the new virtual directory will be created. Alias is the name of the folder as users of the site will see it. The Physical Path setting specifies the full physical location of the content you want to make available.

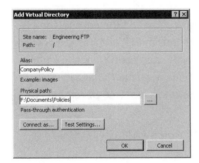

FIGURE 7-6 Adding a new virtual directory to an FTP site.

By default, virtual directories use Pass-Through Authentication for determining whether users have permissions to access the content. This means that the user account used during logon must have permissions on the content folder. You can change this behavior by clicking Connect As and selecting the Specific User option. You will then be able to provide a username and password for a specific account. When the Specific User account option is enabled, all requests for information stored in the physical path you specify will be performed using that user's security context.

Configuring Advanced FTP Site Properties

In addition to the standard properties available in Features View of IIS Manager, you can also configure Advanced Settings options. To access these settings, click Advanced Settings in the Actions pane. Figure 7-7 shows the available options and their default values.

FIGURE 7-7 Configuring Advanced Settings for an FTP site.

The Behavior section includes options for fine-tuning the settings of the FTP site. The Connections section enables you to control data channel timeouts (in seconds) as well as a maximum number of connections. These settings can be helpful for managing performance on busy web and FTP servers. The File Handling section provides options for dealing with partial uploads and allowing a session to perform actions while uploading data.

Managing FTP Site Bindings

The FTP server in Windows Server 2008 R2 provides a simplified method for website administrators to manage their content by using FTP. In previous versions of FTP, administrators were required to configure a new site or virtual directories manually for accessing website content. You can now add a new FTP site binding to a website to provide access automatically to FTP clients. This is useful when you want to allow remote administrators and web developers to access or modify the contents of specific websites.

To add a new FTP binding, select a website in IIS Manager and then click Bindings. Click Add to create a new site binding. (See Figure 7-8.)

FIGURE 7-8 Adding a new FTP site binding to an existing website.

In the Add Site Binding dialog box, you can change the Type setting to FTP. You can then enter IP address, port, and host name information for determining how users access the FTP site. After you have added an FTP binding, you will see a grouping for FTP-related commands in Features View of IIS Manager. You can use these features to modify the settings of the FTP site binding in the same way you would for a stand-alone website. You will also see a new Manage FTP Site section in the Actions pane. An FTP site that is part of a website can be started, stopped, and restarted independently of the website.

> **IMPORTANT FTP PORT NUMBERS AND SECURITY**
>
> Changing the port from the default setting of port 21 can add a little extra security to an FTP server configuration. Casual intruders often attempt to connect to this port to find unprotected FTP servers. In general, however, the idea of security through obscurity is not the best solution. Simply making an FTP server more difficult to find does not address the most important security issues. Always remember to use other security features, such as firewall settings, authentication settings, and authorization rules, in conjunction with site bindings.

WebDAV Publishing

With IIS, you can configure Web-based Distributed Authoring and Versioning (WebDAV) publishing for websites. WebDAV is an extension to HTTP that essentially turns a website into a file server, enabling users to transfer files to and from the site over the HTTP protocol. When you enable and configure WebDAV on a site, remote users can map a network drive to its URL. They can then interact with the site as they would with any network drive. A mapped drive to a website is shown in Figure 7-9.

FIGURE 7-9 A WebDAV-enabled network drive.

Because it provides the same basic services as FTP, a WebDAV-enabled website can serve as an alternative to an FTP server—with two additional benefits. First, unlike FTP, WebDAV uses the same port as HTTP (80), so it reduces the number of ports you need to leave open on your firewall. Second, and again unlike FTP, WebDAV in Windows Server 2008 R2 can use file locking to prevent more than one user at a time from modifying an open file, which can help prevent file version inconsistencies.

To add WebDAV publishing to a site in IIS, you first have to add the following components to your web server by using Server Manager:

- WebDAV Publishing

  This role service component is found in the Common HTTP Features role service group of the Web Server (IIS) server role.
- Windows Authentication

  This role service component is found in the Security role service group of the Web Server (IIS) server role.
- Desktop Experience

  This is a server feature that you need to add with the Add Features Wizard. In Windows Server 2008 R2, this feature facilitates connections to WebDAV folders through URLs that specify fully qualified domain names or IP addresses, such as *http://www.contoso.com* or *http://192.168.10.1*.

After you add these components, perform the following steps on the web server:

1. In IIS Manager, select the website for which you want to configure WebDAV functionality.

2. Use the Authentication feature in IIS Manager to enable Windows Authentication for the website.

3. Use the WebDAV Authoring Rules item in IIS Manager first to enable WebDAV for the site and then to add an authoring rule (or set of rules) allowing access to the site through WebDAV. You can perform these two configuration steps through the Actions pane, as shown in Figure 7-10.

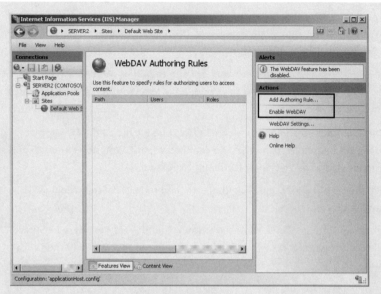

FIGURE 7-10 Configurig WebDAV for a site in IIS.

After you enable WebDAV and click Add Authoring Rule, use the Add Authoring Rule dialog box shown in Figure 7-11 to create an authoring rule that defines the type of access you want for the users you specify. (This step is similar to sharing a folder in Windows Explorer, but it shares the site for WebDAV access only.)

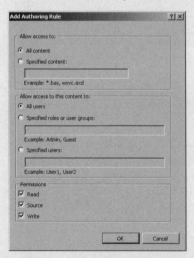

FIGURE 7-11 Creating an authoring rule that defines WebDAV access to a site.

4. Next, configure NTFS permissions on the website folder for the users to whom you want to provide access through WebDAV. For example, if you want all members of Domain Users to be able to cut from and paste to the Default Web Site

through a WebDAV folder, use the Security tab on C:\inetpub\wwwroot to assign the Modify permission to Domain Users. (Note that you don't need to share the folder by using the Sharing tab.)

The next procedure is to map a network drive to the WebDAV folder from the desired client computers. To map a network drive to a WebDAV-enabled website, perform the following steps:

5. If the computer is running Windows Server 2008 R2, install the Desktop Experience feature by using the Add Features Wizard. (You don't need to perform this step if the computer is running Windows 7.)

6. From the Start menu, right-click Computer and then click Map Network Drive from the shortcut menu.

7. In the Map Network Drive Wizard (shown in Figure 7-12), specify a URL that points to the website for which you have configured WebDAV and then click Finish.

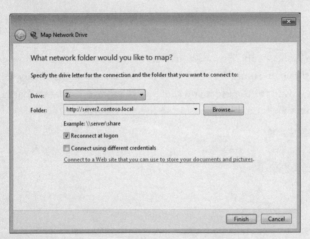

FIGURE 7-12 Mapping a network drive to a URL.

8. When prompted to provide a username and password, specify credentials for a user to whom you have granted access through WebDAV authoring rules and NTFS permissions.

   The Computer window of the Start menu now appears with the new network drive listed beneath Network Locations.

For more information about installing and configuring WebDAV publishing on IIS 7, see *http://learn.iis.net/page.aspx/350/installing-and-configuring-webdav-on-iis-7/.*

Managing FTP User Security

Users can upload and download sensitive data through FTP servers, and you can choose from several methods to control which individuals have access to specific content. In this section, you learn about authentication, authorization, and user isolation settings.

Configuring Authentication Options

You can use Authentication settings for an FTP site to determine how users can access the content stored on the site. There are several built-in methods for managing authentication. To configure these settings in IIS Manager, select the *FTP Site* node and then double-click FTP Authentication in Features View. Figure 7-13 shows an example of authentication options. You can enable or disable various authentication options by using the Actions pane. The *Edit* command in the Actions pane enables you to specify additional details for the selected authentication method.

FIGURE 7-13 Viewing FTP Authentication settings for an FTP site.

Anonymous Authentication allows all users who connect to the site to access content, regardless of the credentials they provide. Use this option when you plan to make the content available to all visitors to the FTP site or when you are using other security methods to restrict access to the site. When an FTP user makes a request to read or write data, Anonymous Authentication uses a specified user account to validate permissions. The default setting is to use the built-in IUSR account for this purpose. You can assign a specific Windows account by clicking Edit in the Actions pane. You can then provide a specific user identity for use by Anonymous Authentication. (See Figure 7-14.)

Basic Authentication requires visitors to the website to provide credentials for a valid Windows user account. The account can be a local Windows username and password or can belong to an Active Directory domain if the server is a member of a domain. It is important to remember that, by default, credentials sent to the FTP server are sent in clear text. This can present a security risk, especially for FTP connections that are made over the Internet. You will use Basic Authentication primarily when you want to restrict FTP-based access to content based on user credentials.

FIGURE 7-14 Modifying Anonymous Authentication Credentials settings.

You can also choose from two other authentication methods by selecting Custom Providers in the Actions pane. IIS Manager Authentication (IISManagerAuth) configures the FTP site to accept credentials for an IIS Manager User. This method is useful when you want to restrict access to the FTP site to specific users who do not have Windows accounts on the local FTP server. The IIS Management role service must be installed and enabled before you can use this authentication method. For more information about creating and managing IIS Manager Users, see Chapter 6, "Managing Server Security." Like Basic Authentication credentials, the username and password information is sent in clear text between the FTP client and the FTP server.

ASP.NET Authentication (AspNetAuth) relies on the .NET user management framework for authentication. It is useful when you have created an ASP.NET website that validates user credentials. It is common for web applications to use credentials data stored in a database to validate access and permissions to the site.

EXAM TIP

You have to understand the purpose of custom providers for the 70-643 exam.

Defining FTP Authorization Rules

You can use FTP Authorization rules to determine which users have access to specific content within the FTP site. Authorization rules can be defined at the level of the FTP site or for specific logical or virtual folders. These capabilities provide you with the flexibility to implement granular authorization rules based on the type of content that should be available to users. There are two types of authorization rules: Allow Rules and Deny Rules. By default, a new FTP site will not have any predefined authorization rules, so no users have access by default. You should use the commands in the Actions pane to create new rules. Figure 7-15 shows the available options when creating a new rule.

FIGURE 7-15 Adding an Allow FTP Authorization rule.

Allow and Deny rules can apply to the following types of users:

- All Users
- All Anonymous Users
- Specified Roles Or User Groups
- Specified Users

After you select the users or groups to which the rule will apply, you can select whether the user will have *read*, *write*, or *read and write* permissions.

Configuring FTP User Isolation Options

When you are managing access permissions and settings for an FTP server, a common requirement is to provide individual users with their own folders and directories. Users should be able to upload and download files from their own folders, but should be prevented from accessing those that belong to other users. The *FTP User Isolation* feature enables you to configure these settings. To modify the settings, select an FTP site in IIS Manager and then open the FTP User Isolation feature, as shown in Figure 7-16.

The default selection for user isolation settings is FTP Root Directory. This option configures the server to start users in the FTP root directory, which you defined when you created the FTP site. This setting is most appropriate when you want all users to be able to access the same content. You can then use authorization rules to define permissions further on specific folders.

The User Name Directory option specifies that every user will have his or her own starting folder based on the username that was provided. If the user-specific folder name does not exist, the user will be placed in the root directory of the FTP site. Remember that this default folder setting is not designed as a security mechanism (at least when used by itself). If your FTP site is configured to allow anonymous authentication, you can create a Default folder for these users.

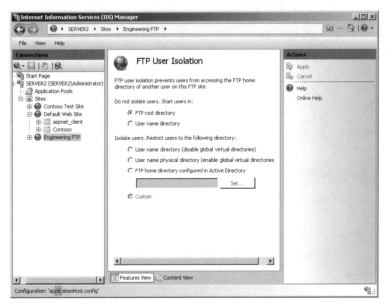

FIGURE 7-16 Viewing FTP User Isolation options.

EXAM TIP

You can manage FTP security settings through various features, including Authentication, Authorization, and IPv4 Address And Domain Restrictions. When you are implementing security for an FTP site, keep in mind that the best solution will likely involve using these features together to meet your goals. For example, you can use FTP User Isolation settings to determine the files and content to which users will have access. You can then use FTP Authorization Rules settings to restrict access to specific content. Keep this in mind when you're working with FTP server security on production servers and when you're taking the 70-643 exam.

The remaining options enable isolation for FTP users. You can use them to restrict access to specific folders within the FTP site. The User Name Directory (Disable Global Virtual Directories) option places users within a designated home directory based on the user account that was used for logon. The user will be unable to navigate to the parent folder and, therefore, will be prevented from accessing other folders. The user will not be able to see any global virtual directories defined for the FTP site. You can enable users to access these directories by instead choosing the User Name Physical Directory (Enable Global Virtual Directories) option.

To support *FTP user isolation* settings, you must create the appropriate folder structure for your users. The folder location for each user can be a physical or virtual directory on the server. The path to the folder is based on several variables:

- **FTPRoot** The root folder for the FTP site.

- **UserName**   The name of the authenticated user as provided by the client during the logon process.
- **UserDomain**   The name of the Windows domain used to validate credentials. This will be the name of the local FTP server or, if the server is a member of a domain, the name of the Active Directory domain.

The specific folder path you create is based on the authentication settings for the site and the type of user who is attempting to access the content. Table 7-1 provides a list of the default locations for each type of user account.

TABLE 7-1 Default FTP Folder Locations for User Accounts

FTP USER ACCOUNT TYPE	HOME DIRECTORY FOLDER LOCATION
Anonymous Users	*%FTPRoot%*\LocalUser\Public
Local Windows Accounts	*%FTPRoot%*\LocalUser*%UserName%*
Domain Windows Accounts	*%FTPRoot%**%UserDomain%**%UserName%*
IIS Manager or ASP.NET User Accounts	*%FTPRoot%**LocalUser**%UserName%*

The next FTP user isolation option is FTP Home Directory Configured In Active Directory. You can use this method to define users' FTP folders within Active Directory by using the *FTPRoot* and *FTPDir* variables. These properties exist in Active Directory domains that are running Windows Server 2003 or later. (You can add the properties manually for Windows 2000 Server–based domains.) The *Set* button enables you to specify the credentials to use to connect to Active Directory. When a user logs on to the FTP server, the FTP server attempts to obtain these properties for the user. If the properties exist and the folder path is valid, the user is placed in that folder. Otherwise, the user will be prevented from accessing the server.

Finally, the FTP User Isolation configuration pane displays a Custom option. This option can be selected only by modifying the FTP configuration settings in the associated ApplicationHost.config file. When this option is selected, it signifies that you have configured the ApplicationHost.config file to specify a custom security provider for your FTP users.

NOTE   **CREATING USER ACCOUNTS BY SCRIPTING**

Creating individual folders for many user accounts at a time can seem like a time-consuming and tedious task at first. Fortunately, this is an ideal job for scripting. You can obtain a list of user accounts by using a variety of methods, including VBScript and Windows PowerShell. You can then use this information to execute commands that create the necessary folders. For more information about scripting, visit the Microsoft TechNet Script Center at *http://technet.microsoft.com/en-us/scriptcenter/.*

Configuring IIS Manager Permissions

In many environments, it is common to have multiple administrators who must be able to connect to and administer FTP sites and their contents. For example, a web and FTP hosting provider might have separate administrators for each FTP site. You can allow other users to access the site by using the IIS Manager Permissions feature. The *Allow User* command enables you to add a new user defined within IIS Manager or based on a Windows account. Authorized users can then use IIS Manager on their computers to connect to an FTP server. For more information about configuring IIS Manager Permissions settings, see Chapter 6.

Configuring FTP Network Security

The FTP server in Windows Server 2008 R2 provides numerous methods for ensuring that only authorized users can access an FTP site. In this section, you learn about using SSL, firewall settings, IP address restrictions, and FTP Request Filtering to control access to FTP sites.

Configuring FTP SSL Settings

By default, all control channel and data channel communications between an FTP server and an *FTP client* are sent in clear text. This is a serious security issue, especially when providing FTP access over the Internet. For example, if packets are intercepted during the authentication process, username and password information can be collected and used to access the site.

Administrators can encrypt communications between an FTP server and an FTP client by using the *FTP over SSL* (commonly referred to as FTP/S or FTPS) standard. To modify these settings, select the appropriate FTP site in IIS Manager and double-click the FTP SSL Settings feature. (See Figure 7-17.)

The first setting enables you to specify which SSL certificate will be used by the FTP site. For more information about creating or obtaining SSL certificates, see Chapter 6. The SSL Policy section provides three options. Allow SSL Connections specifies that users can use SSL connections, but they can also connect to the server by using an unencrypted connection. Require SSL Connections forces all users to use SSL and prevents unencrypted connections. The Custom option enables you to specify different rules for the Control Channel and Data Channel. (See Figure 7-18.) You can use these options to minimize the performance overhead of implementing encryption. For example, by requiring encryption only for credentials, you can prevent usernames and passwords from being sent in clear text but still allow other control commands and data transfer to occur without encryption.

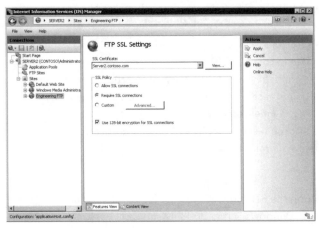

FIGURE 7-17 Configuring FTP SSL settings by using IIS Manager.

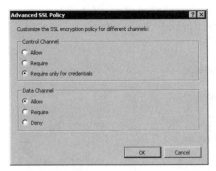

FIGURE 7-18 Configuring an advanced SSL policy for an FTP site.

By default, the FTP SSL functionality uses a 40-bit encryption key strength. This reduces the CPU performance overhead while still maintaining adequate security for most scenarios. You can enable the Use 128-Bit Encryption For SSL Connections option to increase the strength of the encryption (at the expense of performance).

Users typically will configure their SSL settings in their FTP client software. When they attempt to create a new connection, they will see a message that enables them to view and accept the SSL certificate that is installed for the FTP server.

Managing FTP Firewall Options

To access an FTP server, firewalls must allow network traffic to be passed for both the control channel and the data channel. When users connect to a web server, the initial connection uses the port provided in the address. (The default is port 21 if none is provided.) However, for sending data channel information such as directory listings and files, the FTP server can respond by using a range of port numbers. If these ports are not allowed across the firewall, users will be unable to use the full functionality of the site.

> **NOTE TROUBLESHOOTING COMMON FTP CONNECTION ISSUES**
>
> A common FTP connection issue is related to accessing an FTP server from across a firewall. Users might report that they are able to connect to the FTP server and provide their authentication credentials. However, when they attempt to perform an action (such as listing the contents of a directory), they do not receive a response. This is a classic case of an issue with a firewall that is restricting data channel communications. One option for resolving this issue is to enable passive FTP connections on the FTP client. Another option is to reconfigure the firewall. Keep these symptoms in mind when you are troubleshooting FTP connection issues.

You can avoid this problem through the FTP Firewall Support feature in IIS Manager. (See Figure 7-19.) The FTP server feature in Windows Server 2008 R2 supports passive-mode FTP connections to specify the ports on which the FTP server responds to requests. The Data Channel Port Range setting enables you to specify the range of ports that send responses to clients. You should use ports between 1,024 and 65,535. The External IP Address Of Firewall setting enables the FTP server to determine the location from which packets are being sent. This is useful for supporting SSL encryption scenarios.

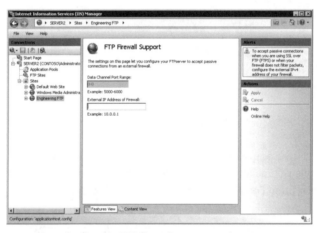

FIGURE 7-19 Configuring FTP firewall support options.

Implementing IP Address and Domain Restrictions

You can increase the security of an FTP server by limiting the network addresses from which specific FTP sites or folders can be accessed. To manage these settings, select an FTP site or folder in IIS Manager and then double-click the FTP IPv4 Address And Domain Restrictions feature. The Actions pane provides two commands for managing rules: *Add Allow Entry* and *Add Deny Entry*. IP address–based rules enable you to specify either a single IP address or a range of IP addresses that is defined by using a subnet mask. (See Figure 7-20.)

Use the *Edit Feature Settings* command in the Actions pane to specify the default action for IP addresses that do not match any of the existing rules. The default setting, Allow, specifies that these IP addresses are allowed to connect. You can restrict access to only those clients that match Allow Entries by selecting the Deny option.

FIGURE 7-20 Adding a new IP address restriction rule for an FTP site.

You can also enable domain name restrictions through the Edit Feature Settings dialog box. Domain name restrictions are based on DNS domain names (such as extranet.contoso. com). Although they can be easier to manage than specific IP address rules, the drawback is that domain name restrictions can reduce performance significantly because rules are evaluated based on performing a reverse DNS lookup operation, which can be time consuming and can create significant load on the DNS infrastructure.

IPv4 Address And Domain Restrictions settings are automatically inherited by child objects. For example, restrictions defined at the level of an FTP site automatically apply to all the folders that are part of that site. You can override this behavior by creating explicit rules for specific folders and virtual directories. You can also use the *Revert To Parent* command in the Actions pane to remove any specific settings.

Configuring FTP Request Filtering

FTP Request Filtering is a security feature that is new to FTP 7. Similar to HTTP Request Filtering in IIS, FTP Request Filtering enables you to define rules that allow or block FTP traffic based on the content of FTP requests. To configure these settings, select an FTP site or folder in IIS Manager and then double-click the FTP Request Filtering feature.

You can filter FTP requests based on the following criteria:

- **File name extensions** You can specify file name extensions that the FTP server specifically allows or blocks in an FTP connection. For example, you can prevent users from uploading files with the *.zip or *.mp3 extension.

- **Hidden segments** You can specify a portion of the FTP site to hide from clients. When such portions are hidden, clients will not see the section displayed in the listing of available directories.

- **Denied URL sequences** You can define a list of URLs to which the FTP server will block access.
- **Commands** You can allow or deny FTP service based on the specific command sent to the FTP server in a request.

Managing FTP Site Settings

The FTP Server role service in Windows Server 2008 R2 includes features for monitoring users and for improving the user experience. In this section, you learn about these configuration options and how you can monitor FTP site usage.

Monitoring FTP Current Sessions

You can use the FTP Current Sessions feature for an FTP site to view which users are currently connected to the server. (See Figure 7-21.) The details that are shown include:

- User Name
- Client IP Address
- Session Start Time
- Current Command
- Previous Command
- Command Start Time
- Bytes Sent
- Bytes Received
- Session ID

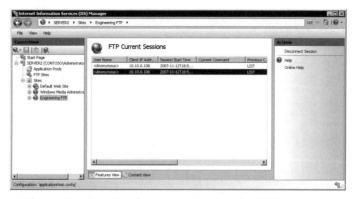

FIGURE 7-21 Viewing a list of current sessions by using IIS Manager.

Managing FTP Messages

You can use the FTP Messages feature to define text-based messages sent to clients. The specific types of text you can define are:

- **Banner**   This is the information presented initially when a user connects to the FTP site.

- **Welcome**   This message is displayed after a user has successfully authenticated to the FTP site.

- **Exit**   This message is displayed after the user chooses to end his or her connection, and it is sent just prior to closing the connection.

- **Maximum Connections**   This message is displayed when the FTP server has reached its maximum number of connections, and the user is unable to access the site.

FTP messages often include warnings related to the intended use of the site and can provide contact information for administrators of the site. (See Figure 7-22.)

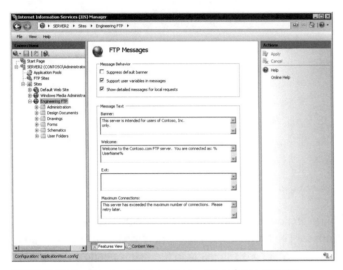

FIGURE 7-22 Configuring FTP messages settings for an FTP site.

You can prevent the default banner from being sent to the user by using the Message Behavior section. This is useful when you do not want to disclose details about the purpose or function of the site until users are authenticated. The Support User Variables In Messages option enables you to use the following string values in your messages:

- *BytesReceived*
- *BytesSent*
- *SessionID*
- *SiteName*
- *UserName*

When the variable name is surrounded by percent symbols (for example, *%UserName%*), the FTP server automatically replaces the information with the appropriate value.

Configuring FTP Logging

The FTP server in Windows Server 2008 R2 can automatically create log files that keep track of the activity of the FTP site. By default, information is stored to text files stored in the %SystemDrive%\Inetpub\Logs\LogFiles folder. Separate folders are created for each FTP site created on the local machine. You can use the FTP Logging option to modify the log file settings.

The *Select W3C Fields* command enables you to specify which types of information are tracked for each command or request sent to the FTP server. Figure 7-23 shows the default options, which are designed to provide a balance between providing detailed information and reducing performance overhead and log file size.

FIGURE 7-23 Selecting which fields are included in FTP log files.

You can use the Log File Rollover section to specify when new log files will be created. You can also enable the Use Local Time For File Naming And Rollover option if you are managing FTP servers in multiple time zones. The *View Logs* command in the Actions pane opens the folder that contains the FTP log files. The files themselves are text documents that contain comma-separated values. They can be viewed in Windows Notepad or by using third-party log analysis software. In general, it is a good idea to review FTP server logs regularly to detect any unauthorized activity or unexpected usage patterns.

Configuring Directory Browsing

One of the most commonly used commands FTP clients send is to request a directory listing. Most FTP client software programs automatically execute a *LIST* command whenever the user changes the current working folder. You can configure options that affect client directory listing by selecting the FTP Directory Browsing feature after selecting a site in IIS Manager. (See Figure 7-24.) The Directory Listing Style options enable you to specify whether information should be returned in MS-DOS (the default style) or UNIX style. The setting specifies how information is presented to an FTP client. Most FTP clients are able to handle both formats.

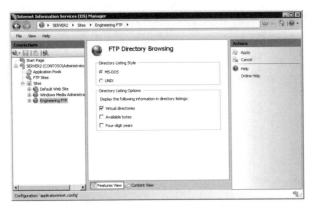

FIGURE 7-24 Configuring FTP Directory Browsing settings.

You can use the Directory Listing Options section to specify which types of information are included in the directory listing. The Virtual Directories option specifies whether the names of virtual directories will be returned to the user. If you want to hide virtual directories from users, disable this option. The Available Bytes option returns the amount of remaining disk space for the FTP site. If disk quotas are enabled, the remaining space will be based on how much storage space is left for the currently connected user. Enabling Four-Digit Years returns all year information in four characters rather than in two.

Using FTP Client Software

Users can use several types of FTP client options for connecting to an FTP server. Windows operating systems include the Ftp.exe command-line utility that provides basic text-based functionality for connecting to an FTP server. This is useful for performing simple operations and for testing website functionality. You can also place Ftp.exe commands within a batch file to automate common operations, such as transferring backup files to a remote server.

In addition, you can use an FTP-capable web browser, such as Internet Explorer, to connect to an FTP site. (See Figure 7-25.) The standard syntax for the URL is *ftp://ServerName*. You can provide logon information and port details in the URL by using the following syntax:

ftp://UserName:Password@ServerName:Port/Path

FTP URLs are helpful for providing quick access to files from websites. It is important to note that, by default, all communications occur by using a clear text connection. Therefore, you should generally use FTP URLs only for FTP sites that are intended for use by anonymous users.

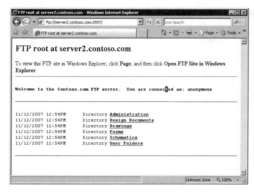

FIGURE 7-25 Connecting to an FTP site by using Internet Explorer 7.

You can also use Windows Explorer to provide graphical access to an FTP site, as shown in Figure 7-26. This method gives you the benefits of using familiar commands and functions, such as drag-and-drop operations. To connect, simply enter the FTP URL in the Address bar of Windows Explorer. You can also use the *Open FTP Site In Windows Explorer* command from the View menu of Internet Explorer 9 if you have already connected to an FTP site. Although some file and folder management features are limited, this is a useful method by which even nontechnical users can access FTP-based content.

Finally, there are numerous third-party FTP client software packages. You can find them by doing a web search for "ftp client software." These products often provide advanced features, such as the ability to script common operations, and automated methods for keeping multiple folders synchronized with the same content.

FIGURE 7-26 Using Windows Explorer to access an FTP site.

Quick Check

1. When using the FTP server in Windows Server 2008 R2, what is the easiest way to prevent a particular group of users from accessing a specific folder that is part of your FTP site?

2. How can you ensure that credentials sent for an Internet-accessible FTP site using Basic Authentication are encrypted during transmission?

Quick Check Answers

1. FTP Authorization Rules can be used to set specific permissions on a portion of an FTP site.

2. Enable FTP Over SSL (FTPS) for the FTP site. The process involves obtaining a server SSL certificate and then requiring SSL for at least passing credentials on the server.

PRACTICE **Configure and Test FTP**

In this practice, you learn about the process of setting up an FTP site in Windows Server 2008 R2. You add the FTP Server role service and an FTP site binding to the Default Web Site, configure security, and, finally, test the connection by using the Ftp.exe command-line utility. For this practice, it is assumed that you have already installed the Web Server (IIS) server role.

EXERCISE Adding an FTP Site Binding to a Website

In this exercise, you add the FTP Server role service and create a new FTP site binding for the Default Web Site by using IIS Manager.

1. Log on to Server2 as a user who has Administrator permissions.

2. In Server Manager, expand the *Roles* node, right-click Web Server (IIS), and click Add Role Services.

3. On the Select Role Services page of the Add Role Services Wizard, click to select FTP Server from the list of available role services.

   Both the FTP Service and FTP Extensibility subcomponents should automatically be selected.

4. Click Next.

5. On the Confirm Installation Selections page, click Install.

6. When the installation is complete, click Close.

7. Open IIS Manager and connect to the local server.

8. Right-click the *Default Web Site* node in the left pane and select Edit Bindings. In the Site Bindings dialog box, click Add.

9. In the Add Site Binding dialog box, select FTP for the Type setting. Use the default IP Address setting of All Unassigned and the default port of port 21. Leave the Host Name section blank and then click OK to add the site binding.

10. Verify that a new site binding for the FTP protocol on port 21 has been created. Click Close in the Site Bindings dialog box.

11. To view the FTP-related options for the Default Web Site, click Refresh on the View menu in IIS Manager.

    You now see an FTP section along with options for configuring FTP settings. The Actions pane also includes commands for managing the FTP site.

12. In the Actions pane, click Advanced Settings in the Manage FTP Site section. The Physical Path setting is mapped to the root directory for the Default Web Site (*%SystemDrive%*\Inetpub\Wwwroot). Click OK to continue.

13. In Features View of IIS Manager, double-click FTP Authentication. By default, no authentication options are enabled. Enable the Basic Authentication and Anonymous Authentication options by selecting them and then clicking the Enable command in the Actions pane.

14. Click Back or the *Default Web Site* node to return to Features View.

15. Open the FTP SSL Settings feature. By default, the server is configured to Require SSL Connections. For the purpose of this practice exercise, change the setting to Allow SSL Connections. Note that you could optionally choose an SSL certificate from the drop-down list. Click Apply to save the settings.

16. Open the FTP Authorization Rules feature. In the Actions pane, click Add Allow Rule.

17. In the Add Allow Authorization Rule dialog box, select the Read and Write check boxes and then click OK. The new rule appears in the center pane of IIS Manager.

18. Next, use the Ftp.exe command-line utility to test access to the FTP site. Open a command prompt by selecting this command from the Start menu. Type **Ftp server2** to connect to the local FTP server. You do not need to provide a port number because the server is bound to the default port, port 21.

19. At the User prompt, enter the name of your Windows user account and enter your password when prompted. At the Ftp.exe prompt, type **dir** and press Enter to retrieve the list of files located in the root folder for Default Web Site. You can also use the *GET* and *PUT* commands to download and upload files. When you are finished, type **quit** to exit the Ftp.exe prompt. Close the command prompt window.

20. Close IIS Manager.

Lesson Summary

- Windows Server 2008 R2 includes a new built-in version of an FTP server, called FTP 7. FTP 7 was available only as an installable download in Windows Server 2008.

- To add FTP server functionality, add the FTP Server role service, which is part of the Web Server (IIS) role. You can then use IIS Manager to manage FTP sites.

- You can add FTP service either by creating a new FTP site or by adding an FTP binding to an existing website.

- Allowing access to an FTP server requires you to configure both authentication and authorization for that server.

- You can apply security to an FTP server by using SSL, IP address, and domain restrictions and request filtering.

Lesson Review

You can use the following questions to test your knowledge of the information in Lesson 1, "Configuring FTP." The questions are also available on the companion CD if you prefer to review them in electronic form.

> **NOTE ANSWERS**
>
> Answers to these questions and explanations of why each answer choice is correct or incorrect are located in the "Answers" section at the end of the book.

1. You are a Windows Server 2008 R2 systems administrator. You want to create an FTP site that is used only by members of the Engineering department. The IIS server is shared by all members of the organization. Which of the following actions best enables you to achieve this goal?

    A. Configure a unique host header in the properties of the Default Web Site.

    B. Assign an alternative IP address to the Default Web Site.

    C. Add a new FTP site and use Basic Authentication.

    D. Add FTP Publishing to the Default Web Site and use Anonymous Authentication.

2. You are a systems administrator who has recently installed and configured FTP on a computer running Windows Server 2008 R2. You have enabled the FTP Over SSL (FTPS) option for the server by obtaining an SSL certificate from a trusted third-party issuer. Recently, the usage of the FTP site has increased, and users are complaining about slow download performance. You want to configure SSL settings to encrypt credentials and commands but not file-related information. You also want to optimize encryption performance. Which of the following settings changes should you make? (Each correct answer presents part of a complete solution. Choose two.)

    A. Select the Allow SSL Connections SSL Policy option.

    B. Disable the Use 128-bit Encryption For SSL Connections option.

    C. Select the Require SSL Connections SSL Policy option.

    D. Select the Custom SSL Policy option.

Lesson 2: Configuring SMTP

The *Simple Mail Transfer Protocol* (SMTP) feature in Windows Server 2008 R2 enables you to relay email messages. The SMTP standard provides a consistent method by which servers can send messages either for internal email traffic or for communicating across the Internet. Individuals and applications often use SMTP functionality to send notifications and other information. In this lesson, you learn how to enable and configure the SMTP Server feature in Windows Server 2008 R2.

> **After this lesson, you will be able to:**
> - Enable the SMTP Server feature in Windows Server 2008 R2.
> - Create a new SMTP virtual server.
> - Configure IP address and port settings for an SMTP virtual server.
> - Secure SMTP services by configuring authentication settings for inbound and outbound connections.
> - Test SMTP services by using an email client application.
>
> **Estimated lesson time: 45 minutes**

Installing the SMTP Server Feature

The Windows Server 2008 R2 SMTP Server feature enables you to support many applications and network connections to send large volumes of messages. For example, a web application can use SMTP to send email notifications to users. The SMTP protocol is designed to send emails that a messaging server, such as Microsoft Exchange Server, can receive. Messages can also be stored in a file system location, so they can be accessed by other applications. Users typically receive these messages by connecting to their mailbox on the messaging server by using a protocol such as the Post Office Protocol (POP).

You can install the SMTP Server feature on a computer running Windows Server 2008 R2 by using Server Manager. To do this, right-click the *Features* node and select Add Features. The SMTP Server has several dependencies. (See Figure 7-27.)

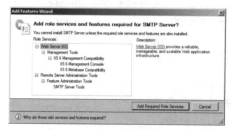

FIGURE 7-27 Viewing dependencies of the SMTP Server feature.

You can also remove the SMTP Server feature by using Server Manager. To do this, right-click the *Features* node and select Remove Features. When you remove the SMTP server, you are no longer able to use the server to transmit or relay email messages.

Configuring SMTP Services

After you have installed the SMTP Server feature on a computer running Windows Server 2008 or Windows Server 2008 R2, you can use IIS 6.0 Manager to configure SMTP settings. To do this, open IIS 6.0 Manager and expand the server object. A default site called SMTP Virtual Server #1 is included automatically when you add the SMTP Server feature.

Creating a New SMTP Virtual Server

You can use the New SMTP Virtual Server Wizard to create a new SMTP virtual server in Windows Server 2008 and Windows Server 2008 R2. Each virtual server has its own set of configuration settings and can be managed independently. To begin the process of creating a new SMTP virtual server by using IIS 6.0 Manager, right-click the *server* node, point to New, and then click SMTP Virtual Server. The first page of the New SMTP Virtual Server Wizard asks you to provide a name for the virtual server. You should use a descriptive name that indicates the purpose of the virtual server because this setting will identify different servers in the IIS 6.0 Manager user interface.

On the Select IP Address page, select the network connections on which the SMTP server will be available. If the server has multiple physical network adapters or multiple IP addresses, you can choose a specific one from the drop-down list. This is useful when you want to limit access to the SMTP server for security reasons. For example, if one or more IP addresses are accessible from the Internet, you might not want the server to respond on that address. The default IP address setting is All Unassigned, which specifies that the SMTP virtual server will respond on any IP address that is configured for the server.

Another reason to change the IP address is that no two SMTP virtual servers can run concurrently if they have the same IP address and port assignment. The default port for SMTP connections is port 25. If you attempt to create a new SMTP virtual server that has the same combination of IP address and port number, you will see the error message shown in Figure 7-28. In this case, you can continue to create the server, but you will have to modify its settings later before you can start it.

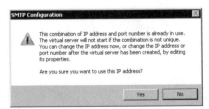

FIGURE 7-28 Viewing a warning about the SMTP configuration.

On the Select Home Directory page, specify the file system location that will serve as the root for the SMTP virtual server. (See Figure 7-29.) Message files and other data will be stored in this location.

FIGURE 7-29 Configuring the home directory location for a new SMTP virtual server.

The Default Domain page is where you specify the fully qualified domain name for which this SMTP virtual server will be responsible. Generally, you use a DNS domain name such as hr.contoso.com. When you finish the New SMTP Virtual Server Wizard, the new server will appear in IIS 6.0 Manager. You can then access the properties of the server to make additional configuration changes.

Configuring General SMTP Server Settings

To access the configuration settings for an SMTP virtual server, right-click it in IIS 6.0 Manager and then select Properties. The General tab includes details that specify the network connection settings for the SMTP server. (See Figure 7-30.) You can select IP Address or All Unassigned from the drop-down list, or you can click Advanced to configure multiple bindings.

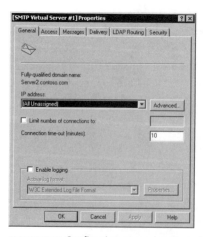

FIGURE 7-30 Configuring general settings for an SMTP virtual server.

The Advanced option also enables you to change the port number on which the SMTP server can be accessed. On the General tab, you can limit the number of connections and set connection timeouts. Configuring these limits can help manage performance for busy SMTP servers. You can also use the Enable Logging option to store information about messages that are transmitted using this SMTP virtual server. The *Properties* button opens the Logging Properties dialog box and gives you options for determining the storage location of the log files. On the Advanced tab of the Logging Properties dialog box, you can specify which types of information will be included in the log file. You can view log files by using a standard text editor, such as Windows Notepad. On busy SMTP servers, enabling logging can decrease performance and increase disk space usage.

Securing Access to an SMTP Virtual Server

To prevent unwanted use of SMTP virtual servers, it is important to configure access rules for sending messages by SMTP. A large portion of unsolicited commercial email (spam) is sent through SMTP relays that are unprotected. You can manage rules for using the SMTP virtual server through the properties on the Access tab, as shown in Figure 7-31.

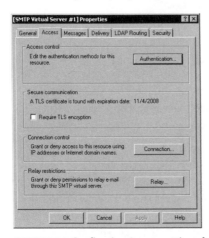

FIGURE 7-31 Configuring Access settings for an SMTP virtual server.

You can use the Authentication settings to determine how potential users of the SMTP virtual server must pass their credentials to the service. Figure 7-32 shows the available options. The default setting is Anonymous Access, which specifies that no credentials are required to connect to the SMTP virtual server. This option is useful when you are using other methods (such as firewalls or trusted network connections) to prevent unauthorized access to the server.

The Basic Authentication option requires a username and password to be sent to the SMTP virtual server. By default, these logon credentials are transmitted in clear text and are, therefore, susceptible to interception. You can also enable Transport Layer Security (TLS) to enable encryption for sent messages. TLS uses a certificate-based approach to create the encrypted connection. Integrated Windows Authentication relies on standard Windows accounts to verify credentials to access the system. This method is most appropriate for applications that will be used by a single Windows account or when all potential users of the SMTP server have Active Directory domain accounts.

FIGURE 7-32 Managing authentication options for an SMTP virtual server.

In addition to configuring authentication settings, you can also restrict access to an SMTP virtual server based on IP addresses or domain names. This can help ensure that only authorized network clients are able to use SMTP services. To add these restrictions, click Connection on the Access tab of the properties of the SMTP virtual server. You can then choose the default behavior for connection attempts.

The Only The List Below option means that only computers that match the entry rules you have configured will be able to use the server. This is most appropriate when all the expected client computers are part of one or a few networks. The All Except The List Below option means that the rules you add are for computers that are not allowed to use the SMTP virtual server. Click Add to create new configuration rules. (See Figure 7-33.) You can configure restrictions by specifying a single IP address or an IP address range.

You can also specify that IP addresses should be resolved automatically based on a domain name. The Domain option instructs the SMTP server to perform a DNS reverse lookup operation when a computer attempts to connect. This method attempts to resolve the IP address of the incoming connection to a DNS name. Enabling this option can reduce performance due to the overhead of performing many DNS queries.

The final set of Access control options are *relay restrictions*. SMTP relaying occurs when a message is sent with both To and From addresses that are not part of the virtual server's domain. Relaying is a common method by which large spammers are able to use unprotected SMTP virtual servers to send unsolicited mail. The Relay Restrictions option enables you to specify which computers can relay messages through the SMTP server. (See Figure 7-34.) The default settings are for all users and computers to be allowed to relay messages, as long as they are able to authenticate. You can use the *Add* command to define which IP addresses, domain names, or both will be allowed to relay messages.

FIGURE 7-33 Creating a new Connection Control rule for an SMTP virtual server.

FIGURE 7-34 Configuring SMTP relay restrictions.

> **NOTE** **HELPING REDUCE SPAM**
>
> In addition to the benefits of reducing load on unprotected networks, there are other good reasons to protect your SMTP virtual server from unauthorized access. Many anti-spam utilities maintain a list of known unprotected SMTP servers and add them to a block list. All messages sent through this SMTP relay might be marked as spam, making it difficult for your users and applications to communicate with individuals outside your organization. When you're setting up a new SMTP virtual server, be sure to take the time to secure the configuration. It is also important to review SMTP server configuration and log files regularly to find potential unauthorized use of the server.

Configuring Messages Options

The Messages tab of the properties of an SMTP virtual server enables you to configure limitations on messages that are sent through the server. (See Figure 7-35.) The first two options enable you to specify the maximum size of a message (including attachments) and the maximum amount of data that can be sent through one connection to the server. You can also limit the number of messages sent per connection and the number of recipients to whom they can be sent. These methods all help reduce unwanted access to the server and preserve resources such as network bandwidth.

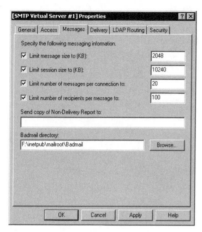

FIGURE 7-35 Configuring messages settings for an SMTP virtual server.

The most common reasons for messaging failures include incorrect addresses or domain names entered by the sending user. The Send Copy Of Non-Delivery Report To option enables you to specify an email address to which undeliverable mail will be forwarded. The Badmail Directory setting specifies the path to the folder into which these messages will be sent. You can review these messages or files to detect undeliverable mail.

Defining Delivery Properties

When communicating on the Internet, network routing issues and server failures can cause service outages. The SMTP standard was designed with reliability in mind. SMTP servers automatically store copies of messages while they are trying to send them to their intended destination. If the destination server is unavailable, the SMTP server retries the operation. You can manage the details of this behavior through the properties of the Delivery tab. (See Figure 7-36.) The Outbound rules define the intervals at which the server retries the transmission of a message if a failure occurs.

You can also configure the Delay Notification and Expiration Timeout options for both the Outbound and Local settings to determine when resending of a message should end.

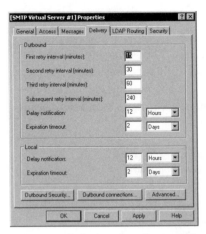

FIGURE 7-36 Default settings for the Delivery properties of an SMTP virtual server.

It is common for SMTP servers to send messages through other SMTP servers before they reach their final destination. Administrators can configure their SMTP servers to require authentication before they relay a message. The *Outbound Security* command on the Delivery tab enables you to specify the authentication information to be used when connecting to another SMTP server. The Outbound Connections settings specify limits on the number of connections to other SMTP servers and how long they will remain active.

The *Advanced* button leads to additional options for managing how messages are processed by the SMTP virtual server. The options include:

- **Maximum Hop Count**   When a message is forwarded to an SMTP server, the message itself includes a hop count to record the number of times it has been forwarded. When a message has exceeded the maximum hop count setting, it will be considered undeliverable.

- **Masquerade Domain**   This setting instructs the SMTP server to rewrite automatically the domain of the From address used for outbound messages. You can use this setting when you want to ensure that outgoing messages have a consistent domain name.

- **Fully Qualified Domain Name**   This setting specifies the DNS address of the SMTP virtual server, based on Address (A) and Mail Exchanger (MX) records. In general, each SMTP server for a domain should have a unique, fully qualified domain name that includes the server name (for example, Server01.mail.contoso.com).

- **Smart Host**   When a server name or IP address is defined for the Smart Host setting, all messages from this SMTP virtual server are routed through the specified server. This option is commonly used when multiple internal servers should route their messages through a specific SMTP server that has access to the Internet. Using a *smart host* configuration can save bandwidth and increase security because only specific servers will require access to external networks. The Attempt Direct Delivery Before Sending To Smart Host option instructs the local SMTP server to attempt to connect directly to the destination SMTP server. If this operation fails, the message will be forwarded to the designated smart host.

- **Perform Reverse DNS Lookup On Incoming Messages** This setting instructs the SMTP server to perform a DNS reverse lookup to verify that the user's domain matches the IP address in the message header. By enabling this option, you can reduce or prevent unauthorized usage of the SMTP server by messages that use inconsistent header information.

EXAM TIP

You need to understand all of these advanced options for the 70-643 exam.

Enabling LDAP Routing

The Lightweight Directory Access Protocol (LDAP) is the primary standard by which different types of directory services software can communicate with each other. Examples of LDAP-compliant directory services are Active Directory Domain Services and Exchange Server. You can enable the LDAP Routing tab to configure an SMTP virtual server to use LDAP queries to resolve To and From addresses in mail messages. The configuration options specify the type of LDAP system to which the SMTP server will be connecting and the address of the server. Other details include authentication information for connecting to and querying the LDAP server.

Managing Security Permissions

You can define which Windows users may manage SMTP Virtual Server settings by using the Security tab. (See Figure 7-37.) The list defines which users should be considered operators. Operators have permissions to change the configuration of the SMTP virtual server. By default, this includes the Administrators group and the Local Service and Network Service built-in accounts. You can click Add to include additional users or groups on the list of operators.

FIGURE 7-37 Configuring security settings for an SMTP virtual server.

Monitoring SMTP Virtual Servers

There are several ways to monitor your SMTP virtual servers after they are properly configured. IIS 6.0 Manager provides the Current Sessions item to view all current connections to the SMTP server. If you are experiencing delays in message transmissions or performance problems on the server, you can use this information to determine the source of messaging traffic.

You can also monitor many Windows Performance Monitor counters that are part of the *SMTP Server* object. Some useful counters for monitoring SMTP server usage include:

- % Recipients Local
- % Recipients Remote
- Inbound Connections Current
- Message Bytes Total
- Messages Delivered/sec
- Messages Sent/sec
- Outbound Connections Total
- Total Connection Errors

In addition to monitoring usage of the server, you should check periodically for undeliverable messages. By default, these messages are stored within the root folder that was defined for the SMTP server. The default SMTP Virtual Server #1 uses the *%SystemDrive%*\Inetpub\ Mailroot folder. Within this folder are several subfolders that can include message details:

- **Badmail**   Messages that are undeliverable due to addressing or security issues
- **Drop**   Storage of all incoming SMTP messages
- **Pickup**   Storage of messages that are waiting to be processed by another program or service
- **Queue**   Messages that are awaiting delivery

In addition, if you have configured undeliverable messages to be forwarded to a specific account, you should review those messages periodically.

Using an SMTP Virtual Server

SMTP virtual servers can be accessed in several ways. Systems administrators can use the Telnet command-line utility to connect to an SMTP server directly and send commands or create messages. In general use, however, the most typical sources of SMTP messages are end-user applications and web applications.

Using Telnet

You can connect to an SMTP server directly by using the *Telnet* command. Telnet Client is an optional Windows Server 2008 and Windows Server 2008 R2 feature that can be added to the server. After you have added this feature, you can use the *Telnet* command from a command prompt to connect to an SMTP virtual server. You can then type manual commands to carry out actions such as sending a new message. Generally, *Telnet* is used only for diagnostic and troubleshooting purposes. End users will most likely rely on user-friendly applications to send and receive email messages.

> **MORE INFO** **TROUBLESHOOTING WITH** *TELNET*
>
> For more information about troubleshooting SMTP by using *Telnet*, see the Microsoft Support article entitled "How to Test SMTP Services Manually in Windows Server 2003" at *http://support.microsoft.com/kb/323350/*.

Using a Client Messaging Application

For end users, the most common method of sending email messages is through a client email application. Examples include Microsoft Outlook, Windows Live Mail, Windows Mail (which is included with the Windows Vista operating system), and Outlook Express (which is included with Windows XP). The specific setup instructions for these applications vary, but users will generally need the following information to configure their SMTP servers properly:

- SMTP server address or hostname
- SMTP server port
- SMTP authentication information (if authentication is required)

Configuring SMTP Settings for ASP.NET

A common requirement for many web applications is the ability to send email messages to users. To complete this task, the web application requires information about an available SMTP server. You can configure these settings for an ASP.NET application that is running on IIS 7 by using IIS Manager. To do this, select the applicable web server, website, or web application in the left pane and then open the SMTP Email setting in the ASP.NET group of features. (See Figure 7-38.)

EXAM TIP

For the exam and in production, don't confuse the SMTP email settings in IIS Manager for IIS 7 with the SMTP virtual server settings that are accessible through IIS 6.0 Manager. The IIS 7 settings simply provide information for use by web applications and will not make any configuration changes to the SMTP virtual server. You must use IIS 6.0 Manager to modify settings and permission for the SMTP Server service.

Web applications can be built to query this information whenever a new email message needs to be sent, thereby reducing deployment configuration. The available options include E-Mail Address, which is the address that will be used in the From field for the message. The SMTP Server and Port settings define details for connecting to an available SMTP virtual server. The Authentication settings can be provided if the SMTP server requires credentials to be passed. Finally, the Store E-Mail In Pickup Directory option is an alternative to forwarding messages to an SMTP server. When you choose this option, outbound messages will be stored as individual files within the folder you have specified.

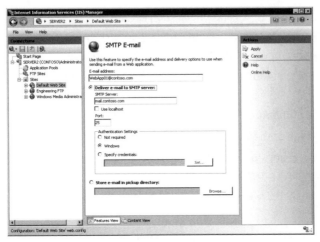

FIGURE 7-38 Configuring SMTP email settings for an IIS 7 website.

Quick Check

1. Which setting should you change to enable SMTP users to send large attachments by using an SMTP virtual server?

2. How can you configure an SMTP virtual server so that only a single web server can send messages to it?

Quick Check Answers

1. The properties on the Messages tab enable you to configure the limits for message size in kilobytes.

2. You can enable the Connection options on the Access tab of the properties of the SMTP virtual server. You should modify the settings to allow only the IP addresses of the web server.

PRACTICE **Configure and Test SMTP Services**

This practice helps you review the process of enabling SMTP services in Windows Server 2008 R2.

EXERCISE Creating a New SMTP Virtual Server

In this exercise, you create a new SMTP virtual server by using IIS 6.0 Manager. The steps assume that you have not yet installed the SMTP Server feature.

1. Log on to Server2.contoso.local as a user with Administrator permissions.
2. Open Server Manager. Right-click Features and select Add Features.
3. On the Select Features page of the Add Features Wizard, select SMTP Server. When the Add Features Wizard dialog box appears, click Add Required Role Services.
4. On the Select Features page of the Add Features Wizard, select Telnet Client and click Next to continue.
5. On the Web Server (IIS) page of the Add Features Wizard, click Next.
6. On the Select Role Services page of the Add Features Wizard, click Next.
7. On the Confirm Installation Selections page, click Install to begin the feature installation process. When the installation process has finished, click Close.
8. Close Server Manager. Launch IIS 6.0 Manager from the Administrative Tools program group.
9. Expand the *Server2* (*Local Computer*) node and note that a default SMTP virtual server called SMTP Virtual Server #1 has already been created.
10. Right-click the *Server2* node, point to New, and then select SMTP Virtual Server.
11. For the Name setting, type **Contoso SMTP**. Click Next.
12. For the Select IP Address setting, keep the default setting and then click Next. Read the warning message and then click Yes to continue.

    You resolve this conflict in later steps.
13. Using Windows Explorer, create a new folder named **Mail** in the root of your system drive. For the Home Directory setting, type or browse to select the path to this folder (for example, C:\Mail). Click Next.
14. In the Default Domain step, type **mail.contoso.local** in the Domain text box and then click Finish. Note that a new SMTP virtual server named Contoso SMTP appears in the left pane of IIS 6.0 Manager.
15. Right-click the *Contoso SMTP* node and select Properties.
16. On the General tab, click Advanced to open the list of IP address and port number settings for the SMTP virtual server. Select (All Unassigned) in the list and then click Edit.
17. Change the TCP Port setting to 2525 and then click OK. This resolves the conflict with the default SMTP Virtual Server. Click OK to close all dialog boxes and save the settings.
18. In IIS 6.0 Manager, right-click the *Contoso SMTP virtual server* node and select Start.
19. Open a command prompt. At the prompt, type **telnet server2 2525**.

You receive output beginning with the code 220, which indicates that the SMTP service is ready on Server2.

20. After you have completed the steps of this exercise, you can use an email client to connect to the SMTP server and send a message. You can attempt to send a message to a known bad email address (such as Recipient@mail.test) to verify the behavior of the SMTP server.

21. When you are finished, close IIS 6.0 Manager. Optionally, you can uninstall the SMTP server on Server2.

Lesson Summary

- You can enable the SMTP Server feature by using Server Manager in Windows Server 2008 and Windows Server 2008 R2.

- Each SMTP virtual server must be configured to use a unique IP address and port combination.

- You can configure authentication to require users to provide credentials to use an SMTP virtual server.

- You can use Relay Restrictions settings to reduce unsolicited commercial email messages.

- You can test the configuration of an SMTP virtual server by using a client email application.

Lesson Review

You can use the following questions to test your knowledge of the information in Lesson 2, "Configuring SMTP." The questions are also available on the companion CD if you prefer to review them in electronic form.

> **NOTE ANSWERS**
>
> Answers to these questions and explanations of why each answer choice is correct or incorrect are located in the "Answers" section at the end of the book.

1. You are a systems administrator responsible for configuring a Windows Server 2008 R2 SMTP server. Your organization is currently using the default SMTP virtual server for sending order notifications from a single web application called ContosoOrderManagement. Recently, you noticed that a large number of messages have been sent to the SMTP virtual server from other computers and users. Which two methods can you use to prevent unauthorized access to the SMTP server? (Each correct answer presents a complete solution. Choose two.)

A. Enable Basic Authentication.

B. Configure a smart host for use by the SMTP virtual server.

C. Add Connection Control entries to limit which IP addresses can use the SMTP server.

D. Modify settings on the Security tab of the properties of the SMTP virtual server.

2. You are a systems administrator responsible for managing a Windows Server 2008 R2 SMTP server. Recently, users have complained that a web application running on the server is experiencing performance problems at specific times of the day. You suspect that the problem might be related to load placed on the SMTP Server service. Which of the following methods should you use to monitor the performance of an SMTP virtual server over time?

A. The Current Sessions section of IIS 6.0 Manager

B. SMTP Server counters collected by Performance Monitor

C. Windows Event Viewer: Application Log

D. Windows Event Viewer: System Log

E. The contents of the Badmail folder for the SMTP virtual server

Chapter Review

To further practice and reinforce the skills you learned in this chapter, you can perform the following tasks:

- Review the chapter summary.
- Review the list of key terms introduced in this chapter.
- Complete the case scenarios. These scenarios set up real-world situations involving the topics of this chapter and ask you to create a solution.
- Complete the suggested practices.
- Take a practice test.

Chapter Summary

- Windows Server 2008 R2 includes a built-in FTP server that provides new features, such as integration with website bindings, administration using IIS manager, and support for FTP Over SSL (FTPS).
- The SMTP service enables Windows Server 2008 and Windows Server 2008 R2 to route email messages securely to other servers or users.

Key Terms

Do you know what these key terms mean? You can check your answers by looking up the terms in the glossary at the end of the book.

- File Transfer Protocol (FTP)
- FTP client
- FTP Over SSL
- FTP server
- FTP user isolation
- masquerade domain
- relay restrictions
- Simple Mail Transfer Protocol (SMTP)
- smart host

Case Scenarios

In these case scenarios, you apply what you have learned about configuring FTP and SMTP services in Windows Server 2008 R2.

Case Scenario 1: Implementing a Secure FTP Site

You are a systems administrator responsible for enabling web developers to manage their web applications on a test server. Some of these users are consultants who do not have accounts in your organization's Active Directory domain. You want to ensure that they are able to access and modify content for specific websites. You also want to minimize the administrative effort required to set up this configuration. Your organization's security policies state that logon credentials such as usernames and passwords should never be sent unencrypted.

1. How can you ensure that logon credentials are encrypted during transmission?

2. What is the easiest method of providing FTP-based access to existing websites?

Case Scenario 2: Configuring an SMTP Virtual Server

You are a systems administrator responsible for securing an SMTP virtual server in Windows Server 2008 R2. The server on which the SMTP virtual server resides currently has two physical network adapters that are attached to separate networks. Your security requirements require the SMTP server to respond on only one of these IP addresses and only to requests on port 8937. Users and applications that require access to the SMTP server must be required to provide credentials. Recently, users have complained that they are unable to send attachments that are over 2MB in size. You want to allow attachments of up to 10MB in size to be sent through the server.

1. How should you configure the SMTP virtual server to respond only to specific network requests?

2. How can you configure the server to require credentials for sending SMTP messages?

3. How can you change the maximum allowable message size?

Suggested Practices

To help you successfully master the exam objectives presented in this chapter, complete the following tasks. The activities in this section enable you to practice the process of creating and managing FTP and SMTP services in Windows Server 2008 R2.

- **Practice 1**   In this practice, you work with FTP features in Windows Server 2008 R2.

    1. Using IIS Manager, create a new FTP site binding for the *Default Web Site* object.

    2. Configure different FTP User Isolation settings and use an FTP client application to test their effects. Pay attention to the default folder location based on each setting and which folders are accessible to the users.

    3. Enable FTP Over SSL (FTPS) by creating a self-signed SSL certificate. Use an FTPS-compatible FTP client application to test the functionality.

- **Practice 2**   In this practice, you test and configure SMTP Services in Windows Server 2008 R2.

  1. Install the SMTP Server feature in Windows Server 2008 R2.

  2. Modify the settings of the default SMTP virtual server to require Basic Authentication to send messages.

  3. Test the SMTP server configuration by sending an email through the SMTP server, using a client application such as Windows Live Mail or Outlook.

  4. Attempt to send a test email message to an email address that is incorrectly formatted or does not exist. Inspect the SMTP server's Badmail folder to attempt to find the message. Also, test whether you receive an undeliverable failure email message.

Take a Practice Test

The practice tests on this book's companion CD offer many options. For example, you can test yourself on just one exam objective, or you can test yourself on all the 70-643 certification exam content. You can set up the test so that it closely simulates the experience of taking a certification exam, or you can set it up in study mode so that you can look at the correct answers and explanations after you answer each question.

> **MORE INFO   PRACTICE TESTS**
>
> For details about all the practice test options available, see the "How to Use the Practice Tests" section in this book's introduction.

CHAPTER 8

Configuring Windows Media Services

M any organizations need to deliver a rich digital media experience efficiently to users. Audio and video files are often available to employees and to external users to communicate important information better. For example, an organization can store archived versions of company meetings and other presentations on an intranet server for later review. Some businesses provide audio and video content to their users as part of their business model. Users have come to expect a seamless experience that provides both live and on-demand access to various types of media. However, the process of sending media information over network connections and the Internet can create significant strains on network bandwidth and tax server resources.

Windows Server 2008 and Windows Server 2008 R2 provide features for efficiently streaming media to users over a public or private network. In this chapter, you learn how to install and configure the Streaming Media Services server role and how you can configure Windows Media Services to provide access to different types of content. You also learn about ways you can secure digital content.

> **MORE INFO**   **OBTAINING WINDOWS MEDIA SERVICES**
>
> The Streaming Media Services server role is available as a downloadable add-on for Windows Server 2008 R2. To download the required file, visit *http://download.microsoft .com* and search for "Windows Media Services 2008 for Windows Server 2008 R2."

Exam objectives in this chapter:

- Manage the Streaming Media Services role.
- Secure streaming media.

Lesson in this chapter:

Before You Begin

To complete the lesson in this chapter, you should have installed and configured the Web Server (IIS) server role on Server2.contoso.local.

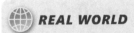 **REAL WORLD**

J.C. Mackin

Streaming Media Services is the only streaming media provider that is covered on the 70-643 exam. However, it's important to note a real-world development currently taking place with streaming media delivery that isn't covered on the exam. Another Microsoft technology —a platform integrated with IIS 7 called IIS Media Services —is seriously challenging Streaming Media Services as the preferred delivery system for streaming media.

IIS Media Services has a number of advantages over Streaming Media Services. For example, IIS Media Services offers an extension called Smooth Streaming that adjusts the bitrate of the media stream delivery in response to the bandwidth available. IIS Media Services is also able to deliver media to a wider range of clients, including, for example, iPhones. Finally, IIS Media Services is integrated with IIS 7 and therefore allows you to consolidate your web server and streaming media services administration.

If you need to set up a streaming media infrastructure in your organization, be sure to look into IIS Media Services before setting up Streaming Media Services. For more information about IIS Media Services, visit *http://www.iis.net/media*.

Lesson 1: Configuring Windows Media Services

The *Streaming Media Services* server role in Windows Server 2008 R2 provides features for managing and presenting audio and video content to users. It also includes administrative tools and configuration options for meeting many business and technical requirements. In this lesson, you learn how to enable and configure the Windows Media Server service. You also learn about methods of improving scalability, performance, security, and reliability.

After this lesson, you will be able to:

- Install the Streaming Media Services server role on a computer running Windows Server 2008 R2.

- Configure Streaming Media Services settings by using the Windows Media Services administrative tool.

- Create publishing points for delivering broadcast and on-demand audio and video content to users.

- Configure authentication and authorization security settings to protect access to content.

- Enable cache/proxy features to increase performance and reliability of Windows Media server services.

- Determine how best to secure streaming media in your organization.

Estimated lesson time: 60 minutes

Understanding Media Services

The technical requirements for providing access to audio and video media can differ significantly from requirements for other types of content. The Web Server (IIS) server role can provide your users with access to many types of files. For example, you can enable users to download Windows Media Audio (.wma) and Windows Media Video (.wmv) files by providing them with the appropriate URL and access permissions. The drawback of this approach, however, is that users typically need to download an entire file before they can start using it. The need to wait for a complete file download offers a poor user experience. Many users will choose not to wait for the media due to this inconvenience. Whenever users request large video and audio files, web servers attempt to send the information as quickly as possible. This reduces the performance of the server for other users and limits overall scalability. The download process can also waste significant resources if users decide they do not want the entire file.

For these reasons, it is preferable to use a specialized service for serving media content. The primary purpose of the Streaming Media Services server role in Windows Server 2008 and Windows Server 2008 R2 is to provide access to both live and on-demand audio and video content over standard communications protocols such as those used on the Internet.

Media can be made available to users in an intranet scenario or over a publicly accessible website. In many cases, a web application will include links that help users easily locate and launch the content they need. Usually, the content can begin playing within seconds, and the media server can throttle network bandwidth automatically, based on the client's connection speed and the desired quality. You can also use Digital Rights Management (DRM) to protect the content provided to users.

Delivering Live vs. Prerecorded Content

Users can use Windows Media Services to access two main types of content. Live broadcasts are typically used for events such as sportscasts, music concerts, and company meetings. The original source for live broadcasts is usually a server or camera that supports the Windows Media Encoder standard. This type of content starts at a specific time, and all users receive the same audio or video content. Because the data is being sent as it is generated, users are unable to pause, fast-forward, or replay the content during the live event. Live broadcasts can, however, be archived so that users can access them on demand at a later time.

Prerecorded content is available to users on demand. Examples include a library of training videos, music videos, television shows, or other content that is available upon request. When users request content, Streaming Media Services starts sending it immediately. As soon as the client computer's media player has buffered enough of the data stream, the playback can begin. The buffering process often takes only a few seconds, so playback usually begins very quickly. Content developers can also create webpages that include an embedded media player to provide easy access to content and associated information. Additionally, users can stop, pause, fast-forward, or rewind the playback when accessing on-demand content.

Understanding Unicast vs. Multicast Streaming

An important goal for providing access to streamed audio and video content is reducing network bandwidth requirements. Both clients and servers often have limitations that can reduce both scalability and the number of users who can access media. Windows Media Services provides two methods of sending data to clients. Unicast streaming is available as a delivery method on all versions of Windows Server 2008 R2. However, Windows Server 2008 R2 Enterprise and Windows Server 2008 R2 Datacenter also offer multicast streaming as an option.

Unicast streaming is based on a direct one-to-one connection between client computers and the media server. This is the most appropriate approach for scenarios in which users should be able to start playing any content on demand. Because the content is sent individually to each client, users can pause, replay, or fast-forward content in their media player. The primary drawback of the unicast approach is that it can consume a significant amount of network bandwidth.

With multicast streaming, many clients can subscribe simultaneously to the same stream from a server. Server bandwidth requirements are minimized because the information is sent only once. As long as the network infrastructure supports multicast routing and distribution, clients can then receive the content without requiring a direct connection to the server. Multicast streaming is most appropriate for delivering live, broadcast-based media because users will be unable to control the playback of the stream. Multicast streaming is also well suited for internal corporate networks where administrators can ensure that the infrastructure supports it.

EXAM TIP

For the exam, remember that although multicast streaming minimizes network traffic, it is only available as an option on Windows Server 2008 R2 Enterprise and Windows Server 2008 R2 Datacenter. You also need to know the address ranges used in multicast transmission: In IPv4 networks, multicast communications use the 224.0.0.0/24 range. In IPv6 networks, FF00::/8 is used.

Comparing Data Transfer Protocols

Content providers must design their streaming media services to ensure accessibility and performance. Windows Media Services supports different protocols based on client and network capabilities. The *Real-Time Streaming Protocol* (RTSP) provides an efficient method to send audio and video content to computers that are running Windows Media Player 9 or later. RTSP can use the User Datagram Protocol (UDP, referred to as RTSPU) if it is supported by the client and network. If UDP is not supported, RTSP can use TCP (RTSPT). The default TCP port for connections is 554, but you can change this setting to support specific firewall requirements. For RTSPU, use ports 5004 and 5005.

The advantage of RTSP and RTSPU is that they minimize network latency. However, if the streaming media traverses any firewalls, you need to configure those firewalls specially to allow RTSP and RTSPU traffic.

EXAM TIP

For the 70-643 exam, you need to know the ports that RTSP and RTSPU use. To enable RTSP and RTSPU traffic through a firewall, configure the firewall to allow traffic through TCP port 554 and UDP ports 5004 and 5005.

Windows Media Services can also stream information by using the HTTP protocol to support clients or networks that do not support RTSP. By default, data is sent on HTTP port 80, but the port can be changed to avoid conflicts with the Web Server (IIS) server role. To simplify the connection process, Windows Media Services provides a feature called automatic protocol rollover. This feature can automatically determine the most appropriate connection type for a particular media player client and send data using that method.

The advantage of HTTP streaming is that it is supported by all client types and typically does not require the special configuration of any firewalls. However, it is slower and less efficient than RTSP and RTSPU are.

Installing Streaming Media Services

Windows Media Services is an optional role server that must be downloaded and installed from Microsoft. You can find the appropriate download update package (MSU file) by browsing to *http://www.microsoft.com/downloads* and searching for "Windows Media Services 2008 for Windows Server 2008 R2." The site provides information about installing the Streaming Media Services server role by using Server Manager. To begin the process, open Server Manager, right-click Roles, and select Add Roles. The Streaming Media Services role will appear in the list. (See Figure 8-1.)

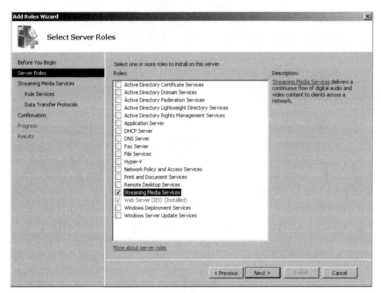

FIGURE 8-1 Adding the Streaming Media Services server role by using Server Manager.

The Streaming Media Services server role includes the following role services:

- **Windows Media Server**   This option installs the basic Windows Media Services service and the Windows Media Services console. You must select this option to be able to stream audio and video to clients from the local server.

- **Web-Based Administration**   Windows Media Services also includes an optional web-based configuration and management website that provides the same functionality as the default Windows Media Services console. This component requires the Web Server (IIS) server role to be enabled on the local computer.

- **Logging Agent**   This component works with web servers to capture information about audio and video streams. It requires the Web Server (IIS) server role. If you install it on the same computer as the Windows Media Services role service, you must change the HTTP port that the Default Web Site or the Logging Agent uses to avoid a binding conflict.

The Select Data Transfer Protocols page provides options for which protocols will be enabled by default. If you have previously installed the Web Server (IIS) server role and have a web server that is bound to HTTP port 80, you will be unable to select the Hypertext Transfer Protocol (HTTP) option. (See Figure 8-2.) You will be able to reconfigure and enable HTTP after the role addition process has completed.

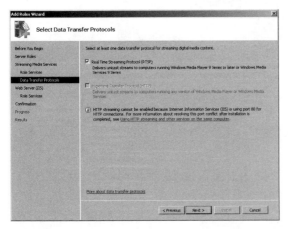

FIGURE 8-2 Configuring data transfer protocol settings for the Streaming Media Services server role.

In addition to these role services, the Windows Media Services console provides features for testing access to content by using Windows Media Player. To make Windows Media Player available for use, you must install the Desktop Experience feature by using Server Manager. This feature is optional, however, and is not necessary if you do not plan to test media streaming on the local computer running Windows Server 2008 or Windows Server 2008 R2.

After you have installed the Streaming Media Services server role on the computer, you can use Server Manager to view additional details. To do this, expand the *Roles* object and select Streaming Media Services. (See Figure 8-3.) Any errors that have been written to the Windows event logs are displayed in the Events section. The Resources And Support section provides numerous recommendations related to the configuration and deployment of streaming media.

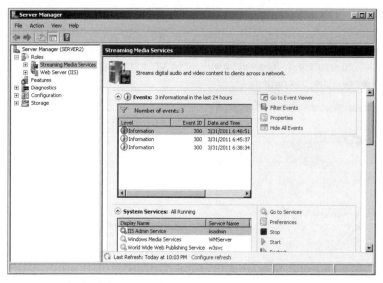

FIGURE 8-3 Viewing information about Streaming Media Services in Server Manager.

Using Windows Media Services Management Tools

Windows Media Services has two main administrative tools. You can launch the Windows Media Services console by selecting Windows Media Services from the Administrative Tools program group. (See Figure 8-4.)

FIGURE 8-4 Using the Windows Media Services console.

If you have chosen to install the Web-Based Administration option, you can also configure Windows Media Services by using a web browser. The default port for the Windows Media Administration website is HTTP port 8080. You can start, stop, and reconfigure the website by using IIS Manager. (See Figure 8-5.)

FIGURE 8-5 Viewing the Windows Media Administration site by using IIS Manager.

After you have started the site, you can access it by launching Windows Media Services (Web) from the Administrative Tools program group or by navigating to its URL directly. The default site bindings do not include an SSL-enabled site binding, so you will receive the warning shown in Figure 8-6. For more information about configuring and enabling Secure Sockets Layer (SSL) for a website, see Chapter 6, "Managing Web Server Security." You can also continue to the Windows Media Services administration website without using an SSL connection.

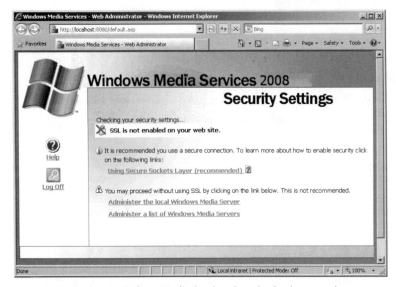

FIGURE 8-6 Viewing a Windows Media Services Security Settings warning.

The Windows Media Services Administration website, shown in Figure 8-7, has been designed to resemble the Windows Media Services console. All the same features and functions are available by using this site. The webpages are configured to refresh automatically at regular intervals to ensure that the information displayed is current. In general, the administration website is more convenient for performing remote management features.

The remainder of the screens and instructions in this lesson focus on using the Windows Media Services console. However, most of the same steps can be completed by using the Windows Media Services Administration website.

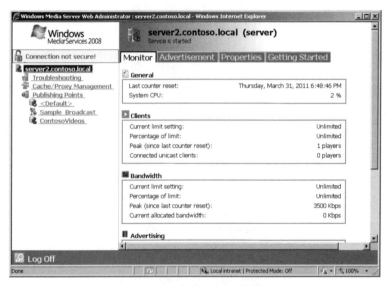

FIGURE 8-7 Viewing the Windows Media Services Administration website.

> *NOTE* **USE LOCAL ADMINISTRATOR PRIVILEGES**
>
> When you connect to the Windows Media Services Administration website, be sure to use the credentials of an account with local administrator privileges on the server.

Managing Publishing Points

To meet the varying requirements of your streaming media, you can configure different publishing points on your Windows Media Server. A *publishing point* defines a file location, content type, delivery type, and other attributes for streaming media that you make available. When you install the Streaming Media Services role, a default publishing point named <Default> (on-demand) is created automatically. The root file system location for this folder is *%SystemDrive%*\Wmpub\Wmroot. This location contains a set of default media files, including sample Windows Media Video (.wmv) video files, playlists, and image files.

Creating a New Publishing Point

When you want to provide access to new content, you can create a new publishing point by using the Windows Media Services console. To start the process, right-click the *Publishing Points* object on the left side of the console and then select the *Add Publishing Point (Wizard)* command. On the Welcome page, click Next. The Publishing Point Name page of the Add Publishing Point Wizard will ask you to provide a name for the new publishing point. (See Figure 8-8.) This name should be brief but also descriptive because it will be part of the URL by which clients connect to content.

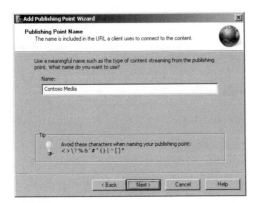

FIGURE 8-8 Providing a name for a new publishing point.

The Content Type page of the wizard prompts you to specify the type of content that will be made available through this publishing point. (See Figure 8-9.) The options are:

- Encoder (A Live Stream)
- Playlist (A Mix Of Files And/Or Live Streams That You Can Combine Into A Continuous Stream)
- One File (Useful For A Broadcast Of An Archived File)
- Files (Digital Media Or Playlists) In A Directory (Useful For Providing Access For On-Demand Playback Through A Single Publishing Point)

The Publishing Point Type page enables you to create either a Broadcast Publishing Point or an On-Demand Publishing Point. (See Figure 8-10.) Based on the option you chose on the previous page, one of the options might be unavailable.

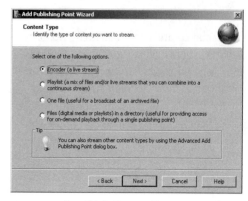

FIGURE 8-9 Specifying Content Type settings for a new publishing point.

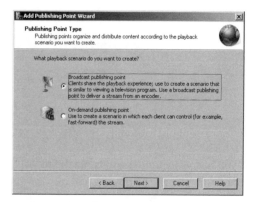

FIGURE 8-10 Specifying Publishing Point Type.

For Windows Server 2008 R2 Enterprise and Windows Server 2008 R2 Datacenter, you also see a Delivery Options For Broadcast Publishing Points page. This page enables you to specify whether you want to use Unicast or Multicast communications. (See Figure 8-11.) The default setting is Unicast, which is the more compatible approach but which also uses more bandwidth. For networks and Windows versions that support multicast, you can choose the Multicast option. When you select Multicast, you also can enable Unicast rollover, a feature that provides unicast transmissions to clients that cannot access the multicast stream.

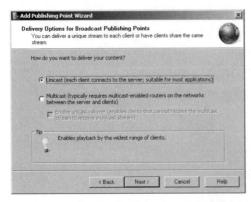

FIGURE 8-11 Selecting the Unicast or Multicast delivery option.

When you are creating a publishing point that provides access to files, you are presented with the Directory Location page as shown in Figure 8-12. The Location Of Directory setting specifies the root folder in which media content is located. You should plan to store all the audio and video files you want to make available within this folder.

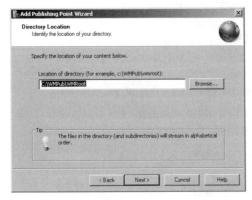

FIGURE 8-12 Configuring Directory Location settings for a new publishing point.

The Enable Access To Directory Content Using Wildcards option enables users to directly access any of the files that are stored in this location. They can do this by manually modifying the URL if they know the name of the file to retrieve. Enabling this option is useful when you have a large number of files to which you want to link directly. However, if you want to ensure that users can access only the files you make available by using links on a website, disable this option.

The Content Playback page provides options related to how playlists will be created and managed for on-demand content. The two options are:

- Loop (Content Plays Continuously)
- Shuffle (Content Plays Randomly)

If you have chosen to create an on-demand publishing point based on a live stream, the Encoder URL page prompts you to provide the URL of the encoder that will provide the media content. (See Figure 8-13.) The URL should include the full path and port number to a server running a Windows Media Services–based encoder.

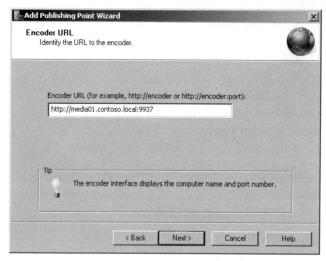

FIGURE 8-13 Providing encoder URL information when creating a broadcast publishing point.

The Unicast Logging page of the Add Publishing Point Wizard enables you to set the collection and storage of usage statistics for Unicast users of the publishing point.

The Publishing Point Summary page provides a list of the selections you have made in the previous steps. (See Figure 8-14.)

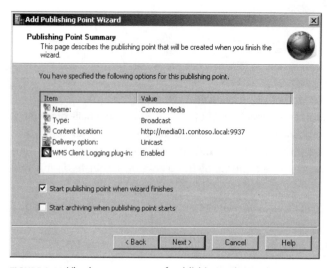

FIGURE 8-14 Viewing a summary of publishing point settings.

The final page of the wizard contains important information about the URL that accesses the publishing point. (See Figure 8-15.) At this point, you can also choose from various files that help make your content accessible to users. You learn more about these options later in this section.

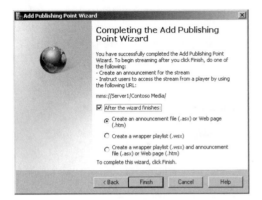

FIGURE 8-15 Completing the Add Publishing Point Wizard.

Administering Publishing Points

You can manage the status of publishing points by using the Windows Media Services console. To manage the status of a publishing point and to perform other administrative functions, right-click the appropriate object. The available commands include:

- *Start*
- *Stop*
- *Allow New Connections*
- *Deny New Connections*
- *Duplicate*
- *Rename*
- *Remove*

Individual publishing points can be started and stopped individually. You can also use the *Duplicate* command to create a new publishing point (with a new name and URL) based on the settings of an existing one. Denying new connections effectively makes the contents of the publishing point inaccessible to new users but continues to send streamed information to users who have already connected. The *Stop* command ends all streams for the publishing point by disconnecting any active users.

Monitoring Publishing Points

The Monitor tab of a publishing point provides an overview of current connections and statistics related to the content currently being served. (See Figure 8-16.) By default, the display is configured to refresh automatically every three seconds. You can use the *Reset All Counters* command (the icon is located at the bottom of the tab) to reset all cumulative-value counters to their initial values.

The *View Performance Monitor* command opens a new window that displays relevant Windows Performance Monitor counters for the publishing point. As with the full Performance Monitor application, you can use the commands on the toolbar to add values or to customize the display. For example, you can add counters related to the *Processor*, *Memory*, and *Network Interface* objects to collect more details about the overall performance of the server.

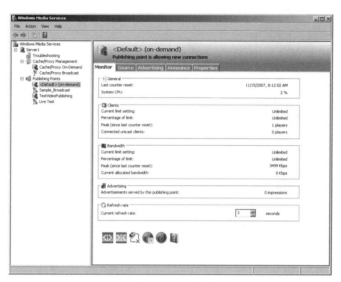

FIGURE 8-16 Monitoring activity for a publishing point by using the Windows Media Services console.

Configuring Source Settings

Every publishing point must have source information to specify which media files will be available to users. As you learned in the previous section, you can specify the default information when you create a new publishing point by using the Add Publishing Point Wizard. You can also use the Windows Media Services console to make changes to the source settings. To do this, select a publishing point and then click the Source tab. (See Figure 8-17.)

The options and details on this page vary based on the type of publishing point you have created. For example, a publishing point that provides access to live broadcast video has information about the URL of the streaming source, whereas on-demand publishing points include playlist and file location information. The Source settings provide an easy way to modify the type of content that is accessible to users without having to create a new publishing point. You can highlight a video and click the *Test Stream* button to access the media automatically by using Windows Media Player directly or by launching Internet Explorer to play the content.

FIGURE 8-17 Configuring Source settings for an on-demand publishing point.

Creating Announcements

After you have prepared a new publishing point for the Windows Media Services server, you need a method to make the content available to users. The Windows Media Services console enables you to create announcements, which are a method of creating links and playlists for the content you want to make available. The last step of the Add Publishing Point Wizard enables you to create the relevant types of announcements automatically. The options include:

- Create An Announcement File (.asx) Or Web Page (.htm)
- Create A Wrapper Playlist (.wsx)
- Create A Wrapper Playlist (.wsx) And Announcement File (.asx) Or Web Page (.htm)

An .asx file directs Windows Media Player to a media file, a .wsx file is a media playlist file, and an .htm file is a webpage that (in this context) includes streaming media content. Depending on which option you select, you will be presented with one or more wizard options. You can also view and modify the announcement settings for an existing publishing point by selecting it in the Windows Media Services console and clicking the Announce tab. (See Figure 8-18.)

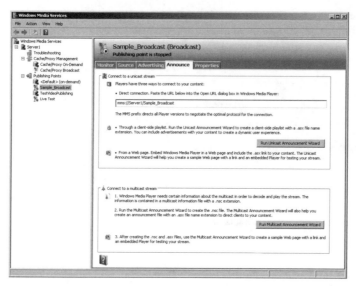

FIGURE 8-18 Viewing Announce settings for a publishing point.

You can use announcements information in your own webpages (for example, by creating a tag that links directly to a publishing point), or you can provide links to the playlist files or wrappers themselves.

EXAM TIP

Remember for the exam that if you have content for which different groups of users require different streaming methods, you can create separate publishing points and announcements for each of these groups. For example, you could define multicast streaming of a file for users inside your network and unicast streaming of the same file for users on the Internet. You could then distribute separate announcements to each group.

Using the Create Wrapper Wizard

The final page of the Add Publishing Point Wizard gives you an option to create a wrapper playlist. When you choose this option, the Create Wrapper Wizard starts automatically. The wrapper playlist you create by using this wizard can include media files and advertisements. (See Figure 8-19.)

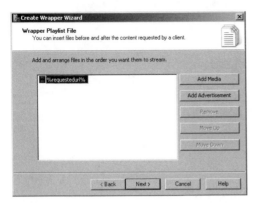

FIGURE 8-19 Using the Create Wrapper Wizard.

Click the *Add Media* button to add new files or other types of content. (See Figure 8-20.) The data can come from other publishing points and can include a mix of on-demand and live encoder-based content. After you have selected the appropriate option, you'll be prompted for the location in which the .wsx file should be stored. Generally, you should place the file within the publishing point's root folder so it will be accessible to users. You can also copy or move the file to another location, such as the root folder of a website.

FIGURE 8-20 Adding media to a wrapper playlist.

Using the Unicast Announcement Wizard

If you have selected to deliver streaming content by using the unicast method, you can use the Unicast Announcement Wizard to configure the appropriate options. By default, unicast URLs are prefixed with the mms content type (for example, *mms://Server2.contoso.local /Media*). Client media players, such as Windows Media Player, are automatically associated with this URL type, so the content can start playback automatically when the user clicks an appropriate hyperlink in a webpage. The Save Announcement Options page of the wizard enables you to specify the location into which the Announcement file (.asx) will be saved. (See Figure 8-21.) The default location is within the root folder of the Web Server (IIS) server role's *Default Web Site* object.

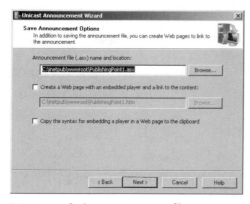

FIGURE 8-21 Saving announcement files.

You can also use this page to create an HTML webpage that includes an embedded player and a link to the content. This method provides a simplified way for web developers to see the HTML and media player tags they need to include in their own code. Later, you can load the webpage directly in Internet Explorer. If you have Windows Media player installed, you can then test the announcement by playing the video. (See Figure 8-22.) If you plan to place the link to the media within an existing webpage, you can use the Copy The Syntax For Embedding A Player In A Web Page To The Clipboard option.

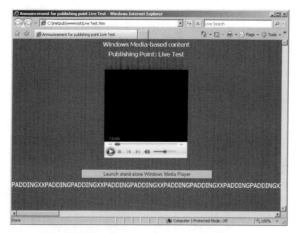

FIGURE 8-22 Viewing an announcement webpage created by using the Unicast Announcement Wizard.

The Edit Announcement Metadata page enables you to specify details related to the title and author of the content and copyright details. This information will be sent to users' media player applications automatically.

To verify the settings you have selected, you can use the buttons in the Test Unicast Announcement window. This window is launched automatically after you have completed the Unicast Announcement Wizard. (See Figure 8-23.) The first *Test* button provides direct access to the playlist and should open Windows Media Player and start playing the content. The Test

Web Page With Embedded Player option *Test* button launches Internet Explorer and loads the test webpage (if one was created).

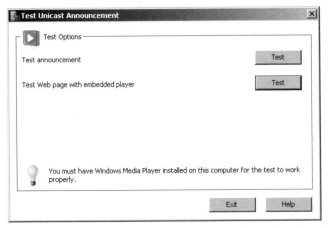

FIGURE 8-23 Testing an announcement after completing the Unicast Announcement Wizard.

Using the Multicast Announcement Wizard

When configuring publishing points that support multicasting of media streams, you can start the Multicast Announcement Wizard to create the necessary files immediately after you complete the Add Publishing Point Wizard. The Specify Files To Create page enables you to select the method by which you will provide links to a multicast stream, as shown in Figure 8-24.

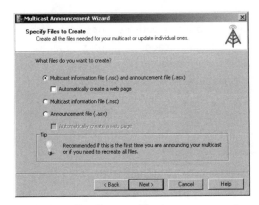

FIGURE 8-24 Creating a multicast announcement.

The default option, Multicast Information File (.nsc) And Announcement File (.asx), creates all the necessary files to provide access to the content. (An .nsc file enables Windows Media Player to decode the streaming media, and an .asx file directs Windows Media Player to the location where the content is stored.) You can also choose an option to create or re-create the .nsc or .asx files individually. The Automatically Create A Web Page option generates an HTML file that includes a link to the multicast content.

EXAM TIP

For the 70-643 exam, you need to understand the roles that .nsc files, .asx files, .wsx files, and .htm files play in streaming media.

The Stream Formats page enables you to define which streams are made available through the announcement. You can provide access to different streams located on various publishing points either on the same server or on another Windows Media Services server. Click Add to access the Add Stream Formats dialog box. (See Figure 8-25.) The Location Of Content setting can point directly to an audio or video file, or it can specify the location of a live media encoder. You can also link to a stream from another publishing point. When you click Next to continue, the Multicast Announcement Wizard automatically attempts to verify the links to the content you specified.

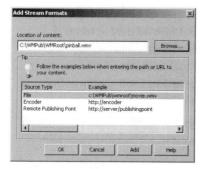

FIGURE 8-25 Adding stream formats by using the Multicast Announcement Wizard.

The Save Multicast Announcement Files page lists the physical path locations into which the selected files will be stored. (See Figure 8-26.) The default location is the root folder for Default Web Site, created when you install the Web Server (IIS) server role. However, you can change the location to make the announcements available from another website.

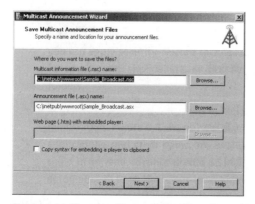

FIGURE 8-26 Choosing file system locations for multicast announcement files.

An announcement can point to a web server location or to a network share for the actual .nsc file that stores the multicast information. You can choose the option in the Specify URL To Multicast Information File page. (See Figure 8-27.) If you are using a shared network location, the Windows Media Services service account must have permissions to read the file. The Network Share option is useful when you want to centralize the creation and management of multicast information files.

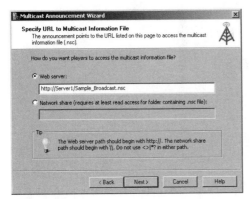

FIGURE 8-27 Specifying the location of multicast information files.

Because multicast streams are designed to provide access to live content, the audio or video stream is not automatically available for replay. You can use the Yes option on the Archive Content page to automatically create an archived video file that can be accessed after the live stream has concluded.

After you have finished the steps of the Multicast Announcement Wizard, you can test the files and settings that were generated in the same way you tested the files and settings that were generated by using the Unicast Announcement Wizard. For example, you can load the web page that contains an embedded player link for the live webcast. You should note, however, that if a live stream has not started from the encoder link you specified, you will not yet be able to view any of the media.

Configuring Publishing Point Properties

Windows Media Services uses a plug-in–based architecture to configure the features and options available for each publishing point. To access these settings, select a publishing point by using the Windows Media Services console and then select the Properties tab. Figure 8-28 shows an overview of the available options.

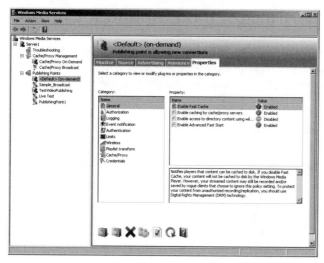

FIGURE 8-28 Viewing properties for an on-demand publishing point.

The specific list of categories and their default properties settings vary based on the decisions you made when you created the publishing point.

For example, the Limits category provides numerous options for managing bandwidth and performance. The options include:

- Limit Player Connections
- Limit Outgoing Distribution Connections
- Limit Aggregate Player Bandwidth (Kbps)
- Limit Aggregate Outgoing Distribution Bandwidth (Kbps)
- Limit Bandwidth Per Player Connection (Kbps)
- Limit Bandwidth Per Outgoing Distribution Connection (Kbps)
- Limit Fast Start Bandwidth Per Player Connection (Kbps)
- Limit Fast Cache Content Delivery Rate

These settings are useful for managing network usage, especially when many Windows Media Services components might be competing for the same resources or when many publishing points are running on the same server. You learn more about other properties settings related to security later in this lesson.

Managing Advertising Settings

For many content providers, audio and video advertisements are a significant source of revenue. You can use the Windows Media Services console to create and manage advertisements automatically. To view and modify settings, select a publishing point and then click the Advertising tab. (See Figure 8-29.)

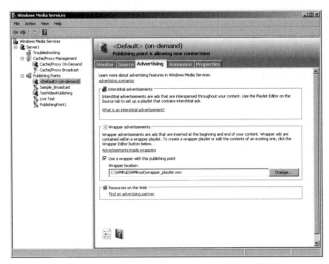

FIGURE 8-29 Configuring Advertising settings for a publishing point.

It is possible to include advertisements manually by inserting the relevant files within a playlist. However, this process can be tedious and time-consuming, especially when users can access many audio and video files from the same publishing point. There are three primary methods of presenting advertisements.

- **Banner ads**   Many webpages that link to video or audio content can include advertisements on the source webpage. For example, the center of the screen might show a video broadcast while the surrounding areas of the page include relevant static image banner ads. This method does not require any special configuration in Windows Media Services.

- **Wrapper ads**   A typical requirement for many organizations is the ability to play a specific audio or video clip automatically before or after any streaming media are accessed. For example, a news video service might want to include a brief splash video whenever a user accesses its media. Wrapper ads point to a playlist that includes this information. These ads will also play automatically for live broadcasts, so they ensure that users who join a stream that has already started will also see the ads.

- **Interstitial ads**   These ads are presented at various times during the streaming of specific content. For example, an online television broadcaster might include a new advertisement after every four on-demand videos are played. You can manually define which ads are shown by modifying playlist settings on the Source tab of the properties of the publishing point. You can also edit playlists manually to achieve the same result.

The Advertising tab also provides a link to the Windows Media Partner Center. Companies listed here are able to provide services such as centralized advertisement distribution and DRM.

Configuring Security for Windows Media Services

As with other types of network-accessible content, it is important to ensure that only authorized users have access to streamed audio and video. Some organizations provide content only to paid or registered users and want to prevent others from using network bandwidth. Unauthorized individuals must also be prevented from directly linking to content or downloading and redistributing media files. Windows Media Services provides several methods for securing Streaming Media Services. Default security settings can be defined at the server level. These settings apply automatically to all publishing points on the server. However, you can also override the settings for each individual publishing point. In this section, you learn about authentication, authorization, and permissions settings that are available within the Properties tab of a publishing point.

Configuring Authentication Options

By default, new publishing points inherit the security-related settings that are defined at the server level. You can define specific settings for different types of content by accessing the Authentication category on the Properties tab of a publishing point. (See Figure 8-30.)

You can authenticate users by using one of three methods. WMS Anonymous User Authentication specifies that Windows Media Services should not prompt users for credentials. However, when this option is enabled, users can access content allowed through NTFS permissions only to a user account specified for anonymous authentication. The default user account is the WMUS_*servername* account, which is automatically created when you install the Streaming Media Services server role. To change the account setting, double-click the WMS Anonymous User Authentication plug-in and provide the appropriate user name and password. Anonymous authentication is useful when you want all the users of the media server to have access to the same set of content.

FIGURE 8-30 Viewing Authentication settings for a publishing point.

WMS Negotiate Authentication uses either NTLM or Kerberos-based methods to determine the identity of the incoming user. This method is useful if you want to restrict access to users who have accounts on the local server or within an Active Directory domain. When users attempt to access content, their Windows credentials determine whether they have permission to access the requested files.

The WMS Digest Authentication option primarily supports Internet users. It relies on the HTTP protocol to request and receive credentials over the network. For security, it does not send the actual password. Instead, it sends a hash that can validate the user's identity.

Configuring Authorization Options

The Authorization properties for a Windows Media Services server or a publishing point specify how permissions are checked before users have access to content. There are three available options. (See Figure 8-31.) WMS NTFS ACL Authorization uses NTFS file system permissions to determine whether a user has access to files. If only anonymous authentication is enabled, the designated anonymous user account must have at least permissions to the content. Otherwise, when user credentials are supplied, the user's effective permissions are checked before a stream is sent.

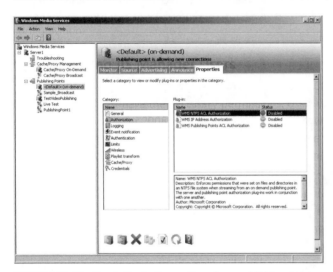

FIGURE 8-31 Viewing Authorization options for a publishing point.

Some Windows Media Services installations are intended for use by only a certain group of computers. For example, an organization might provide company meeting videos that require all users to connect to the organization's local area network (LAN) to obtain access to the content. Administrators can use the WMS IP Address Authorization plug-in to specify which IP addresses can access content. (See Figure 8-32.) Default settings can be configured to automatically allow or deny connections that are not explicitly listed.

FIGURE 8-32 Configuring properties for WMS IP Address Authorization.

You can use the WMS Publishing Points ACL Authorization plug-in to configure which users and groups have access to the publishing point. (See Figure 8-33.) To access content, users must have at least *Read* permissions. By default, the Everyone group has these permissions to the content. Users and groups can also be granted *Write* and *Create* permissions to modify the contents of the publishing point.

FIGURE 8-33 Configuring WMS Publishing Points ACL Authorization settings.

EXAM TIP

For the 70-643 exam, you must understand the differences between all the publishing point authentication and authorization plug-ins.

Using Web Server Permissions

Another method of securing access to streamed audio and video content does not directly involve Windows Media Services. You can use permissions and security options that are available with the Web Server (IIS) server role to secure links and other content that might be accessible to users. For example, you might expose links and playlists for video content only to registered users who are connecting using a secure SSL connection. For more information on configuring security for IIS, see Chapter 6.

Encrypting Media Content

In addition to protecting your media through authentication or authorization settings, you can encrypt media content by using Encrypting File System (EFS) or IPsec.

With EFS, you can encrypt the source media files, but the content is decrypted before it is sent across the network. The purpose of EFS is to prevent unauthorized users from viewing media content that is stolen from its location in storage. Files that are encrypted by EFS can be decrypted only by the user account that has encrypted the file or by any accounts specified as data recovery agents in Group Policy.

EXAM TIP

Remember for the exam that if you use EFS to encrypt media files, you should be sure to designate the service account assigned to the Windows Media Services service as a data recovery agent. Otherwise, Windows Media Services will not be able to read the files.

Another option you can use to encrypt media content is IPsec, which you can implement through IPsec policies or Connection Security Rules in Group Policy. The advantage of IPsec is that it is the only way to protect media content *as it crosses the network*. Unauthorized users who intercept this content as it is streaming are therefore not able to view it.

Enabling Cache/Proxy Features

Managing network bandwidth and server resources when supporting large numbers of users can be difficult when you are using only one Windows Media Services server. The server itself can often become a bottleneck and lead to performance problems for clients. Further, the failure of the server can result in a loss of access to audio and video data. To address these issues, you can use the Windows Media Services Cache/Proxy features.

Caching and proxying are methods by which Windows Media Services can relay streamed information from one publishing point to users who need it. Caching refers to when Windows Media Services copies content from the origin server and stores it locally. The caching server is responsible for obtaining the data from the source and sending it directly to the client. A proxy configuration has multiple computers that are running Windows Media Services send requests to other streaming media servers. Figure 8-34 provides an example of a typical server configuration.

In this diagram, the origin server is providing access directly to only the distribution servers. The distribution servers, in turn, can then send streamed information to the clients that require it. This reduces the network and processing load on the primary Windows Media Services server and enables users to connect to servers that are optimally located, based on their network configuration.

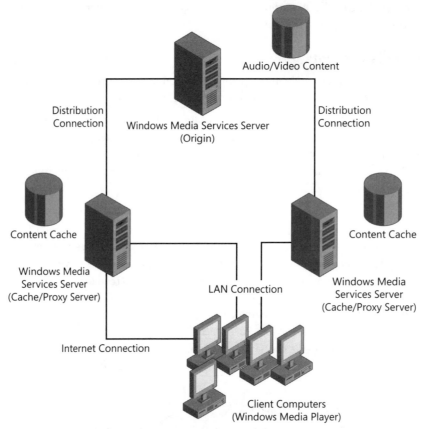

FIGURE 8-34 Using cache/proxy servers to increase scalability and performance.

Enabling Cache/Proxy Settings

By default, Cache/Proxy Management is disabled for new Streaming Media Services installations. To enable this feature for a server, open the Windows Media Services console and select the *server* object. Select the Properties tab and the Cache/Proxy Management category. Right-click the WMS Cache Proxy plug-in and select Enable.

You can also double-click the WMS Cache Proxy plug-in to access the WMS Cache Proxy Properties dialog box. This dialog box presents configuration options for the cache and proxy features.

The General tab of the WMS Cache Proxy Properties dialog box enables you to select which protocol is preferred for streaming media between an origin server and the cache/proxy server. The default setting is to use whichever protocol the client has requested.

Configuring Caching Settings

The Cache tab of the WMS Cache Proxy Properties dialog box enables you to specify storage space locations and limits. (See Figure 8-35.) A proxy/cache server attempts to store as much information as possible to reduce load on the origin server. The default settings do not include any limits on caching, but if you are caching data for a large amount of content, it is recommended that you set some limits.

FIGURE 8-35 Configuring cache settings for a Windows Media server.

The Caching Speed section specifies how quickly data is pulled from the origin server. If you select Maximum Available Bandwidth, the proxy/cache server attempts to transfer content from the origin server as quickly as possible and then to cache it locally. The Content Bit Rate option specifies that data will be transferred from the origin server at the same rate as the bandwidth of the file. This option is useful if many caching servers are accessing the same origin server.

The Prestuff tab provides options related to populating the proxy/cache server's media cache, even when users are not requesting content. (See Figure 8-36.) It is useful when you want to populate server content initially before it goes into production (when the load will be significantly higher). The first option is to pull the information from a stream. This option requires the full URL to a publishing point located on the origin server. You can also limit the amount of bandwidth consumed for the prestuff operation.

FIGURE 8-36 Configuring Prestuff settings for a caching server.

To reduce network load when transferring large amounts of data, you can also load the prestuff data from a file. The Content Path setting can be a local file system location or a network path. The Stream URL validates the files from an existing publishing point. To start the prestuff operation, click the *Prestuff* button.

EXAM TIP

You need to understand prestuff settings for the 70-643 exam.

Configuring Proxy Settings

A Windows Media Services server can also proxy requests from clients to reduce the load on the origin server. The Proxy tab includes settings for three modes of proxy options. They are:

- **Proxy** This is the default proxy functionality in which the server presents content to clients. The server appears to the client as the same computer as the origin Windows Media Services server.

- **Proxy Redirect** This option specifies that client requests should be redirected to another proxy server located on the network. It is most often used in load-balancing configurations when you want to redirect all users to a specific server that has available content.

- **Reverse Proxy** A reverse proxy redirects incoming requests to a specific publishing point. The reverse proxy server verifies authentication for the user and then requests the content from the origin server.

By using proxy servers, you can generally increase the scalability of a Windows Media Services server content distribution point.

Configuring Cache/Proxy Settings for Publishing Points

After you have enabled and configured Cache/Proxy Management settings on the appropriate servers, you can use Windows Media Services to configure caching settings. To do this, select a publishing point and then click the Properties tab. The Cache/Proxy category will include properties for determining how information can be cached. For broadcast-based publication points, the available setting is *Stream Splitting Expiration*. This represents the amount of time the content can be accessed before it must communicate with the origin server to check for content updates. The *Cache Expiration* property has the same effect for on-demand publishing points. The default setting for both is 86,400 seconds (24 hours).

Monitoring Proxy/Cache Servers

The Windows Media Services console includes two objects within the Cache/Proxy Management section. These objects monitor the current performance and usage of proxy services. The Cache/Proxy On-Demand and Cache/Proxy Broadcast sections show information based on the type of publication point on the origin server. You can manage these settings independently. For example, you can deny new connections for on-demand content while still allowing new clients to access broadcast streams. The Monitor tab provides performance statistics and configuration information. (See Figure 8-37.)

You can also configure settings for both types of cache/proxy points on the Properties tab. As with publishing points, you can configure categories such as Authorization, Authentication, and Limits.

FIGURE 8-37 Monitoring cache/proxy settings and performance.

Protecting Digital Content through Rights Management

Organizations that provide valuable content to their users need to ensure that the information is used as it was intended. For example, if a user is able to save a copy of a video file on her computer, she should be restricted from sending it to other users or posting it on a website without the permission of the content provider. *Digital Rights Management* (DRM) enables content providers and content authors to limit the distribution of their information.

Understanding Windows Media DRM

Windows Media DRM is a software infrastructure that supports the licensing of media files. This infrastructure includes the following components:

- A content packager (Windows Media Rights Manager)

    Windows Media Rights Manager packages digital media files. In the packaging process, a secret value called a *key seed* is generated, which then generates a unique key. This key then encrypts the media content and digitally signs a content header, which includes essential licensing information (such as an ID number for the key and the URL where the license can be acquired). As an alternative, multiple files can be encrypted with the same key. In this case, the packaging process specifies the same key ID for the selected files.

    The packaged file, including the encrypted content and signed header, is saved with a .wma, a .wmv, or an .asf extension.

- A content provider (Streaming Media Services)

    This component of the infrastructure stores the media and makes it available to users or consumers.

- A license clearing house (Windows Media License Service)

    Also called a license issuer, the role of the *license clearing house* is to authenticate a request for a license. Licenses are created by using Windows Media License Service. To create the license, the media packager provides the license issuer with the key seed that originally created the encryption key for media content. The key seed then regenerates the same unique key, which can unlock a specific media file or set of files.

    In addition to a key, a license also includes rights and conditions that apply to the content. For example, a license can specify whether users can play or copy the media file, and the expiration date of the license.

- A Windows Media DRM-aware application (Windows Media Player)

    This component typically uses data contained in the media file to download a license. Using the key contained in the license, the application can then decrypt the file and play the associated media if allowed by the license.

Using Active Directory Rights Management Services

In Windows Server 2008 R2, DRM can also be provided by a server role called *Active Directory Rights Management Services* (AD RMS). This server role allows a computer running Windows Server 2008 R2 to issue licenses for creating and protecting content such as media files and documents. To use this infrastructure, content creation applications must be compatible with RMS. Compatible applications include Microsoft Office 2010. You can also use RMS features through Internet Explorer. For more information about AD RMS, search for Active Directory Rights Management on the Microsoft TechNet website at *http://technet.microsoft.com*.

Other Content Protection Methods

There are also other methods of protecting digital audio and video content. For example, you can implement web-based authentication and authorization to ensure that only registered users are permitted to access the content. You can also use network security devices, such as firewalls, to prevent direct access to content files. Overall, the goal of DRM involves several components that must be configured to ensure that only authorized users can access and use content.

 Quick Check

1. Which type of publishing point should you create if you want to enable users to select and stream items from a large library of audio and video files?

2. How can you increase the scalability of a Windows Media Services publishing point that is experiencing network-related bottlenecks frequently?

Quick Check Answers

1. An on-demand publishing point enables users to request the media they wish to access at any time and allows them to fast-forward, pause, and replay the content.

2. Configure additional Streaming Media Services servers as cache/proxy servers to reduce the load on the origin server.

PRACTICE   **Configure the Windows Media Services Server Role**

In this practice, you install and configure the Streaming Media Services server role on a computer running Windows Server 2008 R2. The steps assume that you have already downloaded and installed the necessary Windows Media Services update package (MSU file) as described in the "Installing Streaming Media Services" section of this lesson. You also need to install the Desktop Experience feature on Server2. You must complete the steps in Exercise 1 before you start the steps in Exercise 2.

EXERCISE 1   Installing the Streaming Media Services Server Role

In this exercise, you use Server Manager to add the Streaming Media Services server role to Server2.contoso.local. You must have installed the Windows Media Services 2008 for Windows Server 2008 R2 and restarted the server before beginning this exercise.

1. Log on to Server2 as a user who has *Administrator* permissions.

2. Open Server Manager, right-click the *Roles* object, and select Add Roles.

3. Click Next on the Before You Begin page.

4. On the Select Server Roles page, select Streaming Media Services. Click Next to continue.

5. On the Streaming Media Services page, read all the text on the page and then click Next to continue.

    You can also access more details about configuring this server role by clicking the links in the Additional Information section.

6. On the Select Role Services page, select all three role services: Windows Media Server, Web-Based Administration, and Logging Agent. If you are prompted to add any additional required role services, click Add Required Role Services. After all three role services are selected, click Next to continue on the Select Role Services page.

7. On the Select Data Transfer Protocols page, select Real Time Streaming Protocol (RTSP). You will be unable to add the HTTP protocol if an existing website is already bound to HTTP port 80 on the local server. Click Next to continue.

8. If the Web Server (IIS) page appears, click Next. For more information about this role and its associated role services, see Chapter 5, "Installing and Configuring Web Applications."

9. On the Select Role Services page, click Next.

10. On the Confirm Installation Selections page, verify the summary of options you have selected and then click Install to begin the installation process.

11. When the installation finishes, click Close on the Installation Results page.

12. In Server Manager, expand the *Roles* object and select Streaming Media Services. Note the Events, System Services, Role Services, and Resources And Support information that is available. When you are finished, close Server Manager.

13. Launch Windows Media Services from the Administrative Tools program group. The console automatically connects to the local Windows Media Services service. You can expand the *server* object to view the default configuration of the server. When you are finished, close the Windows Media Services console.

14. Open Windows Explorer and browse to the *%SystemDrive%*\Wmpub folder. Note the default content located here. The wmroot folder contains sample files you can use for testing purposes.

15. When you are finished, close Windows Explorer.

EXERCISE 2 Creating and Testing a New Publishing Point

In this exercise, you create a new Windows Media Services publishing point that provides on-demand access to several of the sample media files that were included with the default Streaming Media Services server role. You then test access to content by connecting to a video file by using Internet Explorer. To perform the test, you must have installed the Windows Desktop Experience feature on Server2 and then restarted the server.

1. If you have not already done so, log on to Server2 as a user with *Administrator* permissions.

2. Open Windows Explorer and create a copy of the wmroot folder within the *%SystemDrive%* \Wmpub folder. Rename the copied folder to **ContosoVideos**. This folder will serve as the root folder for a new publishing point. When you are finished, close Windows Explorer.

3. Open the Windows Media Services console from the Administrator Tools program group.

4. Expand the *Server2.contoso.local* object, right-click Publishing Points, and select Add Publishing Point (Wizard).

5. Click Next to begin the Add Publishing Point Wizard.

6. For Publishing Point Name, type **ContosoVideos**. Click Next.

7. For Content Type, select Files (Digital Media Or Playlists) and then click Next.

8. For Publishing Point Type, select On-Demand Publishing Point.

   This option enables users to access any of the available videos (assuming that they have the appropriate permissions) and to control playback while they are receiving the stream. Click Next.

9. On the Directory Location page, type **C:\WMPub\ContosoVideos** to specify the path to the folder you created in step 2. (If your system drive is not C, you should type the drive letter on your system.) Select the Enable Access To Directory Content Using Wildcards option. This option enables users to type the name of a video manually to access it directly from the server. Click Next.

10. On the Content Playback page, leave the default settings and then click Next.

11. On the Unicast Logging page, leave the default setting and then click Next.

12. Verify the details on the Publishing Point Summary page and then click Next to continue.

13. On the final step of the Add Publishing Point Wizard, keep the default options selected and then click Finish.

14. The Unicast Announcement Wizard opens automatically after the publishing point is created. Click Next to start the wizard.

15. On the On-Demand Directory page, click Browse to select the serverside _playlist.wsx file in the folder you created in step 2. (The full path should be C:\WMPub \ContosoVideos\serverside_playlist.wsx.) Click Next.

16. On the Access The Content page, note the URL you can use to access the content. You use this in a later step to test the announcement. Click Next.

17. On the Save Announcement Options page, keep the default path. This is the location of Default Web Site, installed with the Web Server (IIS) server role. Also, select the option to create a webpage and keep the default path specified. Click Next to continue.

18. On the Edit Announcement Metadata page, type **Contoso Training** for the title. Click Next.

19. On the final page of the Unicast Announcement Wizard, verify that the Test Files When This Wizard Finishes option is selected and then click Finish.

20. In the Test Unicast Announcement dialog box, click the first *Test* button to test the announcement directly. This should launch Windows Media Player and automatically start playing the video from the publishing point. (If this is the first time you have run Windows Media Player, you must first click Recommended Settings and then click Finish.) When the video is finished, close Windows Media Player.

21. In the Test Unicast Announcement dialog box, click the second *Test* button to access a webpage that contains an embedded browser. Verify that the video plays properly and then close Internet Explorer. (If necessary, first enable the browser option in the yellow banner to allow the required ActiveX control.)

22. When you are finished, click Exit in the Test Unicast Announcement dialog box and close the Windows Media Services console.

Lesson Summary

- Windows Media Services is designed to provide users with access to live and on-demand audio and video streams.
- The Streaming Media Services server role includes MMC-based and web-based administrative tools.
- Multicast streaming can reduce bandwidth requirements on networks that support it.
- You can create multiple publishing points on a Windows Media Services server to provide access to different types of content.

- Cache/proxy servers can improve the performance and scalability of Windows Media Services servers.
- You can secure access to publishing points by using Authorization and Authentication plug-in settings.
- Digital Rights Management (DRM) technology enables content producers to protect their intellectual property by retaining control of when and how the media is used.

Lesson Review

You can use the following questions to test your knowledge of the information in this chapter's lesson, "Configuring Windows Media Services." The questions are also available on the companion CD if you prefer to review them in electronic form.

> **NOTE ANSWERS**
>
> Answers to these questions and explanations of why each answer choice is correct or incorrect are located in the "Answers" section at the end of the book.

1. You are a Windows Server 2008 R2 systems administrator responsible for configuring the Streaming Media Services server role. Your organization would like to make numerous human resources training videos available for access by its employees. Employees should be able to pause and fast-forward content as needed. You also want to ensure that users can access the content only while they are connected to your company's LAN. Which actions should you take? (Each correct answer presents part of the complete solution. Choose two.)

   A. Create a new broadcast publishing point.

   B. Create a new on-demand publishing point.

   C. Enable WMS IP Address Authorization for the publishing point.

   D. Enable WMS Negotiate Authentication for the publishing point.

   E. Enable WMS NTFS ACL Authorization for the publishing point.

2. You are a Windows Media Services administrator responsible for configuring the Streaming Media Services server role for access by the public over the Internet. You currently have 200 large video files in a folder that is used by four publishing points on the server. You want to provide users with access to only 100 files, which are training videos. You have created a new on-demand publishing point that uses the folder containing the videos as its root folder. You also want to minimize the amount of storage space used on the server. Users should be able to access any of the 100 training videos on demand without providing credentials. Which of the following actions should you take?

A. Run the Unicast Announcement Wizard to create an HTML page that provides access to the content.

B. Enable WMS NTFS ACL Authorization for the website and set up the appropriate file system permissions.

C. Copy the training videos to another folder and modify the root folder of the publishing point.

D. Disable WMS Anonymous Authentication for the publishing point.

E. Create a new Wrapper Playlist that includes only the training videos.

3. You are a Windows Server 2008 R2 systems administrator responsible for providing access to a large volume of video files to registered users of your organization's public website. All the video files are located within the D:\Public\Videos folder. Content producers often create and modify these videos. Recently, users have complained that they are experiencing poor performance when accessing videos during busy times. During these times, the Windows Media Services server that hosts the content is experiencing high CPU and network bandwidth use. You want to minimize the administrative time and effort required to increase performance. Which of the following actions should you take to resolve the problem?

A. Copy the training videos to another folder on the Windows Media Services server.

B. Install the Streaming Media Services server role on additional servers and configure them as caching servers.

C. Install the Streaming Media Services server role on additional servers and configure them as proxy servers.

D. Enable the Limit Outgoing Distribution Connections option in the properties of the publishing point.

Chapter Review

To further practice and reinforce the skills you learned in this chapter, you can perform the following tasks:

- Review the chapter summary.
- Review the list of key terms introduced in this chapter.
- Complete the case scenarios. These scenarios set up real-world situations involving the topics of this chapter and ask you to create a solution.
- Complete the suggested practices.
- Take a practice test.

Chapter Summary

- Streaming Media Services in Windows Server 2008 R2 provides a scalable method for delivery of on-demand and broadcast audio and video content to users.
- A Windows Media Services server can host many publishing points to provide access to different types of content.
- You can configure cache and proxy servers to improve the performance of Windows Media Services server installations.

Key Terms

Do you know what these key terms mean? You can check your answers by looking up the terms in the glossary at the end of the book.

- Active Directory Rights Management Services (AD RMS)
- Digital Rights Management (DRM)
- interstitial advertisements
- key seed
- license clearing house
- publishing points
- Real-Time Streaming Protocol (RTSP)
- Streaming Media Services (server role)
- Windows Media server announcements
- Windows Media server broadcast
- Windows Media server cache/proxy server
- Windows Media server playlist
- Windows Media server plug-ins
- Windows Media Services

- Windows Media Services multicast
- Windows Media Services unicast
- wrapper playlist advertisements

Case Scenarios

In the following case scenarios, you apply what you've learned in this chapter. You can find answers to these questions in the "Answers" section at the end of this book.

Case Scenario 1: Protecting Streaming Media Content

You are a Windows Server 2008 R2 systems administrator who works for a company that provides IT training services. Your company has recently decided to make training videos available to registered students who are actively enrolled in a specific course. Users should have access only to training videos related to the classes for which they are currently enrolled. Students are given Windows user accounts within your organization's training Active Directory domain. They should be able to access any of the videos at any time and should be able to control the playback. Your training company would like to display a brief splash introduction before the playback of every video.

1. Which type of publishing point should you create to provide access to the media?

2. How can you restrict students' access to only the training videos that are relevant to them?

3. What is the easiest method of implementing the introduction to each video?

Case Scenario 2: Improving Windows Media Services Performance and Scalability

Your organization provides access to streamed audio content to paid users over the Internet. You have configured a single computer running Windows Server 2008 R2 with the Streaming Media Services server role. Initially, this server was able to meet users' demands. However, recently, several thousand additional users have registered for the service, and some are reporting slow playback or other performance problems during certain times of the day. For security and management reasons, you want to avoid manually moving or copying the audio content from the current Windows Media Services server. Your organization also plans to provide access to a live music concert within the next month and would like to support as many client connections as possible.

1. Which type of publishing point should you create for the live music event?

2. How can you reduce the bandwidth requirements for the live event without including additional Windows Media Services servers?

3. How can you configure additional Windows Media Services servers to improve scalability?

Suggested Practices

To help you successfully master the exam objectives presented in this chapter, complete the following tasks. The practices in this section enable you to practice configuring and managing the Streaming Media Services role in Windows Server 2008 R2 and help you learn about creating new publishing points on a Windows Media Services server.

- **Practice 1** Create an on-demand publishing point and provide access to a playlist that includes multiple audio and video files. (You can use the sample media files included with the Streaming Media Services server role if you do not have access to other files.)

  Configure one of the videos to play automatically before any content is sent to users by creating a wrapper advertisement.

  By using a web browser, start playback of content to verify that it is accessible. If you have multiple computers available, attempt to access the video from them simultaneously to test the effects of multiple concurrent connections.

  Access the publishing point's Monitor tab to view statistics and details related to the content playback.

- **Practice 2** Install the Streaming Media Services server role on two computers running Windows Server 2008 R2. Configure one of the servers with an on-demand publishing point.

  Download the Windows Media Load Simulator at *http://technet.microsoft.com/en-us /library/bb676129.aspx*. Use the Windows Media Load Simulator utility to test the performance and scalability of your Windows Media Services server. Attempt to simulate a large number of connections, and use the Monitor tab in the properties of the publishing point to view access statistics.

  Configure the second Windows Media Services server as a cache/proxy server for the publishing point you created on the first Windows Media Services server.

  Repeat the Windows Media Load Simulator tests to measure performance and to see the server from which the content is being served.

  Optionally, configure Limits settings in the properties of the publishing point and measure the effects on the Windows Media Load Simulator tests.

Take a Practice Test

The practice tests on this book's companion CD offer many options. For example, you can test yourself on just one exam objective, or you can test yourself on all the 70-643 certification exam content. You can set up the test so that it closely simulates the experience of taking a certification exam, or you can set it up in study mode so that you can look at the correct answers and explanations after you answer each question.

MORE INFO   PRACTICE TESTS

For details about all the practice test options available, see the "How to Use the Practice Tests" section in this book's introduction.

CHAPTER 9

Configuring Microsoft SharePoint Foundation

SharePoint Foundation 2010 is the latest version of the application previously named Windows SharePoint Services. Like Windows SharePoint Services, SharePoint Foundation is a free download from the Microsoft website and provides a core set of features with which users can share, modify, and discuss content. SharePoint Foundation provides features for centrally creating common types of information, including announcements, tasks, and reminders. Application developers can also use SharePoint Foundation as a platform for their own web-based programs.

In this chapter, you learn about configuring SharePoint Foundation 2010, including steps such as setting up and managing new SharePoint sites and managing operations for a SharePoint server.

Exam objectives in this chapter:

- Configure SharePoint Foundation options.
- Configure SharePoint Foundation integration.

Lesson in this chapter:

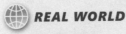 **REAL WORLD**

Anil Desai

All too often, we IT professionals focus on technology rather than on how it can benefit users. When deciding to deploy a product such as SharePoint Foundation, it's important to first consider how it will be used in the production environment. The process of creating a new SharePoint site is simple, but understanding the best implementation approach can take significantly more time and effort. In some cases, it might be appropriate just to deploy a new site, allow users to access it, and see how it evolves on its own. In most cases, however, a little planning and forethought can ensure a successful deployment.

An important part of successful IT application and service deployments is including affected users in the decision process. You need to understand the true objectives of employees throughout the organization. SPF has many powerful features that enable document sharing and collaboration. However, what users ask for is not always what they really want or need. People might ask for a SharePoint site to be created when a similar one already exists, or they might try to use a single site to serve multiple purposes. For this reason, a good initial question to ask users is, "What problems are you trying to solve?" Other considerations for planning SharePoint deployments include the security requirements, the number of users who will actively use the site, and the volume of data expected to be hosted. You can combine this information to determine the best way to make SPF available to users. Having well-defined requirements also helps you verify that the deployment was successful.

Take time to understand the needs and anticipated benefits of SharePoint (or of just about any IT technology, for that matter) for users. For more information and examples, see the Planning Worksheets for SharePoint Foundation 2010 page on Microsoft TechNet by visiting *http://technet.microsoft.com/en-us/library /cc288346.aspx* or searching for "SharePoint Foundation planning worksheets" at *http://technet.microsoft.com.*

Before You Begin

To complete the lesson in this chapter, you must have:

- Added the Web Server (IIS) server role to Server2.contoso.local by using the default options. For more information on installing this role, see Chapter 5, "Installing and Configuring Web Applications."

- Downloaded Microsoft SharePoint Foundation 2010 from the Microsoft Download Center at *http://go.microsoft.com/FWLink/?Linkid=197422* and installed this software on Server2 by specifying the stand-alone option.

Lesson 1: Configuring and Managing SharePoint Foundation

The purpose of SharePoint Foundation (SPF) is to provide a web-based environment in which users can collaborate and share information. Many applications, such as those in the Microsoft Office suite, provide integration with SPF for managing and editing documents. SPF is also a platform that developers can use to write their own web-based applications based on specific business needs.

Because SPF enables many usage scenarios, it is important to configure various options and settings to suit your needs after installation. In this lesson, you learn about the available options and features and how to configure them.

After this lesson, you will be able to:

- Explain the purpose of SharePoint Foundation (SPF).
- Describe the difference between a stand-alone deployment and a server farm deployment of SPF.
- Complete SPF configuration tasks by using the SharePoint Central Administration website.
- Manage SPF operations settings related to security, email, and logging.
- Perform backup and recovery operations for SharePoint sites.
- Deploy and configure new SharePoint sites.
- Manage web application settings for SharePoint sites.

Estimated lesson time: 120 minutes

Understanding SharePoint Foundation 2010

SharePoint Foundation 2010 is a server application that creates collaborative web applications in Windows Server 2008 or Windows Server 2008 R2. After SPF is installed and configured, users can post and maintain content on SPF sites directly.

Specific features and types of content that can be hosted include:

- Announcements
- Libraries (for version control), including those for shared documents
- Lists, including calendars and tasks
- Discussions
- Links
- Contact information

Figure 9-1 shows a view of the user interface of SPF.

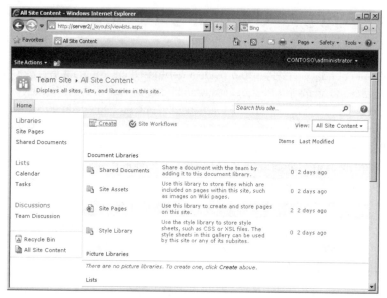

FIGURE 9-1 A team site created in SPF.

Users can directly manage all this information in a web browser after you grant them access through security permissions. SPF sites can also work with email systems to send users notifications of content changes and to get information into and out of SPF. Presence-awareness features can also help distributed teams keep in touch by using instant messaging and other applications. SPF is also an extensible platform so that applications developers can add new functionality. Overall, the features and capabilities of SPF offer an easy way for teams and departments to share information and collaborate.

> **MORE INFO** **SHAREPOINT SERVER 2010**
>
> Although SharePoint Foundation 2010 is free, it offers only a limited set of features compared with the commercial product, SharePoint Server 2010. SharePoint Server 2010 uses SharePoint Foundation 2010 as a core, but then builds on this product by offering many more features related to content management, enterprise search, social networking, Microsoft Office integration, business intelligence, and other areas. Unlike SharePoint Foundation 2010, SharePoint Server 2010 is a paid-for product that requires client access licenses. For more information about SharePoint Server 2010, visit *http://sharepoint .microsoft.com*.

Understanding SPF Deployment Options

To meet different organizational needs for scalability, SPF has two main types of deployment options: a *stand-alone server configuration* and a server farm configuration. You choose between these two deployment options when you run the SharePoint Foundation

2010 installation program. In this section, you learn about these different ways of deploying SharePoint.

> **NOTE** **REQUIREMENTS FOR SHAREPOINT FOUNDATION 2010**
>
> For hardware, the official requirements for SPF include a 64-bit processor with four cores for small deployments and eight cores for a medium deployment, 8 GB of RAM for small deployments and 16 GB for medium deployments, and 80 GB of hard disk space for the system drive.
>
> For software, SPF requires either Windows Server 2008 with SP2 or Windows Server 2008 R2 with SP1. In addition, the server farm deployment of SPF requires the 64-bit edition of Microsoft SQL Server 2008 R2, or the 64-bit edition of Microsoft SQL Server 2008 with SP1 and Cumulative Update 2 or 5, or the 64-bit edition of Microsoft SQL Server 2005 with SP3 and Cumulative Update 3.

Deploying SPF in a Stand-Alone Configuration

The simplest method of getting up and running with SPF is to use a single server configuration. In the stand-alone deployment option, SPF is designed to use a single server that hosts all necessary components and services on the local computer. IIS is required to host the SPF websites. For data storage, the stand-alone configuration uses SQL Express 2008, which has a 4-GB limit.

By running all these services on the same computer, you can complete the setup and deployment process very quickly. To install SPF in a stand-alone configuration, you simply use the SharePoint installation program to install first the SPF software prerequisites and then SPF itself. You can then perform additional setup by using the *SharePoint Central Administration website*.

The primary drawback to a stand-alone configuration is that it does not support multiple SPF servers for scalability in larger environments.

Deploying SPF in a Server Farm Configuration

In many organizations, collaboration features become an important part of the infrastructure. Because SPF provides many useful features, scalability is an important consideration. Its architecture enables systems administrators to divide the front-end functionality (the user and administration websites) from the back-end data storage (the SPF database). This deployment option is known as a *server farm configuration*.

In a server farm, multiple SPF front-end servers can connect to a back-end database server that hosts copies of all documents, settings, and related data. This helps organizations increase performance and provide access in a variety of scenarios. For example, it enables the creation of an extranet scenario that third-party users and organizations (such as business partners or consulting partners) can use. In addition, remote offices might choose to have their own SPF servers for performance and accessibility reasons.

The basic system requirements of each server in a server farm configuration are identical to those of a stand-alone configuration, with the exception of the database application that hosts the SPF databases. To deploy into a server farm configuration, a SQL database must already exist on a computer running Microsoft SQL Server 2005 SP3 or SQL Server 2008 SP1. Although creating this database adds steps to the setup process, organizations can use the expertise of database administrators (DBAs) to handle the SPF database, and use existing SQL Server installations for hosting the database.

The first step of deploying SPF in a server farm is to install and configure the required databases on a computer running SQL Server. Depending on the security and performance requirements for the deployment, SQL Server might or might not be installed and configured on one of the computers running SPF. The next step is to install the SPF software prerequisites and SPF itself on all the front-end servers. (Additional servers can be added later.) The SharePoint Central Administration website will be installed and configured on the first server that is to be part of the server farm.

Using the SharePoint Products Configuration Wizard

After SPF finishes installing, you are immediately given an opportunity to launch the SharePoint Products Configuration Wizard (shown in Figure 9-2). This wizard creates the SPF database and configures the web server or servers. When working in a server farm configuration, you use the SharePoint Products Configuration Wizard to specify the location and logon information for the database server that will be used for the server farm. Finally, you can also use the wizard to repair an installation of SPF if the site is inaccessible or has encountered errors.

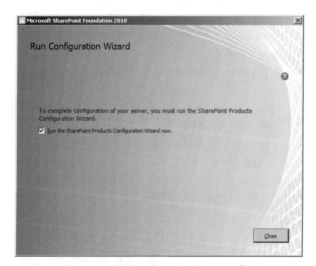

FIGURE 9-2 Running the SharePoint Products Configuration Wizard.

Migration Options from Windows SharePoint Services 3.0

If you are migrating to SPF from Windows SharePoint Services (WSS) 3.0, you can perform the upgrade by performing either an in-place upgrade or a database attach upgrade.

An in-place upgrade migrates all your WSS 3.0 sites to SPF on the same hardware. You can only use this approach if your hardware meets the minimum requirements for SPF 2010. An advantage of this approach is that it simplifies the upgrade process and automatically preserves server and farm-wide settings. A disadvantage is that your servers and farms must remain offline during the upgrade procedure.

A database attach upgrade enables you to migrate your SharePoint installation to new hardware. With this approach, you create a new SPF farm, detach the content databases from your WSS 3.0 farm, and then attach these databases to the new SPF farm. This method enables you to upgrade your hardware, which is faster than an in-place upgrade. However, a database attach upgrade does not update server and farm settings automatically; you have to transfer these settings manually.

For more information about upgrading to SharePoint Foundation 2010, visit *http://technet .microsoft.com/en-us/library/cc303309*.

Verifying the SPF Installation

After you have completed the installation of SPF and run the SharePoint Products Configuration Wizard, you can use the Services console and IIS Manager to verify settings. In this section, you learn how to ensure that SPF is properly installed.

Verify SPF Services

To see the new services that have been added by SPF installation, open the Services console. Figure 9-3 shows these eleven new services, six of which relate to SharePoint and five of which relate to SQL. Not all these services are started or even enabled by default, but you should verify that the services with a startup type set to *Automatic* have started.

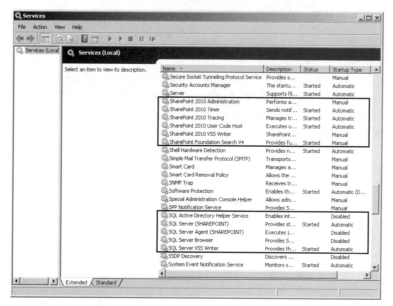

FIGURE 9-3 SharePoint Foundation services.

Verifying SPF Websites

Installing SharePoint Foundation creates three new IIS websites. They are:

- **SharePoint – 80** This is the primary website, created on port 80, that users of SPF will access with their web browser. The default version of this site is shown in Figure 9-4. After the site has been created, users can use *http://ServerName* to access SPF.

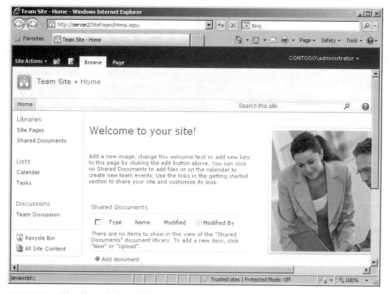

FIGURE 9-4 The SharePoint – 80 website.

- **SharePoint Central Administration v4** This website enables SharePoint administrators to configure SPF-related options. You can access the Central Administration site through the Start menu by clicking All Programs/Microsoft SharePoint 2010 Products/ SharePoint 2010 Central Administration. You can also access the site directly in a browser by navigating to *http://ServerName:PortNumber*, where *PortNumber* represents the random port number assigned to the site. To discover this port number, select the site in IIS Manager and then look for the number assigned beneath Browse Web Site in the Action pane, as shown in Figure 9-5.

FIGURE 9-5 The SharePoint Central Administration v4 website is assigned a unique port number.

The Central Administration website is shown in Figure 9-6.

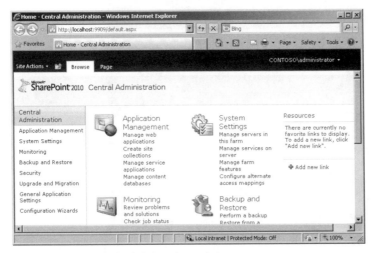

FIGURE 9-6 The Central Administration website.

- **SharePoint Web Services** This website is new to SPF. It is used for Business Data Connectivity, security token management, topology, and other features available only in SharePoint Server 2010.

Note that SPF installation automatically stops any other IIS site configured to use port 80 on the local server. This is necessary because IIS does not allow multiple sites to run concurrently on the same HTTP port without the use of unique host headers. If the local server is hosting another website or web application, consider changing its port settings to ensure that users can still access it. For more information about configuring IIS, see Chapter 5.

Performing SPF Post-Installation Configuration Tasks

To complete the deployment of SPF, you must take certain configuration steps after the SharePoint Foundation 2010 installation program has completed. First, configure email settings for the server and then select the administrators for the entire SPF installation or farm. Finally, if you have installed SPF in a farm configuration, register managed accounts for SharePoint.

SPF uses standard email to send alerts and notifications and to receive messages, so you must specify your outgoing and incoming email server after installation.

Configuring Outgoing Email Settings

To configure the default outgoing email settings for every web application in the farm, open Central Administration and click the System Settings link. Then, on the System Settings page, beneath E-mail And Text Messages (SMS), click Configure Outgoing E-mail Settings. This link is shown in Figure 9-7.

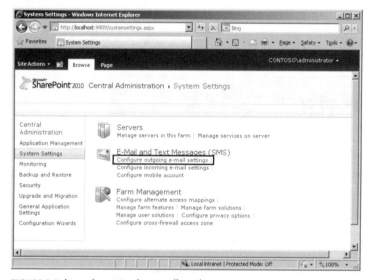

FIGURE 9-7 Accessing outgoing email settings.

The Outgoing E-mail Settings configuration page is shown in Figure 9-8. To complete the configuration, simply specify your chosen outbound SMTP server, the From address you want to appear in email sent from SPF, the Reply-to address you want to appear when users click Reply, and the character set to be used in the email. (The Unicode UTF-8 character set is specified by default.) You can modify these default outgoing email settings for any individual web application in the General Settings for that application.

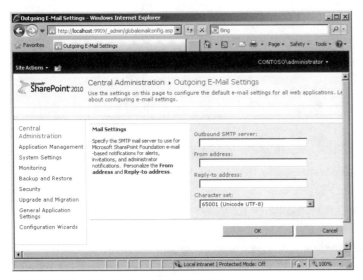

FIGURE 9-8 The Outgoing E-mail Settings page.

EXAM TIP

Remember for the exam that users will not be able to create alerts until you specify an outbound SMTP server on this configuration page. If users do not receive alerts even after you specify an outbound SMTP server in SPF, verify that the relay restrictions set on the SMTP server are not preventing users from receiving the messages.

Configuring Incoming Email Settings

In addition to sending email, SPF can also receive email from users. To enable and configure this feature, first click Configure Incoming E-mail Settings on the System Settings page, as shown in Figure 9-9. This step opens the Configure Incoming E-mail Settings page, shown in Figure 9-10.

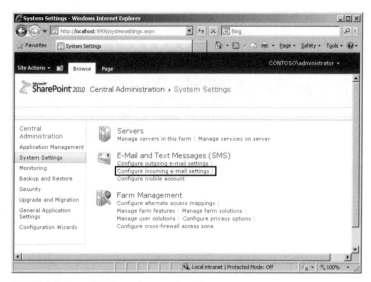

FIGURE 9-9 Accessing incoming email settings.

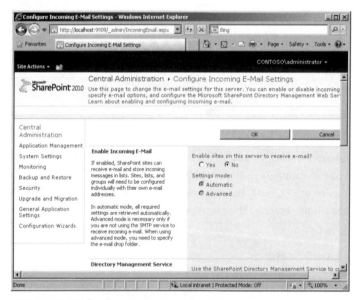

FIGURE 9-10 Configuring incoming email settings.

To enable sites on the server to receive email, select Yes in the Enable Incoming E-mail section. You have two settings modes to choose from: Automatic and Advanced. Automatic mode uses settings you have defined in the Outgoing E-mail Settings page. (Specifically, it uses the SMTP server you have defined.) In this scenario, email is delivered directly to your SMTP server, and SharePoint Foundation 2010 periodically checks for email in the default email drop folder that is automatically configured by the SMTP service. (For more information about configuring SMTP server settings, see Chapter 7, "Configuring FTP and SMTP Services.") With Advanced mode, you don't use the SMTP service to receive incoming email. In this case, you specify a file system location in which new messages will be stored. For both Automatic and Advanced modes, you can also assign an incoming email server display address and configure SPF to accept an email server only through servers that have been designated as safe.

After you configure incoming email on your SPF server, incoming email must also be configured individually on all the particular sites, libraries, lists, and groups for which you want to store incoming email. Each object must be assigned a unique email address in the form of *address@SMTPserveraddress*, for example, sharedfiles@SMTPserver.contoso.com.

EXAM TIP

For the exam, remember that Automatic mode requires you to install and configure a local SMTP server. Also remember that even after you enable and configure incoming email for the SPF server, you still must enable incoming email on each site, library, list, or group that you want to receive and store email.

Configuring Directory Management Service

Another feature you can configure when you enable incoming email is the Microsoft SharePoint Directory Management Service. This service enables you to integrate SharePoint sites with Microsoft Exchange and Active Directory for use with email distribution groups. To enable this service on a server or server farm running SharePoint Foundation 2010, first create a special organizational unit (OU) in Active Directory to store the selected distribution lists and contacts. Then, for that OU, assign *write* access permissions to the SharePoint Central Administration v4 application pool account. (For a stand-alone installation, that account is the Network Service by default.) As an alternative, you can select the Use Remote option, which enables you to configure a server farm to use a remote SharePoint Directory Management Web Service.

EXAM TIP

You need to know the purpose of the Directory Management Service and the basics about configuring it for the 70-643 exam.

Choosing Farm Administrators

Farm Administrators are the user accounts that have full access to the Central Administration website and to all settings in your stand-alone or server farm deployment of SPF. By default, the Farm Administrators group includes only the local administrators and the account used to install SPF. To modify the members of this group, in Central Administration, first click Manage The Farm Administrators Group. (This link is shown in Figure 9-11.) This step opens the Farm Administrators page, which is shown in Figure 9-12.

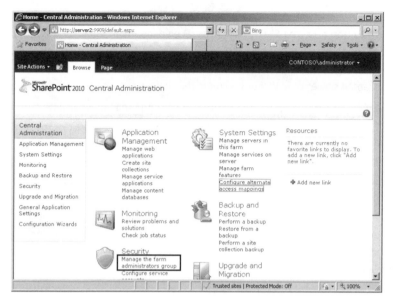

FIGURE 9-11 Accessing the farm administrator settings.

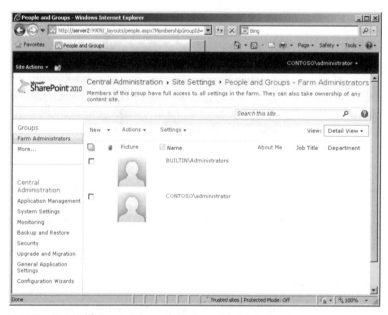

FIGURE 9-12 Modifying members of the Farm Administrators group.

To add users to the Farm Administrators group, select Add Users from the New menu. To remove an identity from the list, select the account and then select Remove Users From Group from the Actions menu.

In general, it's a good idea to use the Farm Administrators group to keep your SharePoint administrators separate from your general network administrators. Using the Farm Administrator group enables you to grant a selected user the rights to administer SharePoint (for instance, to perform SharePoint backups) without granting that user any administrative privileges outside of SharePoint.

Registering Managed Accounts

When you install SharePoint Foundation in a stand-alone configuration, the Local Service, Local System, and Network Service accounts run all the SharePoint services. When you install SPF instead in a server farm configuration, however, you must create and specify dedicated service accounts in the domain with the permissions required to run SPF services on different servers in the farm.

In previous versions of SharePoint, using dedicated service accounts presented a problem regarding password expirations: Either you had to configure the password to never expire for the service account (a security risk), or you had to remember to change the password periodically for each service account before expiration (a management burden). In SharePoint Foundation, you are now required to register most of your SharePoint service accounts in a server farm as managed accounts. A managed account automatically generates new passwords before they expire.

To register a managed account, on the Central Administration website, click Security. Then, beneath General Security, click Configure Managed Accounts. This link is shown in Figure 9-13. On the Managed Accounts page that opens after clicking this link, click Register Managed Account and use the Register Managed Account page shown in Figure 9-14 to specify the service accounts you want to be managed, along with the desired automatic password change settings.

FIGURE 9-13 Accessing managed account settings.

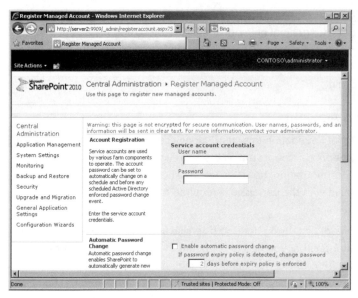

FIGURE 9-14 Registering a managed account.

Managing SPF by Using the SharePoint 2010 Management Shell

Although using the SharePoint Central Administration website is an intuitive and user-friendly way to manage configuration settings, it can be time-consuming to perform common operations on many SPF servers. To help automate the task, SPF includes the SharePoint 2010 Management Shell, an environment that enables you to conduct SharePoint administration by using either the Stsadm command-line utility or PowerShell cmdlets.

To open the SharePoint 2010 Management Shell, click Start, click All Programs, click Microsoft SharePoint 2010 Products, and, finally, click SharePoint 2010 Management Shell.

Using Stsadm

You can use the Stsadm utility to perform common tasks, such as creating or deleting SharePoint sites or performing backups. You can use the –*help* switch to get more details about the syntax and operations the command can perform. Figure 9-15 shows a portion of the command usage.

As mentioned, the SharePoint 2010 Management Shell provides an environment in which you can execute *Stsadm* commands. You can also use *Stsadm* from any command prompt by navigating to *%ProgramFiles%*\Common Files\Microsoft Shared\Web Server Extensions \14\BIN.

```
Administrator: SharePoint 2010 Management Shell                    _ □ X
           upgrade
           upgradesolution
           upgradetargetwebapplication
           userrole

Examples:
stsadm.exe -o addpath -url http://server/sites -type wildcardinclusion
stsadm.exe -o adduser
           -url http://server/site
           -userlogin DOMAIN\name
           -useremail someone@example.com
           -role reader
           -username "Your Name"
           -siteadmin
stsadm.exe -o backup -url http://server/site -filename backup.dat -overwrite
stsadm.exe -o backup -directory c:\backup -backupmethod full
stsadm.exe -o createsite -url http://server/site
           -ownerlogin DOMAIN\name
           -owneremail someone@example.com
stsadm.exe -o createweb -url http://server/site/web
stsadm.exe -o deletesite -url http://server/site
stsadm.exe -o deleteweb -url http://server/site/web
stsadm.exe -o enumsites -url http://server
stsadm.exe -o enumsubwebs -url http://server/site/web
stsadm.exe -o enumusers -url http://server/site/web
stsadm.exe -o extendvs -url http://server:80
           -ownerlogin DOMAIN\name
           -owneremail someone@example.com
stsadm.exe -o renameweb -url http://server/site/web1 -newname web2
stsadm.exe -o restore -url http://server/site -filename backup.dat
stsadm.exe -o restore -directory c:\backup -restoremethod overwrite
stsadm.exe -o setconfigdb -databaseserver server
stsadm.exe -o unextendvs -url http://server

For information about other operations and parameters,
use "stsadm.exe -help" or "stsadm.exe -help <operation>"

PS C:\Users\administrator.CONTOSO> _
```

FIGURE 9-15 Viewing help information for the Stsadm command-line utility.

NOTE THE STSADM UTILITY HAS BEEN DEPRECATED

Although you can use Stsadm to manage SharePoint Foundation 2010, the utility has been deprecated (set on an official path to obsolescence) by Microsoft. It might not work in future releases of SharePoint.

Using PowerShell

New to SharePoint Foundation 2010 are PowerShell-specific cmdlets for SharePoint administration. To enable an account to use these SharePoint administration cmdlets, you use a special PowerShell cmdlet, *Add-SPShellAdmin*, which prompts you to specify the account you want to act as a shell administrator. (You must also add this account to the Farm Administrators group.) Note that SharePoint shell administrators are granted privileges to administer *all* site collections, so you should not elevate administrators of particular site collections to shell administrators. To remove SharePoint shell administrator privileges from an account, you can use the *Remove-SPShellAdmin* cmdlet. To review the list of SharePoint shell administrators, use the *Get-SPShellAdmin* cmdlet.

EXAM TIP

You need to know the function of the Add-SPShellAdmin, Remove-SPShellAdmin, and Get-SPShellAdmin cmdlets for the 70-643 exam.

MORE INFO SHAREPOINT CMDLETS

For a complete list of the SharePoint Foundation 2010 PowerShell cmdlets, visit *http://technet.microsoft.com/en-us/library/ff686791.aspx*.

Overall, command-line administration is most useful when you need to perform the same or similar tasks on multiple computers running SPF or if you need to script commonly performed operations. It is also useful when you do not have web-based access to the SharePoint Central Administration website.

Understanding Backup and Recovery for SPF

Because users in your organization will likely depend on the data stored in SharePoint, it's important to ensure that the content and configuration is protected. The primary reason for performing backups is to prevent against data loss due to hardware failures, accidental modifications, or other issues that might arise. In this section, you learn about ways you can back up and restore SharePoint data.

Creating SharePoint Backups

The SharePoint Central Administration website includes features for creating and scheduling backups. However, before you can perform any backup or restore procedures, you must start the SharePoint 2010 Administration service. To start the service, you can either use the Services console or type the **net start spadminv4** command at an elevated command prompt. By default, this service is configured with a startup type set to *manual*, which means that it will not start automatically after the server restarts unless you change the startup type to *automatic*. Be sure to configure this setting if you want to schedule regular backup jobs.

After you have started the SharePoint 2010 Administration service, you can start the process of performing a backup by clicking the Perform A Backup link in the Backup And Restore administrative group on the main page in Central Administration. The next step to define the backup requires you to select the information that should be stored in the backup set. (See Figure 9-16.)

SPF includes many components, each of which can be included in the backup set. If you are backing up a relatively small SPF deployment or if you want to ensure that all configuration and user data is protected, select the check box at the Farm level. This selects all the other components automatically. In other situations, you might want to back up only a specific site or collection of settings. You can do this by selecting only the appropriate options.

Clicking Next opens the Select Backup Options page (shown in Figure 9-17), which provides options for storing the backup content. The Type Of Backup section offers two options. Full backups include a copy of the latest data for all the selected components. The size of the backup will be based on the amount of content included on the SharePoint site. (An estimate is provided at the bottom of the screen.)

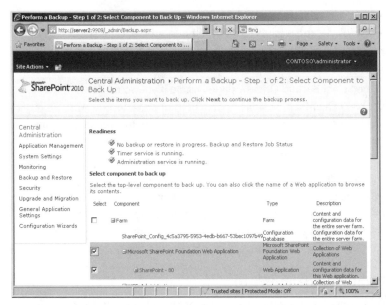

FIGURE 9-16 Selecting which components should be included in a backup.

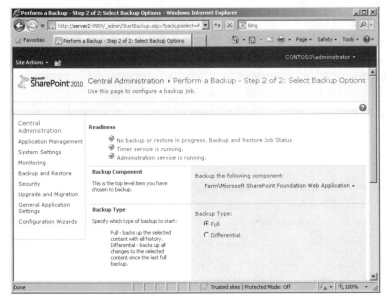

FIGURE 9-17 Selecting backup-related options in the Perform A Backup task.

The other option is to create a differential backup. This backup will store only the data that has changed since the last full backup was performed. Although the backup storage space and resource overhead is less for a differential backup, you will need access to both the Full and Differential backups to perform a complete restore of the SPF system.

The final setting on the Select Backup Options page (visible if you scroll down) is the location for the backup. You can enter a local file system path or provide a network path to a shared folder location. To protect against permanent data loss due to storage hardware failures, backup files should be stored on another computer in the environment.

After you have selected the appropriate options, you can click Start Backup to schedule the backup process. The job will use the built-in timer feature in SPF to start the process as quickly as possible. Backups are performed without any downtime for the site, although users might notice a decrease in SharePoint system performance. The Backup And Restore Job Status page shows the progress of the job along with any additional details. The page refreshes periodically until the job is complete.

Restoring SharePoint Foundation 2010

For several reasons, you might need to perform a restore of SharePoint data. In some cases, a hardware failure or file system corruption might result in an unusable site, or important documents or other content might have been deleted or incorrectly modified. You can start the process by clicking the Restore From A Backup link on the Central Administration site main page. Performing a restore operation requires four steps.

1. **Specify Backup Directory Location**   This text box enables you to type the path of the local or network file system location in which the backup is stored. The default value is the path used for the last backup operation.

2. **Select Backup To Restore**   Based on the path provided in step 1, SPF finds the backups that are stored in the location specified. If the appropriate backup is found, you can select it and then click Next. Otherwise, you can type a different backup directory location and click Refresh.

3. **Select Component To Restore**   This page enables you to select one or more components to restore to the SPF server. The list of components will be based on which components were included in the original backup. (See Figure 9-18.) Select the appropriate items and then click Next.

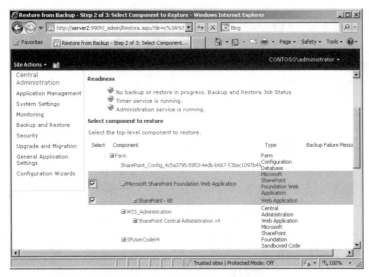

FIGURE 9-18 Specifying which components to restore.

4. **Select Restore Options** On this screen, you can specify the type of restore operation you wish to perform.

    The Same Configuration option is useful when you want to replace all the current components with those stored in the backup. Note that this option will result in the loss of any changes that have been made to the selected components since the time the backup was created.

    The other option, New Configuration, enables you to specify an alternate configuration to which the data will be restored. This option is useful for making a new copy of the site from the backup. It is also a safer option because it will not affect the current SharePoint site. The available options vary based on the selections you made when you created the backup. When you are ready to perform the restore operation, click Start Restore.

Viewing Backup and Restore History

To verify that backups have been properly performed, click Backup And Restore on the Central Administration main page and then click View Backup And Restore History in the Farm Backup And Restore administrative group. Figure 9-19 shows the available information. Details are displayed for the date and time of each job, the contents of the backup, the backup type, and the location of the backup files. It is also possible to start a restore process by selecting a backup and clicking Begin Restore Process.

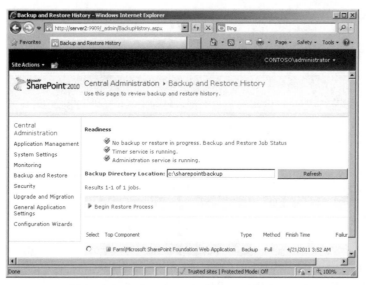

FIGURE 9-19 Viewing information about the history of backup and restore operations.

EXAM TIP

To back up and restore a site collection, you can use the Backup-SPSite and Restore-SPSite PowerShell cmdlets. To back up and restore all SharePoint farm data, you can use Backup-SPFarm and Restore-SPFarm. Remember these techniques for the 70-643 exam.

Deploying and Configuring SharePoint Sites

Because SPF enables you to create many SharePoint sites on the same server, it is important to decide how to divide up content and users. In general, try to limit the purpose and number of users for each type of site. When a single site is used for numerous types of activities and by numerous users, it can become difficult for people to quickly find what they're looking for. Further, organizing the content can become very difficult and time consuming. In this section, you learn about ways to create and manage sites.

Understanding Subsites and Site Collections

A *site collection* is a set of related SharePoint sites that share many settings. For example, all the sites within a site collection share the same navigation bars. This makes it easy for users to access sites within the collection without having to go to a different URL. In addition, details related to content types, search functionality, and security groups are common to all sites in the collection.

There are two main approaches to creating additional sites in SPF. Overall, it is best to add multiple sites to a single site collection if the content of each site is related and the technical requirements are similar. The other option is to create a new top-level SharePoint site in a new site collection. This approach is best used when the requirements for the new site differ significantly from settings in existing site collections. Sites in different site collections can have different configuration settings for security permissions. Other details, such as search scope and quotas, can be managed independently for different site collections. From operations and management standpoints, different site collections can be managed independently. Larger organizations can divide systems administration responsibilities for SPF by using multiple site collections. Also, these sites can be backed up and restored separately, enabling you to make backups more manageable.

Creating Site Collections

You can use the SharePoint Central Administration website to manage site collections, websites, and their related settings. The SharePoint Site Management section enables you to create or delete site collections. The Create Site Collection link, available on the main page in the Application Management administrative group, shows the available options. (The Create Site Collection page is shown in Figure 9-20.)

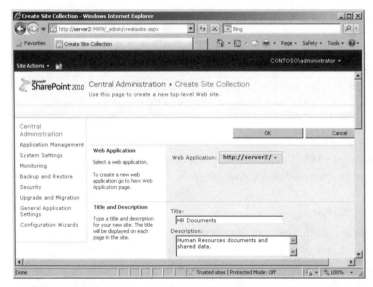

FIGURE 9-20 Creating a new site collection in the SharePoint Central Administration website.

The required information includes:

- **Web Application**   This drop-down list includes all the web applications that have been created in the SharePoint environment. If you have not yet created additional web applications, only the default server URL is shown.

- **Title And Description**   Use this information to identify the site collection. The title will be shown to users and administrators, and the description should include details about the purpose and intended usage of the site collection. In some cases, site collections might be based on the organizational units, such as the marketing or human resources departments.

- **Website Address** Each website created in SPF must have a unique URL. By default, a default URL path called /sites is available. The text box enables you to specify the browser link that accesses the site. Because users must generally type this address, use an abbreviation of the site name and avoid characters such as spaces or other punctuation.

- **Template Selection** Each new SharePoint site collection can be based on a specific template. The default templates are organized into two main categories: Collaboration and Meetings. You can click each option to read a brief description of the purpose of the site. Later in this lesson, you learn how to add new templates to the server.

- **Primary Site Collection Administrator and Secondary Site Collection Administrator** In relatively small SharePoint environments, a single systems administrator might be responsible for managing multiple sites and site collections. These sections enable you to specify which users have permissions to manage the site collection. You can click the Browse icon to view a list of available accounts on either the local computer or the domain (if the computer is a member of a domain).

- **Quota Template** This section enables you to select a quota template that restricts the storage space available for the site collection. You learn more about quota templates later in this section.

The contents and layout of the site will be based on the application template you selected. When you click OK, SPF performs the tasks required to create a new site collection. The resulting message displays the URL of the new top-level site. To verify that the site has been set up properly, either click the link or copy and paste it into a new browser window.

To view a list of all the site collections defined on an SPF server, click Application Management on the main page of the Central Administration website and then click View All Site Collections in the Site Collections administrative group.

Defining Quota Templates

If you have experience with managing data storage, such as the contents of a file server or Microsoft Exchange Server, you know that users can consume large amounts of disk space quickly. SPF is no exception, because users often upload many large documents to their sites. To help manage resource usage, you can create *quota templates*, which can then be assigned to specific SharePoint site collections. By default, no quota templates are included in the SPF configuration. To create a quota template, first click Application Management on the main page of the Central Administration website and then click Specify Quota Templates in the Site Collections administrative group. Figure 9-21 shows the available options.

The first setting is to provide a name for the new quota template. You can edit the settings for any existing quota templates or provide a name for a new one. The name should be a description of the purpose of the template (for example, Engineering Dept. Quota). The Storage Limit Values section enables you to configure two restrictions. The Limit Site Storage To A

Maximum Of field enables you to specify the maximum amount of content storage space that should be available for the site (in megabytes). When this limit is exceeded, users will be unable to add new content. The second option enables sending a warning email notification to the site administrator when the site has reached a certain amount of storage space usage.

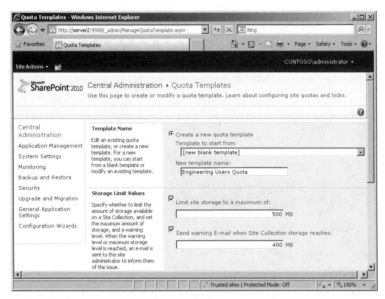

FIGURE 9-21 Defining a new quota template in the SharePoint Central Administration website.

To attach a quota template to a site, click the Site Collection Quotas And Locks link on the Application Management page. This step opens the Site Collection Quotas And Locks page, shown in Figure 9-22. This page enables you to choose a site collection and then specify storage-related options. The Site Lock Information section enables you to specify limitations on content storage for the site. The options include:

- Not Locked
- Adding Content Prevented
- Read-Only (Blocks Additions, Updates, And Deletions)
- No Access

These options are useful when you no longer want to enable users to modify the contents of a SharePoint site, but you want them to be able to view existing data. The Site Quota Information section enables you to select a quota template or to use the Individual Quota option to define specific settings for this site collection. The primary benefit of using a quota template is the ability to centrally modify the storage limitations for numerous site collections without having to edit the settings of each one.

FIGURE 9-22 Configuring quotas and locks for site collections.

Configuring Site Settings

In addition to the basic details that you can provide when creating a new SharePoint site or site collection, numerous settings can be managed for the content of the site itself. To access these settings, first use a browser to navigate to the address of the site you want to administer. All sites have a Site Actions drop-down menu in the top-right section of the screen. The Site Settings option enables you to view a large number of administrative settings. (See Figure 9-23.)

These site settings are organized into the following groups:

- Users And Permissions
- Look And Feel
- Galleries
- Site Actions
- Site Administration
- Reporting Services
- Site Collection Administration

In some cases, systems administrators might be responsible for making changes and managing the site. However, users with basic SharePoint experience (and the necessary permissions) can also administer details based on their organization's requirements.

FIGURE 9-23 Viewing a list of site settings.

Managing Web Applications

Web applications are used to manage the front-end SharePoint sites to which users connect.
By default, only two of the three web applications built into SharePoint Foundation include
content to be managed: The SharePoint – 80 site and the SharePoint Central Administration
v4 site. To manage these and any new web applications you create, click Manage Web
Applications in the Application Management section of Central Administration, as shown
in Figure 9-24. This step opens the Web Applications Management webpage, shown in
Figure 9-25.

FIGURE 9-24 Opening the Web Applications Management page.

FIGURE 9-25 The Web Applications Management page.

The Web Applications Management page enables you to perform many administrative functions on individual web applications, such as creating, extending, and deleting web applications; configuring general settings; defining managed paths; configuring permissions for web applications; managing authentication settings; and enabling self-service site creation. These administrative functions are described in the following sections.

Creating, Extending, and Deleting Web Applications

On the Web Applications Management page, you can see the options for creating, extending, and deleting web applications on the left side of the ribbon, as shown in Figure 9-26.

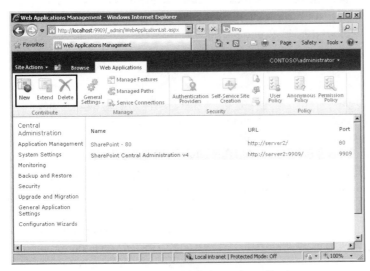

FIGURE 9-26 Creating, extending, and deleting web applications.

Clicking New opens the Create New Web Application window, which is shown in Figure 9-27.

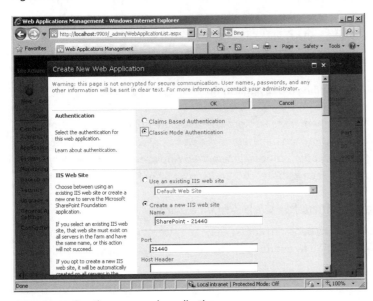

FIGURE 9-27 Creating a new web application.

The Create A New Web Application window enables you to specify the details for a new website and a new database. Note that the Authentication section at the top of this page, visible in Figure 9-27, represents a feature that is new to SharePoint Foundation 2010. This setting provides a configuration choice between Claims Based Authentication or Classic Mode Authentication for the new web application. Classic-mode authentication provides the standard authentication methods used in IIS and previous versions of SharePoint. Claims-based authentication supports these authentication methods and two additional authentication types: forms-based authentication, which SQL and LDAP databases use, and Security Assertion Markup Language (SAML), which Active Directory Federation Services, Windows Live, and other providers use. The main advantage of claims-based authentication is that it can support a very broad range of authentication types, including methods that support user tokens and single–sign on capability for users outside of Windows. Other settings you configure when creating a new web application include specifying a website name, port, optional host header, and file location; security options, including an authentication protocol (Kerberos or NTLM), whether to allow anonymous access, and SSL encryption; and details regarding the public URL, application pool, and associated database.

Clicking Extend on the ribbon on the Web Application Management page provides an option to extend an existing web application. Use this function to provide an additional website that connects to the same back-end database storage system. One scenario that can require this is an extranet configuration. In this setup, multiple URLs are used: one for internal company users and another for users who might access the site from the Internet. Although the content both groups see will be the same, systems administrators can create different configuration settings for an externally accessible website. For example, you might have configured internal users with Kerberos authentication for the original web application but want to use NTLM authentication on an identical site for extranet users.

EXAM TIP

Remember the purpose of extending a web application for the 70-643 exam.

The Web Application Management page also provides a Delete option on the ribbon. You can use this menu to delete the content databases for the web application or the associated website. To delete the entire application, choose Delete Web Application from the Delete menu. If you want to remove only the website, choose Remove SharePoint From IIS website.

Configuring General Settings for Web Applications

The Web Application Management page provides a General Settings menu, as shown in Figure 9-28. You can use this section to define the behavior of the web application you have selected.

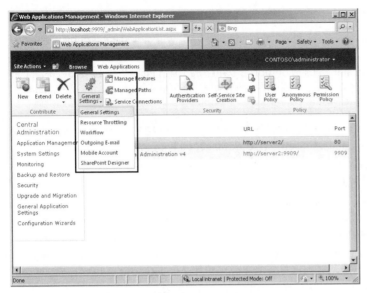

FIGURE 9-28 Configuring General Settings.

The following list briefly describes the six options on this menu.

- **General Settings** This option opens a page on which you can configure many settings, such as the default time zone, default quota template, alerts, maximum upload size, and RSS settings.

- **Resource Throttling** This feature is new to SharePoint Foundation 2010. It enables you to limit the number of items that can be displayed in a list view. Without resource throttling, opening a very large list in SharePoint can degrade performance for other users.

- **Workflow** A workflow is a task that is triggered by an event or change. Choosing this option enables you to determine whether users can generate their own workflows in the web application.

- **Outgoing E-mail** This option enables you to configure an outbound SMTP server, From address, Reply-to address, and Character set that is specific to the web application.

- **Mobile Account** New to SharePoint Foundation 2010, this option enables you to specify a Text Message (SMS) service and user account from which alerts should be sent. Users can then subscribe to alerts and receive updates through SMS when changes are made to a SharePoint list or item.

- **SharePoint Designer** Use this option to determine whether to allow users to edit the web application by using SharePoint Designer. SharePoint Designer is a separate and free product by which you can edit and enhance your SharePoint sites with additional customizations.

Defining Managed Paths

A managed path is a URL or set of URLs that is handled by SharePoint instead of by IIS. By default, SPF includes two managed paths. The *(root)* path is the default location accessed when a user navigates to the default website on port 80. The *sites* path includes a base URL that can include multiple additional sites and web applications, such as *http://server2/sites/engineering* and *http://server2/sites/hr*.

You can add additional managed paths if you want to customize the URLs handled by SharePoint. To access managed path settings, click Managed Paths on the Web Applications Management page, as shown in Figure 9-29. This step opens the Define Managed Paths window, shown in Figure 9-30.

You can add two types of managed paths: an explicit managed path and a wildcard managed path. An explicit managed path defines a specific URL with no subdirectories. You could use this type of path to define a single site collection. A wildcard managed path includes any number of subdirectories after the path you define. (The *sites* managed path is an example of a wildcard managed path.) You could use this type of path if you want to host multiple site collections within a customized URL such as *http://contoso.com/blogs/*.

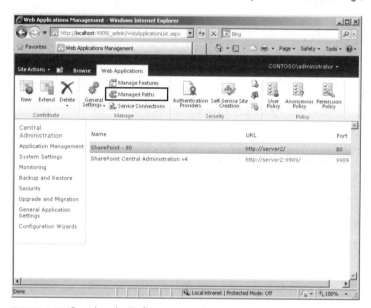

FIGURE 9-29 Opening the Define Managed Paths window.

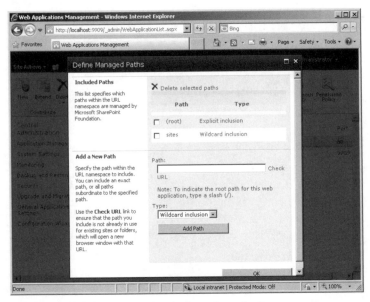

FIGURE 9-30 Defining managed paths for web applications.

Configuring Web Application Permissions

Because organizations often store sensitive information on SharePoint websites, managing security settings is an important concern. You can control user permissions for SharePoint websites by clicking the User Permissions icon on the ribbon of the Web Applications Management page, shown in Figure 9-31. This step opens the User Permissions For Web Applications window, which is shown in Figure 9-32.

FIGURE 9-31 Opening the User Permissions For Web Applications window.

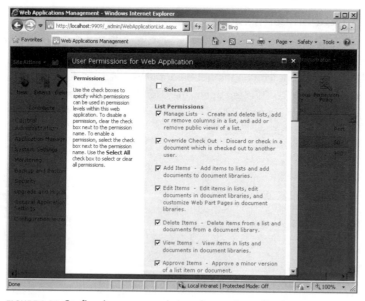

FIGURE 9-32 Configuring user permissions for a web application.

The permissions you configure on this page are not granted to specific users. Instead, the settings here determine which permissions may be granted to users by administrators of the web application. The permissions are divided into three groups:

- **List Permissions** These permissions apply to SharePoint controls that enable adding or removing data. Examples include Announcements, News, and Discussion components. The available permissions include the ability to add, edit, delete, and view items.

- **Site Permissions** Use these permissions to determine which features and operations can be performed by administrators of a SharePoint web application. Examples include the ability to manage permissions for other users, add and customize pages, and view site usage information.

- **Personal Permissions** Users of SharePoint-based websites can create their own customized views of components known as web parts. Users can add, remove, and rearrange these parts based on personal preferences. These permissions determine whether users can create and manage personal views.

To modify the actual permissions to a site assigned to users, first connect to that site as a user with administrator privileges and then select Site Permissions from the Site Actions menu, as shown in Figure 9-33. This step opens the Permissions page, which is shown in Figure 9-34.

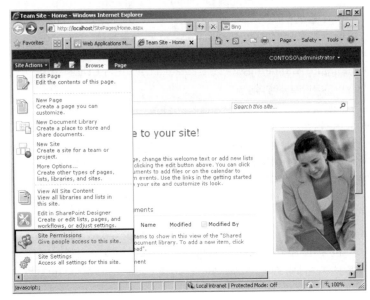

FIGURE 9-33 Accessing site permissions for a site.

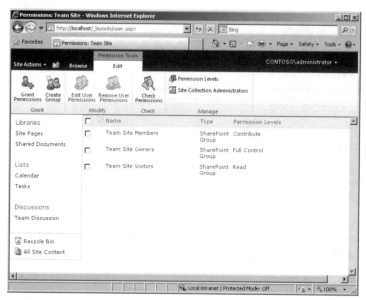

FIGURE 9-34 Permissions page for a SharePoint site.

The SharePoint – 80 website includes three groups by default. The Members group is assigned the *Contribute* permission level, the Owners group is assigned the *Full Control* permission level, and the Visitors group is assigned the *Read* permission level. It is recommended that you assign permissions to users by adding them to one of these groups or to another group that you create and configure with permissions. To create a new group, click Create Group on the ribbon of the Permissions webpage.

You can assign permissions directly to any user or group account by clicking Grant Permissions on the ribbon of the Permissions webpage. This step opens the Grant Permissions window, shown in Figure 9-35. This window reveals four permission levels: *Full Control*, *Design*, *Contribute*, and *Read*. *Design* is more powerful than *Contribute* but less powerful than *Full Control*. In addition to viewing, adding, updating, and deleting site elements like users with the *Contribute* permission level can, users assigned the *Design* permission level can also approve and customize site elements.

If you need to give a user access to an entire web application (as opposed to a site), click User Policy on the ribbon on the Web Applications Management webpage. User Policy provides you with a single access control list that you can configure for all the site collections in the selected web application.

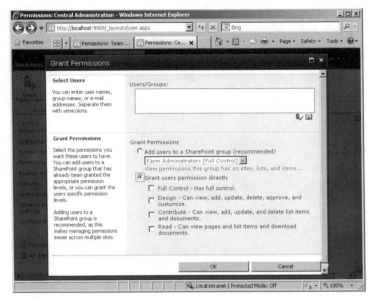

FIGURE 9-35 Granting permissions to a user or group.

EXAM TIP

You have to understand SharePoint permissions and permission levels for the 70-643 exam.

Managing Authentication Settings

A critical aspect of SharePoint security is authenticating user identity. You can configure authentication by first clicking Authentication Providers on the Web Applications Management webpage, shown in Figure 9-36. Then, on the Authentication Providers webpage that opens, select a zone. (Only the Default zone exists by default.) This step opens the Edit Authentication window, shown in Figure 9-37.

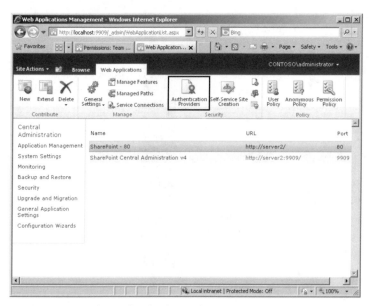

FIGURE 9-36 Accessing authentication settings.

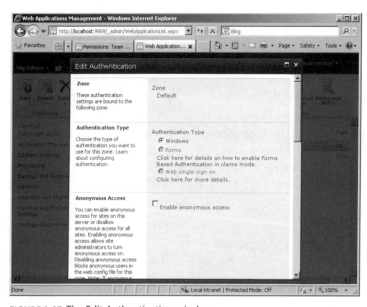

FIGURE 9-37 The Edit Authentication window.

The Edit Authentication window enables you to specify how the authentication process occurs for a given web application.

There are three primary options for the Authentication Type setting.

- **Windows**   This option takes advantage of the standard Windows authentication method, which is the best solution if the primary users of the site will be employees who have accounts either on the local computer or within an Active Directory domain. Apart from using strong security protocols (such as Kerberos), authenticated users might not need to enter a username and password to access the site.

- **Forms**   Forms-based authentication relies on a SQL database separate from Windows and requires users to provide a valid username and password to log on to the site. This setting is most appropriate when Windows-based authentication is not possible. For example, if external business partners or Internet users need access to the SharePoint site, Forms authentication is a viable option.

- **Web Single Sign-On**   The Web Single Sign-On (SSO) option is a standard mechanism by which users can be authenticated against a web service. It is useful when Windows-based authentication is not possible. This is a simplified access method for users who frequently need to access numerous web-based systems and applications. Active Directory Federation Services (ADFS) can provide SSO-based services.

Additional details can be specified, including the option to allow anonymous access to a SharePoint site. This option is useful for sites that contain information that should be available to the public or to all users within an organization. Overall, the ability to choose from several authentication options helps administrators ensure that their SharePoint sites are secure while still maintaining accessibility for users outside the organization.

EXAM TIP

For the 70-643 exam, you need to understand the options made available by configuring Authentication Provider.

Enabling Self-Service Site Creation

In smaller and less dynamic environments, it can make sense for systems administrators to be responsible for creating new sites. In larger environments, however, a better management approach can be to allow users to create their own sites. You can enable this functionality for a site by clicking Self-Service Site Creation on the Web Applications Management webpage, as shown in Figure 9-38. The default setting is for this feature to be disabled for new web applications.

FIGURE 9-38 Enabling Self-Service Site Creation.

Using Office Web Applications with SharePoint Foundation 2010

Office Web Applications (Office Web Apps) enables users to access Microsoft Office applications from anywhere, even when these applications are not installed on the local computer. To install Office Web Apps in a SharePoint server farm or on a stand-alone server, you need a volume license version of Microsoft Office 2010. After you install Office Web Apps, Office files that you open in a SharePoint site open in a browser window by default instead of as a local client application, such as Microsoft Word, by default. This behavior is a result of the Open In Browser setting being enabled by default. You can change this setting by reactivating the Open In Client feature. These settings can be defined at the site collection level or library level.

EXAM TIP

You have to understand the new functionality that Office Web Apps adds to SharePoint for the 70-643 exam.

 Quick Check

1. Which option should you choose to create a new SharePoint site that shares the same navigation and security options as an existing site?

2. How can you limit the amount of storage for several SharePoint sites?

PRACTICE **Configure and Manage SharePoint Foundation**

In this practice, you look at the process of configuring SharePoint Foundation settings and using the backup and restore features that are part of the SharePoint Central Administration website. The steps in these exercises assume that you have downloaded SharePoint Foundation 2010 from the Microsoft website and that on Server2 you have installed the SharePoint Foundation software prerequisites, installed SharePoint Foundation in a stand-alone configuration, and run the SharePoint Products Configuration Wizard. (This wizard starts automatically after you finish installing SharePoint Foundation.)

To perform these exercises, it is also recommended that you assign as much RAM as possible to the Server2 virtual machine. At least 2048 MB is preferred.

EXERCISE 1 Configuring SPF Sites and Site Collections

In this exercise, you walk through the steps required to create a new SharePoint Services site. You then verify the site by connecting to it by using Internet Explorer.

1. Log on to Server2 as a user with Administrator permissions on the computer.

2. Open the SharePoint 2010 Central Administration website by clicking Start, clicking All Programs, clicking Microsoft SharePoint 2010 Products, and then clicking the SharePoint 2010 Central Administration icon.

3. If prompted, provide the credentials you used to log on to the server in step 1. You will now see the Central Administration website in Internet Explorer.

4. In the Application Management section of the Central Administration window, click Manage Web Applications.

5. On the ribbon of the Web Applications tab, click New.

6. In the Create New Web Application window, leave the default settings for the Authentication section and the IIS website section. Note that the Central Administration website has automatically provided a suggested name and port number for the new web application. It has also chosen a Path setting based on the location of existing web content.

7. Scroll down to view the Application Pool section. In the Application Pool section, leave the default selection of Create A New Application Pool. Change the security account

information to Predefined and leave Network Service selected in the drop-down menu.

8. In the Search Server section, choose Server2.

9. To begin the web application creation process, click OK. The web application creation process might take several minutes, depending on the performance of and other activity on the server.

10. When the process has completed, you will see the Application Created window. Click Create Site Collection to begin the process of creating a new site collection.

11. In the Create Site Collection window, type **Contoso Meetings** for Title.

12. In the Template Selection section, select the Meetings tab and then select the Decision Meeting Workspace item in the list.

13. For the User Name setting in the Primary Site Collection Administration section, type the user name you used to log on to the server in step 1.

14. To begin the creation of the site collection, click OK.

15. The Top-Level Site Successfully Created screen provides you with the URL you can use to access the new site. Click this link to access the site, and type your authentication credentials if prompted.

16. Note that you can now access a new SharePoint site titled Contoso Meetings. The default site includes numerous elements, including Objectives, Agenda, Attendees, and Document Library sections. Optionally, you can create new items and upload files to practice working with the site. Also, note the URL for the new site if you plan to revisit it later.

17. When you are finished, close Internet Explorer.

EXERCISE 2   Backing Up and Restoring a Windows SharePoint Site

In this exercise, you create a backup of your SharePoint Foundation server configuration on the local computer. You then restore the Contoso Meetings SharePoint site that you created in Exercise 1. The specific steps assume that you have completed Exercise 1.

1. If you have not done so already, log on to Server2 as a user who has Administrator permissions on the computer.

2. By using Windows Explorer, create a new folder into which you will store the backup. The folder can be located on any volume on the server. Make a note of the full path to this folder because you will be using it in later steps.

   You must start the SharePoint 2010 Administration service before you can perform a backup. This service does not start automatically by default.

3. Open the Services console in the Administrative Tools program group. In the list of services, locate and double-click SharePoint 2010 Administration.

4. In the SharePoint 2010 Administration Properties dialog box, click Start and then click OK. Close the Services console.

5. Open the SharePoint 2010 Central Administration website by clicking Start, clicking All Programs, clicking Microsoft SharePoint 2010 Products, and then clicking the SharePoint 2010 Central Administration icon.

6. If prompted, provide the credentials you used to log on to the server in step 1.

   You now see the Central Administration website in Internet Explorer.

7. On the Central Administration website, click the Perform A Backup link in the Backup And Restore section.

8. In the Select Component To Backup step, select the top-level component entitled Farm. This automatically includes all the content for the entire server, including all SharePoint sites. Click Next.

9. On the Select Backup Options page, leave the default settings for the Backup Component, Backup Type, and Back Up Only Configuration Settings sections. For the Backup File Location, provide the full path to the new folder you created in step 2. Note that the information includes an estimate of the amount of required disk space to store the backup. Click Start Backup to continue.

10. The backup begins automatically. To view the status of the backup, click Refresh. The screen also automatically refreshes every few seconds. Wait until the screen shows that the backup has completed, which should take a few minutes.

11. When the backup is complete, in the Central Administration console, click Backup And Restore.

    The Backup and Restore page appears.

12. On the Backup And Restore page, click Restore From A Backup in the Farm Backup And Restore section.

13. On the Select Backup To Restore page, the Backup Directory Location should automatically have the path of the folder you created in step 2. In the Results list, select the option button for the backup and then click Next.

14. On the Select Component To Restore page, select the new SharePoint web application that you created in Exercise 1. You can identify it based on the name and port number. The Content Database for the web application is also selected automatically. Click Next.

15. On the Select Restore Options page, select Same Configuration in the Restore Options section. Press OK when you receive a message about overwriting the existing site. You could also restore the site to another database if you wanted to make a copy of it without overwriting the current version. Click Start Restore.

16. The restore process begins. You can click Refresh to view the progress of the operation. When the Readiness section shows that the restore has been completed, the entire contents of the Contoso Meetings SharePoint site should be restored to the server. Optionally, you can verify that the site is accessible by opening an instance of Internet Explorer and connecting to the site's URL.

17. When you are finished, close all open browser windows and then log off Server2.

Lesson Summary

- SPF can be deployed in a stand-alone configuration or as part of a server farm.
- The SharePoint Central Administration website provides a location for managing sites, site collections, and related configuration settings.
- After installing SPF, verify or update settings related to email, farm administrators, and managed accounts.
- The SharePoint 2010 Management Shell enables you to use the Stsadm.exe command-line utility and PowerShell cmdlets to perform common administration tasks from the command line.
- You can create multiple subsites and site collections to segment SharePoint content based on users' needs.
- You can use the Web Applications Management page of the Central Administration website to perform many administration tasks, such as creating, extending, and deleting web applications; configuring permissions for web applications; and managing authentication settings.

Lesson Review

You can use the following questions to test your knowledge of the information in the Lesson "Configuring and Managing SharePoint Foundation." The questions are also available on the companion CD if you prefer to review them in electronic form.

> **NOTE ANSWERS**
>
> Answers to these questions and explanations of why each answer choice is correct or incorrect are located in the "Answers" section at the end of the book.

1. You are a systems administrator in charge of installing SharePoint Foundation on a computer running Windows Server 2008 R2. You have completed the initial installation process for the server but have not yet added any roles or features to the installation. Based on your technical requirements, you have decided to install SharePoint Foundation in a server farm configuration. Which of the following is not a dependency of SharePoint Foundation? (Each correct answer presents a complete solution. Choose two.)

   A. SQL Server 2008 Express

   B. Microsoft .NET Framework 3.5

   C. Web Server (IIS) role

   D. File Server role

2. You are a systems administrator responsible for deploying SharePoint Foundation for access by users from an external business partner. You have installed the appropriate server role and have verified that the SharePoint website loads properly from the local server computer. All options are using their installation default values. External users report that they cannot log on to the site. Which of the following changes should you make to resolve the problem?

   A. Create a new site within an existing site collection for the external users.

   B. Create a new site collection for the external users.

   C. Change the authentication mode for the web application to Forms authentication.

   D. Modify the User Permissions For Web Applications settings.

   E. Modify the Quota Template settings for the default web application.

Chapter Review

To further practice and reinforce the skills you learned in this chapter, you can perform the following tasks:

- Review the chapter summary.
- Review the list of key terms introduced in this chapter.
- Complete the case scenarios. These scenarios set up real-world situations involving the topics of this chapter and ask you to create a solution.
- Complete the suggested practices.
- Take a practice test.

Chapter Summary

- SharePoint Foundation includes a default website and the SharePoint Central Administration website.
- SharePoint Foundation can be deployed in a stand-alone configuration or in a server farm configuration.
- Administrators can create and manage sites, site collections, and web applications by using the SharePoint Central Administration website.
- You should configure web applications with customized security and authentication settings that are based on the particular needs of those applications and of your organization.

Key Terms

Do you know what these key terms mean? You can check your answers by looking up the terms in the glossary at the end of the book.

- quota templates (SharePoint Foundation)
- server farm configuration (SharePoint Foundation)
- SharePoint Central Administration website
- site collection (SharePoint Foundation)
- stand-alone server configuration (SharePoint Foundation)
- Stsadm
- web application (SharePoint Foundation)

Case Scenarios

The following case scenarios will help you determine the best way to deploy SharePoint Foundation based on different organizational and technical requirements.

Case Scenario 1: Deploying SharePoint Foundation

You are a systems administrator responsible for enabling SharePoint Foundation on seven computers running Windows Server 2008 R2. Your organization plans to use a single back-end database for storing the site configuration data and contents. On six of the servers, you will need to create several site collections and web applications.

1. Which deployment option should you use when installing SharePoint Foundation on the computers?

2. How can you automate the process of creating the site collections and web applications?

Case Scenario 2: Managing SharePoint Foundation

You are a systems administrator responsible for managing an existing SharePoint Foundation server. The server has been configured with several site collections and sites. The SharePoint Foundation server is part of an Active Directory domain, and all the users have individual accounts. Users have been able to access the site for several months but have reported several problems. Users of some SharePoint Web applications note that they are always required to provide user name and password information when connecting to certain sites. Also, in the past, the SPF server has become unavailable when the computer ran out of available disk space. Finally, some users would like to be able to create their own sites without requiring the involvement of the IT department.

1. How should you configure the authentication settings to meet users' requirements?

2. How can you prevent future disk storage issues from occurring on the SPF server?

3. What is the easiest method of enabling users to create their own SharePoint sites?

Suggested Practices

To help you successfully master the exam objectives presented in this chapter, complete the following tasks. The practice items in this section enable you to practice the process of setting up and managing SPF.

- **Practice 1** Create a new site collection by using the SharePoint Central Administration website. Choose one of the built-in application templates to configure the default content. Add a second site to the same site collection and note the changes to the navigation bar. Create a third site that uses a different template and test the included functionality by using a web browser.

- **Practice 2** On a test SharePoint Foundation server, practice the process of creating and restoring configuration information from backups. First, restore the configuration settings over an existing site and verify that the contents have reverted to the earlier version. Then, use the backup and restore process to create a second copy of a SharePoint site collection by restoring it with different site information.

- **Practice 3** Access additional information at the following URLs:
  - Microsoft SharePoint Foundation 2010 website on TechNet:
    http://technet.microsoft.com/en-us/sharepoint/ee263910.aspx.
  - Microsoft TechNet Virtual Labs: SharePoint Products and Technologies:
    http://technet.microsoft.com/en-us/bb512933.aspx.

Take a Practice Test

The practice tests on this book's companion CD offer many options. For example, you can test yourself on just one exam objective, or you can test yourself on all the 70-643 certification exam content. You can set up the test so that it closely simulates the experience of taking a certification exam, or you can set it up in study mode so that you can look at the correct answers and explanations after you answer each question.

> **MORE INFO** **PRACTICE TESTS**
>
> For details about all the practice test options available, see the "How to Use the Practice Tests" section in this book's introduction.

Answers

Chapter 1: Lesson Review Answers

Lesson 1

1. Correct Answer: C

   A. **Incorrect:** Windows PE is used to boot from a CD to service a hard disk.

   B. **Incorrect:** The ImageX utility captures, modifies, and applies WIM images.

   C. **Correct:** Sysprep prepares a Windows installation to be imaged by removing all unique system information from the Windows installation, for example, by resetting security IDs (SIDs), clearing system restore points, and deleting event logs.

   D. **Incorrect:** Use the Windows System Image Manager (SIM) tool to create unattended Windows Setup answer files.

2. Correct Answer: D

   A. **Incorrect:** The ImageX utility captures, modifies, and applies WIM images.

   B. **Incorrect:** Use the Windows System Image Manager (SIM) tool to create unattended Windows Setup answer files.

   C. **Incorrect:** Windows PE is used to boot from a CD to service a hard disk.

   D. **Correct:** Dism.exe modifies WIM files offline.

3. Correct Answer: A

   A. **Correct:** A public key infrastructure provides encryption. Windows Deployment Services does not require encryption.

   B. **Incorrect:** The server hosting the Deployment Server role of Windows Deployment Services must be a member of an Active Directory Domain Services domain.

   C. **Incorrect:** Clients rely on a DHCP server to locate Windows Deployment Services on the network.

   D. **Incorrect:** A DNS server is required for Windows Deployment Services because DNS is a required feature of Active Directory Domain Services, and Active Directory Domain Services are required for Windows Deployment Services.

Lesson 2

1. **Correct Answer: C**

    A. Incorrect: The image store is found in the *Path*\RemoteInstall folder on your WDS server and is used to contain and manage boot and install images used for deployment.

    B. Incorrect: WDS includes a TFTP server that can respond to a PXE-enabled client computer so that the client can download the WDS client to display the boot menu and begin the installation.

    C. Correct: Although Windows SIM is useful for creating answer files for performing unattended installations using WDS, it is not part of WDS—Windows SIM is included as part of the Windows AIK.

    D. Incorrect: WDS includes a PXE server that can respond to BOOTP requests from PXE-enabled client computers and provide these computers with the location of the WDS client, which is needed to start the installation process.

2. **Correct Answer: A**

    A. Correct: FAT32 volumes are not supported by WDS.

    B. Incorrect: You have not pre-staged any of the computers in the domain, so you must configure the PXE Response settings to respond to all client computers (known and unknown).

    C. Incorrect: You should use the Boot.wim file found on the Windows 7 DVD to act as the boot image for your WDS clients.

    D. Incorrect: You want to deploy Windows 7, so you should use the Install.wim file located on the Windows 7 DVD as the install image for your WDS clients.

3. **Correct Answer: B**

    A. Incorrect: A boot image is used to boot a computer. You want an image that will install an operating system on the WDS clients.

    B. Correct: An install image is used to install an operating system on a WDS client. You want to use a capture image to create an install image based on Win7-01.

    C. Incorrect: A capture image is used to create an image of a computer and upload that image to WDS. You do want to use a capture image to create an install image of Win7-01, but you don't want to create a capture image based on the installation of Win7-01. To create a capture image, you use a boot image file that is already saved to the image store in WDS.

    D. Incorrect: A discover image is used to locate a WDS server. You do not need to create a discover image because the computers in the organization are PXE-compatible.

Lesson 3

1. **Correct Answer: B**

    A. Incorrect: Insufficient RAM would not prevent a PXE-compatible computer from looking for a WDS server.

    B. Correct: If an earlier network adapter is not first in the boot order, another bootable device such as a bootable CD could cause the virtual machine to start without looking for the WDS server.

    C. Incorrect: Only an earlier network adapter is compatible with PXE and WDS.

    D. Incorrect: Although a discover CD helps a computer locate a WDS server, creating a new CD is unnecessary when you need only to adjust the boot order in the BIOS settings.

2. **Correct Answer: C**

    A. Incorrect: An internal network in Hyper-V cannot connect to computers on the external LAN, but it can communicate with the host computer.

    B. Incorrect: A private network in Hyper-V cannot connect to computers on the external LAN or communicate directly with the host computer.

    C. Correct: Only an external network is bound to a physical adapter that allows a virtual machine to communicate with the external LAN.

    D. Incorrect: Neither an internal network nor a private network enables communication with the external LAN.

3. **Correct Answer: A**

    A. Correct: You can use the *attach vdisk* command in the Diskpart utility to mount a VHD file as a drive.

    B. Incorrect: The *create vdisk* command in the Diskpart utility creates a VHD file. You don't need to create a VHD file; you need to mount one as a drive in the file system.

    C. Incorrect: Attaching the VHD files used in Hyper-V as hard disks in Virtual PC is possible but not easy to accomplish. It is also unnecessarily resource intensive compared to using the Diskpart utility.

    D. Incorrect: The expert's system has an x86 processor and cannot run Hyper-V.

Lesson 4

1. **Correct Answer: C**

    A. Incorrect: A total of 25 computers must request activation before Windows 7 clients can be successfully activated. The branch office meets this requirement, but it also meets the requirement for Windows Server 2008 R2 activation.

    B. Incorrect: A total of five computers need to request activation before Windows Server 2008 R2 can be successfully activated through a KMS host. The branch office meets this requirement, but it also meets the requirement for Windows 7 activation.

C. **Correct:** KMS licensing is available for both client types. For Windows 7 clients to be activated through KMS, the KMS host needs to receive activation requests from 25 computers. For Windows Server 2008 R2 installations to be activated, the KMS host needs to receive activation requests from five computers. The branch office meets these requirements.

D. **Incorrect:** The branch office network meets the requirements for KMS licensing for both operating systems.

2. **Correct Answer: B**

A. **Incorrect:** Without Internet access, MAK online activation would require activating each computer by telephone. This process would be very time consuming and inefficient.

B. **Correct:** MAK proxy activation provides the most efficient way to activate fewer than 25 computers that are running Windows 7 and that have no Internet access. In MAK proxy activation, you use an XML file to gather installation IDs from the clients to be activated. You then obtain confirmation IDs from Microsoft on a computer that can connect to the Internet, and these confirmation IDs are used to activate the computers.

C. **Incorrect:** You cannot use KMS licensing or activation in this scenario because there are not enough computers on the research subnet to support a KMS host.

D. **Incorrect:** You cannot perform retail key activation because the question states that volume licenses have been obtained for the 15 client computers.

3. **Correct Answer: D**

A. **Incorrect:** The *slmgr.vbs –ipk* command installs an enterprise volume license key on the KMS server.

B. **Incorrect:** The *slmgr.vbs –ato* command activates the KMS server over the Internet.

C. **Incorrect:** You must configure a firewall exception for TCP port 1688 because KMS clients use this port to activate with the KMS host.

D. **Correct:** TCP port 1723 is used with Point-to-Point Tunneling protocol, which is not required by KMS hosts.

Chapter 1: Case Scenarios Answers

Case Scenario 1: Deploying Servers

1. System Center Configuration Manager 2007 R3.

2. You should migrate the four servers running Windows Server 2003 and SUSE Linux applications to two servers in a virtual environment. This option reduces the costs of running the servers and eliminates the need to purchase additional servers for the Windows Server 2008 R2 deployment.

Case Scenario 2: Creating an Activation Infrastructure

1. At the Headquarters site, use KMS licensing and activation for all computers except those on the research subnet. For the computers on the isolated research subnet, use MAK proxy activation.

2. At the Binghamton site, use KMS licensing and a locally installed KMS host.

3. At the Syracuse site, use MAK licensing.

Chapter 2: Lesson Review Answers

Lesson 1

1. Correct Answer: B

   A. **Incorrect:** No disks will appear in Disk Management unless the vendor solution includes the VDS hardware provider. Even then, they will appear only once LUNs have been created and assigned to the server.

   B. **Correct:** VDS is an API that exposes disk subsystems and SAN hardware to administrative tools in Windows. For built-in storage management tools such as Storage Manager for SANs to connect to disk enclosures produced by independent hardware vendors, the hardware must include a software interface to VDS. This interface is known as the VDS hardware provider.

   C. **Incorrect:** If the vendor software can connect to the disk subsystem, the iSCSI connection to the device is already established. In addition, iSCSI Initiator in Windows will not see the device unless the vendor solution includes the VDS hardware provider.

   D. **Incorrect:** If the vendor software can connect to the disk subsystem, the connection to the device is already established. Configuring an iSNS server will not enable the physical discovery of the device. To enable physical discovery of the device, the vendor solution needs to include the VDS hardware provider.

2. Correct Answer: D

   A. **Incorrect:** A simple volume would use only one of the three disks, and it would not offer the highest read or write performance.

   B. **Incorrect:** A spanned volume could use the maximum space on all three disks, but it would not offer the highest read or write performance.

   C. **Incorrect:** A mirrored volume would use the space equivalent of just one disk. In addition, a mirrored volume would not offer the highest read or write performance.

   D. **Correct:** A striped volume would use the total space available on all three disks. In addition, a striped volume offers the best read and write performance of any volume type.

E. **Incorrect:** A RAID-5 volume would use the space equivalent of two out of the three disks. In addition, although a RAID-5 volume offers excellent read performance, it would also offer relatively poor write performance.

3. **Correct Answer: C**

   A. **Incorrect:** Although this procedure would make the maximum space available through the K drive, it makes this space available through a new separate folder. You want to make more space available in their current folders.

   B. **Incorrect:** This procedure would not maximize the amount of space available to users because it removes the space current available on the E drive.

   C. **Correct:** This procedure makes available through K the space of both the E drive and the new volume. In addition, users can continue to store and share data as they did before.

   D. **Incorrect:** This procedure would not increase the amount of space available. It would merely add fault tolerance to the data stored on E and available through K.

Lesson 2

1. **Correct Answer: B**

   A. **Incorrect:** A more powerful server might be able to meet the performance requirements of the website in the short term, but if traffic is expected to grow for many years, this solution does not provide the best way to meet that demand in the long term.

   B. **Correct:** An NLB cluster (web farm) would enable you to meet the performance demands of the website in the short term and in the long term. As traffic to the website increases, you merely need to add additional servers to meet the increased demand.

   C. **Incorrect:** A failover cluster would not enable a website to sustain an increased workload. A failover cluster merely enables one server to take over for another if that second server fails.

   D. **Incorrect:** Round-robin might be adequate for some small deployments, but it is not the best solution in the long term. In the long term, you do not want web clients to be directed to failed or busy web servers, and you want to be able to control the workload distribution better than round-robin allows.

2. **Correct Answer: B**

   A. **Incorrect:** You don't want to choose the Node Majority quorum configuration because this option is best suited for failover clusters with an odd number of nodes.

   B. **Correct:** Node And Disk Majority is the most suitable quorum configuration for failover clusters that have an even number of nodes and plentiful shared storage options.

   C. **Incorrect:** Node And File Share Majority is the most suitable quorum configuration for a failover cluster that has an even number of nodes but does not have access to a share volume that can be used for a witness disk.

D. **Incorrect:** The No Majority: Disk Only quorum configuration is not generally recommended. It can be used in testing environments or in special circumstances for which no other quorum configuration is suitable.

3. **Correct Answer: A, C**

   A. **Correct:** Cluster shared volumes (CSVs) enable you to store the virtual hard disks (VHDs) of multiple virtual machines on a single logical unit number (LUN) while providing failover service for those same virtual machines. In addition, the failure of one virtual machine stored in a CSV does not trigger a failover procedure of other virtual machines stored in the CSV.

   B. **Incorrect:** A pass-through disk is a disk on a Hyper-V host system that is reserved for use by a single virtual machine. Implementing pass-through disks would not minimize the number of drives appearing in Disk Management on cluster nodes.

   C. **Correct:** Cluster shared volumes (CSVs) can be used only with virtual machines. In addition, this option enables you to meet your goal of minimizing the number of hardware components.

   D. **Incorrect:** If you pursued this option by assigning each application server to a physical server, you would not meet your goal of minimizing the number of hardware components in the cluster. If you pursued this option by running each application server in a virtual machine, you would not meet your goal of minimizing the number of drives appearing in Disk Management.

Chapter 2: Case Scenarios Answers

Case Scenario 1: Designing Storage

1. You should choose an iSCSI-based SAN because this option provides excellent performance while enabling you to draw upon the networking expertise of the IT staff.

2. You should look for vendor solutions that include a hardware provider for VDS.

Case Scenario 2: Designing High Availability

1. You should configure an NLB cluster to host IIS and the web application. This option would maximize performance by load balancing the client requests among servers. In addition, an NLB cluster minimizes downtime by redirecting requests away from inactive servers.

2. You should choose a failover cluster to host the back-end database. Because the data must always be internally consistent, the database needs to reside on a single storage solution. The failover cluster will also minimize downtime by providing failover service if the database server fails.

Chapter 3: Lesson Review Answers

Lesson 1

1. **Correct Answers: A and C**

   A. **Correct:** This command configures a local Server Core installation of Windows Server 2008 or Windows Server 2008 R2 to accept Remote Desktop connections.

   B. **Incorrect:** This command configures a local Server Core installation of Windows Server 2008 or Windows Server 2008 R2 to block Remote Desktop connections.

   C. **Correct:** This command configures a local Server Core installation of Windows Server 2008 or Windows Server 2008 R2 to accept Remote Desktop connections from clients running Windows XP or earlier versions of Windows.

   D. **Incorrect:** This command configures a local Server Core installation of Windows Server 2008 or Windows Server 2008 R2 to block Remote Desktop connections from clients running Windows XP or earlier versions of Windows.

2. **Correct Answer: D**

   A. **Incorrect:** Remote Desktop for Administration is the unlicensed version of Remote Desktop that allows only two concurrent desktop sessions. Two sessions are not enough to support 75 consultants working in the field. In addition, if you were to use Remote Desktop for Administration, you would not need to purchase any licenses.

   B. **Incorrect:** Remote Desktop for Administration is the unlicensed version of Remote Desktop that allows only two concurrent desktop sessions. Two sessions are not enough to support 75 consultants working in the field. In addition, if you were to use Remote Desktop for Administration, you would not need to purchase any licenses.

   C. **Incorrect:** You must install Remote Desktop Services on the application server so that more than two users can connect to it simultaneously. However, it is advisable to use per user CALs because the number of devices exceeds the number of users.

   D. **Correct:** You need to install Remote Desktop Services on the application server so that more than two users can connect to it simultaneously. In addition, although you would have to purchase 75 per user CALs, you would have to purchase many more per device RDS CALs because of the large number of computers from which consultants might connect. Purchasing per user CALs is therefore the best option in this case.

3. **Correct Answer: B**

   A. **Incorrect:** Although this step would fix the problem, it would compromise security by exposing App1 to potential denial-of-service attacks.

   B. **Correct:** You would encounter this problem if you had configured the Remote Desktop server to allow connections only from computers running Remote Desktop with Network-Level Authentication (NLA). Windows XP SP3 does support NLA, but to enable it, you must enable CredSSP in the Registry.

C. Incorrect: This step would solve the problem, but it would not reduce administrative overhead.

D. Incorrect: This step would not solve the problem because computers running Windows XP SP3 already include Remote Desktop Connection 6.1.

Lesson 2

1. **Correct Answer: B**

   A. Incorrect: RD Connection Broker keeps track of user sessions in a farm and is responsible for reconnecting users to disconnected RDP sessions. For the RD Connection Broker to keep track of the sessions on each farm member, each member server needs to be added to the Session Directory Computers local group on the RD Connection Broker server. In this scenario, the Session Broker server is RDCB1.

   B. Correct: For users to be able to reconnect disconnected RDP sessions in a Remote Desktop server farm, each member server must be added to the Session Directory Computers local group on the RD Connection Broker server. In this scenario, the RD Connection Broker server is RDCB1.

   C. Incorrect: This option ensures that only some of the client requests for RDFARM1 will be directed to RDS6. It does not enable the RD Connection Broker to reconnect users to disconnected RDP sessions.

   D. Incorrect: This option ensures that users can connect to RDS6 only by specifying the server directly. It does not enable users who connect through the RDFARM1 farm name to reconnect to disconnected RDP sessions.

2. **Correct Answer: D**

   A. Incorrect: This option would prevent Remote Desktop clients from printing to printers local to the client. It would not configure a fallback printer driver for Remote Desktop clients.

   B. Incorrect: This option would change the default printer within a Remote Desktop session to a printer local to RDS1. It would not configure a fallback printer driver for Remote Desktop clients.

   C. Incorrect: This policy setting improves printing consistency for Remote Desktop clients, but it does not configure a fallback printer driver.

   D. Correct: To configure a fallback printer driver, you must configure this policy setting in Group Policy.

3. **Correct Answer: C**

   A. Incorrect: Network Load Balancing can be used to distribute initial requests to the farm evenly among the servers, but it will not reduce the processing overhead resulting from those initial requests.

B. **Incorrect:** Adding Host records ensures that any specific Remote Desktop Session Host server can be reached by specifying its name. It will not reduce the processing overhead resulting from initial client requests to the farm.

C. **Correct:** By introducing a new server and configuring it as a dedicated redirector, you can offload all the processing related to handling initial client requests from the other 10 farm member servers. The new server will handle all the initial client requests before redirecting them to the Remote Desktop Connection Broker.

D. **Incorrect:** Adding another server to the farm will reduce processing from initial client requests, but not as much as adding a dedicated redirector would.

Chapter 3: Case Scenarios Answers

Case Scenario 1: Choosing an RD Licensing Strategy

1. Yes, you should install Remote Desktop Services, because you need to support many simultaneous connections. You should choose per user CALs because there are fewer users than devices that connect to App1.

2. No, you do not need to install Remote Desktop Services on NS2, because there is no stated need for more than two concurrent desktop sessions. You can merely enable the Remote Desktop feature on the server instead. You do not need to purchase any client access licenses for Remote Desktop.

Case Scenario 2: Troubleshooting a Remote Desktop Services Installation

1. On the General tab of the RDP-Tcp Properties dialog box on App3, clear the check box to allow connections only from computers running Remote Desktop with Network-Level Authentication.

2. On the Sessions tab of the RDP-Tcp Properties dialog box on App2, set the End A Disconnected Session setting to Never.

Chapter 4: Lesson Review Answers

Lesson 1

1. **Correct Answer: B**

A. **Incorrect:** Mandatory profiles are incompatible with the stated requirement that users be able to save their own data.

B. **Correct:** By implementing disk quotas, you can ensure that the size of the user profiles does not exhaust the storage capacity of the disk.

C. **Incorrect:** Roaming user profiles alone will not solve the problem. You would need to store the profiles in a separate location with more storage capacity.

D. **Incorrect:** Profiles for Remote Desktop users are stored on the remote Remote Desktop Session Host server, not on the local computer. Assigning disk quotas to each user's local disks will not address the problem.

2. **Correct Answer: A**

A. **Correct:** Use the *Rwinsta* or *Reset session* command to delete a user session on a Remote Desktop Session Host. Deleting the disconnected, idle sessions will free up server resources for active sessions.

B. **Incorrect:** The *Tdiscon* command disconnects user sessions that are currently connected. You want to delete disconnected sessions, not active ones.

C. **Incorrect:** The *Tskill* command ends an individual process on a Remote Desktop Session Host. It does not end user sessions in general.

D. **Incorrect:** The *Tscon* command connects to a disconnected session. It does not end user sessions.

3. **Correct Answer: D**

A. **Incorrect:** The Equal_Per_Process resource allocation policy divides processor time equally among all processes running on the Remote Desktop Session Host. This policy will not enable you to give higher priority to applications run by users in the Finance department.

B. **Incorrect:** The Equal_Per_User resource allocation policy divides processor time equally among all users connected to the Remote Desktop Session Host. This policy will not enable you to give higher priority to applications run by users in the Finance department.

C. **Incorrect:** The Equal_Per_Session resource allocation policy divides processor time equally among all active sessions. This policy will not enable you to give higher priority to applications run by users in the Finance department.

D. **Correct:** You can use the Weighted_Remote_Sessions resource allocation policy to define users or groups that should receive priority for processor time. In this case, you want to add members of the Finance department to the policy and assign them the Premium priority.

Lesson 2

1. **Correct Answer: C**

A. **Incorrect:** TCP port 25 is used for SMTP traffic. This port is not needed to communicate with RD Gateway.

B. **Incorrect:** TCP port 3389 is used for direct RDP connections without RD Gateway. You want clients to communicate through RD Gateway.

C. Correct: TCP port 443 is the port used for SSL. RD Gateway communicates with clients over SSL.

D. Incorrect: TCP port 80 is used for HTTP traffic. You would need to leave this port open for a client to communicate with a web server hosted behind your company firewall.

2. **Correct Answer: D**

   A. Incorrect: If you enable HTTPS–HTTP bridging, you will not be using Forefront TMG as an SSL endpoint for RD Gateway connections. Communications with RD Gateway will be sent unencrypted through HTTP.

   B. Incorrect: It is necessary to open TCP port 443 on the Forefront TMG server so that external clients can initiate connections to it. However, opening this port will not ensure that Forefront TMG can communicate with RD Gateway.

   C. Incorrect: You need to export the RD Gateway server certificate to Forefront TMG server, not the other way around.

   D. Correct: When Forefront TMG is deployed between external Remote Desktop clients and an internal RD gateway, Forefront TMG acts as a client to RD Gateway. For this reason, the RD Gateway server certificate used for SSL must be installed on the computer running Forefront TMG.

3. **Correct Answer: A**

   A. Correct: This option automatically disconnects users who connect through Remote Desktop Gateway after five hours, regardless of whether the session is active. This is the desired outcome.

   B. Incorrect: This option would disconnect users connecting through Remote Desktop Gateway only if the session is idle for five hours. The desired outcome, however, is to disconnect sessions after five hours regardless of whether they are active.

   C. Incorrect: This option would automatically disconnect users connecting to App1 both from over the local network and through the Remote Desktop Gateway server after five hours. The desired outcome is to set a session limit only for users connecting through the Remote Desktop Gateway server.

   D. Incorrect: This option would automatically disconnect the inactive sessions from users connecting to App1 both from over the local network and through the Remote Desktop Gateway server after five hours. The desired outcome is to set a limit only for users connecting through the Remote Desktop Gateway server. In addition, you don't want to set a limit only on inactive sessions. You want to set a limit on all sessions.

Lesson 3

1. **Correct Answer: B**

   A. Incorrect: The *Chglogon* command enables or disables logons from client sessions on a Remote Desktop Session Host. It will not ensure that an installed application will support multiple users.

B. **Correct:** Use the *Change user/install* command before installing an application to create .ini files for the application in the system directory. This ensures that when users run the application, they will all be able to save personal settings for the application. After installation, use the *Change user/execute* command.

C. **Incorrect:** The *Qappsrv* command displays a list of all the Remote Desktop Session Host servers on the network. You cannot use it to ensure that an installed application will support multiple users.

D. **Incorrect:** The *Mstsc* command launches Remote Desktop Connection (Mstsc.exe). You cannot use this command to ensure that an installed application will support multiple users.

2. **Correct Answers: A and B**

A. **Correct:** The new RD Web Access site will list the RemoteApp program and point to its new location.

B. **Correct:** After the RemoteApp program is migrated, the old RDP file can no longer be used. You must re-create the file and distribute the file to users.

C. **Incorrect:** You can modify some settings in an RDP file, but you cannot modify the location of the RemoteApp program to which it is pointing. If you move an application, you must re-create any associated RDP file.

D. **Incorrect:** You can change the server name in Remote Desktop Session Host Settings, but this step is performed primarily when the local server belongs to a server farm. Changing the name of the server will not enable users to connect to the moved application.

3. **Correct Answer: D**

A. **Incorrect:** If you merely publish RemoteApp programs and virtual desktops to Remote Desktop Web Access, these resources will not be made available through the Start menu.

B. **Incorrect:** An .rdp file can connect to a remote resource, but it does not install itself automatically in the Start menu.

C. **Incorrect:** You can create Windows Installer packages to install RemoteApp programs automatically in the Start menu, but you can't use this method to do the same with virtual desktops.

D. **Correct:** If you use RemoteApp and Desktop Connections to subscribe to a feed from a Remote Desktop Web Access server, both the RemoteApp programs and the virtual desktops available through that server will also be made available through the local Start menu.

Chapter 4: Case Scenarios Answers

Case Scenario 1: Managing Remote Desktop Sessions

1. You can use the *Query session* command to find his session ID. You can use the *Rwinsta* or Reset session command to end (delete) his session.

2. You can use the Remote Control feature to take over her user session and then show her how to use the application.

Case Scenario 2: Publishing Applications

1. You should use Group Policy to publish the RemoteApp program to their desktops. You could achieve this with either an RDP file or an MSI file.

2. Use RemoteApp Manager to add App1 to the list of RemoteApp programs and then to create a Windows Installer package of the application. Configure the MSI file to install a shortcut to the RemoteApp program in the Start menu and to launch the program whenever a file with the associated extension is opened. Deploy the MSI file by using Group Policy.

3. Deploy an RD Gateway server in your company's perimeter network. Use RemoteApp Manager to create an RDP file for App1 that specifies the RD Gateway server. Distribute the RDP file to remote users.

Chapter 5: Lesson Review Answers

Lesson 1

1. **Correct Answer: B**

   A. **Incorrect:** The HTTP Errors role service sends custom error pages to users. Because the server does not appear to be responding, this is unlikely to resolve the problem.

   B. **Correct:** The most likely cause of the problem is that the World Wide Web Publishing Service has been stopped. You can verify the status of the service (and view any related events) by using Server Manager.

   C. **Incorrect:** Because multiple users are having problems accessing the site, it is most likely that the problem is related to a server-side issue.

   D. **Incorrect:** The HTTP Logging role server enables you to collect information about requests to the website. However, because the web server is not responding to requests, adding this role service will not resolve the problem.

   E. **Incorrect:** The IIS Admin Service is required to make configuration changes to the web server. However, even if this service is stopped, the web server should still be able to respond to user requests.

2. **Correct Answer: C**

   A. **Incorrect:** This utility manages Windows Deployment Services. It can't add features to an IIS installation.

   B. **Incorrect:** You can use this utility to back up and restore your system and to back up your website content, but it doesn't help you install IIS features.

   C. **Correct:** You can use Dism.exe to install features to an installation image, including the installation image that is currently online. To install ASP.NET, type **dism /online /enable-feature /featurename:IIS-ASPNET**.

   D. **Incorrect:** You can use this script to manage activations on your server. It can't install IIS features.

3. **Correct Answer: C**

   A. **Incorrect:** Directory Browsing enables users to see directory contents on a web server. It is not necessary to install this feature to enable remote management.

   B. **Incorrect:** ASP.NET provides server-side objects to support web applications written on this platform. It does not enable remote management.

   C. **Correct:** You need to install this feature if you want to enable remote management of an IIS 7 server.

   D. **Incorrect:** This feature allows you to manage IIS 7 locally, not remotely.

Lesson 2

1. **Correct Answers: A and D**

   A. **Correct:** Because both applications must be accessible by using the standard HTTP port, they must be contained within the same website.

   B. **Incorrect:** IIS does not allow multiple websites to share the same site-binding settings; therefore, you cannot start multiple websites that bind to HTTP port 80.

   C. **Incorrect:** Assigning both web applications to the same application pool will not prevent problems in one web application from affecting the other.

   D. **Correct:** By using separate application pools, each web application will run using isolated processes. This helps protect against potential performance and reliability problems.

2. **Correct Answer: A**

   A. **Correct:** After you copy the application to the server, you should select the option to add the application. You can then specify the application by browsing to it.

   B. **Incorrect:** This option will create a virtual directory within a particular website.

   C. **Incorrect:** This option will create an application pool without enabling any application.

   D. **Incorrect:** This option will create a new website. You want to enable an application.

3. **Correct Answer: D**

    A. **Incorrect:** The process of re-creating the websites can be time consuming, and it will be difficult to ensure that all settings have been restored to the correct options.

    B. **Incorrect:** Manually adding settings to the ApplicationHost.config file can be time consuming and risky.

    C. **Incorrect:** Because no manual backups of the IIS configuration have been made, you cannot use AppCmd to restore a backup.

    D. **Correct:** Because each website includes numerous additional settings, and because no additional changes have been made to the server, the quickest method of restoring the sites is to restore the IIS configuration by copying an automatic backup of the ApplicationHost.config file to the working location.

Chapter 5: Case Scenarios Answers

Case Scenario 1: IIS Web Server Administration

1. The IIS Shared Configuration feature enables multiple web servers to use the same configuration files. To do this, export the configuration from one of the servers and configure them all to use the same settings file.

2. You should include all the website content folders (including their Web.config files). The backup should also include the *%SystemDrive%*\Inetpub\History folder because this location contains previous versions of configuration files.

3. You can use the AppCmd.exe utility to create and restore manual backups of the IIS configuration. Making a manual backup is recommended before you make configuration changes to the server. Alternatively, you can restore previous versions of the ApplicationHost.config over the working version to revert to an earlier configuration of the server.

Case Scenario 2: Managing Multiple Websites

1. By adding each web application to a separate application pool, memory and processing errors can be contained to minimize negative effects.

2. You can modify the site bindings for each website to include a different *host name* value. Users will be redirected automatically to the appropriate site based on this information.

3. By adding the IIS 6 Management Compatibility role service, you can provide access to the IIS 6.0 metabase and other features. If the ASP.NET application requires access to the classic pipeline mode, you can create or change the settings for its application pool.

Chapter 6: Lesson Review Answers

Lesson 1

1. **Correct Answer: B**

   A. **Incorrect:** Adding the handler to the entire website will make it available to all web applications and can potentially decrease security.

   B. **Correct:** A managed handler enables you to call a .NET library to process the request. To reduce the attack surface of IIS, make this handler available only to the one web application that requires it.

   C. **Incorrect:** Module mappings are not designed to provide access to .NET libraries.

   D. **Incorrect:** Module mappings are not designed to provide access to .NET libraries.

2. **Correct Answer: C**

   A. **Incorrect:** IIS Manager enables you to configure user permissions for websites even when Management Service has been stopped.

   B. **Incorrect:** File system permissions will not affect whether IIS Manager users can be added to a website.

   C. **Correct:** To add IIS Manager users to the website, Management Service must be configured to accept IIS Manager credentials.

   D. **Incorrect:** Authentication settings only apply to users attempting to access web content by using a web browser or other applications. These settings do not affect remote IIS Manager user settings or connections.

Lesson 2

1. **Correct Answers: A and C**

   A. **Correct:** Windows authentication is designed to enable users with Windows domain or local user accounts to authenticate to the server.

   B. **Incorrect:** Basic authentication is a less secure option than Windows authentication because all required users have Windows accounts.

   C. **Correct:** Anonymous authentication must be disabled for users to be prompted to provide credentials when accessing the site.

   D. **Incorrect:** If anonymous authentication is enabled, users will be able to access the site without presenting credentials.

2. **Correct Answer: C**

   A. **Incorrect:** The site appears to be accepting connections on port 443 because users are receiving a warning message rather than an error message.

B. Incorrect: The requirements specify that users should be able to connect using both HTTP and HTTPS; therefore, you should not require SSL to access the site.

C. Correct: Users are receiving the warning because the server certificate is not issued by a trusted third party. It is likely that a self-signed certificate was installed earlier. You can resolve the issue by generating an Internet certificate request, obtaining a certificate, and then registering it on the server.

D. Incorrect: Because the server certificate appears to be installed properly, exporting and reimporting it will not solve the problem.

E. Incorrect: Because users are receiving a warning message when attempting to connect to the website, firewall issues are not preventing the connection.

Chapter 6: Case Scenarios Answers

Case Scenario 1: Configuring Remote Management for IIS

1. Assuming that you have the necessary permissions, you can create multiple connections (one for each server) within IIS Manager. Optionally, you can provide different credentials for each connection.

2. The most secure option is to enable IIS Manager credentials for the Management Service and create a new IIS Manager user account for the administrator.

3. Feature delegation settings determine which settings IIS Manager administrators can view or modify. Set the Default Document and Directory Browsing settings to Read Only to prevent administrators from making modifications.

Case Scenario 2: Increasing Website Security

1. Because the web application must be able to connect to a remote database server, you must select the High (web_hightrust.config) .NET trust level. This setting should be assigned at the level of the web application.

2. First, use file system permissions to restrict access to the content to only the approved users. You can then use authorization rules to manage which users can access the content.

3. You must first obtain and install an Internet Security Certificate on the web server. Then you can enable SSL connections by using the site bindings settings. Finally, to require encryption, use the SSL Settings feature for the web application.

Chapter 7: Lesson Review Answers

Lesson 1

1. **Correct Answer: C**

   A. Incorrect: You must create a new FTP site. Creating a host header for the Default Web Site will not enable you to add a new FTP site. Host headers enable you to assign more than one site to a single IP address on a web server.

   B. Incorrect: Assigning an alternative address to the Default Web Site would enable users to connect to the Default Web Site by using that alternate address. It would not enable you to create a new FTP site.

   C. Correct: This option would enable you to configure a unique address for the Engineering FTP site and provide authentication that would restrict some users from gaining access to the site.

   D. Incorrect: Adding FTP Publishing to the Default Web Site and using Anonymous Authentication would allow all users to connect to an FTP site with the same anonymous credentials, even though the site is supposed to be for the Engineering department only. It would also use the main IIS server address for the purpose of one department when all members of the organization use this server.

2. **Correct Answers: B and D**

   A. Incorrect: Allowing SSL connections will not require all users to enable encryption. Therefore, this option does not meet the requirement to encrypt credentials and commands.

   B. Correct: Disabling 128-bit encryption instructs the FTP site to use 40-bit encryption for transfers. This will increase FTP server performance while still encrypting data.

   C. Incorrect: The Require SSL Connections policy encrypts all communications between the FTP client and the FTP site.

   D. Correct: The Custom SSL Policy option enables administrators to set Control Channel and Data Channel settings independently.

Lesson 2

1. **Correct Answers: A and C**

   A. Correct: By requiring Basic Authentication, all users or applications must provide credentials to use the SMTP virtual server.

   B. Incorrect: A smart host setting will force the SMTP virtual server to route all new mail messages through a specified server. This will not directly prevent unauthorized access to the server.

C. **Correct:** Connection Control rules can be used to define which computers or IP addresses can use the SMTP virtual server.

D. **Incorrect:** The Security tab is used to determine which users are operators of the SMTP server. This will not directly prevent unauthorized users from sending messages.

2. **Correct Answer: B**

A. **Incorrect:** The Current Sessions section shows only which users and applications are accessing the server at a specific point in time. It does not provide a good method of monitoring performance over time.

B. **Correct:** Performance counters that are part of the *SMTP Server* node can provide details about how many messages are sent and received by the server over time. You can also correlate these statistics with other information such as CPU, memory, and network usage.

C. **Incorrect:** The Windows Event logs will not contain performance-related statistics for the SMTP Server service.

D. **Incorrect:** The Windows Event logs will not contain performance-related statistics for the SMTP Server service.

E. **Incorrect:** Messages that are undeliverable are stored in the Badmail folder, but the performance problems are not necessarily caused by undeliverable messages.

Chapter 7: Case Scenarios Answers

Case Scenario 1: Implementing a Secure FTP Site

1. Obtain a server certificate for the FTP server and then enable FTP Over SSL (FTPS) by using IIS Manager.

2. You can use IIS Manager to add a new FTP site binding to an existing website. This automatically configures the root directory for the site.

Case Scenario 2: Configuring an SMTP Virtual Server

1. You can use the settings on the General tab of the SMTP virtual server to specify the IP addresses and port numbers to which the server will respond.

2. On the Access tab of the properties of the SMTP virtual server, enable the Basic Authentication option.

3. The Limit Message Size option on the Messages tab enables you to specify the maximum size of a single SMTP message.

Chapter 8: Lesson Review Answers

Lesson 1

1. **Correct Answers: B and C**

   A. **Incorrect:** Users will not be able to fast-forward media that is streamed from a broadcast publishing point.

   B. **Correct:** Users can access an on-demand publishing point to select which videos they want to view and can control the playback.

   C. **Correct:** WMS IP Address Authorization settings can allow only computers that are part of the specified LAN to connect to the server.

   D. **Incorrect:** WMS Negotiate Authentication is designed for authenticating users based on Windows accounts, but it will not prevent clients from accessing content from locations other than the LAN.

   E. **Incorrect:** WMS NTFS ACL Authorization verifies users' Windows accounts to determine whether they have access to content, but it will not limit the network locations from which streamed media can be accessed.

2. **Correct Answer: B**

   A. **Incorrect:** The Unicast Announcement Wizard will not prevent users from accessing specific content from the publishing point.

   B. **Correct:** You can use NTFS permissions to determine which content will be available by using the publishing point. You can configure the WMS NTFS ACL Authorization plug-in to specify the user account that should be used.

   C. **Incorrect:** Copying the training videos increases storage space requirements and is not necessary to meet the requirements.

   D. **Incorrect:** Disabling WMS Anonymous Authentication will require users to provide authentication credentials to access the content.

   E. **Incorrect:** Providing users with access to the Wrapper Playlist will not enable them to choose which videos they want to watch.

3. **Correct Answer: B**

   A. **Incorrect:** Copying the training videos will make it more difficult to manage updates and revisions to the content and will use additional disk space on the server.

   B. **Correct:** Caching servers automatically obtain and store copies of the video content from the origin server and will make streams available to users.

   C. **Incorrect:** Proxy servers redirect client requests to other servers. They can increase performance, but they will not improve scalability as much as caching servers will.

   D. **Incorrect:** Limiting distribution connections will not directly increase scalability for supporting client connections.

Chapter 8: Case Scenarios Answers

Case Scenario 1: Protecting Streaming Media Content

1. You should create a single publishing point that provides access to video files on demand. This will enable users to select which videos they want to view and to pause or fast-forward the content during playback.

2. Because the users have Active Directory accounts, you should enable WMS NTFS ACL Authorization. For ease of administration, you can place students in groups based on their class enrollments. You can then apply file system permissions to specify which files are accessible to which users.

3. You can use wrapper advertisements to play a video clip automatically before the playback of specific videos. This is the easiest method because it does not involve the manual creation of individual playlists.

Case Scenario 2: Improving Windows Media Services Performance and Scalability

Your organization provides access to streamed audio content to paid users over the Internet.

1. A broadcast publishing point is most suitable for live events because it can obtain information directly from a Windows Media Services live encoder stream.

2. For networks and operating systems that support it, multicast broadcasts can significantly reduce the bandwidth requirements for the origin server. Users who cannot access the multicast stream can fall back on using the unicast method.

3. Adding cache/proxy Windows Media Services servers can greatly improve performance while enabling content to remain on the origin server.

Chapter 9: Lesson Review Answers

Lesson 1

1. Correct Answers: A and D
   A. **Correct:** Unlike a stand-alone (single server) installation of SharePoint Foundation, a server farm installation does not use SQL Server 2008 Express. All content and configuration information will be stored in the full version of SQL Server 2005 or SQL Server 2008.
   B. **Incorrect:** SharePoint Foundation requires .NET Framework 3.5 for it to run.
   C. **Incorrect:** The Web Server (IIS) server role is required to host the SharePoint user, administration, and web services websites.

D. **Correct:** The File Server role is not a requirement for a server running SharePoint Foundation.

2. **Correct Answer: C**

   A. **Incorrect:** It is not necessary to create a new site to provide access to the default SharePoint site.

   B. **Incorrect:** It is not necessary to create a new site collection to provide access to the default SharePoint site.

   C. **Correct:** The default authentication option for the default SharePoint site is Windows authentication. To connect, users require access to logon information for the local domain. External users who do not have local domain accounts will not be able to access the site unless you change the authentication mode to Forms.

   D. **Incorrect:** User permissions settings apply only to operations that can be performed after a user is connected to the SharePoint site. They do not prevent users from connecting to the site itself.

   E. **Incorrect:** Quota Template settings affect only the maximum amount of storage allowed for a site collection and will not prevent users from connecting to the site.

Chapter 9: Case Scenarios Answers

Case Scenario 1: Deploying SharePoint Foundation

1. Because a single back-end database server will store content, you should deploy the servers by using the server farm configuration option. You can use the SharePoint Products Configuration Wizard later to configure database access settings.

2. You can use the *Stsadm.exe* command-line utility or PowerShell cmdlets to perform tasks such as creating new sites without using the SharePoint Central Administration website. The commands can be placed in a script file to simplify the setup process.

Case Scenario 2: Managing SharePoint Foundation

1. Because the site's users are all part of the same Active Directory domain, Windows authentication will enable them to connect to SharePoint Foundation without requiring additional authentication information.

2. Quota templates can be created and assigned to specific site collections to limit the amount of disk space used by each site. You can also configure email warnings to be sent if specific sites are approaching their limits.

3. The Self-Service Site Creation feature enables users to create their own SharePoint sites. You can enable this option on the Web Applications Management page of the SharePoint Central Administration website.

Glossary

A

Active Directory Rights Management Services (AD RMS) A Windows Server 2008 R2 server role that enables a computer to issue certificates and permissions for creating and editing contents of documents and media files.

AppCmd.exe A command-line utility for managing IIS 7.0 configuration settings and for performing tasks such as configuration backup and restore operations.

Application pools (IIS) A method by which multiple websites can run using separate worker processes in IIS. Application pools minimize the possibility of websites and web applications adversely affecting other sites and applications.

ApplicationHost.config file The primary settings that store server-level configuration details for IIS. The file is based on an XML format that can be edited manually.

ASP.NET impersonation An IIS security method that enables ASP.NET applications to run under a specific security context or the security context of the authenticated user.

ASP.NET Microsoft Web application development technology, based on the Microsoft .NET Framework. ASP.NET applications are supported by IIS.

Attack surface A term that refers to the overall potential security liability of a server or service. The attack surface for a web server, for example, can be reduced by disabling unnecessary features and services.

B

Block-based Direct or unformatted, as opposed to file-based. Block-based access provides fast and direct access to the data needed by operating systems and applications.

Boot image A WIM file you can use to boot a bare-metal computer. The Windows 7 and Windows Server 2008 R2 product DVDs are able to start the computer by using versions of a boot image named Boot.wim.

C

Capture image A special boot image used to start a master computer and upload an image of that computer to WDS.

Certificate authority (CA) An organization or service that generates server certificates. Trusted third-party organizations can issue certificates for web servers accessed by using the Internet.

Client Certificate Authentication A method by which security certificates are installed on client computers and are verified by a web server to confirm the identity of the user or computer.

Cluster A general term that represents any group of servers that act as one. Despite some similarities, Network Load Balancing (NLB) clusters and failover clusters serve very different purposes.

Cluster shared volumes (CSVs) Volumes used to store VHDs of multiple virtual machines in a failover cluster. CSVs allow failover to occur for one application or service without triggering failover for other applications and services stored on the same physical volume.

Console session On a Remote Desktop Session Host, the session of the user who is logged on locally and who has current access to the desktop.

D

Defense in depth A security approach that involves the implementation of multiple layers of security to protect sensitive data such as web server content.

Digital Rights Management (DRM) Technology that enables content producers to prevent unauthorized use of their intellectual property.

Discover image A boot image you can use to enable a bare-metal computer that is not PXE-enabled to locate a WDS server and download a boot menu and image.

Domain restrictions (IIS) A method by which systems administrators can restrict which users can connect to a web server based on the DNS domain of the client computer.

F

Feature delegation (IIS) A method of limiting which configuration settings users can view or change when they connect to a web server by using IIS Manager.

File Transfer Protocol (FTP) A standard protocol for transferring files among computers.

FTP client Software that enables users to connect to an FTP server to upload and download files. Examples include the FTP command-line utility in Windows and FTP features in Internet Explorer.

FTP Over SSL A secure implementation of the FTP protocol that enables server administrators to require or allow encryption of data and control channel information.

FTP server A computer configured to enable users to access, upload, and download files.

FTP user isolation Settings that determine the default folders and the folders to which FTP users will have access.

G

Guest operating system The operating system of a virtual machine.

H

Handler mappings (IIS) Configuration settings that specify which types of content requests are handled by which request handlers.

Home folder The default location in which a user's files are saved.

Host operating system The base operating system installed on a computer in which virtualization technology is being used.

HTTPS HTTP-over-SSL. A commonly used method to encrypt web traffic.

Hypertext Transfer Protocol (HTTP) The primary protocol used for communicating between web browsers and web servers. By default, HTTP uses TCP port 80 for communications.

Hypertext Transfer Protocol Secure (HTTPS) HTTP-over-SSL, a commonly used method to encrypt web traffic.

Hypervisor A small layer of software installed beneath a host operating system that grants the host and all guests equal access to hardware resources (such as the CPU).

I

IIS Management Service A role service for providing remote IIS management to users of the Web Server (IIS) role.

IIS Manager credentials An authentication method that enables web server administrators to define user accounts and passwords to enable remote users to manage IIS.

IIS Manager The primary graphical management tool for configuring IIS.

Install image An image of a Windows installation that you can deploy onto a computer.

Install mode A mode of Remote Desktop Services used to install applications for multiple users.

Internet certificate request (IIS) A request for a server certificate generated on a web server that will be publicly accessible. The request is sent to a certificate authority (CA), which can then generate a server certificate for installation on the computer.

Internet Information Services (IIS) The web server platform included with Windows Server. IIS provides support for HTTP, FTP, SMTP, and other communications protocols. It also supports a wide variety of web development languages and platforms.

Interstitial advertisements Audio or video advertisements that are designed to play back at periodic intervals when users are accessing content.

IP address restrictions (IIS) A method by which systems administrators can restrict which users can connect to a web server, based on IP address information.

iSCSI initiator A software agent that initiates a connection to an iSCSI device on behalf of a computer.

iSCSI target A hardware device with a SCSI interface connected to a computer through an iSCSI adapter and cabling.

K

Key Management Service (KMS) A service and volume licensing option based on a KMS key. In KMS, clients automatically discover a locally installed KMS host and activate themselves without user intervention.

Key seed A secret value that creates a unique encryption key. A key seed is used in Windows Media DRM infrastructure to create a key to encrypt media.

L

License clearing house A server running the Windows Media License Service that stores media licenses and authenticates requests for those licenses.

M

Masquerade domain An SMTP domain name option that rewrites the domain information for all messages sent through an SMTP virtual server.

Modules (IIS) web server code designed to provide additional functionality or capabilities for web services. Modules can be added, removed, and disabled by using the IIS Manager utility.

Multiple Access Key (MAK) A volume-license key that can be activated a specific number of times.

N

.NET trust levels IIS configuration settings that determine the Code Access Security (CAS) rules applied to an application based on the .NET Framework.

Network-Level Authentication (NLA) A feature of Remote Desktop Protocol 6.0 and later that enables user authentication to occur before a connection to a remote computer is established.

P

Parity information Error-checking information based on the evenness (0) or oddness (1) of values. Parity data provides fault tolerance in a RAID-5 volume.

Partition style The basic structure of a disk that defines how partitions are created and used. The most common partition style by far is Master Boot Record (MBR).

Personal virtual desktop A virtual machine that is assigned to a particular user and that is made available to that user remotely through Remote Desktop Web Access, RemoteApp and Desktop Connections, or the Start Menu.

Publish (an application) Make an application available remotely.

Publishing points A Windows Media server endpoint that provides access to either on-demand or broadcast-based content. A single Windows Media Services server can host numerous publishing points.

Q

Quorum configuration In a failover cluster, the chosen rules that determine the number of failures the cluster can sustain before the cluster stops running.

Quota templates (SharePoint Foundation) Settings that control the maximum amount of storage space that a site collection can use. Quota templates can be created and managed by using the SharePoint Central Administration website.

R

RD CAP A type of policy applied to an RD Gateway server and restricting client access to the gateway from external sources.

RD Connection Broker An optional component of Remote Desktop Services that enables a computer to keep track of all user sessions in a Remote Desktop server farm. One benefit of RD Connection Broker is that users who are accidentally disconnected from sessions on a server farm can be reconnected to the same session on the correct server.

RD Gateway A feature in Windows Server 2008 R2 that enables authorized users on the Internet to connect to a Remote Desktop Session Host on a private network.

RD RAP A type of policy applied to an RD Gateway server and used to restrict access to Remote Desktop Services resources in an organization.

RD Web Access A component of a Remote Desktop Session Host that enables a user to access RemoteApp programs and remote desktops through a web page.

Real-Time Streaming Protocol (RTSP) A streaming protocol Windows Media Services uses with compatible players (such as Windows Media Player Series 9 or later). RTSP can function over UDP (RTSPU) or TCP (RTSPT).

Relay restrictions SMTP security settings that specify which users or computers can send messages that are neither from nor to the SMTP domain. Implementing relay restrictions can help reduce the number of unwanted email messages sent through an SMTP server.

Remote Desktop for Administration (RDA) A mode of Remote Desktop Services on Windows Server 2008 R2 that does not require the installation of the Remote Desktop Services server role or the purchase of any RDS CALs. This mode allows only two concurrent desktop sessions on the local server, including the console session.

Remote Desktop Protocol (RDP) The protocol that enables the transport of a desktop from one computer to another through a Remote Desktop connection.

Remote Desktop Services client access licenses (RDS CALs) Licenses you must purchase either for every user or for every device that connects to Remote Desktop Services in Windows Server 2008 R2. Without RDS CALs, Remote Desktop Services ceases to operate after 120 days.

RemoteApp A feature of Remote Desktop Services in Windows Server 2008 R2 that enables a user to run a program installed on a remote server as if that program were installed locally.

RemoteApp and Desktop Connection In Windows 7 and Windows Server 2008 R2, a Control Panel program that enables users to subscribe to an updated feed of resources made available through a Remote Desktop Web Access server.

Request handlers Programs designed to accept incoming IIS requests and generate responses. Request handlers can be enabled or disabled based on the specific needs of web applications.

Round-robin DNS A simple method to distribute client requests for one server among a group of servers.

S

SAN fabric The hardware devices that connect servers and storage in a storage area network (SAN).

Secure Sockets Layer (SSL) A security protocol designed to provide encryption and authentication capabilities for web servers and web browsers. SSL is a predecessor to the Transport Layer Security (TLS) protocol.

Self-signed certificate A security certificate a computer issues to itself, created on a server for development and testing purposes. A self-signed certificate does not provide proof of identity, but it still can be used for encryption. Self-signed certificates do not require the involvement of a certificate authority (CA).

Server certificates A method by which web servers can provide their identity to web users. Server certificates are obtained from a certificate authority (CA).

Server farm configuration (SharePoint Foundation) A SharePoint Foundation deployment option that enables multiple front-end web servers to access back-end database servers for performance, scalability, and reliability improvements.

SharePoint Central Administration website The default management website for SharePoint Foundation. It enables features for completion operations and application management tasks.

Simple Mail Transfer Protocol (SMTP) An Internet standard for sending text-based messages among computers by using the TCP/IP protocol.

Site bindings Information that specifies the types of requests to which an IIS website should respond. The site binding includes a protocol type, IP address settings, port numbers, and, optionally, a host name.

Site collection (SharePoint Foundation) A group of SharePoint sites that share the same navigation and configuration settings. Multiple site collections can be created to allow different options.

Smart host An SMTP virtual server configuration option that specifies that all outbound messages should be forwarded to a specific SMTP server rather than being sent directly. The use of smart hosts can increase performance and security.

SSL A security protocol designed to provide encryption and authentication capabilities for web servers and web browsers. SSL is a predecessor to the Transport Layer Security (TLS) protocol.

Stand-alone server configuration (SharePoint Foundation) A SharePoint Foundation deployment option that includes all the necessary components on the same server.

Streaming Media Services (server role) An optional, downloadable Windows Server 2008 R2 server role that includes Windows Media Services, sample content, and administrative tools and features.

Stsadm A command-line utility for configuring and managing SharePoint Foundation.

U

URL authorization rules IIS server settings that define which content is available to which users based on the path of the URL request.

User profile The collection of data that comprises a user's individual environment, including individual files, application settings, and desktop configuration.

V

Virtual desktop pool A group of identically configured virtual machines running on Remote Desktop Virtualization Hosts that provides a shared desktop interface for many users. Users connecting to a virtual desktop pool are connected to any one of the desktops and are not able to save personal information.

W

Web application (SharePoint Foundation) A SharePoint website that provides functionality for a team or portion of the organization. Web applications can be created to serve the needs of different groups of users.

Web farm An NLB cluster that answers client requests for a website or group of websites.

Web Server (IIS) server role A server role in Windows Server 2008 and Windows Server 2008 R2 that provides support for websites and web applications. This role installs IIS 7.0 and allows administrators to enable a wide array of additional role services.

Web server farms Groups of web servers that work together to provide increased capacity, scalability, performance, and reliability. Generally, the servers within a farm share the same content and configuration settings.

Web.config files Configuring files that can be created within IIS web applications and websites. These files can contain settings that override details specified in the ApplicationHost.config file.

WIM file A file that contains one or more images in the native Windows Imaging format.

Windows Media server announcements A method by which content providers can include links to content available on their servers. Options include creating a web page or special announcement files users can connect to directly.

Windows Media server broadcast A method of sending streamed audio or video to many users at once. Broadcasts are most commonly used for live events and in conjunction with a streaming media encoder.

Windows Media server cache/proxy server A Windows Media server configuration that enables servers to manage client connections and store copies of streamed content to increase performance and scalability.

Windows Media server playlist A file that contains a list of audio and video media scheduled for playback.

Windows Media server plug-ins A method by which Microsoft and third-party providers can extend the functionality of a Windows Media server. Plug-ins are available for managing authentication, authorization, and performance.

Windows Media Services multicast A streaming media delivery method, available only in Windows Server 2008 R2 Enterprise and Datacenter, that involves many clients connecting to a single outbound stream from Windows Media.

Windows Media Services unicast A streaming media delivery method that involves point-to-point connections between a Windows Media Services server and client computers.

Windows Media Services A server service that provides access to broadcast-based and on-demand audio and video content.

Windows PowerShell A Microsoft scripting environment and programming language. Windows PowerShell enables users to create scripts by using object-based programming techniques.

Windows System Resource Manager (WSRM) A utility in Windows Server 2008 and Windows Server 2008 R2 that enables resource management. Administrators can define processor and memory priorities for applications and services running on their servers.

Witness disk In a failover cluster, a disk that contains a copy of the cluster configuration database. The availability of a witness disk is sometimes used to determine whether a cluster should run. Also called a disk witness, a quorum disk, or a quorum witness.

Wrapper playlist advertisements Audio or video advertisements that are designed to play before or after a client requests access to on-demand media.

Index

A

About Remote Desktop Connection dialog box, 176
ACLs (access control lists), 3
activation. *See* Windows activation
Active Directory Certificate Services server role, 383
Active Directory Domain Services. *See* AD DS (Active Directory Domain Services)
Active Directory Rights Management Services (AD RMS), 485
Active Server Pages (ASP) technology, 288
AD DS (Active Directory Domain Services)
    CALs and, 162
    forms authentication, 372
    RD Virtualization Host and, 253
    WDS requirements, 12, 19
AD RMS (Active Directory Rights Management Services), 485
Add Allow Authorization Rule dialog box, 378
Add Allow Entry command, 390, 422
Add Allow Restriction Rule dialog box, 390
Add Allow Rule command, 378
Add Application dialog box, 313
Add Application Pool dialog box, 315
Add Authoring Rule dialog box, 413
Add command, 320, 436
Add Deny Entry command, 390, 422
Add Deny Restriction Rule dialog box, 388
Add Deny Rule command, 378
Add Driver Packages dialog box, 36
Add Features Wizard
    configuring NLB clusters, 121
    Desktop Experience feature, 412, 414
    enabling MPIO, 96
    installing MSAs, 323
ADD FTP Site Wizard

Authentication And Authorization Information page, 407
    Binding and SSL Settings page, 407
    Site Information page, 406
Add Image Wizard
    Image File page, 25
    Image Group page, 25
    launching, 25
    Review Settings page, 26
Add Publishing Point (Wizard) command, 461
Add Publishing Point Wizard
    configuring source settings, 466
    Content Playback page, 463
    Content Type page, 461
    creating wrapper playlist, 468
    Delivery Options For Broadcast Publishing Points page, 462
    Directory Location page, 463
    Encoder URL page, 464
    Publishing Point Name page, 461
    Publishing Point Summary page, 464
    Publishing Point Type page, 461
    Unicast Logging page, 464
Add Role Services command, 405
Add Role Services dialog box, 265
Add Role Services Wizard
    Choose A Server Authentication Certificate for SSL Encryption page, 226, 233
    Confirm Installation Selections page, 233, 265
    Create An RD RAP For RD Gateway page, 229, 233
    Create Authorization Policies For RD Gateway page, 233
    generating self-signed certificates, 226
    Installation Progress page, 234, 265
    Installation Results page, 234, 265
    launching, 226
    Network Policy And Access Services page, 233

X

About the Authors

 J.C. MACKIN (MCITP, MCTS, MCSE, MCDST, MCT) is a writer, editor, and trainer who has been working with Microsoft networks since Windows NT 4.0. Books he has previously authored or coauthored include *MCSA/MCSE Self-Paced Training Kit (Exam 70-291): Implementing, Managing, and Maintaining a Microsoft Windows Server 2003 Network Infrastructure, MCITP Self-Paced Training Kit (Exam 70-443): Designing a Database Server Infrastructure Using Microsoft SQL Server 2005,* and *MCITP Self-Paced Training Kit (Exam 70-685): Windows 7, Enterprise Desktop Support Technician.* He also holds a master's degree in Telecommunication and Network Management. When not working with computers, J.C. can be found with a panoramic camera photographing villages in Italy or France.

ANIL DESAI is an independent consultant based in Austin, Texas. He specializes in evaluating, implementing, and managing information technology (IT) solutions. He has worked extensively with IT management, development, and database technology. Anil holds many certifications and is a Microsoft Most Valuable Professional (MVP) (Windows Server – Virtualization). Anil is the author of numerous technical books focusing on the Windows Server platform, virtualization, databases, and IT management best practices. He is also a frequent contributor to numerous IT publications and conferences. For more information, please see *http://AnilDesai.net.*

Windows Server 2008 Resource Kit—
Your Definitive Resource!

**Windows Server® 2008
Resource Kit**

Microsoft® MVPs with the
Microsoft Windows Server Team

ISBN 9780735623613

Your definitive reference for deployment and operations—from the experts who know the technology best. Get in-depth technical information on Active Directory®, Windows PowerShell® scripting, advanced administration, networking and network access protection, security administration, IIS, and other critical topics—plus an essential toolkit of resources on CD.

ALSO AVAILABLE AS SINGLE VOLUMES

**Windows Server 2008
Security Resource Kit**

Jesper M. Johansson et al. with
Microsoft Security Team

ISBN 9780735625044

**Windows Server 2008
Networking and Network
Access Protection (NAP)**

Joseph Davies, Tony Northrup,
Microsoft Networking Team

ISBN 9780735624221

**Windows Server 2008
Active Directory Resource Kit**

Stan Reimer et al. with
Microsoft Active Directory Team

ISBN 9780735625150

**Windows® Administration
Resource Kit: Productivity
Solutions for IT Professionals**

Dan Holme

ISBN 9780735624313

**Windows Powershell
Scripting Guide**

Ed Wilson

ISBN 9780735622791

**Internet Information
Services (IIS) 7.0
Resource Kit**

Mike Volodarsky et al.
with Microsoft IIS Team

ISBN 9780735624412

microsoft.com/mspress

Windows Server 2008— Resources for Administrators

Windows Server® 2008 Administrator's Companion

Charlie Russel and Sharon Crawford
ISBN 9780735625051

Your comprehensive, one-volume guide to deployment, administration, and support. Delve into core system capabilities and administration topics, including Active Directory®, security issues, disaster planning/recovery, interoperability, IIS 7.0, virtualization, clustering, and performance tuning.

Windows Server 2008 Administrator's Pocket Consultant, Second Edition

William R. Stanek
ISBN 9780735627116

Portable and precise—with the focused information you need for administering server roles, Active Directory, user/group accounts, rights and permissions, file-system management, TCP/IP, DHCP, DNS, printers, network performance, backup, and restoration.

Windows Server 2008 Resource Kit

Microsoft MVPs with Microsoft Windows Server Team
ISBN 9780735623613

Six volumes! Your definitive resource for deployment and operations—from the experts who know the technology best. Get in-depth technical information on Active Directory, Windows PowerShell® scripting, advanced administration, networking and network access protection, security administration, IIS, and more—plus an essential toolkit of resources on CD.

Internet Information Services (IIS) 7.0 Administrator's Pocket Consultant

William R. Stanek
ISBN 9780735623644

This pocket-sized guide delivers immediate answers for administering IIS 7.0. Topics include customizing installation; configuration and XML schema; application management; user access and security; Web sites, directories, and content; and performance, backup, and recovery.

Windows PowerShell 2.0 Administrator's Pocket Consultant

William R. Stanek
ISBN 9780735625952

The practical, portable guide to using *cmdlets* and scripts to automate everyday system administration—including configuring server roles, services, features, and security settings; managing TCP/IP networking; monitoring and tuning performance; and other essential tasks.

ALSO SEE

Windows PowerShell 2.0 Best Practices
ISBN 9780735626461

Windows® Administration Resource Kit: Productivity Solutions for IT Professionals
ISBN 9780735624313

Windows Server 2008 Hyper-V™ Resource Kit
ISBN 9780735625174

Windows Server 2008 Security Resource Kit
ISBN 9780735625044

Microsoft® Press

Get Certified—Windows® 7

Desktop support technicians and administrators—demonstrate your expertise with Windows 7 by earning a Microsoft® Certification focusing on core technical (MCTS) or professional (MCITP) skills. With our 2-in-1 *Self-Paced Training Kits*, you get a comprehensive, cost-effective way to prepare for the certification exams. Combining official exam-prep guides + practice tests, these kits are designed to maximize the impact of your study time.

EXAM 70-680
MCTS Self-Paced Training Kit: Configuring Windows 7
Ian McLean and Orin Thomas
ISBN 9780735627086

EXAM 70-685
MCITP Self-Paced Training Kit: Windows 7 Enterprise Desktop Support Technician
Tony Northrup and J.C. Mackin
ISBN 9780735627093

EXAM 70-686
MCITP Self-Paced Training Kit: Windows 7 Enterprise Desktop Administrator
Craig Zacker and Orin Thomas
ISBN 9780735627178

Great for on the job

Windows 7 Resource Kit
Mitch Tulloch, Tony Northrup, Jerry Honeycutt, Ed Wilson, and the Windows 7 Team at Microsoft
ISBN 9780735627000

Windows 7 Inside Out, Deluxe Edition
Ed Bott, Carl Siechert, Craig Stinson
ISBN 9780735656925

Windows 7 Administrator's Pocket Consultant
William R. Stanek
ISBN 9780735626997

microsoft.com/mspress

What do you think of this book?

We want to hear from you!

To participate in a brief online survey, please visit:

microsoft.com/learning/booksurvey

Tell us how well this book meets your needs—what works effectively, and what we can do better. Your feedback will help us continually improve our books and learning resources for you.

Thank you in advance for your input!